CONSTITUTIONAL LAW
STRUCTURE and PRINCIPLES

THIRD EDITION

By

Bradley W. Joondeph
Jerry A. Kasner Professor
Santa Clara University School of Law

July 2022

ABOUT THE AUTHOR

Bradley W. Joondeph is the Jerry A. Kasner Professor at Santa Clara University School of Law in Santa Clara, California. His research focuses on constitutional federalism, state and local taxation, judicial behavior, and American constitutional development. He served as a judicial clerk to the Honorable Sandra Day O'Connor at the Supreme Court of the United States (1999–2000), and to the Honorable Deanell Reece Tacha at the United States Court of Appeals for the Tenth Circuit (1994–1995). Prior to Santa Clara, he was Associate Professor at Washington University School of Law in St. Louis (1997–1999) and a teaching fellow at Stanford Law School (1995–1997).

Brad Joondeph and James Obergefell

ACKNOWLEDGMENTS

I am grateful to the many people who made this book possible. The research and administrative assistance provided by Trisha Cobb, Sabeena Bali-Dingra, and Nancy Diaz were invaluable. I owe thanks to Santa Clara University School of Law—and all my colleagues—who have generously supported my teaching and research for more than 20 years; Lisa Kloppenberg, Mike Flynn, Eric Goldman, and Michael Kaufman have been especially encouraging and supportive of this project. Justice O'Connor and Judge Tacha patiently guided and shaped me in ways they will never know. Professors Barbara Fried, Robert Rabin, Peter Wiedenbeck, and June Carbone—as well as Chief Judge Sri Srinivasan—made my career in academia possible. I cannot thank my students enough for teaching me so much along the way; I am humbled by the wisdom and insights they have graciously shared. Most of all, I am grateful to my incredible family—Srija and Akhil in particular—for their love and support. I am so blessed.

For any questions regarding the contents of this book (or any accompanying materials), please contact the author at bjoondeph@scu.edu.

CONSTITUTIONAL LAW
STRUCTURE and PRINCIPLES

TABLE OF CONTENTS

Chapter 6: Justiciability: Political Questions and Adequate and Independent State Grounds

Chapter 7: Political Constraints on Federal Courts

PART IV: THE SEPARATION OF POWERS

Chapter 13: The Powers of the President

Chapter 14: The Appointment and Removal of Federal Officers

APPENDIX: FINAL EXAM QUESTIONS & SUGGESTED ANALYSES

PART I

INTRODUCTION

CHAPTER 1
AN INTRODUCTION TO CONSTITUTIONAL LAW

A.   The Nature of Constitutional Law

In some respects, constitutional law is the single most significant course in the law school curriculum. It is foundational, in the sense that the entire American legal system is built on top of it. Every governmental action in the United States—whether federal, state, or local, whether legislative, executive, or judicial—is governed (and thus shaped) by what the Constitution permits. For instance, a state's imposition of tort liability for a given personal injury must consist with the Constitution (for instance, the Due Process Clause's limitations on the damages that may be awarded to the plaintiff); a federal district court's exercise of subject matter jurisdiction must be consistent with the limits set by Article III of the Constitution; and the manner in which the federal or a state government can prosecute a criminal defendant (such as affording the defendant a right to jury trial, and requiring that guilt be proved beyond a reasonable doubt) is determined by the Constitution.

Despite—and perhaps because of—its significance, constitutional law, as an academic subject, can be quite challenging. First, the relevant legal principles or rules are often quite abstract and indeterminate. This is necessarily so when the source of those rules and principles is a *constitution*, which needs to be sufficiently flexible to survive the inevitable social, economic, and political changes to a political community over time. The U.S. Constitution is only a few pages in length, and thus can merely set out the broad outlines of our governmental system. A more detailed charter—that reads more like a statute or administrative regulation—would risk rapidly becoming obsolete. (And amending the Constitution is much more difficult than revising a statute or regulation.) Terms like "due process of law," "commerce among the states," and "necessary and proper" are not self-defining. The text itself, though critical in framing the relevant questions, provides very few definitive answers.

As a result, constitutional law depends heavily on a synthesis of Supreme Court opinions spanning the nation's 230-year history. And those opinions can be dense and complicated. Moreover, understanding the disputes raised in those cases often requires some familiarity with American history, and how our political system has functioned over time. To name a few examples, it is difficult to comprehend the Court's decision in *Marbury v. Madison*, 5 U.S. (1 Cranch) 137 (1803), without understanding the contest in the late 1790s and early 1800s between the Federalists and Jeffersonian-Republicans over the role of the federal government; or to understand *McCulloch v. Maryland*, 17 U.S. (4 Wheat.) 159 (1819), without some understanding of the controversy surrounding the Bank of the United States and the scope of the national government's powers; or to understand the *Slaughter-House Cases*, 83 U.S. 36 (1873), without some grasp of what the Civil War had (or had not) resolved about the relationship between the federal government and the states; or to understand the modern breadth of Congress's enumerated powers without some feel for the intense political fight over President Franklin Roosevelt's New Deal in the 1930s. American constitutional law is inseparable from the broader story of America's political history.

Complicating matters further is that, given the text's indeterminacy—and the stakes for its meaning—constitutional law changes over time. For good or ill, the meaning of the Constitution has evolved. And this evolution, without any corresponding change to the text of the Constitution itself, can be disorienting. It seems to conflict with a conception of law as an objective, concrete set of rules that are set apart from politics. How is it really *law* if it means something on one day and the something quite different soon thereafter?

If it were easier to amend the Constitution, perhaps that would have become the principal mode for constitutional change in the United States. But because amending the Constitution is so difficult—and because constitutional change is inevitable in any society—our system has experienced change mostly through new understandings of what the unchanging text requires. And these new understandings are often triggered, at least proximately, by changes in the identity of the justices serving on the Supreme Court.

While these dynamics can make constitutional law a challenging subject, they can also make it rich and rewarding. Compared to most courses in the law school curriculum, it offers a deeper, richer story about American law—and the political destiny of the United States.

B.   The Functions of the Constitution

The Constitution is essentially the law of *lawmaking*: the law that governs how governments in the United States may govern. It covers all aspects of law creation, law enforcement, and law application. It sets down the rules for the creation of legislation, for the enforcement or execution of the law, and for the adjudication of legal disputes. It creates and delineates the three branches of the national government: Congress (the Legislative Branch), the President (the Executive Branch), and the federal courts (the Judicial Branch). And it assigns to each branch certain responsibilities and imposes limits on their actions. In doing so, it creates a system of separated powers—a distinct assignment of different powers to each branch of government.

Similarly, the Constitution—through its specific enumeration of powers granted to the three branches—limits the authority of the national government as a whole, reserving the balance of authority to the states (or to the People). An essential feature of America's constitutional architecture is that both the federal government *and* the state governments are independent sovereigns. They each have their own, exclusive spheres of authority, and neither is fully answerable to the other.

If a valid federal law conflicts with state law in the context of a legal dispute, Article VI of the Constitution (through the Supremacy Clause) dictates that courts must apply the federal law, at least to the extent of the conflict. But there are areas of human activity the Constitution does not permit the federal government to touch at all, and thus reserves exclusively to the states for their regulation. For instance, with respect to judicial authority, consider a dispute arising under state law between two citizens of the same state. The Constitution generally forbids federal courts from adjudicating such a case, leaving it entirely to the state courts for resolution. This feature of our system—in which both the federal government and the states simultaneously exercise authority over the same territory and residents, with citizens having separate and distinct relationships with each sovereign—is known as *federalism*.

Finally, the Constitution protects a number of individual rights from governmental interference. In general, these rights (such as the freedom of expression protected by the First Amendment, or to marry the person of one's choice protected by the Due Process Clause of the Fourteenth Amendment) are enforceable against *any* governmental action—whether legislative, executive, or judicial, whether federal, state, or local. They are liberties enjoyed against governmental deprivation of any stripe.

These are the three essential functions of our Constitution: to establish and allocate power among the three branches of the national government; to establish the boundaries between the authority of the federal government and the states; and to endow all Americans with various individual rights against governmental action.

C. The Creation of the Constitution of the United States

Every important subject has a narrative to explain its birth—its creation story, if you will. For the Constitution, that story involves the relatively short and unhappy period of the nation's initial independence, governed by the Articles of Confederation. It was the failure of the Articles as a viable charter that forced the fledgling nation's leaders to explore other possibilities. And that exploration ultimately resulted in our present Constitution.

1. The road to Philadelphia

On July 4, 1776, the thirteen original American colonies declared their independence from Great Britain. Five years later, after Yorktown, hostilities between British and American troops ceased. In November 1777, in the midst of the Revolutionary War, the Continental Congress—the existing national legislature—approved the Articles of Confederation. The Articles were officially ratified by the original thirteen states in 1781 and operated as the country's governing constitution for the next seven years.

The Articles created a government quite different from that ordained by our present Constitution. The national government essentially consisted only of a legislature, the Confederation Congress. There was no President or federal executive branch, and the federal judiciary consisted of a single court of extremely limited jurisdiction (the Court of Appeals in Cases of Capture). Moreover, the national government had no authority to regulate the people directly; it could only regulate through the state governments, directing them to take certain actions in the governance of their own citizens. In this way, the national government under the Articles operated much like the United Nations does today, relying on constituent member states to carry out its directives. Given this arrangement, the states tended to operate in practice more as independent nations than as constituent parts of a single republic.

This system was rather ineffectual, at least from the perspective of those desiring a cohesive national union. With no authority to regulate the people directly—and without an executive branch or courts to administer and enforce national laws or treaties—the national government lacked the practical power to make its directives stick. And this was not mere happenstance. Given that the colonies had declared their independence from Britain largely *because* they resented a distant, powerful central government, they were quite hesitant to create a national government possessing much power. During the colonial period, the states had conceived of themselves very much as independent sovereigns. Their uniting in 1776 was more a marriage of convenience, to coordinate their prosecution of the war, than the expression of a desire to form a strong, single nation.

Over the course of the 1780s, many prominent American statesmen grew disheartened by the state of American government. George Washington revealingly wrote the following in a letter to Thomas Jefferson: "That something is necessary, none will deny; for the situation of the general government, if it can be called a government, is shaken to its foundation . . . . [U]nless a remedy is soon applied, anarchy and confusion will inevitably ensue."[1] As an example of how poorly this constitutional system functioned, consider this: In 1786, the Confederation Congress requisitioned $3.8 million from the states to make current payments on the national debt; in response, the thirteen states collectively remitted a total of $663.

Driven by these concerns, a small group of prominent citizens, representing five of the thirteen states, convened in the summer of 1786 in Annapolis, Maryland to discuss possibilities for reform. This 1786 Annapolis Convention did not accomplish anything substantive, but the delegates agreed to reconvene at

---

[1] Lucas A. Powe, Jr., The Supreme Court and the American Elite, 1789–2008 1 (2009).

a formal convention the following summer in Philadelphia. And this subsequent meeting, in 1787, ultimately became the most significant political gathering in American history.

2. The Constitutional Convention

Delegates to the Constitutional Convention debated scores of issues in the summer of 1787, many of which ended in some sort of a compromise. Thus, many of the Constitution's provisions do not reflect some enlightened, forward-looking genius, but instead the hard-nosed horse-trading of competing interests. Moreover, many Americans thought the entire endeavor was a terrible idea. Rhode Island was so opposed to the adoption of a new constitution that it refused to send a delegation to Philadelphia, and several delegates from other states who attended the beginning of the convention (including New York's attendees other than Alexander Hamilton) left midway in protest.

Though the delegates debated many important questions, two related points were central to finding some sort of compromise: state representation in the national legislature and the protection of slavery. Those states where slavery was important economically would not join a union that did not protect their "peculiar institution." Thus, any bargain struck in framing a new constitution would need to ensure the southern states that slavery would not be threatened by the new national government. Though the words "slave" and "slavery" are conspicuously absent from the Constitution's text, evidence of this compromise is found in several places—from the infamous "three-fifths clause" of Article I, §2, clause 3, to the Fugitive Slave Clause, to the rules regarding the election of the President and state representation in the Senate. (This is why abolitionist William Lloyd Garrison called the Constitution "a covenant with death and an agreement with hell.")

After rejecting numerous proposals, the Framers ultimately reached a breakthrough of sorts in July, the most significant part of which was an agreement to split the national legislature between two chambers, one where there would be popular representation (the House of Representatives) and one where the states would have equal representation (the Senate). This is known as the "Connecticut Compromise," as it was originally proposed by Connecticut delegate Roger Sherman. It was approved by the Convention on July 23, 1787.

Structurally, there were two major differences between the new proposed Constitution and the Articles of Confederation. First, under the new Constitution, the national government would govern the people directly; it would not be required to depend on the states. Second (and relatedly), the national government would consist not just of a legislature, but also of an executive branch (headed by the President) and a judiciary (headed by the Supreme Court).

3. Ratification

The Constitutional Convention concluded on September 17, 1787. All the delegates who had remained in Philadelphia—other than George Mason,

Elbridge Gerry, and Edmond Randolph—signed the proposed Constitution. It was then transmitted to the Confederation Congress, which in turn sent it out to the states for ratification.

It is worth noting that the proposed mechanism for ratifying the new Constitution also marked a radical break with existing law. Under the Articles of Confederation—the governing constitution at the time of the Convention—the Articles could only be amended with the unanimous consent of the state legislatures. Specifically, Article XIII of the Articles of Confederation provided:

"Every State shall abide by the determination of the United States in Congress assembled, on all questions which by this confederation are submitted to them. And the Articles of this Confederation shall be inviolably observed by every State, and the Union shall be perpetual; nor shall any alteration at any time hereafter be made in any of them; unless such alteration be agreed to in a Congress of the United States, and be afterwards confirmed by the legislatures of every State."

But Article VII of the proposed Constitution stated that "[t]he Ratification of the Conventions of nine States, shall be sufficient for the Establishment of this Constitution between the States so ratifying the same." The new Constitution was a proposed wholesale amendment (really, a replacement) of the Articles of Confederation. Yet, it proclaimed that merely *nine* of the thirteen states were needed to ratify it, and that the ratification would occur through *conventions* in those states, not state legislatures.

In all events, following contentious votes in New York and Virginia, the necessary nine states ratified the new Constitution in 1788. (It was the ratification debates in New York that produced the *Federalist Papers*—essays by James Madison, Alexander Hamilton, and John Jay, published in New York newspapers, urging ratification.) And once nine states had ratified, it was impractical for the remaining states to stand outside the union as separate nations. (But there was still some foot-dragging; North Carolina and Rhode Island did not ratify until late 1789 and early 1790.) The first Congress convened on March 4, 1789. And one of the first statutes Congress enacted was the Judiciary Act of 1789—the statute that would lie at the heart of perhaps the Supreme Court's single greatest decision, *Marbury v. Madison*.

D. Recurring Themes in Constitutional Law

There are several important, recurring themes in American constitutional law that are worth highlighting at the outset. It may be difficult to grasp their full significance at this juncture, but identifying them now might be helpful as you move through the material.

1. The Constitution and constitutional law

A course on constitutional law focuses principally on decisions handed down by the Supreme Court of the United States. These opinions interpret the text of the Constitution, as well as the Court's own precedent, and construct applicable rules to govern and constrain the operation of American politics and the process of public governance.

These decisions are extremely important: they spell out the doctrinal rules creating most of what we call "constitutional law." But they are not the Constitution *itself*. The doctrinal rules discernable from the Court's decisions practically dictate how the Constitution is to be implemented (at least for the time being), but they lack the legal authority of the Constitution's text. To say that a Supreme Court decision interpreting the Constitution calls for A, B, or C is not *necessarily* to say that the Constitution itself calls for that result. For example, the Supreme Court held in 1857 in *Scott v. Sandford*, 60 U.S. 393 (1857), that, for purposes of the Constitution, African Americans could never be citizens of the United States. But millions of Americans, including soon-to-be President Abraham Lincoln, rightly refused to accept that interpretation, maintaining that the Constitution dictated a contrary result.

More broadly, it is important to understand that the Supreme Court is only one actor within the American constitutional ecosystem. While the Court operates with a fair measure of autonomy—and is formally independent of the other two branches of government—it is hardly immune from political influence. To the contrary, the Court is embedded *within* the American political system, influencing and being influenced by its other component parts.

Moreover, though the Supreme Court is probably the most important arbiter of what the Constitution means on a day-to-day basis, it is hardly the *sole* contributor to the construction of constitutional meaning. Other institutions and actors—the President, Congress, lower courts, state legislatures, state governors, social or political movements, and ordinary citizens—help decide important constitutional questions as well. And on a regular basis.

Even when the Court appears to be the ultimate decider (for instance, in concluding that the Fourteenth Amendment requires every state to recognize same-sex marriages), the outcome may really be the work of other actors (such as the modern LGBTQ rights movement, the President, and the people more generally) who have fostered a political environment in which that decision was possible. So even when the Court nominally decides a particular question (as it did in *Obergefell v. Hodges*, 576 U.S. 644 (2015)), it is hardly doing so on its own, without implicit political supports. A host of forces external to the Court—most notably, the political pressures that led to the appointments of the current justices—are constantly shaping the Court's decision making.

2. The meaning of the Constitution over time

This leads to a related point: the meaning of our Constitution is not static. Justice Scalia famously argued that, as a normative matter, the Constitution's meaning *should* be static, and that any effort to treat the Constitution as "a living, breathing document" that "evolves" is illegitimate—inconsistent with the idea of a binding, written Constitution. But this claim is simply inaccurate factually. It fails to capture what has happened during the course of the nation's existence. Over and over again, the accepted meaning of the Constitution has changed with the times.

Consider a few signal examples. In 1896, the Supreme Court held in *Plessy v. Ferguson*, 163 U.S. 537, that it was consistent with the Fourteenth Amendment's Equal Protection Clause for a state to mandate racial segregation in public accommodations (in *Plessy* specifically, in railroad cars). In *Brown v. Board of Education*, 347 U.S. 483 (1954), the Court held that such racial segregation (this time, in public schools) was unconstitutional. In 1986, the Court held in *Bowers v. Hardwick*, 486 U.S. 186, that it was perfectly constitutional for a state to criminalize same-sex sodomy, even between consenting adults in private. Sixteen years later, in *Lawrence v. Texas*, 539 U.S. 558 (2003)—interpreting the same Due Process Clause—the Court overruled *Bowers* and held that such laws were unconstitutional. In both instances, with respect to highly salient issues, the governing meaning of the Constitution took a complete U-turn, even though the relevant texts (and their "original public meanings") were unchanged.

This evolution in meaning is not a function of Supreme Court justices thinking harder, or solving a long-simmering doctrinal riddle, as if it were a particularly challenging logic puzzle. Rather, it is a function of evolving historical, social, and political forces in American society. The Constitution is foundational to American politics. Every significant political movement in American history has sought to enlist the Constitution as its ally, to ground its basic objectives in the nation's constitutional destiny. Every significant political movement conceptualizes itself as embracing the true, loyal, essential meaning of the Constitution, moving the country closer to the ideal that the document envisions. Thus, in this sense, every generation reinterprets the Constitution for itself to facilitate its own political aspirations.

That is not to say that anything goes—that the text of the Constitution is somehow irrelevant, or that each generation starts with a blank slate. The text—along with history, tradition, inertia, and precedent—are powerful constraining forces. And as the nation matures, it becomes increasingly difficult to alter settled constitutional meanings. Some of our constitutional commitments have become deeply entrenched. And some are so specifically dictated by the text of the Constitution that it is difficult to reconceptualize or reconfigure them, no matter how much a present majority may wish to do so. (Consider the Constitution's command that each state be represented by two senators, or that the President be at least 35 years of age.)

But many constitutional meanings *do* change. The Constitution does not so much provide definitive answers as it creates a framework: a set of institutional ground rules for the resolution of our most fundamental political questions.

3. The many layers of constitutional law

A third important theme is that there are several layers to the study of constitutional law, and moving between them can be confusing. First, there is the doctrinal layer, the common grist of most law school courses. It consists of the black-letter rules, principles, and standards governing constitutional disputes. (For instance—to pick just one example—the Eleventh Amendment deprives federal courts of jurisdiction over private, nonconsenting suits against state governments.) This doctrinal layer will constitute the vast bulk of any course on constitutional law, and it is principally what students are expected to learn for purposes of any state's bar exam.

But the doctrinal rules of constitutional law are only a part of the picture in understanding our constitutional system, for at least two reasons. First, these "rules" are often stated at such a broad level of generality that they hardly help decide difficult cases. For example, knowing that Congress cannot "unduly interfere" with the President's obligation to enforce federal law doesn't resolve whether a particular constraint on the President's removal of an executive officer is unconstitutional. Second, of the different components of constitutional law, the doctrinal layer is the most ephemeral. Again, doctrinal rules—especially in their finer detail—are constantly in flux.

Second, there is a layer of deeper constitutional principles. These are structural, foundational, more lasting and more basic—for instance, that the federal government is a government of "enumerated powers." These are the enduring axioms to which interpreters of the Constitution must resort when the more reticulated doctrinal rules fail to provide answers. They are also the principles to which people will typically appeal when they believe those doctrinal rules need to be refined, altered, or overruled.

Third, there is always the historical, social, and political context in which given constitutional disputes arise. It is difficult to really appreciate the Supreme Court's important decisions—or the doctrinal rules they announce and set down—without a sense of the surrounding circumstances. Again, constitutional law is our collective constitutional history. We cannot fully understand the significance of decisions like *Marbury v. Madison*, *Brown v. Board of Education*, *Obergefell v. Hodges*, or *Dobbs v. Jackson Women's Health* without some sense of American politics. If one approaches American constitutional law as an exercise in purely abstract, formal logic, divorced from the surrounding historical, social, and political forces—as if it were a form of mathematics—it will make no sense. It is only with some appreciation for the broader context that a more coherent understanding of American constitutional law can emerge.

Finally, there is the layer of critical evaluation: what alternatives are possible? Again, the doctrinal rules are ephemeral. The deeper principles are less malleable, but even these are contestable. How might our constitutional order be different? Should it be? Obviously, the framing generation radically reconceived our constitutional possibilities. Should we as well? Can we? This is the grist of the critical evaluation of our existing constitutional order. Every American is responsible for preserving or reconceiving our constitutional destiny, like every generation since 1776.

4. The role of the Supreme Court

Finally, it is important to see constitutional law with an eye toward the proper role of the judiciary in a democratic republic. Again, the Constitution is the law of American government. Thus, a constitutional case only arises after elected representatives (at some level) have made a decision, explicitly or implicitly, about the meaning of the Constitution. The weight we might afford those decisions can obviously differ. (For instance, we might grant much greater deference to the constitutional judgment of Congress in enacting a significant statute than to that of a city police officer in determining how much force is appropriate in apprehending a suspect.) But the critical question, presented to some degree in every constitutional case, is this: *When, in a democracy, should a court overturn the actions of electorally accountable officials in the interpretation of the very indeterminate language of the Constitution?*

It would be one thing if the elected officials and their subordinates were demonstrably wrong about the Constitution's meaning, and thus clearly acting beyond the bounds of what the Constitution permits. (For instance, suppose a President was elected who was twelve years old.) But that is rarely the case. The Constitution is written in broad, open-ended, and vague terms: "due process," "equal protection," "commerce among the states," and the like. These phrases are susceptible to several plausible understandings. In a democracy, when is it proper for the views of unelected judges to prevail over those of officers who are electorally accountable to the People?

This is the so-called "counter-majoritarian difficulty," famously so labeled by Yale law professor Alexander Bickel in the 1960s. What legitimates the Supreme Court's role in dictating for the nation, for instance, that affirmative action is generally illegal? That government generally cannot forbid the possession of handguns? That George W. Bush won the 2000 presidential election? Or that every state must recognize same-sex marriages? In other words, when should the federal judiciary impose *its* view of contestable constitutional language over the views of people who have actually been elected?

It is an extraordinarily difficult question, and one that essentially arises in *every* constitutional case. For in each dispute to reach the Supreme Court, the justices must decide not just what they think about the issue on the merits, but also how much deference they should afford the prior constitutional judgment of some electorally accountable public officials. There are no easy answers. The important point to recognize is that this question of institutional role—and the role of the federal judiciary in particular—is imbedded in every constitutional case you will encounter.

CHAPTER 2

THE CONSTITUTION OF THE UNITED STATES

Preamble

We the People of the United States, in Order to form a more perfect Union, establish Justice, insure domestic Tranquility, provide for the common defence, promote the general Welfare, and secure the Blessings of Liberty to ourselves and our Posterity, do ordain and establish this Constitution for the United States of America.

Article I

Section 1

All legislative Powers herein granted shall be vested in a Congress of the United States, which shall consist of a Senate and House of Representatives.

Section 2

1. The House of Representatives shall be composed of Members chosen every second Year by the People of the several States, and the Electors in each State shall have the Qualifications requisite for Electors of the most numerous Branch of the State Legislature.

2. No Person shall be a Representative who shall not have attained to the Age of twenty five Years, and been seven Years a Citizen of the United States, and who shall not, when elected, be an Inhabitant of that State in which he shall be chosen.

3. Representatives and direct Taxes shall be apportioned among the several States which may be included within this Union, according to their respective Numbers, which shall be determined by adding to the whole Number of free Persons, including those bound to Service for a Term of Years, and excluding Indians not taxed, three fifths of all other Persons. The actual Enumeration shall be made within three Years after the first Meeting of the Congress of the United States, and within every subsequent Term of ten Years, in such Manner as they shall by Law direct. The Number of Representatives shall not exceed one for every thirty Thousand, but each State shall have at Least one Representative; and until such enumeration shall be made, the State of New Hampshire shall be entitled to chuse three, Massachusetts eight, Rhode-Island and Providence Plantations one, Connecticut five, New-York six, New Jersey four, Pennsylvania eight, Delaware one, Maryland six, Virginia ten, North Carolina five, South Carolina five, and Georgia three.

4. When vacancies happen in the Representation from any State, the Executive Authority thereof shall issue Writs of Election to fill such Vacancies.

5. The House of Representatives shall chuse their Speaker and other Officers; and shall have the sole Power of Impeachment.

Section 3

1. The Senate of the United States shall be composed of two Senators from each State, chosen by the Legislature thereof, for six Years; and each Senator shall have one Vote.

2. Immediately after they shall be assembled in Consequence of the first Election, they shall be divided as equally as may be into three Classes. The Seats of the Senators of the first Class shall be vacated at the Expiration of the second Year, of the second Class at the Expiration of the fourth Year, and of the third Class at the Expiration of the sixth Year, so that one third may be chosen every second Year; and if Vacancies happen by Resignation, or otherwise, during the Recess of the Legislature of any State, the Executive thereof may make temporary Appointments until the next Meeting of the Legislature, which shall then fill such Vacancies.

3. No Person shall be a Senator who shall not have attained to the Age of thirty Years, and been nine Years a Citizen of the United States, and who shall not, when elected, be an Inhabitant of that State for which he shall be chosen.

4. The Vice President of the United States shall be President of the Senate, but shall have no Vote, unless they be equally divided.

5. The Senate shall chuse their other Officers, and also a President pro tempore, in the Absence of the Vice President, or when he shall exercise the Office of President of the United States.

6. The Senate shall have the sole Power to try all Impeachments. When sitting for that Purpose, they shall be on Oath or Affirmation. When the President of the United States is tried, the Chief Justice shall preside: And no Person shall be convicted without the Concurrence of two thirds of the Members present.

7. Judgment in Cases of impeachment shall not extend further than to removal from Office, and disqualification to hold and enjoy any Office of honor, Trust or Profit under the United States: but the Party convicted shall nevertheless be liable and subject to Indictment, Trial, Judgment and Punishment, according to Law.

Section 4

1. The Times, Places and Manner of holding Elections for Senators and Representatives, shall be prescribed in each State by the Legislature thereof; but the Congress may at any time by Law make or alter such Regulations, except as to the Places of chusing Senators.

2. The Congress shall assemble at least once in every Year, and such Meeting shall be on the first Monday in December, unless they shall by Law appoint a different Day.

Section 5

1. Each House shall be the Judge of the Elections, Returns and Qualifications of its own Members, and a Majority of each shall constitute a Quorum to do Business; but a smaller Number may adjourn from day to day, and may be authorized to compel the Attendance of absent Members, in such Manner, and under such Penalties as each House may provide.

2. Each House may determine the Rules of its Proceedings, punish its Members for disorderly Behaviour, and, with the Concurrence of two thirds, expel a Member.

3. Each House shall keep a Journal of its Proceedings, and from time to time publish the same, excepting such Parts as may in their Judgment require Secrecy; and the Yeas and Nays of the Members of either House on any question shall, at the Desire of one fifth of those Present, be entered on the Journal.

4. Neither House, during the Session of Congress, shall, without the Consent of the other, adjourn for more than three days, nor to any other Place than that in which the two Houses shall be sitting.

Section 6

1. The Senators and Representatives shall receive a Compensation for their Services, to be ascertained by Law, and paid out of the Treasury of the United States. They shall in all Cases, except Treason, Felony and Breach of the Peace, be privileged from Arrest during their Attendance at the Session of their respective Houses, and in going to and returning from the same; and for any Speech or Debate in either House, they shall not be questioned in any other Place.

2. No Senator or Representative shall, during the Time for which he was elected, be appointed to any civil Office under the Authority of the United States, which shall have been created, or the Emoluments whereof shall have been encreased during such time; and no Person holding any Office under the United States, shall be a Member of either House during his Continuance in Office.

Section 7

1. All Bills for raising Revenue shall originate in the House of Representatives; but the Senate may propose or concur with Amendments as on other Bills.

2. Every Bill which shall have passed the House of Representatives and the Senate, shall, before it become a Law, be presented to the President of the United States; If he approve he shall sign it, but if not he shall return it, with his Objections to that House in which it shall have originated, who shall enter

the Objections at large on their Journal, and proceed to reconsider it. If after such Reconsideration two thirds of that House shall agree to pass the Bill, it shall be sent, together with the Objections, to the other House, by which it shall likewise be reconsidered, and if approved by two thirds of that House, it shall become a Law. But in all such Cases the Votes of both Houses shall be determined by yeas and Nays, and the Names of the Persons voting for and against the Bill shall be entered on the Journal of each House respectively. If any Bill shall not be returned by the President within ten Days (Sundays excepted) after it shall have been presented to him, the Same shall be a Law, in like Manner as if he had signed it, unless the Congress by their Adjournment prevent its Return, in which Case it shall not be a Law.

3. Every Order, Resolution, or Vote to which the Concurrence of the Senate and House of Representatives may be necessary (except on a question of Adjournment) shall be presented to the President of the United States; and before the Same shall take Effect, shall be approved by him, or being disapproved by him, shall be repassed by two thirds of the Senate and House of Representatives, according to the Rules and Limitations prescribed in the Case of a Bill.

Section 8

1. The Congress shall have Power To lay and collect Taxes, Duties, Imposts and Excises, to pay the Debts and provide for the common Defence and general Welfare of the United States; but all Duties, Imposts and Excises shall be uniform throughout the United States;

2. To borrow Money on the credit of the United States;

3. To regulate Commerce with foreign Nations, and among the several States, and with the Indian Tribes;

4. To establish an uniform Rule of Naturalization, and uniform Laws on the subject of Bankruptcies throughout the United States;

5. To coin Money, regulate the Value thereof, and of foreign Coin, and fix the Standard of Weights and Measures;

6. To provide for the Punishment of counterfeiting the Securities and current Coin of the United States;

7. To establish Post Offices and post Roads;

8. To promote the Progress of Science and useful Arts, by securing for limited Times to Authors and Inventors the exclusive Right to their respective Writings and Discoveries;

9. To constitute Tribunals inferior to the supreme Court;

10. To define and punish Piracies and Felonies committed on the high Seas, and Offences against the Law of Nations;

11. To declare War, grant Letters of Marque and Reprisal, and make Rules concerning Captures on Land and Water;

12. To raise and support Armies, but no Appropriation of Money to that Use shall be for a longer Term than two Years;

13. To provide and maintain a Navy;

14. To make Rules for the Government and Regulation of the land and naval Forces;

15. To provide for calling forth the Militia to execute the Laws of the Union, suppress Insurrections and repel Invasions;

16. To provide for organizing, arming, and disciplining, the Militia, and for governing such Part of them as may be employed in the Service of the United States, reserving to the States respectively, the Appointment of the Officers, and the Authority of training the Militia according to the discipline prescribed by Congress;

17. To exercise exclusive Legislation in all Cases whatsoever, over such District (not exceeding ten Miles square) as may, by Cession of particular States, and the Acceptance of Congress, become the Seat of the Government of the United States, and to exercise like Authority over all Places purchased by the Consent of the Legislature of the State in which the Same shall be, for the Erection of Forts, Magazines, Arsenals, dock-Yards, and other needful Buildings;—And

18. To make all Laws which shall be necessary and proper for carrying into Execution the foregoing Powers, and all other Powers vested by this Constitution in the Government of the United States, or in any Department or Officer thereof.

Section 9

1. The Migration or Importation of such Persons as any of the States now existing shall think proper to admit, shall not be prohibited by the Congress prior to the Year one thousand eight hundred and eight, but a Tax or duty may be imposed on such Importation, not exceeding ten dollars for each Person.

2. The Privilege of the Writ of Habeas Corpus shall not be suspended, unless when in Cases of Rebellion or Invasion the public Safety may require it.

3. No Bill of Attainder or ex post facto Law shall be passed.

4. No Capitation, or other direct, Tax shall be laid, unless in Proportion to the Census or Enumeration herein before directed to be taken.

5. No Tax or Duty shall be laid on Articles exported from any State.

6. No Preference shall be given by any Regulation of Commerce or Revenue to the Ports of one State over those of another: nor shall Vessels bound to, or from, one State, be obliged to enter, clear, or pay Duties in another.

7. No Money shall be drawn from the Treasury, but in Consequence of Appropriations made by Law; and a regular Statement and Account of the Receipts and Expenditures of all public Money shall be published from time to time.

8. No Title of Nobility shall be granted by the United States: And no Person holding any Office of Profit or Trust under them, shall, without the Consent of the Congress, accept of any present, Emolument, Office, or Title, of any kind whatever, from any King, Prince, or foreign State.

Section 10

1. No State shall enter into any Treaty, Alliance, or Confederation; grant Letters of Marque and Reprisal; coin Money; emit Bills of Credit; make any Thing but gold and silver Coin a Tender in Payment of Debts; pass any Bill of Attainder, ex post facto Law, or Law impairing the Obligation of Contracts, or grant any Title of Nobility.

2. No State shall, without the Consent of the Congress, lay any Imposts or Duties on Imports or Exports, except what may be absolutely necessary for executing it's inspection Laws: and the net Produce of all Duties and Imposts, laid by any State on Imports or Exports, shall be for the Use of the Treasury of the United States; and all such Laws shall be subject to the Revision and Controul of the Congress.

3. No State shall, without the Consent of Congress, lay any Duty of Tonnage, keep Troops, or Ships of War in time of Peace, enter into any Agreement or Compact with another State, or with a foreign Power, or engage in War, unless actually invaded, or in such imminent Danger as will not admit of delay.

Article II

Section 1

1. The executive Power shall be vested in a President of the United States of America. He shall hold his Office during the Term of four Years, and, together with the Vice President, chosen for the same Term, be elected, as follows

2. Each State shall appoint, in such Manner as the Legislature thereof may direct, a Number of Electors, equal to the whole Number of Senators and Representatives to which the State may be entitled in the Congress: but no Senator or Representative, or Person holding an Office of Trust or Profit under the United States, shall be appointed an Elector.

3. The Electors shall meet in their respective States, and vote by Ballot for two Persons, of whom one at least shall not be an Inhabitant of the same State with themselves. And they shall make a List of all the Persons voted for, and of the Number of Votes for each; which List they shall sign and certify, and transmit sealed to the Seat of the Government of the United States, directed to the President of the Senate. The President of the Senate shall, in the Presence of the Senate and House of Representatives, open all the Certificates, and the Votes

shall then be counted. The Person having the greatest Number of Votes shall be the President, if such Number be a Majority of the whole Number of Electors appointed; and if there be more than one who have such Majority, and have an equal Number of Votes, then the House of Representatives shall immediately chuse by Ballot one of them for President; and if no Person have a Majority, then from the five highest on the List the said House shall in like Manner chuse the President. But in chusing the President, the Votes shall be taken by States, the Representation from each State having one Vote; A quorum for this Purpose shall consist of a Member or Members from two thirds of the States, and a Majority of all the States shall be necessary to a Choice. In every Case, after the Choice of the President, the Person having the greatest Number of Votes of the Electors shall be the Vice President. But if there should remain two or more who have equal Votes, the Senate shall chuse from them by Ballot the Vice President.

4. The Congress may determine the Time of chusing the Electors, and the Day on which they shall give their Votes; which Day shall be the same throughout the United States.

5. No Person except a natural born Citizen, or a Citizen of the United States, at the time of the Adoption of this Constitution, shall be eligible to the Office of President; neither shall any Person be eligible to that Office who shall not have attained to the Age of thirty five Years, and been fourteen Years a Resident within the United States.

6. In Case of the Removal of the President from Office, or of his Death, Resignation, or Inability to discharge the Powers and Duties of the said Office,9 the Same shall devolve on the VicePresident, and the Congress may by Law provide for the Case of Removal, Death, Resignation or Inability, both of the President and Vice President, declaring what Officer shall then act as President, and such Officer shall act accordingly, until the Disability be removed, or a President shall be elected.

7. The President shall, at stated Times, receive for his Services, a Compensation, which shall neither be encreased nor diminished during the Period for which he shall have been elected, and he shall not receive within that Period any other Emolument from the United States, or any of them.

8. Before he enter on the Execution of his Office, he shall take the following Oath or Affirmation:—"I do solemnly swear (or affirm) that I will faithfully execute the Office of President of the United States, and will to the best of my Ability, preserve, protect and defend the Constitution of the United States."

Section 2

1. The President shall be Commander in Chief of the Army and Navy of the United States, and of the Militia of the several States, when called into the actual Service of the United States; he may require the Opinion, in writing, of the principal Officer in each of the executive Departments, upon any Subject

relating to the Duties of their respective Offices, and he shall have Power to grant Reprieves and Pardons for Offences against the United States, except in Cases of Impeachment.

2. He shall have Power, by and with the Advice and Consent of the Senate, to make Treaties, provided two thirds of the Senators present concur; and he shall nominate, and by and with the Advice and Consent of the Senate, shall appoint Ambassadors, other public Ministers and Consuls, Judges of the supreme Court, and all other Officers of the United States, whose Appointments are not herein otherwise provided for, and which shall be established by Law: but the Congress may by Law vest the Appointment of such inferior Officers, as they think proper, in the President alone, in the Courts of Law, or in the Heads of Departments.

3. The President shall have Power to fill up all Vacancies that may happen during the Recess of the Senate, by granting Commissions which shall expire at the End of their next Session.

Section 3

He shall from time to time give to the Congress Information of the State of the Union, and recommend to their Consideration such Measures as he shall judge necessary and expedient; he may, on extraordinary Occasions, convene both Houses, or either of them, and in Case of Disagreement between them, with Respect to the Time of Adjournment, he may adjourn them to such Time as he shall think proper; he shall receive Ambassadors and other public Ministers; he shall take Care that the Laws be faithfully executed, and shall Commission all the Officers of the United States.

Section 4

The President, Vice President and all civil Officers of the United States, shall be removed from Office on Impeachment for, and Conviction of, Treason, Bribery, or other high Crimes and Misdemeanors.

Article III

Section 1

The judicial Power of the United States, shall be vested in one supreme Court, and in such inferior Courts as the Congress may from time to time ordain and establish. The Judges, both of the supreme and inferior Courts, shall hold their Offices during good Behaviour, and shall, at stated Times, receive for their Services, a Compensation, which shall not be diminished during their Continuance in Office.

Section 2

1. The judicial Power shall extend to all Cases, in Law and Equity, arising under this Constitution, the Laws of the United States, and Treaties made, or

which shall be made, under their Authority;—to all Cases affecting Ambassadors, other public Ministers and Consuls;—to all Cases of admiralty and maritime Jurisdiction;—to Controversies to which the United States shall be a Party;—to Controversies between two or more States;—between a State and Citizens of another State;[10]—between Citizens of different States,—between Citizens of the same State claiming Lands under Grants of different States, and between a State, or the Citizens thereof, and foreign States, Citizens or Subjects.

2. In all Cases affecting Ambassadors, other public Ministers and Consuls, and those in which a State shall be Party, the supreme Court shall have original Jurisdiction. In all the other Cases before mentioned, the supreme Court shall have appellate Jurisdiction, both as to Law and Fact, with such Exceptions, and under such Regulations as the Congress shall make.

3. The Trial of all Crimes, except in Cases of Impeachment, shall be by Jury; and such Trial shall be held in the State where the said Crimes shall have been committed; but when not committed within any State, the Trial shall be at such Place or Places as the Congress may by Law have directed.

Section 3

1. Treason against the United States, shall consist only in levying War against them, or in adhering to their Enemies, giving them Aid and Comfort. No Person shall be convicted of Treason unless on the Testimony of two Witnesses to the same overt Act, or on Confession in open Court.

2. The Congress shall have Power to declare the Punishment of Treason, but no Attainder of Treason shall work Corruption of Blood, or Forfeiture except during the Life of the Person attainted.

Article IV

Section 1

Full Faith and Credit shall be given in each State to the public Acts, Records, and judicial Proceedings of every other State. And the Congress may by general Laws prescribe the Manner in which such Acts, Records and Proceedings shall be proved, and the Effect thereof.

Section 2

1. The Citizens of each State shall be entitled to all Privileges and Immunities of Citizens in the several States.

2. A Person charged in any State with Treason, Felony, or other Crime, who shall flee from Justice, and be found in another State, shall on Demand of the executive Authority of the State from which he fled, be delivered up, to be removed to the State having Jurisdiction of the Crime.

3. No Person held to Service or Labour in one State, under the Laws thereof, escaping into another, shall, in Consequence of any Law or Regulation therein, be discharged from such Service or Labour, but shall be delivered up on Claim of the Party to whom such Service or Labour may be due.

Section 3

1. New States may be admitted by the Congress into this Union; but no new State shall be formed or erected within the Jurisdiction of any other State; nor any State be formed by the Junction of two or more States, or Parts of States, without the Consent of the Legislatures of the States concerned as well as of the Congress.

2. The Congress shall have Power to dispose of and make all needful Rules and Regulations respecting the Territory or other Property belonging to the United States; and nothing in this Constitution shall be so construed as to Prejudice any Claims of the United States, or of any particular State.

Section 4

The United States shall guarantee to every State in this Union a Republican Form of Government, and shall protect each of them against Invasion; and on Application of the Legislature, or of the Executive (when the Legislature cannot be convened) against domestic Violence.

Article V

The Congress, whenever two thirds of both Houses shall deem it necessary, shall propose Amendments to this Constitution, or, on the Application of the Legislatures of two thirds of the several States, shall call a Convention for proposing Amendments, which, in either Case, shall be valid to all Intents and Purposes, as Part of this Constitution, when ratified by the Legislatures of three fourths of the several States, or by Conventions in three fourths thereof, as the one or the other Mode of Ratification may be proposed by the Congress; Provided that no Amendment which may be made prior to the Year One thousand eight hundred and eight shall in any Manner affect the first and fourth Clauses in the Ninth Section of the first Article; and that no State, without its Consent, shall be deprived of its equal Suffrage in the Senate.

Article VI

1. All Debts contracted and Engagements entered into, before the Adoption of this Constitution, shall be as valid against the United States under this Constitution, as under the Confederation.

2. This Constitution, and the Laws of the United States which shall be made in Pursuance thereof; and all Treaties made, or which shall be made, under the Authority of the United States, shall be the supreme Law of the Land; and the

Judges in every State shall be bound thereby, any Thing in the Constitution or Laws of any State to the Contrary notwithstanding.

3. The Senators and Representatives before mentioned, and the Members of the several State Legislatures, and all executive and judicial Officers, both of the United States and of the several States, shall be bound by Oath or Affirmation, to support this Constitution; but no religious Test shall ever be required as a Qualification to any Office or public Trust under the United States.

Article VII

The Ratification of the Conventions of nine States, shall be sufficient for the Establishment of this Constitution between the States so ratifying the Same.

* * *

Amendment I

Congress shall make no law respecting an establishment of religion, or prohibiting the free exercise thereof; or abridging the freedom of speech, or of the press; or the right of the people peaceably to assemble, and to petition the Government for a redress of grievances.

Amendment II

A well regulated Militia, being necessary to the security of a free State, the right of the people to keep and bear Arms, shall not be infringed.

Amendment III

No Soldier shall, in time of peace be quartered in any house, without the consent of the Owner, nor in time of war, but in a manner to be prescribed by law.

Amendment IV

The right of the people to be secure in their persons, houses, papers, and effects, against unreasonable searches and seizures, shall not be violated, and no Warrants shall issue, but upon probable cause, supported by Oath or affirmation, and particularly describing the place to be searched, and the persons or things to be seized.

Amendment V

No person shall be held to answer for a capital, or otherwise infamous crime, unless on a presentment or indictment of a Grand Jury, except in cases arising in the land or naval forces, or in the Militia, when in actual service in time of War or public danger; nor shall any person be subject for the same offence to be twice put in jeopardy of life or limb; nor shall be compelled in any criminal case to be a witness against himself, nor be deprived of life, liberty, or property, without due process of law; nor shall private property be taken for public use, without just compensation.

Amendment VI

In all criminal prosecutions, the accused shall enjoy the right to a speedy and public trial, by an impartial jury of the State and district wherein the crime shall have been committed, which district shall have been previously ascertained by law, and to be informed of the nature and cause of the accusation; to be confronted with the witnesses against him; to have compulsory process for obtaining witnesses in his favor, and to have the Assistance of Counsel for his defence.

Amendment VII

In Suits at common law, where the value in controversy shall exceed twenty dollars, the right of trial by jury shall be preserved, and no fact tried by a jury, shall be otherwise re-examined in any Court of the United States, than according to the rules of the common law.

Amendment VIII

Excessive bail shall not be required, nor excessive fines imposed, nor cruel and unusual punishments inflicted.

Amendment IX

The enumeration in the Constitution, of certain rights, shall not be construed to deny or disparage others retained by the people.

Amendment X

The powers not delegated to the United States by the Constitution, nor prohibited by it to the States, are reserved to the States respectively, or to the people.

Amendment XI

The Judicial power of the United States shall not be construed to extend to any suit in law or equity, commenced or prosecuted against one of the United States by Citizens of another State, or by Citizens or Subjects of any Foreign State.

Amendment XII

The Electors shall meet in their respective states, and vote by ballot for President and Vice-President, one of whom, at least, shall not be an inhabitant of the same state with themselves; they shall name in their ballots the person voted for as President, and in distinct ballots the person voted for as Vice-President, and they shall make distinct lists of all persons voted for as President, and of all persons voted for as Vice-President, and of the number of votes for each, which lists they shall sign and certify, and transmit sealed to the seat of the government of the United States, directed to the President of the Senate;—The President of the Senate shall, in the presence of the Senate and House of Representatives, open all the certificates and the votes shall then be counted;—The person having the greatest number of votes for President, shall be the President, if such number be a majority of the whole number of Electors appointed; and if no person have such majority, then from the persons having the highest numbers not exceeding three on the list of those voted for as President, the House of Representatives shall choose immediately, by ballot, the President. But in choosing the President, the votes shall be taken by states, the representation from each state having one vote; a quorum for this purpose shall consist of a member or members from two-thirds of the states, and a majority of all the states shall be necessary to a choice. And if the House of Representatives shall not choose a President whenever the right of choice shall devolve upon them, before the fourth day of March next following, then the Vice-President shall act as President, as in the case of the death or other constitutional disability of the President.—The person having the greatest number of votes as Vice-President, shall be the Vice-President, if such number be a majority of the whole number of Electors appointed, and if no person have a majority, then from the two highest numbers on the list, the Senate shall choose the Vice-President; a quorum for the purpose shall consist of two-thirds of the whole number of Senators, and a majority of the whole number shall be necessary to a choice. But no person constitutionally ineligible to the office of President shall be eligible to that of Vice-President of the United States.

Amendment XIII

Section 1

Neither slavery nor involuntary servitude, except as a punishment for crime whereof the party shall have been duly convicted, shall exist within the United States, or any place subject to their jurisdiction.

Section 2

Congress shall have power to enforce this article by appropriate legislation.

Amendment XIV

Section 1

All persons born or naturalized in the United States, and subject to the jurisdiction thereof, are citizens of the United States and of the State wherein they reside. No State shall make or enforce any law which shall abridge the privileges or immunities of citizens of the United States; nor shall any State deprive any person of life, liberty, or property, without due process of law; nor deny to any person within its jurisdiction the equal protection of the laws.

Section 2

Representatives shall be apportioned among the several States according to their respective numbers, counting the whole number of persons in each State, excluding Indians not taxed. But when the right to vote at any election for the choice of electors for President and Vice President of the United States, Representatives in Congress, the Executive and Judicial officers of a State, or the members of the Legislature thereof, is denied to any of the male inhabitants of such State, being twenty-one years of age, and citizens of the United States, or in any way abridged, except for participation in rebellion, or other crime, the basis of representation therein shall be reduced in the proportion which the number of such male citizens shall bear to the whole number of male citizens twenty-one years of age in such State.

Section 3

No person shall be a Senator or Representative in Congress, or elector of President and Vice President, or hold any office, civil or military, under the United States, or under any State, who, having previously taken an oath, as a member of Congress, or as an officer of the United States, or as a member of any State legislature, or as an executive or judicial officer of any State, to support the Constitution of the United States, shall have engaged in insurrection or rebellion against the same, or given aid or comfort to the enemies thereof. But Congress may by a vote of two-thirds of each House, remove such disability.

Section 4

The validity of the public debt of the United States, authorized by law, including debts incurred for payment of pensions and bounties for services in suppressing insurrection or rebellion, shall not be questioned. But neither the United States nor any State shall assume or pay any debt or obligation incurred in aid of insurrection or rebellion against the United States, or any claim for the loss or emancipation of any slave; but all such debts, obligations and claims shall be held illegal and void.

Section 5

The Congress shall have power to enforce, by appropriate legislation, the provisions of this article.

Amendment XV

Section 1

The right of citizens of the United States to vote shall not be denied or abridged by the United States or by any State on account of race, color, or previous condition of servitude.

Section 2

The Congress shall have power to enforce this article by appropriate legislation.

Amendment XVI

The Congress shall have power to lay and collect taxes on incomes, from whatever source derived, without apportionment among the several States, and without regard to any census or enumeration.

Amendment XVII

Section 1

The Senate of the United States shall be composed of two Senators from each State, elected by the people thereof, for six years; and each Senator shall have one vote. The electors in each State shall have the qualifications requisite for electors of the most numerous branch of the State legislatures.

Section 2

When vacancies happen in the representation of any State in the Senate, the executive authority of such State shall issue writs of election to fill such vacancies: Provided, That the legislature of any State may empower the executive thereof to make temporary appointments until the people fill the vacancies by election as the legislature may direct.

Section 3

This amendment shall not be so construed as to affect the election or term of any Senator chosen before it becomes valid as part of the Constitution.

Amendment XVIII

Section 1

After one year from the ratification of this article the manufacture, sale, or transportation of intoxicating liquors within, the importation thereof into, or the exportation thereof from the United States and all territory subject to the jurisdiction thereof for beverage purposes is hereby prohibited.

Section 2

The Congress and the several States shall have concurrent power to enforce this article by appropriate legislation.

Section 3

This article shall be inoperative unless it shall have been ratified as an amendment to the Constitution by the legislatures of the several States, as provided in the Constitution, within seven years from the date of the submission hereof to the States by the Congress.

Amendment XIX

Section 1

The right of citizens of the United States to vote shall not be denied or abridged by the United States or by any State on account of sex.

Section 2

Congress shall have power to enforce this article by appropriate legislation.

Amendment XX

Section 1

The terms of the President and Vice President shall end at noon on the 20th day of January, and the terms of Senators and Representatives at noon on the 3d day of January, of the years in which such terms would have ended if this article had not been ratified; and the terms of their successors shall then begin.

Section 2

The Congress shall assemble at least once in every year, and such meeting shall begin at noon on the 3d day of January, unless they shall by law appoint a different day.

Section 3

If, at the time fixed for the beginning of the term of the President, the President elect shall have died, the Vice President elect shall become President. If a President shall not have been chosen before the time fixed for the beginning of his term, or if the President elect shall have failed to qualify, then the Vice President elect shall act as President until a President shall have qualified; and the Congress may by law provide for the case wherein neither a President elect nor a Vice President elect shall have qualified, declaring who shall then act as President, or the manner in which one who is to act shall be selected, and such person shall act accordingly until a President or Vice President shall have qualified.

Section 4

The Congress may by law provide for the case of the death of any of the persons from whom the House of Representatives may choose a President whenever the right of choice shall have devolved upon them, and for the case of the death of any of the persons from whom the Senate may choose a Vice President whenever the right of choice shall have devolved upon them.

Section 5

Sections 1 and 2 shall take effect on the 15th day of October following the ratification of this article.

Section 6

This article shall be inoperative unless it shall have been ratified as an amendment to the Constitution by the legislatures of three-fourths of the several States within seven years from the date of its submission.

Amendment XXI

Section 1

The eighteenth article of amendment to the Constitution of the United States is hereby repealed.

Section 2

The transportation or importation into any State, Territory, or possession of the United States for delivery or use therein of intoxicating liquors, in violation of the laws thereof, is hereby prohibited.

Section 3

This article shall be inoperative unless it shall have been ratified as an amendment to the Constitution by conventions in the several States, as provided in the Constitution, within seven years from the date of the submission hereof to the States by the Congress.

Amendment XXII

Section 1

No person shall be elected to the office of the President more than twice, and no person who has held the office of President, or acted as President, for more than two years of a term to which some other person was elected President shall be elected to the office of the President more than once. But this article shall not apply to any person holding the office of President when this article was proposed by the Congress, and shall not prevent any person who may be holding the office of President, or acting as President, during the term within which this article becomes operative from holding the office of President or acting as President during the remainder of such term.

Section 2

This article shall be inoperative unless it shall have been ratified as an amendment to the Constitution by the legislatures of three-fourths of the several states within seven years from the date of its submission to the states by the Congress.

Amendment XXIII

Section 1

The District constituting the seat of government of the United States shall appoint in such manner as the Congress may direct: A number of electors of President and Vice President equal to the whole number of Senators and Representatives in Congress to which the District would be entitled if it were a state, but in no event more than the least populous state; they shall be in addition to those appointed by the states, but they shall be considered, for the purposes of the election of President and Vice President, to be electors appointed by a state; and they shall meet in the District and perform such duties as provided by the twelfth article of amendment.

Section 2

The Congress shall have power to enforce this article by appropriate legislation.

Amendment XXIV

Section 1

The right of citizens of the United States to vote in any primary or other election for President or Vice President, for electors for President or Vice President, or for Senator or Representative in Congress, shall not be denied or abridged by the United States or any state by reason of failure to pay any poll tax or other tax.

Section 2

The Congress shall have power to enforce this article by appropriate legislation.

Amendment XXV

Section 1

In case of the removal of the President from office or of his death or resignation, the Vice President shall become President.

Section 2

Whenever there is a vacancy in the office of the Vice President, the President shall nominate a Vice President who shall take office upon confirmation by a majority vote of both Houses of Congress.

Section 3

Whenever the President transmits to the President pro tempore of the Senate and the Speaker of the House of Representatives his written declaration that he is unable to discharge the powers and duties of his office, and until he transmits to them a written declaration to the contrary, such powers and duties shall be discharged by the Vice President as Acting President.

Section 4

Whenever the Vice President and a majority of either the principal officers of the executive departments or of such other body as Congress may by law provide, transmit to the President pro tempore of the Senate and the Speaker of the House of Representatives their written declaration that the President is unable to discharge the powers and duties of his office, the Vice President shall immediately assume the powers and duties of the office as Acting President.

Thereafter, when the President transmits to the President pro tempore of the Senate and the Speaker of the House of Representatives his written declaration that no inability exists, he shall resume the powers and duties of his office unless the Vice President and a majority of either the principal officers of the executive department or of such other body as Congress may by law provide, transmit within four days to the President pro tempore of the Senate and the Speaker of the House of Representatives their written declaration that the President is unable to discharge the powers and duties of his office. Thereupon Congress shall decide the issue, assembling within forty-eight hours for that purpose if not in session. If the Congress, within twenty-one days after receipt of the latter written declaration, or, if Congress is not in session, within twenty-one days after Congress is required to assemble, determines by two-thirds vote of both Houses that the President is unable to discharge the powers and duties of his office, the Vice President shall continue to discharge the same as Acting President; otherwise, the President shall resume the powers and duties of his office.

Amendment XXVI

Section 1

The right of citizens of the United States, who are 18 years of age or older, to vote, shall not be denied or abridged by the United States or any state on account of age.

Section 2

The Congress shall have the power to enforce this article by appropriate legislation.

Amendment XXVII

No law varying the compensation for the services of the Senators and Representatives shall take effect until an election of Representatives shall have intervened.

PART II

THE FEDERAL JUDICIAL POWER

CHAPTER 3
THE POWER OF JUDICIAL REVIEW

A. Introduction

Though the Constitution plays a significant role in protecting individual rights, its central object is to divide and allocate governmental power. It does this principally along two dimensions. The first is that of *federalism*, the division of authority between the national government and the states. In our constitutional system, the federal government and the states constitute independent sovereigns. They operate independently of one another, with distinct bases for their authority to govern. American residents and citizens (and the territory within each state) are simultaneously governed by two distinct governments, neither of which is fully controlled by the other. Under the Supremacy Clause of Article VI, when valid federal and state laws conflict, a court must apply the federal law. But the scope of federal power is limited to that authority specified (or "enumerated") in the Constitution. Thus, though the federal government is supreme within its assigned sphere, that sphere has limits. Those matters not within the federal government's authority are left exclusively to the states.

The second dimension to the division of governmental power is that of separated national powers. The Constitution divides power among the three branches of the federal government: Congress (which exercises the legislative power), the President (who exercises the executive power), and the federal courts (which exercise the judicial power). Each branch is obligated to perform its assigned functions, and none is permitted to unduly interfere with the others.

These two features of our constitutional architecture—federalism and the separation of powers—are perhaps the most foundational attributes of our constitutional system. They were conceived by the Framers as the principal means for protecting individual liberty. As James Madison famously wrote in The Federalist No. 51, "[i]n the compound republic of America, the power surrendered by the people is first divided between two distinct governments, and then the portion allotted to each subdivided among distinct and separate departments. Hence a double security arises to the rights of the people." In an important sense, *every* question concerning the allocation of governmental power in the United States is about federalism, the separation of powers, or both.

We begin the exploration of these issues by examining the powers the Constitution grants to the federal judiciary. In doing so, we necessarily explore the boundaries of the federal judicial power vis-à-vis state judicial systems (matters of federalism) and the other branches of the national government (matters concerning the separation of powers). And the first question we take up is perhaps the most basic: whether the Constitution grants federal courts the power of judicial review.

B.   Reviewing the Acts of Congress or the President

Article III of the Constitution addresses the authority of the federal judiciary. Section 1 of Article III provides as follows:

> "The judicial power of the United States, shall be vested in one Supreme Court, and in such inferior courts as the Congress may from time to time ordain and establish. The judges, both of the supreme and inferior courts, shall hold their offices during good behaviour, and shall, at stated times, receive for their services, a compensation, which shall not be diminished during their continuance in office."

This paragraph does four important things: (1) it mandates the existence of the Supreme Court; (2) it grants Congress the authority to create lower federal courts (if it so desires); (3) it invests federal courts with "[t]he judicial power of the United States"; and (4) by guaranteeing that federal judges shall "hold their offices during good behavior" (and protecting their salaries from being reduced), it effectively grants those judges life tenure.

Section 2 of Article III specifies the "cases" and "controversies" the federal courts are empowered to decide, and further defines the original and appellate jurisdictions of the Supreme Court:

> "The judicial power shall extend to all cases, in law and equity, arising under this Constitution, the laws of the United States, and treaties made, or which shall be made, under their authority;—to all cases affecting ambassadors, other public ministers and consuls;—to all cases of admiralty and maritime jurisdiction;—to controversies to which the United States shall be a party;—to controversies between two or more states;—between a state and citizens of another state;—between citizens of different states;—between citizens of the same state claiming lands under grants of different states, and between a state, or the citizens thereof, and foreign states, citizens or subjects.

> "In all cases affecting ambassadors, other public ministers and consuls, and those in which a state shall be party, the Supreme Court shall have original jurisdiction. In all the other cases before mentioned, the Supreme Court shall have appellate jurisdiction, both as to law and fact, with such exceptions, and under such regulations as the Congress shall make."

Chapter 4 will explore the details of the federal judiciary's subject matter jurisdiction. Here we take up a question that traditionally comes first: if a case is filed in federal court in which one of the litigants asserts that a federal statute is invalid (at least as applied to her), may the court declare that the statute (again, at least as applied to the claimant) is unconstitutional? And if the President or one of his agents (such as the Secretary of State) takes action that a litigant claims violates federal law, may a federal court hold that the President or his agent has acted unlawfully?

These questions are critical to the role of the federal courts in our constitutional system—and particularly to whether the judiciary might act as a check on the other branches. It is therefore somewhat surprising that they were not expressly addressed in the text of the Constitution. Given the centrality of these questions, though, it was not long after the Constitution's ratification that they came to the Supreme Court. And Court's pronouncements on these questions occurred in what is arguably the single most famous decision in American law, *Marbury v. Madison*, 5 U.S. (1 Cranch) 137 (1803). The fame of *Marbury* is attributable to the principle for which it has come to stand: that the federal judiciary has the authority to adjudge acts of Congress and the President unconstitutional (or otherwise unlawful). This is the power of *judicial review*.

Marbury was the first decision in which the Supreme Court explicitly asserted and defended the power of judicial review. For this reason, it has become an icon of American law. It is important to note, though, that by 1803 judicial review (though not uncontroversial) had been accepted by many American jurists and political actors. Indeed, the Supreme Court had effectively invalidated a federal statute a few years earlier in an unpublished opinion. And in another case prior to *Marbury*, the justices had upheld a federal statute against a challenge to its constitutionality—a holding that presumed the Court's power to rule the other way.

In many respects, what is most extraordinary about *Marbury* is its backstory, the political and historical context in which the Court exercised this power. That backstory reveals as much about the brilliance of Chief Justice John Marshall—and the Court's practical weakness in the early years of the Republic—as it does about the role of the federal judiciary in our constitutional system.

C. *Marbury v. Madison*

George Washington was the nation's first President, and he enjoyed nearly universal adoration. While he remained in office, political differences about the direction of the nation—that is, normal politics—remained somewhat muted. But those differences were simmering. And when Washington decided not to seek a third term in 1796, they emerged forcefully.

To oversimplify a bit, there were two predominant, competing schools of political thought in the late 1790s: the Federalists (led by John Adams, Alexander Hamilton, and John Marshall) and the Republicans (or the Democratic Republicans, led by Thomas Jefferson and James Madison). The Federalists generally favored stronger, more centralized national power. And the federal courts were a critical aspect of this potential national power, as the courts were perceived as the only national institution (at least at that time) capable of effectively constraining the centrifugal tendencies of the states. The Jeffersonian Republicans, by contrast, believed in the greater diffusion and decentralization of power: more state autonomy and a smaller national government.

Adams defeated Jefferson in the presidential election in 1796. But according to Article II of the original Constitution, the person receiving the second-most votes in the electoral college became Vice President. Jefferson thus became Vice President. And he, along with James Madison, opposed and undermined Adams throughout his presidency, diluting the effectiveness of his administration whenever possible. The political sniping was nasty. Indeed, the Federalist Congress enacted the infamous Alien and Sedition Acts of 1798, and the Adams administration jailed many Republicans for criticizing the government. Adams then faced Jefferson again in the presidential election of 1800, and Aaron Burr effectively ran as Jefferson's running mate.

Jefferson defeated Adams soundly in their rematch, but he tied with Burr in the electoral college. Again, Article II at that time provided that each elector was entitled to two votes for President, and that the candidate with the second-most electoral votes became Vice President. Thus, all of the presidential electors who sided with the Republicans voted both for Jefferson and Burr, resulting in a tie. (Apparently there had been a plan for one Republican elector to abstain from voting for Burr with his second ballot, but the plan was botched. The episode led Congress to propose the Twelfth Amendment, calling for separate electoral college ballots for President and Vice President, which was ratified in 1804.) In February 1801, the House of Representatives—still controlled by the Federalists, as the new Congress would not convene until December 1801—ultimately decided the election in favor of Jefferson, though it took 36 ballots to do so.

Meanwhile, President Adams's term was set to expire at midnight on March 3, 1801. This left some time—though not much—for the Federalists to attempt to entrench themselves and their policies. They would soon lose control of the White House, the Senate, and the House of Representatives, all of which would go to Jeffersonian Republicans. Thus, Adams and the Federalists moved to consolidate their power in the one branch through which they might still exert power: the judiciary.

On January 20, 1801—six weeks before leaving office—Adams nominated John Marshall, then Secretary of State, to be the next Chief Justice. The Federalist-controlled Senate confirmed Marshall, and he took the oath of office on February 4, 1801. On February 13, the still-Federalist-controlled Congress passed the Circuit Courts Act. The Act established six federal courts of appeals—and sixteen new appellate judgeships to staff those six courts. Until this point, there had been no federal courts of appeals; appeals taken from the judgments of district courts were heard by *ad hoc* groups of district court judges and Supreme Court justices. President Adams quickly nominated sixteen Federalists to fill these new judgeships, and the Senate confirmed them on March 2, 1801, the penultimate day of Adams's presidency. The Circuit Courts Act also reduced the size of the Supreme Court from six to five justices but made that change effective upon the retirement of the next justice, prospectively depriving President Jefferson of an appointment to the Court. (Justice Cushing, a Federalist, was ill and likely to retire or die in the near future.)

Finally, on February 27, 1801—five days before the expiration of Adams' term—Congress enacted the Organic Act of the District of Columbia. This statute authorized the President to appoint magistrates for the newly created District of Columbia. (The nation's capital was initially located in New York and Philadelphia before moving to Washington in 1800.) Adams nominated 42 such magistrates, all of whom were confirmed by the Senate on March 3, Adams's last day in office.

The commissions—the documents formally stating that the magistrates were entitled to their appointments—were made out in the office of the Secretary of State, occupied then (still) by John Marshall. (Marshall was serving both as Chief Justice and Secretary of State for the last four weeks of Adams's presidency.) President Adams signed the commissions, and Marshall affixed to them the official seal of the United States. But when the clock struck midnight, four of the 42 commissions had not yet been delivered to the magistrates-to-be. One of the four undelivered commissions belonged to a staunch Federalist named William Marbury. And when Jefferson took office the next day, he ordered his administration *not* to deliver those four undelivered commissions.

After waiting eight months without receiving his commission, Marbury filed suit against the Secretary of State, James Madison, on December 12, 1801. What is more—and this is critical to understanding the case—Marbury filed his complaint *directly* in the Supreme Court of the United States as an *original* action. The remedy he sought was a writ of mandamus compelling Madison to deliver his commission.

At an initial hearing in December 1801, the Supreme Court issued to Madison an order to "show cause"—effectively, an order to the Jefferson administration to explain why it had not delivered Marbury's commission. The Court thus scheduled the case for oral argument during the Court's 1802 term. Before that argument could take place, however, the Jeffersonian Republicans—now in control of both houses of Congress and the White House—acted to unwind much of the Federalists' work.

First, the Republicans repealed the Circuit Courts Act. In doing so, they reestablished the old circuit court system and completely eliminated the sixteen new judgeships that President Adams had filled with Federalist jurists. Given that Article III seems to grant federal judges life tenure, and that the sole method for removing federal judges prescribed in the Constitution is through impeachment, there were significant doubts about whether this statutory elimination of the judgeships was constitutional.

Concerned that the Supreme Court might declare this Repeal Act unconstitutional—and uncertain about what Chief Justice Marshall might do in the *Marbury* case now pending at the Court—the Republican Congress also enacted a statute canceling the 1802 term of the Supreme Court. As a result, the Court was not legally permitted to convene again until February 1803, fourteen months after Marbury had filed his suit.

Further, a week before the Supreme Court reconvened in February 1803, the House of Representatives initiated impeachment proceedings against a Federalist U.S. district court judge in New Hampshire, John Pickering, who had been appointed by President Adams. Judge Pickering was an alcoholic, and probably mentally ill, so there were nonpartisan reasons for his removal from office. But the Republicans were deliberately sending Federalist judges (and justices) a message, one that was only partially veiled: they needed to mind themselves. Many Republicans were already stating publicly that Supreme Court justices—including Chief Justice Marshall—would be next on the impeachment block once Pickering had been removed from office.

The specific legal question presented in *Marbury v. Madison* was whether William Marbury was entitled to an order from the Supreme Court requiring the Secretary of State, James Madison, to deliver his commission to become a justice of the peace for the District of Columbia. The Court's ultimate answer was no. Marbury *lost* the case. Madison (and the Jefferson administration) prevailed, at least as a formal legal matter. The Supreme Court concluded that it lacked jurisdiction over the action and thus dismissed Marbury's suit.

But this nominal outcome is not why *Marbury v. Madison* is remembered. *Marbury* has become an icon of American law because it stands for the proposition that the federal judiciary possesses the power of judicial review—the power to declare acts of Congress and the Executive Branch unconstitutional. And what makes *Marbury* a truly great case is the cunning Marshall deployed in reaching this result. It is Marshall's deft maneuvering, in the face of danger from all sides, that renders *Marbury* perhaps the greatest decision in all of American law.

As you read the opinion, please consider the following questions:

1. Did the Supreme Court hold that the Jefferson administration (and specifically, Secretary of State Madison) had acted lawfully in withholding Marbury's commission from him? Why or why not?

2. What did the Court say in *Marbury* about the judiciary's authority to declare an action of the Executive Branch unlawful?

3. Did the Judiciary Act of 1789 grant the Supreme Court subject matter jurisdiction over Marbury's action? Why or why not? Why do you suppose Chief Justice Marshall interpreted the Judiciary Act as he did?

4. On what basis, precisely, did the Court conclude that the Judiciary Act (at least as applied in Marbury's case) was inconsistent with the Constitution?

5. What was the Court's rationale for concluding that the Constitution gives the federal judiciary the authority to decide that an act of Congress is unconstitutional, and thus not apply it in a given case? Do you find the Court's rationale convincing?

To understand the legal arguments in *Marbury*, one important detail needs elaboration. Article III, §2, clause 2 of the Constitution provides that "[i]n all cases affecting ambassadors, other public ministers and consuls, and those in which a state shall be party, the Supreme Court shall have original jurisdiction." Neither William Marbury nor James Madison was a "public minister" or "consul" within the meaning of this provision. As all agreed, these terms (at least as used in Article III) only encompass officials of *foreign* governments.

Marbury v. Madison
5 U.S. (1 Cranch) 137 (1803)

Mr. CHIEF JUSTICE MARSHALL delivered the opinion of the Court.

The peculiar delicacy of this case, the novelty of some of its circumstances, and the real difficulty attending the points which occur in it require a complete exposition of the principles on which the opinion to be given by the Court is founded. In the order in which the Court has viewed this subject, the following questions have been considered and decided.

1. Has the applicant a right to the commission he demands?

2. If he has a right, and that right has been violated, do the laws of his country afford him a remedy?

3. If they do afford him a remedy, is it a mandamus issuing from this court?

1. Has the applicant a right to the commission he demands?

It appears from the affidavits that, in compliance with this law, a commission for William Marbury as a justice of peace for the County of Washington was signed by John Adams, then President of the United States, after which the seal of the United States was affixed to it, but the commission has never reached the person for whom it was made out. . . . The transmission of the commission is a practice directed by convenience, but not by law. It cannot therefore be necessary to constitute the appointment, which must precede it and which is the mere act of the President. . . . It is therefore decidedly the opinion of the Court that, when a commission has been signed by the President, the appointment is made, and that the commission is complete when the seal of the United States has been affixed to it by the Secretary of State. . . . Mr. Marbury, then, since his commission was signed by the President and sealed by the Secretary of State, was appointed, and as the law creating the office gave the officer a right to hold for five years independent of the Executive, the appointment was not revocable, but vested in the officer legal rights which are protected by the laws of his country. To withhold the commission, therefore, is an act deemed by the Court not warranted by law, but violative of a vested legal right.

2. If he has a right, and that right has been violated, do the laws of his country afford him a remedy?

The very essence of civil liberty certainly consists in the right of every individual to claim the protection of the laws whenever he receives an injury. One of the first duties of government is to afford that protection. . . . Blackstone states two cases in which a remedy is afforded by mere operation of law. "In all other cases," he says, "it is a general and indisputable rule that where there is a legal right, there is also a legal remedy by suit or action at law whenever that right is invaded."

The Government of the United States has been emphatically termed a government of laws, and not of men. It will certainly cease to deserve this high appellation if the laws furnish no remedy for the violation of a vested legal right. . . . It behooves us, then, to inquire whether there be in its composition any ingredient which shall exempt from legal investigation or exclude the injured party from legal redress.

[T]he question whether the legality of an act of the head of a department be examinable in a court of justice or not must always depend on the nature of that act. . . . By the Constitution of the United States, the President is invested with certain important political powers, in the exercise of which he is to use his own discretion, and is accountable only to his country in his political character and to his own conscience. To aid him in the performance of these duties, he is authorized to appoint certain officers, who act by his authority and in conformity with his orders.

In such cases, their acts are his acts; and whatever opinion may be entertained of the manner in which executive discretion may be used, still there exists, and can exist, no power to control that discretion. The subjects are political. They respect the nation, not individual rights, and, being entrusted to the Executive, the decision of the Executive is conclusive. . . . But when the Legislature proceeds to impose on that officer other duties; when he is directed peremptorily to perform certain acts; when the rights of individuals are dependent on the performance of those acts; he is so far the officer of the law, is amenable to the laws for his conduct, and cannot at his discretion, sport away the vested rights of others.

The conclusion from this reasoning is that, where the heads of departments are the political or confidential agents of the Executive, merely to execute the will of the President, or rather to act in cases in which the Executive possesses a constitutional or legal discretion, nothing can be more perfectly clear than that their acts are only politically examinable. But where a specific duty is assigned by law, and individual rights depend upon the performance of that duty, it seems equally clear that the individual who considers himself injured has a right to resort to the laws of his country for a remedy. . . .

It is then the opinion of the Court:

1. That, by signing the commission of Mr. Marbury, the President of the United States appointed him a justice of peace for the County of Washington in the District of Columbia, and that the seal of the United States, affixed thereto by the Secretary of State, is conclusive testimony of the verity of the signature, and of the completion of the appointment, and that the appointment conferred on him a legal right to the office for the space of five years.

2. That, having this legal title to the office, he has a consequent right to the commission, a refusal to deliver which is a plain violation of that right, for which the laws of his country afford him a remedy.

It remains to be inquired whether,

3. He is entitled to the remedy for which he applies. This depends on:

1. The nature of the writ applied for, and

2. The power of this court.

1. The nature of the writ.

Blackstone, in the third volume of his Commentaries, page 110, defines a mandamus to be "a command issuing in the King's name from the Court of King's Bench, and directed to any person, corporation, or inferior court of judicature within the King's dominions requiring them to do some particular thing therein specified which appertains to their office and duty, and which the Court of King's Bench has previously determined, or at least supposes, to be consonant to right and justice." . . .

Still, to render the mandamus a proper remedy, the officer to whom it is to be directed must be one to whom, on legal principles, such writ may be directed, and the person applying for it must be without any other specific and legal remedy. . . .

The province of the Court is solely to decide on the rights of individuals, not to inquire how the Executive or Executive officers perform duties in which they have a discretion. Questions, in their nature political or which are, by the Constitution and laws, submitted to the Executive, can never be made in this court.

But, if this be not such a question; if so far from being an intrusion into the secrets of the cabinet, it respects a paper which, according to law, is upon record, and to a copy of which the law gives a right, on the payment of ten cents; if it be no intermeddling with a subject over which the Executive can be considered as having exercised any control; what is there in the exalted station of the officer which shall bar a citizen from asserting in a court of justice his legal rights, or shall forbid a court to listen to the claim or to issue a mandamus directing the performance of a duty not depending on Executive discretion, but on particular acts of Congress and the general principles of law?

If one of the heads of departments commits any illegal act under colour of his office by which an individual sustains an injury, it cannot be pretended that his office alone exempts him from being sued in the ordinary mode of proceeding, and being compelled to obey the judgment of the law. How then can his office exempt him from this particular mode of deciding on the legality of his conduct if the case be such a case as would, were any other individual the party complained of, authorize the process?

It is not by the office of the person to whom the writ is directed, but the nature of the thing to be done, that the propriety or impropriety of issuing a mandamus is to be determined. Where the head of a department . . . is directed by law to do a certain act affecting the absolute rights of individuals, in the performance of which he is not placed under the particular direction of the President, and the performance of which the President cannot lawfully forbid, and therefore is never presumed to have forbidden . . . , it is not perceived on what ground the Courts of the country are further excused from the duty of giving judgment that right to be done to an injured individual than if the same services were to be performed by a person not the head of a department. . . .

This, then, is a plain case of a mandamus, either to deliver the commission or a copy of it from the record, and it only remains to be inquired:

Whether it can issue from this Court.

The act to establish the judicial courts of the United States authorizes the Supreme Court "to issue writs of mandamus, in cases warranted by the principles and usages of law, to any courts appointed, or persons holding office, under the authority of the United States."

The Secretary of State, being a person, holding an office under the authority of the United States, is precisely within the letter of the description, and if this Court is not authorized to issue a writ of mandamus to such an officer, it must be because the law is unconstitutional, and therefore absolutely incapable of conferring the authority and assigning the duties which its words purport to confer and assign.

The Constitution vests the whole judicial power of the United States in one Supreme Court, and such inferior courts as Congress shall, from time to time, ordain and establish. This power is expressly extended to all cases arising under the laws of the United States; and consequently, in some form, may be exercised over the present case, because the right claimed is given by a law of the United States.

In the distribution of this power, it is declared that "The Supreme Court shall have original jurisdiction in all cases affecting ambassadors, other public ministers and consuls, and those in which a state shall be a party. In all other cases, the Supreme Court shall have appellate jurisdiction."

It has been insisted at the bar, that, as the original grant of jurisdiction to the Supreme and inferior courts is general, and the clause assigning original jurisdiction to the Supreme Court contains no negative or restrictive words, the power remains to the Legislature to assign original jurisdiction to that Court in other cases than those specified in the article which has been recited, provided those cases belong to the judicial power of the United States.

If it had been intended to leave it in the discretion of the Legislature to apportion the judicial power between the Supreme and inferior courts according to the will of that body, it would certainly have been useless to have proceeded further than to have defined the judicial power and the tribunals in which it should be vested. The subsequent part of the section is mere surplusage—is entirely without meaning—if such is to be the construction. If Congress remains at liberty to give this court appellate jurisdiction where the Constitution has declared their jurisdiction shall be original, and original jurisdiction where the Constitution has declared it shall be appellate, the distribution of jurisdiction made in the Constitution, is form without substance. . . . It cannot be presumed that any clause in the Constitution is intended to be without effect, and therefore such construction is inadmissible unless the words require it. . . .

When an instrument organizing fundamentally a judicial system divides it into one Supreme and so many inferior courts as the Legislature may ordain and establish, then enumerates its powers, and proceeds so far to distribute them as to define the jurisdiction of the Supreme Court by declaring the cases in which it shall take original jurisdiction, and that in others it shall take appellate jurisdiction, the plain import of the words seems to be that, in one class of cases, its jurisdiction is original, and not appellate; in the other, it is appellate, and not original. If any other construction would render the clause inoperative, that is an additional reason for rejecting such other construction, and for adhering to the obvious meaning.

To enable this court then to issue a mandamus, it must be shown to be an exercise of appellate jurisdiction, or to be necessary to enable them to exercise appellate jurisdiction. . . .

It is the essential criterion of appellate jurisdiction that it revises and corrects the proceedings in a cause already instituted, and does not create that case. Although, therefore, a mandamus may be directed to courts, yet to issue such a writ to an officer for the delivery of a paper is, in effect, the same as to sustain an original action for that paper, and therefore seems not to belong to appellate, but to original jurisdiction. . . .

The authority, therefore, given to the Supreme Court by the act establishing the judicial courts of the United States to issue writs of mandamus to public officers appears not to be warranted by the Constitution, and it becomes necessary to inquire whether a jurisdiction so conferred can be exercised.

The question whether an act repugnant to the Constitution can become the law of the land is a question deeply interesting to the United States, but, happily, not of an intricacy proportioned to its interest. It seems only necessary to recognise certain principles, supposed to have been long and well established, to decide it.

That the people have an original right to establish for their future government such principles as, in their opinion, shall most conduce to their own happiness is the basis on which the whole American fabric has been erected. The exercise of this original right is a very great exertion; nor can it nor ought it to be frequently repeated. The principles, therefore, so established are deemed fundamental. And as the authority from which they proceed, is supreme, and can seldom act, they are designed to be permanent.

This original and supreme will organizes the government and assigns to different departments their respective powers. It may either stop here or establish certain limits not to be transcended by those departments.

The Government of the United States is of the latter description. The powers of the Legislature are defined and limited; and that those limits may not be mistaken or forgotten, the Constitution is written. To what purpose are powers limited, and to what purpose is that limitation committed to writing, if these limits may at any time be passed by those intended to be restrained? The distinction between a government with limited and unlimited powers is abolished if those limits do not confine the persons on whom they are imposed, and if acts prohibited and acts allowed are of equal obligation. It is a proposition too plain to be contested that the Constitution controls any legislative act repugnant to it, or that the Legislature may alter the Constitution by an ordinary act.

Between these alternatives there is no middle ground. The Constitution is either a superior, paramount law, unchangeable by ordinary means, or it is on a level with ordinary legislative acts, and, like other acts, is alterable when the legislature shall please to alter it.

If the former part of the alternative be true, then a legislative act contrary to the Constitution is not law; if the latter part be true, then written Constitutions are absurd attempts on the part of the people to limit a power in its own nature illimitable.

Certainly all those who have framed written Constitutions contemplate them as forming the fundamental and paramount law of the nation, and consequently the theory of every such government must be that an act of the Legislature repugnant to the Constitution is void.

This theory is essentially attached to a written Constitution, and is consequently to be considered by this Court as one of the fundamental principles of our society. It is not, therefore, to be lost sight of in the further consideration of this subject.

If an act of the Legislature repugnant to the Constitution is void, does it, notwithstanding its invalidity, bind the Courts and oblige them to give it effect? Or, in other words, though it be not law, does it constitute a rule as operative as if it was a law? This would be to overthrow in fact what was established in theory, and would seem, at first view, an absurdity too gross to be insisted on. It shall, however, receive a more attentive consideration.

It is emphatically the province and duty of the Judicial Department to say what the law is. Those who apply the rule to particular cases must, of necessity, expound and interpret that rule. If two laws conflict with each other, the Courts must decide on the operation of each.

So, if a law be in opposition to the Constitution, if both the law and the Constitution apply to a particular case, so that the Court must either decide that case conformably to the law, disregarding the Constitution, or conformably to the Constitution, disregarding the law, the Court must determine which of these conflicting rules governs the case. This is of the very essence of judicial duty.

If, then, the Courts are to regard the Constitution, and the Constitution is superior to any ordinary act of the Legislature, the Constitution, and not such ordinary act, must govern the case to which they both apply.

Those, then, who controvert the principle that the Constitution is to be considered in court as a paramount law are reduced to the necessity of maintaining that courts must close their eyes on the Constitution, and see only the law.

This doctrine would subvert the very foundation of all written Constitutions. It would declare that an act which, according to the principles and theory of our government, is entirely void, is yet, in practice, completely obligatory. It would declare that, if the Legislature shall do what is expressly forbidden, such act, notwithstanding the express prohibition, is in reality effectual. It would be giving to the Legislature a practical and real omnipotence with the same breath which professes to restrict their powers within narrow limits. It is prescribing limits, and declaring that those limits may be passed at pleasure.

That it thus reduces to nothing what we have deemed the greatest improvement on political institutions—a written Constitution, would of itself be sufficient, in America where written Constitutions have been viewed with so much reverence, for rejecting the construction. But the peculiar expressions of the Constitution of the United States furnish additional arguments in favour of its rejection.

The judicial power of the United States is extended to all cases arising under the Constitution.

Could it be the intention of those who gave this power to say that, in using it, the Constitution should not be looked into? That a case arising under the Constitution should be decided without examining the instrument under which it arises?

This is too extravagant to be maintained.

In some cases then, the Constitution must be looked into by the judges. And if they can open it at all, what part of it are they forbidden to read or to obey?

There are many other parts of the Constitution which serve to illustrate this subject.

It is declared that "no tax or duty shall be laid on articles exported from any State." Suppose a duty on the export of cotton, of tobacco, or of flour, and a suit instituted to recover it. Ought judgment to be rendered in such a case? ought the judges to close their eyes on the Constitution, and only see the law?

The Constitution declares that "no bill of attainder or *ex post facto* law shall be passed."

If, however, such a bill should be passed and a person should be prosecuted under it, must the Court condemn to death those victims whom the Constitution endeavours to preserve?

"No person," says the Constitution, "shall be convicted of treason unless on the testimony of two witnesses to the same overt act, or on confession in open court."

Here, the language of the Constitution is addressed especially to the Courts. It prescribes, directly for them, a rule of evidence not to be departed from. If the Legislature should change that rule, and declare one witness, or a confession out of court, sufficient for conviction, must the constitutional principle yield to the legislative act?

From these and many other selections which might be made, it is apparent that the framers of the Constitution contemplated that instrument as a rule for the government of courts, as well as of the Legislature.

Why otherwise does it direct the judges to take an oath to support it? This oath certainly applies in an especial manner to their conduct in their official character. How immoral to impose it on them if they were to be used as the instruments, and the knowing instruments, for violating what they swear to support!

The oath of office, too, imposed by the Legislature, is completely demonstrative of the legislative opinion on this subject. It is in these words: "I do solemnly swear that I will administer justice without respect to persons, and do equal right to the poor and to the rich; and that I will faithfully and impartially discharge all the duties incumbent on me as according to the best of my abilities and understanding, agreeably to the Constitution and laws of the United States."

Why does a judge swear to discharge his duties agreeably to the Constitution of the United States if that Constitution forms no rule for his government? if it is closed upon him and cannot be inspected by him?

If such be the real state of things, this is worse than solemn mockery. To prescribe or to take this oath becomes equally a crime.

It is also not entirely unworthy of observation that, in declaring what shall be the supreme law of the land, the Constitution itself is first mentioned, and not the laws of the United States generally, but those only which shall be made in pursuance of the Constitution, have that rank.

Thus, the particular phraseology of the Constitution of the United States confirms and strengthens the principle, supposed to be essential to all written Constitutions, that a law repugnant to the Constitution is void, and that courts, as well as other departments, are bound by that instrument.

The rule must be discharged.

* * *

Notes on *Marbury v. Madison*

1. *The steps to Marshall's analysis*: Given its significance, it is worth carefully examining each step in the Court's opinion.

a. *Was Marbury entitled to his commission?*: The first question Marshall addressed was whether Marbury was legally entitled to his commission. His answer was yes, because Marbury had been nominated by the President and confirmed by the Senate. The last *material* act was either the signing of the commission by the President or the affixing of the official seal by the Secretary of State. Because President Adams had signed the commission and Marshall himself had affixed the seal, Marbury had a legal right to his commission.[2] Notice also that Marshall jumped straight to the merits, even though he ultimately concluded that the Supreme Court lacked jurisdiction. Was this proper? One could rightly call most of the opinion dicta. But of course, addressing the jurisdictional question first would have deprived Marshall of the

---

[2] Given Marshall's own involvement in this case, you might ask why he did not recuse himself. A good question—Marshall arguably should have stepped aside given that he was essential figure in the underlying dispute.

opportunity to make some important statements about the role of the judiciary—and to declare publicly that the Jefferson administration had acted unlawfully.

b. *Did Marbury have a remedy for the denial of this right?*: Presumptively, Marshall wrote, all violations of law should have a remedy; this is the essence of the rule of law. Nonetheless, Marshall conceded that this is only a presumption, and that there may be cases in which there is no remedy—or at least no *judicial* remedy. According to Marshall, these are cases where the challenged action is a "mere political act," one "belonging to the executive department alone, for the performance of which entire confidence is placed by our constitution in the supreme executive." There is no judicial remedy in these circumstances, either because the law creates no legal entitlement, or because the Constitution vests these decisions in the discretionary judgment of the Executive Branch (ultimately, the President).

These paragraphs in *Marbury* presage the "political questions" doctrine (discussed in Chapter 6). That doctrine's animating idea is that the Constitution vests the resolution of certain constitutional questions exclusively in the elected (or "political") branches. This does not mean there is no remedy whatsoever; it means the matter is not subject to *judicial* scrutiny. If a remedy is available, it must be found elsewhere in our constitutional system.

Did Marbury's claim constitute such a "political question"? No, concluded Marshall. The act being challenged—Madison's refusal to deliver Marbury's commission—concerned an individual legal entitlement rather than a discretionary political decision. And Congress, by statute, had imposed a legal duty on an executive official. At least under these circumstances, the Executive Branch's refusal to deliver the commission was subject to judicial scrutiny.

Notice what is implicit in this reasoning. Marshall effectively asserts that the judiciary has the authority to declare acts of the Executive Branch—indeed, acts of officials as elevated as the Secretary of State—unlawful, whether by virtue of violating a federal statute or the Constitution. This means federal courts have the authority to order such executive officers to take particular actions, such as delivering a magistrate's commission. In February 1803, this holding may have been the most controversial aspect of the *Marbury* opinion. (Indeed, it was the point that made President Jefferson most furious—though given Marshall's maneuverings, there was nothing for Jefferson to do in protest other than rant about it.)

c. *Was mandamus the proper remedy?*: Given that Marbury had a legal right that had been violated by the Executive Branch, and that the law offered Marbury a remedy, the remaining question was whether the Supreme Court could provide that remedy. The first part of this question was rather simple: whether a writ of mandamus was the appropriate remedy for Marbury to seek. A writ of mandamus is a court order directed to a government official to perform a mandatory act. This was a proper remedy here: Madison's duty to deliver the commission was nondiscretionary; everything involving the exercise of discretion—Marbury's appointment by the President and his subsequent confirmation by the Senate—had already occurred.

d. *Was the statute granting the Supreme Court jurisdiction constitutional?*: This gets closer to the crux of the matter. Article III, §2, clause 1 generally sets out those "cases" or "controversies" that federal courts are constitutionally permitted to adjudicate. But it does not *require* Congress to confer the full breadth of this subject matter jurisdiction on the federal judiciary. For a federal court to have the authority to adjudicate a claim, it is insufficient that it fall within the subject matter jurisdiction specified in Article III; additionally, Congress must confer jurisdiction over the claim by statute. And any statutorily conferred subject matter jurisdiction must, of course, be consistent with Article III. The Constitution sets the boundary around the jurisdiction Congress is permitted to confer on the federal courts.

The statute Marbury argued conferred subject matter jurisdiction on the Supreme Court was §13 of the Judiciary Act of 1789. As relevant here, §13 provided that

> "[t]he Supreme Court shall also have appellate jurisdiction from the circuit courts and courts of the several states, in the cases herein after specially provided for; and shall have the power to issue writs of mandamus, in cases warranted by the principles and usages of law, to any courts appointed, or persons holding office, under the authority of the United States."

Crucially, Marshall interpreted §13 as granting the Supreme Court subject matter jurisdiction in *any case in which mandamus is a proper remedy*. If the litigant was appropriately seeking mandamus (and the case otherwise satisfied the Constitution's subject matter jurisdiction requirements set out in Article III, §2, clause 1), reasoned Marshall, the Supreme Court had jurisdiction under §13.

This was not the only way to interpret §13. One might have construed it as only granting the Supreme Court the power to issue writs of mandamus in cases in which the Court already possessed appellate jurisdiction. Or §13 might have meant that, in any case in which the Court already had jurisdiction, it was authorized to issue a writ of mandamus as appropriate. But Marshall eschewed those readings to conclude that §13 itself *conferred jurisdiction* on the Court in all cases in which mandamus was the proper remedy.

So construed, the question was whether §13 was constitutional. Marshall concluded that it was not because it contravened Article III, §2, clause 2. That provision states as follows:

> "In all cases affecting Ambassadors, other public Ministers and Consuls, and those in which a State shall be a Party, the supreme Court shall have original jurisdiction. In all other cases before mentioned, the supreme Court

shall have appellate Jurisdiction, both as to Law and Fact, with such Exceptions, and under such Regulations as the Congress shall make."

Neither Marbury nor Madison were "Ambassadors" or "other public Ministers and Consuls." (Again, those terms refer to *foreign* officials.) Nor did this dispute involve a state as a party. So for the Supreme Court to have jurisdiction over Marbury's claim, the case needed to come to the Court as part of its "appellate Jurisdiction"—on appeal from a lower court.

But Marbury had filed his lawsuit directly in the Supreme Court as an original action. And Marshall had interpreted §13 as purporting to grant the Supreme Court original jurisdiction in *all* cases in which mandamus was a proper remedy. Section 13 was thus unconstitutional, at least as applied to a case like Marbury's. That is, it was inconsistent with Article III, §2, clause 2 for Congress to confer original jurisdiction on the Supreme Court in cases other than those "affecting Ambassadors, other public Ministers and Consuls, and those in which a State shall be a Party." In conferring original jurisdiction on the Supreme Court in a case like this, §13 was unconstitutional.

It is not obvious that Article III, §2, clause 2 sets a hard ceiling on the Supreme Court's original jurisdiction. It is possible to understand that clause as merely setting a starting point that Congress could subsequently alter as it saw fit. (Indeed, the next sentence gives Congress the authority to regulate the appellate jurisdiction of the Supreme Court). But Marshall read Article III, §2, clause 2 as setting out the full universe of cases in which the Supreme Court was constitutionally permitted to exercise original jurisdiction. Insofar as §13 expanded the Court's original jurisdiction beyond those cases and controversies, it was unconstitutional.

e. *Does the Supreme Court have the authority to declare an act of Congress unconstitutional?*: Here, finally, is the point for which *Marbury* is famous: the Supreme Court's power to declare an act of Congress (like §13) unconstitutional, at least as applied in a given case.

Notice how Marshall framed his analysis: "The question, whether an act, repugnant to the constitution, can become the law of the land, is a question deeply interesting to the United States." Marshall rhetorically posed the question as whether an unconstitutional law can still be binding law. All agreed the answer to *this* question is no. But that was not the real question. The real question was *who has the authority* to decide whether a given federal statute is unconstitutional.

In enacting the Judiciary Act, Congress had determined that §13 was consistent with Article III. And President Washington, in signing the Act into law, had agreed. Thus, the issue was whether the federal judiciary possessed the authority to exercise its own independent judgment as to whether §13 was consistent with Article III—or whether, instead, it was required to defer to the judgments reached by Congress and the President. By opining first that §13 was unconstitutional as applied to Marbury's lawsuit—and *then* asking whether §13 was nonetheless binding on the Court despite being unconstitutional—Marshall essentially assumed the answer to the pertinent question.

Still, Marshall ultimately offered several justifications for the principle that the federal judiciary has the power of judicial review. He set them out roughly as follows:

i. ***The Constitution is fundamental.*** The entire point of a constitution is to set down fundamental principles that cannot be transcended by ordinary legislation. The Constitution is meant to limit or constrain Congress. If Congress could exceed those limits with impunity through the enactment of ordinary legislation, the whole point of a written constitution would be subverted; the Constitution would effectively stand on the same plane as an ordinary statute. But the Constitution is supposed to be more than that. It is fundamental or foundational, standing above ordinary law. (But this begs the most important question: whether the Constitution empowers the federal judiciary to hold Congress accountable, or whether that power instead belongs to the voters through the political process.)

ii. ***The Constitution is written law.*** A written constitution is a form of law. And in Marshall's famous words, "[i]t is emphatically the province and duty of the judicial department to say what the law is." This is the essence of the judicial function, to interpret written law. If two laws are in conflict, and one is superior to the other, it is a court's essential obligation to declare that the superior law trumps the inferior. (But one could argue that a constitution is a different sort of law: It is not law in the ordinary sense, but a foundational charter for "We the People" to enforce through the operation of politics.)

iii. ***The Constitution directs the Court to decide all cases "arising under" the Constitution.*** Article III grants federal courts the authority to hear all cases "arising under" the Constitution. Marshall reasoned that it would be strange if the Court had jurisdiction over cases "arising under" the Constitution, yet was not empowered to examine what the Constitution actually meant in deciding those cases. (This is a reasonably strong textual point in favor of judicial review.)

iv. ***The Constitution requires judges to uphold the Constitution.*** Article VI, clause 3 directs judges to take an oath to uphold the Constitution. Why demand that judges take an oath to uphold the Constitution, asked Marshall, if they are not permitted to examine and interpret the Constitution in discharging their judicial duties? (A possible rejoinder is that members of Congress, the President, state legislators, and state governors have also taken oaths to uphold the Constitution.)

v. ***Article VI makes the Constitution supreme.*** The Supremacy Clause, found in Article VI, lists the Constitution first in rank among the laws that are supreme over state law. A natural inference is that judges are to examine and interpret the Constitution in enforcing the Supremacy Clause. And if they are to examine and interpret the Constitution to determine whether a state law is valid, why not also in passing judgment on the lawfulness of a federal statute? (This is another solid textual point in favor of judicial review.)

vi. *Absent judicial review, absurd consequences would result.* What if Congress enacted laws that were plainly unconstitutional? Several constitutional rules are fairly clear; what if Congress blatantly disobeyed them? For instance, what if Congress enacted a federal statute providing that a person could be convicted of treason on the testimony of only one witness, or on a confession made out of court? Would a federal court be required to ignore the text of the Constitution? (Of course, constitutional cases are almost never so easy. As discussed earlier, the text is typically vague or ambiguous. Moreover, this again seems to beg the relevant question: Is this a problem for the courts to solve, or instead for the People to resolve through politics and elections?)

2. *Marbury's* brilliance in broader context: So that is *Marbury v. Madison*. And there are certainly some questionable steps in Marshall's analysis. Most notable is his interpretation of §13, which was hardly the most obvious, especially since it forced the Court to answer a huge constitutional question. (A general canon of statutory interpretation—the canon of constitutional avoidance—dictates that, when possible, courts should construe laws in a manner that avoids difficult constitutional questions.) Why would Marshall have interpreted §13 as he did, when "saving" constructions were readily available? The best explanation is that it permitted the Court to decide whether §13 was constitutional, which in turn gave the Court a platform for staking its claim to the power of judicial review.

Again, the surrounding political context is critical. At stake—at least in the minds of the participants—was nothing short of the nation's survival. Marshall and Jefferson personified the competing visions of the Federalists and the Republicans. Jefferson staunchly opposed increasing national authority, including judicial authority: "Nothing should be spared to eradicate this spirit of Marshallism." He was the intellectual and political leader of those seeking to augment the power of the states. He had helped author the Virginia and Kentucky Resolutions in 1798, which asserted that the states (and *not* the federal courts) possessed the authority to declare acts of Congress unconstitutional.

Marshall, by contrast, thought Jefferson was a dangerous demagogue who was placing the nation's survival in jeopardy. Marshall believed the federal government needed sufficient power to control the centrifugal forces of the states, which, if left unchecked, would pull the country apart. To him, the federal judiciary in particular needed the authority to decide whether acts of Congress (and those of state legislatures) violated the Constitution. As R. Kent Newmyer explained in his excellent biography of Marshall,

"It was Jefferson and Marshall . . . who symbolized and personalized the competing constitutional persuasions of the age and brought them into explosive focus. Each had taken a stand on the great foreign and domestic issues of the 1790s; each had conflated those issues into a dispute over the meaning of the Constitution. When fate and ambition made Jefferson president and Marshall chief justice, the institutional stage was set for what is one of the most creative confrontations in American constitutional history. At stake was not just the position of the Supreme Court in American government but the place of law in republican culture. Neither of these great issues had been settled by the Constitution; both would be influenced significantly by the personalities of Jefferson and Marshall—and by their unrelenting mutual hatred."[3]

Marshall's interpretation of §13 gave the Court the chance to assert a significant power for the federal government generally, and for the federal judiciary in particular.

Even more remarkable is that Marshall managed this trick in the face of an incredibly hostile political environment. As a matter of political reality, had the Court ordered the Jefferson administration to deliver Marbury his commission, the order almost certainly would have been disobeyed. And such open defiance of the Court—to which the justices would lacked any effective response—would have exposed the judiciary as meek. At the same time, had the justices simply caved on their principles and ruled in favor of Madison on all the contested issues, the Court likewise would have appeared feeble.

The genius of *Marbury* lies in how Marshall somehow threaded this needle. He managed to author an opinion that reached the only outcome politically feasible—denying Marbury his right to the commission—but nonetheless held that the Jefferson administration had acted illegally in denying Marbury his commission. More important, Marshall found a way to assert for the federal courts the authority to order important officers in the Executive Branch to follow the Court's interpretation of the law, and to declare acts of Congress unconstitutional. These claims to power would (at least in theory) make the judiciary a vital branch of the national government. Further, Marshall staked these claims by holding that a law purporting to give the Court *more* power (that is, more subject matter jurisdiction) was unconstitutional. As Robert McCloskey has written, *Marbury* "was a masterwork of indirection, a brilliant example of Marshall's capacity to sidestep danger while seeming to court it, to advance in one direction while his opponents are looking in another."[4]

3. *Why didn't Marbury just file his lawsuit in a federal district court?* The answer is unclear. Given the rationale of the Supreme Court's

---

[3] R. Kent Newmyer, John Marshall and the Heroic Age of the Supreme Court 147–48 (2001)

[4] Robert C. McClosky, The American Supreme Court 25 (4th ed. 2005).

decision, Marbury could have filed (or re-filed) his case in federal district court and avoided the jurisdictional problem. (And the Supreme Court would have had appellate jurisdiction over a judgment against Marbury by a lower federal court.) But it is uncertain whether Marbury actually cared about his commission, at least by the time he filed suit. The suit was filed in the Supreme Court by Charles Lee, a Federalist attorney who had served as Attorney General for both Presidents Washington and Adams. And it was filed precisely at the time Congress (then controlled by the Jeffersonian Republicans) was debating the Repeal Act of 1802. The stakes in the Repeal Act debate were much weightier than those concerning four unfilled magistrate positions for the District of Columbia. Perhaps the goal of the suit was to establish a precedent that would have complicated the constitutionality of the Repeal Act. Or perhaps it was just to be a thorn in the side of the Jeffersonians. If so, obtaining an opinion authored by Chief Justice Marshall as quickly as possible was likely more important than actually prevailing on the merits.

4. *The meaning of a judicial decision "declaring a statute unconstitutional"*: It is important to understand that, when the Court decided in *Marbury* that §13 of the Judiciary Act of 1789 was unconstitutional, it merely held that that the statute was unconstitutional *as applied in Marbury's case*. To the extent §13 conferred original jurisdiction on the Supreme Court in cases "affecting Ambassadors, other public Ministers and Consuls, and those in which a State shall be a Party," it remained entirely constitutional. Thus, the Court's decision did not invalidate §13 in its entirety, or somehow erase it from the United States Code. Rather, *Marbury* merely held that, in Marbury's case, §13 could not be applied—consistent with the Constitution—to grant the Supreme Court subject matter jurisdiction.

More generally, when a court declares a statute unconstitutional, it typically is not declaring that the statute is facially invalid in every one of its possible applications. This occurs on occasion, but that can only be discerned through an examination of the opinion's rationale. (For example, because the Constitution makes it impermissible for a legislature to enact a statute for the purpose of persecuting people on the basis of their religion, any law enacted for this purpose would be unconstitutional in *all* of its applications. The law is simply invalid from its inception.) More typically—as in *Marbury*—a court's holding is that the challenged law is unconstitutional in its application to the litigant in the case (or to the class of persons of which she is a part). The law is not entirely invalid, but unconstitutional *as applied* to the person raising the challenge.

Further, even when the Supreme Court holds that a law is facially invalid, there is no obligation for the legislature that enacted the law to repeal it. Often unconstitutional laws remain on the books for scores (if not hundreds) of years. (Consider that Mississippi did not officially abolish slavery until 2013.) Rather, such a judicial decision means that, if the government attempted to enforce that law again in a future case, the opposing party could invoke as precedent the decision declaring the law unconstitutional.

In short, a judicial decision "declaring a law unconstitutional" does not somehow make that law disappear. It means that the Constitution does not permit the court to apply the law in the case before the court. All other implications flowing from the decision are a matter of precedent, which will necessarily turn on the opinion's rationale.

5. *Judicial review in a democracy: the "counter-majoritarian difficulty"*: Again, *Marbury* is famous for staking the federal judiciary's claim to the power of judicial review. In the twenty-first century, we largely take this authority for granted as a fundamental aspect of our system of "checks and balances." But it is worth noting that not everyone thinks judicial review is such a good thing. As many have noted, it stands in some tension with some basic democratic commitments. In a democratic republic, in which the People are the ultimate sovereign, how does it make sense to invest such a preemptive power—essentially, the power to decide some of our most vital political questions—in a small group of unelected judges? Why should their views about affirmative action, abortion, the free exercise of religion, or the fairness of various election procedures take precedence over those of our elected representatives? This is the so-called "counter-majoritarian difficulty."

Perhaps an even more interesting question—or at least the more pertinent one today, given that judicial review is so firmly established—is how far this power extends. That is, when the Supreme Court declares a law unconstitutional, is that the end of the matter? Are the rest of us bound by that interpretation? Or does the Court's decision merely amount to a holding in a particular case, which the President, Congress, state governments, and the nation's citizens can fight to overrule, narrow, or alter—in future cases or through the political process?

6. *Judicial review—in theory and in fact*: One last point: it can be quite misleading to read *Marbury* in isolation and assume the Supreme Court, from that point forward, had the capacity to exercise substantial power, much as it does today. It had *some* power, to be sure, but that power was constrained. First, consider that Marshall (as a matter of practical reality) had no choice but to rule in favor of Madison in *Marbury* itself; had the Court ordered that Marbury be delivered his commission, the Jefferson administration would have almost certainly defied its ruling. (Indeed, no one appeared on behalf of the government in *Marbury*, on the ground that doing so would have lent the proceeding a semblance of legitimacy.) Second, perhaps more telling than *Marbury* is a decision the Court handed down only one week later, *Stuart v. Laird*, 5 U.S. (1 Cranch) 299 (1803). That case was more practically significant, as it involved a challenge to the constitutionality of the Repeal Act of 1802. (Again, the Repeal Act was the statute that eliminated the newly created federal courts of appeals and their sixteen federal judgeships.) Declaring the Repeal Act unconstitutional plainly would have provoked a showdown with President Jefferson and Congress. Unsurprisingly, then, the Court quietly held, in a two-paragraph opinion, that the act was constitutional. (Notably, Marshall recused himself from the decision.)

Moreover, the Republicans went on (after *Marbury*) to impeach the Federalist Supreme Court Justice Samuel Chase. Indeed, in the midst of Chase's impeachment, Chief Justice Marshall went so far as to suggest that Congress should be granted the authority to overrule some Supreme Court decisions by statute. Thus, we should not overestimate the Court's assertion of power in *Marbury*. In some ways, it was quite tentative. But given all the surrounding circumstances, it was bold. And it planted a seed that eventually grew into a foundational aspect of our constitutional system.

*   *   *

D.   Judicial Review of State Laws by Federal Courts

At issue in *Marbury* were (1) the constitutionality of a federal statute (specifically, §13 of the Judiciary Act of 1789); (2) the lawfulness of acts by the federal Executive Branch (in denying Marbury his commission); and (3) the power of the Supreme Court to pass judgment—that is, to judicially review—these acts. Thus, there were no federalism issues in *Marbury*. The case did not involve the division of authority between the federal government and the states. Rather, *Marbury* concerned the powers of the three component parts of the national government: Congress, the Executive Branch, and the judiciary. In this sense, it was a national separation of powers case.

Seven years after *Marbury*, in *Fletcher v. Peck*, 10 U.S. (6 Cranch) 87 (1810) (also known as the "Yazoo lands" case), the Supreme Court invalidated a *state* law as unconstitutional. The underlying merits of the case are unimportant here. Georgia controlled a vast territory to its west, known as the Yazoo lands, which now comprise much of Alabama and Mississippi. The Georgia legislature had enacted laws granting much of that land to individual claimants, but it did so after having been bribed by investors and land speculators. At the subsequent legislative session, once the bribes had come to light, the Georgia legislature repealed the corrupt land grants. A recipient of one of the repealed land grants then brought suit in federal district court claiming that that the repealing statute violated the Contracts Clause of Article I, §10, clause 1, which provides that "[n]o State shall . . . pass any . . . Law impairing the Obligation of Contracts."

On appeal, the Supreme Court vindicated the plaintiff-grantee's claim and ruled that the Georgia statute repealing the land grants violated the Contracts Clause. Again, the details of the Court's decision on the merits are unimportant here. What matters is that *Fletcher v. Peck* was the first decision in which the Supreme Court exercised its authority of judicial review to hold that a state law violated the Constitution.

To this day, much of the Supreme Court's docket involves cases in which one of the parties contends that a state law—whether a statute, regulation, common law rule, or constitutional provision—violates the Constitution or another form of federal law. (For instance, that was the claim in *Obergefell v. Hodges*, 576 U.S. 644 (2015)—namely, that the laws of Ohio, Kentucky, Tennessee, and Michigan, by limiting marriage to opposite-sex couples, violated the Fourteenth Amendment.)

E. Supreme Court Review of State Court Judgments

Fletcher v. Peck established that the federal courts possess the authority to declare the actions of state governments unconstitutional. That is, a plaintiff could bring an action in federal district court claiming that a state had violated the Constitution, and the courts could decide whether the state's action was impermissible. More controversial was whether the Supreme Court of the United States could, on appeal, review the judgment of a state court on a question of federal law. Such was the question presented in *Martin v. Hunter's Lessee*, 14 U.S. (1 Wheat.) 304 (1816).

1. *Martin v. Hunter's Lessee*

Martin arose out of a dispute over the land previously held by Lord Fairfax in the Commonwealth of Virginia (what is now Fairfax County) just outside the District of Columbia. Virginia—and, in turn, Mr. Hunter—claimed that the Commonwealth had validly confiscated a portion of the Fairfax estate before 1783 as "unappropriated" land belonging to a British subject. (A Virginia statute purported to give Virginia the authority to confiscate such land.) Hunter contended that, because Virginia had validly secured title to the land, he possessed title as a subsequent grantee.

By contrast, Martin claimed the land as a devise from Fairfax. That is, he argued that his title to the land was protected by the Peace Treaty of 1783 and the Jay Treaty of 1794—treaties entered into by the United States and Great Britain following the war's conclusion. If Virginia had not perfected title to the land by 1783, the property at issue belonged to Martin by the operation of federal law—specifically the aforementioned treaties, which are supreme to state law under Article VI of the Constitution. (Under the Supremacy Clause of Article VI, a valid treaty preempts a state law to the extent the two come into conflict.)

Here, unlike in *Fletcher v. Peck*, the lawsuit originated in *state* court (as Hunter had filed an action for ejectment in a Virginia state trial court). In 1810, the Virginia Court of Appeals (the highest court in the Virginia state court system) held that Virginia had validly seized the land prior to 1783, and that the federal treaties therefore did not protect Martin's claim. In the Virginia court's view, the land was now Hunter's. Martin appealed this decision to the Supreme Court of the United States. In 1813, the Supreme Court reversed, holding that the treaties protected the title of the Fairfax heirs. Regardless of what Virginia state law dictated, federal law (in the form of the two treaties) meant that the land now belonged to Martin. The Supreme Court accordingly remanded the case, directing the Virginia Court of Appeals to enter judgment in favor of Martin.

On remand, the Virginia Court of Appeals refused to follow the Supreme Court's instructions, essentially reasoning as follows. When a case is brought in federal court challenging the validity of a state law, the Supreme Court has the power to declare that state law unconstitutional; the matter is simply moving up through the hierarchy of the federal judiciary. But when a case is brought in *state* court, the Supreme Court of the United States has no authority of review. Rather, the state supreme court is the final arbiter of that dispute, no matter the dispute's subject matter.

Permitting the Supreme Court to review the judgments of the Virginia Court of Appeals, reasoned the Virginia judges, was incompatible with Virginia's independent sovereignty. Again, though the Constitution created the federal government, it also left in place the states as independent sovereigns. And the basic idea of sovereignty is that the sovereign is *answerable to no one*. If the Constitution truly retained the states' sovereignty—a point no one disputed, at least in the abstract—then the decision of a state's highest court could not be reviewed in any other court. Or so the Virginia Court of Appeals contended. The Commonwealth of Virginia conceived of itself as independent of the United States in the same way that the United States, today, would conceive itself independent of the United Nations. (If a litigant loses at the Supreme Court of the United States today, she cannot appeal that decision to the UN's International Court of Justice (ICJ); the ICJ lacks the authority to review the Supreme Court's decisions, even on questions of international law. Or perhaps more to the point, if the ICJ happened to hear such a case, no United States court would be required to treat that decision as controlling.)

Martin *again* appealed to the Supreme Court of the United States. And unlike in *Marbury*, there was no question as to what the Judiciary Act of 1789 specified. Congress had plainly conferred jurisdiction on the Supreme Court in cases like Martin's, where the claimant had invoked a right arising under a federal treaty that had been denied by the state court. Section 25 of the Judiciary Act stated that

> "a final judgment or decree in any suit, in the highest court of law or equity of a State in which a decision in the suit could be had, where is drawn in question the validity of a treaty or statute of, or an authority exercised under the United States, and the decision is against their validity; or where is drawn in question the validity of a statute of, or an authority exercised under any State, on the ground of their being repugnant to the constitution, treaties or laws of the United States, and the decision is in favour of such their validity, . . . may be re-examined and reversed or affirmed in the Supreme Court of the United States upon a writ of error . . . ."

As a matter of statutory authorization, this clearly granted the Supreme Court the power to review the Virginia Court of Appeals' decision. The question, then, was whether §25 of the Judiciary Act—in conferring this power of appellate review over state court judgments on the Supreme Court—was constitutional.

In an opinion by Justice Joseph Story, the Supreme Court held that it was. (Chief Justice Marshall recused himself because he owned a sizable portion of the land affected by the decision.) The Court offered three basic reasons for its conclusion:

a. *The structure of Constitution.* Justice Story's first argument concerned the federal judicial structure created by the Constitution, and what it necessarily implied. The only federal court Article III *requires* to exist is the Supreme Court of the United States. If Congress decided not to create any lower federal courts, and the Supreme Court did *not* have the power to review appeals from state court judgments (as Virginia contended), the Supreme Court would have no appellate jurisdiction whatsoever; it would be left only to hear the very few cases falling within its original jurisdiction. Justice Story reasoned that this would be an exceptionally odd result. Why mandate the existence of a court—the head of one of the three branches of the national government—if it might only hear a handful of cases? Thus, Justice Story reasoned, Article III should be construed to avoid making such an odd result possible.

b. *Policies related to a federal system.* Next, Justice Story noted that uniformity in the interpretation of federal law is quite important. And if state court judgments on questions of federal law were unreviewable by the Supreme Court, there would potentially be as many different interpretations of the Constitution (and federal law more generally) as there are states. Moreover, because Congress has, in fact, created lower federal courts, the Constitution could have different meanings within the same state, depending on whether a case is brought in state or federal court. This would be bizarre, or at least quite unfair. And it would undermine a central reason for having national laws. (A similar concern led the Court, at least in part, to jettison the "general federal common law" in *Erie Railroad Co. v. Tompkins*, 304 U.S. 64 (1938).)

c. *Safeguarding federal rights.* Finally, Justice Story suggested that the protection of federal rights requires the provision of a federal forum in which to vindicate those rights. State courts—through the normal operation of political forces—are apt to favor local interests in the protection of federal rights. In other words, state courts cannot be fully trusted, in the long run, to protect the provisions of federal law against state encroachments. Federal rights generally require a federal forum for robust protection and vindication.

2. **The lingering controversy surrounding §25 of the Judiciary Act**

The Supreme Court's decision in *Martin* was hardly the end of this controversy. Section 25 of the Judiciary Act of 1789 remained hotly contested all the way up until the Civil War in 1861. Many states continued to maintain that §25 was unconstitutional, and there were several efforts in Congress to effectuate its repeal (though none was successful).

Moreover, though *Marbury* is certainly more famous than *Fletcher v. Peck* and *Martin v. Hunter's Lessee*, the federal judiciary's power to review the constitutionality of state laws and state court judgments is probably more important to the functioning of our constitutional system. As a purely statistical matter, the states (since there are fifty of them) are far more likely to run off the constitutional rails than is the federal government. This is also true because states are more politically homogenous than the nation as a whole. It requires a certain level of national consensus to enact federal legislation, which makes federal law less likely to veer too far from the constitutional mainstream. That is not necessarily true of laws or judgments coming from the states or their political subdivisions. A political majority in a given state or municipality can diverge substantially from national norms. Reflecting these concerns, Justice Oliver Wendell Holmes once noted that he did "not think the United States would come to an end if we lost our power to declare an Act of Congress void. I do think the Union would be imperiled if we could not make that declaration as to the laws of the several States."

3. A concluding note: *Cohens v. Virginia*

The Supreme Court's decision in *Cohens v. Virginia*, 19 U.S. (6 Wheat.) 264 (1821), reaffirmed and slightly extended the holding of *Martin v. Hunter's Lessee*. Specifically, *Cohens* extended the principle to cases in which the state itself was a party. Following *Martin*, some argued that, because of the principles of state sovereign immunity—the idea that the sovereign is immune from unconsenting suits brought by private parties—a state could not be forced to appear against its will in federal court, even at the Supreme Court of the United States. But the Supreme Court held in *Cohens* that, in ratifying the Constitution, the states effectively agreed to subject themselves to the power of the Supreme Court in cases appealed from state courts when the case falls within the subject matter jurisdiction spelled out in Article III.

The Court's opinion in *Cohens*, like that in *Marbury*, represented another stroke of strategic brilliance by Chief Justice Marshall (if you admire Marshall) or another set of "twistifications" (if you, like Thomas Jefferson, do not). The underlying legal question concerned the conviction of two Virginia residents for selling lottery tickets in Virginia, tickets they had purchased in the District of Columbia. It was fairly clear that the federal statute authorizing the national lottery intended to authorize the sale of those tickets throughout the United States. Marshall, however, construed the statute as only authorizing the sale of the tickets in Washington, D.C. This construction of the statute allowed Marshall to assert the Supreme Court's authority to adjudge the constitutionality of Virginia's actions, but then proceed to hold that Virginia had nonetheless acted lawfully. Thus, Virginia—though it disagreed vigorously with the Court's assertion of jurisdiction—could not actually do anything to protest the decision. It was left without a judicial order to defy.

Like *Marbury*, *Cohens* is a lesson in Marshall's strategic maneuvering, as well as the underlying vulnerability of the Court. Nonetheless, *Cohens* marked another important step in embedding §25 of the Judiciary Act into our constitutional fabric (despite the Court's evident weakness in 1821 to enforce it).

*   *   *

PROBLEMS ON THE POWER OF JUDICIAL REVIEW

In each of the following scenarios, please assess whether the court in question would have the authority to resolve the relevant legal dispute. Where possible, identify the legal authority supporting your conclusion.

1. California enacts a statute that prohibits any person from posting on social media any communication expressing "hatred based on race, ethnicity, religion, national origin, gender, or sexual orientation" and which a reasonable person would find "personally threatening." Plaintiff, a citizen of California, files suit in California Superior Court (a state trial court of general jurisdiction) against the California attorney general—the officer with the ultimate responsibility of enforcing the statute—claiming the law violates the Free Speech Clause of the First Amendment to the U.S. Constitution. The superior court awards summary judgment to the attorney general on the merits of the claim; its judgment is affirmed by the California Court of Appeal and the California Supreme Court. May Plaintiff now seek review of the California Supreme Court's decision in the Supreme Court of the United States?

2. The facts are the same as in (1), except Plaintiff files the action in the U.S. District Court for the Northern District of California. The district court grants summary judgment to the attorney general on the merits of the claim, which is affirmed by the U.S. Court of Appeals for the Ninth Circuit. The Supreme Court of the United States then grants Plaintiff's petition for a writ of certiorari (the procedural device necessary to obtain the Supreme Court's discretionary review of a lower court decision). Would the Supreme Court have the authority to hold that applying the California statute to Plaintiff violates the federal Constitution?

3. The facts are the same as in (2), except the law challenged by Plaintiff is a federal statute that has been enacted by Congress. Would the Supreme Court have the authority to declare the statute unconstitutional (at least as applied to Plaintiff)? What precedent would you cite as authority?

4. Suppose a transgender member of the U.S. military files suit in federal district court against the Secretary of Defense, asserting that a policy recently announced by the Secretary (which would exclude all transgender persons from military service) is unconstitutional. Could the district court hold that the Secretary's actions were unlawful and enjoin the Secretary from enforcing the policy? What precedent would you cite as authority for your answer?

5. The facts are the same as in (4). Assume the district court finds in favor of the plaintiff and issues a permanent injunction barring the Secretary from discharging the plaintiff from military service, and this judgment is ultimately upheld by the Supreme Court.

   a. Could the Secretary (as directed by the President) nonetheless discharge the plaintiff from the military?

   b. Suppose the Secretary obeys the injunction with respect to the named plaintiff, but nonetheless discharges several other transgender persons based purely on their being transgender. Are the Secretary's actions permissible? (As you think about this question, consider the difference between a court order and binding precedent. How are they different? What legal obligations do they create?)

CHAPTER 4
THE JURISDICTION OF THE FEDERAL COURTS

A foundational principle of our constitutional system is that the federal government is one of "enumerated powers." This means the Constitution must affirmatively grant the federal government the relevant authority—expressly or implicitly—for its actions to be valid; the power must be "enumerated" somewhere in the Constitution. All "residuary" powers are reserved to the states (or to the People, if no part of any government is permitted to exercise them).

Historically, the breadth of the national government's enumerated powers has been contested most fiercely with respect to Congress's legislative powers. For instance, the question whether Congress could charter a national bank led to *McCulloch v. Maryland*, 17 U.S. (4 Wheat.) 159 (1819); the question whether Congress could prohibit slavery in the territories precipitated *Scott v. Sandford*, 60 U.S. 393 (1857), and then the Civil War; and more recently, the question whether Congress could require individuals to acquire minimally adequate health insurance culminated in the Supreme Court's decision in *NFIB v. Sebelius*, 567 U.S. 519 (2012).

But this basic principle applies equally to the federal courts: they may only act pursuant to an authority granted by the Constitution. Thus, a critical part of understanding our governmental structure concerns the scope of the jurisdiction that the Constitution grants the federal judiciary.

A. The Subject Matter Jurisdiction of the Federal Courts

Article III defines the breadth of the federal courts' constitutionally permissible authority. The first section of Article III provides that

> "[t]he judicial power of the United States, shall be vested in one Supreme Court, and in such inferior courts as the Congress may from time to time ordain and establish. The judges, both of the supreme and inferior courts, shall hold their offices during good behaviour, and shall, at stated times, receive for their services, a compensation, which shall not be diminished during their continuance in office."

This text mandates the existence of only the Supreme Court, while leaving the creation of any lower federal courts to the discretion of Congress. This arrangement was the product of a compromise at the Constitutional Convention, between those who felt a robust federal judiciary was necessary to preserve a viable Union and those who felt state courts were sufficient as courts of original jurisdiction (with a right of appeal to the Supreme Court). The command that federal judges "shall hold their offices during good behaviour" has been understood as protecting them from removal from office, except through impeachment. And the final sentence of this section protects federal judges from political retaliation through a reduction in their pay.

Article III, §2, clause 1 sets out the constitutionally allowable subject matter jurisdiction of the federal courts:

"The judicial power shall extend to all cases, in law and equity, arising under this Constitution, the laws of the United States, and treaties made, or which shall be made, under their authority;—to all cases affecting ambassadors, other public ministers and consuls;—to all cases of admiralty and maritime jurisdiction;—to controversies to which the United States shall be a party;—to controversies between two or more states;—between a state and citizens of another state;—between citizens of different states;—between citizens of the same state claiming lands under grants of different states, and between a state, or the citizens thereof, and foreign states, citizens or subjects."

At least two of these categories of "cases" or "controversies" are familiar to those who have taken Civil Procedure: cases "arising under this Constitution, the laws of the United States, and treaties made, or which shall be made, under their authority"—so-called "federal questions"—and cases "between citizens of different states" or "between a state, or the citizens thereof, and foreign states, citizens or subjects"—the federal courts' "diversity jurisdiction." But Article III also contains a handful of other "cases" or "controversies": "all cases affecting ambassadors, other public ministers and consuls"; "all cases of admiralty and maritime jurisdiction"; "controversies to which the United States shall be a party"; "controversies between two or more states"; controversies "between a state and citizens of another state"; and controversies "between citizens of the same state claiming lands under grants of different states." Together, this list of disputes constitutes the outer limit of the federal courts' subject matter jurisdiction. Congress may not confer jurisdiction exceeding these boundaries.

But enumeration in Article III is insufficient, by itself, for a particular case or controversy to be one that a federal court can adjudicate. In addition, Congress must affirmatively grant subject matter jurisdiction by statute—for instance, as it has in 28 U.S.C. §1331 for questions arising under federal law.

* * *

EXAMPLE

Article III, §2, clause 1 specifies that the "judicial power shall extend to all cases . . . between citizens of different states." In *State Farm Fire & Casualty Co. v. Tashire*, 386 U.S. 523 (1967), the Supreme Court explained that a case is "between citizens of different states" for purposes of Article III so long as at least one plaintiff is a citizen of a different state than at least one defendant—that is, there exists "minimal diversity" among the parties. Thus, if a California citizen sued both a

Nevada citizen and a California citizen as co-defendants in federal court, the case would meet the constitutional standard for diversity. But in 28 U.S.C. §1332(a)(1) (as interpreted by the Supreme Court in *Strawbridge v. Curtiss*, 7 U.S. (3 Cranch) 267 (1806)), Congress has granted federal district courts subject matter jurisdiction only in cases with "complete diversity" of state citizenship among the parties: when all plaintiffs are citizens of different states than all defendants. Thus, a district court would lack subject matter jurisdiction under §1332(a) over a state-law claim brought by a Californian against a Nevadan and a Californian as co-defendants. The action would be within the constitutionally permissible limits of Article III, but not within the jurisdiction statutorily granted by Congress (unless some other statutory grant of jurisdiction applied).

* * *

As may be obvious, there is no constitutional *obligation* for Congress to confer on the federal courts the entirety of the subject matter jurisdiction permitted by Article III. Indeed, Congress has never done so. Again, consider the federal district courts' diversity jurisdiction under §1332(a). As discussed, though Article III authorizes such jurisdiction whenever there is minimal diversity among the parties, Congress has only conferred such jurisdiction (at least as a general matter) when there is complete diversity. Further, Article III contains no requirement concerning the amount in controversy in diversity cases, but Congress has granted jurisdiction in such cases (under current law) only when the amount in controversy exceeds $75,000. The broader point is that the scope of jurisdiction permitted by Article III is (and has always been) substantially broader than the jurisdiction Congress has conferred by statute.

With respect to the Supreme Court in particular (as opposed to the lower federal courts), its subject matter jurisdiction comes directly from the Constitution. Thus, as a formal matter, Congress need not confer subject matter jurisdiction on the Court for it to have the authority to decide a case or controversy. But this is just a technical point. As the Court explained in *Ex parte McCardle*, 74 U.S. 506 (1869), one of the very first statutes ever enacted by Congress was the Judiciary Act of 1789, which set out the terms of the Supreme Court's subject matter jurisdiction. And comprehensive exposition of the Court's jurisdiction in the Judiciary Act has always been understood to imply the withdrawal of those cases or controversies not specified in the statute. (As explored below, the Exceptions Clause of Article III gives Congress the authority to make "exceptions" and "regulations" regarding the Supreme Court's appellate jurisdiction.) Thus, as a practical matter, the Supreme Court must also be granted subject matter jurisdiction statutorily by Congress, except in those rare cases falling within its original jurisdiction.

B. The Nature of Subject Matter Jurisdiction

Subject matter jurisdiction speaks to the authority of a court to adjudicate a particular type of dispute. It is quite unlike *personal* jurisdiction. The requirement that a court have personal jurisdiction derives from the Due Process Clause; it is an *individual* right that (like most personal constitutional rights) can be waived or forfeited. By contrast, subject matter jurisdiction concerns the power granted to the court, and thus the constitutional legitimacy of the judicial proceeding. It can never be waived or forfeited by the parties. Indeed, the contention that a federal court lacks subject matter jurisdiction can be raised at any time, and the court's jurisdiction must continue to exist until its judgment becomes final. A federal court is obligated to ensure itself of its own subject matter jurisdiction before proceeding to the merits of a dispute, even if the question is never pressed by the parties.

Again, given the structure of government created by the Constitution, federal courts are courts of *limited* subject matter jurisdiction. This reflects the Constitution's system of "enumerated powers," by which the federal government's powers are "few and defined." By contrast, there are no federal constitutional limits on state courts' subject matter jurisdiction. (This is why they are often called courts of "general jurisdiction.") As a matter of state law, states typically regulate the subject matter jurisdiction of their own courts. (For instance, state law might dictate that state superior courts lack original jurisdiction over certain family law or landlord-tenant matters, diverting those disputes into specialized trial courts instead.) Moreover, Congress—in exercising one of its enumerated legislative powers—can dictate that certain questions of federal law *must* be litigated in federal court. (It has done so, for instance, with respect to "any claim for relief arising under any Act of Congress relating to patents, plant variety protection, or copyrights." 28 U.S.C. §1338(a).) But these are legislative policy choices. As a matter of federal constitutional law, there are no limits to state courts' subject matter jurisdiction.

* * *

PROBLEMS ON SUBJECT MATTER JURISDICTION

In each of the following examples, please evaluate whether it would be constitutional for the court in question to exercise subject matter jurisdiction over the case being litigated. (Please ignore any statutes that have been enacted by Congress and focus exclusively on whether the court's exercise of subject matter jurisdiction would be consistent with the Constitution.)

1. California enacts a statute that prohibits any person from posting on social media any communication that expresses "hatred based on race, ethnicity, religion, national origin, gender, or sexual orientation," and which a reasonable person would find "personally threatening." Plaintiff, a citizen of California, files suit in California Superior Court (a state trial court of general jurisdiction) against the California attorney general—the officer with responsibility for enforcing the statute—asserting that the law violates the California state constitution. The plaintiff seeks an injunction proscribing enforcement of the statute.

2. The facts are the same as in (1), except Plaintiff files the action in the U.S. District Court for the Northern District of California.

3. The facts are the same as in (1), except Plaintiff contends that the California statute violates the Free Speech Clause of the First Amendment to the U.S. Constitution.

4. The facts are the same as in (3), except that Plaintiff files the lawsuit (as an original action) directly in the Supreme Court of the United States.

5. Would the following federal statutes, if enacted by Congress, be constitutional?

   a. A statute that permits the Supreme Court to exercise original jurisdiction in all cases in which a party claims that the President has acted unconstitutionally.

   b. A statute that permits federal district courts to exercise original jurisdiction in any case in which a state is a plaintiff and the claim arises under federal law.

*   *   *

C. Congress's Authority to Regulate the Jurisdiction of the Federal Courts

The preceding section addressed the scope of the federal courts' subject matter jurisdiction as permitted by Article III. Yet to be explored, at least in detail, is Congress's authority to regulate or adjust that subject matter jurisdiction. Importantly, this involves two discrete powers: (1) Congress's authority to regulate the jurisdiction of the lower federal courts (*i.e.*, of the U.S. District Courts and the U.S. Courts of Appeals), and (2) Congress's authority to regulate the jurisdiction of the Supreme Court. These powers derive from different constitutional provisions, have different constitutional pedigrees, and possess different constitutional implications.

1. Congress's regulation of the lower federal courts' jurisdiction

On this subject, it is critical to appreciate that Congress has no constitutional obligation to create *any* lower federal courts at all. Again, the first sentence of Article III provides that "[t]he judicial power of the United States, shall be vested in one Supreme Court, *and in such inferior courts as the Congress may from time to time ordain and establish*" (emphasis added). Congress *may* ordain and establish lower federal courts—or it may not. At the Constitutional Convention, those favoring a stronger national government sought to mandate the existence of lower federal lower courts, while those more resistant to strong national authority argued that all cases could be brought in state court (with a right of appeal to the Supreme Court). Their compromise was to leave the decision to Congress. (In this regard, notice that Article I, §8, clause 9 specifically lists among Congress's enumerated powers the authority "[t]o constitute tribunals inferior to the Supreme Court.")

Given that Congress plainly possesses the greater power to not create any lower federal courts, it has always been understood to have the lesser power—

if it chooses to create such courts—to define the scope of their subject matter jurisdiction. As many have explained, it would be odd if Congress was not constitutionally obligated to create any lower federal courts, but once it did so it had no choice but to invest them with *all* the subject matter jurisdiction permitted by Article III, §2, clause 1. That is, it would be strange to read Article III as presenting Congress with only two choices: either (1) vesting the lower courts with jurisdiction over every single "case" or "controversy" listed in Article III, or (2) not creating lower federal courts at all.

Second, it was generally understood by those involved in the framing and ratification of the Constitution that Congress would have the discretion to decide which sorts of "cases" and "controversies" specified in Article III could be originally litigated in lower federal courts, and which instead need to be brought in state court. Again, state courts are courts of general jurisdiction. Thus, there is no constitutional problem with state courts adjudicating claims arising under federal law (including the federal Constitution) and those cases later reaching the Supreme Court on appeal. (That is precisely what occurred in *Martin v. Hunter's Lessee* and *Cohens v. Virginia*.)

Third, the unbroken practice since the Constitution's ratification has reflected this understanding. Congress has never granted the lower federal courts jurisdiction over all the cases and controversies enumerated in Article III, §2, clause 1. Indeed, Congress did not give the federal district courts general federal question jurisdiction (what is now codified in 28 U.S.C. §1331) until 1875. Instead, Congress has always worked well within the outer limits of the subject matter jurisdiction authorized by Article III.

Thus, as the Supreme Court explained in *Kline v. Burke Construction Co.*, 260 U.S. 226, 233–34 (1922), the effect of Article III, §2, clause 1

> "is not to vest jurisdiction in the inferior courts over the designated cases and controversies but to delimit those in respect of which Congress may confer jurisdiction upon such courts as it creates. . . . Every [lower] court created by the general government derives its jurisdiction wholly from the authority of Congress. That body may give, withhold or restrict such jurisdiction at its discretion, provided it be not extended beyond the boundaries fixed by the Constitution. The Constitution simply gives to the inferior courts the capacity to take jurisdiction in the enumerated cases, but it requires an act of Congress to confer it. And the jurisdiction having been conferred may, at the will of Congress, be taken away in whole or in part."

Today, there are numerous regulations or exceptions to the lower federal courts' jurisdiction in the U.S. Code, ensuring that those courts' subject matter jurisdiction falls well short of that authorized by Article III:

* Federal district courts lack general diversity jurisdiction over actions where the amount in controversy is $75,000 or less, even when the constitutional requirements of diversity jurisdiction are satisfied.

* Federal district courts lack general diversity jurisdiction over actions that lack complete diversity among the parties, even though Article III requires only minimal diversity.

* Federal district courts generally only have federal question jurisdiction when a claim created by federal law is part of the plaintiff's well-pleaded complaint, whereas Article III permits federal question jurisdiction over any case in which federal law forms "an ingredient"—including by virtue of a defendant's counterclaim or affirmative defense.

* The Johnson Act deprives lower federal courts of jurisdiction in cases where a litigant is challenging certain state regulatory actions.

* The Tax Injunction Act deprives lower federal courts of subject matter jurisdiction over cases in which a taxpayer claims that a state or local tax violates federal law, so long as state law offers an "adequate" and "efficient" remedy.

Of course, a statute that regulates the lower courts' jurisdiction might run afoul of other constitutional provisions. For example, a federal law depriving district courts of jurisdiction in cases brought by registered Republicans would violate the Free Speech Clause, as it would constitute an impermissible restriction on free expression. But that limitation would come from the First Amendment—a cross-cutting limitation on all governmental action in the interest of protecting individual rights—not from those provisions that define the powers of Congress (Article I) or of the federal courts (Article III).

2. Congress's regulation of the Supreme Court's jurisdiction

Article III, §2, clause 2 provides as follows:

"In all Cases affecting Ambassadors, other public Ministers and Consuls, and those in which a State shall be a Party, the supreme Court shall have original jurisdiction. In all other Cases before mentioned, the supreme Court shall have appellate jurisdiction, both as to Law and Fact, *with such Exceptions, and under such Regulations as Congress shall make*" (emphasis added).

That emphasized phrase is known as the Exceptions Clause, granting Congress the authority to "regulate" and make "exceptions" to the Supreme Court's appellate jurisdiction. What does this power entail?

Recall that the immediately preceding clause—Article III, §2, clause 1—sets out all the "cases" or "controversies" the federal courts are authorized to adjudicate. But the Exceptions Clause plainly indicates that Congress need not grant the Supreme Court appellate jurisdiction over all such disputes. And that has been borne out in practice, from the first days of the republic. The Judiciary Act of 1789, for instance, in granting the Supreme Court appellate jurisdiction over the judgments of state supreme courts, only conferred such jurisdiction where the state supreme court's judgment *denied* a claim grounded in federal law; a state supreme court decision *upholding* a claim arising under federal law could not be appealed to the Supreme Court, even though it presented a question arising under federal law under Article III.

How far does this authority extend? The most important decision addressing the scope of the Exceptions Clause is *Ex parte McCardle*, 74 U.S. 506 (1869). Unfortunately, the decision remains an enigma, leaving many of the most important questions unanswered.

The Supreme Court decided *Ex parte McCardle* at the height of Reconstruction, the period following the Civil War in which the victorious Union (and the Radical Republicans in Congress) sought to "reconstruct" the defeated South. Reconstruction was a massive domestic program. Quite controversially, it involved the governance of the South by the U.S. Army, necessary to protect the rights and personal safety of the recently freed slaves. This ongoing military occupation—along with the exercise of civil and political rights by African Americans—was deeply resisted in the South. McCardle was the publisher of a newspaper in Vicksburg, Mississippi (the *Vicksburg Daily Times*), who was highly critical of the federal government's Reconstruction policies. He was arrested by military officials and charged (under the authority of the Military Reconstruction Act enacted by Congress in 1867) with disturbing the peace, inciting insurrection, criminal libel, and impeding Reconstruction.[5] McCardle argued that his arrest was unlawful, relying largely on the claim that—by authorizing American civilians to be arrested and tried by military officials and commissions—the Military Reconstruction Act was unconstitutional. He thus filed suit seeking a writ of habeas corpus in federal circuit court.[6] (This was a statutorily permissible court in which to seek a writ of habeas corpus.)

The federal circuit court denied McCardle's petition. McCardle then appealed that judgment to the Supreme Court. In doing so, he relied on a new federal statute, the Habeas Corpus Act of 1867, that granted the Supreme Court jurisdiction to hear appeals from lower federal court judgments denying writs of habeas corpus. Prior to the passage of the Habeas Corpus Act, the Supreme Court could potentially hear appeals like McCardle's—from prisoners being held in federal custody—under §22 of the Judiciary Act of 1789. But it was unclear whether that provision would apply in McCardle's case. The 1867 Act's jurisdictional provision plainly applied to McCardle's appeal, and thus offered a surer basis for invoking the Supreme Court's appellate jurisdiction.

---

[5] *See* Daniel J. Meltzer, *The Story of* Ex parte McCardle: *The Power of Congress to Limit the Supreme Court's Appellate Jurisdiction, in* FEDERAL COURTS STORIES 57, 64–65 (Vicki C. Jackson & Judith Resnick eds., 2010).

[6] A writ of habeas corpus is a longstanding remedy dating at least to the Habeas Corpus Act of 1679, adopted by the British Parliament. It is a means of challenging the lawfulness of one's detention by the executive, and it literally means "to produce the body." The purpose of the writ is to require the government to demonstrate its justifications for detaining the person.

In December 1867, the Supreme Court held a hearing to determine whether it had jurisdiction over McCardle's appeal under the Habeas Corpus Act of 1867. The Court unanimously concluded it did and set the case down for oral argument. In early March 1868, the Court heard argument on the merits of McCardle's constitutional claims. Many who attended the argument surmised the Court was poised to grant McCardle relief and declare significant portions of the Military Reconstruction Act unconstitutional. But while McCardle's case was still pending—after oral argument, but before the Court had handed down its opinion—Congress enacted the Repeal Act of 1868 (over President Andrew Johnson's veto). The Repeal Act repealed the provision in the Habeas Corpus Act of 1867 granting the Supreme Court appellate jurisdiction in cases like McCardle's—that is, the act on which McCardle had relied in asserting the Court had jurisdiction over his appeal. The Court now needed to address whether it still had subject matter jurisdiction—or instead whether the Repeal Act of 1868 stripped the Court of authority to decide the merits of McCardle's claims (even though it plainly had jurisdiction when it took the case and heard oral argument).

As you read *McCardle*, please consider the following questions:

1. Why do you suppose Congress repealed the provision in the Habeas Corpus Act of 1867 granting the Supreme Court jurisdiction over appeals like McCardle's? Did Congress's motive matter?

2. Was the Repeal Act of 1868, which purported to repeal the Supreme Court's jurisdiction in cases like McCardle's, constitutional? Why or why not?

3. What was the ultimate outcome for McCardle in this case?

4. In enacting the Repeal Act of 1868, had Congress completely foreclosed any avenue for McCardle to present his constitutional claims to the Supreme Court? What is the significance of the opinion's final paragraph?

Ex parte McCardle
74 U.S. 506 (1869)

CHIEF JUSTICE CHASE delivered the opinion of the court.

The first question necessarily is that of jurisdiction, for if the act of March, 1868, takes away the jurisdiction defined by the act of February, 1867, it is useless, if not improper, to enter into any discussion of other questions.

It is quite true, as was argued by the counsel for the petitioner, that the appellate jurisdiction of this court is not derived from acts of Congress. It is, strictly speaking, conferred by the Constitution. But it is conferred "with such exceptions and under such regulations as Congress shall make."

It is unnecessary to consider whether, if Congress had made no exceptions and no regulations, this court might not have exercised general appellate jurisdiction under rules prescribed by itself. For among the earliest acts of the first Congress, at its first session, was the act of September 24th, 1789, to establish the judicial courts of the United States. That act provided for the organization of this court, and prescribed regulations for the exercise of its jurisdiction.

The source of that jurisdiction, and the limitations of it by the Constitution and by statute, have been on several occasions subjects of consideration here. In the case of *Durousseau v. The United States* particularly, the whole matter was carefully examined, and the court held that, while "the appellate powers of this court are not given by the judicial act, but are given by the Constitution," they are, nevertheless, "limited and regulated by that act, and by such other acts as have been passed on the subject." The court said further that the judicial act was an exercise of the power given by the Constitution to Congress "of making exceptions to the appellate jurisdiction of the Supreme Court." "They have described affirmatively," said the court, "its jurisdiction, and this affirmative description has been understood to imply a negation of the exercise of such appellate power as is not comprehended within it."

The principle that the affirmation of appellate jurisdiction implies the negation of all such jurisdiction not affirmed having been thus established, it was an almost necessary consequence that acts of Congress, providing for the exercise of jurisdiction, should come to be spoken of as acts granting jurisdiction, and not as acts making exceptions to the constitutional grant of it.

The exception to appellate jurisdiction in the case before us, however, is not an inference from the affirmation of other appellate jurisdiction. It is made in terms. The provision of the act of 1867 affirming the appellate jurisdiction of this court in cases of habeas corpus is expressly repealed. It is hardly possible to imagine a plainer instance of positive exception.

We are not at liberty to inquire into the motives of the legislature. We can only examine into its power under the Constitution, and the power to make exceptions to the appellate jurisdiction of this court is given by express words.

What, then, is the effect of the repealing act upon the case before us? We cannot doubt as to this. Without jurisdiction, the court cannot proceed at all in any cause. Jurisdiction is power to declare the law, and, when it ceases to exist, the only function remaining to the court is that of announcing the fact and dismissing the cause. And this is not less clear upon authority than upon principle. . . .

[T]he general rule, supported by the best elementary writers, is that, "when an act of the legislature is repealed, it must be considered, except as to transactions past and closed, as if it never existed." And the effect of repealing acts upon suits under acts repealed has been determined by the adjudications of this court. The subject was fully considered in *Norris v. Crecker,* and more recently in *Insurance Company v. Ritchie.* In both of these cases, it was held that no judgment could be rendered in a suit after the repeal of the act under which it was brought and prosecuted.

It is quite clear, therefore, that this court cannot proceed to pronounce judgment in this case, for it has no longer jurisdiction of the appeal, and judicial duty is not less fitly performed by declining ungranted jurisdiction than in exercising firmly that which the Constitution and the laws confer.

Counsel seem to have supposed, if effect be given to the repealing act in question, that the whole appellate power of the court, in cases of habeas corpus, is denied. But this is an error. The act of 1868 does not except from that jurisdiction any cases but appeals from Circuit Courts under the act of 1867. It does not affect the jurisdiction which was previously exercised.

The appeal of the petitioner in this case must be

DISMISSED FOR WANT OF JURISDICTION.

* * *

Notes on *Ex parte McCardle*

1. *Congress's purpose in repealing the Court's jurisdiction*: The reason Congress enacted the Repeal Act of 1868 was obvious: it feared the Supreme Court would decide in *McCardle* that the Military Reconstruction Act was unconstitutional. Congress acted specifically to deprive the Court of the opportunity to decide this enormously important constitutional question. Congress therefore had a particular outcome for the litigation in mind and sought to engineer that outcome by repealing the Court's jurisdiction. But the Supreme Court held that this underlying intent was immaterial: "We are not at liberty to inquire into the motives of the legislature. We can only examine into its power under the Constitution; and the power to make exceptions to the appellate jurisdiction of this court is given by express words." Even though Congress was seeking to produce a specific result in a pending case, the Repeal Act was constitutional because it was within the authority granted by the Exceptions Clause.

2. *A limit on regulating the Court's jurisdiction to produce desired outcomes*: United States v. Klein: Despite the rationale of *McCardle*—which seems to affirm Congress's broad authority to regulate the Supreme Court's appellate jurisdiction—there are limits to Congress's power under the Exceptions Clause. One such limit was enforced in *United States v. Klein,* 80 U.S. 128 (1872). At issue in *Klein* were the circumstances under which former confederates could take back title to land they had owned before the Civil War. In a decision before *Klein,* the Supreme Court had held that, under the relevant statute, a person who had received a presidential pardon was entitled to repossess his land. The Republican-controlled Congress did not like this result and thus enacted a statute providing that, in any case in which a litigant had proved that he had received a presidential pardon, the presiding federal court would immediately lose jurisdiction over the case and be required to enter judgment against the claimant. The Supreme Court held in *Klein* that this latter statute was unconstitutional.

According to the Court, the statute violated separation of powers principles. Congress cannot prescribe a "rule of decision" for the courts: it cannot dictate that the courts rule for a particular party or class of parties in pending litigation. It can be *motivated* to effectuate a particular outcome, as it plainly was in *McCardle*. But a statute cannot formally direct the judiciary, in so many words, to enter judgment for a party in a pending action. A law that does so encroaches on the province of the judiciary under Article III; it assumes for Congress the role of adjudicating live cases, a responsibility that belongs to the courts.

As *McCardle* shows, though, Congress can remove the Supreme Court's appellate jurisdiction in a neutral way, even if its underlying *intent* is to preserve a particular outcome in a particular case. That is what distinguishes *McCardle* from *Klein*. Regardless of Congress's intent, the Repeal Act of 1868 did not prescribe a rule of decision in a pending case. At least in form, it repealed a general grant of jurisdiction previously given (in the Habeas Corpus Act of 1867)—jurisdiction in all appeals from decisions by the circuit courts denying writs of habeas corpus. The 1868 Repeal Act applied in a neutral fashion, to all such cases, across the board.

3. *Regulations of the Supreme Court's original jurisdiction*: By its terms, the Exceptions Clause only allows Congress to regulate or make exceptions to the Supreme Court's *appellate* jurisdiction. By implication, Congress has no authority to regulate or make exceptions to the Supreme Court's *original* jurisdiction. As you might recall from *Marbury*, Article III, §2, clause 2 provides that "[i]n all Cases affecting Ambassadors, other public Ministers and Consuls, and those in which a State shall be a Party, the supreme Court shall have original jurisdiction." Congress cannot deprive the Supreme Court of original jurisdiction in any of these "cases" or "controversies." Nevertheless, the Supreme Court has held that Congress may confer original jurisdiction over these same disputes to the district courts as well, such that they may be brought originally either in district courts or the Supreme Court. This means that the Supreme Court can hear these cases as part of its appellate jurisdiction, and not just as part of its original jurisdiction (despite the portion of the opinion in *Marbury* suggesting otherwise). Moreover, Congress can grant the Supreme Court discretion whether to review such cases as an original matter—such that the justices can effectively force litigants (by declining discretionary review) to bring their actions originally in a district court. Under current federal law, the only category of cases that litigants *must* bring originally in the

Supreme Court (that is, where the Supreme Court's original jurisdiction is exclusive) is those in which one state is suing another state.

4. *Can Congress completely eliminate any avenue for Supreme Court review of a constitutional claim?*: A crucial question in understanding what *McCardle* does and does not resolve is this: there was another route for litigants like McCardle, whose petitions for a writ of habeas corpus had been denied, to seek review in the Supreme Court. As the last paragraph of *McCardle* cryptically referenced, §14 of the Judiciary Act of 1789 granted the Supreme Court jurisdiction over petitions for writs of habeas corpus filed directly in the Supreme Court (a so-called "original writ"). The 1868 Repeal Act only repealed the appellate jurisdiction granted by the Habeas Corpus Act of 1867; it left intact this other route for obtaining Supreme Court review of a habeas petitioner's constitutional claim.

This fact—and the way in which the Court referred to this fact in the opinion's final paragraph—renders *McCardle* an enigma. If Congress in 1868 had completely removed the Supreme Court's jurisdiction in habeas corpus cases like McCardle's—such that the McCardles of the world had no jurisdictional path to presenting their constitutional claims to the Supreme Court—would that have been a constitutional regulation of the Court's appellate jurisdiction? The reasoning of the *McCardle* opinion up until its last paragraph seems to indicate yes, that Congress has nearly unlimited authority to regulate the Court's appellate jurisdiction. But the last paragraph muddles things. It can be interpreted as indicating that such exceptions are permissible only if there is another way to obtain Supreme Court review of the petitioner's claims. At a minimum, the last paragraph means that *McCardle* does not conclusively resolve the question.

On the one hand, the text of Article III does not seem to impose any limits. The words are "with such Exceptions, and under such Regulations as the Congress shall make." On its face, the power seems limitless, at least with respect to any constraints coming from Article III. On the other hand, one could understand the availability of judicial review at the Supreme Court—at least on constitutional questions—as a foundational aspect of the Constitution's structure. In light of *Marbury v. Madison* and *Martin v. Hunter's Lessee*, one could argue that one of the Court's essential purposes is to operate as a check on the elected branches, at least with respect to individual constitutional rights. Reading the Exceptions Clause to grant Congress the authority to completely eliminate the Court's power to review particular constitutional claims would violate this structural principle.

But it is important to distinguish what is unconstitutional from what might be unwise. Perhaps the real brake on Congress's stripping the Supreme Court of appellate jurisdiction in certain cases is not the Constitution but the political process. Historically, politicians have paid a steep price when the public has perceived them as interfering with the judiciary's capacity to decide constitutional questions independently. (President Franklin Roosevelt's ill-fated Court-packing plan in 1937 is a signal example.) This is likely why almost all of the jurisdiction-stripping bills proposed in Congress—even when introduced in response to very unpopular Supreme Court opinions—have failed to win passage.

*   *   *

PROBLEMS ON CONGRESS'S POWER TO REGULATE JURISDICTION

In each of the following scenarios, please assess whether Congress has the authority to enact the statute in question. Please identify the relevant source of authority, and why you believe it confers (or does not confer) the power to enact the law in question.

1. A statute that limits the original jurisdiction of the federal district courts in cases "arising under" federal law (under 28 U.S.C. §1331) to those disputes in which the amount in controversy exceeds $75,000.

2. A statute that expands the original jurisdiction of the federal district courts in cases "arising under" federal law (under 28 U.S.C. §1331) to any case in which there is a "federal ingredient," including those in which the federal legal question arises in a counterclaim or an affirmative defense.

3. A statute providing that the federal district courts shall have jurisdiction over cases between citizens of different states (under 28 U.S.C. §1332) only if the amount in controversy exceeds $75,000.

4. A statute providing that the Supreme Court shall have jurisdiction over appeals from the judgments of state supreme courts only when the judgment in question denied a claim, right, or protection provided by federal law.

5. A statute providing that no federal district court shall have jurisdiction over any claim that a state tax violates federal law (unless the state court with subject matter jurisdiction over the case would not provide a meaningful avenue for judicial review).

6. A statute providing that the federal district courts shall have jurisdiction over any case arising under federal law brought by a state government against a private party.

7. A statute abolishing the federal district courts. (What about a statute abolishing the federal courts of appeals?)

8. A statute prohibiting the federal district courts from exercising jurisdiction over any case in which the plaintiff asserts that a state law regulating gender-affirming medical care is unconstitutional.

9. A statute prohibiting the Supreme Court from exercising appellate jurisdiction over any case in which the plaintiff asserts a right protected by the Second Amendment.

10. Imagine that the House of Representatives has subpoenaed certain documents from the Secretary of Commerce, who has refused to comply with the subpoena (due to the assertion of executive privilege by the President). The House of Representatives

sues the Secretary of Commerce in federal district court and obtains an injunction ordering the Secretary to comply with the subpoena. The Secretary then appeals the district court's judgment to the Supreme Court, invoking a specific statute that permits the Court to hear appeals directly from federal district courts. (There is also a statute that permits the Supreme Court to hear appeals from federal courts of appeals, but that would require litigation and a final judgment from the court appeals first.) The Supreme Court agrees to hear the case. At oral argument, a majority of the justices appear poised to reverse the district court's judgment (and quash the subpoena). Before the Supreme Court hands down its decision, however, Congress enacts a new statute that repeals the statutory provision granting the Supreme Court jurisdiction over appeals directly from district courts—the provision on which the Court's subject matter jurisdiction is predicated in the pending case. Is the repealing statute constitutional? What should the Supreme Court do?

*   *   *

D.   The Eleventh Amendment

The text of the Eleventh Amendment provides that "[t]he Judicial power of the United States shall not be construed to extend to any suit in law or equity, commenced or prosecuted against one of the United States by Citizens of another State, or by Citizens or Subjects of any Foreign State." By the amendment's express terms, it deprives federal courts of subject matter jurisdiction over suits "commenced or prosecuted against one of the United States" by certain parties. Stated differently, the amendment confers immunity from suit in federal court on state governments in particular circumstances. But care is necessary in sorting out precisely when this bar applies. This section summarizes the contours of Eleventh Amendment doctrine; Chapter 12 will revisit the related topic of when Congress can use its legislative powers to abrogate states' sovereign immunity.

Importantly, the Eleventh Amendment only concerns the jurisdiction of *federal* courts. The Constitution poses no bar to private suits against state governments in state court. To be sure, states typically enjoy sovereign immunity in their own courts as a matter of *state* law (though states have enacted laws waiving that immunity in particular contexts, just as the United States has done for certain types of suits brought in federal court). But those laws reflect the states' own choices, not the dictates of the federal Constitution.

1. History and background

"Sovereign immunity" refers to a government's immunity from legal proceedings. It is an immunity from *suit*, not just from being held liable. Its roots lie in British law stemming from the notion that "the king can do no wrong." The doctrine now rests partly on the Eleventh Amendment, as well as a number of structural presuppositions the Eleventh Amendment confirms.

In drafting the Constitution, the Framers debated whether the Constitution should embrace any form of sovereign immunity. During ratification, they puzzled over how to reconcile sovereign immunity with the language of Article III. Again, Article III, §2, clause 1 provides that

> "[t]he judicial power shall extend . . . to controversies between two or more states; between a state and citizens of another state; between citizens of different states; between citizens of the same state claiming lands under grants of different states; and between a state, or the citizens thereof, and foreign states, citizens or subjects."

This text explicitly grants the federal judiciary the authority to adjudicate suits in which states are parties. But those suits might only be those in which the state is a *plaintiff*. Could a federal court hear a suit prosecuted by a private party *against* a state government without its consent? George Mason opposed ratification of the Constitution for precisely this reason; he understood Article III to render states vulnerable to unconsenting suits in federal court. By contrast, Alexander Hamilton and James Madison read Article III as leaving the states' sovereign immunity intact. Hamilton reasoned that the states' immunity from such suits was inherent in their retained sovereignty; Madison likewise thought Article III only permitted federal courts to hear cases in which states were plaintiffs.

In 1793, the Supreme Court addressed the issue in *Chisholm v. Georgia*, 2 U.S. (2 Dall.) 419. Robert Farquhar, a citizen of South Carolina, had supplied materials to Georgia during the Revolutionary War. After the war, Georgia refused to pay Farquhar's invoice. Farquhar sued in federal court, but Georgia refused to appear, believing it was immune from suit absent its consent. In *Chisholm*, the Supreme Court held that Article III, §2 rendered the states amenable to unconsenting actions in federal court brought by citizens of other states. The Court reasoned that a plain reading of the Constitution dictates federal courts can adjudicate controversies "between" states and citizens of another state. In dissent, Justice Iredell contended that the nature of sovereignty meant only a *consenting* sovereign could be sued; the federal judiciary thus exceeded its constitutional powers by adjudicating an unconsenting suit brought against a state by a private plaintiff.

In the wake of the Revolutionary War, states feared plaintiffs might sue them to recover unpaid war debts, and the judgment in *Chisholm* heightened those concerns. (Indeed, Georgia enacted a statute providing that anyone attempting to enforce the Court's holding in *Chisholm* would be "hereby declared to be guilty of a felony, and shall suffer death, without the benefit of clergy, by being hanged."[7]) This backlash to *Chisholm* resulted in the prompt swift ratification of the Eleventh Amendment.

2. Suits against states by their own citizens: *Hans v. Louisiana*

The text of the Eleventh Amendment would seem only to bar subject matter jurisdiction over suits brought against a state government "by Citizens of another State, or by Citizens or Subjects of any Foreign State." But in *Hans v. Louisiana*, 134 U.S. 1 (1890), the Supreme Court held it extends to nonconsenting private suits against states when brought by their own citizens. Hans, a Louisiana citizen, had purchased bonds issued by Louisiana. Louisiana then amended its constitution to forbid the state from making interest payments on the bonds. Hans sued Louisiana in federal court, alleging the state's constitutional amendment (and its consequent failure to make the interest payments) violated the Contracts Clause of Article I, §10, clause 1.

The Supreme Court held that, despite Hans being a citizen of the state he had sued, the Eleventh Amendment deprived the district court of subject matter jurisdiction. To the Court, those who had drafted and ratified the Eleventh Amendment surely must have assumed that states were *already* constitutionally immune from suits commenced by their own citizens, and thus saw no need to address the matter in the text of the amendment:

> "Can we suppose that, when the Eleventh Amendment was adopted, it was understood to be left open for citizens of a State to sue their own state in federal courts, whilst the idea of suits by citizens of other states, or of foreign states, was indignantly repelled? . . . The supposition that it would is almost an absurdity on its face."

Thus, it is not so much the Eleventh Amendment itself, but the structural principles the Amendment presupposes, that prescribed the result in *Hans*. And since *Hans*, it has been accepted doctrine that the Constitution bars federal courts from adjudicating private unconsenting suits commenced against a state, regardless of the plaintiff's state of citizenship. The precise constitutional source of this rule is largely a theoretical question, of no practical consequence. The states' constitutional immunity extends to *all* private unconsenting actions brought in federal court.

3. "Unconsenting" suits

When applicable, the Eleventh Amendment only deprives federal courts of jurisdiction over suits brought by private plaintiffs to which a state has not *consented*. State governments can waive or forfeit their Eleventh Amendment immunity by making themselves amenable to suit. This makes the Eleventh Amendment a misfit among the rules of federal subject matter jurisdiction, as it's a basic axiom that a federal court's lack of subject matter jurisdiction *can*

---

[7] PETER W. LOW & JOHN C. JEFFRIES, JR., FEDERAL COURTS AND THE LAW OF FEDERAL-STATE RELATIONS 810 (5th Ed. 2004).

never be waived by a party. The immunity afforded by the Eleventh Amendment is different: though it defines the contours of the federal courts' subject matter jurisdiction, it nonetheless can be waived (due to its origins in the doctrine of sovereign immunity, an immunity that has always be waivable).

a. *Waiver by state statute*

One way a state can effect such a waiver is by enacting a statute proclaiming the state's amenability to suit. For example, a state might enact a law providing that "any plaintiff may sue the state government, and seek any form of appropriate relief (including damages), in state or federal court, for the state government's violation of any applicable anti-discrimination law." Such statutory waivers are uncommon, but they exist, and they grant federal courts jurisdiction over suits otherwise barred by the Eleventh Amendment. Still, the Supreme Court has emphasized that the test for determining whether a state has waived its Eleventh Amendment immunity in this fashion "is a stringent one." *Atascadero State Hosp. v. Scanlon*, 473 U.S. 234, 241 (1985). As the Court explained in *Port Authority Trans-Hudson Corp. v. Feeney*, 495 U.S. 299 (1990), a federal court should interpret a state statute as effectuating such a waiver "only where stated by the most express language or by such overwhelming implication from the text as [will] leave no room for any other reasonable construction." For example, a state "does not waive its Eleventh Amendment immunity by consenting to suit only in its own courts." Instead, it must "specify the State's intention to subject itself to suit in *federal* court."

b. *Waiver through participation in a federal spending program*

Similarly, a state can waive its Eleventh Amendment immunity by agreeing to participate in a federal spending program, where a condition of participation is being amenable to private suits in federal court. For example, the federal Religious Land Use and Institutionalized Persons Act (RLUIPA) provides that states that accept federal funds covered by the Act may not "impose a substantial burden on the religious exercise" of an institutionalized person (*e.g.*, a person incarcerated in a state prison), and persons subjected to such "substantial burdens" may assert a cause of action in "a judicial proceeding and obtain appropriate relief against a [state] government." In *Sossamon v. Texas*, 563 U.S. 277 (2011), the Supreme Court held that this language did not mean that states accepting RLUIPA funds had waived their Eleventh Amendment immunity in federal court because RLUIPA's authorization of "appropriate relief against a government" was not an "unequivocal expression of state consent. . . . 'Appropriate relief' does not so clearly and unambiguously waive sovereign immunity to private suits for damages that we can 'be certain that the State in fact consents' to such a suit." But if the text of RLUIPA had constituted a "clear" and "unambiguous" waiver of immunity from suit in federal court, a states' participation in the program would have been sufficient to eliminate the Eleventh Amendment bar to private suits.

c. *Waiver through litigation conduct*

States can also forfeit their Eleventh Amendment immunity (at least in a particular case) through their conduct in litigation. First, when a state itself files a claim in federal court, it necessarily forfeits its immunity from being subjected to the federal court's jurisdiction. *See Gardner v. New Jersey*, 329 U.S. 565 (1947). Second, if a private plaintiff sues a state government in state court, and the state then removes the case to federal court—thereby invoking the federal court's jurisdiction—it forfeits its right to assert Eleventh Amendment immunity. As the Supreme Court explained in *Lapides v. Board of Regents*, 535 U.S. 613 (2002),

> "It would seem anomalous or inconsistent for a State both (1) to invoke federal jurisdiction, thereby contending that the 'Judicial power of the United States' extends to the case at hand, and (2) to claim Eleventh Amendment immunity, thereby denying that the 'Judicial power of the United States' extends to the case at hand. And a Constitution that permitted States to follow their litigation interests by freely asserting both claims in the same case could generate seriously unfair results."

Still, the voluntary appearance of a state in federal court, without more, will generally not constitute a waiver of Eleventh Amendment immunity. In this respect, a state does not waive this immunity nearly so easily as the defense of a lack of personal jurisdiction (which is generally waived by a party if it fails to raise the defense in its first responsive filing).

4. Implicit consent through the "plan of the Convention"

The Eleventh Amendment also does not afford states any immunity from those suits to which they implicitly consented by entering the Union upon ratification of the Constitution. The idea is that "the plan of the Convention" was for states to be amenable to certain kinds suits, and the Eleventh Amendment did nothing to disturb this arrangement. As the Supreme Court recently explained in *PennEast Pipeline Co. v. New Jersey*, 141 S. Ct. 2244 (2021), "where the States agreed in the plan of the Convention not to assert any sovereign immunity defense, no congressional abrogation is needed." What sorts of suits does this include? The Court has identified five categories: (1) actions brought by other states, at least when the state plaintiff is seeking to vindicate its own interests (rather than the private interests of its citizens), *see, e.g., Colorado v. New Mexico,* 459 U.S. 176 (1982); (2) actions brought by the federal government, *see, e.g., United States v. Mississippi,* 380 U.S. 128 (1965); (3) claims against states arising in bankruptcy proceedings, *see, e.g., Central Va. Community College v. Katz,* 546 U. S. 356, 379 (2006); (4) cases where the federal government has validly exercised its eminent domain power, "including in condemnation proceedings brought by private delegates," *PennEast Pipeline,* 141 S. Ct. at 2259; and (5) actions brought under federal statutes enacted by

Congress under its authority "to build and keep a national military," *Torres v. Texas Dept. of Public Safety*, No. 20–603 (2022), slip op. at 2.

Importantly, these categories do not include *all* actions brought by governmental (or sovereign-like) plaintiffs. The Eleventh Amendment still deprives federal courts of jurisdiction over unconsenting actions against states brought by foreign nations, *see Principality of Monaco v. Mississippi*, 292 U.S. 313 (1934), or by Native American tribes, *see Seminole Tribe of Florida v. Florida*, 517 U.S. 44, 56 (1996).

5. Appeals of state court judgments to the Supreme Court

It is well settled that the Eleventh Amendment poses no barrier to the Supreme Court's hearing appeals from a state's highest court in cases originally brought by a state as a plaintiff. This was first resolved in *Cohens v. Virginia*, 19 U.S. 264 (1821) (discussed in Chapter 3). Virginia had criminally prosecuted the Cohen brothers in Virginia state court for violating a state law forbidding the sale of lottery tickets. The Cohens were convicted, and their convictions were upheld by the Virginia Court of Appeals (the state's highest court). The Cohens then appealed to the Supreme Court, contending their convictions were invalid under federal law. In response, Virginia argued that the Supreme Court's jurisdiction over the appeal was barred by the Eleventh Amendment. In an opinion by Chief Justice Marshall, the Court held that the Eleventh Amendment was beside the point because it only bars jurisdiction over actions "commenced or prosecuted *against*" a state. When a state *initiates* a suit in state court—and the party sued later seeks review at the Supreme Court—the appeal does not meet this definition. As Marshall explained, a litigant who appeals "a judgment rendered against him by a State court into this Court for the purpose of reexamining the question whether that judgment be in violation of the Constitution or laws of the United States does not commence or prosecute a suit against the State."

6. Suits against local or municipal governments

Unlike all other aspects of constitutional law—under which local and municipal governments are considered extensions of the states—only *state* governments proper are considered "one of the United States" under the Eleventh Amendment. Thus, Eleventh Amendment immunity does not extend to local governments, whether they be cities, counties, school districts, utility districts, or the like. Nonetheless, where a state is so involved in the matter that a suit against the local government effectively constitutes a suit against the state itself, the Eleventh Amendment applies. *See Pennhurst State School & Hospital v. Halderman*, 465 U.S. 89 (1984). And Eleventh Amendment immunity extends to all "arms of the state." This means state agencies and executive departments are clearly protected by the Eleventh Amendment, and so often (but not always) are entities like state universities. Whether state boards, corporations, and various other entities enjoy Eleventh Amendment immunity depends on the nature of the relationship between the relevant entity and the state in question. Factors courts have examined in determining whether a governmental entity constitutes an "arm of the state" include (1) whether a judgment against the entity would be paid by funds drawn from the state treasury; (2) whether the state government exerts significant control over the entity's actions; (3) whether the state executive or legislative branch appoints the entity's policymakers; and (4) how state law formally characterizes the entity. *See* Erwin Chemerinsky, Federal Jurisdiction, at 456 (7th ed. 2016).

7. Official capacity suits against state officers: *Ex parte Young*

The most significant "exception" to the immunity conferred by the Eleventh Amendment is that recognized in *Ex parte Young*, 209 U.S. 123 (1908). *Ex parte Young* establishes that—though a private plaintiff cannot sue a state itself in federal court without the state's consent—it can sue the relevant *state officer* in her official capacity for prospective relief. In an *Ex parte Young* action, the appropriate defendant is the officer responsible for enforcing or implementing the challenged state law or executive action.

Ex parte Young involved a Minnesota law that set the maximum rates railroads could charge freight customers. Northern Pacific Railway shareholders brought suit in federal court against Minnesota's attorney general (Edward Young) to prohibit him from enforcing the statute. The district court issued a preliminary injunction forbidding Young from enforcing the law, but Young defied the court's order. The district court thus placed Young in federal custody for contempt of court. Young then petitioned for a writ of habeas corpus, claiming the shareholders' suit was barred by the Eleventh Amendment.

The Supreme Court concluded that the Eleventh Amendment did not divest the district court of jurisdiction over the shareholders' suit. The Court's rather creative rationale went as follows. State officers lack the constitutional authority to violate federal law. Indeed, all governmental officials in the U.S. are obligated by their offices to act consistent with the federal Constitution and any applicable federal statutes. Thus, when a state officer violates federal law (and thus acts beyond the scope of his authority), he is no longer technically acting on behalf of the state (though he is still acting with governmental authority for purposes of the state action doctrine). Therefore, a lawsuit seeking only to bring a state officer's actions within the boundaries permitted by federal law is not *actually* a suit against the state, since no state is permitted to violate federal law. (Such, at least, is the theory of *Ex parte Young*.)

More realistically, *Ex parte Young* created a legal fiction—albeit a fiction with enormous practical consequences. So long as a private plaintiff names the appropriate state officer (and not the state itself) as the defendant in her complaint, the plaintiff's claim for prospective relief will not be barred by the Eleventh Amendment. This means federal courts can adjudicate all sorts of claims that state governments are acting unconstitutionally—for instance, in denying individuals the right to vote, limiting marriage licenses to opposite-sex couples, or depriving people of their reproductive freedoms. Indeed, many of the most significant decisions in modern constitutional history have been predicated on *Ex parte Young*.

*   *   *

EXAMPLE

Suppose a New York law only permits gun owners (who legally possess guns with a license) to transport those firearms to a handful of designated firing ranges within the state. Any other transportation of firearms within the state—even if only to transport the gun to a second residence—is prohibited. A private citizen who owns a gun believes the New York law violates the Constitution's Second Amendment. The Eleventh Amendment would prohibit the gun owner from suing the State of New York in federal court. But the gun owner could sue the New York state officer responsible for enforcing the law (most likely, the state's attorney general) in federal court seeking an injunction that would forbid the officer from enforcing the law against him. In this way, private plaintiffs can, as a practical matter, sue to prevent state governments from violating federal law. But they can only obtain a change in the state government's conduct *going forward*, and not any damages or compensation for prior violations (unless the state has waived its Eleventh Amendment immunity.)

*   *   *

8. Distinguishing prospective from retrospective relief

Ex parte Young only applies when a plaintiff seeks prospective relief. The most common forms of prospective relief are injunctions and declaratory judgments. *Ex parte Young* does not permit actions for retrospective relief, relief that seeks compensation to make a plaintiff whole for past wrongs. The most common form of retrospective relief is damages, but it includes other forms of compensatory remedies (such as restitution).

When deciding whether a particular form of relief is prospective or retrospective, courts will examine the relief's practical effects, not just the plaintiff's formal pleading. Thus, if a private suit seeks relief that effectively seeks funds paid out of the state's treasury based on prior actions or inactions, the relief will be considered retrospective. For instance, the plaintiff in *Edelman v. Jordan*, 415 U.S. 651 (1974), claimed the State of Illinois was violating federal law in its processing of residents' welfare applications. He brought suit against the Illinois Commissioner of the Department of Public Welfare, seeking two injunctions. One injunction would have required the state to comply with the existing federal welfare guidelines going forward; the other would have required the commissioner to pay funds it had previously withheld (allegedly in violation of federal law). The Supreme Court held that, because the second injunction would have required monetary relief to be drawn from the state's treasury for past violations, it constituted retrospective relief. As such, the claim for the second injunction exceeded the doctrine of *Ex parte Young* and was barred by Eleventh Amendment.

Nonetheless, a prospective injunction or declaratory judgment may portend significant financial consequences for a state. For example, in *Edelman v. Jordan*, Illinois's compliance with federal welfare law might have meant much larger welfare payments in the future, costing the state millions of dollars. But such an injunction is still permissible under *Ex parte Young* because the relief only concerns the future behavior of the state official; it does not seek any compensation for past acts.

9. Congress's authority to abrogate states' sovereign immunity

A final detail concerns Congress's authority, in limited circumstances, to pierce the immunity provided by the Eleventh Amendment. Specifically, Congress can enact a statute that *abrogates* states' Eleventh Amendment immunity, and thus subjects them to unconsenting private suits in federal court. But Congress can do so only if the statute is within the legislative authority granted by §5 of the Fourteenth Amendment.[8] Statutes enacted pursuant to Congress's other legislative powers—though they still constitute valid federal laws—cannot strip the states of their sovereign immunity.

As will be discussed in Chapter 12, the scope of Congress's §5 power is relatively narrow. But when a federal statute fits within this power, Congress can choose to subject state governments to private unconsenting suits in federal court. For example, in enacting Title VII of the Civil Rights Act of 1964, Congress has prohibited all employers—including state governments—from discriminating based on race in the terms and conditions of employment. And Title VII subjects employers violating this prohibition to private suits for damages. As applied to state governments, Title VII is a valid exercise of Congress's power under §5 of the Fourteenth Amendment. As a result, Title VII abrogates the states' Eleventh Amendment immunity and subjects the states to private unconsenting suits in federal court—for damages and any other form of appropriate relief. *See Fitzpatrick v. Bitzer*, 427 U.S. 445 (1976).

For Congress to successfully abrogate states' Eleventh Amendment immunity, two conditions must hold. First, again, the statute purporting to abrogate the states' immunity must be valid under §5 of the Fourteenth Amendment; it is insufficient that the law would be valid under one of Congress's other

---

[8] As explained in section D.5 *supra*, states are not protected from unconsenting claims brought against them in bankruptcy proceedings. And Congress has enacted federal bankruptcy law pursuant to its authority under Article I, §8, clause 4 to establish "uniform laws on the subject of Bankruptcies throughout the United States." But as the Court recently explained, Congress has not actually abrogated states' sovereign immunity through federal bankruptcy statutes. Instead, the states implicitly agreed at the Framing to waive any immunity from claims asserted against them in bankruptcy proceedings. *See PennEast Pipeline*, 141 S. Ct. at 2259.

enumerated powers.[9] Second, the statute must express Congress's intent to do so in "unmistakably clear" terms. Any ambiguity in the statute's text will be construed against abrogation.

* * *

QUESTION: Suppose Oregon enacts a state statute that forbids the sale of gasoline-powered vehicles in the state beginning in 2025. In 2024, General Motors (GM) files a lawsuit in federal district court against the State of Oregon asserting the new law is preempted by federal statutes regulating the sale of automobiles nationwide. GM seeks an injunction prohibiting the state from enforcing the new law. Does the court have subject matter jurisdiction?

ANSWER: No. This is a suit brought by a private party against a state in federal court to which the state has not consented. The Eleventh Amendment bars a federal court from hearing such a suit.

QUESTION: Suppose that GM instead sues the Director of the Oregon Department of Environmental Quality, the officer responsible for enforcing the new state law. Would the answer change?

ANSWER: Yes. In this case, GM's suit fits within the doctrine of *Ex parte Young*, which permits private unconsenting suits in federal court against state officers so long as the action seeks prospective relief. The suit must be against the officer in her official capacity, but a claim seeking an injunction against the enforcement of a state law will meet this requirement. Such actions inherently target the officer's official responsibilities. Thus, the district court would have subject matter jurisdiction.

QUESTION: Suppose GM instead files the suit in 2026, again against the Director, seeking both an injunction and damages (for GM's lost revenue in 2025 and 2026 due to the operation of the state law).

ANSWER: The district court would have subject matter jurisdiction to adjudicate the claim for an injunction. But GM's claim seeking damages falls outside *Ex parte Young* because damages are a form of retrospective (rather than prospective) relief. Thus, the court would need to dismiss the claim for damages, but it would retain jurisdiction over the claim for an injunction.

* * *

---

[9] It is conceivable that the Court could decide in the future that some other enumerated power also gives Congress the authority to abrogate states' immunity. But that seems unlikely. In the recent decision of *Allen v. Cooper*, 140 S. Ct. 994 (2020), for instance, the Court held that Congress lacks the power to abrogate states' sovereign immunity using its power to regulate intellectual property.

PROBLEMS ON THE ELEVENTH AMENDMENT

For each of the following scenarios, please evaluate whether the Eleventh Amendment forbids the court where the action has been filed from exercising subject matter jurisdiction. Please explain the source of authority supporting your conclusion.

1. California enacts a statute prohibiting the sale to minors of video games containing "ultra-violent" content. (The statute provides a lengthy definition of what constitutes such content.) Plaintiff, a citizen of Arizona, is a producer of video games that meet the statutory definition of "ultra-violent," and she regularly sells these games to California consumers. Plaintiff files suit against California in the U.S. District Court for the Northern District of California. In her complaint, Plaintiff seeks an injunction prohibiting the state from enforcing the statute against her.

2. The facts are the same as (1), except Plaintiff is a citizen of California.

3. The facts are the same as in (2), except Plaintiff names California's attorney general as the defendant in the action (rather than the state). The action is against the attorney general in his official capacity.

4. The facts are the same as (3), except Plaintiff, in addition to seeking an injunction against the attorney general, also seeks $500,000 in damages for the loss of revenue she has suffered attributable to the enactment of the statute.

5. The facts are the same as (4), except Plaintiff files her action in California Superior Court for the County of Santa Clara.

6. Illinois enacts a so-called "sanctuary law" that forbids Illinois state or local law enforcement officers from cooperating with federal Immigration and Customs Enforcement (ICE) officials in ICE's efforts to detain or deport persons suspected of being undocumented. The United States files suit against Illinois in federal district court, seeking an injunction that would forbid the state from enforcing its sanctuary law.

7. The facts are the same as (6), except the suit is brought by Indiana. (Assume Indiana can show that it has suffered an injury that is fairly traceable to the enactment of Illinois's sanctuary law.) Please look closely at 28 U.S.C. §1251(a).

8. The facts are the same as in (6), except the suit is brought by an Illinois private citizen. (Again, assume that the plaintiff can establish that she has suffered an injury that is fairly traceable to the enactment of the Illinois law.)

9. The facts are the same as in (8), except the "sanctuary law" at issue—instead of being enacted by Illinois—was enacted by the city of Chicago, and thus the action is brought against the city of Chicago in federal district court.

10. A professor at UC-Berkeley was accused by the university of using the university's name in an unauthorized fashion, in connection with the professor's extra-professional political activities. The university sued the professor in California Superior Court, seeking an injunction prohibiting the professor from using the university's name in connection with his political activities. The superior court granted the

injunction, and its judgment was affirmed by the California Court of Appeal and the California Supreme Court. The professor has now appealed to the Supreme Court of the United States, on the ground that the university's efforts to suppress his political activities violate his federal constitutional right to free speech. (Assume the University of California is an arm of the state for purposes of the Eleventh Amendment.) May the Supreme Court exercise jurisdiction over the professor's appeal?

11. The facts are the same as in (10), except the university files suit against the professor in federal district court, asserting that his actions violated a federal statute. Again, as a defense to liability, the professor asserts that the university's conduct violated the First Amendment. The university files a motion to strike the professor's defense on the ground that the Eleventh Amendment deprives the district court of jurisdiction to adjudicate the professor's defense that the university is violating his free speech rights.

12. A federal statute (the Age Discrimination in Employment Act) prohibits discrimination on the basis of age in the terms or conditions of employment. The statute is a valid exercise of Congress's power to regulate "commerce among the states" under Article I, §8, clause 3. Plaintiff is 60 years old and a former employee of the Oregon state government. She sues Oregon in federal district court, seeking damages for her lost wages, on the ground that the state violated the statute by terminating her due to her age.

13. The facts are the same as in (12), except Plaintiff sues the Oregon attorney general in her official capacity. In her demand for relief, Plaintiff seeks an injunction requiring the attorney general to grant her "back pay" for the time she has been unlawfully deprived of her position.

14. The facts are the same as in (12), except Plaintiff instead claims that she was terminated due to her race in violation of a federal statute (Title VII of the Civil Rights Act of 1964)—a law Congress has the authority to enact under the power granted by §5 of the Fourteenth Amendment.

CHAPTER 5

JUSTICIABILITY: ADVISORY OPINIONS, STANDING, RIPENESS and MOOTNESS

An important constraint on the federal courts is that the Constitution only permits them to decide disputes that are "justiciable." While subject matter jurisdiction tends to focus on the topic of the dispute (*e.g.*, whether it arises under federal law) or the identity of the litigants (*e.g.*, whether they are citizens of different states), *justiciability* focuses on the nature of the dispute or a party's personal stake in the litigation. The most basic justiciability limitation is that Article III forbids federal courts from issuing so-called "advisory opinions." This prohibition goes to the core of the judiciary's proper role in our constitutional scheme. Stated differently, whenever a federal court adjudicates a nonjusticiable dispute—a dispute that is nonjusticiable for any reason—it issues an impermissible "advisory opinion."

A. The Prohibition on Advisory Opinions

The prohibition on advisory opinions was established by some famous precedents quite early in the nation's history. There are two basic criteria that determine whether a judicial opinion is impermissibly "advisory." Specifically, a judicial decision constitutes a prohibited advisory opinion if (1) there is not an actual legal dispute between adverse parties, or (2) there is not a substantial likelihood the decision will have a binding legal effect on the parties.

1. An actual legal dispute between adverse parties

To constitute a "case" or "controversy" under Article III, there must be an actual, concrete legal dispute between adverse parties. It is insufficient that the parties seeking the court's intervention care deeply about the answer to the legal question they have posed.

This principle was firmly established shortly after ratification, during the presidential administration of George Washington. Washington's Secretary of State, Thomas Jefferson, sought the advice of the Supreme Court concerning the justices' interpretation of federal statutes that required the United States to remain neutral in an ongoing war between France and Great Britain. The justices politely refused Jefferson's request, explaining that it was beyond their constitutional authority—other than in the context of actual case before the Court—to announce an opinion about the meaning of federal law. Article III does not permit federal courts to offer such "advice," however helpful or desirable. Pronouncing such views is not part of the "judicial power" granted by the Constitution.

* * *

QUESTION: Suppose, while Congress is debating a federal statute regulating the possession of semi-automatic weapons and large ammunition magazines, Congress seeks the Supreme Court's view on whether the bill would violate the Second Amendment's right to "keep and bear arms." Members of Congress seek the Court's opinion because it would be an enormous waste of time (and political capital) for Congress to enact the law, only to have it ultimately invalidated as unconstitutional a few years later. May the Court respond to Congress's query?

ANSWER: No. For the Court to answer this question, in this posture, would be to issue an advisory opinion, as there would be no concrete legal proceeding between adverse parties. What Congress would be asking the Court to decide—though clearly a question "arising under [the] Constitution"—is not a "case" or "controversy" within the meaning of Article III.

QUESTION: Suppose the exact same facts, but instead the bill is a proposed Massachusetts state statute being debated among lawmakers in the Massachusetts legislature, and the legislature asks the Massachusetts Supreme Judicial Court (the state's highest court) to decide whether the law would be constitutional.

ANSWER: This would be fully consistent with the federal Constitution. Article III only governs the authority of the *federal* judiciary—and specifically, what "cases" or "controversies" federal courts are empowered to decide. This hypothetical potentially raises a question about the authority granted to the Massachusetts Supreme Judicial Court as a matter of Massachusetts state law. But many states—including Massachusetts—permit their highest courts to issue advisory opinions under circumstances like these. These state procedures are perfectly consistent with Article III and the federal Constitution.

* * *

2. Decisions lacking binding legal effect

A judicial decision will also constitute an advisory opinion if it lacks a substantial likelihood of having a binding legal effect on the parties. The most famous example of a statute attempting to grant the federal courts such authority was the law at issue in *Hayburn's Case*, 2 U.S. (2 Dall.) 409 (1792). A statute enacted by Congress shortly after the Revolutionary War required federal courts to reach initial judgments as to the validity of pension claims submitted by war veterans. The Secretary of War would then take the courts' decisions under advisement but was not bound to follow their rulings. Under the statute, the Secretary's independent judgment as to whether to pay a given veteran's claim was final, regardless of what the court had previously decided.

Five different Supreme Court justices (sitting as circuit judges in different cases) concluded that this scheme violated Article III. And the Supreme Court later summarily dismissed a case—a form of decision on the merits—in a manner consistent with that view. Because the statute called for federal courts to

104

issue decisions that were advisory in every sense—merely to be taken under advisement by the Secretary of War—it was unconstitutional. Since *Hayburn's Case*, it has been understood that Article III precludes federal courts from issuing decisions that lack a substantial likelihood of having a binding legal effect on the parties.

3. The constitutional basis for the prohibition

Again, the justiciability limitations imposed by Article III only apply to federal courts. Article III establishes the federal judicial power. States, on the other hand, are free to organize their courts however they wish, so long as they do not run afoul of any constitutional prohibitions that apply to the states.

Moreover, it is worth recognizing that the issuance of advisory opinions could be fully consistent with various understandings of democratic government and the separation of powers. Indeed, there might be several advantages to permitting federal courts to render advisory opinions. It might be more efficient, as we would not need to wait for a party with a concrete interest to file a lawsuit and have the case wind its way through the lower courts before the question is settled. Many unconstitutional laws probably are never challenged because of the hassle and expense of litigating; perhaps the availability of advisory opinions would keep some of these laws off of the books. And it might be better for federal courts to examine difficult legal questions when they are still in a relatively abstract form, before the parties' concrete interests (and the decision's political consequences) could bias the courts' reasoning.

But that is not the system created by Article III. The prohibition on advisory opinions has long been considered a foundational constraint on the federal judiciary. With the power of judicial review, federal courts effectively have the power to override the constitutional judgments of both Congress and the President. This is strong medicine—especially in a democracy, given that the federal judiciary is the only branch that is not electorally accountable. An important constraint on this power is that it may only be used *reactively*, when legal question are brought before the courts by adverse parties with concrete legal disputes. If federal courts were not required to wait passively for issues to be brought before them—and could instead decide important legal questions proactively, on their own initiative—the counter-majoritarian tensions inherent in judicial review would be aggravated considerably.

B. Standing

The most frequently litigated justiciability requirement—and therefore likely the most practically significant—is that of *standing*. For a legal dispute to constitute a "case" or "controversy" under Article III, §2, the party invoking the power of the federal judiciary must have standing. While subject matter jurisdiction generally refers to the *topic* of a given dispute, standing concerns a litigant's *personal stake* in the outcome.

Article III demands that a litigant meet three distinct requirements to establish standing in federal court:

1. The litigant must demonstrate she has suffered an "injury in fact"—a harm that is concrete, particularized, and either actual or imminent.

2. She must demonstrate there is a causal connection between her injury and the allegedly unlawful action—that her injury is "fairly [traceable] to the challenged action of the defendant, and [not] the result [of] the independent action of some third party not before the court."

3. She must show it is "likely," and not merely "speculative," that her injury will be redressed by a favorable decision from the court.

Standing must exist until a federal court enters final judgment. Thus, the plaintiff must have standing when she files her complaint, and through the moment the district court finally disposes of the case. If there is an appeal, the appellant—the party who is invoking the power of the appellate court—must have standing to bring the appeal, and until the court of appeals hands down its decision. And if either party appeals to the Supreme Court, standing must still exist while the Court decides the case. If standing is somehow lost, the case (or the appeal) must at that point be dismissed.

1. Injury in fact

The first and most basic element of standing is the requirement that the party enlisting a federal court to exercise its adjudicatory authority must demonstrate an "injury in fact." In the district court, this burden falls on the plaintiff—the party asking the court to use its power—who must make a plausible showing of her injury in her complaint. The injury must be "concrete," "particularized," and either "actual or imminent."

The Supreme Court's decision in *Summers v. Earth Island Institute*, 555 U.S. 488 (2009), is not especially important in terms of the precise question it resolves. But it is a nice example of a typical standing dispute, one challenging enough to reach the Supreme Court. At issue was a regulation promulgated by the U.S. Forest Service that exempted certain projects (fire-rehabilitation activities on areas of less than 4,200 acres and salvage-timber sales of 250 acres or less) from the requirement to file an environmental impact statement or environmental assessment. This meant that, under the regulation, these projects were not subject to the notice, comment, and appeal processes available for larger projects. Earth Island Institute and several other groups challenged the regulation as inconsistent with the Forest Service Decisionmaking and Appeals Reform Act. Before reaching the merits of that claim, however, the Court first needed to resolve whether the plaintiff had standing to bring its suit. As you read the Court's decision, please consider the following questions:

1. Which of the standing requirements did Earth Island Institute have difficulty meeting? Why?

2. What injury (or injuries) did it assert it had suffered (or would suffer) as a result of the Forest Service's actions? In practical terms, how did it attempt to make this demonstration?

3. In the view of the Court, why was the plaintiff's showing insufficient to support standing?

4. Given the Court's analysis, what sort of showing would have been sufficient under the circumstances for the plaintiff to have established its standing to bring suit?

Summers v. Earth Island Institute
555 U.S. 488 (2009)

JUSTICE SCALIA delivered the opinion of the Court.

Respondents are a group of organizations dedicated to protecting the environment. (We will refer to them collectively as "Earth Island.") They seek to prevent the United States Forest Service from enforcing regulations that exempt small fire-rehabilitation and timber-salvage projects from the notice, comment, and appeal process used by the Forest Service for more significant land management decisions. We must determine whether respondents have standing to challenge the regulations in the absence of a live dispute over a concrete application of those regulations.

I

In 1992, Congress enacted the Forest Service Decisionmaking and Appeals Reform Act. Among other things, this required the Forest Service to establish a notice, comment, and appeal process for "proposed actions of the Forest Service concerning projects and activities implementing land and resource management plans developed under the Forest and Rangeland Renewable Resources Planning Act of 1974."

The Forest Service's regulations implementing the Act provided that certain of its procedures would not be applied to projects that the Service considered categorically excluded from the requirement to file an environmental impact statement (EIS) or environmental assessment (EA). Later amendments to the Forest Service's manual of implementing procedures, adopted by rule after notice and comment, provided that fire-rehabilitation activities on areas of less than 4,200 acres, and salvage-timber sales of 250 acres or less, did not cause a significant environmental impact and thus would be categorically exempt from the requirement to file an EIS or EA. This had the effect of excluding these projects from the notice, comment, and appeal process.

In the summer of 2002, fire burned a significant area of the Sequoia National Forest. In September 2003, the Service issued a decision memo approving the Burnt Ridge Project, a salvage sale of timber on 238 acres damaged by that fire. Pursuant to its categorical exclusion of salvage sales of less than 250 acres, the Forest Service did not provide notice in a form consistent with the Appeals Reform Act, did not provide a period of public comment, and did not make an appeal process available.

In December 2003, respondents filed a complaint in the Eastern District of California, challenging the failure of the Forest Service to apply to the Burnt Ridge Project §215.4(a) of its regulations implementing the Appeals Reform Act (requiring prior notice and comment), and §215.12(f) of the regulations (setting forth an appeal procedure). . . .

The District Court granted a preliminary injunction against the Burnt Ridge salvage-timber sale. Soon thereafter, the parties settled their dispute over the Burnt Ridge Project and the District Court concluded that the Burnt Ridge timber sale is not at issue in this case. The Government argued that, with the Burnt Ridge dispute settled, and with no other project before the court in which respondents were threatened with injury in fact, respondents lacked standing to challenge the regulations; and that absent a concrete dispute over a particular project a challenge to the regulations would not be ripe. The District Court proceeded, however, to adjudicate the merits of Earth Island's challenges. It invalidated five of the regulations (including §§ 215.4(a) and 215.12(f)) and entered a nationwide injunction against their application.

The Ninth Circuit . . . affirmed the District Court's determination that §§ 215.4(a) and 215.12(f), which were applicable to the Burnt Ridge Project, were contrary to law, and upheld the nationwide injunction against their application.

The Government sought review of the question whether Earth Island could challenge the regulations at issue in the Burnt Ridge Project, and if so whether a nationwide injunction was appropriate relief. We granted certiorari.

II

In limiting the judicial power to "Cases" and "Controversies," Article III of the Constitution restricts it to the traditional role of Anglo-American courts, which is to redress or prevent actual or imminently threatened injury to persons caused by private or official violation of law. Except when necessary in the execution of that function, courts have no charter to review and revise legislative and executive action. See *Lujan v. Defenders of Wildlife*, 504 U.S. 555, 559–560 (1992); *Los Angeles v. Lyons*, 461 U.S. 95, 111–112 (1983). This limitation "is founded in concern about the proper—and properly limited—role of the courts in a democratic society." *Warth v. Seldin*, 422 U.S. 490, 498 (1975).

The doctrine of standing is one of several doctrines that reflect this fundamental limitation. It requires federal courts to satisfy themselves that "the plaintiff has alleged such a personal stake in the outcome of the controversy as to warrant his invocation of federal-court jurisdiction." *Warth, supra*, at 498–499. He bears the burden of showing that he has standing for each type of relief sought. To seek injunctive relief, a plaintiff must show that he is under threat of suffering "injury in fact" that is concrete and particularized; the threat must be actual and imminent, not conjectural or hypothetical; it must be fairly traceable to the challenged action of the defendant; and it must be likely that a favorable judicial decision will prevent or redress the injury. This requirement assures that "there is a real need to exercise the power of judicial review in order to protect the interests of the complaining party," *Schlesinger v. Reservists Comm. to Stop the War*, 418 U.S. 208, 221 (1974). Where that need does not exist, allowing courts to oversee legislative or executive action "would significantly alter the allocation of power . . . away from a democratic form of government," *Richardson*, supra, at 188.

The regulations under challenge here neither require nor forbid any action on the part of respondents. The standards and procedures that they prescribe for Forest Service appeals govern only the conduct of Forest Service officials engaged in project planning. "[W]hen the plaintiff is not himself the object of the government action or inaction he challenges, standing is not precluded, but it is ordinarily 'substantially more difficult' to establish." *Defenders of Wildlife*, supra, at 562. Here, respondents can demonstrate standing only if application of the regulations by the Government will affect them in the manner described above.

It is common ground that the respondent organizations can assert the standing of their members. To establish the concrete and particularized injury that standing requires, respondents point to their members' recreational interests in the national forests. While generalized harm to the forest or the environment will not alone support standing, if that harm in fact affects the recreational or even the mere esthetic interests of the plaintiff, that will suffice. *Sierra Club v. Morton*, 405 U.S. 727, 734–736 (1972).

Affidavits submitted to the District Court alleged that organization member Ara Marderosian had repeatedly visited the Burnt Ridge site, that he had imminent plans to do so again, and that his interests in viewing the flora and fauna of the area would be harmed if the Burnt Ridge Project went forward without incorporation of the ideas he would have suggested if the Forest Service had provided him an opportunity to comment. The Government concedes this was sufficient to establish Article III standing with respect to Burnt Ridge. Marderosian's threatened injury with regard to that project was originally one of the bases for the present suit. After the District Court had issued a preliminary injunction, however, the parties settled their differences on that score. Marderosian's injury in fact with regard to that project has been remedied, and it is, as the District Court pronounced, "not at issue in this case." We know of no precedent for the proposition that when a plaintiff has sued to challenge the lawfulness of certain action or threatened action but has settled that suit, he retains standing to challenge the basis for that action (here, the regulation in the abstract), apart from any concrete application that threatens imminent harm to his interests. Such a holding would fly in the face of Article III's injury-in-fact requirement.

Respondents have identified no other application of the invalidated regulations that threatens imminent and concrete harm to the interests of their members. The only other affidavit relied on was that of Jim Bensman. He asserted, first, that he had suffered injury in the past from development on Forest Service land. That does not suffice for several reasons: because it was not tied to application of the challenged regulations, because it does not identify any particular site, and because it relates to past injury rather than imminent future injury that is sought to be enjoined.

Bensman's affidavit further asserts that he has visited many national forests and plans to visit several unnamed national forests in the future. Respondents describe this as a mere failure to "provide the name of each timber sale that affected [Bensman's] interests." It is much more (or much less) than that. It is a failure to allege that any particular timber sale or other project claimed to be unlawfully subject to the regulations will impede a specific and concrete plan of Bensman's to enjoy the national forests. The national forests occupy more than 190 million acres, an area larger than Texas. There may be a chance, but is hardly a likelihood, that Bensman's wanderings will bring him to a parcel about to be affected by a project unlawfully subject to the regulations. Indeed, without further specification it is impossible to tell which projects are (in respondents' view) unlawfully subject to the regulations. The allegations here present a weaker likelihood of concrete harm than that which we found insufficient in *Lyons*, 461 U.S. 95, where a plaintiff who alleged that he had been injured by an improper police chokehold sought injunctive relief barring use of the hold in the future. We said it was "no more than conjecture" that Lyons would be subjected to that chokehold upon a later encounter. *Id.*, at 108. Here we are asked to assume not only that Bensman will stumble across a project tract unlawfully subject to the regulations, but also that the tract is about to be developed by the Forest Service in a way that harms his recreational interests, and that he would have commented on the project but for the regulation. Accepting an intention to visit the national forests as adequate to confer standing to challenge any Government action affecting any portion of those forests would be tantamount to eliminating the requirement of concrete, particularized injury in fact.

The Bensman affidavit does refer specifically to a series of projects in the Allegheny National Forest that are subject to the challenged regulations. It does not assert, however, any firm intention to visit their locations, saying only that Bensman "want[s] to" go there. This vague desire to return is insufficient to satisfy the requirement of imminent injury: "Such 'some day' intentions—without any description of concrete plans, or indeed even any specification of when the some day will be—

110

do not support a finding of the 'actual or imminent' injury that our cases require." *Defenders of Wildlife*, 504 U.S., at 564.

Respondents argue that they have standing to bring their challenge because they have suffered procedural injury, namely that they have been denied the ability to file comments on some Forest Service actions and will continue to be so denied. But deprivation of a procedural right without some concrete interest that is affected by the deprivation—a procedural right *in vacuo*—is insufficient to create Article III standing. Only a "person who has been accorded a procedural right to protect his concrete interests can assert that right without meeting all the normal standards for redressability and immediacy." *Id.*, at 572, n. 7. Respondents alleged such injury in their challenge to the Burnt Ridge Project, claiming that but for the allegedly unlawful abridged procedures they would have been able to oppose the project that threatened to impinge on their concrete plans to observe nature in that specific area. But Burnt Ridge is now off the table.

It makes no difference that the procedural right has been accorded by Congress. That can loosen the strictures of the redressability prong of our standing inquiry—so that standing existed with regard to the Burnt Ridge Project, for example, despite the possibility that Earth Island's allegedly guaranteed right to comment would not be successful in persuading the Forest Service to avoid impairment of Earth Island's concrete interests. Unlike redressability, however, the requirement of injury in fact is a hard floor of Article III jurisdiction that cannot be removed by statute.

"[I]t would exceed [Article III's] limitations if, at the behest of Congress and in the absence of any showing of concrete injury, we were to entertain citizen suits to vindicate the public's nonconcrete interest in the proper administration of the laws. . . . [T]he party bringing suit must show that the action injures him in a concrete and personal way." *Id.*, at 580–581 (KENNEDY, J., concurring in part and concurring in judgment).

*   *   *

Notes on *Summers v. Earth Island Institute*

1. *The precise standing problem for the plaintiffs in* Summers: The difficulty for the plaintiff in *Summers* was not that it had never alleged an injury that was sufficient under Article III. As the Court explained,

"[a]ffidavits submitted to the District Court alleged that organization member Ara Marderosian had repeatedly visited the Burnt Ridge site, that he had imminent plans to do so again, and that his interests in viewing the flora and fauna of the area would be harmed if the Burnt Ridge Project went forward without incorporation of the ideas he would have suggested if the Forest Service had provided him an opportunity to comment."

The government conceded that these allegations were sufficient to demonstrate an injury in fact with respect to the application of the regulations to Burnt Ridge. The problem was that the parties had settled their dispute regarding the Burnt Ridge Project, such that it was no longer a part of the case. As a result, the plaintiff could not rely on a member's potential deprivation of the enjoyment of Burnt Ridge as an injury in fact fairly traceable to the challenged regulations. As the Court observed, the plaintiffs "ha[d] identified no other application of the invalidated regulations that threatens imminent and concrete harm to the interests of their members."

2. *The difficulty with the alleged harm from projects other than Burnt Ridge*: Once the alleged harm from the Burnt Ridge Project was set aside, the plaintiff's allegations with respect to a member's injuries from the regulations were thin. The only other affidavit on which it relied was that of Jim Bensman. Bensman first averred that he had visited forests potentially affected by the regulations in the past. But that could not establish any injury from the *future* application of the regulations; such an injury would only be possible if he credibly alleged that he would be visiting affected areas in the future. Bensman did aver that he "plan[ned] to visit several unnamed national forests in the future." But this allegation failed "to allege that any particular timber sale or other project claimed to be unlawfully subject to the regulations will impede a specific and concrete plan of Bensman's to enjoy the national forests." To constitute a concrete and particularized injury that was either actual or imminent, the allegation needed to be much more specific about how, precisely, Bensman was likely to be harmed by the Forest Service's application of the challenged regulation. Finally, although Bensman referred specifically "to a series of projects in the Allegheny National Forest that are subject to the regulations," he had not asserted "any firm intention to visit their locations." Thus, though the allegations with respect to the Allegheny National Forest may have been sufficiently specific, they included no showing that Bensman would "actually" or "imminently" suffer the injury he alleged. To the Court, Bensman's "vague desire to return [to the forest] is insufficient to satisfy the requirement of imminent injury."

3. *How might Earth Island Institute have cured its standing problem?*: It needed a member who had actual, concrete plans to visit areas that would be affected by the challenged Forest Service regulations, and it needed to demonstrate that the projects planned for those areas (and affected by the challenged regulations) would interfere with the member's enjoyment of those areas. The Court's analysis of Bensman's allegations regarding the Allegheny National Forest is revealing. The precise problem, said the Court, was that Bensman only alleged mere "some day intentions—without any description of concrete plans, or indeed even any specification of when the some day will be." Presumably, Earth Island Institute would have had standing if Bensman could have described concrete plans to visit areas affected by the regulations, and

how the regulations (if they allowed the projects to go forward) would have interfered with his recreational or aesthetic interests in the affected areas.

4. *Intangible injuries*: It is important to see that the Institute could have established standing even though its members' injuries were entirely intangible: the deprivation of the recreational and aesthetic enjoyment of various national forests. As the Court explained, "[w]hile generalized harm to the forest or the environment will not alone support standing, *if that harm in fact affects the recreational or even the mere esthetic interests of the plaintiff, that will suffice.*" All sorts of intangible injuries can be sufficient to support standing; these include the inability to display a monument of one's choice in a public park, *see Pleasant Grove City v. Summum*, 555 U.S. 460 (2009), or to engage in religious ceremonies, *see Church of Lukumi Babalu Aye, Inc. v. Hialeah*, 508 U.S. 520 (1993). More to the point here, the Court noted in *Lujan v. Defenders of Wildlife*, 504 U.S. 555 (1992), that "the desire to use or observe an animal species, even for purely aesthetic purposes," can constitute a sufficient harm to constitute an Article III injury. But when the plaintiff's alleged injury is intangible—a harm not traditionally recognized at common law, like a physical or economic injury—it can be more difficult to establish that it is sufficiently "concrete." (This issue is explored further below.)

5. *Organizational standing*: Notice that Earth Island Institute and a group of other organizations were the actual plaintiffs in this lawsuit, not any individuals. Yet in analyzing whether the Institute had standing, the Court focused on the injuries alleged by particular individuals (namely, Ara Marderosian and Jim Bensman). The reason is that an organization of individuals will have standing if (a) at least one of its members has standing in her own right, and (b) the lawsuit is germane to the association's purpose. (An organization can also establish standing, like any other party, when it suffers an injury itself, to its own institutional interests.) In practice, organizations generally do not file lawsuits that are not germane to their reason for being. Hence, the Court begins its analysis by just referring to the first requirement—"[i]t is common ground that the respondent organizations can assert the standing of their members"—and proceeding to analyze whether any of the group's members had standing as individuals.

6. *The jurisdictional nature of standing*: A fundamental point about standing is that it is *jurisdictional*. It is essentially a component of subject matter jurisdiction, and this has several important implications. First, it means that standing must exist at every point in the litigation, until the last appeal has been exhausted and the case is closed. Even if standing existed at the time the plaintiff filed her complaint, the case must be dismissed if standing disappears before the judgment is final. Second, the requirement cannot be waived by the parties. Indeed, federal courts are obligated to assure themselves that whichever party is invoking the court's power has standing to do so. Third, if a federal court determines at any point that standing is lacking, it must dismiss the action for want of jurisdiction. In some instances, this means vacating the entire proceeding, as if it had never occurred. On other occasions—when standing only poses a problem on appeal—the appeal might be dismissed, leaving the district court's judgment in place. Finally, a federal court must resolve that standing exists before addressing the merits of the dispute. Even if the merits question is easy, the court cannot assume standing *arguendo* and conclude the plaintiff would lose regardless. Such a decision—based on so-called "hypothetical standing"—would constitute an impermissible advisory opinion. As the Court explained in *Steel Co. v. Citizens for a Better Environment*, 523 U.S. 83 (1998), "[h]ypothetical jurisdiction produces nothing more than a hypothetical judgment—which comes to the same thing as an advisory opinion, disapproved by this Court from the beginning."

*   *   *

2. "Concrete and particularized" injuries

As the test articulated by the Supreme Court in *Earth Island Institute* makes clear, an Article III injury-in-fact must be "concrete," "particularized," and either "actual" or "imminent." The Court recently addressed the "concrete" and "particularized" requirements in *Spokeo v. Robins*, 578 U.S. 330 (2016). The plaintiff in *Spokeo* had filed a class action in federal district court alleging that Spokeo, a company operating a "people search engine," had violated the federal Fair Credit Reporting Act. As you read the opinion, please consider the following questions:

1. What exactly was the injury that had Robins alleged?

2. Of what relevance to the standing question was the fact that, in the Fair Credit Reporting Act, Congress had created an individual cause of action (that is, a statutory right to sue) for persons like Robins?

3. Did Robins's injury satisfy the "particularized" requirement? Did it satisfy the "concreteness" requirement? Why or why not?

4. What is the legal standard for determining whether an injury is sufficiently "particularized" to the plaintiff to support standing? For determining whether an injury is sufficiently "concrete"?

Spokeo, Inc. v. Robins
578 U.S. 330 (2016)

JUSTICE ALITO delivered the opinion of the Court.

This case presents the question whether respondent Robins has standing to maintain an action in federal court against petitioner Spokeo under the Fair Credit Reporting Act of 1970.

Spokeo operates a "people search engine." If an individual visits Spokeo's Web site and inputs a person's name, a phone number, or an e-mail address, Spokeo conducts a computerized search in a wide variety of databases and provides information about the subject of the search. Spokeo performed such a search for information about Robins, and some of the information it gathered and then disseminated was incorrect. When Robins learned of these inaccuracies, he filed a complaint on his own behalf and on behalf of a class of similarly situated individuals.

The District Court dismissed Robins' complaint for lack of standing, but a panel of the Ninth Circuit reversed. The Ninth Circuit noted, first, that Robins had alleged that "Spokeo violated his statutory rights, not just the statutory rights of other people," and, second, that "Robins's personal interests in the handling of his credit information are individualized rather than collective." Based on these two observations, the Ninth Circuit held that Robins had adequately alleged injury in fact, a requirement for standing under Article III of the Constitution.

This analysis was incomplete. As we have explained in our prior opinions, the injury-in-fact requirement requires a plaintiff to allege an injury that is both "concrete *and* particularized." *Friends of the Earth, Inc. v. Laidlaw Environmental Services (TOC), Inc.*, 528 U.S. 167, 180–181 (2000) (emphasis added). The Ninth Circuit's analysis focused on the second characteristic (particularity), but it overlooked the first (concreteness). We therefore vacate the decision below and remand for the Ninth Circuit to consider both aspects of the injury-in-fact requirement.

I

The FCRA seeks to ensure "fair and accurate credit reporting." To achieve this end, the Act regulates the creation and the use of "consumer report[s]" by "consumer reporting agenc[ies]" for certain specified purposes, including credit transactions, insurance, licensing, consumer-initiated business transactions, and employment. Enacted long before the advent of the Internet, the FCRA applies to companies that regularly disseminate information bearing on an individual's "credit worthiness, credit standing, credit capacity, character, general reputation, personal characteristics, or mode of living."

The FCRA imposes a host of requirements concerning the creation and use of consumer reports. As relevant here, the Act requires consumer reporting agencies to "follow reasonable procedures to assure maximum possible accuracy of" consumer reports; to notify providers and users of consumer information of their responsibilities under the Act; to limit the circumstances in which such agencies provide consumer reports "for employment purposes"; and to post toll-free numbers for consumers to request reports.

The Act also provides that "[a]ny person who willfully fails to comply with any requirement [of the Act] with respect to any [individual] is liable to that [individual]" for, among other things, either "actual damages" or statutory damages of $100 to $1,000 per violation, costs of the action and attorney's fees, and possibly punitive damages.

Spokeo is alleged to qualify as a "consumer reporting agency" under the FCRA. It operates a Web site that allows users to search for information about other individuals by name, e-mail address, or phone number. In response to an inquiry submitted online, Spokeo searches a wide spectrum of databases and gathers and provides information such as the individual's address, phone number, marital status, approximate age, occupation, hobbies, finances, shopping habits, and musical preferences. According to Robins, Spokeo markets its services to a variety of users, including not only "employers who want to evaluate prospective employees," but also "those who want to investigate prospective romantic partners or seek other personal information." Persons wishing to perform a Spokeo search need not disclose their identities, and much information is available for free.

At some point in time, someone . . . made a Spokeo search request for information about Robins, and Spokeo trawled its sources and generated a profile. . . . [Robins] became aware of the contents of that profile and discovered that it contained inaccurate information. His profile, he asserts, states that he is married, has children, is in his 50's, has a job, is relatively affluent, and holds a graduate degree. According to Robins' complaint, all of this information is incorrect.

Robins filed a class-action complaint . . . , claiming, among other things, that Spokeo willfully failed to comply with the FCRA requirements enumerated above.

The District Court initially denied Spokeo's motion to dismiss the complaint for lack of jurisdiction, but later reconsidered and dismissed the complaint with prejudice. The court found that Robins had not "properly pled" an injury in fact, as required by Article III.

The Court of Appeals for the Ninth Circuit reversed. Relying on Circuit precedent, the court began by stating that "the violation of a statutory right is usually a sufficient injury in fact to confer standing." The court recognized that "the Constitution limits the power of Congress to confer standing." But the court held that those limits were honored in this case because Robins alleged that "Spokeo violated *his* statutory rights, not just the statutory rights of other people," and because his "personal interests in the handling of his credit information are individualized rather than collective." The court thus concluded that Robins' "alleged violations of [his] statutory rights [were] sufficient to satisfy the injury-in-fact requirement of Article III." . . .

II

A

The Constitution confers limited authority on each branch of the Federal Government. It vests Congress with enumerated "legislative Powers," Art. I, § 1; it confers upon the President "[t]he executive Power," Art. II, § 1, cl. 1; and it endows the federal courts with "[t]he judicial Power of the United States," Art. III, § 1. In order to remain faithful to this tripartite structure, the power of the Federal Judiciary may not be permitted to intrude upon the powers given to the other branches. See *DaimlerChrysler Corp. v. Cuno*, 547 U.S. 332, 341 (2006); *Lujan v. Defenders of Wildlife*, 504 U.S. 555, 559–560 (1992).

Although the Constitution does not fully explain what is meant by "[t]he judicial Power of the United States," Art. III, § 1, it does specify that this power extends only to "Cases" and "Controversies," Art. III, § 2. And "[n]o principle is more fundamental to the judiciary's proper role in our system of government than the constitutional limitation of federal-court jurisdiction to actual cases or controversies." *Raines v. Byrd*, 521 U.S. 811, 818 (1997).

Standing to sue is a doctrine rooted in the traditional understanding of a case or controversy. The doctrine developed in our case law to ensure that federal courts do not exceed their authority as it has been traditionally understood. The doctrine limits the category of litigants empowered to maintain a lawsuit in federal court to seek redress for a legal wrong. In this way, "[t]he law of Article III standing . . . serves to prevent the judicial process from being used to usurp the powers of the political branches," *Clapper v. Amnesty Int'l USA*, 568 U.S. 398, 408 (2013), and confines the federal courts to a properly judicial role.

Our cases have established that the "irreducible constitutional minimum" of standing consists of three elements. *Lujan*, 504 U.S., at 560. The plaintiff must have (1) suffered an injury in fact, (2) that is fairly traceable to the challenged conduct of the defendant, and (3) that is likely to be redressed by a favorable judicial decision. Id., at 560–561. The plaintiff, as the party invoking federal jurisdiction, bears the burden of establishing these elements. *FW/PBS, Inc. v. Dallas*, 493 U.S. 215, 231 (1990). Where, as here, a case is at the pleading stage, the plaintiff must "clearly . . . allege facts demonstrating" each element. *Warth*, supra, at 518.

B

This case primarily concerns injury in fact, the "[f]irst and foremost" of standing's three elements. *Steel Co. v. Citizens for Better Environment*, 523 U.S. 83, 103 (1998). Injury in fact is a constitutional requirement, and "[i]t is settled that Congress cannot erase Article III's standing requirements by statutorily granting the right to sue to a plaintiff who would not otherwise have standing." *Raines*, supra, at 820, n. 3; see *Summers v. Earth Island Institute*, 555 U.S. 488, 497 (2009); *Gladstone, Realtors v. Village of Bellwood*, 441 U.S. 91, 100 (1979) ("In no event . . . may Congress abrogate the Art. III minima").

To establish injury in fact, a plaintiff must show that he or she suffered "an invasion of a legally protected interest" that is "concrete and particularized" and "actual or imminent, not conjectural or hypothetical." *Lujan*, 504 U.S., at 560. We discuss the particularization and concreteness requirements below.

For an injury to be "particularized," it "must affect the plaintiff in a personal and individual way." Ibid., n. 1; see also, e.g., *Cuno*, supra, at 342 ("plaintiff must allege personal injury"); *Whitmore v. Arkansas*, 495 U.S. 149, 155 (1990) ("distinct"); *Allen v. Wright*, 468 U.S. 737, 751 (1984) ("personal"); *Valley Forge*, supra, at 472 (standing requires that the plaintiff "personally has suffered some actual or threatened injury"); *United States v. Richardson*, 418 U.S. 166, 177 (1974) (not "undifferentiated").[10]

Particularization is necessary to establish injury in fact, but it is not sufficient. An injury in fact must also be "concrete." Under the Ninth Circuit's analysis, however, that independent requirement was elided. As previously noted, the Ninth Circuit concluded that Robins' complaint alleges "concrete, de facto" injuries for essentially two reasons. First, the court noted that Robins "alleges that Spokeo violated his statutory rights, not just the statutory rights of other people." Second, the court wrote that "Robins's personal interests in the handling of his credit information are *individualized rather than collective*." Both of these observations concern particularization, not concreteness. We have made it clear time and time again that an injury in fact must be both concrete and particularized.

A "concrete" injury must be "de facto"; that is, it must actually exist. See Black's Law Dictionary 479 (9th ed. 2009). When we have used the adjective "concrete," we have meant to convey the usual meaning of the term—"real," and not "abstract." Webster's Third New International Dictionary 472 (1971); Random House Dictionary of the English Language 305 (1967). Concreteness, therefore, is quite different from particularization.

2

"Concrete" is not, however, necessarily synonymous with "tangible." Although tangible injuries are perhaps easier to recognize, we have confirmed in many of our previous cases that intangible injuries can nevertheless be concrete. See, e.g., *Pleasant Grove City v. Summum*, 555 U.S. 460 (2009) (free speech); *Church of Lukumi Babalu Aye, Inc. v. Hialeah*, 508 U.S. 520 (1993) (free exercise).

In determining whether an intangible harm constitutes injury in fact, both history and the judgment of Congress play important roles. Because the doctrine of standing derives from the case-or-controversy requirement, and because that requirement in turn is grounded in historical practice, it is instructive to consider whether an alleged intangible harm has a close relationship to a harm that has traditionally been regarded as providing a basis for a lawsuit in English or American courts.

---

[10] The fact that an injury may be suffered by a large number of people does not of itself make that injury a nonjusticiable generalized grievance. The victims' injuries from a mass tort, for example, are widely shared, to be sure, but each individual suffers a particularized harm.

See *Vermont Agency of Natural Resources v. United States ex rel. Stevens*, 529 U.S. 765, 775–777 (2000). In addition, because Congress is well positioned to identify intangible harms that meet minimum Article III requirements, its judgment is also instructive and important. Thus, we said in *Lujan* that Congress may "elevat[e] to the status of legally cognizable injuries concrete, de facto injuries that were previously inadequate in law." 504 U.S., at 578. Similarly, Justice Kennedy's concurrence in that case explained that "Congress has the power to define injuries and articulate chains of causation that will give rise to a case or controversy where none existed before." *Id.*, at 580.

Congress' role in identifying and elevating intangible harms does not mean that a plaintiff automatically satisfies the injury-in-fact requirement whenever a statute grants a person a statutory right and purports to authorize that person to sue to vindicate that right. Article III standing requires a concrete injury even in the context of a statutory violation. For that reason, Robins could not, for example, allege a bare procedural violation, divorced from any concrete harm, and satisfy the injury-in-fact requirement of Article III. See *Summers*, 555 U.S., at 496 ("[D]eprivation of a procedural right without some concrete interest that is affected by the deprivation . . . is insufficient to create Article III standing").

This does not mean, however, that the risk of real harm cannot satisfy the requirement of concreteness. See, e.g., *Clapper v. Amnesty Int'l USA*, 568 U.S. 398. For example, the law has long permitted recovery by certain tort victims even if their harms may be difficult to prove or measure. See, e.g., Restatement (First) of Torts §§ 569 (libel), 570 (slander per se) (1938). Just as the common law permitted suit in such instances, the violation of a procedural right granted by statute can be sufficient in some circumstances to constitute injury in fact. In other words, a plaintiff in such a case need not allege any additional harm beyond the one Congress has identified. See *Federal Election Comm'n v. Akins*, 524 U.S. 11, 20–25 (1998) (confirming that a group of voters' "inability to obtain information" that Congress had decided to make public is a sufficient injury in fact to satisfy Article III); *Public Citizen v. Department of Justice*, 491 U.S. 440, 449 (1989) (holding that two advocacy organizations' failure to obtain information subject to disclosure under the Federal Advisory Committee Act "constitutes a sufficiently distinct injury to provide standing to sue").

In the context of this particular case, these general principles tell us two things: On the one hand, Congress plainly sought to curb the dissemination of false information by adopting procedures designed to decrease that risk. On the other hand, Robins cannot satisfy the demands of Article III by alleging a bare procedural violation. A violation of one of the FCRA's procedural requirements may result in no harm. For example, even if a consumer reporting agency fails to provide the required notice to a user of the agency's consumer information, that information regardless may be entirely accurate. In addition, not all inaccuracies cause harm or present any material risk of harm. An example that comes readily to mind is an incorrect zip code. It is difficult to imagine how the dissemination of an incorrect zip code, without more, could work any concrete harm.

Because the Ninth Circuit failed to fully appreciate the distinction between concreteness and particularization, its standing analysis was incomplete. It did not address the question framed by our discussion, namely, whether the particular procedural violations alleged in this case entail a degree of risk sufficient to meet the concreteness requirement. We take no position as to whether the Ninth Circuit's ultimate conclusion—that Robins adequately alleged an injury in fact—was correct.

* * *

Notes on *Spokeo, Inc. v. Robins*

1. *Particularity*: The problem for the plaintiff in *Spokeo* was not that he had failed to allege an injury that was sufficiently particularized. Robins's allegation was that Spokeo had constructed a profile of *him* that contained inaccurate information. "His profile, he asserts, states that he is married, has children, is in his 50's, has a job, is relatively affluent, and holds a graduate degree. According to Robins' complaint, all of this information is incorrect." This alleged harm was plainly particular to Robins.

2. *Distinguished from concreteness*: Instead, the issue was whether Robins's alleged injury was sufficiently concrete. As the Court explained, the Ninth Circuit had effectively conflated the concreteness and particularity requirements: "First, the court noted that Robins 'alleges that Spokeo violated his statutory rights, not just the statutory rights of other people.' Second, the court wrote that 'Robins's personal interests in the handling of his credit information are *individualized rather than collective*.' Both of these observations concern particularization, not concreteness."

Notice that the Court did not hold that Robins had failed to show a sufficiently concrete harm. Rather, after explaining the inquiry—and, in particular, how concreteness and particularity are distinct—the Court remanded the case to the Ninth Circuit so that court could conduct the proper analysis in the first instance. As the justices are wont to say, the Supreme Court is "a court of final review, not first view." *Cutter v. Wilkinson*, 544 U.S. 709, 718 n.7 (2005).

3. *What makes an injury sufficiently "concrete"?*: This may be the single most difficult question regarding standing. The Court in *Spokeo* stated that "[a] 'concrete' injury must be 'de facto'; that is, it must actually exist. When we have used the adjective 'concrete,' we have meant to convey the usual meaning of the term—'real,' and not 'abstract.'" Thus, part of the answer is that the injury must be "real," and "not 'abstract.'" But that only takes us so far.

More recently, the Court in *TransUnion LLC v. Ramirez*, 141 S. Ct. 2190 (2021), attempted to explain the concreteness requirement in greater detail. Writing for the Court, Justice Kavanaugh set out the contours of the requirement as follows:

> "What makes a harm concrete for purposes of Article III? As a general matter, the Court has explained that 'history and tradition offer a meaningful guide to the types of cases that Article III empowers federal courts to consider.' *Sprint Communications Co.* v. *APCC Services, Inc.*, 554 U.S. 269, 274 (2008). And with respect to the concrete-harm requirement in particular, this Court's opinion in *Spokeo* v. *Robins* indicated that courts should assess whether the alleged injury to the plaintiff has a 'close relationship' to a harm 'traditionally' recognized as providing a basis for a lawsuit in American courts. 578 U.S., at 341. That inquiry asks whether plaintiffs have identified a close historical or common-law analogue for their asserted injury. *Spokeo* does not require an exact duplicate in American history and tradition. But *Spokeo* is not an open-ended invitation for federal courts to loosen Article III based on contemporary, evolving beliefs about what kinds of suits should be heard in federal courts.

> "As *Spokeo* explained, certain harms readily qualify as concrete injuries under Article III. The most obvious are traditional tangible harms, such as physical harms and monetary harms. If a defendant has caused physical or monetary injury to the plaintiff, the plaintiff has suffered a concrete injury in fact under Article III.

> "Various intangible harms can also be concrete. Chief among them are injuries with a close relationship to harms traditionally recognized as providing a basis for lawsuits in American courts. Those include, for example, reputational harms, disclosure of private information, and intrusion upon seclusion. And those traditional harms may also include harms specified by the Constitution itself. See, *e.g.*, *Spokeo*, 578 U.S., at 340 (citing *Pleasant Grove City v. Summum*, 555 U.S. 460 (2009) (abridgment of free speech), and *Church of Lukumi Babalu Aye, Inc. v. Hialeah*, 508 U.S. 520 (1993) (infringement of free exercise))."

Thus, the inquiry centers on whether the plaintiff's alleged injury is one that has been "traditionally recognized as providing a basis for a lawsuit in American courts": whether there is "a close historical or common-law analogue for their asserted injury." Again, the injury need not be *tangible*. But the harm must be one that is at least analogous to an injury that American courts have traditionally recognized as forming the basis for a lawsuit.

4. *Can Congress render a particular injury "concrete and particularized" for purposes of Article III?* If Congress enacts a statute prohibiting certain acts, and grants a class of persons the right to sue defendants who violate that prohibition, does a person within that class—a person Congress has granted a federal legal right and a private right of action—necessarily have Article III standing?

Setting aside the question of standing, there are at least two legal prerequisites for a plaintiff to assert a claim arising under federal law in federal court: (1) the law must plausibly prohibit the act the plaintiff claims to be unlawful, and (2) the law must grant the plaintiff a *cause of action*—a right to file a lawsuit. (Many federal statutes impose legal obligations without granting private plaintiffs the right to sue to enforce those legal obligations, instead leaving enforcement entirely to the Executive Branch.) Is the satisfaction of these two preconditions necessarily *sufficient* for a plaintiff to have standing under Article III?

The Court in *TransUnion* (echoing what it had previously said in *Spokeo*) emphatically answered *no*: a plaintiff must *also* demonstrate a concrete and particularized injury. While Congress's judgment (through its creation of a legal right and a cause of action) warrants consideration by courts in deciding whether an injury is sufficiently "concrete," Congress's view cannot be determinative. As the Court reasoned in *TransUnion*,

> "[i]n determining whether a harm is sufficiently concrete to qualify as an injury in fact, the Court in *Spokeo* said that Congress's views may be 'instructive.' Courts must afford due respect to Congress's decision to impose a statutory prohibition or obligation on a defendant, and to grant a plaintiff a cause of action to sue over the defendant's violation of that statutory prohibition or obligation. In that way, Congress may 'elevate to the status of legally cognizable injuries concrete, *de facto* injuries that were previously inadequate in law.' But even though 'Congress may elevate harms that exist in the real world before Congress recognized them to actionable legal status, it may not simply enact an injury into existence, using its lawmaking power to transform something that is not remotely harmful into something that is.' *Hagy v. Demers & Adams*, 882 F.3d 616, 622 (CA6 2018).

> "Importantly, this Court has rejected the proposition that 'a plaintiff automatically satisfies the injury-in-fact requirement whenever a statute grants a person a statutory right and purports to authorize that person to sue to vindicate that right.' *Spokeo*, 578 U.S., at 341. As the Court emphasized in *Spokeo*, 'Article III standing requires a concrete injury even in the context of a statutory violation.' *Ibid.*

> "Congress's creation of a statutory prohibition or obligation and a cause of action does not relieve courts of their responsibility to independently decide whether a plaintiff has suffered a concrete harm under Article III any more than, for example, Congress's enactment of a law regulating speech relieves courts of their responsibility to independently decide whether the law violates the First Amendment. As Judge Katsas has rightly stated, 'we cannot treat an injury as "concrete" for Article III purposes based only on

Congress's say-so.' *Trichell v. Midland Credit Mgmt., Inc.*, 964 F.3d 990, 999, n.2 (CA11 2020).

"For standing purposes, therefore, an important difference exists between (i) a plaintiff's statutory cause of action to sue a defendant over the defendant's violation of federal law, and (ii) a plaintiff's suffering concrete harm because of the defendant's violation of federal law. Congress may enact legal prohibitions and obligations. And Congress may create causes of action for plaintiffs to sue defendants who violate those legal prohibitions or obligations. But under Article III, an injury in law is not an injury in fact. Only those plaintiffs who have been *concretely harmed* by a defendant's statutory violation may sue that private defendant over that violation in federal court. . . .

"To appreciate how the Article III 'concrete harm' principle operates in practice, consider two different hypothetical plaintiffs. Suppose first that a Maine citizen's land is polluted by a nearby factory. She sues the company, alleging that it violated a federal environmental law and damaged her property. Suppose also that a second plaintiff in Hawaii files a federal lawsuit alleging that the same company in Maine violated that same environmental law by polluting land in Maine. The violation did not personally harm the plaintiff in Hawaii.

"Even if Congress affords both hypothetical plaintiffs a cause of action (with statutory damages available) to sue over the defendant's legal violation, Article III standing doctrine sharply distinguishes between those two scenarios. The first lawsuit may of course proceed in federal court because the plaintiff has suffered concrete harm to her property. But the second lawsuit may not proceed because that plaintiff has not suffered any physical, monetary, or cognizable intangible harm traditionally recognized as providing a basis for a lawsuit in American courts. An uninjured plaintiff who sues in those circumstances is, by definition, not seeking to remedy any harm to herself but instead is merely seeking to ensure a defendant's 'compliance with regulatory law' (and, of course, to obtain some money via the statutory damages). Those are not grounds for Article III standing.

"As those examples illustrate, if the law of Article III did not require plaintiffs to demonstrate a 'concrete harm,' Congress could authorize virtually any citizen to bring a statutory damages suit against virtually any defendant who violated virtually any federal law. Such an expansive understanding of Article III would flout constitutional text, history, and precedent. In our view, the public interest that private entities comply with the law cannot 'be converted into an individual right by a statute that denominates it as such, and that permits all citizens (or, for that matter, a subclass of citizens who suffer no distinctive concrete harm) to sue.' *Lujan*, 504 U.S., at 576–577.[11]

"A regime where Congress could freely authorize *unharmed* plaintiffs to sue defendants who violate federal law not only would violate Article III but also would infringe on the Executive Branch's Article II authority. We accept the 'displacement of the democratically elected branches when necessary to decide an actual case.' Roberts, 42 Duke L.J., at 1230. But otherwise, the choice of how to prioritize and how aggressively to pursue legal actions against defendants who violate the law falls within the discretion of the Executive Branch, not within the purview of private plaintiffs (and their attorneys). Private plaintiffs are not accountable to the people and are not charged with pursuing the public interest in enforcing a defendant's general compliance with regulatory law."

Thus, Article III ultimately controls whether a given plaintiff has standing, and Congress cannot alter this constitutional requirement by statute. Congress cannot simply deem certain people to have suffered a concrete and particularized harm sufficient to support standing. Its judgment is certainly relevant, and courts must give its views respect. But Congress's determination is not dispositive.

5. *Third-party standing*: As a general rule, a plaintiff cannot "rest his claim to relief on the legal rights or interests of third parties." *Kowalski v. Tesmer*, 543 U. S. 125, 129 (2004). This is the so-called presumption against third-party standing. As an example, suppose a state in 2018 adopted a law requiring any physician performing an abortion to have admitting privileges at a hospital within 30 miles, and this substantially reduced the number of qualified abortion providers in the state. Before June 24, 2022, the Due Process Clause protected a woman's right to terminate a pregnancy before the fetus was viable, and this law arguably infringed that right. But the law made it illegal for a *physician* to perform an abortion without the necessary admitting privileges, and physicians had no constitutional right to perform abortions. So if a physician (or clinic) filed suit seeking to have the law declared unconstitutional, she would have been a "third party" for purposes of standing: she would have been claiming the law violates *someone else*'s constitutional rights.

Two points about third-party standing bear emphasis. First, the presumption against third-party standing is purely *prudential*, meaning it is not dictated by the Constitution. Article III requires an injury in fact. Litigants like

---

[11] "A plaintiff must show that the injury is not only concrete but also particularized. But if there were no concrete-harm requirement, the requirement of a particularized injury would do little or nothing to constrain Congress from freely creating causes of action for vast classes of *unharmed* plaintiffs to sue any defendants who violate any federal law. (Congress might, for example, provide that everyone has an individual right to clean air and can sue any defendant who violates any air-pollution law.) That is one reason why the Court has been careful to emphasize that concreteness and particularization are separate requirements."

the physician in this example plainly had an injury in fact that was actual or imminent, as they ran the risk of prosecution if they performed a prohibited abortion. Thus, if there is a standing problem, it is not one created by Article III, but instead by judicial practice. Second, this prudential bar to third-party standing is well short of absolute. As the Supreme Court recognized in *June Medical Services LLC v. Russo*, 140 S. Ct. 2103 (2020), the Court has "long permitted abortion providers to invoke the rights of their actual or potential patients in challenges to abortion-related regulations." Thus, while a plaintiff suing to vindicate the rights of a third party may need to demonstrate why it would be *prudential* for the court to permit her to do so, there is no *constitutional* bar to third-party standing.

* * *

PROBLEMS ON STANDING: INJURY IN FACT

1. Plaintiff files a complaint in federal district court against Defendant, asserting a claim arising under a federal statute. Defendant timely files a motion to dismiss under Rules 12(b)(1) and 12(b)(6), making two assertions: (1) that the district court lacks subject matter jurisdiction because Plaintiff has failed to allege sufficient facts to establish Article III standing; and (2) that even if Plaintiff has alleged sufficient facts to establish standing, she has failed to allege sufficient facts to render her substantive claim plausible. The district court concludes that the standing question is a close one, but that Plaintiff clearly has failed to state a claim for relief, and thus grants Defendant's Rule 12(b)(6) motion. Is the district court's judgment proper? Why or why not?

2. Please assess whether the plaintiff has satisfied the Article III injury-in-fact requirement (necessary to establish standing) in each of the following circumstances. Assume the action in question has been filed in federal district court.

   a. Worker is discharged from her job by Employer. Worker files an action asserting that, in firing her, Employer violated the federal Age Discrimination in Employment Act. Employee seeks back pay and reinstatement to her job with Employer.

   b. Plaintiff files a complaint asserting that Lumber Co. has violated the federal Wildlife Protection Act (WPA) by clearcutting thousands of old growth redwood trees from the Shasta Trinity National Forest. Plaintiff lives 10 miles from Shasta Trinity National Forest and has visited it several times. But she has not visited the forest in the past two years, and she has no specific plans to visit in the future.

   c. The facts are the same as in (b), except that, in the WPA, Congress expressly specified that "any person may bring suit for a violation of this Act's provisions."

   d. The facts are the same as in (b), except that Plaintiff visits the forest once a week and files a declaration stating she highly values the aesthetics of the park as a pristine forest and plans to visit the park weekly for the indefinite future (attaching the declaration to her memorandum opposing Lumber Co.'s motion for summary judgment).

e. Plaintiff is a U.S. taxpayer and fierce critic of American foreign policy. The U.S. Department of Defense annually spends more than $500 billion on the military. Plaintiff sues the Secretary of Defense, claiming that, in one of its major weapons procurement programs, the Department has violated federal law by failing to solicit the requisite number of bids from potential manufacturers. In her complaint, Plaintiff asserts that she is injured by having to pay her tax dollars to contribute to a spending program, which Department of Defense has implemented unlawfully.

f. Plaintiff is a U.S. taxpayer who, like millions of other taxpayers, has been required to pay a recently-enacted federal tax on all persons who lack "minimally adequate health coverage." Plaintiff argues that the tax exceeds Congress's enumerated powers and is thus unconstitutional.

g. Plaintiff is a regular user of Google. Plaintiff sued Google asserting that, in violation of the federal Stored Communications Act (SCA), Google saved and transmitted the search terms that Plaintiff used to the owners of the web sites that Plaintiff ultimately visited, after using those search terms. (Plaintiff does not allege she has suffered any other harm from this disclosure of her search terms.) The SCA entitles any "person aggrieved by any violation" to "recover from the person or entity that committed such violation such relief as may be appropriate."

h. The facts are the same as in (g), except the SCA also entitles any person aggrieved by a violation of the Act to recover $500 from the defendant per violation.

i. Plaintiff is a committed atheist who regularly attends city council meetings. The city council begins each of its meetings with a sectarian prayer. Plaintiff sues the city, asserting that its practice of beginning city council meetings with a sectarian prayer violates the Establishment Clause of the First Amendment to the U.S. Constitution. In her complaint, Plaintiff alleges that, on several occasions, her being forced as a captive audience member to listen to these prayers offended her own beliefs and makes her feel excluded and ostracized from the community.

j. Power Co. experienced a meltdown at the Springfield Nuclear Power Plant, exposing tens of millions of people downwind of the power plant (across several states) to substantial amounts of radioactive material. Millions of people later develop symptoms of radiation sickness. One of those persons sues Power Co., asserting various violations of state and federal law. Power Co. moves to dismiss the complaint because the plaintiff's injury is not sufficiently "particularized."

k. Plaintiff owns a convenience store in San Jose, at which she sells a large stock of vaping devices and products. The California legislature recently enacted a statute that makes it a felony, punishable by up to two years in prison, to knowingly sell a vaping device to any person younger than 24 years old. The law will go into effect in three months. Plaintiff files suit against the California attorney general, asserting the law is unconstitutional and seeking an injunction against its enforcement. (What might you advise Plaintiff to include in her complaint in the statement of the grounds for the court's jurisdiction?)

3. Plaintiff is an Arizona citizen who pays taxes annually to the state. The Arizona legislature has recently enacted a state law declaring itself a "sanctuary state" and appropriating $5 million from the state budget to rescue, clothe, and feed needy migrants found crossing the Arizona desert. Plaintiff sues the State of Arizona in Arizona state court asserting that Arizona's program violates federal law. (Specifically, she contends that the state law frustrates the purposes of federal immigration statutes and is therefore preempted by federal law.) The injury she alleges is the unlawful expenditure of her state tax dollars.

*   *   *

3. Causation and redressability

Establishing an Article III injury in fact—one that is concrete, particularized, and either actual or imminent—does not itself mean a litigant has standing. She must also plausibly demonstrate that her injury is fairly traceable to the defendant's allegedly unlawful conduct, and that a favorable judicial decision will redress or eliminate her injury. These are the requirements of *causation* and *redressability*. In most cases, the two are linked, such that the existence of causation will also entail the existence of redressability. But that is not always the case. As the Supreme Court has emphasized, they are distinct requirements, and both must be satisfied under Article III.

When the defendant's allegedly unlawful actions directly harm the plaintiff, the plaintiff's showing of causation and redressability is relatively straightforward. For instance, an entity subject to a newly promulgated regulation—assuming it can show an injury from that regulation—should have no difficulty showing that the regulation has caused that harm, or that the relief it seeks (typically an injunction against the regulation's enforcement) would redress its injury. But demonstrating causation and redressability is often problematic when the plaintiff's injury depends on the intervening acts of third parties who are not before the court.

A seminal example is *Allen v. Wright*, 468 U.S. 737 (1984). The plaintiffs in *Allen* were the parents of African American children attending schools in public school districts undergoing racial desegregation. The plaintiffs sued the Internal Revenue Service (IRS) asserting the IRS had not adequately enforced a federal tax regulation denying tax-exempt status to racially discriminatory private schools. The plaintiffs claimed that, in cities across the U.S., the ability of private schools simultaneously to racially discriminate and retain their tax-exempt status enabled them to enroll more white students—undermining desegregation efforts in those cities, and thus depriving the plaintiffs' children of their right to attend desegregated public schools. As you read *Allen v. Wright*, consider the following questions:

1. What was the precise injury in fact the plaintiffs alleged (in the portion of the opinion presented)? Was that injury sufficiently concrete, particularized, and either actual or imminent?

2. On what basis did the plaintiffs contend that this injury had been caused by the government's allegedly unlawful actions? On whose actions did this causal link depend?

3. How would the relief sought by the plaintiffs have redressed their injury? Was this certain? Likely? Merely conceivable?

4. What could the plaintiffs have done in to successfully establish standing? Or were the obstacles to their doing so essentially insuperable?

Allen v. Wright
468 U.S. 737 (1984)

JUSTICE O'CONNOR delivered the opinion of the Court.

Parents of black public school children allege in this nationwide class action that the Internal Revenue Service (IRS) has not adopted sufficient standards and procedures to fulfill its obligation to deny tax-exempt status to racially discriminatory private schools. They assert that the IRS thereby . . . interferes with the ability of their children to receive an education in desegregated public schools. The issue before us is whether plaintiffs have standing to bring this suit. We hold that they do not.

I

The IRS denies tax-exempt status under §§ 501(a) and (c)(3) of the Internal Revenue Code—and hence eligibility to receive charitable contributions deductible from income taxes under §§ 170(a)(1) and (c)(2) of the Code—to racially discriminatory private schools. The IRS policy requires that a school applying for tax-exempt status show that it "admits the students of any race to all the rights, privileges, programs, and activities generally accorded or made available to students at that school and that the school does not discriminate on the basis of race in administration of its educational policies, admissions policies, scholarship and loan programs, and athletic and other school-administered programs." To carry out this policy, the IRS has established guidelines and procedures for determining whether a particular school is in fact racially nondiscriminatory. Failure to comply with the guidelines "will ordinarily result in the proposed revocation of" tax-exempt status. . . .

In 1976 respondents challenged these guidelines and procedures in a suit filed in Federal District Court against the Secretary of the Treasury and the Commissioner of Internal Revenue. The plaintiffs named in the complaint are parents of black children who, at the time the complaint was filed, were attending public schools in seven States in school districts undergoing desegregation. They brought this nationwide class action "on behalf of themselves and their children, and . . . on behalf of all other parents of black children attending public school systems undergoing, or which may in the future undergo, desegregation pursuant to court order [or] HEW regulations and guidelines, under state law, or voluntarily." They estimated that the class they seek to represent includes several million persons.

Respondents allege in their complaint that many racially segregated private schools were created or expanded in their communities at the time the public schools were undergoing desegregation. . . . Respondents allege that, despite the IRS policy of denying tax-exempt status to racially discriminatory private schools and despite the IRS guidelines and procedures for implementing that policy, some of the tax-exempt racially segregated private schools created or expanded in desegregating districts in fact have racially discriminatory policies. Respondents allege that the IRS grant of tax exemptions to such racially discriminatory schools is unlawful.

Respondents allege that the challenged Government conduct harms them in [that it]

> "fosters and encourages the organization, operation and expansion of institutions providing racially segregated educational opportunities for white children avoiding attendance in desegregating public school districts and thereby interferes with the efforts of federal courts, HEW and local school authorities to desegregate public school districts which have been operating racially dual school systems."

Thus, respondents do not allege that their children have been the victims of discriminatory exclusion from the schools whose tax exemptions they challenge as unlawful. Indeed, they have not alleged at any stage of this litigation that their children have ever applied or would ever apply to any private school. Rather, respondents claim a direct injury from the mere fact of the challenged Government conduct and, as indicated by the restriction of the plaintiff class to parents of children in desegregating school districts, injury to their children's opportunity to receive a desegregated education. The latter injury is traceable to the IRS grant of tax exemptions to racially discriminatory schools, respondents allege, chiefly because contributions to such schools are deductible from income taxes under §§ 170(a)(1) and (c)(2) of the Internal Revenue Code and the "deductions facilitate the raising of funds to organize new schools and expand existing schools in order to accommodate white students avoiding attendance in desegregating public school districts."

Respondents request only prospective relief. They ask for a declaratory judgment that the challenged IRS tax-exemption practices are unlawful. . . .

II

A

Article III of the Constitution confines the federal courts to adjudicating actual "cases" and "controversies." As the Court explained in *Valley Forge Christian College v. Americans United for Separation of Church and State*, 454 U.S. 464, 471–476 (1982), the "case or controversy" requirement defines with respect to the Judicial Branch the idea of separation of powers on which the Federal Government is founded. The several doctrines that have grown up to elaborate that requirement are "founded in concern about the proper—and properly limited—role of the courts in a democratic society." *Warth v. Seldin*, 422 U.S. 490, 498 (1975).

> "All of the doctrines that cluster about Article III—not only standing but mootness, ripeness, political question, and the like—relate in part, and in different though overlapping ways, to an idea, which is more than an intuition but less than a rigorous and explicit theory, about the constitutional and prudential limits to the powers of an unelected, unrepresentative judiciary in our kind of government." *Vander Jagt v. O'Neill*, 699 F.2d 1166, 1178–1179 (D.C. Cir. 1983) (Bork, J., concurring).

The case-or-controversy doctrines state fundamental limits on federal judicial power in our system of government.

The Art. III doctrine that requires a litigant to have "standing" to invoke the power of a federal court is perhaps the most important of these doctrines. "In essence the question of standing is whether the litigant is entitled to have the court decide the merits of the dispute or of particular issues." *Warth v. Seldin, supra*, at 498. . . . A plaintiff must allege personal injury fairly traceable to the defendant's allegedly unlawful conduct and likely to be redressed by the requested relief. . . .

[T]he constitutional component of standing doctrine incorporates concepts concededly not susceptible of precise definition. The injury alleged must be, for example, "distinct and palpable," and not "abstract" or "conjectural" or "hypothetical." The injury must be "fairly" traceable to the challenged action, and relief from the injury must be "likely" to follow from a favorable decision. These terms cannot be defined so as to make application of the constitutional standing requirement a mechanical exercise.

The absence of precise definitions, however, as this Court's extensive body of case law on standing illustrates, hardly leaves courts at sea in applying the law of standing. Like most legal notions, the standing concepts have gained considerable definition from developing case law. In many cases the standing question can be answered chiefly by comparing the allegations of the particular complaint to those made in prior standing cases. More important, the law of Art. III standing is built on a single basic idea—the idea of separation of powers. It is this fact which makes possible the gradual clarification of the law through judicial application. Of course, both federal and state courts have long experience in applying and elaborating in numerous contexts the pervasive and fundamental notion of separation of powers.

Determining standing in a particular case may be facilitated by clarifying principles or even clear rules developed in prior cases. Typically, however, the standing inquiry requires careful judicial examination of a complaint's allegations to ascertain whether the particular plaintiff is entitled to an adjudication of the particular claims asserted. Is the injury too abstract, or otherwise not appropriate, to be considered judicially cognizable? Is the line of causation between the illegal conduct and injury too attenuated? Is the prospect of obtaining relief from the injury as a result of a favorable ruling too speculative? These questions and any others relevant to the standing inquiry must be answered by reference to the Art. III notion that federal courts may exercise power only "in the last resort, and as a necessity," *Chicago & Grand Trunk R. Co. v. Wellman*, 143 U.S. 339, 345 (1892), and only when adjudication is "consistent with a system of separated powers and [the dispute is one] traditionally thought to be capable of resolution through the judicial process," *Flast v. Cohen*, 392 U.S. 83, 97 (1968).

B

Respondents . . . say that the federal tax exemptions to racially discriminatory private schools in their communities impair their ability to have their public schools desegregated. . . . We conclude that [this does not suffice] to support respondents' standing. . . .

* * *

2

The injury they identify—their children's diminished ability to receive an education in a racially integrated school—is, beyond any doubt, not only judicially cognizable but . . . one of the most serious injuries recognized in our legal system. Despite the constitutional importance of curing the injury alleged by respondents, however, the federal judiciary may not redress it unless standing requirements are met. In this case, respondents' second claim of injury cannot support standing because the injury alleged is not fairly traceable to the Government conduct respondents challenge as unlawful.

The illegal conduct challenged by respondents is the IRS's grant of tax exemptions to some racially discriminatory schools. The line of causation between that conduct and desegregation of respondents' schools is attenuated at best. From the perspective of the IRS, the injury to respondents is highly indirect and "results from the independent action of some third party not before the court," *Simon v. Eastern Kentucky Welfare Rights Org.*, 426 U.S., at 42. As the Court pointed out in *Warth v. Seldin*, 422 U.S. at 505, "the indirectness of the injury . . . may make it substantially more difficult to meet the minimum requirement of Art. III . . . ."

The diminished ability of respondents' children to receive a desegregated education would be fairly traceable to unlawful IRS grants of tax exemptions only if there were enough racially discriminatory private schools receiving tax exemptions in respondents' communities for withdrawal of those exemptions to make an appreciable difference in public school integration. Respondents have made no such allegation. It is, first, uncertain how many racially discriminatory private schools are in fact receiving tax exemptions. Moreover, it is entirely speculative, as respondents themselves conceded in the Court of Appeals, whether withdrawal of a tax exemption from any particular school would lead the school to change its policies. It is just as speculative whether any given parent of a child attending such a private school would decide to transfer the child to public school as a result of any changes in educational or financial policy made by the private school once it was threatened with loss of tax-exempt status. It is also pure speculation whether, in a particular community, a large enough number of the numerous relevant school officials and parents would reach decisions that collectively would have a significant impact on the racial composition of the public schools.

The links in the chain of causation between the challenged Government conduct and the asserted injury are far too weak for the chain as a whole to sustain respondents' standing. In *Simon v. Eastern Kentucky Welfare Rights Org.*, the Court held that standing to challenge a Government grant of a tax exemption to hospitals could not be founded on the asserted connection between the grant of tax-exempt status and the hospitals' policy concerning the provision of medical services to indigents. The causal connection depended on the decisions hospitals would make in response to withdrawal of tax-exempt status, and those decisions were sufficiently uncertain to break the chain of causation between the plaintiffs' injury and the challenged Government action. *Id.*, at 40–46. The chain of causation is even weaker in this case. It involves numerous third parties (officials of racially discriminatory schools receiving tax exemptions and the parents of children attending such schools) who may not even exist in respondents' communities and whose independent decisions may not collectively have a significant effect on the ability of public school students to receive a desegregated education.

The idea of separation of powers that underlies standing doctrine explains why our cases preclude the conclusion that respondents' alleged injury "fairly can be traced to the challenged action" of the IRS. That conclusion would pave the way generally for suits challenging, not specifically identifiable Government violations of law, but the particular programs agencies establish to carry out their legal obligations. Such suits, even when premised on allegations of several instances of violations of law, are rarely if ever appropriate for federal-court adjudication.

> "Carried to its logical end, [respondents'] approach would have the federal courts as virtually continuing monitors of the wisdom and soundness of Executive action; such a role is appropriate for the Congress acting through its committees and the 'power of the purse'; it is not the role of the judiciary, absent actual present or immediately threatened injury resulting from unlawful governmental action." *Laird v. Tatum*, 408 U.S. at 15.

. . . . Animating this Court's holdings [is] the principle that "[a] federal court . . . is not the proper forum to press" general complaints about the way in which government goes about its business. *Id.,* at 112. . . . When transported into the Art. III context, that principle, grounded as it is in the idea of separation of powers, counsels against recognizing standing in a case brought, not to enforce specific legal obligations whose violation works a direct harm, but to seek a restructuring of the apparatus established by the Executive Branch to fulfill its legal duties. The Constitution, after all, assigns to the Executive Branch, and not to the Judicial Branch, the duty to "take Care that the Laws be faithfully executed." U. S. Const., Art. II, § 3. We could not recognize respondents' standing in this case without running afoul of that structural principle.

* * *

III

"The necessity that the plaintiff who seeks to invoke judicial power stand to profit in some personal interest remains an Art. III requirement." *Simon v. Eastern Kentucky Welfare Rights Org.,* 426 U.S., at 39. Respondents have not met this fundamental requirement. The judgment of the Court of Appeals is accordingly reversed, and the injunction issued by that court is vacated.

* * *

Notes on *Allen v. Wright*

1. *The plaintiffs' injury*: As the Court acknowledged, the plaintiffs' alleged injury (at least that discussed in this excerpt) was sufficient to satisfy the injury-in-fact requirement. "The injury they identify—their children's diminished ability to receive an education in a racially integrated school—is, beyond any doubt, not only judicially cognizable but . . . one of the most serious injuries recognized in our legal system." Instead, the plaintiffs' standing problem (with respect to this harm) was one of causation and redressability.

2. *The link between the injury and the allegedly unlawful action*: The specific problem for the plaintiffs was the various steps necessary—involving the behavior of third parties not before the court—to trace their harm to the allegedly unlawful action by the IRS. Again, the plaintiffs' claim was that the IRS unlawfully failing to deny tax-exempt status to racially discriminatory private schools. Their claim that this deprived their children of the opportunity to attend desegregated public schools depended on several links in a causal chain: that the IRS's stiffer enforcement of the policy would lead to the withdrawal of several private schools' tax-exempt status in the plaintiff's communities; that the denial of this tax-exempt status would lead the affected private schools either to cease discriminating, to increase their tuition, or to reduce their offers of admission to white students; that this change in the private schools' policies would prompt white parents to withdraw their children from these private schools and enroll them in public schools in districts undergoing desegregation; and that the number of white parents making such decisions would be sufficient to have an appreciable impact on the racial composition of the schools attended by the plaintiffs' children. Such a chain of events was certainly conceivable. But to the Court, the causal connection was "attenuated at best": the "links in the chain of causation between the challenged Government conduct and the asserted injury are far too weak for the chain as a whole to sustain respondents' standing."

3. ***The legal standards for causation and redressability***: Justice O'Connor's opinion sets out what plaintiffs must demonstrate to establish causation and redressability sufficient to support Article III standing. With respect to causation, "[t]he injury must be fairly traceable to the challenged action." This presumably means something more than just but-for causation; it must be "fair" to trace the injury to the allegedly unlawful action. With respect to redressability, the opinion states that "relief from the injury must be likely to follow from a favorable decision." The mere possibility that the relief sought will redress the plaintiff's harm is insufficient; "likely" indicates it must be more probable than not.

4. ***The relief-specific nature of standing***: An important implication of the redressability requirement is that standing is *relief-specific*. Under a given set of facts, a litigant might have standing to pursue one form of relief (such as damages) but not another (such as an injunction or a declaratory judgment). One form of relief might redress the plaintiff's harm while another might not.

The crucial case on this point is *Los Angeles v. Lyons*, 461 U. S. 95 (1983). The plaintiff in *Lyons* had been subjected to a chokehold while being arrested by Los Angeles police officers. Lyons sued the LAPD seeking two forms of relief: (1) compensatory damages, and (2) an injunction forbidding Los Angeles police officers from using chokeholds under similar circumstances. The Supreme Court held that, while Lyons plainly had standing to seek damages, he lacked standing to seek an injunction because he could not establish that such relief would redress his injury. Lyons had been subjected to a chokehold; damages would redress this injury by compensating him for his pain and suffering. But an injunction prohibiting the *future* use of chokeholds by police officers would provide him no redress unless he could somehow show he was likely to be subjected to a chokehold by an LAPD officer in the future.

The larger point is that standing must be established for each form of relief sought. As a result, from the same set of facts and claims, a plaintiff might have standing to seek one type of relief but not another.

5. ***So-called "procedural" injuries***: Many laws impose various procedural requirements and grant individuals the right to sue when the required procedure is not followed. (Indeed, this was the case in both *Earth Island Institute* and *Spokeo*.) Taken to their logical conclusion, the requirements of causation and redressability might make it nearly impossible for a plaintiff to

establish standing to challenge a defendant's failure to follow such a mandated procedure. The reason is that, except in rare cases, it is impossible to demonstrate that, had the defendant followed the legally required procedure, the ultimate result would have been different. For example, it would have been extremely difficult for Earth Island Institute to establish that, had the U.S. Forest Service submitted the various proposed logging projects to the notice, comment, and appeal processes, the projects would have been rejected and the relevant portions of the forests would have remained un-logged.

As both *Earth Island* and *Spokeo* explain, the causation and redressability requirements are not so demanding, at least with respect to "procedural injuries." Plaintiffs *can* have standing to challenge a defendant's failure to follow a legally mandated procedure even if the plaintiff cannot show that the ultimate result would have been different. But to establish Article III standing based on such an injury, the plaintiff must demonstrate an *underlying concrete interest* affected by the failure to follow the required procedure. As the Court explained in *Earth Island Institute*,

"deprivation of a procedural right without some concrete interest that is affected by the deprivation—a procedural right *in vacuo*—is insufficient to create Article III standing. Only a 'person who has been accorded a procedural right to protect his concrete interests can assert that right without meeting all the normal standards for redressability and immediacy.'"

*   *   *

EXAMPLE

Suppose the federal government, to build a new military installation, plans to use its power of eminent domain to seize a person's property. And suppose a federal statute requires the government to prepare and publish an environmental impact study before seizing any property for such a purpose. Finally, suppose the government fails to conduct the required environmental impact study, and plaintiff sues to enjoin the taking of her property on the ground that the government has acted illegally in failing to follow the statutorily mandated procedures. The plaintiff likely cannot demonstrate that, had the government conducted the environmental impact study, the government would not have seized her property (or decided to go forward with constructing the military installation). Nonetheless, the plaintiff has standing to assert her "procedural injury" of the government's failure to follow the mandated process. The reason is that, under these circumstances, the procedural right she invokes—the right to have the government complete the environmental impact study—is connected to her underlying, concrete interest in her property. By contrast, a plaintiff who lacked such an underlying interest protected by the challenged procedure—who merely asserts "a procedural right *in vacuo*"—would lack standing.

*   *   *

6. *Redressability and nominal damages*: Can an award of nominal damages, standing alone, redress a past injury and thus satisfy the redressability requirement for standing under Article III? Nominal damages are a de minimis sum awarded to a plaintiff when her legal rights have been violated, often because it is difficult for the plaintiff to demonstrate economic loss. In *Uzuegbunam v. Preczewski*, 141 S. Ct. 792 (2021), the Supreme Court held that the award of such damages is sufficient to redress a completed injury.

The plaintiff in *Uzuegbunam* was an evangelical Christian who sought to share his faith with passers-by on the campus of Georgia Gwinnett College, a public college where he was enrolled as a student. Though he limited his activities to a designated "free speech zone," he nonetheless was prevented from speaking by campus police officers because his speech "disturbed the peace." He then sued several of the college's officers in federal district court; he sought an injunction against the enforcement of their campus speech policies and nominal damages. The college subsequently withdrew the challenged speech policies, rendering the claim for an injunction moot. But the plaintiff still sought nominal damages for the incident in which the officials enforced the college's speech policies against him.

Writing for the Court, Justice Thomas explained that,

> "[i]n determining whether nominal damages can redress a past injury, we look to the forms of relief awarded at common law. Article III's restriction of the judicial power to 'Cases' and 'Controversies' is properly understood to mean 'cases and controversies of the sort traditionally amenable to, and resolved by, the judicial process.'"

And the prevailing rule at common law, reasoned the Court, was that a party whose rights are invaded can always recover nominal damages without furnishing evidence of actual damage. By permitting plaintiffs to pursue nominal damages whenever they suffered a personal legal injury, the common law avoided the oddity of privileging small economic rights over important, but not easily quantifiable, nonpecuniary rights.

Importantly, the common law did not require a plea for compensatory damages as a prerequisite to an award of nominal damages. Nominal damages are not purely symbolic, but instead the damages awarded by default until the plaintiff establishes entitlement to some other form of damages. So even if a single dollar often will not provide the plaintiff full redress, it is a partial remedy that satisfies Article III's redressability requirement. And unlike an award of attorney's fees and costs—which may be the byproduct of a successful suit but not redress the plaintiff's injury—an award of nominal damages is relief on the merits.

Chief Justice Roberts dissented for himself alone. He contended that "an award of nominal damages does not alleviate the harms suffered by a plaintiff, and is not intended to. If nominal damages can preserve a live controversy, then federal courts will be required to give advisory opinions whenever a plaintiff tacks on a request for a dollar."

*   *   *

PROBLEMS ON STANDING: CAUSATION AND REDRESSIBILITY

In each of the following circumstances, please assess whether the plaintiff has satisfied the causation and redressability components necessary to establish standing under Article III. Assume the lawsuit has been filed in federal district court and the plaintiff has alleged a constitutionally sufficient injury in fact.

1. After the local basketball team won a championship, Plaintiff celebrated in the streets of Everytown. The Everytown police department has adopted a policy of using tasers on persons who disobey an order from an officer more than twice. During the celebration, an officer twice ordered Plaintiff to stop climbing a lamp post, but she ignored the officer and continued to climb the post. The officer then tased Plaintiff, causing her to fall from the post and suffer injuries. Plaintiff has filed suit against Everytown, asserting that the officer's use of the taser was unlawful.

   a. In her demand for relief, Plaintiff seeks damages (for pain and suffering and her medical expenses) attributable to her injuries suffered in the incident.

   b. In her demand for relief, Plaintiff seeks an injunction that forbids the Everytown police department from maintaining its policy on taser use.

2. Plaintiff is a low-income resident in the San Francisco Bay Area. He has not been able to find decent low-income housing for several months, but instead has been forced to live in his automobile. A California law requires property developers, in developments with at least 20 new residential units, to devote at least 15 percent of the units to affordable housing (to be rented at below-market rates). The state, however, has not aggressively enforced the law, and the number of new affordable units in the Bay Area has remained largely unchanged. Plaintiff has sued the California attorney general asserting the lax enforcement of the law is illegal. In his complaint, Plaintiff alleges he has been personally harmed by the lack of access to affordable housing.

*   *   *

REVIEW ESSAY QUESTION 1

On November 4, 2008, the voters of California approved Proposition 8, amending the California constitution to provide as follows: "Only marriage between a man and a woman is valid or recognized in California." In May 2009, two same-sex couples (plaintiffs Kristin Perry and Sandra Stier, and Paul Katami and Jeffrey Zarrillo) filed suit in the U.S. District Court for the Northern District of California claiming that Proposition 8 violated the Equal Protection and Due Process Clauses of the Fourteenth Amendment. They sought a declaration of its unconstitutionality and an injunction barring its enforcement.

The lawsuit properly named the governor, the state attorney general, and two county clerks (all in their official capacities) as defendants, as these were the officers responsible for enforcing and implementing Proposition 8. But all of the named defendants refused to defend Proposition 8's constitutionality, publicly agreeing with the plaintiffs that Proposition 8 was unconstitutional. Nonetheless, these state and county officials continued to enforce Proposition 8, believing it was their legal responsibility to do so until a court directed otherwise.

Given the defendants' unwillingness to defend Proposition 8 in court, the proposition's official proponents—the private citizens who, as California voters, were responsible for placing the proposition on the ballot—moved to intervene under Rule 24 of the Federal Rules of Civil Procedure to defend Proposition 8's validity. The district court granted their motion, and the proponents presented briefs and oral arguments in favor of the proposition's constitutionality.

In August 2010, following a bench trial, the district court held that Proposition 8, by denying same-sex couples the right to marry, violated the Fourteenth Amendment. The court thus enjoined the named defendants from enforcing it. *Perry v. Schwarzenegger*, 704 F. Supp. 2d 291 (N.D. Cal. 2010). The nominal defendants—again, the governor, the attorney general, and two county clerks—agreed with the district court's decision, agreed to abide by the injunction and did not appeal the judgment. The injunction was stayed pending appeal, however, so the defendants continued to enforce Proposition 8.

The proponents of Proposition 8 immediately appealed the district court's judgment to the U.S. Court of Appeals for the Ninth Circuit. In February 2012, the Ninth Circuit affirmed, though based on different reasoning. *Perry v. Brown*, 671 F.3d 1052 (9th Cir. 2012). The proponents then filed a petition for a writ of certiorari at the Supreme Court of the United States. The Court granted their petition, and ultimately decided the case in June 2013 (in *Hollingsworth v. Perry*, 570 U.S. 693 (2013)).

For purposes of this problem, ignore the underlying merits of the constitutional dispute. Instead, please address the following questions concerning the case's jusiticiability under Article III:

1. Was there a standing problem that should have prevented the district court from deciding the case? Why or why not?

2. Was there a standing problem that should have prevented the Ninth Circuit Court of Appeals from deciding the case? Why or why not?

3. Was there a standing problem that should have prevented the Supreme Court of the United States from deciding the case? Why or why not?

*   *   *

SUGGESTED ANALYSIS

1. No, there was no standing problem in the district court. The plaintiffs sued the two state officials responsible for enforcing Proposition 8, claiming that the law had deprived them of something they value very much: the right to be married. First, the deprivation of a marriage license is clearly an injury in fact; not only does it have economic

ramifications for the couple, but it has all sorts of other, less tangible impacts. This is sufficiently concrete, and it is particularized to the plaintiffs (as they have been specifically deprived of the right to marry). Second, the injury the plaintiffs have alleged has been caused by the enforcement of the law the plaintiffs challenge as unlawful. The causal connection is direct and straightforward. Third, the relief the plaintiffs seek—an injunction forbidding the relevant officials from discriminating against same-sex couples in the issuance of marriage licenses—would presumably redress their injury, as there is no indication that these couples would not otherwise be entitled to marry under California law. Because the plaintiffs could show injury in fact, causation, and redressability—and because the would-be married couples were the party seeking to invoke the federal judicial power in the district court—there was no standing problem. (Recall that only the party invoking the power of the federal courts must establish standing; the party against whom relief is sought need not.)

2. Yes, there was a potentially serious standing problem once the litigation proceeded to the court of appeals. Because the plaintiffs won in the district court, it was the official proponents of Proposition 8 who appealed the decision. But is unclear whether the proponents could demonstrate an injury in fact. The State of California could easily demonstrate an injury in fact; its law has been declared unconstitutional, which is an injury to its sovereignty as a state. Thus, had the California governor or attorney general appealed the decision—the state officers with the authority to enforce and litigate on behalf of the state—there would have been no standing problem. As state officers, they could assert the state's injury, which was caused by the district court's judgment (declaring California's law unconstitutional) and would be redressed by the court of appeals' reversal of the decision. But the state officials chose *not* to appeal. The question, then, is whether the proponents of Proposition 8 had standing to prosecute the appeal.

To answer this question, we have to address two distinct questions. First, did the proponents have standing *in their own right*, as supporters of Proposition 8? The answer seems pretty clearly no. Even if their injury were particularized (which seems questionable), it does not seem sufficiently concrete. They have a rather abstract, ideological interest in the content of the law, but nothing more. They might feel strongly, but that is insufficient. Second, even if the proponents lacked standing in their own right, were they entitled to stand in for the State of California and assert the state's injury in these circumstances, where the officials with the authority to litigate for the state have declined to do so? It is conceivable in circumstances like this—where the *People* of California have enacted a voter initiative and the elected officials have declined to defend that initiative in court—that some group of the populace would have the right assert the interests of the State of California. If so, the proponents would "stand in" for the state, and thus be able to assert the state's injury as grounds for having standing. (In other words, they would have the same right to assert standing as the governor or the attorney general.) This is plausible, and it would be the only way the proponents could have had standing to pursue this appeal. (Ultimately, the Supreme Court concluded in *Hollingsworth v. Perry* that the proponents of Proposition 8 could *not* represent the state in this fashion in federal court.)

3. Yes, there was the same serious standing problem that existed in the court of appeals. Again, the original plaintiffs (that is, the would-be married couples) prevailed in the Ninth Circuit. Thus, it was the proponents of Proposition 8 who sought review from the Supreme Court. Thus, the same issue existed as existed in the court of appeals—namely, what injury could the proponents assert that was sufficiently "concrete" and "particularized" under Article III? The only plausible injury was that suffered as a sovereign by the State of California, which the proponents could then claim to represent (since the relevant public officials had stepped aside). But the Supreme Court held that this was not permissible under Article III. That is, a state is not permitted to deputize citizens to litigate on behalf of the state in federal court when those citizens' injury is really no different than that suffered by the public at large. As a result, the Court concluded that the proponents lacked standing in the Supreme Court, and they had likewise lacked standing before the Ninth Circuit. The appeal was therefore dismissed, leaving the district court's judgment in place—the only point in the litigation in which there was standing.

* * *

C. Timing Questions: Ripeness and Mootness

In many respects, the issues of ripeness and mootness are specific applications of the doctrine of standing. They address circumstances in which standing may not yet—or may no longer—exist. Stated simply, a case is unripe if it is brought too soon, and it is moot if it has become too late. There is an important twist with respect to mootness, however, as the Supreme Court has created some minor exceptions that can permit a case to continue even when it appears the relevant injury has vanished.

1. Ripeness

Ripeness presents the question whether the plaintiff has yet suffered an "injury in fact." More specifically, the question is whether the plaintiff's injury is sufficiently "imminent." Again, a plaintiff need not have yet suffered any *actual* harm to establish an injury in fact under Article III; it is sufficient that the alleged injury be *imminent*. For instance, suppose a plaintiff credibly alleges that, but for the existence of a statute, she would engage in a particular activity. Suppose the activity is now criminally proscribed, and there is a substantial likelihood that, were the plaintiff to violate the statute, she would be prosecuted for that violation. The plaintiff need not commit the act and be criminally prosecuted for the case to be *ripe*.

More generally, it is well established that a plaintiff need not subject herself to legal liability—criminal or civil—to have standing to challenge a law she contends is invalid. It is enough that the law is currently preventing her, or will imminently prevent her, from doing something she would otherwise do. To make such a showing, she will need to demonstrate that there is a "credible threat" that, if she engaged in the prohibited activity, she would be prosecuted or subjected to an enforcement action. As the Supreme Court explained in *Susan B. Anthony List* v. *Driehaus*, 573 U.S. 149 (2014), "a plaintiff satisfies the injury-in-fact requirement where he alleges an intention to engage in a course of conduct arguably affected with a constitutional interest, but proscribed by a statute, and there exists a credible threat of prosecution thereunder." *Id.* at 159.

But the plaintiff's injury must, at a minimum, be *imminent*. A case is unripe when the alleged injury remains merely "hypothetical" or "conjectural." The more speculative the future harm, the more likely the case is unripe. And the "speculativeness" of an injury turns both on how distant it is in time and how uncertain it is to ultimately occur. The more uncertain the future harm will come to fruition, the more apt the case is to be deemed unripe. Conversely, the more certain the injury, the further into the future it can be while still satisfying the injury-in-fact requirement. This is largely why federal courts concluded that the plaintiffs in the various cases challenging the constitutionality of the Affordable Care Act's "minimum essential coverage provision"—which required all Americans to obtain minimally adequate health coverage or face a "tax penalty"—had standing when they brought their cases in 2010, even though the individual mandate was not set to take effect until 2013. There was almost no doubt the plaintiffs would be subjected to the mandate, even if that would not occur for three years.

2. Mootness

Mootness is slightly more complicated. Generally, a case is moot when one of the components necessary for standing has disappeared during the course of the litigation. It might be that the plaintiff's injury no longer exists, or that the defendant's conduct is no longer causing the injury, or that the court can no longer redress the alleged harm. For whatever reason, one of the essential requirements for standing no longer exists, though it existed when the suit was filed.

A case can become moot in a variety of circumstances. The legislature might have repealed or amended the law being challenged; or the parties might have settled their dispute; or the defendant might have provided the plaintiff with complete relief; or the defendant might no longer exist (for instance, if it is a business entity, it may have dissolved). In each of these instances, the injury in fact, the causal connection to the defendant's allegedly unlawful actions, or the court's capacity to redress the alleged harm has evaporated during the course of the litigation.

What makes mootness tricky is that, even though mootness is effectively a subspecies of standing doctrine—and though standing must exist at every point in the litigation—the Supreme Court has articulated some limited "exceptions." That is, in a narrow set of circumstances, a federal court still has jurisdiction to decide a case or controversy under Article III even though the dispute might otherwise appear moot.

a. *Voluntary cessation by the defendant*

One exception is when the dispute has purportedly been mooted by the defendant's voluntary cessation of the challenged conduct, but it is uncertain the change in conduct is permanent. The rationale behind this exception is that the defendant's voluntary cessation might be more strategic than sincere—an effort to obtain the suit's dismissal before the court issues any decision on the merits, thus permitting the defendant to resume the activity in the future. Indeed, this cycle could go on indefinitely without a court ever adjudicating the legality of the defendant's actions. Given the understandable skepticism of the defendant's motives under these circumstances, the Supreme Court has held that such cases generally are not moot. Though the plaintiff's alleged injury may no longer exist (at least at that moment), the plaintiff nonetheless has standing, and the court still has jurisdiction to decide the merits of the case.

b. *Capable of repetition yet evading review*

A second exception is when the question in dispute is capable of repetition while evading judicial review. This refers to circumstances in which the legal issue is otherwise justiciable, but there is something about its factual circumstances that precludes judicial review. This precise problem arose with respect to regulations of abortion. Due to the biological fact that a human pregnancy only lasts nine months (and that a fetus becomes viable by the fifth month), it would be nearly impossible for a pregnant woman to challenge a law regulating the abortion procedure before her particular dispute became moot. The Supreme Court therefore allowed such challenges to be brought by pregnant women, even though the plaintiff was no longer immediately affected by the law she was challenging.

CHAPTER 6
JUSTICIABILITY: POLITICAL QUESTIONS AND ADEQUATE AND INDEPENDENT STATE GROUNDS

A.   The "Political Questions" Doctrine

The political questions doctrine is another aspect of justiciability. Specifically, an otherwise-justiciable "case" or "controversy" will still lie beyond a federal court's adjudicative authority if the dispute constitutes a so-called "political question": an issue that the Constitution vests for its resolution in the elected (or "political") branches.

Two initial points are worth clarifying. First, the term "political questions" does *not* refer to cases that involve political subject matter, or that have political implications. (If it did, it would encompass much of the Supreme Court's docket.) Rather, it refers to a narrow category of disputes the Constitution leaves for decision to the political process, unreviewable by the federal courts. Second, cases presenting "political questions" still present questions of *constitutional law*. But they are questions that the federal courts are not empowered to answer, even when all the other requirements of Article III are satisfied.

What makes a dispute a non-justiciable "political question"? Unfortunately, the answer is often unclear. The criteria identified by the Supreme Court are fairly amorphous, making their application in any given case uncertain. Relatedly, several of those criteria would seem to apply to a large proportion of the Court's cases. Yet the Court has actually held that a dispute presented a non-justiciable political question in a vanishingly small number of instances. (We can basically count them on our hands.)

To be sure, the political questions doctrine remains an important aspect of constitutional law, as it forms one of the lines demarking the boundary to the federal judiciary's Article III authority. But it is important to keep in mind that, as a practical matter, the doctrine only affects a small number of disputes. As the Supreme Court recently explained, the political questions doctrine represents a "narrow exception" to the general rule that "the Judiciary has a responsibility to decide cases properly before it."

1.   A recent exploration: the recognition power

The Supreme Court has decided two important cases about the scope of the political questions doctrine in the past decade. The first was *Zivotofsky v.*

Clinton, 566 U.S. 189 (2012), which concerned the constitutionality of §214(d) of the Foreign Relations Authorization Act, Fiscal Year 2003. For many years, the State Department (a part of the Executive Branch, with the Secretary of State reporting directly to the President) directed its employees to record the place of birth of U.S. citizens born in Jerusalem simply as "Jerusalem," without reference to any country. Section 214(d) disrupted this longstanding practice by directing the Secretary of State, when requested by the citizen or the citizen's guardian, to record the place of birth as "Israel."

Congress generally can direct the President or other members of the Executive Branch to carry out specified actions. This is an uncontroversial feature of many (or most) federal statutes. (Indeed, carrying out the directions contained in federal statutes is, in many respects, the crux of the President's constitutional duty under Article II.) But this case was atypical. Two presidential administrations contended that §214(d) unconstitutionally trenched on a power that the Constitution reserves *exclusively* to the President (or to his representatives in the Executive Branch): the power to recognize foreign governments. Thus, the Bush and Obama administrations argued that §214(d)'s attempt effectively to direct the Secretary to recognize Jerusalem as lying within the territorial sovereignty of Israel was unconstitutional. In their view, the statute appropriated a power to Congress that the Constitution confers exclusively on the President. (Congress, of course, thought differently.)

The dispute raised fascinating questions about the powers of the President, the authority of Congress, and the separation of powers. But no federal court could resolve the dispute if it presented a nonjusticiable political question. Both the district court and the court of appeals so held, concluding that there was no "case" or "controversy" under Article III. As you read the case, please consider the following questions:

1. According to the Court's opinion, when will a dispute present a nonjusticiable political question?

2. Why did the Court conclude that the dispute in *Zivotofsky* did not constitute a political question? What related question, in the view of the Court, *would* have presented a nonjusticiable political question? How are those questions different?

3. How would you phrase the justiciability question presented in *Zivotofsky*? How would you phrase the underlying merits question? What exactly distinguishes the two questions from one another?

Zivotofsky v. Clinton
566 U.S. 189 (2012)

CHIEF JUSTICE ROBERTS delivered the opinion of the Court.

Congress enacted a statute providing that Americans born in Jerusalem may elect to have "Israel" listed as the place of birth on their passports. The State Department declined to follow that law, citing its longstanding policy of not taking a position on the political status of Jerusalem. When sued by an American who invoked the statute, the Secretary of State argued that the courts lacked authority to decide the case because it presented a political question. The Court of Appeals so held.

We disagree. The courts are fully capable of determining whether this statute may be given effect, or instead must be struck down in light of authority conferred on the Executive by the Constitution.

I

In 2002, Congress enacted the Foreign Relations Authorization Act, Fiscal Year 2003. . . . [Section] 214(d) is the only [provision] at stake in this case. Entitled "Record of Place of Birth as Israel for Passport Purposes," it provides that "[f]or purposes of the registration of birth, certification of nationality, or issuance of a passport of a United States citizen born in the city of Jerusalem, the Secretary shall, upon the request of the citizen or the citizen's legal guardian, record the place of birth as Israel."

The State Department's Foreign Affairs Manual states that "[w]here the birthplace of the applicant is located in territory disputed by another country, the city or area of birth may be written in the passport." The manual specifically directs that passport officials should enter "JERUSALEM" and should "not write Israel or Jordan" when recording the birthplace of a person born in Jerusalem on a passport.

Section 214(d) sought to override this instruction by allowing citizens born in Jerusalem to have "Israel" recorded on their passports if they wish. . . .

Petitioner Menachem Binyamin Zivotofsky was born in Jerusalem on October 17, 2002, shortly after §214(d) was enacted. Zivotofsky's parents were American citizens and he accordingly was as well, by virtue of congressional enactment. Zivotofsky's mother filed an application for a consular report of birth abroad and a United States passport. She requested that his place of birth be listed as "Jerusalem, Israel" on both documents. U. S. officials informed Zivotofsky's mother that State Department policy prohibits recording "Israel" as Zivotofsky's place of birth. Pursuant to that policy, Zivotofsky was issued a passport and consular report of birth abroad listing only "Jerusalem."

Zivotofsky's parents filed a complaint on his behalf against the Secretary of State. Zivotofsky sought a declaratory judgment and a permanent injunction ordering the Secretary to identify his place of birth as "Jerusalem, Israel" in the official documents. . . . The District Court . . . found that the case was not justiciable. It explained that "[r]esolving [Zivotofsky's] claim on the merits would necessarily require the Court to decide the political status of Jerusalem." Concluding that the claim therefore presented a political question, the District Court dismissed the case for lack of subject matter jurisdiction.

The D.C. Circuit affirmed. It reasoned that the Constitution gives the Executive the exclusive power to recognize foreign sovereigns, and that the exercise of this power cannot be reviewed by the courts. Therefore, "deciding whether the Secretary of State must mark a passport . . . as Zivotofsky requests would necessarily draw [the court] into an area of decisionmaking the Constitution leaves to the Executive alone." The D.C. Circuit held that the political question doctrine prohibits such an intrusion by the courts, and rejected any suggestion that Congress's decision to take "a position on the status of Jerusalem" could change the analysis. . . .

II

The lower courts concluded that Zivotofsky's claim presents a political question and therefore cannot be adjudicated. We disagree.

In general, the Judiciary has a responsibility to decide cases properly before it, even those it "would gladly avoid." *Cohens* v. *Virginia*, 6 Wheat. 264, 404 (1821). Our precedents have identified a narrow exception to that rule, known as the "political question" doctrine. We have explained that a controversy "involves a political question . . . where there is a textually demonstrable constitutional commitment of the issue to a coordinate political department; or a lack of judicially discoverable and manageable standards for resolving it." *Nixon* v. *United States*, 506 U.S. 224, 228 (1993). In such a case, we have held that a court lacks the authority to decide the dispute before it.

The lower courts ruled that this case involves a political question because deciding Zivotofsky's claim would force the Judicial Branch to interfere with the President's exercise of constitutional power committed to him alone. The District Court understood Zivotofsky to ask the courts to "decide the political status of Jerusalem." This misunderstands the issue presented. Zivotofsky does not ask the courts to determine whether Jerusalem is the capital of Israel. He instead seeks to determine whether he may vindicate his statutory right, under §214(d), to choose to have Israel recorded on his passport as his place of birth.

For its part, the D.C. Circuit treated the two questions as one and the same. That court concluded that "[o]nly the Executive—not Congress and not the courts—has the power to define U. S. policy regarding Israel's sovereignty over Jerusalem," and also to "decide how best to implement that policy." Because the Department's passport rule was adopted to implement the President's "exclusive and unreviewable constitutional power to keep the United States out of the debate over the status of Jerusalem," the validity of that rule was itself a "nonjusticiable political question" that "the Constitution leaves to the Executive alone." Indeed, the D.C. Circuit's opinion does not even mention §214(d) until the fifth of its six paragraphs of analysis, and then only to dismiss it as irrelevant: "That Congress took a position on the status of Jerusalem and gave Zivotofsky a statutory cause of action . . . is of no moment to whether the judiciary has [the] authority to resolve this dispute."

The existence of a statutory right, however, is certainly relevant to the Judiciary's power to decide Zivotofsky's claim. The federal courts are not being asked to supplant a foreign policy decision of the political branches with the courts' own unmoored determination of what United States policy toward Jerusalem should be. Instead, Zivotofsky requests that the courts enforce a specific statutory right. To resolve his claim, the Judiciary must decide if Zivotofsky's interpretation of the statute is correct, and whether the statute is constitutional. This is a familiar judicial exercise.

Moreover, because the parties do not dispute the interpretation of §214(d), the only real question for the courts is whether the statute is constitutional. At least since *Marbury* v. *Madison*, 1 Cranch 137 (1803), we have recognized that when an Act of Congress is alleged to conflict with the Constitution, "[i]t is emphatically the province and duty of the judicial department to say what the law is." *Id.,* at 177. That duty will sometimes involve the "[r]esolution of litigation challenging the constitutional authority of one of the three branches," but courts cannot avoid their responsibility merely "because the issues have political implications." *INS* v. *Chadha*, 462 U.S. 919, 943 (1983).

In this case, determining the constitutionality of §214(d) involves deciding whether the statute impermissibly intrudes upon Presidential powers under the Constitution. If so, the law must be invalidated and Zivotofsky's case should be dismissed for failure to state a claim. If, on the other hand, the statute does not trench on the President's powers, then the Secretary must be ordered to issue Zivotofsky a passport that complies with §214(d). Either way, the political question doctrine is not implicated. "No policy underlying the political question doctrine suggests that Congress or the Executive . . . can decide the constitutionality of a statute; that is a decision for the courts." *Id.,* at 941–942.

The Secretary contends that "there is a textually demonstrable constitutional commitment" to the President of the sole power to recognize foreign sovereigns and, as a corollary, to determine whether an American born in Jerusalem may choose to have Israel listed as his place of birth on his passport. *Nixon*, 506 U. S., at 228. Perhaps. But there is, of course, no exclusive commitment to the Executive of the power to determine the constitutionality of a statute. The Judicial Branch appropriately exercises that authority, including in a case such as this, where the question is whether Congress or the Executive is "aggrandizing its power at the expense of another branch." *Freytag v. Commissioner*, 501 U.S. 868, 878 (1991).

Our precedents have also found the political question doctrine implicated when there is "a lack of judicially discoverable and manageable standards for resolving" the question before the court. *Nixon*, 506 U.S. at 228. Framing the issue as the lower courts did, in terms of whether the Judiciary may decide the political status of Jerusalem, certainly raises those concerns. They dissipate, however, when the issue is recognized to be the more focused one of the constitutionality of §214(d).

Indeed, both sides offer detailed legal arguments regarding whether §214(d) is constitutional in light of powers committed to the Executive, and whether Congress's own powers with respect to passports must be weighed in analyzing this question.

For example, the Secretary reprises on the merits her argument on the political question issue, claiming that the Constitution gives the Executive the exclusive power to formulate recognition policy. . . . For his part, Zivotofsky argues that, far from being an exercise of the recognition power, §214(d) is instead a "legitimate and permissible" exercise of Congress's "authority to legislate on the form and content of a passport." . . . Recitation of these arguments—which sound in familiar principles of constitutional interpretation—is enough to establish that this case does not "turn on standards that defy judicial application." *Baker*, 369 U. S. at 211. Resolution of Zivotofsky's claim demands careful examination of the textual, structural, and historical evidence put forward by the parties regarding the nature of the statute and of the passport and recognition powers. This is what courts do. The political question doctrine poses no bar to judicial review of this case.

III

To say that Zivotofsky's claim presents issues the Judiciary is competent to resolve is not to say that reaching a decision in this case is simple. Because the District Court and the D.C. Circuit believed that review was barred by the political question doctrine, we are without the benefit of thorough lower court opinions to guide our analysis of the merits. . . . Having determined that this case is justiciable, we leave it to the lower courts to consider the merits in the first instance.

The judgment of the Court of Appeals for the D. C. Circuit is vacated, and the case is remanded for further proceedings consistent with this opinion.

*   *   *

Notes on *Zivotofsky v. Clinton*

1. The "merits" question and the "political question" question: In analyzing any justiciability issue, it is critical to keep the matter of justiciability distinct from the case's underlying merits. In *Zivotofsky*, the underlying merits question was whether the Constitution commits the decision to record a country's name (such as Israel) on a government-issued document (such as a passport) to the sole discretion of the Executive Branch. Stated slightly differently, the merits issue was whether §214(d) impermissibly infringed on the President's power to recognize foreign governments and their territorial sovereignty. The "political question" question, by contrast, was whether this merits question was, itself, committed to the political branches to resolve, and thus unreviewable by the federal courts. In *Zivotofsky*, the Supreme Court ruled that the merits question was justiciable—that it did not present a nonjusticiable political question. In the opinion's critical passage, Chief Justice Roberts reasoned that

> "determining the constitutionality of §214(d) involves deciding whether the statute impermissibly intrudes upon Presidential powers under the Constitution. If so, the law must be invalidated and Zivotofsky's case should be dismissed for failure to state a claim. If, on the other hand, the statute does not trench on the President's powers, then the Secretary must be ordered to issue Zivotofsky a passport that complies with §214(d). Either way, the political question doctrine is not implicated. 'No policy underlying the political question doctrine suggests that Congress or the Executive . . . can decide the constitutionality of a statute; that is a decision for the courts.'"

As it turns out, the Executive Branch ultimately prevailed on the underlying merits. Following the Court's decision in *Zivotofksy v. Clinton*, the case was remanded to the D.C. Circuit, which held in favor of the government. Zivotofsky again appealed to the Supreme Court. And in *Zivotofsky v. Kerry*, 576 U.S. 1 (2015), the Court held that "the power to recognize or decline to recognize a foreign state and its territorial bounds resides in the President alone," and §214(d) unconstitutionally interfered with that power.

2. *The doctrinal test for identifying a political question*: *Zivotofsky* concisely states the standard for when an otherwise justiciable dispute presents a political question: "a controversy involves a political question . . . where there is a textually demonstrable constitutional commitment of the issue to a coordinate political department; or a lack of judicially discoverable and manageable standards for resolving it." This definition is much more focused than some of the Court's prior statements. (In *Baker v. Carr*, 396 U.S. 186 (1962), for instance, the Court suggested six different attributes that have characterized cases found to present political questions.) *Zivotofsky* cleared much of the doctrinal underbrush, such that there now appear to be just two questions to address: (1) whether the Constitution commits the resolution of the issue to a branch other than the judiciary, and (2) whether the court lacks judicially discoverable and manageable standards for resolving the dispute.

3. *A "textually demonstrable constitutional commitment of the issue to a coordinate political department"*: The plainest example of a textually demonstrable commitment of a constitutional question to the political branches are the two clauses concerning the impeachment and removal of federal officers. Article I, § 2, clause 5 states that "[t]he House of Representatives . . . shall have the sole Power of Impeachment." Article I, § 3, clause 6 similarly states that "[t]he Senate shall have the sole Power to try all Impeachments."

At issue in *Nixon v. United States*, 503 U.S. 224 (1993), was the impeachment of a U.S. District Judge Walter Nixon. Nixon had been impeached by the House of Representatives for accepting bribes, and the matter moved to a trial in the Senate. Rather than conduct the trial before the full body of 100

Senators, the Senate decided to conduct the proceeding before a special committee, which then referred its conclusions to the full Senate. Following this process, the Senate voted to convict Nixon by the necessary two-thirds majority, and he was removed from office. Nixon then sued in federal court, contending the Constitution requires impeachment trials to occur before the full Senate. The Court held that the case presented a nonjusticiable political question:

> "We think that the word 'sole' is of considerable significance. Indeed, the word 'sole' appears only one other time in the Constitution—with respect to the House of Representatives' '*sole* Power of Impeachment.' Art. I, § 2, cl. 5 (emphasis added). The commonsense meaning of the word 'sole' is that the Senate alone shall have authority to determine whether an individual should be acquitted or convicted. The dictionary definition bears this out. 'Sole' is defined as 'having no companion,' 'solitary,' 'being the only one,' and 'functioning . . . independently and without assistance or interference.' Webster's Third New International Dictionary 2168 (1971). If the courts may review the actions of the Senate in order to determine whether that body 'tried' an impeached official, it is difficult to see how the Senate would be 'functioning . . . independently and without assistance or interference.'"

4. *A lack of judicially discoverable or manageable standards*: The plainest example of a constitutional dispute that lacks a judicially manageable or discoverable standard is a claim grounded in the Guarantee Clause. Article IV, § 4 provides that "[t]he United States shall guarantee to every State in this Union a Republican Form of Government." In several decisions, the Supreme Court has held that this clause leaves the judiciary with no manageable standard to discover or apply. As a result, claims based on the Guarantee Clause have long been considered to present nonjusticable political questions. For example, in *Pacific States Telephone & Telegraph Co. v. Oregon*, 223 U.S. 118 (1912), the plaintiff challenged a state tax imposed on corporations that had been adopted by voter initiative (rather than being enacted by the state legislature). The plaintiff contended that lawmaking by voters, rather than the state legislature, constituted something other than "a Republican Form of Government." The Court held that the claim was nonjusticiable, explaining that "when a State has ceased to be republican in form" was a question that had "long since been determined . . . to be political in character, and therefore not cognizable by the judicial power, but solely committed by the Constitution to the judgment of Congress."

5. *When are judicial standards "discoverable" and "manageable"?*: In practice, the answer is nearly always. To be sure, the text of the Guarantee Clause is somewhat vague and open-ended. But so is the language of the Due Process Clause of the Fourteenth Amendment ("nor shall any State deprive any person of life, liberty, or property, without due process of law"), of the Equal Protection Clause of the Fourteenth Amendment ("nor deny to any person within its jurisdiction the equal protection of the laws"), and of scores of

150

other provisions under which the Supreme Court has forged ahead to discover manageable judicial standards. The Guarantee Clause is really the exception that proves the rule: the Supreme Court will be able to discern a judicially manageable standard to enforce almost all of the Constitution's provisions.

6. *Some additional examples*: In *Roudebush v. Hartke*, 405 U.S. 15 (1972), the Court stated, following a contested election, "[w]hich candidate is entitled to be seated in the Senate is, to be sure, a nonjusticiable political question." In *Coleman v. Miller*, 307 U.S. 433 (1932), a plurality (but not a majority) of the justices concluded that a claim that a state legislature had not properly ratified a proposed constitutional amendment presented a nonjusticiable political question. And a plurality (but again not a majority) held in *Goldwater v. Carter*, 444 U.S. 996 (1979), that a challenge to the President's unilateral rescission of a treaty, without any concurrence by the Senate (as is necessary for treaty ratification), presented a nonjusticiable political question.

*   *   *

QUESTION: Suppose Congress enacted a law stating as follows: "The District Courts of the United States shall not exercise jurisdiction over any case or controversy in which the lawfulness of an action of the President or a member of the Executive Branch regarding the topic of immigration is challenged." A plaintiff brings suit in federal court, arguing that this jurisdiction-stripping statute is unconstitutional. The United States responds by filing a motion to dismiss (under Rule 12(b)(1) of the Federal Rules of Civil Procedure) contending that the court lacks jurisdiction because the plaintiff's claim presents a nonjusticiable "political question." Should the district court grant the government's motion?

ANSWER: No. And the easiest way to see this is by recalling that we have already seen the Supreme Court (in *Ex parte McCardle*, for instance) reach the merits of whether a federal statute stripping the federal courts of jurisdiction was constitutional. To be sure, the Court in *McCardle* ultimately concluded that the Supreme Court lacked jurisdiction to adjudicate the underlying dispute (about the constitutionality of McCardle's detention). But the Court reached that holding by first concluding that the Repeal Act was constitutional. Necessarily, then, the Court found that the question whether the Repeal Act was constitutional was justiciable. Further, *Zivotofsky* bluntly stated that "[a]t least since *Marbury* v. *Madison*, we have recognized that when an Act of Congress is alleged to conflict with the Constitution, '[i]t is emphatically the province and duty of the judicial department to say what the law is.'" In this hypothetical, Congress has enacted a statute, and the plaintiff has claimed that the statute is unconstitutional. *Zivotofsky* seems to hold that this sort of a claim (assuming all other aspects of Article III are satisfied) will always be justiciable, unless for some reason the nature of the claim leaves the Court without judicially discoverable or manageable standards.

QUESTION: Suppose the House of Representatives votes articles of impeachment against the President of the United States on the ground that he obstructed justice (by interfering in a Department of Justice investigation), and two-thirds of the Senate vote to convict, resulting in the President's removal from office. The President immediately files an action in a federal district court seeking to enjoin his removal on the ground that the President (as head of the Executive Branch, and thus ultimately in charge of all federal criminal investigations) cannot obstruct justice, and thus could not have committed a "high crime or misdemeanor" justifying impeachment (or removal). Can the district court hear the President's claim?

ANSWER: Almost certainly not. The Supreme Court held in *Nixon* that the Constitution's two Impeachment Clauses place the decision of whether to impeach or to convict a federal officer (and thus remove her from office) "solely" in the hands of the House of Representatives and the Senate, respectively. The wording of those clauses constitutes a textually demonstrable commitment of these questions to the elected branches, precluding judicial review. Hence, this case would almost certainly not present a "case" or "controversy" within the meaning of Article III and could not be decided by a federal court.

* * *

2. Partisan gerrymandering: *Rucho v. Common Cause*

The most recent Supreme Court decision addressing the political question doctrine is *Rucho v. Common Cause*, 139 S. Ct. 2484 (2019). And it may well be the most significant political question decision in the nation's history.

At issue in *Rucho* was the justiciability of claims that the drawing of the boundaries of electoral districts had been excessively—and thus unconstitutionally—partisan. Every ten years, following the publication of the decennial census, state legislatures draw the lines that define their state's electoral districts, both for the House of Representatives and for the state's own legislature. The party that controls the legislature typically draws those district lines in ways that maximize the party's electoral chances. Using huge sums of granular, block-level voter data, and deploying sophisticated computer programs, they attempt to "pack" the opposing party's voters into certain districts, and to "crack" them among others. In this way, the party in power gives its own candidates "safe" margins in as many districts as possible. ("Cracking" the opposing party's voters into multiple districts, for instance, can ensure that those voters constitute somewhere between 40 and 45 percent of the registered, party-affiliated voters in the district. And "packing" those voters into districts that the ruling party is bound to lose regardless can render them as much as 90 percent of the registered, party-affiliated voters in a given district). In short, the aim is to maximize the impact of any votes for the party in power and render practically useless as many votes as possible for the opposing party.

This "partisan gerrymandering" had provoked constitutional challenges for several years, though the precise nature of those claims varied. Some plaintiffs had claimed the practice violates the Equal Protection Clause of the Fourteenth Amendment. Others had claimed it violates the First Amendment (by penalizing voters based on their political views). And still others had claimed it violates the Elections Clause, which grants Congress the authority to regulate elections for federal office. Regardless of the precise claim, a federal court could not adjudicate the merits of any such constitutional challenge if it presented a nonjusticiable political question.

No one really defends partisan gerrymanders as a matter of policy. They can distort the results of elections, facilitating representations in Congress or state legislatures that diverge substantially from the proportion of votes earned by the parties as a whole. (For instance, the North Carolina map at issue in *Rucho* resulted in the state's congressional delegation consisting of ten Republicans and three Democrats, even though the statewide vote for the House of Representatives was split almost evenly between the parties.) Further, the practice reeks of corruption and self-dealing: those in power seem to be "rigging" the election rules to ensure their own reelection and preserve their own party's prerogatives, despite the preferences of the voters. Perhaps most important, partisan gerrymanders tend to result in an excessive number of uncompetitive districts, where the prevailing party is essentially predetermined. This means that few districts are truly contested in the general election, and representatives need only to worry about their party's primary election to be reelected. This, in turn, fuels political polarization. It gives representatives no incentive to "play to the middle" and every incentive to play to their party's political base (especially since the voters who tend to vote in primary contests are disproportionately party loyalists).

But the question for the Supreme Court in *Rucho* was not whether partisan gerrymanders are a good idea, or even whether they are constitutional. The question was whether a federal court has the authority to adjudicate whether they are constitutional. Dividing along party lines, the Court held 5-to-4 that it does not.

Writing for the Court, Chief Justice Roberts began by explaining that partisan gerrymandering claims have proved very difficult to adjudicate—more difficult than other sorts of election disputes—partly because "a jurisdiction may engage in constitutional political gerrymandering." To hold that legislators cannot take their partisan interests into account when drawing district lines would essentially countermand the Framers' decision to entrust districting to political entities. The "central problem" is "determining when political gerrymandering has gone too far."

The Court further reasoned that any standard for resolving partisan gerrymandering claims must be grounded in a "limited and precise rationale" and be "clear, manageable, and politically neutral." The question is one of degree: how to "provide a standard for deciding how much partisan dominance is too much." Partisan gerrymandering claims rest on an instinct that groups with a certain level of political support should enjoy a commensurate level of political power and influence. Such claims invariably sound in a desire for proportional representation, but the Constitution does not require proportional representation, and federal courts are neither equipped nor authorized to apportion political power as a matter of fairness. It is not even clear, stated the Chief Justice, what fairness looks like in this context. It may mean achieving a greater number of competitive districts by undoing packing and cracking so that supporters of the disadvantaged party have a better shot at electing their preferred candidates. But it could mean engaging in cracking and packing to ensure each party its "appropriate" share of "safe" seats. Or perhaps it should be measured by adherence to "traditional" districting criteria.

The Court thus concluded that deciding among those different visions of fairness poses questions that are *political*, not *legal*. There are no legal standards discernible in the Constitution for making such judgments. And it is only after determining how to define fairness that one can even begin to answer the determinative question, "How much is too much?"

The Court thus rejected each of the proposed tests for determining the constitutionality of partisan gerrymanders, concluding that none met the need for a limited and precise standard that is judicially discernible and manageable. Some lower courts had found these claims justiciable under the First Amendment, coalescing around a basic three-part test: proof of intent to burden individuals based on their voting history or party affiliation, an actual burden on political speech or associational rights, and a causal link between the invidious intent and the actual burden. But this analysis, concluded the Court, offered no "clear" and "manageable" way of distinguishing permissible from impermissible partisan motivation. And it stated that using a state's own districting criteria as a baseline from which to measure how extreme a partisan gerrymander is would be indeterminate and arbitrary; it would still leave open the question of how much political motivation and effect is too much.

The Court noted there remained other solutions to the problem. Numerous states have addressed the issue through state constitutional amendments and legislation placing power to draw electoral districts in the hands of independent commissions, mandating particular districting criteria for their mapmakers, or prohibiting drawing district lines for partisan advantage. The Framers also gave Congress the power to do something about partisan gerrymandering through the enactment of federal legislation under the Elections Clause. That avenue for reform established by the Framers, and used by Congress in the past, remains open. But the federal courts lack the authority to adjudicate claims that partisan gerrymanders are unconstitutional.

Justice Kagan, joined by Justices Ginsburg, Breyer, and Sotomayor, dissented:

"For the first time ever, this Court refuses to remedy a constitutional violation because it thinks the task beyond judicial capabilities. And not just any constitutional violation. The partisan gerrymanders in these cases deprived citizens of the most fundamental of their constitutional rights: the rights to participate equally in the political process, to join with others to advance political beliefs, and to choose their political representatives. In so doing, the partisan gerrymanders here debased and dishonored our democracy, turning upside-down the core American idea that all governmental power derives from the people. These gerrymanders enabled politicians to entrench themselves in office as against voters' preferences. They promoted partisanship above respect for the popular will. They encouraged a politics of polarization and dysfunction. If left unchecked, gerrymanders like the ones here may irreparably damage our system of government."

The dissent lamented that

"gerrymandering is, as so many Justices have emphasized before, anti-democratic in the most profound sense. In our government, 'all political power flows from the people.' And that means, as Alexander Hamilton once said, 'that the people should choose whom they please to govern them.' But in Maryland and North Carolina they cannot do so. In Maryland, election in and election out, there are 7 Democrats and 1 Republican in the congressional delegation. In North Carolina, however the political winds blow, there are 10 Republicans and 3 Democrats. Is it conceivable that someday voters will be able to break out of that prefabricated box? Sure. But everything possible has been done to make that hard. To create a world in which power does not flow from the people because they do not choose their governors."

The dissent concluded that, "[o]f all times to abandon the Court's duty to declare the law, this was not the one. The practices challenged in these cases imperil our system of government. Part of the Court's role in that system is to defend its foundations. None is more important than free and fair elections."

B.   Adequate and Independent State Grounds

1. The essence of the doctrine

The doctrine of adequate and independent state grounds represents a limited but important constraint on when the Supreme Court of the United States will have jurisdiction to review the judgment of a state court. The doctrine does not constitute a distinct or new jurisdictional principle, but instead describes a situation in which two other limitations converge.

The essence of the doctrine of adequate and independent state grounds is that the Supreme Court lacks the authority to review a state court's judgment when that judgment rests on a state-law holding that is both (1) *adequate* to support the judgment and (2) *independent* of any holding on a federal question (even if the state court's decision *also* resolves a question of federal law). In such a circumstance, the Supreme Court cannot review the state court's judgment because (a) it lacks subject matter jurisdiction over the state-law question and (b) its review of the federal question lacks the capacity to alter the ultimate outcome of the case, making it purely advisory.

* * *

EXAMPLE

Suppose the State of California prosecutes a criminal defendant in state court for possessing heroin with the intent to distribute the narcotic. The police had previously discovered the heroin during a warrantless search of the defendant's apartment. At trial, the defendant files a motion to exclude the heroin from evidence, asserting two distinct legal bases for its exclusion: (1) that the search of his apartment violated the Fourth Amendment to the federal Constitution, and (2) that the search violated a provision of the California state constitution. (If either of the defendant's claims prevails, the trial court would be required to exclude the heroin from evidence, and given its importance to the prosecution, the case against the defendant would have to be dismissed.)

The trial court rejects both of defendant's arguments and the heroin is admitted into evidence. The jury then renders a verdict convicting defendant. The defendant then appeals, first to the California Court of Appeal and then to the California Supreme Court. The California Supreme Court holds that the police officers' search of the defendant's apartment violated *both* the federal Constitution and the California state constitution. It thus orders that the defendant's conviction to be vacated.

QUESTION: If the State of California then seeks review of the California Supreme Court's judgment in the Supreme Court of the United States, would the Supreme Court of the United States have the authority to review the California Supreme Court's decision?

ANSWER: No, because the judgment rests on adequate and independent state grounds. In these circumstances, the California Supreme Court's decision rests on a state-law ground—that the search of the defendant's apartment violated the state constitution—that is *adequate* to support the judgment. (It is adequate to support the judgment because this aspect of the holding, standing alone, is sufficient to justify the outcome of vacating the defendant's conviction.) And the California Supreme Court's judgment is *independent* of any holding with respect to federal law. The California Supreme Court's judgment may be incorrect with respect to its Fourth Amendment holding, but this would not affect its judgment on the state-law question. As a result, the Supreme Court of the United States may not review California Supreme Court's judgment.

* * *

2. Understanding the doctrine

Properly understood, the doctrine of adequate and independent state grounds reflects a confluence of two distinct limitations on the federal judicial power. First, under Article III, the federal courts lack subject matter jurisdiction over questions of state law except in special circumstances (such as when the parties are diverse in state citizenship). Thus, as a general matter, the Supreme Court cannot review state court judgments on questions of state law. In the example discussed above, for instance, the Supreme Court of the United States could not review the defendant's claim on appeal that the search of his apartment violated the California constitution. This claim lies outside the federal courts' subject matter jurisdiction defined by Article III, §2, clause 1.

Of course, the defendant's claim that the search of his apartment violated the Fourth Amendment to the federal Constitution arises under federal law, and thus plainly fits within the federal courts' subject matter jurisdiction. But to qualify as a "case" or "controversy" under Article II, §2, clause 1, there must be a substantial likelihood that the court's decision would have a binding legal effect on the parties. Without this—if the decision lacks any potential to alter the legal rights of the parties—the Supreme Court's decision on the federal question would be purely advisory. And as we have covered, Article III forbids federal courts from issuing advisory opinions.

When a state court's decision rests on adequate and independent state-law grounds—such that the ultimate outcome of the case would remain unchanged no matter what the Supreme Court of the United States decided on appellate review—any opinion the Supreme Court might render on the federal question would be purely advisory. The state court might have wrongly decided the federal question, and an opinion from the Supreme Court so stating would affect the law on that subject as a matter of precedent. *But such an opinion would have no impact on the legal rights of the parties before the Court.* In the example discussed above, no matter what the Supreme Court of the United States held with respect to whether the search of the defendant's apartment violated the Fourth Amendment, the California Supreme Court's decision ensures that the defendant's conviction will be vacated. Because the California Supreme Court's decision rested adequately and independently on that court's interpretation of state law—a question over which the Supreme Court of the United States lacks subject matter jurisdiction—any opinion from the Supreme Court of the United States on appellate review would be purely advisory.

3. Deciphering state court judgments: *Michigan v. Long*

Suppose a litigant presses independent federal and state law claims in her appeal before a state supreme court. And suppose the state supreme court holds in favor of the litigant, discussing both the federal and state law arguments in its opinion. But suppose the state supreme court's opinion is unclear as to whether its judgment was based on the state-law claim, the federal-law claim, or both. Does the court's judgment rest on adequate and independent state grounds, precluding review by the Supreme Court of the United States?

The Supreme Court addressed this question in *Michigan v. Long*, 463 U.S. 1032 (1983). In an opinion authored by Justice O'Connor, the Court held that, if the state court's opinion is unclear on the matter, the Supreme Court would presume that the state supreme court's decision was based on *federal* law unless the state court's opinion contains a "plain statement" that it rests on independent state-law grounds.

David Long had been arrested by Barry County sheriff's deputies somewhere in the State of Michigan. The deputies stopped Long in his car over after Long had been driving erratically. The deputies peered inside Long's car with a flashlight and saw a pouch protruding from the armrest between the two front seats. As it turned out, the pouch contained marijuana. Long was then prosecuted by the State of Michigan in Michigan state court for the possession of a controlled substance.

Long filed a motion to exclude the marijuana from evidence on the ground that the police had seized it illegally. He made two independent claims as to why the search was unlawful: (1) it violated the Fourth Amendment to the federal Constitution, and (2) it violated Article I, § 11 of the Michigan Constitution, which provides that "[t]he person, houses, papers and possessions of every person shall be secure from unreasonable searches and seizures." The trial court denied Long's motion, and Long was convicted. On appeal, the Michigan Supreme Court reversed his conviction, and the State of Michigan sought review in the Supreme Court of the United States.

Before reaching whether the search of Long's car was constitutional, the justices needed to resolve whether they had jurisdiction to decide the case—specifically, whether the Michigan Supreme Court's decision rested on an adequate and independent state-law ground. Unfortunately, the Michigan Supreme Court's opinion was unclear as to the degree to which that court's judgment had relied on the Michigan Constitution or the Fourth Amendment.

Justice O'Connor's opinion for the Court articulated a new approach for resolving such quandaries:

"[W]hen, as in this case, a state court decision fairly appears to rest primarily on federal law, or to be interwoven with the federal law, and when the adequacy and independence of any possible state law ground is not clear from the face of the opinion, we will accept as the most reasonable explanation that the state court decided the case the way it did because it believed that federal law required it to do so. If a state court chooses merely to rely on federal precedents as it would on the precedents of all other jurisdictions, then it need only make clear by a plain statement in its judgment or opinion that the federal cases are being used only for the purpose of guidance, and do not themselves compel the result that the court has reached. In this way, both justice and judicial administration will be greatly improved. If the state court decision indicates clearly and expressly that it is alternatively based on bona fide separate, adequate, and independent grounds, we, of course, will not undertake to review the decision."

Thus, when confronted with a state court decision that might rest on either state-law or federal-law grounds, the Court will presume that the state court's judgment rested on federal law unless the opinion contains a "plain statement" to the contrary.

There were other possible solutions to the problem. And one might criticize the Court's "plain statement" rule as not sufficiently solicitous of the states' role as independent sovereigns. But the plain-statement rule is simple to administer, as it relieves the Supreme Court of having to delve too deeply into unpacking a state court's opinion. Perhaps more important, once the Court announced the plain-statement standard in *Long*, state supreme courts were on notice as to how to write their opinions if they wished to signal a judgment's grounding in an adequate and independent state-law basis.

In the long run, then, the rule of *Michigan v. Long* may simply force state supreme courts to more clearly explain the rationales of their judgments, at least when litigants press both state-law and federal-law arguments. Assuming state court judges do not forget to include such plain statements in their opinions, the rule should not actually alter any substantive results.

* * *

PROBLEMS ON ADEQUATE AND INDEPENDENT STATE GROUNDS

The state of Ohio has recently enacted the "Save Adolescents from Experimentation Act" (SAFE Act), which makes it unlawful for a physician to perform certain procedures to alter a minor child's sex. A physician who regularly treats teenagers who are transitioning has filed suit against the Ohio attorney general in Ohio state court. In her complaint, the physician has asserted two distinct claims: (1) that the SAFE Act violates the Equal Protection Clause of the Fourteenth Amendment to the U.S. Constitution; and (2) that the SAFE Act violates the right to personal autonomy enshrined in the Ohio state constitution. The physician seeks an injunction forbidding the attorney general from enforcing the statute.

Suppose the trial court's decision has been appealed to the Ohio Supreme Court. In which of the following circumstances would the Supreme Court of the United States—if petitioned to do so—have the authority to hear an appeal from the Ohio Supreme Court's judgment?

1. The Ohio Supreme Court holds that the SAFE Act is consistent with the Ohio Constitution, but that it violates the Equal Protection Clause of the Fourteenth Amendment.

2. The Ohio Supreme Court holds that the SAFE Act is consistent with the Equal Protection Clause of the Fourteenth Amendment, but that it violates the Ohio Constitution.

3. The Ohio Supreme Court holds that the SAFE Act violates both the Equal Protection Clause of the Fourteenth Amendment and the Ohio Constitution.

4. The Ohio Supreme Court holds that the SAFE Act is consistent with both the Equal Protection Clause of the Fourteenth Amendment and the Ohio Constitution.

*   *   *

MULTIPLE-CHOICE REVIEW QUESTIONS ON THE JUDICIAL POWER

1. Plaintiff lives in Texas, where the state legislature has recently redrawn the state's legislative districting map so as to strongly favor Republican candidates. Though Republicans outnumber Democrats by roughly 8 percent in the state (President Biden lost the state by 5.6 percent in 2020), the districting map ensures that registered Republicans will constitute a majority in more than 75 percent of the state's legislative districts. Plaintiff files suit in Texas state court asserting that the districting map violates various provisions in the Texas state constitution and the U.S. Constitution. The Texas trial court dismisses the case as nonjusticiable, holding that the Supreme Court's decision in *Rucho v. Common Cause* commands that result. Plaintiff has now appealed the trial court's ruling. Based on these facts alone, the court of appeals should:

   (a) Affirm the trial court's judgment, because the case p resents a political question.

   (b) Affirm the trial court's judgment, because it is based on adequate and independent state-law grounds.

   (c) Reverse the trial court's judgment, because state courts are obligated to decide questions of federal law.

   (d) Reverse the trial court's judgment, because *Rucho* concerned the meaning of Article III, which is inapplicable in this case.

2. Protester was injured by a police officer while taking part in a Black Lives Matter march in downtown Salt Lake City, Utah. The police officer who injured Protester works for Salt Lake City, but her actions at the time of the march were supervised and directed by a state officer, the Utah State Director of Public Security.

   Protester files suit in federal district court. She asserts one claim against Salt Lake City and one claim against the State of Utah. In each claim, Protester seeks damages for her injuries. (Assume that the federal statute creating Protester's cause of action is a valid exercise of Congress's Article I powers.) Which of the following statements is most accurate?

   (a) The district court lacks jurisdiction over either claim.

   (b) The district court has jurisdiction over both claims.

   (c) The district court has jurisdiction over Protester's claim against Salt Lake City but lacks jurisdiction over her claim against the State of Utah.

   (d) The district court has jurisdiction over Protester's claim against the State of Utah but lacks jurisdiction over her claim against Salt Lake City.

3. Suppose that, instead of Protester filing a lawsuit, the U.S. Department of Justice (DOJ) files an action in federal district court against the State of Utah for its handling of the protest. For relief, DOJ seeks both an injunction (requiring the State to reform the way it polices similar protests) and the imposition of civil penalties (payable to the U.S. government). If the State of Utah files a motion to dismiss for lack of jurisdiction, which of the following is most likely?

   (a) The district court will grant the motion, because the United States lacks standing.

   (b) The district court will grant the motion, because the case presents a nonjusticiable political question.

   (c) The district court will grant the motion, because the Eleventh Amendment deprives the court of subject matter jurisdiction.

   (d) The district court will deny the motion.

4. The Supreme Court's decision in *Martin v. Hunter's Lessee* stands for the fundamental principle that the Supreme Court of the United States has the authority:

   (a) To review the final judgments of state courts on questions of federal law.

   (b) To review the constitutionality of state statutes and state executive actions.

   (c) To review the final judgments of state courts on questions of state law.

   (d) To review the constitutionality of federal statutes or federal executive actions.

5. Responding to a downturn in the state's economy, the Nebraska legislature enacts a statute requiring every business with annual sales to Nebraska customers exceeding $1 million to purchase goods and services from vendors in Nebraska equaling at least half of the business's Nebraska sales. (For instance, a business with $2 million in sales to Nebraska customers must purchase at least $1 million in goods or services from Nebraska vendors.) Among the following, which has the *strongest* claim to have standing to challenge the constitutionality of the Nebraska statute in federal court?

   (a) A business located in Kansas that provides 95 percent of the goods and services purchased by Acme Co, a Nebraska business that has $20 million in annual sales to Nebraska customers.

   (b) A business that presently makes $300,000 in sales to Nebraska customers but that only purchases $10,000 in goods and services each year from Nebraska vendors.

   (c) The State of Kansas, on behalf of the businesses and taxpayers located there.

   (d) A bank that has lent money to ABC Corp., a business with $10 million in sales to Nebraska customers but which only purchases $1 million in goods and services each year from Nebraska vendors.

6. Vermont enacts a statute making it a crime to post (on a site accessible via the internet) a video or audio clip that expresses any form of "racial hatred." Plaintiff brings suit against the Vermont attorney general—the officer responsible for enforcing the statute—asserting that the statute violates the First Amendment to the U.S. Constitution. Plaintiff files her action in a Vermont state court, seeking an injunction against the statute's enforcement. (Assume Plaintiff has standing.) Does the federal Constitution permit the state trial court to adjudicate the case?

   (a) No, because the case presents a purely federal question under Article III.

   (b) Yes, because as a matter of federal constitutional law, state courts are courts of general subject matter jurisdiction.

   (c) No, because Article III only concerns the jurisdiction of the federal courts.

   (d) Yes, because federal law does not preempt the Vermont statute being challenged.

CHAPTER 7

POLITICAL CONSTRAINTS ON THE FEDERAL COURTS

A final subject to address before leaving Article III is how the political system, as created by the Constitution, shapes the federal judiciary's decision making. Federal courts are powerful actors in our constitutional framework, particularly given their authority to declare acts of the other branches—as well as those of state and local governments—unlawful. Moreover, federal judges enjoy a fair measure of independence from political reprisal. Under Article III, §1, federal judges generally enjoy life tenure and protection from a reduction in their salaries. As a norm, judicial independence is deeply embedded in the nation's political fabric, perceived by many as a critical component of the rule of law.

Thus, it is easy to miss the ways that federal courts can be—and often are—influenced by surrounding political pressures. No doubt, the federal judiciary is independent in a particular sense. But the federal courts are also part of a broader political system, constructed by the Constitution, from which they can never be separated. The courts' decisions always emerge from, and thus are a part of, this ecosystem. Stated differently, whatever formal powers the federal courts enjoy, their exercise of those powers is necessarily constrained by the political forces surrounding them.

Moreover, it is a mistake to think that, just because some of these constraints have not actually been deployed for many years, they do not still operate to limit the courts' actions. Even unused, they still pose a threat—a Sword of Damocles, if you will—that likely affects how the courts discharge their responsibilities.

A.   The Powers of Congress

As discussed in prior chapters, an important means by which the elected branches might exercise influence over the federal courts is by regulating their subject matter jurisdiction. Congress has broad authority to regulate the appellate jurisdiction of the Supreme Court under the Exceptions Clause, and it has virtually unlimited authority to regulate the jurisdiction of the lower federal courts (or eliminate those courts altogether). To date—though Congress has often regulated and made exceptions to the federal courts' jurisdiction—Congress has done so quite rarely as a means of "disciplining" the judiciary. That is not to say that the threat of such discipline has not mattered, but only that Congress has mostly kept this sword in its sheath.

There are a wide variety of other tools at Congress's disposal to influence the judiciary. Some of them have been used at critical junctures in constitutional history, and to significant effect.

1. Budget and appropriations

All money spent by the federal government must be appropriated by Congress. As Article I, §9, clause 7 specifies, "No money shall be drawn from the Treasury, but in consequence of Appropriations made by Law." Thus, any funds spent by the federal judiciary (including the Supreme Court), for any purpose, must first be approved by Congress through the enactment of a federal statute. As part of this process, two justices appear before the relevant congressional committees to defend the Supreme Court's proposed budget each year. And Congress, if it so wished, could reduce that budget dramatically as a way of sending the Court a message. Indeed, these hearings have often served as a forum for Senators and Representatives to express their disapproval of recent Supreme Court decisions.

2. The size of the Supreme Court

Nine justices currently sit on the Supreme Court. This number is not dictated by the Constitution, which merely requires the existence of a Supreme Court generally. Instead, the size of the Court rests solely with the discretion of Congress. *See* 28 U.S.C. §1. Originally, the Judiciary Act of 1789 created only six seats on the Supreme Court. The Federalist-controlled Congress reduced the number to five in 1801 (in the waning days of the Adams administration, to deprive President Jefferson of an appointment to the Court), but the Jeffersonian-controlled Congress restored the number to six before the change took effect. Congress increased the size of the Court to seven justices in 1807; to nine in 1837; and to ten in 1863. In 1866, Congress enacted a law providing that the next three justices, as they retired, would not be replaced. After two retirements, this took the size of the Court to eight in 1867. But in 1869, Congress enacted the Circuit Judges Act, which increased the size of the Court to nine justices again. The number has remained nine ever since, though recent events have brought this into question. On April 9, 2021, President Biden announced the creation of a commission to examine whether, among other things, Congress should add seats to the Court.

These adjustments to the Court's size, of course, have often been accomplished precisely to influence the outcome of the Court's decisions—even in specific cases. The Federalists had this in mind in 1801 when they reduced the Court from six to five justices. The Republicans sought to ensure the Court was hospitable to President Lincoln's prosecution of the Civil War in 1863 when it expanded the Court to ten justices. And the Republican-controlled Congress in 1869 specifically had the gold standard dispute in mind when it expanded the Court from eight to nine justices—a change in personnel that, with the appointment of a new Republican justice, led the Court to overrule a decision that was only three years old. The very point of President Roosevelt's proposed Court-packing plan in 1937 (which would have potentially expanded the Court to fifteen justices) was to change the Court's decisions regarding the constitutionality of various New Deal programs. Roosevelt's plan was tabled in Congress, but the Court may well have been influenced into changing the direction of its decisions.

In all events, there is nothing in the Constitution that prevents Congress from changing the size of the Supreme Court. And when Congress has done so, it has generally been to affect the outcomes of the Court's decisions.

3. Amending the Constitution

The most direct and straightforward means to "overruling" the Supreme Court's interpretation of the Constitution is to amend the Constitution. Article V sets out the procedure for doing so:

> "The Congress, whenever two thirds of both Houses shall deem it necessary, shall propose Amendments to this Constitution, or, on the Application of the Legislatures of two thirds of the several States, shall call a Convention for proposing Amendments, which, in either Case, shall be valid to all Intents and Purposes, as Part of this Constitution, when ratified by the Legislatures of three fourths of the several States, or by Conventions in three fourths thereof, as the one or the other Mode of Ratification may be proposed by the Congress."

There have been 27 amendments to the Constitution since its original ratification, but there have only been 17 since 1791 (when the Bill of Rights was added, which was really just an extension of the ratification process, as a promise to add these amendments was necessary to win ratification of the Constitution in some important states). Four of those 17 amendments have been in direct response to controversial Supreme Court decisions:

* The Eleventh Amendment overruled *Chisholm v. Georgia*, 2 U.S. (2 Dall.) 419 (1793), which had held that federal courts could exercise jurisdiction over a lawsuit brought against a state government by a private citizen of another state.

* The Fourteenth Amendment (among other things) overruled *Scott v. Sandford*, 60 U.S. (19 How.) 393 (1857), which had held (again, among other things) that persons of African descent could not be citizens of the United States.

* The Sixteenth Amendment effectively overruled most of *Pollock v. Farmers Loan & Trust Co.*, 157 U.S. 429 (1895), which had held that a federal personal income tax was a "direct tax" under Article I, § 9, and therefore must be apportioned according to a state's population (making the imposition of such a tax practically impossible).

* The Twenty-sixth Amendment overruled *Oregon v. Mitchell*, 400 U.S. 112 (1970), which had held that Congress could not require the states to allow all citizens 18 years or older to vote in state elections.

Thus far, all constitutional amendments have been proposed by Congress rather than by a convention. And it is unclear whether a convention called for the purpose of proposing amendments could actually be limited to the subjects prompting the convention. As a result, many fear that any such gathering runs the risk of morphing into a "runaway convention" at which the entire Constitution might be reconsidered or re-written. (On this point, it is worth remembering what happened in 1787.)

4. Impeachment and removal from office

Supreme Court justices may be removed from office through the process of impeachment for "Treason, Bribery or Other High Crimes and Misdemeanors." The House of Representatives has impeached only one Supreme Court justice: Justice Samuel Chase in 1804. Chase was a Federalist who had been involved in enforcing the Alien and Sedition Acts during the administration of President John Adams, and the Jeffersonian Republicans sought retribution. Though Chase was impeached by the House, he was not convicted by the Senate. (They fell short of the necessary two-thirds majority at the impeachment trial in March 1805.) There have been some rumblings about impeaching other justices, but none has ever come close to success. Several lower court judges, however, have been impeached and removed from office, typically for the commission of crimes (such as accepting bribes).

B.   The Powers of the President

What can the President do to influence the federal courts or to shape the meaning of the Constitution? Perhaps most importantly, the President is the leader of the nation, the only official elected by the People as a whole. He therefore owns an unrivaled capacity to shape public opinion—and thus potentially to turn that opinion against the Supreme Court or its decisions. (For instance, President Obama used his State of the Union address in 2010 to criticize the Court's decision in *Citizens United v. FEC*, 558 U.S. 310 (2010)—with the justices seated only a few feet in front of him during the speech.) But the President has other tools at his disposal as well.

1. Control over the enforcement of federal law

As revealed by the sordid story of President Andrew Jackson's removal of the Cherokees from Georgia (on the Trail of Tears)—essentially in defiance of the Supreme Court's decision in *Worcester v. Georgia*, 31 U.S. (6 Pet.) 515 (1832)—the courts are utterly dependent on the Executive Branch for the enforcement of many of their rulings. If the President decides not to implement the judiciary's decisions, there is really nothing the courts can do about it, other than perhaps hold the relevant executive officers in contempt. If the American public supports the President in an interbranch showdown, the judiciary is largely powerless. In this way, the courts ultimately depend on the public's faith in the rule of law, the persuasiveness of their judgments, and the public's faith that the judiciary is acting in a principled fashion. The President, with all the authority of the Executive Branch, has a great deal of practical power over the way in which Supreme Court decisions are actually enforced (or not).

2. Appointments to the judiciary

Another obvious political influence on the judiciary is that provided by the appointments and confirmation process. The President—through Article II, §2, clause 2—has the authority to nominate all Article III judges. The Senate has the authority to confirm those judges; after presidential nomination, Article III judges are appointed "[w]ith the Advice and Consent of the Senate." Thus, the political commitments of both the President and the Senate affect the composition of the federal judiciary—and the Supreme Court especially, where ideology is particularly important in the selection of justices.

This is probably the single most common mechanism by which we experience constitutional change over time. The replacement of Justice Sandra Day O'Connor with Justice Samuel Alito in 2006, the replacement of Justice Anthony Kennedy with Justice Brett Kavanaugh in 2018, and the replacement of Justice Ruth Bader Ginsburg with Justice Amy Coney Barrett in 2020 all have produced significant changes in the Court's decisions and likely future direction—on high-profile issues such as abortion, religious liberty, campaign finance regulation, gun safety, the death penalty, and partisan gerrymandering.

PART III

THE POWERS OF CONGRESS

CHAPTER 8
THE BASIC FRAMEWORK FOR CONGRESSIONAL POWER

A. Introduction to the Powers of Congress

We now turn to the authority the Constitution grants Congress, the national legislature. Congress consists of two chambers: the House of Representatives and the Senate. Its powers are principally spelled out in Article I, though there are a handful of other relevant provisions elsewhere in the Constitution.

Before delving into the details, it is important understand the basic framework for Congress's powers in our constitutional system. An essential principle—maybe *the* essential principle—is that Congress's authority is *limited*: Congress can only act pursuant to those powers *enumerated* in the Constitution, either expressly or implicitly. It lacks the authority to legislate merely because the law would be in the national interest or would promote the "general welfare." As it is often said, Congress lacks a "general police power"—a power to regulate as it sees fit to further the nation's interests. Instead, the Constitution must affirmatively grant Congress the power to enact any statute it enacts. The grant of power need not be express, but it must be somewhere in the Constitution.

This principle is underscored by the phrasing of the first sentence of Article I: "All legislative Powers *herein granted* shall be vested in a Congress of the United States which shall consist of a Senate and a House of Representatives." And it is confirmed by the text of the Tenth Amendment: "The powers not delegated to the United States by the Constitution, nor prohibited by it to the States, are reserved to the States respectively, or to the people." As James Madison wrote in The Federalist No. 45, "[t]he powers delegated by the proposed constitution to the federal government, are few and defined." Chief Justice Marshall reiterated this principle in the great case of *McCulloch v. Maryland*, 17 U.S. (4 Wheat.) 159 (1819): "This government is acknowledged by all to be one of enumerated powers. The principle, that it can exercise only the powers granted to it, [is] now universally admitted."

The converse of this principle governs the legislative powers of the states. State governments can presumptively act (at least as a matter of federal constitutional law) unless they are prohibited from doing so by valid federal law. Stated differently, states enjoy all *residuary powers*. This authority is often referred to as the "police power"—the presumptive power to enact laws or otherwise regulate in a matter that provides for the health, safety, and welfare of their citizens. Again, to quote Madison in The Federalist No. 45: "Those [powers] which are to remain in the state government, are numerous and indefinite." To be sure, there may be relevant state-law constraints, such as those that a state imposes on itself through its own state constitution. But those are constraints states have adopted of their own accord. They do not come from the federal Constitution.

This structural relationship between the respective legislative authorities of the federal government and the states mirrors that between the federal and state judiciaries. Recall that, pursuant to Article III, federal courts are courts of *limited* jurisdiction: federal courts can only decide those "cases" or "controversies" enumerated in Article III, §2, clause 1. By contrast, state courts are courts of *general* jurisdiction; they can hear any cases unless affirmatively prohibited from doing so by federal law.

The principal means by which the Constitution accomplishes this system of limited legislative powers is through its specific enumeration of Congress's powers. During the Constitutional Convention, the Framers rejected proposals that would have granted Congress a more open-ended power, such as the authority to enact legislation "in all areas in which the states are not competent." Instead, the document endows Congress with a very specific list of powers, from that "to lay and collect Taxes," to the power "[t]o establish Post Offices and post Roads," to the power "[t]o raise and support Armies." (There are several others.) Most of these powers are set out in Article I, §8.

Importantly, the last clause of Article I, §8 authorizes Congress "[t]o make all Laws which shall be necessary and proper for carrying into Execution the foregoing Powers, and all other Powers vested by this Constitution in the Government of the United States, or in any Department of Officer thereof." This provision concerns not the *ends* Congress can pursue through federal statutes, but the *means*. The scope of Congress's latitude in choosing the appropriate means for accomplishing various enumerated objectives largely determines how broadly or narrowly those enumerated powers will operate in practice. This is largely why the Court's decision in *McCulloch v. Maryland* is so significant.

Given this structure, every case about the breadth of Congress's enumerated powers is also a case about federalism. That is, the breadth of Congress's legislative authority necessarily determines the breadth of the authority left exclusively to the states. It is a zero-sum game: the broader Congress's power to regulate "commerce among the States," for instance, the smaller the zone left solely to state control.

Another critical point is that just because Congress has the power to regulate a certain activity does not mean that the states cannot regulate that same activity, too. The federal government's legislative authority is not *exclusive*—unless Congress, by law, chooses to make it so. (For example, Congress has made the patent and bankruptcy systems in the U.S. exclusively federal. But this is by congressional choice; it is not mandated by the Constitution.) Indeed, most areas of American life are regulated in some way by both the federal government and the states. Because federal law is supreme, however, in these vast areas where both the national government and the states can regulate, Congress can always decide to preempt state law. That is, to the extent federal and state law conflict—and the federal law is within Congress's enumerated powers—federal law will displace state law to the extent of the conflict. (This rule is dictated by the Supremacy Clause of Article VI.)

The critical point here is that, to define the breadth of Congress's powers is necessarily to define what is left *exclusively* to the states. In this way, every dispute about the breadth of Congress's enumerated powers also concerns the contours of federalism.

B.   The Basic Framework: *McCulloch v. Maryland*

1. Introduction

The Supreme Court's decision in *McCulloch v. Maryland* may be the most significant in U.S. history, even exceeding *Marbury v. Madison*. Its understanding of Congress' legislative authority, and its interpretation of the Necessary and Proper Clause, were critical in defining the breadth of the federal government's power. Further, *McCulloch* articulated an essential principle about the legitimate spheres of state and federal sovereignty—that states are constitutionally forbidden from interfering with the operation of valid federal law—which has proved vital to binding the nation together as a union.

McCulloch presented two distinct constitutional questions. The first was whether Congress possessed the power to charter a national bank, a question that turned principally on the scope and meaning of the Necessary and Proper Clause. The second was, if Congress had such authority, whether Maryland could impose a state-level tax on the bank's operations. Both issues were vitally important in 1819, but they raised even larger questions with more lasting constitutional consequences. *McCulloch*'s answers to these questions profoundly shaped the direction of the nation.

2. The historical context

Before discussing those issues, however, some background is useful. Following much debate—and over the objections of James Madison, then a leader in the House of Representatives—the very first Congress passed a bill to charter the first Bank of the United States. Before signing the bill into law, President George Washington sought the opinions of two cabinet members, Alexander Hamilton and Thomas Jefferson, as to whether Congress's creation of a national bank was constitutional. Hamilton, the Federalist, believed it was. He thought Congress's enumerated powers should be construed broadly so as to facilitate a more robust national power. Jefferson, meanwhile, thought the bank bill was unconstitutional. He thought Congress's powers should be more narrowly understood so as to constrain the national government and leave greater power with the states. Washington ultimately sided with Hamilton and signed the bill into law, creating the first Bank of the United States in 1790.

Twenty years later, in 1810, the first bank's charter expired, and the bank ceased to exist. Following some economic and financial turbulence—precipitated largely by the War of 1812—Congress rechartered the Bank in 1815. (Then-President James Madison urged the bill's passage, having changed his view about its constitutionality since 1790.) From 1815 to 1818, a brief economic boom ensued, fueled partly by some speculative lending by the Bank.

In the fall of 1818, however, the nation was struck by a financial panic. The Bank was forced to call many of its loans due, at a time when borrowers generally lacked the funds to repay them. This led to a popular uprising against the Bank. In fact, many of the borrowers holding loans called due by the Bank were state governments, making the Bank especially unpopular among state legislators. Soon, a number of states enacted laws openly hostile to the Bank. Some states, like Maryland, imposed taxes on the Bank's operations. Other states went further, enacting laws that purported to forbid the Bank from operating within their borders, effectively nullifying the operation of federal law inside their states.

3. *McCulloch v. Maryland*

In April 1818, Maryland enacted a law imposing a tax on all banks with branches located in the state that had not been chartered by the Maryland legislature. In practical effect, the tax applied to exactly one bank, the Bank of the United States. The law also created what is known as an informer action, which permitted a private citizen to bring suit against violators of the law and keep half of any penalty imposed. McCulloch was the cashier of the Baltimore branch of Bank of the United States. John James, a private citizen, brought an informer action against McCulloch on behalf of State of Maryland for the Bank's failure to pay the state tax due on all deposits. The Maryland state courts decided the case in favor of James (and Maryland). McCulloch then appealed to the Supreme Court. As you read *McCulloch*, please consider the following questions:

1. Where did Maryland contend "ultimate sovereignty" was located within the system of government created by the Constitution? Who did the Supreme Court conclude is the "ultimate sovereign" under the Constitution? Why does this matter?

2. According to Chief Justice Marshall, would Congress have the discretion, through legislation, to adopt "appropriate means" to pursue its enumerated powers even if the Necessary and Proper Clause had not been included in the Constitution? If so, what are the implications to understanding the purpose of the Necessary and Proper Clause?

3. How did Maryland understand the word "necessary" in the Necessary and Proper Clause? What was Chief Justice Marshall's response?

4. What standard does the Court articulate for the breadth of Congress's authority to enact laws implementing its enumerated powers under the Necessary and Proper Clause? Would you characterize this standard as exacting or deferential to Congress?

5. Which taxpayers, in an economic sense, would ultimately pay the tax that Maryland attempted to impose? Which taxpayers would derive the benefit of the revenue produced by the tax?

6. What would be the long-term danger in permitting states to enact laws—whether taxes or regulations—that interfered with the full operation of valid federal law within their borders? What sort of constitutional system would that represent?

McCulloch v. Maryland
17 U.S. (4 Wheat.) 159 (1819)

Mr. CHIEF JUSTICE MARSHALL delivered the opinion of the Court.

In the case now to be determined, the defendant, a sovereign state, denies the obligation of a law enacted by the legislature of the Union, and the plaintiff, on his part, contests the validity of an act which has been passed by the legislature of that state. The constitution of our country, in its most interesting and vital parts, is to be considered; the conflicting powers of the government of the Union and of its members, as marked in that constitution, are to be discussed; and an opinion given, which may essentially influence the great operations of the government. No tribunal can approach such a question without a deep sense of its importance, and of the awful responsibility involved in its decision. But it must be decided peacefully, or remain a source of hostile legislation, perhaps, of hostility of a still more serious nature; and if it is to be so decided, by this tribunal alone can the decision be made. On the supreme court of the United States has the constitution of our country devolved this important duty.

The first question made in the cause is—has congress power to incorporate a bank? It has been truly said, that this can scarcely be considered as an open question, entirely unprejudiced by the former proceedings of the nation respecting it. The principle now contested was introduced at a very early period of our history, has been recognised by many successive legislatures, and has been acted upon by the judicial department, in cases of peculiar delicacy, as a law of undoubted obligation.

It will not be denied, that a bold and daring usurpation might be resisted, after an acquiescence still longer and more complete than this. . . .

The power now contested was exercised by the first congress elected under the present constitution. The bill for incorporating the Bank of the United States did not steal upon an unsuspecting legislature, and pass unobserved. Its principle was completely understood, and was opposed with equal zeal and ability. After being resisted, first, in the fair and open field of debate, and afterwards, in the executive cabinet, with as much persevering talent as any measure has ever experienced, and being supported by arguments which convinced minds as pure and as intelligent as this country can boast, it became a law. The original act was permitted to expire; but a short experience of the embarrassments to which the refusal to revive it exposed the government, convinced those who were most prejudiced against the measure of its necessity, and induced the passage of the present law. It would require no ordinary share of intrepidity, to assert that a measure adopted under these circumstances, was a bold and plain usurpation, to which the constitution gave no countenance.

In discussing this question, the counsel for the state of Maryland have deemed it of some importance, in the construction of the constitution, to consider that instrument, not as emanating from the people, but as the act of sovereign and independent states. The powers of the general government, it has been said, are delegated by the states, who alone are truly sovereign; and must be exercised in subordination to the states, who alone possess supreme dominion. It would be difficult to sustain this proposition. The convention which framed the constitution was indeed elected by the state legislatures. But the instrument, when it came from their hands, was a mere proposal, without obligation, or pretensions to it. It was reported to the then existing congress of the United States, with a request that it might "be submitted to a convention of delegates, chosen in each state by the people thereof, under the recommendation of its legislature, for their assent and ratification." This mode of proceeding was adopted; and by the convention, by congress, and by the state legislatures, the instrument was submitted to the people. They acted upon it in the only manner in which they can act safely, effectively and wisely, on such a subject, by assembling in convention. It is true, they assembled in their several states—and where else should they have assembled? No political dreamer was ever wild enough to think of breaking down the lines which separate the states, and of compounding the American people into one common mass. Of consequence, when they act, they act in their states. But the measures they adopt do not, on that account, cease to be the measures of the people themselves, or become the measures of the state governments.

From these conventions, the constitution derives its whole authority. The government proceeds directly from the people; is "ordained and established," in the name of the people; and is declared to be ordained, "in order to form a more perfect union, establish justice, insure domestic tranquility, and secure the blessings of liberty to themselves and to their posterity." The assent of the states, in their sovereign capacity, is implied, in calling a convention, and thus submitting that instrument to the people. But the people were at perfect liberty to accept, or reject it; and their act was final. It required not the affirmance, and could not be negatived, by the state governments. The constitution, when thus adopted, was of complete obligation, and bound the state sovereignties. . . .

The government of the Union, then (whatever may be the influence of this fact on the case), is, emphatically and truly, a government of the people. In form, and in substance, it emanates from them. Its powers are granted by them and are to be exercised directly on them, and for their benefit.

This government is acknowledged by all, to be one of enumerated powers. The principle, that it can exercise only the powers granted to it, would seem too apparent, to have required to be enforced by all those arguments, which its enlightened friends, while it was depending before the people, found it necessary to urge; that principle is now universally admitted. But the question respecting the extent of the powers actually granted, is perpetually arising, and will probably continue to arise, so long as our system shall exist. In discussing these questions, the conflicting powers of the general and state governments must be brought into view, and the supremacy of their respective laws, when they are in opposition, must be settled.

If any one proposition could command the universal assent of mankind, we might expect it would be this—that the government of the Union, though limited in its powers, is supreme within its sphere of action. This would seem to result, necessarily, from its nature. It is the government of all; its powers are delegated by all; it represents all, and acts for all. Though any one state may be willing to control its operations, no state is willing to allow others to control them. The nation, on those subjects on which it can act, must necessarily bind its component parts. But this question is not left to mere reason: the people have, in express terms, decided it, by saying, "this constitution, and the laws of the United States, which shall be made in pursuance thereof," "shall be the supreme law of the land," and by requiring that the members of the state legislatures, and the officers of the executive and judicial departments of the states, shall take the oath of fidelity to it. The government of the United States, then, though limited in its powers, is supreme; and its laws, when made in pursuance of the constitution, form the supreme law of the land, "anything in the constitution or laws of any state to the contrary notwithstanding."

Among the enumerated powers, we do not find that of establishing a bank or creating a corporation. But there is no phrase in the instrument which, like the articles of confederation, excludes incidental or implied powers; and which requires that everything granted shall be expressly and minutely described. . . . A constitution, to contain an accurate detail of all the subdivisions of which its great powers will admit, and of all the means by which they may be carried into execution, would partake of the prolixity of a legal code, and could scarcely be embraced by the human mind. It would, probably, never be understood by the public. Its nature, therefore, requires, that only its great outlines should be marked, its important objects designated, and the minor ingredients which compose those objects, be deduced from the nature of the objects themselves. . . . . In considering this question, then, we must never forget that it is a constitution we are expounding.

Although, among the enumerated powers of government, we do not find the word "bank" or "incorporation," we find the great powers, to lay and collect taxes; to borrow money; to regulate commerce; to declare and conduct a war; and to raise and support armies and navies. The sword and the purse, all the external relations, and no inconsiderable portion of the industry of the nation, are intrusted to its government. It can never be pretended, that these vast powers draw after them others of inferior importance, merely because they are inferior. Such an idea can never be advanced. But it may with great reason be contended, that a government, intrusted with such ample powers, on the due execution of which the happiness and prosperity of the nation so vitally depends, must also be intrusted with ample means for their execution. The power being given, it is the interest of the nation to facilitate its execution. It can never be their interest, and cannot be presumed to have been their intention, to clog and embarrass its execution, by withholding the most appropriate means. . . . Can we adopt that construction (unless the words imperiously require it), which would impute to the framers of that instrument, when granting these powers for the public good, the intention of impeding their exercise, by withholding a choice of means? If, indeed, such be the mandate of the constitution, we have only to obey; but that instrument does not profess to enumerate the means by which the powers it confers may be executed; nor does it prohibit the creation of a corporation, if the existence of such a being be essential, to the beneficial exercise of those powers. It is, then, the subject of fair inquiry, how far such means may be employed.

It is not denied, that the powers given to the government imply the ordinary means of execution. . . . The government which has a right to do an act, and has imposed on it, the duty of performing that act, must, according to the dictates of reason, be allowed to select the means; and those who contend that it may not select any appropriate means, that one particular mode of effecting the object is excepted, take upon themselves the burden of establishing that exception. . . .

The power of creating a corporation, though appertaining to sovereignty, is not, like the power of making war, or levying taxes, or of regulating commerce, a great substantive and independent power, which cannot be implied as incidental to other powers, or used as a means of executing them. It is never the end for which other powers are exercised, but a means by which other objects are accomplished. . . . The power of creating a corporation is never used for its own sake, but for the purpose of effecting something else. No sufficient reason is, therefore, perceived, why it may not pass as incidental to those powers which are expressly given, if it be a direct mode of executing them.

But the constitution of the United States has not left the right of congress to employ the necessary means, for the execution of the powers conferred on the government, to general reasoning. To its enumeration of powers is added, that of making "all laws which shall be necessary and proper, for carrying into execution the foregoing powers, and all other powers vested by this constitution, in the government of the United States, or in any department thereof." The counsel for the state of Maryland have urged various arguments, to prove that this clause, though, in terms, a grant of power, is not so, in effect; but is really restrictive of the general right, which might otherwise be implied, of selecting means for executing the enumerated powers. . . .

[T]he argument on which most reliance is placed, is drawn from that peculiar language of this clause. Congress is not empowered by it to make all laws, which may have relation to the powers conferred on the government, but such only as may be "necessary and proper" for carrying them into execution. The word "necessary" is considered as controlling the whole sentence, and as limiting the right to pass laws for the execution of the granted powers, to such as are indispensable, and without which the power would be nugatory. That it excludes the choice of means, and leaves to congress, in each case, that only which is most direct and simple.

Is it true, that this is the sense in which the word "necessary" is always used? Does it always import an absolute physical necessity, so strong, that one thing to which another may be termed necessary, cannot exist without that other? We think it does not. If reference be had to its use, in the common affairs of the world, or in approved authors, we find that it frequently imports no more than that one thing is convenient, or useful, or essential to another. To employ the means necessary to an end, is generally understood as employing any means calculated to produce the end, and not as being confined to those single means, without which the end would be entirely unattainable. Such is the character of human language, that no word conveys to the mind, in all situations, one single definite idea; and nothing is more common than to use words in a figurative sense. Almost all compositions contain words, which, taken in a their rigorous sense, would convey a meaning different from that which is obviously intended. It is essential to just construction, that many words which import something excessive, should be understood in a more mitigated sense—in that sense which common usage justifies. The word "necessary" is of this description. It has not a fixed character, peculiar to itself. It admits of all degrees of comparison; and is often connected with other words, which increase or diminish the impression the mind receives of the urgency it imports. A thing may be necessary, very necessary, absolutely or indispensably necessary. To no mind would the same idea be conveyed by these several phrases. The comment on the word is well illustrated by the passage cited at the bar, from the 10th section of the 1st article of the constitution. It is, we think, impossible to compare the sentence which prohibits a state from laying "imposts, or duties on imports or exports,

179

except what may be absolutely necessary for executing its inspection laws," with that which authorizes congress "to make all laws which shall be necessary and proper for carrying into execution" the powers of the general government, without feeling a conviction, that the convention understood itself to change materially the meaning of the word "necessary," by prefixing the word "absolutely." This word, then, like others, is used in various senses; and, in its construction, the subject, the context, the intention of the person using them, are all to be taken into view.

Let this be done in the case under consideration. The subject is the execution of those great powers on which the welfare of a nation essentially depends. It must have been the intention of those who gave these powers, to insure, so far as human prudence could insure, their beneficial execution. This could not be done, by confiding the choice of means to such narrow limits as not to leave it in the power of congress to adopt any which might be appropriate, and which were conducive to the end. This provision is made in a constitution, intended to endure for ages to come, and consequently, to be adapted to the various crises of human affairs. To have prescribed the means by which government should, in all future time, execute its powers, would have been to change, entirely, the character of the instrument, and give it the properties of a legal code. It would have been an unwise attempt to provide, by immutable rules, for exigencies which, if foreseen at all, must have been seen dimly, and which can be best provided for as they occur. To have declared, that the best means shall not be used, but those alone, without which the power given would be nugatory, would have been to deprive the legislature of the capacity to avail itself of experience, to exercise its reason, and to accommodate its legislation to circumstances. If we apply this principle of construction to any of the powers of the government, we shall find it so pernicious in its operation that we shall be compelled to discard it. . . .

So, with respect to the whole penal code of the United States: whence arises the power to punish, in cases not prescribed by the constitution? All admit, that the government may, legitimately, punish any violation of its laws; and yet, this is not among the enumerated powers of congress. The right to enforce the observance of law, by punishing its infraction, might be denied, with the more plausibility, because it is expressly given in some cases. Congress is empowered "to provide for the punishment of counterfeiting the securities and current coin of the United States," and "to define and punish piracies and felonies committed on the high seas, and offences against the law of nations." The several powers of congress may exist, in a very imperfect state, to be sure, but they may exist and be carried into execution, although no punishment should be inflicted, in cases where the right to punish is not expressly given.

Take, for example, the power "to establish post-offices and post-roads." This power is executed, by the single act of making the establishment. But, from this has been inferred the power and duty of carrying the mail along the post-road, from one post-office to another. And from this implied power, has again been inferred the right to punish those who steal letters from the post-office, or rob the mail. It may be said, with some plausibility, that the right to carry the mail, and to punish those who rob it, is not indispensably necessary to the establishment of a post-office and post-road. This right is indeed essential to the beneficial exercise of the power, but not indispensably necessary to its existence. So, of the punishment of the crimes of stealing or falsifying a record or process of a court of the United States, or of perjury in such court. To punish these offences, is certainly conducive to the due administration of justice. But courts may exist, and may decide the causes brought before them, though such crimes escape punishment.

The baneful influence of this narrow construction on all the operations of the government, and the absolute impracticability of maintaining it, without rendering the government incompetent to its great objects, might be illustrated by numerous examples drawn from the constitution, and from our laws. The good sense of the public has pronounced, without hesitation, that the power of punishment appertains to sovereignty, and may be exercised, whenever the sovereign has a right to act, as incidental to his constitutional powers. It is a means for carrying into execution all sovereign powers, and may be used, although not indispensably necessary. It is a right incidental to the power, and conducive to its beneficial exercise.

If this limited construction of the word "necessary" must be abandoned, in order to punish, whence is derived the rule which would reinstate it, when the government would carry its powers into execution, by means not vindictive in their nature? If the word "necessary" means "needful," "requisite," "essential," "conducive to," in order to let in the power of punishment for the infraction of law; why is it not equally comprehensive, when required to authorize the use of means which facilitate the execution of the powers of government, without the infliction of punishment?

In ascertaining the sense in which the word "necessary" is used in this clause of the constitution, we may derive some aid from that with which it is associated. Congress shall have power "to make all laws which shall be necessary and proper to carry into execution" the powers of the government. If the word "necessary" was used in that strict and rigorous sense for which the counsel for the state of Maryland contend, it would be an extraordinary departure from the usual course of the human mind, as exhibited in composition, to add a word, the only possible effect of which is, to qualify that strict and rigorous meaning; to present to the mind the idea of some choice of means of legislation, not strained and compressed within the narrow limits for which gentlemen contend.

But the argument which most conclusively demonstrates the error of the construction contended for by the counsel for the state of Maryland, is founded on the intention of the convention, as manifested in the whole clause. To waste time and argument in proving that, without it, congress might carry its powers into execution, would be not much less idle, than to hold a lighted taper to the sun. As little can it be required to prove, that in the absence of this clause, congress would have some choice of means. That it might employ those which, in its judgment, would most advantageously effect the object to be accomplished. That any means adapted to the end, any means which tended directly to the execution of the constitutional powers of the government, were in themselves constitutional. This clause, as construed by the state of Maryland, would abridge, and almost annihilate, this useful and necessary right of the legislature to select its means. That this could not be intended, is, we should think, had it not been already controverted, too apparent for controversy.

We think so for the following reasons: 1st. The clause is placed among the powers of congress, not among the limitations on those powers. 2d. Its terms purport to enlarge, not to diminish the powers vested in the government. It purports to be an additional power, not a restriction on those already granted. No reason has been, or can be assigned, for thus concealing an intention to narrow the discretion of the national legislature, under words which purport to enlarge it. The framers of the constitution wished its adoption, and well knew that it would be endangered by its strength, not by its weakness. Had they been capable of using language which would convey to the eye one idea, and, after deep reflection, impress on the mind, another, they would rather have disguised the grant of power, than its limitation. If, then, their intention had been, by this clause, to restrain the free use of means which might otherwise have been implied, that intention would have been inserted in another place, and would have been expressed in terms resembling these. "In carrying into execution the foregoing powers, and all others," &c., "no laws shall be passed but such as are necessary and proper." Had the intention been to make this clause restrictive, it would unquestionably have been so in form as well as in effect.

The result of the most careful and attentive consideration bestowed upon this clause is, that if it does not enlarge, it cannot be construed to restrain the powers of congress, or to impair the right of the legislature to exercise its best judgment in the selection of measures to carry into execution the constitutional powers of the government. If no other motive for its insertion can be suggested, a sufficient one is found in the desire to remove all doubts respecting the right to legislate on that vast mass of incidental powers which must be involved in the constitution, if that instrument be not a splendid bauble.

We admit, as all must admit, that the powers of the government are limited, and that its limits are not to be transcended, But we think the sound construction of the constitution must allow to the national legislature that discretion, with respect to the means by which the powers it confers are to be carried into execution, which will enable that body to perform the high duties assigned to it, in the manner most beneficial to the people. *Let the end be legitimate, let it be within the scope of the constitution, and all means which are appropriate, which are plainly adapted to that end, which are not prohibited, but consist with the letter and spirit of the constitution, are constitutional.*

That a corporation must be considered as a means not less usual, not of higher dignity, not more requiring a particular specification than other means, has been sufficiently proved. If we look to the origin of corporations, to the manner in which they have been framed in that government from which we have derived most of our legal principles and ideas, or to the uses to which they have been applied, we find no reason to suppose, that a constitution, omitting, and wisely omitting, to enumerate all the means for carrying into execution the great powers vested in government, ought to have specified this. . . .

If a corporation may be employed, indiscriminately with other means, to carry into execution the powers of the government, no particular reason can be assigned for excluding the use of a bank, if required for its fiscal operations. To use one, must be within the discretion of congress, if it be an appropriate mode of executing the powers of government. That it is a convenient, a useful, and essential instrument in the prosecution of its fiscal operations, is not now a subject of controversy. All those who have been concerned in the administration of our finances, have concurred in representing its importance and necessity; and so strongly have they been felt, that statesmen of the first class, whose previous opinions against it had been confirmed by every circumstance which can fix the human judgment, have yielded those opinions to the exigencies of the nation. Under the confederation, congress, justifying the measure by its necessity, transcended, perhaps, its powers, to obtain the advantage of a bank; and our own legislation attests the universal conviction of the utility of this measure. The time has passed away, when it can be necessary to enter into any discussion, in order to prove the importance of this instrument, as a means to effect the legitimate objects of the government.

But were its necessity less apparent, none can deny its being an appropriate measure; and if it is, the decree of its necessity, as has been very justly observed, is to be discussed in another place. Should congress, in the execution of its powers, adopt measures which are prohibited by the constitution; or should congress, under the pretext of executing its powers, pass laws for the accomplishment of objects not intrusted to the government; it would become the painful duty of this tribunal, should a case requiring such a decision come before it, to say, that such an act was not the law of the land. But where the law is not prohibited, and is really calculated to effect any of the objects intrusted to the government, to undertake here to inquire into the decree of its necessity, would be to pass the line which circumscribes the judicial department, and to tread on legislative ground. This court disclaims all pretensions to such a power.

After this declaration, it can scarcely be necessary to say, that the existence of state banks can have no possible influence on the question. No trace is to be found in the constitution, of an intention to create a dependence of the government of the Union on those of the states, for the execution of the great powers assigned to it. Its means are adequate to its ends; and on those means alone was it expected to rely for the accomplishment of its ends. To impose on it the necessity of resorting to means which it cannot control, which another government may furnish or withhold, would render its course precarious, the result of its measures uncertain, and create a dependence on other governments, which might disappoint its most important designs, and is incompatible with the language of the constitution. But were it otherwise, the choice of means implies a right to choose a national bank in preference to state banks, and congress alone can make the election.

After the most deliberate consideration, it is the unanimous and decided opinion of this court, that the act to incorporate the Bank of the United States is a law made in pursuance of the constitution, and is a part of the supreme law of the land. . . .

2. Whether the state of Maryland may, without violating the constitution, tax that branch? That the power of taxation is one of vital importance; that it is retained by the states; that it is not abridged by the grant of a similar power to the government of the Union; that it is to be concurrently exercised by the two governments—are truths which have never been denied. But such is the paramount character of the constitution, that its capacity to withdraw any subject from the action of even this power, is admitted. The states are expressly forbidden to lay any duties on imports or exports, except what may be absolutely necessary for executing their inspection laws. If the obligation of this prohibition must be conceded—if it may restrain a state from the exercise of its taxing power on imports and exports—the same paramount character would seem to restrain, as it certainly may restrain, a state from such other exercise of this power, as is in its nature incompatible with, and repugnant to, the constitutional laws of the Union. A law, absolutely repugnant to another, as entirely repeals that other as if express terms of repeal were used.

On this ground, the counsel for the bank place its claim to be exempted from the power of a state to tax its operations. There is no express provision for the case, but the claim has been sustained on a principle which so entirely pervades the constitution, is so intermixed with the materials which compose it, so interwoven with its web, so blended with its texture, as to be incapable of being separated from it, without rending it into shreds. This great principle is, that the constitution and the laws made in pursuance thereof are supreme; that they control the constitution and laws of the respective states, and cannot be controlled by them. From this, which may be almost termed an axiom, other propositions are deduced as corollaries, on the truth or error of which, and on their application to this case, the cause has been supposed to depend.

These are, 1st. That a power to create implies a power to preserve: 2d. That a power to destroy, if wielded by a different hand, is hostile to, and incompatible with these powers to create and to preserve: 3d. That where this repugnancy exists, that authority which is supreme must control, not yield to that over which it is supreme.

These propositions, as abstract truths, would, perhaps, never be controverted. Their application to this case, however, has been denied; and both in maintaining the affirmative and the negative, a splendor of eloquence, and strength of argument, seldom, if ever, surpassed, have been displayed.

The power of congress to create, and of course, to continue, the bank, was the subject of the preceding part of this opinion; and is no longer to be considered as questionable. That the power of taxing it by the states may be exercised so as to destroy it, is too obvious to be denied. But taxation is said to be an absolute power, which acknowledges no other limits than those expressly prescribed in the constitution and like sovereign power of every other description, is intrusted to the discretion of those who use it. But the very terms of this argument admit, that the sovereignty of the state, in the article of taxation itself, is subordinate to, and may be controlled by the constitution of the United States. How far it has been controlled by that instrument, must be a question of construction. In making this construction, no principle, not declared, can be admissible, which would defeat the legitimate operations of a supreme government. It is of the very essence of supremacy, to remove all obstacles to its action within its own sphere, and so to modify every power vested in subordinate governments, as to exempt its own operations from their own influence. This effect need not be stated in terms. It is so involved in the declaration of supremacy, so necessarily implied in it, that the expression of it could not make it more certain. We must, therefore, keep it in view, while construing the constitution.

The argument on the part of the state of Maryland, is, not that the states may directly resist a law of congress, but that they may exercise their acknowledged powers upon it, and that the constitution leaves them, this right, in the confidence that they will not abuse it. Before we proceed to examine this argument, and to subject it to test of the constitution, we must be permitted to bestow a few considerations on the nature and extent of this original right of taxation, which is acknowledged to remain with the states. It is admitted, that the power of taxing the people and their property, is essential to the very existence of government, and may be legitimately exercised on the objects to which it is applicable, to the utmost extent to which the government may choose to carry it. The only security against the abuse of this power, is found, in the structure of the government itself. In imposing a tax, the legislature acts upon its constituents. This is, in general, a sufficient security against erroneous and oppressive taxation.

The people of a state, therefore, give to their government a right of taxing themselves and their property, and as the exigencies of government cannot be limited, they prescribe no limits to the exercise of this right, resting confidently on the interest of the legislator, and on the influence of the constituent over their representative, to guard them against its abuse. But the means employed by the government of the Union have no such security, nor is the right of a state to tax them sustained by the same theory. Those means are not given by the people of a particular state, not given by the constituents of the legislature, which claim the right to tax them, but by the people of all the states. They are given by all, for the benefit of all—and upon theory, should be subjected to that government only which belongs to all.

It may be objected to this definition, that the power of taxation is not confined to the people and property of a state. It may be exercised upon every object brought within its jurisdiction. This is true. But to what source do wo trace this right? It is obvious, that it is an incident of sovereignty, and is co-extensive with that to which it is an incident. All subjects over which the sovereign power of a state extends, are objects of taxation; but those over which it does not extend, are, upon the soundest principles, exempt from taxation. This proposition may almost be pronounced self-evident.

The sovereignty of a state extends to everything which exists by its own authority, or is introduced by its permission; but does it extend to those means which are employed by congress to carry into execution powers conferred on that body by the people of the United States? We think it demonstrable, that it does not. Those powers are not given by the people of a single state. They are given by the people of the United States, to a government whose laws, made in pursuance of the constitution, are declared to be supreme. Consequently, the people of a single state cannot confer a sovereignty which will extend over them.

If we measure the power of taxation residing in a state, by the extent of sovereignty which the people of a single state possess, and can confer on its government, we have an intelligible standard, applicable to every case to which the power may be applied. We have a principle which leaves the power of taxing the people and property of a state unimpaired; which leaves to a state the command of all its resources, and which places beyond its reach, all those powers which are conferred by the people of the United States on the government of the Union, and all those means which are given for the purpose of carrying those powers into execution. We have a principle which is safe for the states, and safe for the Union. We are relieved, as we ought to be, from clashing sovereignty; from interfering powers; from a repugnancy between a right in one government to pull down, what there is an acknowledged right in another to build up; from the incompatibility of a right in one government to destroy, what there is a right in another to preserve. We are not driven to the perplexing inquiry, so unfit for the judicial department, what degree of taxation is the legitimate use, and what degree may amount to the abuse of the power. The attempt to use it on the means employed by the government of the Union, in pursuance of the constitution, is itself an abuse, because it is the usurpation of a power which the people of a single state cannot give. We find, then, on just theory, a total failure of this original right to tax the means employed by the government of the Union, for the execution of its powers. The right never existed, and the question whether it has been surrendered, cannot arise.

But, waiving this theory for the present, let us resume the inquiry, whether this power can be exercised by the respective states, consistently with a fair construction of the constitution? That the power to tax involves the power to destroy; that the power to destroy may defeat and render useless the power to create; that there is a plain repugnance in conferring on one government a power to control the constitutional measures of another, which other, with respect to those very measures, is declared to be supreme over that which exerts the control, are propositions not to be denied. But all inconsistencies are to be reconciled by the magic of the word confidence. Taxation, it is said, does not necessarily and unavoidably destroy. To carry it to the excess of destruction, would be an abuse, to presume which, would banish that confidence which is essential to all government. But is this a case of confidence? Would the people of any one state trust those of another with a power to control the most insignificant operations of their state government? We know they would not. Why, then, should we suppose, that the people of any one state should be willing to trust those of another with a power to control the operations of a government to which they have confided their most important and most valuable interests? In the legislature of the Union alone, are all represented. The legislature of the Union alone, therefore, can be trusted by the people with the power of controlling measures which concern all, in the confidence that it will not be abused. This, then, is not a case of confidence, and we must consider it is as it really is.

If we apply the principle for which the state of Maryland contends, to the constitution, generally, we shall find it capable of changing totally the character of that instrument. We shall find it capable of arresting all the measures of the government, and of prostrating it at the foot of the states. The American people have declared their constitution and the laws made in pursuance thereof, to be supreme; but this principle would transfer the supremacy, in fact, to the states. If the states may tax one instrument, employed by the government in the execution of its powers, they may tax any and every other instrument. They may tax the mail; they may tax the mint; they may tax patent-rights; they may tax the papers of the custom-house; they may tax judicial process; they may tax all the means employed by the government, to an excess which would defeat all the ends of government. This was not intended by the American people. They did not design to make their government dependent on the states.

Gentlemen say, they do not claim the right to extend state taxation to these objects. They limit their pretensions to property. But on what principle, is this distinction made? Those who make it have furnished no reason for it, and the principle for which they contend denies it. They contend, that the power of taxation has no other limit than is found in the 10th section of the 1st article of the constitution; that, with respect to everything else, the power of the states is supreme, and admits of no control. If this be true, the distinction between property and other subjects to which the power of taxation is applicable, is merely arbitrary, and can never be sustained. This is not all. If the controlling power of the states be established; if their supremacy as to taxation be acknowledged; what is to restrain their exercising control in any shape they may please to give it? Their sovereignty is not confined to taxation; that is not the only mode in which it might be displayed. The question is, in truth, a question of supremacy; and if the right of the states to tax the means employed by the general government be conceded, the declaration that the constitution, and the laws made in pursuance thereof, shall be the supreme law of the land, is empty and unmeaning declamation.

In the course of the argument, the Federalist has been quoted; and the opinions expressed by the authors of that work have been justly supposed to be entitled to great respect in expounding the constitution. No tribute can be paid to them which exceeds their merit; but in applying their opinions to the cases which may arise in the progress of our government, a right to judge of their correctness must be retained; and to understand the argument, we must examine the proposition it maintains, and the objections against which it is directed. The subject of those numbers, from which passages have been cited, is the unlimited power of taxation which is vested in the general government. The objection to this unlimited power, which the argument seeks to remove, is stated with fulness and clearness. It is, "that an indefinite power of taxation in the latter (the government of the Union) might, and probably would, in time, deprive the former (the government of the states) of the means of providing for their own necessities; and would subject them entirely to the mercy of the national legislature. As the laws of the Union are to become the supreme law of the land; as it is to have power to pass all laws that may necessary for carrying into execution the authorities with which it is proposed to vest it; the national government might, at any time, abolish the taxes imposed for state objects, upon the pretence of an interference with its own. It might allege a necessity for doing this, in order to give efficacy to the national revenues; and thus, all the resources of taxation might, by degrees, become the subjects of federal monopoly, to the entire exclusion and destruction of the state governments."

The objections to the constitution which are noticed in these numbers, were to the undefined power of the government to tax, not to the incidental privilege of exempting its own measures from state taxation. The consequences apprehended from this undefined power were, that it would absorb all the objects of taxation, "to the exclusion and destruction of the state governments." The arguments of the Federalist are intended to prove the fallacy of these apprehensions; not to prove that the government was incapable of executing any of its powers, without exposing the means it employed to the embarrassments of state taxation. Arguments urged against these objections, and these apprehensions, are to be understood as relating to the points they mean to prove. Had the authors of those excellent essays been asked, whether they contended for that construction of the constitution, which would place within the reach of the states those measures which the government might adopt for the execution of its powers; no man, who has read their instructive pages, will hesitate to admit, that their answer must have been in the negative.

It has also been insisted, that, as the power of taxation in the general and state governments is acknowledged to be concurrent, every argument which would sustain the right of the general government to tax banks chartered by the states, will equally sustain the right of the states to tax banks chartered by the general government. But the two cases are not on the same reason. The people of all the states have created the general government, and have conferred upon it the general power of taxation. The people of all the states, and the states themselves, are represented in congress, and, by their representatives, exercise this power. When they tax the chartered institutions of the states, they tax their constituents; and these taxes must be uniform. But when a state taxes the operations of the government of the United States, it acts upon institutions created, not by their own constituents, but by people over whom they claim no control. It acts upon the measures of a government created by others as well as themselves, for the benefit of others in common with themselves. The difference is that which always exists, and always must exist, between the action of the whole on a part, and the action of a part on the whole — between the laws of a government declared to be supreme, and those of a government which, when in opposition to those laws, is not supreme.

But if the full application of this argument could be admitted, it night bring into question the right of congress to tax the state banks, and could not prove the rights of the states to tax the Bank of the United States.

The court has bestowed on this subject its most deliberate consideration. The result is a conviction that the states have no power, by taxation or otherwise, to retard, impede, burden, or in any manner control, the operations of the constitutional laws enacted by congress to carry into execution the powers vested in the general government. This is, we think, the unavoidable consequence of that supremacy which the constitution has declared. We are unanimously of opinion, that the law passed by the legislature of Maryland, imposing a tax on the Bank of the United States, is unconstitutional and void.

This opinion does not deprive the states of any resources which they originally possessed. It does not extend to a tax paid by the real property of the bank, in common with the other real property within the state, nor to a tax imposed on the interest which the citizens of Maryland may hold in this institution, in common with other property of the same description throughout the state. But this is a tax on the operations of the bank, and is, consequently, a tax on the operation of an instrument employed by the government of the Union to carry its powers into execution. Such a tax must be unconstitutional.

* * *

Notes on *McCulloch v. Maryland*

1. *State sovereignty:* The first question in *McCulloch* was whether Congress had the authority under Article I to charter a national bank. And Maryland's first argument as to why the statute chartering the bank exceeded Congress's enumerated powers centered on the nature of state sovereignty under the Constitution. Maryland contended that "[t]he powers of the general government . . . are delegated by the states, who alone are truly sovereign; and must be exercised in subordination to the States, who alone possess supreme dominion." In other words, Maryland's view was that the federal government possesses only those powers the states decided to relinquish when ratifying the Constitution; the states remain the sole, true sovereigns.

This argument was not new. Recall the position of the Virginia Court of Appeals in *Martin v. Hunter's Lessee* (decided a few years before *McCulloch*). There, Virginia effectively argued that, because Virginia was an independent sovereign, its state-court judgments (even on questions of federal law) were unreviewable by the Supreme Court, such that §25 of the Judiciary Act of 1789 was unconstitutional. Virginia took the position that being sovereign means being answerable to no one. This was the traditional, eighteenth-century conception of sovereignty: it must ultimately rest in one place, and by its nature it cannot be split.

The Supreme Court's response to this argument was that—though the Constitutional Convention was composed of representatives of the states, and the ratifying conventions took place in the respective states—the Constitution was actually ratified by *the People*, not the states (as entities). Through Article VII, the Framers effectively went over the heads of the state legislatures and sought ratification directly from the People. The Constitution was ratified by popular conventions, comprised of elected representatives in their respective states. Thus, the states—just like the federal government—are bound by the terms of the Constitution, and the Constitution owes its legitimacy to its ratification by the People. This means the states, no different than the federal government, enjoy the measure of sovereignty left to them by the People in the text of the Constitution.

Why does this seemingly academic point about "ultimate sovereignty" matter? If Maryland's conception of the Constitution were valid—essentially, as a "compact" among state governments—only those powers the states had agreed to relinquish would belong to the federal government. Moreover, and perhaps more importantly, it would mean, as in any contractual relationship, that a state could choose to withdraw from the compact if it no longer found the terms to its liking. But if the Constitution is premised on the principle that the People are the ultimate sovereign—as the opinion in *McCulloch* concluded—neither of these propositions could hold. Instead, the states are *bound* by whatever obligations the People imposed on them in the Constitution. The ratification of the Constitution imposed those terms on the states, including the surrender of certain powers to the federal government. Further, the states have no capacity to withdraw from the union, as they never were parties to the relevant bargain. The People agreed to the document themselves. The states, by contrast, are simply part of the governmental structure that the People created through the Constitution; the states have no authority to withdraw from this arrangement unless the People validly authorize them to do so.

2. *Enumerated powers:* Chief Justice Marshall conceded that, under the Constitution, the federal government is one of enumerated powers, and that the power to incorporate a bank is nowhere *expressly* enumerated in the Constitution. But Marshall also emphasized that there is no phrase in the Constitution requiring that the powers exercised by Congress be explicitly spelled out in the Constitution's text. This omission was noteworthy, because Article II of the Articles of Confederation had stated that "[e]ach State retains its sovereignty, freedom and independence, and every power, jurisdiction, and right, which is not by this confederation *expressly* delegated to the United States, in Congress assembled" (emphasis added). By contrast, the Tenth Amendment omits the word "expressly": "The powers not delegated to the United States by the Constitution, nor prohibited by it to the States, are reserved to the States respectively, or to the people." Marshall reasoned that this omission—made by those who had lived under the Articles and their shortcomings—could not have been accidental: "[T]he men who drew and adopted this amendment had experienced the embarrassments resulting from the insertion of this word in their articles of confederation, and probably omitted it, to avoid those embarrassments."

Marshall then invoked the nature of a constitution, contrasting it with other sources of law: "A constitution, to contain an accurate detail of all the subdivisions of which its great powers will admit, and of all the means by which they may be carried into execution, would partake of the prolixity of a legal code, and could scarcely be embraced by the human mind." By design, a constitution is a broad framework; "only its great outlines should be marked." Unlike a statute, a constitution is intended to last in perpetuity; if expressed in great detail, it would quickly become obsolete. (Imagine if the Framers had spelled out the meaning of "interstate commerce" in 1787 in fine detail, instead of simply granting Congress the authority to regulate "commerce among the states." The evolving nature of that commerce would have rendered the clause obsolete within a generation.)

Thus, reasoned Marshall, it would be silly to expect the finer points of Congress's powers to be spelled out explicitly in the Constitution. And we should not infer that Congress lacks a particular power (such as the authority to charter a national bank) simply because it is not *specifically* and *expressly* enumerated in the Constitution's text.

3. ***Implied powers:*** According to the Court, then, the question was whether Congress has *this* power—the power to charter a national bank—that was not expressly enumerated. And Chief Justice Marshall approached this question by engaging in a thought experiment. Suppose the Constitution did not include the Necessary and Proper Clause. Imagine instead that Article I, §8 ended with clause 17. Would Congress still have had the authority to use the means it deemed appropriate to carry out the objectives set out in those 17 clauses of Article I, §8? Yes, reasoned Marshall:

> "The government which has a right to do an act, and has imposed on it, the duty of performing that act, must, according to the dictates of reason, be allowed to select the means; and those who contend that it may not select any appropriate means, that one particular mode of effecting the object is excepted, take upon themselves the burden of establishing the exception."

In other words, we must presume that the Constitution, in granting Congress broad legislative powers, also implied the power to enact those means most conducive to carrying out those powers. It would be strange if the Framers endowed this new national government with all of these powers but then, at the same time, hamstrung its capacity to deploy those powers by giving Congress very little discretion in deciding how to pursue them. One arguing otherwise, reasoned Marshall, must overcome this logical presumption.

4. ***The meaning of the word "necessary":*** Maryland's principal argument turned on the meaning of the word "necessary." Maryland contended that "necessary" means *absolutely* necessary—not merely convenient, but *indispensable* to exercising the power in question. (This had been Thomas Jefferson's argument in opposing the chartering of the first national bank in 1790.)

It is important to see exactly what was at stake on this point, as its significance can hardly be overstated. Had Maryland's (and Jefferson's) understanding of the Necessary and Proper Clause prevailed, the Constitution would have afforded the national government a much, *much* narrower range of action. There is a gaping chasm between these two visions for the scope of the federal government's authority: one in which Congress only has the authority to enact laws that are indispensable to the exercise its enumerated powers, and one in which Congress can enact all laws it deems helpful or convenient for doing so.

The Court rejected Maryland's understanding of "necessary," and Chief Justice Marshall offered two bases for doing so. The first was intratextual, relying on a nearby provision in Article I, §10, clause 2. In that cluse, the Constitution contains the phrase "absolutely necessary": "No state shall, without the consent of the Congress, lay any imposts or duties on imports or exports, except what may be absolutely necessary for executing it's inspection laws." If "necessary" standing alone meant *indispensable*, as Maryland contended, then the "absolutely" in Article I, §10, clause 2 would be superfluous. Viewed as a whole, then, the Constitution's text contemplates degrees of necessity, and the unmodified "necessary" in the Necessary and Proper Clause must connote a looser meaning, not the stricter one advocated by Maryland.

Marshall's second argument was grounded in practical consequences, and he used the power granted to Congress regarding the mail as an illustration. Article I, §8, clause 7 gives Congress the power "[t]o establish Post Offices and post Roads." It does not expressly grant Congress the power to enact laws that, for instance, prohibit the theft of the mail. Under Maryland's interpretation of the Necessary and Proper Clause, Congress could not enact such a statute, as doing so is not *absolutely necessary* to the effectuation of the constitutionally granted power to establish post offices and post roads. (One can run a post office without punishing persons who steal letters and packages, though it might make the operation much less efficient.) Marshall argued that such a construction would make very little sense. The Framers certainly intended the new government to be effective. Thus, they must have intended the term necessary to mean something short of *absolutely necessary*.

5. *The role of the Necessary and Proper Clause:* Marshall's capstone argument concerned the role of the Necessary and Proper Clause in the Constitution. Consider first where it appears, as the very last clause in Article I, §8. Marshall's reasoning proceeded as follows. Article I, §8 functions to grant Congress a series of powers; it is the principal section of the Constitution endowing Congress with authority. Thus, each provision in that list should be understood as *expanding*, rather than constricting, Congress's authority.

Why does that matter? If the Constitution would have implicitly granted Congress the power to employ appropriate means to effectuate the powers spelled out in Article I, §8 clauses 1 through 17 even if it had omitted the Necessary and Proper Clause—and if the Necessary and Proper Clause (being placed in the same section) was intended to *expand* Congress's powers beyond what they otherwise would have been—then Maryland's understanding just did not work. Maryland's argument effectively posited that the Necessary and Proper Clause functioned to reduce or constrict Congress's powers—to render them narrower than they would have been had the Framers neglected to include the Necessary and Proper Clause. Again, given the clause's placement in Article I, § 8, such a construction could not have been what the Framers had intended.

This was really a *purposive* (rather than a textual) argument. Regardless of what definitions might exist in dictionaries for the word "necessary," Marshall reasoned, it would make no sense to read the term too literally in this particular context.

6. *The legal standard for evaluating Congress's choice of means*: To be clear, Marshall's broad reading of the Necessary and Proper Clause in *McCulloch* did not mean Congress could do whatever it pleased. But the standard the Court articulated was quite deferential to Congress's choice of legislative means. Specifically, the Court (in one of the most frequently quoted sentences in American law) phrased the relevant constitutional standard as follows: "Let the end be legitimate, let it be within the scope of the constitution, and all means which are appropriate, which are plainly adapted to that end, which are not prohibited, but consist with the letter and spirit of the constitution, are constitutional." So long as the Constitution grants Congress the power to pursue a certain end or objective (such as to regulate "commerce among the states"), Congress also has the power to employ any reasonable or "appropriate" means to accomplish that end. The Necessary and Proper Clause gives Congress a wide berth to use reasonable means to accomplish a constitutionally granted objective.

Returning to the precise question presented in *McCulloch*, why was the incorporation of a national bank an "appropriate" and "plainly adapted" means to accomplish one of Congress' enumerated powers? Marshall did not explain this in much detail. One can see how a national bank was a reasonable means for the federal government to "pay the Debts" of the United States (as it obviated the need to rely smaller, less accountable, state-chartered banks), or "[t]o borrow Money on the credit of the United States" (for the same reason). A national bank made it easier for the federal government to move money around the country for purposes of executing a number of Congress's specifically enumerated powers. Combining those powers with the Necessary and Proper Clause, Congress had the authority to charter the bank.

7. McCulloch *as a foundation for understanding the breadth of Congress's powers*: This construction of the Necessary and Proper Clause, first articulated in *McCulloch*, is foundational to understanding the breadth of Congress's legislative authority. Congress has the power to use all "appropriate" means to pursue those powers enumerated in Article I, §8. So long as a federal law is justifiable as creating means that are "plainly adapted" to the achievement of one of Congress's enumerated powers, the legislation is constitutional.

Rarely do courts explicitly refer to *McCulloch* or the Necessary and Proper Clause—though it happens occasionally, when a federal law's justification is plainly as a means to an enumerated end, rather than as an enumerated end itself. Rather, the Necessary and Proper Clause has generally become a background premise to our understanding of the breadth of Congress's powers, much as *Marbury* has with respect to the judicial power. Consider the most significant power granted to Congress by Article I, the authority to regulate "commerce . . . among the States." This gives Congress the power to regulate interstate commerce itself. But it also gives Congress the power to regulate "activities substantially affecting" interstate commerce. By definition, this goes *beyond* the enumerated power itself, and extends to other, albeit connected activities. Why? In essence, it is because regulating this broader scope of activities (those with a substantial effect on interstate commerce) is "necessary and proper" to the regulation of interstate commerce itself. That is, the "substantial effects" prong of the scope of the commerce power incorporates the teaching of *McCulloch*—namely, that legislation plainly adapted to an objective is within the grant of authority to Congress.

* * *

EXAMPLE

Suppose Congress seeks to eliminate the market for fentanyl in the United States. (Fentanyl is a synthetic opioid that has led to tens of thousands of overdose deaths in the U.S.) As will be discussed in the Chapter 9, Congress would plainly have the authority under the Commerce Clause to proscribe the sale or distribution of fentanyl; these are economic or commercial activities, and thus fit within the power granted to Congress by that clause. But Congress might well lack the authority to prohibit simple *possession* of fentanyl under the Commerce Clause, as the possession of a controlled substance likely is not an economic or commercial activity. Nonetheless, criminalizing the possession of fentanyl might well be conducive—that is, "appropriate" and "plainly adapted"—to prohibiting all sales or distribution of the drug. That is, Congress might find it practically impossible to regulate the commercial market in fentanyl without making the drug illegal to possess. As a result, though a statute forbidding the possession of fentanyl might exceed the power granted by the Commerce Clause, it likely falls within Congress's power considering the Commerce and Necessary and Proper Clauses together.

* * *

8. ***The Constitutionality of Maryland's tax on the bank*:** Because the Court concluded that Congress had the power to incorporate the national bank, the justices needed to address the second question presented: whether Maryland could impose a tax on the bank's operations. Importantly, though the Constitution granted Congress the power to impose federal taxes, the states plainly retained the power to impose their own state-level taxes. Without this power, the states could hardly exist; a government must raise revenue, and taxes are the most common (and typically a necessary) means for doing so. In this way, taxation is an area in which the federal and state governments exercise *concurrent* legislative authority. (There are many others, from criminal law to environmental regulation to employment law.) Thus, there was no problem *generally* in Maryland's imposing a state tax.

Moreover, McCulloch could not point to any particular textual provision in the Constitution that Maryland's tax violated. There are a number of provisions in the Constitution (such as the dormant Commerce Clause and the Import-Export Clause) that place constraints on the states' taxing authority. But Maryland's tax did not run afoul of any of these prohibitions.

Instead, McCulloch made a purely *structural* argument, which the Court embraced. Chief Justice Marshall began with the admonition that the power to tax is "the power to destroy." What he meant was that a government that has the power to tax something necessarily has the power to drive that something out of existence. In general, this does not happen, as the taxation of certain activities generally just makes them more expensive (and thus discourages them). But if one were to impose, for instance, a 2000 percent tax on an activity (such as purchasing cigarettes), it would effectively prevent that activity from occurring.

Marshall then explained that, when a state ordinarily imposes a tax, there is a natural check on the abuse of that power. His term for this was "confidence." "Confidence" in this context is the government's electoral accountability and the ordinary workings of the political process. If a state imposes overly burdensome taxes, legislators will be voted out of office and taxes will be lowered. (Or, in anticipation of the electorate's reaction, the legislature will not impose excessive taxes in the first place.) In an important sense, the people of a state determine how much they want to be taxed—that is, how much they want to tax themselves for the public goods and services they receive in return. The voters impose burdens on themselves in the form of taxes, and they receive the benefit of those taxes in the form of public schools, public health systems, and the like.

The problem posed by Maryland's tax on the national bank was that this political check—this "confidence"—did not exist. This tax was imposed only on the Bank of the United States. By taxing the national bank, Maryland was able to raise revenue only for itself (as it received all the revenue), while imposing the cost on the nation as a whole. The bank would be forced to pay the tax out of the United States treasury, with monies raised through the taxation of all Americans, and Maryland residents would only pay a small portion of that tax burden. But Maryland would collect all the revenue generated by the tax. Thus, the normal check on excessive taxation did not exist; the burden and the benefit were not coextensive. We might call this an *externality* problem: Maryland was seeking to *externalize* the costs of supporting its own state government. Marshall thus concluded that this was "not a case of confidence, and we must consider it is as it really is." There was a disconnect between the government imposing the tax burden (Maryland) and those paying the tax (all Americans).

This was purely *structural* reasoning. But Marshall concluded that this sort of state action was simply incompatible with the federal structure created by the Constitution. For the nation to operate as the Constitution contemplates, states cannot not possess such a power. As Marshall explained, without such a rule, individual states would essentially have a veto power over the federal government's ability to pursue initiatives like the Bank of the United States. Again, the "power to tax is the power to destroy." Had Maryland's tax been permissible, the Constitution would have permitted states to nullify or impede valid federal laws—to "destroy" initiatives like the national bank. Even if Maryland only did so with respect to the Bank's operations within Maryland, this would instantiate a state veto power not contemplated by the Constitution. So long as Congress's laws are constitutionally valid, they are the law of the *entire* United States—and no state has the power to interfere with its operation.

The Constitution permits states to destroy their own governmental institutions. But they cannot, on their own, destroy or (even impede) *national* institutions or legislative programs. Permitting states such authority, reasoned *McCulloch*, would simply be incompatible with the federal structure created by the Constitution.

9. *The birth of federal immunity doctrine*: The holding in *McCulloch* that Maryland's tax was inconsistent with the basic postulates of the federal structure created by the Constitution marked the beginning of what is known today as the "federal immunity doctrine." Stated simply, states may not (absent congressional authorization) impose taxes or regulations directly on the federal government or its instrumentalities. That is precisely what Maryland had attempted to do in *McCulloch*: impose a tax directly on the Bank of the United States, an instrumentality of the federal government. The federal immunity doctrine also forbids states from imposing taxes or regulations that discriminate against the federal government, even when those taxes or regulations are imposed on private persons (rather than the United States itself). For instance, though California could impose a personal income tax on all persons earning income in the state—including federal government employees— it could not impose a more onerous tax on federal employees than it imposed on other California residents.

The present-day contours of the federal immunity doctrine are explored in more detail in Chapter 16.

* * *

PROBLEMS ON THE MEANING OF *McCULLOCH*

In each of the following circumstances, please assess whether the state's actions are unconstitutional in light of the Supreme Court's decision in *McCulloch v. Maryland*. Be sure to explain the rationale for your answers.

1. On December 24, 1860, an elected convention of South Carolina citizens officially declared that South Carolina was seceding from the Union. It asserted that the federal government had failed to uphold its constitutional obligations to South Carolina—specifically, its obligation to enforce the Fugitive Slave Act and those clauses in the Constitution protecting the institution of slavery. (Ignore the provisions of the Constitution added after the Civil War.)

2. In 2010, the Commonwealth of Virginia enacted the Virginia Health Care Freedom Act. The relevant portion of the Act provided that "[n]o resident of this Commonwealth,

regardless of whether he has or is eligible for health insurance coverage under any policy or program provided by or through his employer, or a plan sponsored by the Commonwealth or the federal government, shall be required to obtain or maintain a policy of individual insurance coverage." The federal Affordable Care Act (ACA) had just been enacted by Congress. The ACA required all Americans to acquire "minimally adequate" health coverage, on pain of paying a "tax penalty" to the federal government. The Virginia legislature intended the Virginia Health Care Freedom Act to apply to the mandate imposed by the ACA.

3. Suppose that, in November 2021—frustrated by the slow pace of COVID vaccinations in particular states—the federal government established several free mass vaccination sites in various states, including Alabama. Suppose that the Alabama legislature enacted a statute imposing a state excise tax of $100 per dose on "any government" providing free COVID vaccinations within the state. The tax was to be imposed on the governmental entity administering the vaccine. (Assume the federal government was the only government still administering free vaccines in Alabama.)

4. Assume the facts are the same as in (3), except that several Alabama county health departments were also providing free COVID vaccinations in November 2021, and thus were also subject to the Alabama state tax of $100 per dose.

5. The federal Controlled Substances Act makes it a crime to possess a controlled substance. *See* 21 U.S.C. §844. Any person violating §844 "may be sentenced to a term of imprisonment of not more than 1 year, and shall be fined a minimum of $1,000, or both." Other portions of the Act define marijuana as a "controlled substance" for purposes of §844. In 2016, California adopted the "Control, Regulate and Tax Adult Use of Marijuana Act." Under the terms of that Act, it is no longer a violation of California law for adults 21 years of age and over to possess and grow specified amounts of marijuana for recreational use.

CHAPTER 9
THE COMMERCE POWER

We now turn to examining the specific powers granted to the national legislature: Congress's "enumerated powers," the powers that authorize Congress to enact legislation. Article I, §8 contains the vast bulk of these powers, listed in clauses 1 through 17. Additionally, as we just saw in *McCulloch*, clause 18 gives Congress the authority "[t]o make all laws which shall be necessary and proper for carrying into execution the foregoing powers, and all other powers vested by this Constitution in the government of the United States, or in any department or officer thereof." Chapter 11 covers a handful of other constitutional provisions that grant Congress legislative authority outside Article I, §8.

The most consequential of Congress's powers to *regulate* activity—to impose mandatory norms of conduct, to which persons must conform their actions—is its authority to regulate commerce "among the several States." This *commerce power* underwrites a huge proportion of current federal law, perhaps exceeding all the other enumerated powers combined. Thus, understanding the scope of this power is critical to discerning the metes and bounds of Congress's legislative authority.[12]

A. Background and History

1. From the Framing to 1936

For the nation's first century, the breadth of Congress's authority to regulate interstate commerce was relatively uncontroversial. Most commerce was *intrastate*, occurring entirely within a single state's borders. Naturally, almost all commercial regulation emanated from state and local governments. This began to change—at first gradually, and then rapidly—following the industrial and communications revolutions of the nineteenth century, and the simultaneous emergence of interstate railroads and multistate businesses. In the late 1800s, Congress began to enact laws addressing national commercial concerns. Two statutes in particular were landmarks: the Interstate Commerce Act of

---

[12] As a matter of constitutional doctrine, the Interstate Commerce Clause contains two distinct, entirely different components. The more obvious is its so-called "positive" side, which serves as a grant of power to Congress to regulate commerce among the several states. The less intuitive component is the Commerce Clause's "negative" or "dormant" side, by which the clause functions as a *prohibition* on state or local laws that discriminate against or unduly burden interstate commerce. In this chapter, we examine the clause's former aspect: the legislative authority it affirmatively confers on Congress. Chapter 17 covers the dormant Commerce Clause.

1887 and the Sherman Antitrust Act of 1890. These were Congress's first major forays into the nationwide regulation of commercial activity.

This new, national regulation of commerce forced the Supreme Court to develop rules of constitutional law defining the breadth of Congress's commerce power, which proved no simple task. American society was changing rapidly, and the Court found it difficult to reconcile existing constitutional doctrine with these changing realities. Largely borrowing from its *dormant* Commerce Clause rules (a topic covered in detail in Chapter 17), the Court created several formalistic distinctions that separated activities Congress could regulate from those exceeding its authority. Specifically, the Court distinguished "commerce" and "commercial intercourse" (appropriate subjects of national legislation) from "manufacturing" and "production" (activities beyond Congress's power). Similarly, the Court distinguished the "direct" regulation of interstate commerce (within Congress's authority) from its "indirect" regulation (beyond the commerce power).

Given the malleability of these doctrinal categories, many contemporary observers complained that the Court's decisions were unpredictable and untethered to practical reality. The problems were (at least) twofold. First, many felt the Court was too aggressive in its review of Congress's statutes—that the justices were insufficiently deferential to Congress's judgments about sound policy in the commercial and economic spheres. As a matter of institutional competence, many argued Congress was better positioned to judge whether a particular activity was, in fact, a part of "interstate commerce." Second, the Court faced real challenges in deriving judicially manageable standards that could be defended as principled and objective—that appeared to be *law* rather than political preferences. The formalistic distinctions drawn by the Court seemed open to manipulation, leading many observers to label the Court's decisions insincere: post-hoc rationalizations covering for the justices' conservative, *laissez-faire*, anti-regulatory views.

2. The New Deal

This controversy surrounding the Supreme Court's approach to Congress's commerce power—and the power of the government to regulate the economy more generally—came to a climax in the 1930s. The Great Depression began in 1929, and President Franklin Delano Roosevelt assumed office in March 1933. His domestic legislative program, known as the New Deal, marked a fundamental shift in the role of the federal government. It embraced a much more robust involvement of the federal government in the lives of Americans, both to address the immediate economic crisis and (in the longer run) to create a modern administrative state: a nation in which the government was more a guarantor of the people's welfare. Prompted by FDR, Congress enacted a raft of new regulatory and spending programs, and it created a host of new administrative agencies to implement those programs.

At the time of the New Deal, four justices were known to be politically conservative and generally opposed the New Deal: Justices McReynolds, Van Devanter, Sutherland, and Butler. These four consistently voted to invalidate various aspects of the New Deal and its expansion of the federal government. So long as one additional justice joined them (typically Justice Owen Roberts), the Court would invalidate challenged law as unconstitutional. Thus, the Court struck down some of the most significant statutes Congress enacted between 1933 and 1937, such as the Child Labor Act, the National Industrial Recovery Act, and the Bituminous Coal Act. In doing so, the Court construed the commerce power narrowly, at least compared to present understandings. The Court simultaneously invalidated a number of *state* laws under the Due Process Clause—as infringing on an individuals' right to contract without government interference—creating what FDR called a "no man's land," where neither the states nor the federal government could regulate.

This clash between the Court and the political branches precipitated a full-blown constitutional crisis. The Court invalidating popular and significant legislation designed to provide relief to millions of Americans (when the unemployment rate was 25 percent and millions of people were roaming the country homeless). And it was doing so on highly formalistic grounds. Again, many saw the Court's decisions—rightly or wrongly—as a manipulation of legal doctrine to achieve the *laissez-faire* policy results it preferred.

The crisis reached a boiling point in January 1937, when FDR—having just been reelected to his second term by a landslide—announced a plan to expand the size of the Supreme Court. Under Roosevelt's proposal, if a justice had served on the Court for more than ten years, and he waited more than six months after his seventieth birthday to retire, the President could appoint (with the Senate's advice and consent) a new justice. The plan would have permitted the President to add up to six new justices, expanding the Court to fifteen members. FDR explained his plan to the public as necessary to promote "efficiency," citing the fact that the Court had recently denied certiorari in 87 percent of the cases in which a party had sought review. But his "Court-packing plan" (as it soon became known) was a transparent attempt to change the ideological composition of the Court. Roosevelt wanted a Supreme Court that would uphold Congress's authority to enact New Deal legislation.

3. The "switch in time"

The crisis dissipated due to the famous "the switch in time that saved the nine." Nine weeks after Roosevelt announced his Court-packing plan, Justice Owen Roberts effectively switched sides. In the March 1937 decision of *West Coast Hotel v. Parrish*, 300 U.S. 379, the Court upheld a Washington state minimum wage law against a challenge that it violated the Due Process Clause. *West Coast Hotel* did not involve the scope of Congress's commerce power, but it did concern the broader question of the government's authority to regulate in the commercial sphere. And the justices' alignments were typically the same on these sorts of questions.

Shortly thereafter, in a series of commerce power decisions, the Court abandoned the formalistic distinctions between "manufacturing" and "commerce," and between "direct" and "indirect" regulations of commerce, to uphold very broad exercises of the power by Congress. The first critical decision was in *NLRB v. Jones & Laughlin Steel*, 301 U.S. 1 (1937), decided only two weeks after *West Coast Hotel*. There, the Court upheld the National Labor Relations Act's regulation of employment practices "affecting commerce." Not long thereafter, in *United States v. Darby*, 312 U.S. 400 (1941), the Court turned back challenges to two critical provisions of the Fair Labor Standards Act: one that forbid the shipment in interstate commerce of goods produced using certain wage conditions, and one directly regulating the hours and wages of employees. In both *Jones & Laughlin* and *Darby*, the Court applied a much more capacious understanding of Congress's commerce power than had prevailed before 1937. The Court was suddenly much more deferential to Congress's judgment as to what constituted "commerce among the states."

4. The landmark decision of *Wickard v. Filburn*

Wickard v. Filburn, 317 U.S. 111 (1942), is perhaps the best example of the Supreme Court's deferential, post-New Deal approach to reviewing whether a federal statute fits within Congress's commerce power, the approach that prevailed from 1937 until 1995. The dispute in *Wickard* arose because, through the Agricultural Adjustment Act (AAA), Congress sought to regulate the production of wheat everywhere in the U.S. The principal objective of the AAA was to reduce the supply of crops in the commercial market, and thus increase their price (and hence, the incomes of farmers). Roscoe Filburn was an Ohio farmer who grew wheat, both for sale and for use on his own farm to feed livestock. Under the AAA, each farmer was allowed a quota of wheat they were permitted to grow. It was stipulated that Filburn had not exceeded his quota with the wheat he had grown for sale; but Filburn had exceeded the quota if one included the wheat he had grown for consumption on his own farm. Thus, the question was whether the commerce power permitted Congress to regulate a farmer's growing of wheat for his own use. The Court held this was within Congress's authority.

In upholding the application of the AAA to Filburn, the Court articulated a very broad understanding of the commerce power: "[E]ven if [Filburn]'s activity be local and though it may not be regarded as commerce, it may still, whatever its nature, be reached by Congress if it exerts a substantial economic effect on interstate commerce." Moreover, the relevant question was not whether Filburn's *own* production of wheat produced a substantial effect on interstate commerce. Rather, the issue was the *aggregate effect of all persons similarly situated in the nation as whole*—that is, whether the production of wheat for home consumption in the U.S., collectively, substantially affected interstate commerce. "That appellee's own contribution to the demand for wheat may be trivial by itself is not enough to remove him from the scope of federal regulation where, as here, his contribution, taken together with that of many others similarly situated, is far from trivial."

To the Court, the AAA was within the commerce power because the total amount of wheat produced for home consumption throughout the U.S. had substantial economic effects. Such wheat reduced the demand for wheat in commercial markets due to the substitution effect: farmers who grew wheat for themselves necessarily purchased less wheat in the commercial market. And this, in turn, depressed the price for wheat, frustrating the central purpose of the AAA: to prop up crop prices through the constriction of supply. In aggregate, then, the economic effect of farmers' growing wheat for their own consumption was substantial, which meant that the application of the AAA to people like Filburn was within the commerce power.

Wickard held that the relevant question in determining whether Congress could regulate a given activity under the commerce power was whether that activity had a *substantial effect* on interstate commerce, even if the activity itself was not interstate commerce. (Certainly Wickard's growing of wheat for consumption by his livestock was not "commerce" in the traditional sense, nor was it "interstate.") And this substantial effect was to be evaluated by considering the activity in aggregate throughout the U.S., not just the activity of a particular individual in isolation.

5. The Civil Rights Act of 1964

The Supreme Court's deferential approach to reviewing legislation enacted under the commerce power continued unabated until 1995, when the Court decided *United States v. Lopez* (discussed below). Before reaching *Lopez*, though, it is worth exploring two historically significant decisions handed down on the same day in 1964: *Heart of Atlanta Motel v. United States*, 379 U.S. 241, and *Katzenbach v. McClung*, 379 U.S. 294. Both cases further illustrate the Supreme Court's then-prevailing approach to commerce power questions. More important, they sustained the constitutionality of the Civil Rights Act of 1964, one of the most significant federal statutes ever enacted.

Title II of the Civil Rights Act prohibits racial discrimination in any "public accommodation," which the Act defines to include hotels and restaurants. Congress specifically justified the Act as an exercise of its commerce power. (Congress is not required to identify the enumerated power sustaining a statute, but it did so on this occasion.) Congress might have relied on a different power—specifically, that granted by §5 of the Fourteenth Amendment. That provision gives Congress the "power to enforce, by appropriate legislation, the provisions of" the Fourteenth Amendment. And the Fourteenth Amendment includes the Equal Protection Clause, which forbids any state from "deny[ing] to any person within its jurisdiction the equal protection of the laws." But justifying the Civil Rights Act as an exercise of the §5 power would have required the Supreme Court to overrule a century-old decision holding that Congress can only use its §5 power to regulate the conduct of *governmental* actors (and not private persons). Congress thus chose the path of less resistance, even though its central *purpose* in enacting the Civil Rights Act was moral or social (rather than economic or commercial).

a. *Heart of Atlanta Motel v. United States*

Under Title II of the Civil Rights Act, all hotels and motels offering rooms to transient guests were deemed to affect commerce *per se*, and thus were prohibited from discriminating based on race. In *Heart of Atlanta Motel*, the Court held that this prohibition was within the commerce power. The Court reasoned that Congress had found racial discrimination to impede the capacity of African Americans to travel interstate, and thus interfered with interstate commerce. It also happened that the Heart of Atlanta Motel advertised nationally, and 75 percent of its guests were residents of other states. Under the logic of the Court's holding, though, these case-specific facts did not matter. The relevant frame was the problem of racial discrimination by hotels in the aggregate, not its individual incidents. As stated in *Wickard*, the relevant question is whether discrimination by these establishments *collectively* has a substantial effect on interstate commerce.

b. *Katzenbach v. McClung*

This was a companion case to *Heart of Atlanta Motel* involving a restaurant, Ollie's Barbecue. The Civil Rights Act covers a restaurant when either (a) it serves or offers to serve interstate travelers, or (b) "a substantial portion of the food which it serves . . . has moved in commerce." There was scant evidence that Ollie's Barbecue itself significantly affected interstate commerce; though the restaurant purchased roughly $70,000 of meat annually from outside Alabama, there was no evidence it served travelers in interstate commerce. But the Court again applied the aggregation principle, and it largely deferred to Congress's judgment about the impact of the regulated activity on interstate commerce. The justices only asked whether Congress had a rational basis for concluding that the regulated activity substantially affected interstate commerce: "[W]here we find that the legislators, in light of the facts and testimony before them have a rational basis for finding a chosen regulatory scheme necessary to the protection of commerce, our investigation is at an end."

B. The Modern Era: *United States v. Lopez*

Heart of Atlanta Motel and *Katzenbach v. McClung* were entirely consistent with the conception of the commerce power expressed in *Wickard*. In that era, when faced with a challenge to a federal statute on the ground it exceeded Congress's commerce power, the Supreme Court only asked whether Congress could rationally have concluded that the regulated activity, in aggregate, substantially affected interstate commerce. This standard was very deferential, and the results were predictable: from 1937 to 1995, the Court did not invalidate a single federal statute as exceeding Congress's commerce power.

Matters changed in 1995, when the Court handed down *United States v. Lopez*. As you read *Lopez*, please consider the following questions:

1. What are the three categories of activity Congress can regulate with its commerce power? Can you think of examples of federal statutes falling into each category?

2. What, precisely, was the activity that the Gun Free School Zones Act of 1990 (GFSZA) regulated? Which of the three aforementioned categories could the GFSZA have plausibly fit within?

3. What did the Court examine in evaluating whether the GFSZA constituted a regulation of an activity "substantially affecting interstate commerce"?

4. What other factors did the Court mention in *Lopez* that might have affected the GFSZA's constitutionality? Why were each of them ultimately unavailing?

5. According to the Court, what was the essential problem with the federal government's argument in support of the GFSZA's constitutionality?

United States v. Lopez
514 U.S. 549 (1995)

CHIEF JUSTICE REHNQUIST delivered the opinion of the Court.

In the Gun Free School Zones Act of 1990, Congress made it a federal offense "for any individual knowingly to possess a firearm at a place that the individual knows, or has reasonable cause to believe, is a school zone." The Act neither regulates a commercial activity nor contains a requirement that the possession be connected in any way to interstate commerce. We hold that the Act exceeds the authority of Congress "[t]o regulate Commerce . . . among the several States." U. S. Const., Art. I, §8, cl. 3.

On March 10, 1992, respondent, who was then a 12th grade student, arrived at Edison High School in San Antonio, Texas, carrying a concealed .38 caliber handgun and five bullets. Acting upon an anonymous tip, school authorities confronted respondent, who admitted that he was carrying the weapon. He was arrested and charged under Texas law with firearm possession on school premises. See Tex. Penal Code Ann. §46.03(a)(1). The next day, the state charges were dismissed after federal agents charged respondent by complaint with violating the Gun Free School Zones Act of 1990.

A federal grand jury indicted respondent on one count of knowing possession of a firearm at a school zone, in violation of §922(q). Respondent moved to dismiss his federal indictment on the ground that §922(q) "is unconstitutional as it is beyond the power of Congress to legislate control over our public schools." The District Court denied the motion, concluding that §922(q) "is a constitutional exercise of Congress' well defined power to regulate activities in and affecting commerce, and the 'business' of elementary, middle and high schools . . . affects interstate commerce." Respondent waived his right to a jury trial. The District Court conducted a bench trial, found him guilty of violating §922(q), and sentenced him to six months' imprisonment and two years' supervised release.

On appeal, respondent challenged his conviction based on his claim that §922(q) exceeded Congress' power to legislate under the Commerce Clause. The Court of Appeals for the Fifth Circuit agreed and reversed respondent's conviction. It held that, in light of what it characterized as insufficient congressional findings and legislative history, "section 922(q), in the full reach of its terms, is invalid as beyond the power of Congress under the Commerce Clause." Because of the importance of the issue, we granted certiorari, and we now affirm.

We start with first principles. The Constitution creates a Federal Government of enumerated powers. See U. S. Const., Art. I, §8. As James Madison wrote, "[t]he powers delegated by the proposed Constitution to the federal government are few and defined. Those which are to remain in the State governments are numerous and indefinite." The Federalist No. 45, pp. 292–293 (C. Rossiter ed. 1961). This constitutionally mandated division of authority "was adopted by the Framers to ensure protection of our fundamental liberties." *Gregory* v. *Ashcroft*, 501 U.S. 452, 458 (1991). "Just as the separation and independence of the coordinate branches of the Federal Government serves to prevent the accumulation of excessive power in any one branch, a healthy balance of power between the States and the Federal Government will reduce the risk of tyranny and abuse from either front." *Ibid.*

The Constitution delegates to Congress the power "[t]o regulate Commerce with foreign Nations, and among the several States, and with the Indian Tribes." U. S. Const., Art. I, §8, cl. 3. . . .

[W]e have identified three broad categories of activity that Congress may regulate under its commerce power. First, Congress may regulate the use of the channels of interstate commerce. See, *e.g., Darby*, 312 U. S., at 114; *Heart of Atlanta Motel, supra*, at 256 ("[T]he authority of Congress to keep the channels of interstate commerce free from immoral and injurious uses has been frequently sustained, and is no longer open to question."). Second, Congress is empowered to regulate and protect the instrumentalities of interstate commerce, or persons or things in interstate commerce, even though the threat may come only from intrastate activities. See, *e.g., Shreveport Rate Cases*, 234 U.S. 342 (1914); *Southern R. Co.* v. *United States*, 222 U.S. 20 (1911) (upholding amendments to Safety Appliance Act as applied to vehicles used in intrastate commerce); *Perez, supra*, at 150 ("[F]or example, the destruction of an aircraft, or . . . thefts from interstate shipments"). Finally, Congress' commerce authority includes the power to regulate those activities having a substantial relation to interstate commerce, *Jones & Laughlin Steel*, 301 U. S., at 37, *i.e.,* those activities that substantially affect interstate commerce. *Wirtz,* supra, at 196, n. 27.

Within this final category, admittedly, our case law has not been clear whether an activity must "affect" or "substantially affect" interstate commerce in order to be within Congress' power to regulate it under the Commerce Clause. We conclude, consistent with the great weight of our case law, that the proper test requires an analysis of whether the regulated activity "substantially affects" interstate commerce.

We now turn to consider the power of Congress, in the light of this framework, to enact §922(q). The first two categories of authority may be quickly disposed of: §922(q) is not a regulation of the use of the channels of interstate commerce, nor is it an attempt to prohibit the interstate transportation of a commodity through the channels of commerce; nor can §922(q) be justified as a regulation by which Congress has sought to protect an instrumentality of interstate commerce or a thing in interstate commerce. Thus, if §922(q) is to be sustained, it must be under the third category as a regulation of an activity that substantially affects interstate commerce.

First, we have upheld a wide variety of congressional Acts regulating intrastate economic activity where we have concluded that the activity substantially affected interstate commerce. Examples include the regulation of intrastate coal mining; *Hodel, supra,* intrastate extortionate credit transactions, *Perez, supra,* restaurants utilizing substantial interstate supplies, *McClung, supra,* inns and hotels catering to interstate guests, *Heart of Atlanta Motel, supra,* and production and consumption of home-grown wheat, *Wickard* v. *Filburn,* 317 U.S. 111 (1942). These examples are by no means exhaustive, but the pattern is clear. Where economic activity substantially affects interstate commerce, legislation regulating that activity will be sustained.

Even *Wickard,* which is perhaps the most far reaching example of Commerce Clause authority over intrastate activity, involved economic activity in a way that the possession of a gun in a school zone does not. Roscoe Filburn operated a small farm in Ohio, on which, in the year involved, he raised 23 acres of wheat. It was his practice to sow winter wheat in the fall, and after harvesting it in July to sell a portion of the crop, to feed part of it to poultry and livestock on the farm, to use some in making flour for home consumption, and to keep the remainder for seeding future crops. The Secretary of Agriculture assessed a penalty against him under the Agricultural Adjustment Act of 1938 because he harvested about 12 acres more wheat than his allotment under the Act permitted. The Act was designed to regulate the volume of wheat moving in interstate and foreign commerce in order to avoid surpluses and shortages, and concomitant fluctuation in wheat prices, which had previously obtained. The Court said, in an opinion sustaining the application of the Act to Filburn's activity:

"One of the primary purposes of the Act in question was to increase the market price of wheat and to that end to limit the volume thereof that could affect the market. It can hardly be denied that a factor of such volume and variability as home consumed wheat would have a substantial influence on price and market conditions. This may arise because being in marketable condition such wheat overhangs the market and, if induced by rising prices, tends to flow into the market and check price increases. But if we assume that it is never marketed, it supplies a need of the man who grew it which would otherwise be reflected by purchases in the open market. Home grown wheat in this sense competes with wheat in commerce." 317 U. S., at 128.

Section 922(q) is a criminal statute that by its terms has nothing to do with "commerce" or any sort of economic enterprise, however broadly one might define those terms. Section 922(q) is not an essential part of a larger regulation of economic activity, in which the regulatory scheme could be undercut unless the intrastate activity were regulated. It cannot, therefore, be sustained under our cases upholding regulations of activities that arise out of or are connected with a commercial transaction, which viewed in the aggregate, substantially affects interstate commerce.

Second, §922(q) contains no jurisdictional element which would ensure, through case by case inquiry, that the firearm possession in question affects interstate commerce. For example, in *United States* v. *Bass*, 404 U.S. 336 (1971), the Court interpreted former 18 U.S.C. §1202(a), which made it a crime for a felon to "receiv[e], posses[s], or transpor[t] in commerce or affecting commerce . . . any firearm." 404 U. S., at 337. The Court interpreted the possession component of §1202(a) to require an additional nexus to interstate commerce both because the statute was ambiguous and because "unless Congress conveys its purpose clearly, it will not be deemed to have significantly changed the federal state balance." *Id.*, at 349. The *Bass* Court set aside the conviction because although the Government had demonstrated that Bass had possessed a firearm, it had failed "to show the requisite nexus with interstate commerce." *Id.*, at 347. The Court thus interpreted the statute to reserve the constitutional question whether Congress could regulate, without more, the "mere possession" of firearms. Unlike the statute in *Bass*, §922(q) has no express jurisdictional element which might limit its reach to a discrete set of firearm possessions that additionally have an explicit connection with or effect on interstate commerce.

Although as part of our independent evaluation of constitutionality under the Commerce Clause we of course consider legislative findings, and indeed even congressional committee findings, regarding effect on interstate commerce, see, *e.g., Preseault* v. *ICC*, 494 U.S. 1, 17 (1990), the Government concedes that "[n]either the statute nor its legislative history contain[s] express congressional findings regarding the effects upon interstate commerce of gun possession in a school zone." We agree with the Government that Congress normally is not required to make formal findings as to the substantial burdens that an activity has on interstate commerce. But to the extent that congressional findings would enable us to evaluate the legislative judgment that the activity in question substantially affected interstate commerce, even though no such substantial effect was visible to the naked eye, they are lacking here. . . .

The Government's essential contention, *in fine,* is that we may determine here that §922(q) is valid because possession of a firearm in a local school zone does indeed substantially affect interstate commerce. The Government argues that possession of a firearm in a school zone may result in violent crime and that violent crime can be expected to affect the functioning of the national economy in two ways. First, the costs of violent crime are substantial, and, through the mechanism of insurance, those costs are spread throughout the population. Second, violent crime reduces the willingness of individuals to travel to areas within the country that are perceived to be unsafe. The Government also argues that the presence of guns in schools poses a substantial threat to the educational process by threatening the learning environment. A handicapped educational process, in turn, will result in a less productive citizenry. That, in turn, would have an adverse effect on the Nation's economic well being. As a result, the Government argues that Congress could rationally have concluded that §922(q) substantially affects interstate commerce.

We pause to consider the implications of the Government's arguments. The Government admits, under its "costs of crime" reasoning, that Congress could regulate not only all violent crime, but all activities that might lead to violent crime, regardless of how tenuously they relate to interstate commerce. Similarly, under the Government's "national productivity" reasoning, Congress could regulate any activity that it found was related to the economic productivity of individual citizens: family law (including marriage, divorce, and child custody), for example. Under the theories that the Government presents in support of §922(q), it is difficult to perceive any limitation on federal power, even in areas such as criminal law enforcement or education where States historically have been sovereign. Thus, if we were to accept the Government's arguments, we are hard pressed to posit any activity by an individual that Congress is without power to regulate.

Although Justice Breyer argues that acceptance of the Government's rationales would not authorize a general federal police power, he is unable to identify any activity that the States may regulate but Congress may not. Justice Breyer posits that there might be some limitations on Congress' commerce power such as family law or certain aspects of education. These suggested limitations, when viewed in light of the dissent's expansive analysis, are devoid of substance. . . .

Admittedly, a determination whether an intrastate activity is commercial or noncommercial may in some cases result in legal uncertainty. But, so long as Congress' authority is limited to those powers enumerated in the Constitution, and so long as those enumerated powers are interpreted as having judicially enforceable outer limits, congressional legislation under the Commerce Clause always will engender "legal uncertainty." As Chief Justice Marshall stated in *McCulloch* v. *Maryland*, 4 Wheat. 316 (1819):

> "The [federal] government is acknowledged by all to be one of enumerated powers. The principle, that it can exercise only the powers granted to it . . . is now universally admitted. But the question respecting the extent of the powers actually granted, is perpetually arising, and will probably continue to arise, as long as our system shall exist." *Id.*, at 405.

The Constitution mandates this uncertainty by withholding from Congress a plenary police power that would authorize enactment of every type of legislation. Congress has operated within this framework of legal uncertainty ever since this Court determined that it was the judiciary's duty "to say what the law is." *Marbury* v. *Madison*, 1 Cranch. 137, 177 (1803) (Marshall, C. J.). Any possible benefit from eliminating this "legal uncertainty" would be at the expense of the Constitution's system of enumerated powers. . . .

The possession of a gun in a local school zone is in no sense an economic activity that might, through repetition elsewhere, substantially affect any sort of interstate commerce. Respondent was a local student at a local school; there is no indication that he had recently moved in interstate commerce, and there is no requirement that his possession of the firearm have any concrete tie to interstate commerce.

To uphold the Government's contentions here, we would have to pile inference upon inference in a manner that would bid fair to convert congressional authority under the Commerce Clause to a general police power of the sort retained by the States. Admittedly, some of our prior cases have taken long steps down that road, giving great deference to congressional action. The broad language in these opinions has suggested the possibility of additional expansion, but we decline here to proceed any further. To do so would require us to conclude that the Constitution's enumeration of powers does not presuppose something not enumerated, and that there never will be a distinction between what is truly national and what is truly local. This we are unwilling to do.

*   *   *

Notes on *United States v. Lopez*

1. *The three categories of activity Congress can regulate using its commerce power*: Any analysis of *Lopez* should begin with a careful examination of the doctrinal framework it establishes, which has governed all commerce power questions since 1995. Chief Justice Rehnquist wrote that, pursuant to its commerce power, Congress can regulate three "broad categories of activity": (1) it can regulate "the use of the channels of interstate commerce";

(2) it can "regulate and protect the instrumentalities of interstate commerce, or persons or things in interstate commerce"; and (3) it can regulate "those activities that substantially affect interstate commerce." Notice that the scope of these three categories of activity goes beyond the regulation of interstate commerce *itself*. (An activity "substantially affecting" interstate commerce, for example, may not itself be "interstate commerce.") In essence, these three categories—to the extent they go beyond "commerce among the States"— reflect Congress's authority to select "appropriate" means (under the Necessary and Proper Clause) to deploy the power granted by the Commerce Clause.

2. The "use of the channels of interstate commerce": *Lopez*'s first category is relatively straightforward. It includes activities that constitute the use of those mechanisms through which interstate commerce flows: the mail, interstate shipping, interstate railroad networks, interstate highways, navigable waterways, cables and wires carrying telecommunications, and the like. Congress can regulate how these channels are used, even when the regulated activity is not commercial in nature; it can regulate the use of these channels for *any* reason. For example, Congress in the early 1900s sought to prescribe the terms of employment by federal statute, but the Court invalidated these laws on the ground that regulating labor relations exceeded the commerce power. *See Hammer v. Dagenhart*, 247 U.S. 251 (1918). (This would no longer be the case; regulating the terms of employment falls within *Lopez*'s third category, as an activity substantially affecting interstate commerce.) Congress then sought to regulate these matters indirectly—for instance, by prohibiting the shipment in interstate commerce of items manufactured with employees who had not been paid a prescribed minimum wage. *See United States v. Darby*, 312 U.S. 100 (1941). The Court found these latter statutes to be within the commerce power because the precise activity they regulated was the use of the channels of interstate commerce.

3. Regulating or protecting "the instrumentalities of, or persons or things in, interstate commerce": An instrumentality of interstate commerce is an item used to conduct commerce. It encompasses such things as airplanes, ships, railroad cars, telecommunications towers, and trucks. Thus, a federal statute requiring commercial airliners to use flame retardant fabric in its seat cushions would constitute a regulation of an instrumentality of interstate commerce. The category of "persons or things in" interstate commerce seems to overlap a good deal with the first category—the use of the channels of interstate commerce. That is, a statute that regulates persons or things while they are "in" interstate commerce would seem also, at least in most circumstances, to regulate the use of the channels of interstate commerce. But this category also permits Congress to enact laws "protecting" persons or things in the flow of commerce, even when the activity regulated does not constitute a "use of the channels" of interstate commerce. Thus, a law that forbid the possession of a gun within a certain distance of an airport would likely fit within this category, even though it could not be described as regulating the "use of a channel" of interstate commerce.

4. *Activities that "substantially affect interstate commerce"*: By far the broadest of *Lopez*'s three categories is the third: activities "substantially affecting" interstate commerce. Taken literally—especially when combined with the *Wickard*'s aggregation principle—this category would seem to give Congress almost unlimited regulatory power. As an empirical matter, almost any activity Congress would ever bother to regulate (when considering all of its instances) has a "substantial effect" on interstate commerce. Thus, if there is to be a judicially enforced limit to the commerce power, this test cannot be taken literally.

To construct such a limit, the Court in *Lopez* made a critical analytic move. Specifically, in summarizing the Court's commerce power precedent, Chief Justice Rehnquist wrote as follows: "These examples are by no means exhaustive, but the pattern is clear. Where *economic activity* substantially affects interstate commerce, legislation regulating that activity will be sustained."[13] As the Court remarked, "[e]ven *Wickard*, which is perhaps the most far reaching example of Commerce Clause authority over intrastate activity, involved economic activity in a way that the possession of a gun in a school zone does not."

This means that the critical inquiry in determining whether a federal statute fits within this category is whether the regulated activity is "economic" or "commercial" in nature. If not, *Lopez* suggests that reviewing courts should be unwilling to aggregate the activity's impact, which will mean that its effect on interstate commerce almost certainly will not be "substantial." As the Court explained, a law regulating activity that is not commercial or economic in nature "cannot . . . be sustained under our cases upholding regulations of activities that arise out of or are connected with a commercial transaction, which viewed in the aggregate, substantially affect interstate commerce."

5. *A "jurisdictional element"*: In further explaining why the GFSZA exceeded the commerce power, the Court mentioned a handful of other factors that might have been relevant had they been present. One was that the GFSZA lacked a "jurisdictional element," language "which would ensure, through case-by-case inquiry, that the firearm in question affects interstate commerce." As used here, "jurisdictional" does not refer to a court's adjudicatory jurisdiction, the more typical usage in law. Instead, it refers to Congress's *legislative* jurisdiction. In essence, a jurisdictional element (sometimes called a "jurisdictional hook") is statutory language that narrows the scope of the regulated activity so that the statute only reaches those instances of the activity with a closer

---

[13] This interpretation might have harmonized the Court's precedent, but neither *Wickard* nor *Heart of Atlanta Motel* nor *McClung* actually indicated that the "economic nature" of the regulated activity mattered. In this respect, the Court's interpretation of *Wickard* in *Lopez* was creative and somewhat revisionist.

connection to interstate commerce. (The idea is to narrow the statute's coverage so as to keep it within Congress's legislative jurisdiction.) For instance, a jurisdictional element might limit a statute's application to only those instances of a particular activity having "a substantial effect on interstate commerce," or where the relevant object has "traveled in interstate commerce."

* * *

EXAMPLE

Consider how Congress might have written the GFSZA with a jurisdictional element so as not to exceed the commerce power. Instead of regulating *every* possession of a gun in a school zone, Congress might have limited the law's coverage to only the possession of those guns "that had traveled in interstate commerce," or to only when the possession of the gun had "a substantial effect on interstate commerce," or even to only when the possession was accomplished "for commercial purposes." Indeed, following the decision in *Lopez*, Congress amended 18 U.S.C. §922(q)(2)(A) to read as follows: "It shall be unlawful for any individual knowingly to possess a firearm that has moved in or that otherwise affects interstate or foreign commerce at a place that the individual knows, or has reasonable cause to believe, is a school zone." Thus far, federal courts of appeals have upheld the revised §922(q)(2)(A) as falling within Congress's commerce power. The Supreme Court has not taken up the question.

* * *

It is unclear exactly when a statute's inclusion of a jurisdictional "hook" will be sufficient to render a statute constitutional that would otherwise exceed the commerce power. (Since *Lopez*, the Court has yet to hear a commerce power case that turned on the presence of a jurisdictional element in the statute.) To be sure, language narrowing the scope of the regulated activity is certainly *relevant* to whether the statute is within the commerce power. And the tighter the connection the statute requires between the regulated activity and the impact on interstate commerce, the more likely the law will be constitutional. But the proper question is whether the regulated activity—defined and narrowed by the jurisdictional element—falls within one of the three categories of activity identified in *Lopez*. The existence of a jurisdictional element in the statute *by itself* cannot guarantee the statute's validity. The ultimate question is whether the Constitution empowers Congress to reach the regulated activity, however the statute exactly defines that activity.

6. *Congressional findings*: Another potentially relevant factor identified in *Lopez* is whether Congress has made factual findings regarding the regulated activity's impact on interstate commerce. Such findings would represent a conclusion by Congress—institutionally better positioned than the judiciary to make such empirical judgments—that the regulated activity has a substantial effect on interstate commerce. Presumably, such findings should be entitled to some deference from the courts. Notice, though, that the Court in *Lopez* stopped well short of stating that such findings would be *sufficient* to render a statute like the GFSZA constitutional. (And the point was academic in *Lopez* itself, as Congress had made no such findings.)

7. *An essential part of a broader regulatory scheme*: Notice, too, that the Court conspicuously mentioned that "Section 922(q) is not an essential part of a larger regulation of economic activity, in which the regulatory scheme could be undercut unless the intrastate activity were regulated." This suggests that a statutory provision that—when viewed in isolation—would fall outside *Lopez*'s three categories might nonetheless fit within the commerce power (with the help of the Necessary and Proper Clause) if it was essential to a broader regulatory scheme (if that scheme as a whole is within the commerce power). Though this reasoning was not applicable in *Lopez*—as the GFSZA was essentially a stand-alone statute, not part of any broader scheme—it would prove crucial five years later in *Gonzales v. Raich* (discussed below).

8. *The government's (futile) argument*: To fully appreciate the Court's analysis in *Lopez*, it is constructive to consider the Court's response to the government's defense of the GFSZA. The federal government made three distinct arguments as to why the act was within Congress's commerce power. First, it argued that the "costs of crime" caused by the possession of guns at schools are substantial, and that these costs, through insurance, are spread throughout the national economy. Second, it argued that violent crime (facilitated in part by the possession of guns in school zones) prevents persons from traveling interstate, and thereby inhibits interstate commerce. Third, it argued that the possession of guns at schools interferes with the educational process, which in turn reduces students' capacity to learn and, ultimately, their economic productivity, which then acts as a drag on the national economy.

Looking carefully at the Court's response, one sees that Chief Justice Rehnquist did not dispute the government's *factual* assertion that, in these various ways, the possession of guns in school zones has an impact on interstate commerce. Instead, the Court reasoned from the other direction: "We pause to consider the implications of the Government's arguments. . . . Under the theories that the Government presents in support of §922(q), it is difficult to perceive any limitation on federal power, even in areas such as criminal law enforcement or education, where States historically have been sovereign." In other words, if the Constitution dictates that the federal government is one of "enumerated powers," those powers must have some *limit*, some logical stopping point. But accepting the government's arguments in *Lopez* would have effectively granted Congress unlimited authority—a "police power" that resides only in the states, that the Framers denied the federal government.

Implicitly, then, the Court rejected an understanding of the "substantial effects" inquiry that is factual or empirical, as most any activity (in aggregate) has a "substantial effect" on interstate commerce in that sense. Accepting this as the constitutional test, wrote the Court, "would require us to conclude that the Constitution's enumeration of powers does not presuppose something not enumerated, and that there never will be a distinction between what is truly national and what is truly local."

9. *Areas in which "States have historically been sovereign" or "of traditional state concern"*: A last notable point in *Lopez* was the Court's reference to areas in which "States historically have been sovereign." Justice Kennedy also emphasized this point in his concurring opinion in *Lopez*:

> "In a sense any conduct in this interdependent world of ours has an ultimate commercial origin or consequence, but we have not yet said the commerce power may reach so far. If Congress attempts that extension, then at least we must inquire whether the exercise of national power seeks to intrude upon an area of traditional state concern."

Why does this matter? Again, *Lopez* indicates that whether an activity "substantially affects interstate commerce" (and thus falls within the commerce power) is *not* a factual question. Instead, the test looks to other, more formalistic attributes of the regulated activity. The most important of those attributes is whether the activity is "economic" or "commercial" in nature. Here, the Court indicated that it may also be relevant whether the federal law intrudes on an area that has historically been regulated (largely or exclusively) by the states.

* * *

C.   Reaffirming *Lopez*: *United States v. Morrison*

Immediately following *Lopez*, it was unclear whether the Supreme Court was serious about reinvigorating the limits on Congress's commerce power. The GFSZA was trivial as a matter of public policy; as a matter of state law, it was already illegal to possess a firearm on school grounds in all fifty states. Would the Court really invalidate a federal statute as exceeding Congress's enumerated powers when a significant number of Americans cared about it? The Court's decision years after *Lopez*, in *United States v. Morrison*, 529 U.S. 598 (2000), in showed yes, it would.

Morrison struck down the civil remedy provision of the Violence Against Women Act (VAWA). VAWA contained hundreds of provisions, almost all of which were constitutionally unremarkable. But §13981 was controversial. It provided survivors of gender-motivated violence a private right of action against those who assaulted them. Christy Brzonkala, a student at Virginia Tech and the survivor of a rape perpetrated by Antonio Morrison, brought suit against Morrison under §13981 in federal district court seeking damages. (The federal government intervened in support of Brzonkala.) As a defense, Morrison contended §13981 exceeded Congress's enumerated powers. The Supreme Court split 5-to-4 (just as it had in *Lopez*) and invalidated §13981.

The government argued that Congress had two distinct bases for enacting §13981: the commerce power and the power granted by §5 of the Fourteenth

Amendment. (The §5 portion of the opinion is addressed in Chapter 11.) The Court's commerce power analysis was a carbon copy of *Lopez*. Like the GFSZA, §13981 could not be justified as a regulation of the use of the channels of interstate commerce. Nor was it plausibly a regulation of the instrumentalities of, or persons or things in, interstate commerce. So the question, as in *Lopez*, was whether the statute was justifiable as a regulation of activity "substantially affecting" interstate commerce.

Again, the first and most important aspect of the "substantial effects" inquiry is whether the regulated activity is "economic or commercial in nature." According to the Court, it was not: "[Gender-motivated] crimes of violence are not, in any sense of the phrase, economic activity." Even more explicitly than in *Lopez*, *Morrison* reasoned that if the regulated activity is not economic or commercial in nature, then

> "Congress generally cannot rely on its aggregate effects to conclude that the activity has a substantial effect on interstate commerce. . . . While we need not adopt a categorical rule against aggregating the effects of any noneconomic activity in order to decide these cases, thus far in our Nation's history our cases have upheld Commerce Clause regulation of intrastate activity only where the activity is economic in nature."

Nor did §13981 contain a jurisdictional element limiting its application to instances of gender-motivated violence with a connection to interstate commerce. Instead, it regulated *all* acts of gender-motivated violence.

The VAWA did contain copious findings by Congress about the effects of gender-motivated violence on interstate commerce. But to the Court, those findings were ultimately beside the point. Congressional findings that merely support an attenuated connection between the regulated activity and the effect on interstate commerce, the Court concluded, are effectively irrelevant.

Lastly, like the GFSZA, §13981 regulated in an area of "traditional state concern":

> "The regulation and punishment of intrastate violence that is not directed at the instrumentalities, channels, or goods involved in interstate commerce has always been the province of the States. Indeed, we can think of no better example of the police power, which the Founders denied the national government and reposed in the States, than the suppression of violent crime and the vindication of its victims."

Analytically, then, *Morrison* was a replay of *Lopez*, with the only difference being the existence of congressional findings—findings the Court found unimportant. Most important in both cases, the Court concluded that the regulated activity was not economic or commercial in nature, and hence it would not consider the activity's aggregate effects in all of its instances nationwide. As the Court explained in *Morrison*, "[w]e . . . reject the argument that Congress may regulate noneconomic, violent criminal conduct based solely on that conduct's aggregate effect on interstate commerce."

*   *   *

PROBLEMS ON THE COMMERCE POWER: BUILDING BLOCKS

1. Please assess whether the following activities constitute a "use of a channel of interstate commerce."

   a. The shipping of coal by railroad from Wyoming to California.

   b. The shipping of coal on the same railroad tracks from Sacramento, California, to Benicia, California.

   c. Possessing marijuana.

   d. Driving from Sacramento to Reno with marijuana in the car.

   e. Driving with marijuana in the car from San Francisco to Berkeley on Interstate 80.

   f. Posting a photograph on Instagram.

   g. Committing an assault.

2. Please evaluate whether the following items constitute an "instrumentality of interstate commerce," the protection or regulation of which falls within Congress's commerce power?

   a. A tractor-trailer truck used for transporting goods.

   b. A commercial jetliner.

   c. Clothes that are sold at a retail store in California, which were shipped to that store from a manufacturer in Bangladesh.

   d. Those same clothes, during the period of time they are being transported on a ship from Bangladesh and California.

   e. The container in which those same clothes were shipped across the Pacific Ocean.

   f. A cell phone tower.

3. Please assess whether the following activities would be considered "economic or commercial in nature" for purposes of determining whether they "substantially affect" interstate commerce.

   a. An act of violence against another person.

   b. The provision by a hotel of a room to a guest (in exchange for a fee).

   c. Renting a room in one's home to a guest through Airbnb.

   d. Allowing a friend to stay several nights in one's home.

   e. Growing marijuana.

   f. Growing marijuana in one's own garden, for personal consumption.

g. The possession of a gun.

h. The sale of a gun.

4. Among the following, please identify those definitions of the regulated activity that contain a "jurisdictional element" (and what language represents the jurisdictional element).

a. "Knowingly to possess a firearm at a place that the individual knows, or has reasonable cause to believe, is a school zone."

b. "Knowingly to possess a firearm that has moved in or that otherwise affects interstate or foreign commerce at a place that the individual knows, or has reasonable cause to believe, is a school zone."

c. "Any physician who, in or affecting interstate or foreign commerce, knowingly performs a partial-birth abortion and thereby kills a human fetus shall be fined under this title or imprisoned not more than 2 years, or both."

5. Please evaluate whether the following activities likely constitute areas in which "States have historically been sovereign" or areas "of traditional state concern" for purposes of analyzing whether their regulation exceeds Congress's commerce power.

a. Marriage and divorce.

b. Immigration and naturalization.

c. Crimes of violence against the person (such as murder and assault).

d. The creation and emission of pollutants capable of making the air unsafe for humans to breathe.

e. The content of the curriculum in public elementary, middle, and high schools.

*   *   *

D.   Integral to a Broader Regulatory Scheme

Lopez and *Morrison* reinvigorated the judicial enforcement of the limits to Congress's commerce power. But only five years after *Morrison*, the Supreme Court decided *Gonzales v. Raich*, 545 U.S. (2005), which demonstrated the commerce power—despite some narrowing at the margins—remains quite broad. In *Raich*, the Court upheld the application of the federal Controlled Substances Act (CSA) to persons who themselves were engaged in largely non-commercial, noneconomic, and purely intrastate activity: the growing of marijuana on their own property for their own use. *Lopez* and *Morrison* had seemed to hold that noncommercial, noneconomic activity not involving the use of the channels of interstate commerce, the instrumentalities of interstate commerce, or persons or things in interstate commerce exceeds what Congress can regulate with the commerce power. But *Raich* illustrates the rule is more complicated than that.

As you read *Gonzales v. Raich*, please consider the following questions:

1. What activity did the relevant portion of the CSA regulate? What activity did Angel Raich and Diana Monson engage in?

2. Did the CSA, as written by Congress, regulate activity that is "economic or commercial in nature"? If so, what was the nature of Raich's claim?

3. According to the Court's opinion, when does the commerce power permit Congress to regulate activity that, in particular instances, is not economic or commercial in nature (or even interstate)? Why?

4. Given *Raich's* rationale, can Congress regulate the simple possession of controlled substances? Why or why not? How is that activity different (in a constitutional sense) from the possession of a gun in a school zone?

Gonzales v. Raich
545 U.S. 1 (2005)

JUSTICE STEVENS delivered the opinion of the Court.

California is one of at least nine States that authorize the use of marijuana for medicinal purposes. The question presented in this case is whether the power vested in Congress by Article I, §8, of the Constitution "[t]o make all Laws which shall be necessary and proper for carrying into Execution" its authority to "regulate Commerce with foreign Nations, and among the several States" includes the power to prohibit the local cultivation and use of marijuana in compliance with California law.

I

In 1996, California voters passed Proposition 215, now codified as the Compassionate Use Act of 1996. The proposition was designed to ensure that "seriously ill" residents of the State have access to marijuana for medical purposes . . . . The Act creates an exemption from criminal prosecution for physicians, as well as for patients and primary caregivers who possess or cultivate marijuana for medicinal purposes with the recommendation or approval of a physician.

Respondents Angel Raich and Diane Monson are California residents who suffer from a variety of serious medical conditions and have sought to avail themselves of medical marijuana pursuant to the terms of the Compassionate Use Act. They are being treated by licensed, board-certified family practitioners, who have concluded, after prescribing a host of conventional medicines to treat respondents' conditions and to alleviate their associated symptoms, that marijuana is the only drug available that provides effective treatment. Both women have been using marijuana as a medication for several years pursuant to their doctors' recommendation, and both rely heavily on cannabis to function on a daily basis. . . .

II

[I]n 1970, . . . prompted by a perceived need to consolidate the growing number of piecemeal drug laws and to enhance federal drug enforcement powers, Congress enacted the Comprehensive Drug Abuse Prevention and Control Act. Title II of that Act, the [Controlled Substances Act, or CSA], repealed most of the earlier antidrug laws in favor of a comprehensive regime to combat the international and interstate traffic in illicit drugs. The main objectives of the CSA were to conquer drug abuse and to control the legitimate and illegitimate traffic in controlled substances. Congress was particularly concerned with the need to prevent the diversion of drugs from legitimate to illicit channels.

To effectuate these goals, Congress devised a closed regulatory system making it unlawful to manufacture, distribute, dispense, or possess any controlled substance except in a manner authorized by the CSA. The CSA categorizes all controlled substances into five schedules. The drugs are grouped together based on their accepted medical uses, the potential for abuse, and their psychological and physical effects on the body. Each schedule is associated with a distinct set of controls regarding the manufacture, distribution, and use of the substances listed therein. . . . In enacting the CSA, Congress classified marijuana as a Schedule I drug. . . . By classifying marijuana as a Schedule I drug, as opposed to listing it on a lesser schedule, the manufacture, distribution, or possession of marijuana became a criminal offense, with the sole exception being use of the drug as part of a Food and Drug Administration pre-approved research study. . . .

III

Respondents in this case do not dispute that passage of the CSA, as part of the Comprehensive Drug Abuse Prevention and Control Act, was well within Congress' commerce power. Nor do they contend that any provision or section of the CSA amounts to an unconstitutional exercise of congressional authority. Rather, respondents' challenge is actually quite limited; they argue that the CSA's categorical prohibition of the manufacture and possession of marijuana as applied to the intrastate manufacture and possession of marijuana for medical purposes pursuant to California law exceeds Congress' authority under the Commerce Clause. . . .

Our case law firmly establishes Congress' power to regulate purely local activities that are part of an economic "class of activities" that have a substantial effect on interstate commerce. . . . [*Wickard v. Filburn*] establishes that Congress can regulate purely intrastate activity that is not itself "commercial," in that it is not produced for sale, if it concludes that failure to regulate that class of activity would undercut the regulation of the interstate market in that commodity.

The similarities between this case and *Wickard* are striking. Like the farmer in *Wickard*, respondents are cultivating, for home consumption, a fungible commodity for which there is an established, albeit illegal, interstate market. Just as the Agricultural Adjustment Act was designed "to control the volume [of wheat] moving in interstate and foreign commerce in order to avoid surpluses" and consequently control the market price, a primary purpose of the CSA is to control the supply and demand of controlled substances in both lawful and unlawful drug markets. In *Wickard*, we had no difficulty concluding that Congress had a rational basis for believing that, when viewed in the aggregate, leaving home-consumed wheat outside the regulatory scheme would have a substantial influence on price and market conditions. Here too, Congress had a rational basis for concluding that leaving home-consumed marijuana outside federal control would similarly affect price and market conditions.

More concretely, one concern prompting inclusion of wheat grown for home consumption in the 1938 Act was that rising market prices could draw such wheat into the interstate market, resulting in lower market prices. *Wickard*, 317 U.S., at 128. The parallel concern making it appropriate to include marijuana grown for home consumption in the CSA is the likelihood that the high demand in the interstate market will draw such marijuana into that market. While the diversion of homegrown wheat tended to frustrate the federal interest in stabilizing prices by regulating the volume of commercial transactions in the interstate market, the diversion of homegrown marijuana tends to frustrate the federal interest in eliminating commercial transactions in the interstate market in their entirety. In both cases, the regulation is squarely within Congress' commerce power because production of the commodity meant for home consumption, be it wheat or marijuana, has a substantial effect on supply and demand in the national market for that commodity. . . .

The fact that Wickard's own impact on the market was "trivial by itself" was not a sufficient reason for removing him from the scope of federal regulation. That the Secretary of Agriculture elected to exempt even smaller farms from regulation does not speak to his power to regulate all those whose aggregated production was significant, nor did that fact play any role in the Court's analysis. Moreover, even though Wickard was indeed a commercial farmer, the activity he was engaged in—the cultivation of wheat for home consumption—was not treated by the Court as part of his commercial farming operation. And while it is true that the record in the *Wickard* case itself established the causal connection between the production for local use and the national market, we have before us findings by Congress to the same effect. . . .

Given the enforcement difficulties that attend distinguishing between marijuana cultivated locally and marijuana grown elsewhere, and concerns about diversion into illicit channels, we have no difficulty concluding that Congress had a rational basis for believing that failure to regulate the intrastate manufacture and possession of marijuana would leave a gaping hole in the CSA. Thus, as in *Wickard*, when it enacted comprehensive legislation to regulate the interstate market in a fungible commodity, Congress was acting well within its authority to "make all Laws which shall be necessary and proper" to "regulate Commerce . . . among the several States." U.S. Const., Art. I, §8. That the regulation ensnares some purely intrastate activity is of no moment. As we have done many times before, we refuse to excise individual components of that larger scheme.

IV

To support their contrary submission, respondents rely heavily on two of our more recent Commerce Clause cases. In their myopic focus, they overlook the larger context of modern-era Commerce Clause jurisprudence preserved by those cases. Moreover, even in the narrow prism of respondents' creation, they read those cases far too broadly. Those two cases, of course, are *Lopez* and *Morrison*. As an initial matter, the statutory challenges at issue in those cases were markedly different from the challenge respondents pursue in the case at hand. Here, respondents ask us to excise individual applications of a concededly valid statutory scheme. In contrast, in both *Lopez* and *Morrison*, the parties asserted that a particular statute or provision fell outside Congress' commerce power in its entirety. This distinction is pivotal, for we have often reiterated that "[w]here the class of activities is regulated and that class is within the reach of federal power, the courts have no power 'to excise, as trivial, individual instances' of the class.". . .

* * *

Notes on *Gonzales v. Raich*

1. *The precise nature of the challenge to the CSA in* Raich: To understand the Court's holding in *Raich*, it is critical to appreciate the precise nature of the plaintiffs' challenge to the CSA. They did not allege that the CSA, on its face, exceeded Congress's commerce power. Indeed, they effectively conceded that the vast majority of the applications of the CSA—in prohibiting the manufacture and possession of schedule 1 substances—were constitutional. Rather, as the Court explained, their challenge was "quite limited"; they contended "the CSA's categorical prohibition of the manufacture and possession of marijuana *as applied* to the intrastate manufacture and possession of marijuana for medical purposes pursuant to California law exceeds Congress' authority under the Commerce Clause" (emphasis added). That is, they argued that, although the CSA was generally within Congress's authority, it was unconstitutional as applied to them because they were engaged in purely noncommercial, intrastate activity.

2. *The steps to the Court's analysis*: Again, a critical first step in analyzing whether a statute is within Congress's commerce power is to identify the precise activity the provision regulates. Here, that was the manufacture and possession of a schedule 1 controlled substance (namely, marijuana). *Lopez* and *Morrison* teach that Congress can regulate activities "substantially affecting" interstate commerce. And they further hold that the most important factor in determining whether an activity fits into this category is whether it is "economic or commercial in nature."

Relying a fair amount on *Wickard,* the *Raich* Court concluded that the cultivation and possession of marijuana are economic or commercial activities. (Indeed, the plaintiffs acknowledged as much in conceding the CSA was constitutional on its face.) Thus, the CSA's regulation of these activities fit within the commerce power, at least as a general matter, as a regulation of an activity "substantially affecting" interstate commerce. The complication was that Raich's and Monson's *particular instances* of engaging in these activities were noncommercial and intrastate. The activities—when considered as a class—were economic or commercial in nature; but Raich and Monson individually were not doing anything related to interstate commerce. The question in *Raich,* then, was whether Congress was obligated to create an exception in the CSA for instances of the regulated activity that were noncommercial and intrastate.

Rather emphatically, the Court said no: "Congress can regulate purely intrastate activity that is not itself 'commercial,' in that it is not produced for sale, if it concludes that failure to regulate that class of activity would undercut the regulation of the interstate market in that commodity." So long as the statute, considered on its face, falls within the commerce power, then Congress has no obligation to exempt from the statute's coverage particular instances of that activity that are not a part of interstate commerce—so long as Congress has a reasonable basis for concluding that such an exemption would undercut the effectiveness of the broader scheme. In the Court's words, "[t]hat the regulation ensnares some purely intrastate activity is of no moment. As we have done many times before, we refuse to excise individual components of that larger scheme."

3. *How far does the logic of* Raich *extend?*: Again, the plaintiffs in *Raich* conceded the facial validity of the CSA's prohibition on the cultivation and possession of controlled substances (such as marijuana). Their claim presented an *as-applied* challenge to the statute: that the CSA was unconstitutional *as applied to them* because they, in their particular conduct, had not engaged in activity that Congress could reach with the commerce power. *Raich* holds that when Congress enacts a statute regulating activity that, considered as a class, is economic or commercial in nature—thus constituting a facially valid exercise of the commerce power—Congress is not obligated to exempt from the statute's coverage those instances of the activity that are not economic or commercial in nature (and purely intrastate) if Congress has a rational basis for concluding that exempting those instances of the activity would undermine the effectiveness of the statutory scheme.

But how far does this rationale extend? What if the challenged provision, viewed in isolation, had *zero* constitutional applications as a stand-alone statute? Suppose, for instance, that the plaintiffs in *Raich* had only challenged the provision in the CSA forbidding simple possession of a controlled substance, and they had not conceded the provision was facially constitutional. Unlike the CSA's prohibition on manufacturing, the ban on simple possession *always* applies to activity that is not economic or commercial in nature. (After all, *Lopez* makes clear that the simple possession of an object—other than perhaps something like currency or a security—is not economic nor commercial in nature.) But Congress might well have a rational basis for concluding that prohibiting the possession of Schedule 1 substances is necessary to render effective the CSA's broader statutory scheme, whose aim is to completely stamp out the market for illicit drugs. Does *Raich* mean that Congress can use its commerce power to enact a provision criminalizing simple possession?

The logic of *Raich* suggests it can. And *Raich* itself upheld the prohibition on possession as applied to the plaintiffs. But the plaintiffs conceded the facial validity of the statute in *Raich*, so the question was not squarely presented.

More generally, the Supreme Court's decisions have not conclusively answered this question. One could read *Raich* more narrowly, as only addressing those circumstances where the statutory provision is facially valid and the challenger merely contends the statute exceeds Congress's enumerated powers as applied to her. That was the precise circumstance in *Raich*. At the same time, scores of federal statutes prohibit the simple possession of various objects, from controlled substances to firearms to pornographic images. If the rationale of *Raich* does not apply to these statutes (making them susceptible to constitutional challenge), a significant number of important federal statutes would be constitutionally vulnerable. Thus far, lower courts have upheld these statutes prohibiting simple possession of, and the Court has not addressed them post-*Raich*.

4. *The relevance of state law to the breadth of Congress's enumerated powers*: The activity in which Raich and Monson had engaged—the cultivation and possession of marijuana for personal use—was legal as a matter of California law. But this was *completely irrelevant* to whether the CSA was within Congress's commerce power. Whether Congress has the constitutional authority to regulate a given activity never depends on the content of state law. A state might decide not to regulate an activity, such as the possession and use of marijuana or wagering on sporting events. But Congress is free to reach a different conclusion, so long as its regulation of that activity falls within its enumerated powers. The possession and use of marijuana might be "legal" in California *as a matter of California law*, but it remains a federal crime.

5. *Why was the GFSZA not "an essential part of broader federal regulatory scheme"?*: How come the rationale of *Raich* did not save the GFSZA in *Lopez*? Because the GFSZA was not an integral part of a broader statutory scheme (which itself regulated interstate commerce). Congress had not enacted a statute similar to the CSA that comprehensively regulated the sale, distribution, and possession of handguns in the United States. The GFSZA was a stand-alone statute that regulated nothing other than the possession of guns in school zones. As the Court stated in *Lopez* itself, "Section 922(q) is not an essential part of a larger regulation of economic activity, in which the regulatory scheme could be undercut unless the intrastate activity were regulated."

* * *

QUESTION: Did *Raich* hold that California's Compassionate Use Act was unconstitutional?

ANSWER: No. California law had legalized the possession and use of marijuana for medicinal purposes as a matter of state law. But the fact that an activity is legal under state law—unregulated by the state—says nothing about whether that same activity is legal as a matter of federal law, or whether it is *regulable* by Congress. This is how federalism works. Some activities are regulated by both the states and the federal government. Some activities are regulated by neither. Some activities are regulated by the states but not the federal government. And some activities—such as the possession and use of marijuana for personal purposes within California—are regulated by the federal government but not the states.

* * *

E.   The Authority to Regulate Inactivity: *NFIB v. Sebelius*

1. The constitutional challenges to the Affordable Care Act

In many ways, the Affordable Care Act (ACA) was the most significant federal statute in a generation, expanding access to health insurance for millions of Americans. But the ACA was (and remains) very controversial. Minutes after it was signed into law by President Obama, several lawsuits were filed in district courts across the country challenging its constitutionality. These actions raised a range of arguments, but a common claim was that 26 U.S.C. §5000A—the ACA's so-called "minimum essential coverage provision" (or "individual mandate")—exceeded Congress's enumerated powers.

The minimum coverage provision contained two functionally distinct subsections. One stated that any individual who is not otherwise exempt shall maintain minimally adequate health insurance. The other provided that an individual failing to do so would be required to remit a "penalty" payment on their annual income tax return. The challengers' central claim was that Congress lacked the authority to require "every American to buy a good or service on the private market or face a penalty." In particular, they argued that §5000A did not regulate economic or commercial activity because it did not regulate *activity* of any sort. Instead, it regulated *inactivity*, "the non-purchase of health insurance." And by regulating the decision to abstain from commerce—to decline to obtain minimally adequate health coverage—Congress had exceeded its enumerated powers.

2. The commerce power holding in *NFIB*

In *NFIB v. Sebelius*, 567 U.S. 519 (2012), the Supreme Court (in a portion of the opinion representing only the views of Chief Justice Roberts, but which mirrored the reasoning of Justices Scalia, Kennedy, Thomas, and Alito, and thus has been taken as the Court's views) held that the minimum coverage provision exceeded the commerce power. The central precept of the Chief Justice's opinion was that the commerce power gives Congress the authority to *regulate* commerce, and the very idea of *regulation* presupposes the existence of an activity to regulate. That is, the power to regulate is distinct from the power to create or to call into being. Yet, the creation of commerce is precisely what the individual mandate attempted to accomplish: it did not "regulate existing commercial activity," but instead "compel[led] individuals to *become* active in commerce by purchasing a product, on the ground that the failure to do so affects interstate commerce."

To the Chief Justice, *Wickard v. Filburn* was instructive. At least in *Wickard*, the farmer had been "actively engaged in the production of wheat," which gave the Congress the authority to regulate that activity based on its impact on interstate commerce. In contrast, §5000A regulated individuals merely because they existed, before they voluntarily entered the market Congress sought to regulate. Thus, sustaining the individual mandate would have meant "that individuals may be regulated under the Commerce Clause whenever enough of them are not doing something the Government would have them do."

The Chief Justice reasoned that the government's theory had no logical stopping point: it would permit Congress to impose purchasing mandates "to solve almost any problem." The problem of cost-shifting to which the government pointed, explained Roberts, is not unique to the health insurance market. For example, people with poor diets generally have higher healthcare costs, and they shift much of these costs to others. Thus, "[u]nder the Government's theory, Congress could address the diet problem by ordering everyone to buy vegetables." More broadly, upholding §5000A would "authorize[] Congress to use its commerce power to compel citizens to act as the Government would have them act." To Roberts, that "is not the country the Framers of our Constitution envisioned." Although the commerce power surely has grown as the nation's economy has expanded, one of the Constitution's foundational principles is that there are limits to the national government's authority. "The Government's theory would erode those limits," said the Chief Justice, "fundamentally changing the relation between the citizen and the Federal Government."

Furthermore, Congress could not justify §5000A as an integral component of the ACA's broader regulation of the individual insurance market. True enough, the Chief Justice conceded, *McCulloch* authoritatively construed the concept of "necessity" under the Necessary and Proper Clause quite broadly, permitting Congress to select any legislative means that are "appropriate" or "conducive" to a constitutionally authorized end. Still, no matter how *necessary* a federal law might be, it cannot "undermine the structure of government established by the Constitution." The individual mandate did so, explained Roberts, because instead of merely invoking an "authority derivative of, and in service to, a granted power," it attempted to vest "Congress with the extraordinary ability to create the necessary predicate to the exercise of an enumerated power." As such, §5000A sought to "reach beyond the natural limit of [Congress's] authority and draw within its regulatory scope those who otherwise would be outside of it." Such a law, concluded the Chief Justice, simply could not be "proper" under the Necessary and Proper Clause.

3. The limitations to the commerce power holding in *NFIB*

While the ACA was (and remains) hugely significant as a matter of policy and politics, the Court's commerce power holding in *NFIB* was actually quite narrow. It stands for the principle that Congress cannot use its commerce power to "compel[] individuals to *become* active in commerce by purchasing a product, on the ground that the failure to do so affects interstate commerce."

It is important to see what this principle leaves unaffected. First, it does not disturb laws that compel individuals into commercial transactions when those individuals have already voluntarily entered the relevant market. Under the rationale of *NFIB*, once an individual voluntarily enters a particular market, there exists commercial activity that Congress is free to regulate. For example, Congress still can require all individual health insurance policies sold in the U.S. to offer a defined, baseline scope of coverage, even though some consumers might wish to purchase a policy containing fewer benefits (and in this sense are compelled to purchase something they would rather not). Because the relevant economic activity already exists—the transaction between the insurer and the insured—Congress is entitled to regulate its terms.

Second, Congress still can *forbid* various forms of behavior, even when those prohibitions might be described as compelling individuals to engage in particular transactions. As an example, consider Title II of the Civil Rights Act, which forbids persons who operate places of public accommodation from discriminating on the basis of race, color, ethnicity, or national origin (the statute upheld in *Heart of Atlanta Motel* and *Katzenbach v. McClung*). Title II effectively compels restaurants, hotels, and various other service providers to sell their goods or services to specific customers, even when they might prefer to remain "inactive." But Title II only reaches the conduct of those who are voluntarily operating a business—a restaurant, hotel, medical clinic, or the like—and thus are already engaged in the relevant economic activity.

Third, and relatedly, *NFIB* does not endanger federal laws that might have the foreseeable, practical effect of forcing consumers to enter into unwanted commercial transactions. As the Chief Justice noted, *Wickard v. Filburn* is instructive. Again, *Wickard* upheld Congress's regulation of how much wheat a farmer could grow for his own consumption. The point of that regulation was to increase demand for wheat in the commercial market so as to prop up its market price. Thus, as *Wickard* itself explained, Congress's objective was to "forc[e] some farmers into the market to buy what they could provide for themselves." But again, the Chief Justice expressly distinguished the law sustained in *Wickard* from the ACA's individual mandate on the ground that Roscoe Filburn had been "actively engaged in the production of wheat." This gave Congress the authority to regulate his activity based on its impact on interstate commerce, even though Congress's regulation had the foreseeable effect of forcing farmers like Filburn to make purchases they preferred to avoid—indeed, forcing them to participate in a market they never wished to enter.

Given these limits to its rationale, the commerce power holding of *NFIB* did not jeopardize any existing federal laws. Indeed, the Chief Justice and the joint dissenters took pains to emphasize that the individual mandate was unlike any law Congress had previously enacted. In Roberts's words, never before had Congress "attempted to rely on [the commerce] power to compel individuals not engaged in commerce to purchase an unwanted product." Rather, §5000A was a "[l]egislative novelty" that represented a "new conception[] of federal power." Likewise, the joint dissent underscored that Congress "has never before used the Commerce Clause to compel entry into commerce." Almost by definition, then, the majority's conclusion that §5000A exceeded Congress's commerce power could threaten no laws other than the individual mandate itself.

* * *

PROBLEMS ON THE COMMERCE POWER: COMPLEX APPLICATIONS

1. Consider the following hypothetical (or not-so-hypothetical) federal statutes. In each instance, please assess (1) whether the statute is within the authority granted by Article I to Congress to regulate "commerce among the states," and (2) if so, under what precise rationale (*e.g.*, as a regulation of the use of the channels of interstate commerce, as an activity substantially affecting interstate commerce, or something else).

   a. A statute forbidding any employer from discriminating against any of its employees, with respect to the terms or conditions of their employment, on the basis of an employee's sexual orientation.

   b. A statute forbidding any person from discharging hazardous materials into any navigable waterway of the United States.

   c. A statute forbidding any person from discharging hazardous materials into any ecologically sensitive natural areas in the United States.

   d. A statute forbidding any for-profit business from discharging hazardous materials into any ecologically sensitive natural areas in the United States.

   e. A statute forbidding any passenger from bringing onto a commercial airliner, except in checked luggage, a container with more than 3.4 ounces of liquid.

   f. A statute requiring all newly constructed railroad tracks in the United States be built to the standard gauge of 4 feet, 8.5 inches.

g. A statute that criminalizes the e-mailing of any image that constitutes "child pornography." (Ignore any potential issues under the Free Speech Clause of the First Amendment.)

h. A statute that criminalizes the possession of any image constituting "child pornography." (Again, ignore any potential First Amendment issues.)

i. A statute that criminalizes using any telecommunication device (such as a phone or computer) to threaten violence towards an intimate partner. (Again, ignore any potential First Amendment issues.)

j. A statute forbidding any person previously convicted of a violent felony from possessing a firearm "that has traveled in interstate commerce."

k. A statute forbidding any person previously convicted of a violent felony from possessing a firearm if "any component part of the firearm, at any point in its existence, has traveled in interstate commerce."

l. A statute that forbids the sale of mifepristone and misoprostol, the two-drug regimen most commonly used for medical abortions. (Ignore any potential issues under the Due Process Clause.)

m. A statute that forbids the crossing of state lines for the purpose of obtaining an abortion. (Again, ignore any potential issues under the Due Process Clause.)

2. Suppose that, in addition to holding that the Affordable Care Act's minimum coverage provision exceeded Congress's commerce power, the Supreme Court in *NFIB v. Sebelius* also held (counterfactually) that the provision exceeded Congress's taxing power. Suppose further that Congress now wishes to enact a new Affordable Care Act, with a new minimum coverage provision, which accomplishes largely the same objectives in a manner consistent with the Supreme Court's commerce power holding in *NFIB*. Pursuant to this end, a Senator has proposed legislation that contains (as relevant) the following provision:

> Purchase of Health Care —Required Financing
>
> (a) It shall be unlawful for any person to purchase health care services (such as those provided by a hospital, physician, pharmacist, nurse, or other health care provider) except with minimally adequate health insurance (unless the service in question is not covered by such insurance).
>
> (b) A person violating subsection (a) shall pay a penalty to the United States Treasury, to be submitted on her annual income tax return, equal to the annual cost of minimally adequate health insurance.

In your view, would the Senator's proposal fall within Congress's power to regulate interstate commerce as construed by the Supreme Court in *NFIB*? Why or why not?

CHAPTER 10
THE TAXING AND SPENDING POWERS

The General Welfare Clause of Article I, §8, clause 1 provides that "[t]he Congress shall have the Power To lay and collect Taxes, Duties, Imposts and Excises, to pay the Debts and provide for the common Defence and general Welfare of the United States." The first part grants Congress the authority to impose taxes, while the second gives it the power to spend. The former is known as the taxing power, and the latter as the spending power.

To be clear, the General Welfare Clause does not grant Congress the power to enact all legislation to "provide for the . . . general welfare." Congress has no license to *regulate*—to impose mandatory rules governing conduct, the violation of which triggers some kind of legal sanction—for this purpose. Of course, Congress often enacts regulatory laws it believes promotes the nation's "general welfare." But the Constitution only allows Congress to enact regulatory statutes that, naturally enough, fit within one of the powers granting it the power to regulate. The General Welfare Clause is not such a power; it only gives Congress the powers to tax and spend.

A.   The Taxing Power

To understand the significance of the taxing power, it is important to see when the distinction between a tax and a regulation might matter. As already covered, Congress's regulatory authority has its limits. *Lopez*, *Morrison*, and *NFIB* reinforce this basic principle: some activities (or inactivities) are beyond Congress's power to regulate. But Congress might still have the authority to *influence* those behaviors through the imposition of an exaction, so long as the exaction falls within the taxing power.

* * *

EXAMPLE

Suppose Congress enacts a law requiring any person possessing a gun in a school zone to pay $1,000 to the federal government in the year in which the possession occurs. As *Lopez* makes clear, such a law would exceed Congress's authority to *regulate*—to forbid people from possessing a gun in a school zone, such that doing so would be unlawful. Thus, this law—as a *regulation* of behavior, with a $1,000 penalty imposed on violators—would be unconstitutional under *Lopez*. But the law would be constitutional if it were a *tax*: an exaction imposed on persons who engage in the taxed activity, but which does not make any activity impermissible. Just as Congress can impose a tax on persons who earn income, transfer property at death, or purchase gasoline, Congress could tax people for possessing guns in school zones. (Of course, implementing and enforcing such a tax might be hopelessly impractical—but the law would be within Congress's enumerated powers.)

* * *

The Constitution imposes no subject matter limitations on Congress's taxing power. But to fall within this authority, the statute must actually impose a tax—and *not* a financial penalty for violating a regulation. When, exactly, does a federal statutory provision constitute a "tax"? As it turns out, the constitutionality of the Affordable Care Act turned on this precise question.

As discussed in Chapter 9, the linchpin provision of the Affordable Care Act (or ACA) was the Minimum Essential Coverage Provision (the "individual mandate"). One of the ACA's principal objectives was to make health insurance market more affordable and accessible to individuals who lack coverage from their employer or the government. A critical component of that goal—designed to mitigate the adverse selection problem within the individual insurance market—was the individual mandate, which required all Americans (with a handful of exceptions) to obtain minimally adequate health insurance. If they did not, they were required to make a "shared responsibility payment" on their annual tax return. The relevant section of the ACA provided as follows:

"(1) In general — If a taxpayer who is an applicable individual, or an applicable individual for whom the taxpayer is liable under paragraph (3), fails to meet the requirement of subsection (a) for 1 or more months, then, except as provided in subsection (e), there is hereby imposed on the taxpayer a penalty with respect to such failures in the amount determined under subsection (c).

(2) Inclusion with return — Any penalty imposed by this section with respect to any month shall be included with a taxpayer's return under chapter 1 for the taxable year which includes such month."

Five justices concluded in *NFIB v. Sebelius* that this provision exceeded Congress's commerce power, and thus was unconstitutional as a *regulation*: Congress could not require individuals to purchase health insurance and penalize those violating this regulation. But the government also defended the individual mandate on an alternative ground: that it constituted a permissible exercise of the taxing power.

NFIB v. Sebelius is the most significant decision to construe the taxing power in American history. As you read this portion of the Court's opinion, please consider the following questions:

1. In what ways is Congress's power to tax broader than its power to regulate? In what ways is it narrower?

2. How would you articulate the constitutional test for distinguishing a "tax" from a "regulatory penalty" for purposes of the Constitution? When, exactly, will this distinction matter?

3. What is the significance of Congress's terminology—in denominating the provision either a "tax" or a "penalty"—to the analysis? Of Congress's express invocation of one of its enumerated powers?

4. Why did the Court conclude the "shared responsibility provision" fell within the taxing power? How was it distinguishable from the exaction the Court had invalidated in *Drexel Furniture*?

NFIB v. Sebelius
567 U.S. 519 (2012)

CHIEF JUSTICE ROBERTS delivered the opinion of the Court.

* * *

III

B

Because the Commerce Clause does not support the individual mandate, it is necessary to turn to the Government's second argument: that the mandate may be upheld as within Congress's enumerated power to "lay and collect Taxes." Art. I, §8, cl. 1.

The Government's tax power argument asks us to view the statute differently than we did in considering its commerce power theory. In making its Commerce Clause argument, the Government defended the mandate as a regulation requiring individuals to purchase health insurance. The Government does not claim that the taxing power allows Congress to issue such a command. Instead, the Government asks us to read the mandate not as ordering individuals to buy insurance, but rather as imposing a tax on those who do not buy that product. . . .

Under the mandate, if an individual does not maintain health insurance, the only consequence is that he must make an additional payment to the IRS when he pays his taxes. That, according to the Government, means the mandate can be regarded as establishing a condition—not owning health insurance—that triggers a tax—the required payment to the IRS. Under that theory, the mandate is not a legal command to buy insurance. Rather, it makes going without insurance just another thing the Government taxes, like buying gasoline or earning income. And if the mandate is in effect just a tax hike on certain taxpayers who do not have health insurance, it may be within Congress's constitutional power to tax.

The question is not whether that is the most natural interpretation of the mandate, but only whether it is a "fairly possible" one. As we have explained, "every reasonable construction must be resorted to, in order to save a statute from unconstitutionality." *Hooper v. California*, 155 U.S. 648, 657 (1895). . . .

C

The exaction the Affordable Care Act imposes on those without health insurance looks like a tax in many respects. The "[s]hared responsibility

233

payment," as the statute entitles it, is paid into the Treasury by "taxpayer[s]" when they file their tax returns. It does not apply to individuals who do not pay federal income taxes because their household income is less than the filing threshold in the Internal Revenue Code. For taxpayers who do owe the payment, its amount is determined by such familiar factors as taxable income, number of dependents, and joint filing status. The requirement to pay is found in the Internal Revenue Code and enforced by the IRS, which . . . must assess and collect it "in the same manner as taxes." This process yields the essential feature of any tax: it produces at least some revenue for the Government. *United States v. Kahriger*, 345 U.S. 22, n.4 (1953). Indeed, the payment is expected to raise about $4 billion per year by 2017.

It is of course true that the Act describes the payment as a "penalty," not a "tax." But [that label] does not determine whether the payment may be viewed as an exercise of Congress's taxing power. [Congress's choice of label] does not control whether an exaction is within Congress's constitutional power to tax.

Our precedent reflects this: In 1922, we decided two challenges to the "Child Labor Tax" on the same day. In the first, we held that a suit to enjoin collection of the so-called tax was barred by the Anti-Injunction Act. *George*, 259 U. S., at 20. Congress knew that suits to obstruct taxes had to await payment under the Anti-Injunction Act; Congress called the child labor tax a tax; Congress therefore intended the Anti-Injunction Act to apply. In the second case, however, we held that the same exaction, although labeled a tax, was not in fact authorized by Congress's taxing power. *Drexel Furniture*, 259 U. S., at 38. That constitutional question was not controlled by Congress's choice of label.

We have similarly held that exactions not labeled taxes nonetheless were authorized by Congress's power to tax. In the *License Tax Cases*, for example, we held that federal licenses to sell liquor and lottery tickets—for which the licensee had to pay a fee—could be sustained as exercises of the taxing power. 5 Wall., at 471. And in *New York v. United States* we upheld as a tax a "surcharge" on out-of-state nuclear waste shipments, a portion of which was paid to the Federal Treasury. 505 U. S., at 171. We thus ask whether the shared responsibility payment falls within Congress's taxing power, "[d]isregarding the designation of the exaction, and viewing its substance and application." *United States v. Constantine*, 296 U.S. 287, 294 (1935).

Our cases confirm this functional approach. For example, in *Drexel Furniture*, we focused on three practical characteristics of the so-called tax on employing child laborers that convinced us the "tax" was actually a penalty. First, the tax imposed an exceedingly heavy burden—10 percent of a company's net income—on those who employed children, no matter how small their infraction. Second, it imposed that exaction only on those who knowingly employed underage laborers. Such scienter requirements are typical of punitive statutes, because Congress often wishes to punish only those who intentionally break the law. Third, this "tax" was enforced in part by the Department of Labor, an agency responsible for punishing violations of labor laws, not collecting revenue. 259 U. S., at 36–37; see also, e.g., *Kurth Ranch*, 511 U. S., at 780–782 (considering, *inter alia*, the amount of the exaction, and the fact that it was imposed for violation of a separate criminal law).

The same analysis here suggests that the shared responsibility payment may for constitutional purposes be considered a tax, not a penalty: First, for most Americans the amount due will be far less than the price of insurance, and, by statute, it can never be more.[14] It may often be a reasonable financial decision to make the payment rather than purchase insurance, unlike the "prohibitory" financial punishment in *Drexel Furniture*. 259 U. S., at 37. Second, the individual mandate contains no scienter requirement. Third, the payment is collected solely by the IRS through the normal means of taxation—except that the Service is not allowed to use those means most suggestive of a punitive sanction, such as criminal prosecution. The reasons the Court in *Drexel Furniture* held that what was called a "tax" there was a penalty support the conclusion that what is called a "penalty" here may be viewed as a tax.[15]

None of this is to say that the payment is not intended to affect individual conduct. Although the payment will raise considerable revenue, it is plainly designed to expand health insurance coverage. But taxes that seek to influence conduct are nothing new. Some of our earliest federal taxes sought to deter the purchase of imported manufactured goods in order to foster the growth of domestic industry. Today, federal and state taxes can compose more than half the retail price of cigarettes, not just to raise more money, but to encourage people to quit smoking. And we have upheld such obviously regulatory measures as taxes on selling marijuana and sawed-off shotguns. See *United States v. Sanchez*, 340 U.S. 42–45 (1950); *Sonzinsky v. United States*, 300 U.S. 506, 513 (1937). Indeed, "[e]very tax is in some measure regulatory. To some extent it interposes an economic impediment to the activity taxed as compared with others not taxed." *Sonzinsky*, supra, at 513. That §5000A seeks to shape decisions about whether to buy health insurance does not mean that it cannot be a valid exercise of the taxing

---

[14] In 2016, for example, individuals making $35,000 a year are expected to owe the IRS about $60 for any month in which they do not have health insurance. Someone with an annual income of $100,000 a year would likely owe about $200. The price of a qualifying insurance policy is projected to be around $400 per month.

[15] We do not suggest that any exaction lacking a scienter requirement and enforced by the IRS is within the taxing power. Congress could not, for example, expand its authority to impose criminal fines by creating strict liability offenses enforced by the IRS rather than the FBI. But the fact the exaction here is paid like a tax, to the agency that collects taxes—rather than, for example, exacted by Department of Labor inspectors after ferreting out willful malfeasance—suggests that this exaction may be viewed as a tax.

power.

In distinguishing penalties from taxes, this Court has explained that "if the concept of penalty means anything, it means punishment for an unlawful act or omission." *United States v. Reorganized CF&I Fabricators of Utah, Inc.*, 518 U.S. 213, 224 (1996); see also *United States v. La Franca*, 282 U.S. 568, 572 (1931) ("[A] penalty, as the word is here used, is an exaction imposed by statute as punishment for an unlawful act"). While the individual mandate clearly aims to induce the purchase of health insurance, it need not be read to declare that failing to do so is unlawful. Neither the Act nor any other law attaches negative legal consequences to not buying health insurance, beyond requiring a payment to the IRS. The Government agrees with that reading, confirming that if someone chooses to pay rather than obtain health insurance, they have fully complied with the law.

Indeed, it is estimated that four million people each year will choose to pay the IRS rather than buy insurance. We would expect Congress to be troubled by that prospect if such conduct were unlawful. That Congress apparently regards such extensive failure to comply with the mandate as tolerable suggests that Congress did not think it was creating four million outlaws. It suggests instead that the shared responsibility payment merely imposes a tax citizens may lawfully choose to pay in lieu of buying health insurance.

The plaintiffs contend that Congress's choice of language—stating that individuals "shall" obtain insurance or pay a "penalty"—requires reading §5000A as punishing unlawful conduct, even if that interpretation would render the law unconstitutional. We have rejected a similar argument before. In *New York v. United States* we examined a statute providing that "[e]ach State shall be responsible for providing . . . for the disposal of . . . low-level radioactive waste." 505 U. S., at 169. A State that shipped its waste to another State was exposed to surcharges by the receiving State, a portion of which would be paid over to the Federal Government. And a State that did not adhere to the statutory scheme faced "[p]enalties for failure to comply," including increases in the surcharge. *New York*, 505 U. S., at 152–153. New York urged us to read the statute as a federal command that the state legislature enact legislation to dispose of its waste, which would have violated the Constitution. To avoid that outcome, we interpreted the statute to impose only "a series of incentives" for the State to take responsibility for its waste. We then sustained the charge paid to the Federal Government as an exercise of the taxing power. *Id.*, at 169–174. We see no insurmountable obstacle to a similar approach here.

The joint dissenters argue that we cannot uphold §5000A as a tax because Congress did not "frame" it as such. In effect, they contend that even if the Constitution permits Congress to do exactly what we interpret this statute to do, the law must be struck down because Congress used the wrong labels. An example may help illustrate why labels should not control here. Suppose Congress enacted a statute providing that every taxpayer who owns a house without energy efficient windows must pay $50 to the IRS. The amount due is adjusted based on factors such as taxable income and joint filing status, and is paid along with the taxpayer's income tax return. Those whose income is below the filing threshold need not pay. The required payment is not called a "tax," a "penalty," or anything else. No one would doubt that this law imposed a tax, and was within Congress's power to tax. That conclusion should not change simply because Congress used the word "penalty" to describe the payment. Interpreting such a law to be a tax would hardly "[i]mpos[e] a tax through judicial legislation." Rather, it would give practical effect to the Legislature's enactment.

Our precedent demonstrates that Congress had the power to impose the exaction in §5000A under the taxing power, and that §5000A need not be read to do more than impose a tax. That is sufficient to sustain it. The "question of the constitutionality of action taken by Congress does not depend on recitals of the power which it undertakes to exercise." *Woods v. Cloyd W. Miller Co.*, 333 U. S. 138, 144 (1948). . . .

There may, however, be a more fundamental objection to a tax on those who lack health insurance. Even if only a tax, the payment under §5000A(b) remains a burden that the Federal Government imposes for an omission, not an act. If it is troubling to interpret the Commerce Clause as authorizing Congress to regulate those who abstain from commerce, perhaps it should be similarly troubling to permit Congress to impose a tax for not doing something.

Three considerations allay this concern. First, and most importantly, it is abundantly clear the Constitution does not guarantee that individuals may avoid taxation through inactivity. A capitation, after all, is a tax that every-one must pay simply for existing, and capitations are expressly contemplated by the Constitution. The Court today holds that our Constitution protects us from federal regulation under the Commerce Clause so long as we abstain from the regulated activity. But from its creation, the Constitution has made no such promise with respect to taxes.

Whether the mandate can be upheld under the Commerce Clause is a question about the scope of federal authority. Its answer depends on whether Congress can exercise what all acknowledge to be the novel course of directing individuals to purchase insurance. Congress's use of the Taxing Clause to encourage buying something is, by contrast, not new. Tax incentives already promote, for example, purchasing homes and professional educations. Sustaining the mandate as a tax depends only on whether Congress has properly exercised its taxing power to encourage purchasing health insurance, not whether it can. Upholding the individual mandate under the Taxing Clause thus does not recognize any new federal power. It determines that Congress has used an existing one.

Second, Congress's ability to use its taxing power to influence conduct is not without limits. A few of our cases policed these limits aggressively, invalidating punitive exactions obviously designed to regulate behavior otherwise regarded at the time as beyond federal authority. See, e.g., *United States v. Butler*, 297 U.S. 1 (1936); *Drexel Furniture*, 259 U.S. 20. More often and more recently we have declined to closely examine the regulatory motive or effect of revenue-raising measures. See *Kahriger*, 345 U. S., at 27–31. We have nonetheless maintained that "there comes a time in the extension of the penalizing features of the so-called tax when it loses its character as such and becomes a mere penalty with the characteristics of regulation and punishment." *Kurth Ranch*, 511 U. S., at 779.

We have already explained that the shared responsibility payment's practical characteristics pass muster as a tax under our narrowest interpretations of the taxing power. Because the tax at hand is within even those strict limits, we need not here decide the precise point at which an exaction becomes so punitive that the taxing power does not authorize it. It remains true, however, that the "power to tax is not the power to destroy while this Court sits." *Oklahoma Tax Comm'n v. Texas Co.*, 336 U.S. 342, 364 (1949).

Third, although the breadth of Congress's power to tax is greater than its power to regulate commerce, the taxing power does not give Congress the same degree of control over individual behavior. Once we recognize that Congress may regulate a particular decision under the Commerce Clause, the Federal Government can bring its full weight to bear. Congress may simply command individuals to do as it directs. An individual who disobeys may be subjected to criminal sanctions. Those sanctions can include not only fines and imprisonment, but all the attendant consequences of being branded a criminal: deprivation of otherwise protected civil rights, such as the right to bear arms or vote in elections; loss of employment opportunities; social stigma; and severe disabilities in other controversies, such as custody or immigration disputes.

By contrast, Congress's authority under the taxing power is limited to requiring an individual to pay money into the Federal Treasury, no more. If a tax is properly paid, the Government has no power to compel or punish individuals subject to it. We do not make light of the severe burden that taxation—especially taxation motivated by a regulatory purpose—can impose. But imposition of a tax nonetheless leaves an individual with a lawful choice to do or not do a certain act, so long as he is willing to pay a tax levied on that choice.[11]

---

[11] Of course, individuals do not have a lawful choice not to pay a tax due, and may sometimes face prosecution for failing to do so (although not for declining to make the shared responsibility payment). But that does not show that the tax restricts the lawful choice whether to undertake or forgo the activity on which the tax is predicated. Those subject to the individual mandate may lawfully forgo health insurance and pay higher taxes, or buy health insurance and

The Affordable Care Act's requirement that certain individuals pay a financial penalty for not obtaining health insurance may reasonably be characterized as a tax. Because the Constitution permits such a tax, it is not our role to forbid it, or to pass upon its wisdom or fairness.

D

The Federal Government does not have the power to order people to buy health insurance. Section 5000A would therefore be unconstitutional if read as a command. The Federal Government does have the power to impose a tax on those without health insurance. Section 5000A is therefore constitutional, because it can reasonably be read as a tax.

*   *   *

Notes on *NFIB v. Sebelius*

1. *The difference between a "tax" and a "regulatory penalty"*: Because five justices had concluded that the minimum essential coverage provision exceeded the commerce power, the constitutionality of §5000A hinged on whether it could be justified as a constitutional exercise of the taxing power. That is, the question was whether §5000A—though impermissible as a "regulatory penalty"—could nonetheless qualify as a "tax" for purposes of the taxing power. A regulatory penalty is a sanction (whether civil or criminal) imposed for violating a *regulation*—a coercive rule governing conduct that deems a violation of that rule unlawful. For example, the federal Fair Debt Collection Practices Act prohibits various practices that Congress has deemed "unfair" and grants the Federal Trade Commission (FTC) the authority to enforce the Act. If the FTC concludes a debt collector has violated the Act and orders the debt collector to pay some amount to the U.S. government as a sanction for its violations, the payment would constitute a regulatory penalty. The Act makes unfair debt collection practices *unlawful*, and it authorizes the FTC to impose financial penalties for transgressing its terms.

By contrast, a tax is a financial liability triggered by a certain act (or failure to act)—an act (or failure to act) that generally is *completely lawful*. A tax is *not* triggered by the violation of a governing, coercive rule of conduct. For instance, when a person earns income in the United States, she typically owes an income tax to the federal government. If a single person earns $100,000 in 2022, she will owe roughly $18,000 in federal income taxes; earning the $100,000 is entirely lawful, but it triggers a tax liability. The $18,000 she must remit to the U.S. Treasury is considered a tax (and not a penalty) because that $18,000 liability is not triggered by the taxpayer's having done anything prohibited by law. Of course, the failure to pay a valid tax liability is itself unlawful—but that is distinct from the initial imposition of the tax. To

---

pay lower taxes. The only thing they may not lawfully do is not buy health insurance and not pay the resulting tax.

continue this example, the taxpayer's failure to pay the $18,000 to the IRS would be unlawful, but the earning of the $100,000 (which triggered the $18,000 tax liability) would not be.

In this example, the difference between a tax and a penalty is relatively clear. In cases like *NFIB v. Sebelius* (and many of the cases cited by the Court in its opinion), the line between the two was less obvious.

2. *Comparing the breadth of Congress's regulatory and taxing powers*: When Congress regulates activity, it must act within one of the enumerated powers granting it regulatory authority, such as the power "[t]o regulate Commerce . . . among the several States" or "[t]o make Rules for the Government and Regulation of the land and naval Forces." These powers each have a textually-based subject-matter limitation. For example, Congress cannot use its power "[t]o provide for the Punishment of counterfeiting the Securities and Current Coin of the United States" to regulate the provision of abortions; any legislation enacted pursuant to this power must have some relationship to counterfeiting. By contrast, the taxing power has no subject-matter constraints. Its only limitation concerns the *means* Congress has employed: *the provision must actually be a tax.* Congress can tax any activity, provided the tax does not run afoul of one of the Constitution's other protections, such as the Free Speech Clause. (A tax that targets newspapers, for instance, might well be unconstitutional—not because it exceeds the taxing power, but because it violates the First Amendment.)

3. *Comparing the depth of Congress's regulatory and taxing powers*: At the same time, the *depth* of the taxing power is much shallower than Congress's regulatory powers. When Congress validly regulates an activity, it can attach nearly any kind of consequence to the violation of that regulation. As the Court recognized in *NFIB*, "[o]nce we recognize that Congress may regulate a particular decision under the Commerce Clause, the Federal Government can bring its full weight to bear. Congress may simply command individuals to do as it directs." This includes attaching harsh criminal penalties, such as lengthy prison terms and the loss of various civil rights. By contrast, when Congress imposes a tax, the only action it can demand is the remittance of a payment: "Congress's authority under the taxing power is limited to requiring an individual to pay money into the Federal Treasury, no more. If a tax is properly paid, the Government has no power to compel or punish individuals subject to it."

4. *What made §5000A a "tax" for constitutional purposes?*: Why did the Court ultimately conclude that the ACA's shared responsibility provision qualified as a "tax" for purposes of the taxing power? There appear to be two basic steps to the analysis. First, there are two *essential* characteristics that all taxes share: they do not render the taxed activity unlawful, and they raise at least *some* revenue for the government. The shares responsibility provision met this standard; no legal consequences attached to the failure to obtain health insurance other than the obligation to make the payment, and it was expected to produce roughly $4 billion in revenue annually.

Second, the Court explained that whether a given provision constitutes a tax depends not the label Congress has affixed to it, but on its "practical characteristics." Congress had plainly labeled the exaction imposed by §5000A a "penalty," but this was not determinative. What mattered was how the provision operated in practice. And the Court observed that the shared responsibility payment resembled a tax "in many respects." It was paid by "taxpayers" to the U.S. Treasury on their annual income tax returns; it was codified in the Internal Revenue Code; it was enforced by the Internal Revenue Service; it was assessed and collected by the IRS "in the same manner as taxes"; the amount owed was computed using several criteria familiar to the computation of tax liabilities, including adjusted gross income, and the size of the taxpayer's household, and the number of the taxpayer's dependents; and, again, it was projected to generate considerable revenue. Collectively, these "practical characteristics" indicated that the shared responsibility payment qualified as a "tax" for purposes of the taxing power.

5. *The significance of Congress's motive*: All knew that Congress's true reason for including the shared responsibility provision in the ACA was to alter individuals' behavior. Specifically, the ACA's other important provisions regulating the private insurance market—requiring insurers to sell coverage based on a community's characteristics (rather than an individual's health status) and prohibiting insurers from excluding coverage of preexisting conditions—were vulnerable to failing if only unhealthy people purchased the regulated insurance plans. (There would have been an adverse selection problem, potentially leading to a "death spiral" in the individual insurance market.) The ACA needed to create an incentive for healthy people to purchase insurance in order to balance out the risk pool and make it financially viable for private insurers to offer individual policies at affordable prices. In this sense, Congress's primary purpose in enacting the provision had nothing to do with raising revenue, the typical reason for imposing a tax.

But the Court in *NFIB* held that this fact was beside the point. All taxes—by making the taxed activity more expensive—affect taxpayers' behavior. And surely Congress is aware of these behavioral effects when it decides to impose an exaction. Thus, every tax provision will have a mix of purposes to alter behavior and raise revenue. (Consider taxes on cigarettes or gasoline, which plainly are intended *both* to raise revenue and reduce the prevalence of the taxed activity.) The fact that Congress, in enacting §5000A, was chiefly interested in creating an incentive for individuals to acquire health coverage did not disqualify the provision from being a "tax."

6. *Distinguishing* **Drexel Furniture**: The most difficult analytic step for the Court was to distinguish the shared responsibility payment from the so-called "child labor tax" in *Drexel Furniture*, which the Court had invalidated as exceeding Congress's taxing power. The provision in *Drexel Furniture* required entities using child labor in their manufacturing operations to remit 10 percent of their gross revenue to the federal government. The Court in *NFIB* distinguished §5000A from that provision on three grounds:

1. The exaction in *Drexel Furniture* imposed an "exceedingly heavy burden," whereas the shared responsibility payment did not. Indeed, the shared responsibility payment could never exceed the cost of actually purchasing health insurance, and thus was permanently capped at a reasonable level. By contrast, the exaction in *Drexel Furniture* was 10 percent of the violator's gross revenues for the year, an amount that could be *huge* most businesses.

2. The shared responsibility payment contained no scienter requirement; it was due regardless of the taxpayer's knowledge or intent. By contrast, the exaction in *Drexel Furniture* was imposed only on the "knowing" use of child labor—a feature that indicated the exaction was intended to be a *punishment* for the violation of a regulation. (Taxes generally do not require the taxpayer to have knowingly engaged in the taxed activity.)

3. The shared responsibility payment was assessed, collected, and enforced by the IRS, the agency generally charged with enforcing the federal tax laws. By contrast, the exaction in *Drexel Furniture* was enforced by the Department of Labor, the arm of the Executive Branch charged with enforcing federal labor regulations.

Together, these three attributes—again, practical characteristics of the provision—distinguished §5000A from the exaction invalidated in *Drexel Furniture*. And because the shared responsibility payment possessed the essential attributes of a tax and practically operated like a tax, it constituted a permissible use of Congress's taxing power.

   7. *A postscript*: California v. Texas: Five years after the Court decided *NFIB* and upheld the minimum coverage provision as within the taxing power, Congress amended the ACA to reduce the shared responsibility payment to $0. (Congress did so after failing to repeal the ACA in its entirety.) Led by Texas, several states and two private individuals then filed suit seeking a declaration that the ACA was unconstitutional. They contended that, since the "tax penalty" for failing to acquire minimally adequate health coverage was $0, §5000A could no longer constitute a "tax." A constitutional tax, they argued, raised revenue, and §5000A no longer does so. The plaintiffs further argued that, because the minimum coverage provision was essential to the functioning of the ACA as a whole—such that Congress would not have wanted the ACA to become law absent §5000A—it was inseverable from the Act, such that the entire ACA must be declared unconstitutional.

   The Supreme Court turned away the challenge by holding that the plaintiffs lacked standing. *See California v. Texas*, 141 S. Ct. 2104 (2021). The private individuals lacked standing because they could not identify a judicial remedy that would redress their alleged injury—their felt obligation to purchase minimally adequate health coverage according to §5000A's apparent command. Congress's reduction of the tax penalty to $0 meant §5000A was unenforceable. The government could take no action against the plaintiffs for failing to comply, so there was no remedy a court could provide that would redress their asserted harm.

The states had alleged two distinct injuries. First, they claimed that §5000A induced more of their residents to enroll in state-run health insurance programs, thus imposing additional costs on them. The Court held, however, that the states had failed to produce any evidence that the now-unenforceable §5000A actually had any such impact. Alternatively, the states contended that—though they might not be harmed by §5000A itself—§5000A was inseverable from the rest of the ACA, and other provisions of the ACA (such as the requirement that employers provide health insurance to their employees) directly imposed additional costs on them. But the Court rejected this standing-through-inseverability theory, under which a plaintiff who is harmed by any provision of a statute would have standing to challenge every provision of the same statute, provided she contended the challenged provision was inseverable from the rest of the act. The injuries identified by the states all stemmed from provisions of the ACA that operated entirely independently of §5000A. The states would have standing to challenge those ACA provisions that directly affected them, but that did not mean they had any Article III injury traceable to §5000A.

* * *

PROBLEMS ON THE TAXING POWER

Please evaluate whether each of the following hypothetical (or not-so-hypothetical) federal statutes would fall within Congress's taxing power. Please ignore any complications arising from Article I, §2, clause 3 ("direct Taxes shall be apportioned among the several States which may be included within this Union, according to their respective Numbers") or Article I, §9, clause 4 ("No Capitation, or other direct, Tax shall be laid, unless in Proportion to the Census or Enumeration").

1. A federal statute requires passengers to wear approved face coverings on commercial flights within the United States, except when actively eating or drinking (or when doing so would pose a risk to the person's health). Under the statute, the knowing failure to do so is punishable by up to one year in prison, or a fine of $1,000, or both. A passenger who refused to wear a mask is determined to have violated the statute and ordered to pay $1,000 to the federal government.

2. A federal statute provides that every American 12 years of age or older "shall be vaccinated with a COVID vaccine that has been approved by the Food and Drug Administration." Under the terms of the statute, every U.S. resident shall submit proof of

vaccination (for themselves and their dependents) with their annual income tax return. (Persons with a health condition that prevents them from being vaccinated, or who have a sincere religious objection, are exempt from the requirement.) Persons failing to submit valid proof of vaccination are assessed an additional $250 on their tax return. The assessment is enforced by the Internal Revenue Service.

3. A federal statute imposes a new "wealth tax." Individuals with a total net worth exceeding $10 million are required to pay an annual tax equaling 1 percent of the current net value of all their assets, to the extent that value exceeds $10 million.

4. In 2023, Congress enacts a statute amending the Internal Revenue Code to increase the marginal income tax rates imposed on the highest-earning taxpayers. Under the revised code, taxpayers who earn more than $20 million in a year are subject to a tax of 75 percent on the portion of their income exceeding $20 million.

5. A federal statute forbids the "knowing substantial understatement of income" in filing an income tax return. (A "substantial understatement of income" is one that results in the taxpayer paying at least 20 percent less than what she actually owes.) Violation of the statute is punishable by up to 5 years in federal prison, penalties equal to 5 times the resulting underpayment of taxes, or both. Is this provision within the taxing power? Is it within Congress's enumerated powers? Explain.

* * *

B. The Spending Power

In addition to granting Congress the taxing power, the General Welfare Clause confers on Congress the authority to spend funds from the federal treasury: "The Congress shall have the Power . . . to pay the Debts and provide for the common Defence and general Welfare of the United States." In terms of pure practical impact, the spending power may be the most significant of Congress's enumerated powers. It supports much (or even most) of the federal government's actions, from Social Security to Medicaid to maintaining the U.S. military forces to the $1.9 trillion America Rescue Plan Act of 2021. And through conditional spending programs—by which Congress attaches conditions to the receipt of federal largesse—Congress has a means of accomplishing indirectly (through financial enticement) what it cannot do directly (through coercive regulation).

The Constitution also makes clear that the power to authorize the expenditure of federal funding is *exclusively* Congress's. Article I, §9, clause 7 states that "[n]o money shall be drawn from the treasury, but in consequence of appropriations made by law." Any dollar spent by the U.S. government must be "appropriate[d]" "by law," meaning pursuant to a statute enacted by Congress. The President, in administering the federal government, cannot spend any money that has not first been authorized by Congress. (This principle was at the core of the recent dispute between Congress and President Trump regarding the expenditure of funds to construct a physical barrier along the southern border.) Congress need not appropriate funds for the *precise purpose* for which it is used; the level of specificity necessary in the statute is governed by the nondelegation doctrine (discussed in Chapter 15). But the Executive Branch cannot spend a cent that Congress has not appropriated.

1. The Hamilton-Madison debate

At the time of the Constitution's framing, there was a lively debate between James Madison and Alexander Hamilton concerning the breadth of Congress's spending power. Madison contended that the spending power only permitted Congress to spend money to pursue those objectives otherwise enumerated in Article I, §8, such as to regulate interstate commerce or to establish post offices and post roads. Hamilton, by contrast, argued that the spending power constituted a separate and distinct legislative authority, limited only by the requirement that it be exercised by Congress for the nation's "general welfare."

The Supreme Court did not squarely address the question until 1936, when it embraced the Hamiltonian view: "[T]he power of Congress to authorize expenditure of public moneys for public purposes is not limited by the direct grants of legislative power found in the Constitution." *United States v. Butler*, 297 U.S. 1 (1936). The Court reaffirmed *Butler* a year later in *Steward Machine Co. v. Davis*, 301 U.S. 548 (1937), where it upheld the constitutionality of the Social Security Act—and has adhered to this understanding ever since. Thus, like the taxing power, the spending power is not constrained to the ends Congress is empowered to pursue through its *regulatory* powers. Rather, Congress can spend to pursue "the general welfare" without any connection to one of its other enumerated powers.

2. Federal spending for private individuals or entities

The majority of spending programs enacted by Congress are uncontroversial, at least as a constitutional matter (though many are hotly contested politically). Because Congress has the authority to spend for "the general welfare," there are almost no constitutional constraints on Congress's decisions regarding how to spend the public fisc. This is certainly true when the government is directly purchasing goods or services for its own use. If the federal government wishes to purchase 250 helicopters, it can generally negotiate whatever terms it pleases, just as any other purchaser could.

It is also generally true that, when the federal government provides funds to private individuals or organizations—whether to purchase goods or services, or merely to pursue the public good (for instance, by reducing poverty)—the government can dictate the terms of how those dollars are to be spent. For instance, if the federal government wishes to make grants to medical providers for purposes of family planning, it can specify that none of those funds are to be spent on procedures that terminate a pregnancy. (Medical providers, of course, can decide not to accept federal dollars with these sorts of strings attached; participation in a federal spending program is, by definition, voluntary.)

Some spending conditions have been held to violate individual rights protected by the Constitution. For instance, the Supreme Court recently held that a federal spending program violated the Free Speech Clause of the First Amendment when it required American non-governmental organizations—in order to qualify for federal funding for HIV and AIDS prevention work in foreign countries—to publicly state their support for the criminalization of prostitution. *Agency for Int'l Development v. Alliance for Open Society Int'l, Inc.*, 570 U. S. 205 (2013). The condition trenched on the organizations' right to free speech, and its relationship to the purposes of the underlying spending program was attenuated. It thus amounted to an "unconstitutional condition."

But a constitutional problem like that in *Alliance for Open Society* more concerns the individual right in question (such as the right to free speech), and not so much the breadth of the spending power. From an Article I perspective, the only limitation on the provision of federal funding to private parties is that it further the "general welfare." As a practical matter, this is not really a limitation at all.

3. Conditional spending programs and the states

The most interesting constitutional questions regarding the spending power arise when Congress uses federal funds to encourage state or local governments to take certain actions. As we will see, the so-called "anti-commandeering principle" forbids Congress from directly commanding states or their political subdivisions to enact or enforce regulations conforming to federal instructions. That is, Congress cannot simply command states to enact laws, or to regulate their citizens, in a particular fashion. But the spending power offers Congress a mechanism for eliding this limitation: Congress can induce states to govern in a particular way by dangling the enticement of federal funds in front of them—with conditions attached.

The decision setting out the framework for analyzing the constitutionality of such conditional spending programs are *South Dakota v. Dole*, 483 U.S. 203 (1987). At issue in *Dole* was the National Minimum Drinking Age Amendment, which added a new condition to the federal government's provision of funding to state governments for highway construction. (Congress grants this money to states through annual appropriations, which the states then spend on road construction and improvements.) The Act provided that the federal government would withhold 5 percent of a state's otherwise available federal highway dollars if the state failed to increase its legal drinking age to at least 21. South Dakota—which permitted residents 19 and older to purchase low-alcohol-content beer—argued that this condition exceeded Congress's spending power.

To be clear, the question in *Dole* was not whether Congress could simply *mandate* that the states raise their drinking ages to 21. Nor was the question whether Congress could impose a national drinking age of 21 as a matter of federal law. (Either of those alternatives would have constituted *regulation*.) Rather, the statute in *Dole* presented the states with a choice, at least in form, that entailed some financial consequences. As you read *Dole*, please consider the following questions:

1. What are the "several general restrictions" on Congress's authority to enact a conditional spending program involving the states? What is the rationale for each of those requirements?

2. Which of these requirements were at issue in *Dole*? Why?

3. Why did the Court conclude that the spending condition was "germane" to the purpose of the federal spending program? Are you convinced?

4. How did Justice O'Connor's test for the constitutionality of conditional spending programs differ from the majority's? Would it have produced a different result in *Dole*?

5. Millions of dollars were at stake for a state that did not comply with the spending condition at issue in *Dole*. Why was that not sufficient to render the condition impermissibly "coercive"?

South Dakota v. Dole
483 U.S. 203 (1987)

CHIEF JUSTICE REHNQUIST delivered the opinion of the Court.

Petitioner South Dakota permits persons 19 years of age or older to purchase beer containing up to 3.2% alcohol. In 1984 Congress enacted 23 U.S.C. §158, which directs the Secretary of Transportation to withhold a percentage of federal highway funds otherwise allocable from States "in which the purchase or public possession . . . of any alcoholic beverage by a person who is less than twenty-one years of age is lawful." The State sued in United States District Court seeking a declaratory judgment that §158 violates the constitutional limitations on congressional exercise of the spending power. . . . Congress has acted indirectly under its spending power to encourage uniformity in the States' drinking ages. As we explain below, we find this legislative effort within constitutional bounds even if Congress may not regulate drinking ages directly.

The Constitution empowers Congress to "lay and collect Taxes, Duties, Imposts, and Excises, to pay the Debts and provide for the common Defence and general Welfare of the United States." Art. I, § 8, cl. 1. Incident to this power, Congress may attach conditions on the receipt of federal funds, and has repeatedly employed the power "to further broad policy objectives by conditioning receipt of federal moneys upon compliance by the recipient with federal statutory and administrative directives." *Fullilove v. Klutznick*, 448 U.S. 448, 474 (1980) (opinion of Burger, C. J.). The breadth of this power was made clear in *United States v. Butler*, 297 U.S. 1, 66 (1936), where the Court, resolving a longstanding debate over the scope of the Spending Clause, determined that "the power of Congress to authorize expenditure of public moneys for public purposes is not limited by the direct grants of legislative power found in the Constitution." Thus, objectives not thought to be within Article I's "enumerated legislative fields," may nevertheless be attained through the use of the spending power and the conditional grant of federal funds.

The spending power is of course not unlimited, but is instead subject to several general restrictions articulated in our cases. The first of these limitations is derived from the language of the Constitution itself: the exercise of the spending power must be in pursuit of "the general welfare." See *Helvering v. Davis*, 301 U.S. 619, 640–641 (1937); *United States v. Butler*, supra, at 65. In considering whether a particular expenditure is intended to serve general public purposes, courts should defer substantially to the judgment of Congress. *Helvering v. Davis*, supra, at 640, 645.[2] Second, we have required that if Congress desires to condition the States' receipt of federal funds, it "must do so unambiguously . . . , enabl[ing] the States to exercise their choice knowingly, cognizant of the consequences of their participation." *Pennhurst State School and Hospital v. Halderman*, supra, at 17. Third, our cases have suggested (without significant elaboration) that conditions on federal grants might be illegitimate if they are unrelated "to the federal interest in particular national projects or programs." *Massachusetts v. United States*, 435 U.S. 444, 461 (1978) (plurality opinion). Finally, we have noted that other constitutional provisions may provide an independent bar to the conditional grant of federal funds. *Lawrence County v. Lead-Deadwood School Dist.*, 469 U.S. 256, 269–270 (1985); *Buckley v. Valeo*, 424 U.S. 1, 91 (1976) (per curiam); *King v. Smith*, 392 U.S. 309, 333, n. 34 (1968).

South Dakota does not seriously claim that §158 is inconsistent with any of the first three restrictions mentioned above. We can readily conclude that the provision is designed to serve the general welfare, especially in light of the fact that "the concept of welfare or the opposite is shaped by Congress." *Helvering v. Davis*, supra, at 645. Congress found that the differing drinking ages in the States created particular incentives for young persons to combine their desire to drink with their ability to drive, and that this interstate problem required a national solution. The means it chose to address this dangerous situation were reasonably calculated to advance the general welfare. The conditions upon which States receive the funds, moreover, could not be more clearly stated by Congress. And the State itself, rather than challenging the germaneness of the condition to federal purposes, admits that it "has never contended that the congressional action was . . . unrelated to a national concern in the absence of the Twenty-first Amendment."

---

[2] The level of deference to the congressional decision is such that the Court has more recently questioned whether "general welfare" is a judicially enforceable restriction at all.

Indeed, the condition imposed by Congress is directly related to one of the main purposes for which highway funds are expended—safe interstate travel.[3] This goal of the interstate highway system had been frustrated by varying drinking ages among the States. A Presidential commission appointed to study alcohol-related accidents and fatalities on the Nation's highways concluded that the lack of uniformity in the States' drinking ages created "an incentive to drink and drive" because "young persons commut[e] to border States where the drinking age is lower." Presidential Commission on Drunk Driving, Final Report 11 (1983). By enacting §158, Congress conditioned the receipt of federal funds in a way reasonably calculated to address this particular impediment to a purpose for which the funds are expended.

The remaining question about the validity of §158—and the basic point of disagreement between the parties—is whether the Twenty-first Amendment constitutes an "independent constitutional bar" to the conditional grant of federal funds. Petitioner, relying on its view that the Twenty-first Amendment prohibits direct regulation of drinking ages by Congress, asserts that "Congress may not use the spending power to regulate that which it is prohibited from regulating directly under the Twenty-first Amendment." But our cases show that this "independent constitutional bar" limitation on the spending power is not of the kind petitioner suggests. *United States v. Butler*, supra, at 66, for example, established that the constitutional limitations on Congress when exercising its spending power are less exacting than those on its authority to regulate directly.

We have also held that a perceived Tenth Amendment limitation on congressional regulation of state affairs did not concomitantly limit the range of conditions legitimately placed on federal grants. In *Oklahoma v. Civil Service Comm'n*, 330 U.S. 127 (1947), the Court considered the validity of the Hatch Act insofar as it was applied to political activities of state officials whose employment was financed in whole or in part with federal funds. The State contended that an order under this provision to withhold certain federal funds unless a state official was removed invaded its sovereignty in violation of the Tenth Amendment. Though finding that "the United States is not concerned with, and has no power to regulate, local political activities as such of state officials," the Court nevertheless held that the Federal Government "does have power to fix the terms upon which its money allotments to states shall be disbursed." *Id.*, at 143. The Court found no violation of the State's

---

[3] Our cases have not required that we define the outer bounds of the "germaneness" or "relatedness" limitation on the imposition of conditions under the spending power. *Amici* urge that we take this occasion to establish that a condition on federal funds is legitimate only if it relates directly to the purpose of the expenditure to which it is attached. Because petitioner has not sought such a restriction, and because we find any such limitation on conditional federal grants satisfied in this case in any event, we do not address whether conditions less directly related to the particular purpose of the expenditure might be outside the bounds of the spending power.

sovereignty because the State could, and did, adopt "the 'simple expedient' of not yielding to what she urges is federal coercion. The offer of benefits to a state by the United States dependent upon cooperation by the state with federal plans, assumedly for the general welfare, is not unusual." *Id.*, at 143–144.

These cases establish that the "independent constitutional bar" limitation on the spending power is not, as petitioner suggests, a prohibition on the indirect achievement of objectives which Congress is not empowered to achieve directly. Instead, we think that the language in our earlier opinions stands for the unexceptionable proposition that the power may not be used to induce the States to engage in activities that would themselves be unconstitutional. Thus, for example, a grant of federal funds conditioned on invidiously discriminatory state action or the infliction of cruel and unusual punishment would be an illegitimate exercise of the Congress' broad spending power. But no such claim can be or is made here. Were South Dakota to succumb to the blandishments offered by Congress and raise its drinking age to 21, the State's action in so doing would not violate the constitutional rights of anyone.

Our decisions have recognized that in some circumstances the financial inducement offered by Congress might be so coercive as to pass the point at which "pressure turns into compulsion." *Steward Machine Co. v. Davis*, supra, at 590. Here, however, Congress has directed only that a State desiring to establish a minimum drinking age lower than 21 lose a relatively small percentage of certain federal highway funds. Petitioner contends that the coercive nature of this program is evident from the degree of success it has achieved. We cannot conclude, however, that a conditional grant of federal money of this sort is unconstitutional simply by reason of its success in achieving the congressional objective.

When we consider, for a moment, that all South Dakota would lose if she adheres to her chosen course as to a suitable minimum drinking age is 5% of the funds otherwise obtainable under specified highway grant programs, the argument as to coercion is shown to be more rhetoric than fact. As we said a half century ago in *Steward Machine Co. v. Davis*:

> "[E]very rebate from a tax when conditioned upon conduct is in some measure a temptation. But to hold that motive or temptation is equivalent to coercion is to plunge the law in endless difficulties. The outcome of such a doctrine is the acceptance of a philosophical determinism by which choice becomes impossible. Till now the law has been guided by a robust common sense which assumes the freedom of the will as a working hypothesis in the solution of its problems." 301 U.S., at 589–590.

Here Congress has offered relatively mild encouragement to the States to enact higher minimum drinking ages than they would otherwise choose. But the enactment of such laws remains the prerogative of the States not merely in theory but in fact. Even if Congress might lack the power to impose a national minimum drinking age directly, we conclude that encouragement to state action found in §158 is a valid use of the spending power. . . .

JUSTICE O'CONNOR, dissenting.

The Court today upholds the National Minimum Drinking Age Amendment as a valid exercise of the spending power conferred by Article I, §8. But §158 is not a condition on spending reasonably related to the expenditure of federal funds and cannot be justified on that ground. . . .

My disagreement with the Court is relatively narrow on the spending power issue: it is a disagreement about the application of a principle rather than a disagreement on the principle itself. [In particular,] the Court's application of the requirement that the condition imposed be reasonably related to the purpose for which the funds are expended is cursory and unconvincing. We have repeatedly said that Congress may condition grants under the spending power only in ways reasonably related to the purpose of the federal program. In my view, establishment of a minimum drinking age of 21 is not sufficiently related to interstate highway construction to justify so conditioning funds appropriated for that purpose. . . .

[T]he Court asserts the reasonableness of the relationship between the supposed purpose of the expenditure—"safe interstate travel"—and the drinking age condition. The Court reasons that Congress wishes that the roads it builds may be used safely, that drunken drivers threaten highway safety, and that young people are more likely to drive while under the influence of alcohol under existing law than would be the case if there were a uniform national drinking age of 21. It hardly needs saying, however, that if the purpose of §158 is to deter drunken driving, it is far too over- and under-inclusive. It is over-inclusive because it stops teenagers from drinking even when they are not about to drive on interstate highways. It is under-inclusive because teenagers pose only a small part of the drunken driving problem in this Nation.

When Congress appropriates money to build a highway, it is entitled to insist that the highway be a safe one. But it is not entitled to insist as a condition of the use of highway funds that the State impose or change regulations in other areas of the State's social and economic life because of an attenuated or tangential relationship to highway use or safety. Indeed, if the rule were otherwise, the Congress could effectively regulate almost any area of a State's social, political, or economic life on the theory that use of the interstate transportation system is somehow enhanced. If, for example, the United States were to condition highway moneys upon moving the state capital, I suppose it might argue that interstate transportation is facilitated by locating local governments in places easily accessible to interstate highways—or, conversely, that highways might become overburdened if they had to carry traffic to and from the state capital. In my mind, such a relationship is hardly more attenuated than the one which the Court finds supports §158.

251

There is a clear place at which the Court can draw the line between permissible and impermissible conditions on federal grants. . . .

The appropriate inquiry . . . is whether the spending requirement or prohibition is a condition on a grant or whether it is regulation. The difference turns on whether the requirement specifies in some way how the money should be spent, so that Congress' intent in making the grant will be effectuated. Congress has no power under the Spending Clause to impose requirements on a grant that go beyond specifying how the money should be spent. A requirement that is not such a specification is not a condition, but a regulation, which is valid only if it falls within one of Congress' delegated regulatory powers. . . .

If the spending power is to be limited only by Congress' notion of the general welfare, the reality, given the vast financial resources of the Federal Government, is that the Spending Clause gives "power to the Congress to tear down the barriers, to invade the states' jurisdiction, and to become a parliament of the whole people, subject to no restrictions save such as are self-imposed." *United States v. Butler*. This, of course, as *Butler* held, was not the Framers' plan and it is not the meaning of the Spending Clause. . . .

[A] condition that a State will raise its drinking age to 21 cannot fairly be said to be reasonably related to the expenditure of funds for highway construction. The only possible connection, highway safety, has nothing to do with how the funds Congress has appropriated are expended. Rather than a condition determining how federal highway money shall be expended, it is a regulation determining who shall be able to drink liquor. As such it is not justified by the spending power. . . .

* * *

Notes on *South Dakota v. Dole*

1. The constitutional test for conditional spending programs involving the states: In *Dole*, the Court articulated four (or really five) criteria that federal conditional spending programs involving the states must meet to constitute a valid exercise of the spending power: (1) the spending program must be in pursuit of the "general welfare"; (2) the conditions placed on states to receive the federal funds must be "unambiguous"; (3) the conditions must be "germane" to the purpose of the federal spending program; and (4) the conditions cannot independently violate any other constitutional provision. Near the conclusion of the *Dole* opinion, the Court also mentioned an additional criterion: (5) no spending condition can be "so coercive as to pass the point at which pressure turns into compulsion." A condition coercing states into taking particular actions would not be a valid exercise of the spending power because the essential characteristic that makes such conditions constitutional—and *not* regulations—is that that they are assumed *voluntarily* in exchange for federal funds. If the condition *compels* the states to take particular actions, they no longer meet this definition. Instead, they are *regulations*—mandates imposed on states to conform their behavior to a particular federal standard. As such, they would need to fall within an enumerated power giving Congress *regulatory* power. The power to spend would not suffice.

2. *The "general welfare"*: When does a federal spending program pursue the general welfare? Basically always. As the Court stated in *Dole*, "courts should defer substantially to the judgment of Congress" on this question. Indeed, a footnote in *Dole* suggested that the issue is effectively a nonjusticiable political question: "The level of deference to the congressional decision is such that the Court has more recently questioned whether 'general welfare' is a judicially enforceable restriction at all."

3. *"Unambiguous" conditions*: The Constitution also requires that conditions imposed on states as part of a federal spending program be "unambiguous." The idea is that the exchange of federal funds for the states' compliance with certain conditions is like a contract. Just as a contract requires a "meeting of the minds," so, too, must states be fully aware of any obligations they are undertaking when accepting federal dollars. This is especially true because of the constitutional stakes: states need to be apprised of the strings attached to federal funds before surrendering a portion of their independent sovereignty. This requirement is probably best understood as a rule of statutory interpretation—a rule about construing language in a statute (creating a spending program) that arguably imposes a condition. An ambiguously phrased condition would not render the program unconstitutional; it would just mean that the condition is unenforceable, not part of the "bargain." Congress would then be free to make the condition unambiguous (by amending the statute).

4. *Germaneness*: Perhaps the most important restriction on spending conditions is that they be "germane" to the spending program to which they are attached. The Court did not really explain the rationale behind this requirement. But the idea must be that, if there is no meaningful connection between the condition and the spending program, the condition cannot be justified as safeguarding the purposes of the spending program (or somehow ensuring that federal dollars be spent to pursue Congress's goals). Instead, "nongermane" spending conditions look like an opportunistic use of financial leverage, and thus should be treated as *regulations*.

Whatever the justification, the germaneness requirement appears to lack much bite. Consider its application in *Dole* itself. The Court concluded that the condition of increasing the state's drinking age to 21 was germane to the construction of highways because Congress had appropriated the highway funds not just to build roads, but to facilitate "safe interstate travel." And this purpose would be frustrated by drunk driving. More specifically, the lack of uniform state drinking ages creates an incentive for young adults to drive to other states to consume alcohol and then drive back to their home states on interstate highways. Thus, concluded the Court, the drinking-age condition was germane to the underlying purpose of constructing interstate highways. (Never mind that 18-to-20-year-olds in states with drinking ages of 18 were, at best, a tiny percentage of the drunk driving problem on interstate highways.)

In her dissent, Justice O'Connor argued that the germaneness requirement should be more exacting. To be sufficiently germane, she contended, the condition must be imposed on how the federal funds are actually spent: "The appropriate inquiry, then, is whether the spending requirement or prohibition is a condition on the grant or whether it is regulation. The difference turns on whether the requirement specifies in some way how the money should be spent, so that Congress' intent in making the grant will be effectuated." Notably, Justice O'Connor lost 8–1 on this point.

5. ***An "independent constitutional bar" to the conditional grant of federal funds***: The fourth criterion is whether there is an "independent constitutional bar" to the spending condition. As the Court explained in *Dole*, this factor does not prohibit Congress from achieving certain objectives that it would be unable to pursue directly. Rather, it merely

> "stands for the unexceptionable proposition that the power may not be used to induce the States to engage in activities that would themselves be unconstitutional. Thus, for example, a grant of federal funds conditioned on invidiously discriminatory state action or the infliction of cruel and unusual punishment would be an illegitimate exercise of the Congress' broad spending power."

This factor is thus largely superfluous; if a state were to comply with such a condition and violate the Constitution in the process, the state's action itself could be directly challenged as unconstitutional. This factor merely adds that Congress's imposition of such a condition exceeds the spending power.

6. ***"Coercive" spending conditions***: The final requirement mentioned in *Dole* is that the financial inducement offered by the federal government cannot rise to the level of "coercion." For if the condition is coercive, it crosses the line from being an inducement to being a mandate. And the constitutional legitimacy of conditional spending depends on states' having a choice; their participation must be *voluntary*. If the states have no choice—if they have been compelled by Congress—then the statute is really a command. The Court concluded that the condition in *Dole* was not coercive because those states refusing to increase their drinking ages to 21 only stood to lose 5 percent of their otherwise obtainable federal highway funds. To be sure, this was *millions* of dollars in federal funding. But to the Court, it was still just "relatively mild encouragement." South Dakota remained free to keep its drinking age at 18 and retain 95 percent of its federal highway funds.

Importantly, if a condition is coercive, this does not necessarily mean it is *unconstitutional*. Instead, it means the condition constitutes a *regulation* (because it is compelled). At that point, the question is whether the provision is valid under one of Congress's enumerated *regulatory* powers. (As we will see, though, the "anti-commandeering principle" generally dictates that Congress cannot command the states to take affirmative steps to regulate their citizens according to federal directives.)

*　*　*

4. Coercion: *NFIB v. Sebelius* and the ACA's Medicaid expansion

The most recent Supreme Court decision regarding Congress's spending power was yet another section of *NFIB v. Sebelius*, this part addressing the Affordable Care Act's expansion of the federal Medicaid program. In *NFIB*, the Court held for the first time in U.S. history that a federal spending condition was "coercive" and thus exceeded the spending power.

Medicaid is the joint federal-state spending program that offers health insurance to the indigent and the disabled. States are not required to participate in the program. But if they do, they must abide by a variety of standards to qualify for the associated federal funding. Medicaid is the single largest federal aid program to the states, accounting for roughly 45 percent of all federal grant-in-aid to state governments. It is the third largest federal domestic spending program (behind only Social Security and Medicare), and its present role in the states' finances is enormous. In fiscal year 2016, state governments collectively spent 15.9 percent of their general fund dollars on Medicaid, and the program accounted for 28.7 percent of state spending in total.

The Medicaid program imposes numerous requirements on participating states, and the ACA expansion of Medicaid imposed additional obligations (concerning those persons who needed to be covered and the scope of covered benefits). If a state fails to comply with these requirements,

> "the Secretary [of Health and Human Services] shall notify such State agency that further payments will not be made to the State (or, in his discretion, that payments will be limited to categories under or parts of the State plan not affected by such failure), until the Secretary is satisfied that there will no longer be any such failure to comply."

In their challenge to the ACA, 26 state governments claimed their existing, pre-ACA Medicaid funding streams were simply too massive for them to have any real option of withdrawing from Medicaid. As a result, they argued, the new conditions "crossed the line" into being compulsion.

By a margin of 7-to-2, the Supreme Court agreed. (Because Chief Justice Roberts's opinion articulated the narrowest rationale for sustaining the Court's judgment on this point, it is considered controlling.) The Chief Justice explained that Congress could certainly "condition the receipt of funds on the States' complying with restrictions on the use of those funds, because that is the means by which Congress ensures that the funds are spent according to its view of the 'general Welfare.'" Under the ACA, though, the states' failure to comply with the new conditions did not just jeopardize the funds the federal

255

government was offering the states to expand their Medicaid programs. Instead, the conditions took "the form of threats to terminate other significant independent grants": the states' preexisting Medicaid dollars. Consequently, "the conditions are properly viewed as a means of pressuring the States to accept policy changes."

Such pressuring, achieved through the tool of conditional spending, is generally no more than "encouragement," and thus perfectly constitutional. (Indeed, this was the case in *Dole*; the statute there placed a condition on the states' preexisting federal highway funding.) But in the ACA, explained Roberts, this pressure amounted to compulsion: it was "a gun to the head."

Again, the Medicaid statute gives the Secretary of HHS the authority to terminate the *entirety* of a state's federal Medicaid reimbursement if the state fails to comply with any of the Act's requirements. Thus, a state choosing not to expand its Medicaid coverage as prescribed by the ACA stood "to lose not merely 'a relatively small percentage' of its existing Medicaid funding, but *all* of it." And the states' practical dependence on the existing Medicaid program was undeniable. This dependence, reasoned the Chief Justice, meant Congress was effectively leaving the states with no choice: "The threatened loss of over 10 percent of a State's overall budget, in contrast [to the funds at issue in *Dole*], is economic dragooning that leaves the States with no real option but to acquiesce in the Medicaid expansion."

Importantly, reasoned Roberts, the Act's Medicaid expansion did not simply constitute "a modification of the existing Medicaid program[.]" Instead, it represented "a new program[,]" a "shift in kind, not merely degree." Thus, Congress was not merely amending the terms under which states could spend dollars provided by the federal government. Rather, Congress was effectively forcing the states to implement the ACA's distinct Medicaid-expansion program by "threatening the funds for the existing Medicaid program."

This conclusion did not render the ACA's expansion of Medicaid unconstitutional in its entirety, however. It only meant that Congress could not "penalize States that choose not to participate in that new program by taking away their existing Medicaid funding." Hence, forbidding the Secretary "to withdraw existing [pre-ACA] Medicaid funds for failure to comply with the requirements set out in the expansion" fully remedied the constitutional violation. The Court therefore validated Congress's authority to attach conditions to the ACA's *new* funding: "Nothing in our opinion precludes Congress from offering funds under the Affordable Care Act to expand the availability of health care, and requiring that States accepting such funds comply with the conditions on their use."

After *NFIB v. Sebelius*, then, the states were left with a choice—or, really, two choices. They could choose whether to continue participating in the pre-ACA Medicaid program, according to the conditions previously laid down by

Congress. And they could choose whether to participate in the Act's expansion of Medicaid, according to the terms set out in the ACA.

More broadly, *NFIB v. Sebelius* holds that a federal spending condition imposed on a state will be coercive when two conditions are *both* met: (1) the condition is not merely attached to participation in a new program, but threatens funding that states' are already receiving under an existing spending program; *and* (2) the amount of dollars at stake is substantial—much more than the mere "mild encouragement" at issue in *Dole*, and something closer to the 10 percent of a state's total budget that was at stake under the ACA's expansion of Medicaid.

*   *   *

PROBLEMS ON THE SPENDING POWER

In each of the following circumstances, please evaluate whether the federal statute at issue would constitute a valid exercise of Congress's spending power. In doing so, carefully consider your precise rationale.

1. Congress enacts a statute appropriating funding for the Department of Homeland Security. Within that appropriations law, Congress specifically authorizes DHS to spend $2 billion on the construction of physical barriers related to border security. (Assume no other appropriations within the statute could be construed as authorizing spending for this particular purpose.) The President orders the Department of Homeland Security to spend $7 billion on the construction of a physical barrier along the nation's southern border.

2. Congress enacts a statute entitling any person residing in the United States who has an annual income of less than $15,000 to temporary cash assistance. The disbursements are made monthly to qualifying individuals.

3. Congress enacts a law appropriating $250 million for the acquisition of real property that will be the home of a new military base. The Department of Defense uses the $250 million to acquire the property from private landowners.

4. Congress enacts a statute appropriating funds to provide medical services to indigent persons. Specifically, the law provides funding to eligible private, non-profit health clinics who serve indigent patients. Under the terms of the law, to participate as a health care provider in the program, a health clinic must agree not spend any of the federal funds on gender-affirming medical care.

5. Congress enacts a law appropriating funds to assist elementary, middle, and high schools around the country. Every state may apply to receive funding under the law. To be eligible to receive funding, a state must enact a law criminalizing the possession of a gun within 1,000 feet of any school.

6. The facts are the same as (5), except that the law—instead of requiring that states enact a law criminalizing the possession of a gun within 1,000 feet of any school—requires states accepting funds under the program to "guarantee each student a safe

environment in which to attend school." The federal government decides Texas is ineligible to receive funds under the program because Texas has failed to criminalize the possession of a gun within 1,000 feet of any school. Texas objects.

7. Under existing law, the federal government provides billions of dollars to states every year as part of Chapter 1, a spending program providing aid to economically disadvantaged school districts. To participate, states must comply with a number of rules imposed by Congress. Suppose Congress enacts a new school funding law, which substantially increases the funding available to the states under Chapter 1, making scores of millions of dollars available to every state. To qualify for the new funds, states must comply with a wide range of requirements concerning equity, standardized testing, and the investigation of sexual harassment or assault allegations. If a state refuses to participate in the new, expanded version of the program, however, the Department of Education has the authority to withhold the state's funding for the new funds. (Participation in the new program does not affect a state's eligibility to participate in the existing Chapter 1 program.)

CHAPTER 11
CONGRESS'S OTHER LEGISLATIVE POWERS

A. The Reconstruction Amendment Powers

The vast bulk of Congress's legislative powers are located in Article I, but a handful are found elsewhere in the Constitution. The most important congressional powers added to the original Constitution are those contained in the Thirteenth, Fourteenth, and Fifteenth Amendments—the Reconstruction Amendments, added immediately after the Civil War. Each of these amendments, in addition to containing important substantive prohibitions, contains a grant of power to Congress "to enforce" those prohibitions "by appropriate legislation." They are like clause-specific necessary and proper clauses, enabling Congress to enact statutes that enforce the substantive guarantees of the Reconstruction Amendments. The two most significant of these powers are those in §5 of the Fourteenth Amendment and §2 of the Thirteenth Amendment.

1. Section 5 of the Fourteenth Amendment

Under §1 of the Fourteenth Amendment, "[n]o State shall make or enforce any law which shall abridge the privileges or immunities of citizens of the United States; nor shall any State deprive any person of life, liberty, or property, without due process of law; nor deny to any person within its jurisdiction the equal protection of the laws." Section 5 provides that "[t]he Congress shall have power to enforce, by appropriate legislation, the provisions of this article." Thus, the §5 power is necessarily tethered to what §1 of the Fourteenth Amendment forbids; it is a power to *enforce* the Amendment's prohibitions.

a. *United States v. Morrison*

Critical to understanding the breadth of the §5 power is the Supreme Court's decision in *United States v. Morrison*, 529 U.S. 598 (2000). As discussed in Chapter 9, §13981 of the Violence Against Women Act (VAWA) provided the survivors of gender-motivated violence a private right of action against their assailants. After Christy Brzonkala sued Antonio Morrison for damages under the statute, Morrison asserted as an affirmative defense that §13981 exceeded Congress's enumerated powers. The federal government intervened in the case to defend the statute's constitutionality, and it proffered two arguments. First, it contended that §13981 was within the commerce power, an argument the Court rejected (on the ground that the activity it regulated—acts of gender-motivated violence—fell outside the three categories spelled out in *Lopez*).

Alternatively, the government contended that §13981 constituted "appropriate legislation" under §5 of the Fourteenth Amendment. As the text of §5 suggests, legislation Congress enacts under this authority must in some way *remedy* or *correct* violations of the Fourteenth Amendment's substantive prohibitions; the power it confers is to "enforce" the Fourteenth Amendment's guarantees. Thus, for legislation to fit within the §5 power, there must plausibly be some constitutional violations—either ongoing or prone to occur—that the federal statute seeks to prevent or correct.

The constitutional violations that Congress targeted through §13981 were acts of intentional gender discrimination in the enforcement of state law—acts that violate the Equal Protection Clause of the Fourteenth Amendment. The constitutional problem identified by Congress was the systematic underenforcement of the law by state and local officials with respect to gender-motivated crimes. And this was attributable to gender stereotypes and sex discrimination by state and local police, prosecutors, probation officers, judges, and even public university officials. Intentional discrimination by governmental actors on the basis of gender nearly always a violates the Equal Protection Clause, so a law targeting such acts would plausibly fit within the §5 power.

Importantly, the alleged constitutional violations that the federal government asserted formed the predicate for Congress to enact §13981 had been committed by *government* officials—so-called "state actors." Under the *state action doctrine*, this is necessary: with the exception of the Thirteenth Amendment (which flatly prohibits slavery), the Constitution only regulates the behavior of *government* and *government officials*. This is especially clear in the text of the Fourteenth Amendment, which provides that "No *State* . . . shall deny to any person within its jurisdiction the equal protection of the laws" (emphasis added). The Constitution does not prohibit everyone from discriminating on the basis of sex, but only *government*. This is why the United States's defense of §13981 as a valid exercise of Congress's §5 power pointed to the acts gender discrimination committed by state and local government officials, not private individuals.

But this created a problem: §13981 authorized survivors of gender-motivated violence (such as Christy Brzonkala) to recover damages from the perpetrator, *not* the state and local officials who had arguably violated the Fourteenth Amendment. And perpetrators like Antonio Morrison—no matter how despicable their acts—cannot violate the Fourteenth Amendment. They are *private persons*, not state actors. That is, §13981 regulated persons (through the imposition of liability) who had committed acts of gender-motivated violence. But it did not regulate the actions of state officers who had potentially violated the Constitution—the police, prosecutors, judges, and the like who had made decisions infected with unlawful gender discrimination. To the Supreme Court, this disconnect meant that §13981 was "incongruent" with the constitutional violations Congress was seeking to remedy. As a result, the statute exceeded Congress's §5 power, as it did not logically "enforce" the Fourteenth Amendment's prohibitions.

This somewhat narrow conception of the §5 power—as only permitting Congress to regulate the behavior of persons or entities themselves capable of violating the Constitution—was not inevitable. To be sure, §5 legislation must "enforce" the Fourteenth Amendment's substantive prohibitions. But conceivably, a right to sue private individuals could enforce the command that state and local governments provide all persons the equal protection of the laws. Granting survivors a right to recover from private perpetrators could ensure that those survivors are made whole in a way that state and local governments' unconstitutional discrimination was rendering unlikely. It might also help create legal norms that would lead states to modify their conduct, remedying the problem of gender-biased underenforcement. (Indeed, this is precisely what Congress articulated as its rationale for invoking its §5 power in the legislative history accompanying VAWA.)

But there was a century-old Supreme Court decision directly on point. In the *Civil Rights Cases*, 109 U.S. 3 (1883), the Court had invalidated the public accommodations provision of the Civil Rights Act of 1875 on the ground that it exceeded Congress's §5 power. (Today, such a statute would fit within Congress's commerce power, as *Heart of Atlanta Motel* and *Katzenbach v. McClung* illustrate.) And the floor debates in Congress regarding the 1875 Act revealed that it had been based on precisely the same §5 rationale that Congress was asserting justified §13981. The Civil Rights Act of 1875 was not principally addressed at the problem of formal inequality under the law. Rather, it was aimed at the ways state and local governments tended to enforce those laws in a racially discriminatory manner. As Representative James Garfield related,

> "[t]he chief complaint is not that the laws of the State are unequal, but that even where the laws are just and equal on their face, yet, by a systematic maladministration of them, or a neglect or refusal to enforce their provisions, a portion of the people are denied equal protection under them."

And Senator Charles Sumner noted that

> "[t]he Legislature of South Carolina has passed a law giving precisely the rights contained in your 'supplementary civil rights bill.' But such a law remains a dead letter on her statute-books, because the State courts, comprised largely of those whom the Senator wishes to obtain amnesty for, refuse to enforce it."

In the *Civil Rights Cases*, the Supreme Court rejected precisely this rationale as justifying Congress's use of the §5 power. The Court held that Congress could not use the states' unconstitutional, discriminatory underenforcement of the law (in permitting blatant racial discrimination) as a justification for regulating the actions of private persons under §5. Because the Civil Rights Act of 1875 regulated the actions of private persons—persons who themselves were incapable of violating the Constitution—it exceeded Congress's §5 power. In *Morrison*, the Court reaffirmed this central holding of the *Civil Rights Cases*, concluding that §13981 was unconstitutional for precisely the same reason.

b. *"Congruence" and "proportionality"*

More generally, the test for whether a federal statute is within Congress's §5 power is whether it is "congruent" and "proportional" to the constitutional violations it seeks to remedy or prohibit. Without first covering what the Fourteenth Amendment substantively proscribes, it is difficult to fully grasp what this test means in practice. Still, we can discern its basic outlines.

First, Congress clearly can prohibit conduct that itself violates the Fourteenth Amendment. Thus, Congress can use its §5 power to enact a statute that permits any individual to recover from a defendant who has violated her constitutional rights. This is essentially the effect of 42 U.S.C. §1983, which provides as follows:

> "Every person who, under color of any statute, ordinance, regulation, custom, or usage, of any State or Territory or the District of Columbia, subjects, or causes to be subjected, any citizen of the United States or other person within the jurisdiction thereof to the deprivation of any rights, privileges, or immunities secured by the Constitution and laws, shall be liable to the party injured in an action at law, suit in equity, or other proper proceeding for redress. . . ."

Section 1983 is necessarily "congruent" and "proportional" because its prohibitions are exactly coterminous with those of the Constitution. It regulates conduct that itself is unconstitutional but goes no further.

Second, Congress can go slightly beyond what the Fourteenth Amendment itself proscribes and regulate a "somewhat broader swath" of conduct. For instance, Congress invoked its §5 power in 1965 to forbid the use of literacy tests to determine a person's eligibility to vote. Literacy tests were principally used by jurisdictions in the South to prevent African Americans from voting, a practice that violated the Equal Protection Clause (because it constituted intentional discrimination on the basis of race). Thus, most uses of literacy tests were unconstitutional. Still, some jurisdictions in the United States had adopted literacy tests for benign reasons, such that they were perfectly constitutional. Nonetheless, Congress's flat ban on *all* literacy tests in voting was within the §5 power because a majority of those tests were unconstitutional. The statutory ban went beyond what the Fourteenth Amendment itself proscribed, but it was nonetheless "congruent" and "proportional" to the constitutional rule Congress was seeking to enforce: the Equal Protection Clause's prohibition of all racial discrimination.

Third, *Morrison* and the *Civil Rights Cases* clearly teach that legislation regulating the conduct of private persons—actors who themselves cannot violate the Fourteenth Amendment—is categorically "incongruent," and thus exceeds Congress's §5 power. Congress may only use the §5 power to regulate the behavior of governmental actors, as they are the only persons capable of transgressing the Fourteenth Amendment's substantive prohibitions.

2. Section 2 of the Thirteenth Amendment

The power granted to Congress by §2 of the Thirteenth Amendment is narrower in scope—but deeper in strength—than that granted by §5 of the Fourteenth Amendment. It is narrower in scope due to what the Thirteenth Amendment proscribes. Unlike the Fourteenth Amendment—which guarantees a broad range of fundamental rights—§1 of the Thirteenth Amendment contains one very specific proscription: "Neither slavery nor involuntary servitude, except as a punishment for crime whereof the party shall have been duly convicted, shall exist within the United States, or any place subject to their jurisdiction."

Given the scope of this prohibition, legislation enforcing the Thirteenth Amendment is limited to addressing slavery or the "badges of servitude." According to the Supreme Court, this means §2 only permits Congress to enact laws regulating *racial discrimination*. But the §2 power is not limited to legislation addressing discrimination against African Americans, the group most obviously top of mind when the nation added the Thirteenth Amendment to the Constitution. Rather, Congress can use the §2 power to regulate racial discrimination of any sort.

Moreover, the §2 power is deeper in strength than that granted by §5 of the Fourteenth Amendment in that, when applicable, it permits Congress to regulate the acts of any persons, public or private. As the Court held in *Runyon v. McCrary*, 427 U.S. 160 (1976) (reaffirming its decision in *Jones v. Alfred H. Mayer Co.*, 392 U.S. 409 (1968)), "[i]t has never been doubted . . . 'that the power vested in Congress to enforce (the Thirteenth Amendment) by appropriate legislation' . . . includes the power to enact laws 'direct and primary, operating upon the acts of individuals, whether sanctioned by State legislation or not.'" Congress can regulate private persons with its §2 power because §1 of the Thirteenth Amendment flatly prohibits slavery of any kind, whether practiced by public or private actors. Logically, then, Congress can enforce this proscription by regulating the acts of both public and private persons.

*   *   *

PROBLEMS ON THE RECONSTRUCTION AMENDMENT POWERS

In each of the following scenarios, please evaluate whether the federal statute would constitute a valid exercise of Congress's power under either §2 of the Thirteenth Amendment or §5 of the Fourteenth Amendment.

1. A federal statute forbids commercial lenders from discriminating on the basis of race in the provision of home mortgage loans.

2. A federal statute proscribes discrimination on the basis of religion by private employers in the terms and conditions of employment.

3. The facts are the same as in (2), except the statute applies to *all* employers, including state and local governments. (Assume that intentional discrimination on the basis of religion violates the Equal Protection Clause in §1 of the Fourteenth Amendment.)

4. A statute that creates a private right of action against any state or local government official who fails to prosecute or investigate an allegation of gender-motivated violence, when that failure is the result of intentional gender discrimination.

*　*　*

B.　Other Legislative Powers

The material to this point has covered Congress's most significant legislative powers. Those grants of power, combined with the Necessary and Proper Clause's allowance for Congress to use all "appropriate" means to effectuate those powers, account for the vast bulk of all federal statutes. But before moving on, it is worth noting the other legislative powers the Constitution grants to Congress, though they are generally much narrower scope.

To be clear, many federal statutes are probably justifiable (from the standpoint of Congress's authority) on multiple grounds. For instance, various immigration statutes might simultaneously be valid exercises of the immigration and naturalization power, the foreign affairs power, and the international commerce power. There is no need for federal laws to fit within one particular congressional power. And Congress has no obligation to *specify* which power it is invoking to justify its enactment of a statute. The burden always rests with a litigant challenging an act of Congress as unconstitutional to demonstrate that the law exceeds Congress's enumerated powers.

1.　Other powers in Article I, §8

Article I, §8, clause 2 grants Congress the power "[t]o borrow Money on the credit of the United States." Rather straightforwardly, this permits Congress to borrow money as it deems necessary and appropriate. The Supreme Court has not decided any cases construing this authority for roughly one hundred years, and there have not been any significant disagreements about the scope of this authority in quite some time.

Article I, §8, clause 3, in addition to granting Congress authority to regulate commerce "among the states," also gives Congress the power to regulate "Commerce with foreign Nations, . . . and with the Indian Tribes." The scope of these powers has been litigated frequently throughout U.S. history. But the term "commerce" means the same thing, whether in the interstate, international, or tribal context. Thus, the same framework can generally be applied, at least with respect to what constitutes "commerce."

Article I, §8, clause 4 gives Congress two distinct and independently significant powers: "[t]o establish an uniform Rule of Naturalization" and to establish "uniform Laws on the subject of Bankruptcies throughout the United States." The immigration and naturalization power is quite broad. Recently, in *Arizona v. United States*, 567 U.S. 387 (2012), the Supreme Court stated

> "[t]he Government of the United States has broad, undoubted power over the subject of immigration and the status of aliens. . . . This authority rests, in part, on the National Government's constitutional power to 'establish an uniform Rule of Naturalization,' and its inherent power as sovereign to control and conduct relations with foreign nations."

Most anything related to immigration or naturalization will fall within this power, even if it is unrelated to international commerce, and even if it arguably has no more than a *de minimis* impact on foreign relations. Further, even more so in this area than others, Congress can exercise this power so as to preclude any state regulation touching on the same subject. The typical presumption against the federal preemption of state law does not apply to legislation addressing immigration and naturalization.

Likewise, the bankruptcy power gives Congress wide authority to legislate on the subject of bankruptcies. Pursuant to this power, Congress has enacted an elaborate federal statutory structure, including non-Article III bankruptcy courts to adjudicate bankruptcies.

Article I, §8, clause 5 grants Congress the power "[t]o coin money, regulate the value thereof, and of foreign coin, and fix the standard of weights and measures." This requires little further exploration, much like the power granted in the next clause, which gives Congress the authority "[t]o provide for the punishment of counterfeiting the securities and current coin of the United States." As with many powers listed in Article I, §8, given modern understandings of the commerce power, Congress could likely pursue these objectives under the Commerce Clause (with the additional help of the Necessary and Proper Clause) even if these more specific grants of power were not listed in the Constitution.

Article I, §8, clause 7 gives Congress the power "[t]o establish post offices and post roads." This is the power by which the national government has always maintained the postal service, along with its various instrumentalities.

Article I, §8, clause 8 is what gives Congress its principal power to regulate intellectual property: the power "[t]o promote the progress of science and useful arts, by securing for limited times to authors and inventors the exclusive right to their respective writings and discoveries." The rights Congress has granted to authors are copyrights, while the rights granted to inventors are patents. Each is the subject of detailed federal statutory schemes. Moreover, both fields likely could be regulated by Congress under the commerce power, even if this clause were not included in the Constitution.

As discussed previously, Article I, §8, clause 9 grants Congress the power "[t]o constitute tribunals inferior to the Supreme Court." This reinforces what is recognized in Article III: "The judicial power of the United States, shall be vested in one Supreme Court, and in such inferior courts as the Congress may from time to time ordain and establish." Part of the compromise at the Framing was that the only federal court required to exist by the Constitution is the Supreme Court. It is left to Congress as to whether to create lower federal courts—and if so, how many, and with what jurisdiction.

The next seven clauses—Article I, §8, clauses 9 through 16—concern Congress's authority to legislate with respect to matters of foreign affairs and the military. In this way, the Constitution is clear that Congress has an important, constitutionally prescribed role to play in these fields, despite the heightened role of the President in such matters. Specifically, these clauses grant Congress the power:

* "To define and punish piracies and felonies committed on the high seas, and offences against the law of nations" in clause 10.

* "To declare war, grant letters of marque and reprisal, and make rules concerning captures on land and water" in clause 11.

* "To raise and support armies, but no appropriation of money to that use shall be for a longer term than two years" in clause 12.

* "To provide and maintain a navy" in clause 13.

* "To make rules for the government and regulation of the land and naval forces" in clause 14.

* "To provide for calling forth the militia to execute the laws of the union, suppress insurrections and repel invasions" in clause 15.

* "To provide for organizing, arming, and disciplining, the militia, and for governing such part of them as may be employed in the service of the United States, reserving to the states respectively, the appointment of the officers, and the authority of training the militia according to the discipline prescribed by Congress" in clause 16.

As Chapter 13 will illustrate, the precise boundary between the powers of the President and Congress in these spheres remains hazy and disputed. But those disputes are typically resolved through the political process rather than litigation. Thus, the case law on these questions is sparse. Suffice it to say that both Congress and the President have important constitutional roles in these matters, and each dispute will turn on the precise question presented. Legislation that seems to interfere with an authority granted exclusively to the President (such as the power to recognize foreign sovereigns or to act as Commander in Chief) are more likely to be unconstitutional. But matters that the Constitution leaves *exclusively* to the President are few and far between. More often, there is room for both branches to act.

Article I, §8, clause 17 effectively grants Congress a genuine police power over the District of Columbia. The clause gives Congress the authority

"[t]o exercise exclusive legislation in all cases whatsoever, over such District (not exceeding ten miles square) as may, by cession of particular states, and the acceptance of Congress, become the seat of the government of the United States, and to exercise like authority over all places purchased by the consent of the legislature of the state in which the same shall be, for the erection of forts, magazines, arsenals, dockyards, and other needful buildings."

In other words, for the District of Columbia, Congress is effectively the state government—meaning all the rules about "enumerated powers" are basically turned off. Congress has plenary authority to enact laws governing the District, subject to the same constitutional limitations any state would face.

2. Powers found elsewhere in the original Constitution

The original Constitution grants Congress two other powers not listed in Article I, §8. One is the Elections Clause, located in Article I, §4, clause 1. It provides that "[t]he Times, Places and Manner of holding Elections for Senators and Representatives, shall be prescribed in each State by the Legislature thereof; but the Congress may at any time by Law make or alter such Regulations, except as to the Places of chusing Senators." The Supreme Court explained in *Foster v. Love*, 522 U.S. 67, 69 (1997) that this clause

"grants Congress the power to override state regulations by establishing uniform rules for federal elections, binding on the States. The regulations made by Congress are paramount to those made by the State legislature; and if they conflict therewith, the latter, so far as the conflict extends, ceases to be operative."

As the Court recently clarified, this power indisputably grants Congress the authority to "draw a State's congressional-district boundaries." *Arizona State Legislature v. Arizona Indep. Redistricting Comm'n*, 576 U.S. 787 (2015).

In addition, the Property Clause, located in Article IV, §3, clause 2, states that "[t]he Congress shall have Power to dispose of and make all needful Rules and Regulations respecting the Territory or other Property belonging to the United States." The Court has described this authority in expansive terms, stating that "[t]he power of Congress over public lands . . . is without limitations." *Fed. Power Comm'n v. Idaho Power Co.*, 344 U.S. 17, 21 (1952).

The Property Clause can be understood as granting two distinct powers. One is the authority of the federal government as proprietor, with the rights any owner would have over the property to which it holds title. As the Court has explained, "Congress may deal with such lands precisely as an ordinary individual may deal with [their] property," such as choosing to sell or not to sell it. *Alabama v. Texas*, 347 U.S. 272 (1954). The other is the legislative power to regulate all activity occurring on such lands. In this way, the federal government enjoys a "police power" over lands held by the federal government, even though most of those lands lie within the boundaries of existing states. (For example, the federal government holds title to roughly 28 percent of the land in New Mexico and roughly 60 percent of the land in Alaska.)

3. The treaty power

Finally, Congress—through the combination of the power granted to the President to make treaties, to the Senate to ratify treaties, and to the Congress to make all laws "necessary and proper" to effectuate any powers granted in the Constitution—has long been understood to possess a "treaty power." The precise wording of the Necessary and Proper Clause gives Congress the authority to enact legislation appropriate to carrying out not just those powers granted to Congress itself, but to any part of the national government: "To make all Laws which shall be necessary and proper for carrying into Execution the foregoing Powers, and all other Powers vested by this Constitution in the Government of the United States, or in any Department or Officer thereof." Article II, §2, clause 2, meanwhile, grants the President the "Power, by and with the Advice and Consent of the Senate, to make Treaties, provided two thirds of the Senators present concur." The Necessary and Proper Clause thus gives Congress the authority to enact legislation appropriate for carrying into execution the President's power to make (and the Senate's power to ratify) treaties with other nations.

The most controversial question raised by the treaty power is whether it permits Congress to enact legislation that, absent the relevant treaty, would otherwise be unconstitutional. That is, can a treaty effectively expand Congress's legislative authority? The critical case on this issue is *Missouri v. Holland*, 252 U.S. 416 (1920). The State of Missouri filed an action seeking to prevent the federal game warden from enforcing the terms of the Migratory Bird Treaty Act of 1918 (and regulations that had been promulgated by the Executive Branch to implement the Act). Missouri contended that the Act and the regulations unconstitutionally interfered with the legislative authority reserved to the states—that the Act exceeded Congress's enumerated powers. Congress enacted the Migratory Bird Treaty Act to enforce a validly ratified treaty between the United States and Great Britain regarding, naturally enough, the protection of migratory birds.

Some treaties are self-executing. This means that no federal legislation is necessary to make them effective and controlling of conduct in the United States. Self-executing treaties are, of their own force, enforceable in an American court. The Migratory Bird Treaty was *not* self-executing; by its terms, the party nations agreed to take steps domestically to fulfill their pledged obligations. Thus, the treaty required federal legislation (prohibiting certain conduct) to restrict or bind the actions of American citizens so as to protect migratory birds according to the treaty's terms.

Crucial to understanding the significance of *Missouri v. Holland* is Justice Holmes' brief analysis of whether Congress could have enacted the statute absent the Migratory Bird Treaty. (The case was decided in the 1920s, when the governing conception of Congress's commerce power was quite narrow compared to today.) Holmes wrote that "[t]he fact that an earlier act of Congress that attempted by itself and not in pursuance of a treaty to regulate the killing of migratory birds within the States had been held bad [in two lower court decisions] cannot be accepted as a test of the treaty power." That is, the fact that federal courts had previously held that a nearly identical statute—enacted before the existence of the Migratory Bird Treaty—exceeded Congress's enumerated powers was of no matter. "It is obvious that there may be matters of the sharpest exigency for the national wellbeing that an act of Congress could not deal with but that a treaty followed by such an act could." Under *Holland*, then, Congress can enact legislation pursuant to its treaty power that would otherwise exceed its enumerated powers. The treaty power *augments* Congress's legislative authority.

Notice the implications here. Suppose the United States entered into a treaty concerning the protection of children, part of which required all signatory nations to prohibit the possession of guns in school zones. Could Congress reenact the Gun-Free School Zones Act of 1990 (the version invalidated in *Lopez*) pursuant to its treaty power, even if it would exceed its commerce power? The holding of *Missouri v. Holland* suggests that it could.

Perhaps the more difficult question, though, is determining when a federal statute is actually "necessary and proper" to effectuate certain treaty obligations. Suppose, for instance, that the treaty merely required all signatory nations to "maintain healthy and safe school environments." Assume, again, that Congress reenacted the Gun-Free School Zones Act of 1990. Would that be permissible? Would such a law be sufficiently "necessary"? Would it be "proper"? The Supreme Court's decision in *Bond v. United States*, 564 U.S. 211 (2011), reveals that, at least for the time being, the justices are inclined to construe statutes enacted under Congress's treaty power narrowly when, absent the relevant treaty, they would apparently exceed Congress's enumerated powers.

Suppose that, rather than potentially expanding the authority of Congress to enact legislation, the United States entered into a treaty that empowered the government to infringe on otherwise protected individual rights. For instance, suppose by treaty the U.S. agreed to afford American citizens accused of terrorist-related offenses something less than the full panoply of criminal procedure rights set out in the Fourth, Fifth, Sixth, and Seventh Amendments. Would that be constitutional? One could certainly read *Missouri v. Holland* to permit such restrictions. But the Supreme Court held otherwise in *Reid v. Covert*, 354 U.S. 1 (1957). There, a civilian member of a military family was accused of committing murder on a military base overseas. Congress had enacted legislation, pursuant to an executive agreement with the host nation (an agreement quite similar to a treaty, and indistinguishable for these purposes) requiring that such suspects be tried before a military court rather than an ordinary civilian court. Importantly, military courts generally do not afford defendants all of the rights guaranteed by the Bill of Rights to criminal defendants. In *Reid v. Covert*, the Court held that the legislation at issue, to the extent it permitted such trials of U.S. citizens, was unconstitutional: "[No] agreement with a foreign nation can confer power on the Congress, or on any other branch of Government, which is free from the restraints of the Constitution."

Thus, there is an important distinction between (1) treaties that arguably enable Congress to enact statutes that would otherwise exceed its enumerated powers, and (2) treaties that require (or which themselves) violate the Constitution's express guarantees concerning individual rights. The former arguably expand Congress's legislative powers, enabling Congress to take actions that would otherwise be unconstitutional. The latter, by contrast, are never permissible.

* * *

MULTIPLE-CHOICE REVIEW QUESTIONS ON THE POWERS OF CONGRESS

1. Suppose Congress enacts the Gun Free School Zones Act of 2023. The Act provides that any person who possesses a gun within 500 feet of a school must pay a $1,000 "tax penalty" to the federal government for each violation. (The penalty is to be submitted on the person's federal income tax return, as an addition to the income tax they otherwise owe.) Based on these facts alone, is the Act constitutional?

   (a) No, because the activity it regulates indistinguishable from that regulated by the statute the Supreme Court held was unconstitutional in *United States v. Lopez*.

   (b) Yes, because it is a valid exercise of Congress's authority under the commerce power.

   (c) Yes, because it is a valid exercise of Congress's taxing power.

   (d) Yes, because it is valid exercise of Congress's authority under the Necessary and Proper Clause.

2. Suppose Congress enacts a statute proscribing racial discrimination in the sale, transfer, or leasing of real estate. The statute applies to private individuals and entities, as well as state and local governments. Which of the following constitutional provisions provides the *strongest* basis for Congress's authority to enact the law?

   (a) The Necessary and Proper Clause.

   (b) Section 2 of the Thirteenth Amendment.

   (c) Section 5 of the Fourteenth Amendment.

   (d) The Equal Protection Clause.

3. Imagine Congress enacts a new statute making it a federal crime to sell, or to use in any transaction, a counterfeit COVID-19 vaccination card (whether digital or physical). The only sanction imposed under the statute for committing this crime is that the violator must pay $5,000 per violation to federal government. The *strongest* basis for Congress's authority to enact this statute is:

   (a) Section 5 of the Fourteenth Amendment.

   (b) The taxing power.

   (c) The commerce power.

   (d) The spending power.

4. In the cartoon series *Schoolhouse Rock*, an episode entitled "I'm Just a Bill" focuses on the national legislative process. It follows a federal bill from its initial proposal by a citizen to its enactment into law by Congress. The hypothetical statute used in the episode states provides as follows: "Every school bus in the United States must come to a complete stop before crossing a working railroad track." The *best* argument as to why this statute would be constitutional is that:

   (a) The federal government provides the majority of funding for roads and highways in the United States, making the statute a valid exercise of Congress's spending power.

   (b) The statute is within Congress's commerce power.

   (c) The statute is a valid condition on the provision of federal funding to public schools in the United States.

   (d) The statute is a valid exercise of the states' police powers in primary education, an area in which they have historically been sovereign.

5. Congress enacts a statute providing for federal grants to state governments, to be distributed by the states to transportation agencies within their borders for the purpose of purchasing gas-efficient mass transit vehicles. One of the statute's objectives is to reduce the nation's dependency on oil imported from foreign nations, and thus make economic sanctions imposed on certain nations (such as Russia) more effective. Which of the following offers the *strongest* constitutional basis for Congress's authority to enact the stature?

   (a) The commerce power.

   (b) The General Welfare Clause.

   (c) The Necessary and Proper Clause.

   (d) The foreign relations power.

6. Suppose in 2024 the President negotiates and commits the United States to an international, multilateral treaty on the rights of women. The treaty is then ratified by the Senate. Under the terms of the treaty, every signatory nation must ensure that the survivors of sexual violence within their borders are provided with a personal legal remedy. With the treaty now in effect, Congress enacts a new federal statute that provides every survivor of gender-motivated violence with a private right of action against the person who committed the act of violence against them. Suppose a survivor of an attack covered by the new statute sues the perpetrator, asserting a claim for damages under the statute. The defendant files a motion to dismiss, asserting that the statute exceeds Congress's enumerated powers. How is the district court most likely to rule on the defendant's motion?

    (a) Deny the motion, because the statute is likely a valid exercise of Congress's commerce power.

    (b) Deny the motion, because the statute is likely a valid exercise of Congress's power under §5 of the Fourteenth Amendment.

    (c) Deny the motion, because the statute is likely a valid exercise of Congress's treaty power.

    (d) Grant the motion, because the statute exceeds Congress's enumerated powers.

CHAPTER 12
CONGRESS'S AUTHORITY TO REGULATE THE STATES

Thus far, our examination of Congress's authority has explored the scope of its legislative powers, clause by clause, without regard to how Congress's use of those powers might run afoul of other constitutional principles. That is, we have examined the "internal" limits on each of those enumerated powers—the limits that come from those clauses themselves, rather than other parts of the Constitution. We now turn to some "external," cross-cutting limitations on Congress's authority. In particular, we examine the constraints on Congress's authority to use its powers to regulate the actions of state or local governments.

In this context, the question is not which *activities* are beyond Congress's powers. Rather, the limit on Congress's authority stems from *whose conduct* Congress is attempting to regulate. As we will see, state governments and their political subdivisions enjoy a degree of immunity from federal regulation given their status as independent sovereigns. A particular activity might be within Congress's authority to regulate—for instance, an activity substantially affecting interstate commerce—but Congress's regulation of that activity, when engaged in by state or local governments, might nonetheless transgress the structural principles of federalism.

Many people refer to these structural principles as limits imposed by the Tenth Amendment. As a shorthand, this seems harmless enough. But if we are sticklers, this is not quite correct. The text of the Tenth Amendment itself imposes no limits on Congress. Instead, it reminds us of the federalism-based limits created by the Constitution's structure: "The powers not delegated to the United States by the Constitution, nor prohibited by it to the States, are reserved to the States respectively, or to the people." As the Supreme Court itself has explained, the Tenth Amendment is but a truism. Best understood, these limits derive from the Constitution's structural principles. The Tenth Amendment merely confirms that such limits indeed exist.

As with other topics we have covered, there is an older history, and there is the current doctrine. Also like other topics, the rationales of some of the Court's earlier decisions have been substantially modified (if not discarded altogether), though their precise *holdings* remain intact. The trick is to construct an understanding of present doctrine that can accommodate the outcomes—if not the rationales—of those older decisions.

A. The Anti-Commandeering Principle

1. Before 1992: *National League of Cities* and *Garcia*

In 1976, the Supreme Court decided *National League of Cities v. Usery*, 426 U.S. 833. At issue was a federal law that extended the requirements of the Fair Labor Standards Act (which imposes various minimum wage, maximum hour, and overtime pay requirements on employers) to state and local governments. (For federal constitutional purposes, local or municipal governments are political subdivisions of the states. Congress's regulation of their actions thus constitutes regulation of the states themselves.[16]) The question presented was whether Congress could impose these obligations on the states in their capacity as employers. The Court held this was impermissible. When federal statutes "operate to directly displace the States' freedom to structure integral operations in areas of traditional governmental functions, they are not within the authority granted Congress."

But this ruling was short-lived. Only nine years later, the Court overruled *National League of Cities* in *Garcia v. San Antonio Metropolitan Trans. Auth.*, 469 U.S. 528 (1985), concluding that it had proved unworkable. A "rule of state immunity that looks to the 'traditional,' 'integral,' or 'necessary' nature of governmental functions inevitably invites an unelected federal judiciary to make decisions about which state policies it favors and which one it dislikes." Instead, reasoned the Court in *Garcia*, the real brake on Congress's unduly burdening the states with regulation should be the operation of the political process. State governments are represented in Congress and in the presidential election process; they can represent their own interests—and their desire to be free from regulation—through the normal operation of politics. In essence, *Garcia* suggested that issues concerning Congress's power to regulate the states constitute non-justiciable political questions. The Court thus upheld the constitutionality of Congress's imposition of the Fair Labor Standards Act on state and local governments in their capacities as employers, forcing them to pay their employees a minimum wage, extra pay for overtime, and the like.

The four justices who dissented in *Garcia* argued that they had merely lost this battle, and the war was not over. And they were right, at least in part. Seven years later, the Court handed down *New York v. United States*, 505 U.S. 144 (1992), in which the Court held that whether a federal statute regulating the conduct of states violates the structural principles of federalism is a justiciable question. Further, the Court in *New York* invalidated a portion of the challenged federal statute, announcing a new constitutional limitation on Congress's regulation of the states: the anti-commandeering principle.

---

[16] The only place where this principle does not hold is with respect to the immunity provided by the Eleventh Amendment, which only protects state governments themselves or "arms of the state"—not city, county, or municipal governments.

2. *New York* and *Printz*

The principle that the Supreme Court announced in *New York* (and later reaffirmed in *Printz v. United States*, 521 U.S. 898 (1997)) is this: *Congress lacks the power to command the states (or their political subdivisions) to take affirmative steps to govern their residents according to federal directives.* As the Court explained, any such "commandeering" of state governments is "inconsistent with the federal structure of our Government established by the Constitution." This is the so-called anti-commandeering principle.

In *New York*, the Court invalidated the "take title" provision of the Low-Level Radioactive Waste Policy Amendments of 1985, which had directed the states to do one of two things: either (1) regulate low-level radioactive waste generated by private or public actors within their borders "according to the instructions of Congress[,]" or (2) accept title to all such waste (which would constitute an enormous financial liability). The Court held that Congress's posing of this "choice" to the states was unconstitutional. Importantly, the Court did not conclude that the *activity* Congress was seeking to regulate was beyond Congress's enumerated powers:

> "Petitioners do not contend that Congress lacks the power to regulate the disposal of low level radioactive waste. Space in radioactive waste disposal sites is frequently sold by residents of one State to residents of another. Regulation of the resulting interstate market in waste disposal is therefore well within Congress' authority under the Commerce Clause."

Instead, the constitutional problem was the *manner* in which Congress sought to regulate that activity. As the Court explained,

> "Congress may not simply commandeer the legislative processes of the States by directly compelling them to enact and enforce a federal regulatory program. . . . While Congress has substantial powers to govern the Nation directly, including in areas of intimate concern to the States, the Constitution has never been understood to confer upon Congress the ability to require the States to govern according to Congress' instructions. . . . We have always understood that even where Congress has the authority under the Constitution to pass laws requiring or prohibiting certain acts, it lacks the power directly to compel the States to require or prohibit those acts. The allocation of power contained in the Commerce Clause, for example, authorizes Congress to regulate interstate commerce directly; it does not authorize Congress to regulate state governments' regulation of interstate commerce."

Applying this logic to the take title provision of the statute, the Court held that it was unconstitutional:

> "The take title provision offers state governments a 'choice' of either accepting ownership of waste or regulating according to the instructions of Congress. Respondents do not claim that the Constitution would authorize

Congress to impose either option as a freestanding requirement. On one hand, the Constitution would not permit Congress simply to transfer radioactive waste from generators to state governments. Such a forced transfer, standing alone, would in principle be no different than a congressionally compelled subsidy from state governments to radioactive waste producers. The same is true of the provision requiring the States to become liable for the generators' damages. Standing alone, this provision would be indistinguishable from an Act of Congress directing the States to assume the liabilities of certain state residents. Either type of federal action would 'commandeer' state governments into the service of federal regulatory purposes, and would for this reason be inconsistent with the Constitution's division of authority between federal and state governments. On the other hand, the second alternative held out to state governments— regulating pursuant to Congress' direction—would, standing alone, present a simple command to state governments to implement legislation enacted by Congress. As we have seen, the Constitution does not empower Congress to subject state governments to this type of instruction. Because an instruction to state governments to take title to waste, standing alone, would be beyond the authority of Congress, and because a direct order to regulate, standing alone, would also be beyond the authority of Congress, it follows that Congress lacks the power to offer the States a choice between the two."

The Court's decision in *Printz* was quite similar, with the only salient difference being that the challenged federal statute commanded state and local *executive officials* to implement federal legislation (rather than commanding state legislatures to enact and implement legislation). Interim provisions of the federal Brady Handgun Violence Prevention Act directed state or local chief law enforcement officers (CLEOs) to conduct background checks on all persons seeking to purchase handguns. The Supreme Court held this provision, like the take-title provision in *New York*, violated the anti-commandeering principle:

"[T]he Brady Act purports to direct state law enforcement officers to participate, albeit only temporarily, in the administration of a federally enacted regulatory scheme. Regulated firearms dealers are required to forward Brady Forms not to a federal officer or employee, but to the CLEOs, whose obligation to accept those forms is implicit in the duty imposed upon them to make 'reasonable efforts' within five days to determine whether the sales reflected in the forms are lawful. . . .We held in *New York* that Congress cannot compel the States to enact or enforce a federal regulatory program. Today we hold that Congress cannot circumvent that prohibition by conscripting the States' officers directly. The Federal Government may neither issue directives requiring the States to address particular problems, nor command the States' officers, or those of their political subdivisions, to administer or enforce a federal regulatory program."

Importantly, the Court in *Printz* explained that this prohibition on Congress's commandeering of the states was absolute, not subject to any sort of balancing with respect to the importance of the activity regulated or the weight of the federal government's interest: "It matters not whether policymaking is involved, and no case-by-case weighing of the burdens or benefits is necessary; such commands are fundamentally incompatible with our constitutional system of dual sovereignty."

3. The contours of the anti-commandeering principle

Though important—perhaps even foundational—the anti-commandeering principle is narrower than might first appear. By its nature, there are three important limits to its reach. First, it only applies to federal statutes regulating the states in their *sovereign capacities*—that is, as regulators or governors of their inhabitants, and not as entities acting in their proprietary capacities (when they engage in activities that private parties can engage in as well). Second, the anti-commandeering principle only forbids federal laws that require the states to take *affirmative acts*, not those that merely *prohibit* states from acting. (Federal statutes forbidding states from regulating in a particular way are the commonplace stuff of preemption.) And third, the anti-commandeering principle does not forbid Congress from encouraging the states to regulate or govern according to federal instructions, even if Congress could not command the states to do the same. The following notes explore each of these points in turn.

a. *States acting in their sovereign vs. proprietary capacities*

A critical limit on the anti-commandeering principle is that it only forbids federal laws that dictate how states *regulate* or *govern*. To regulate or govern is to impose mandatory, coercive rules of conduct through the power of sovereignty. It can be distinguished from a government's *proprietary* actions: the actions it takes that are no different in kind or nature from those that any other private entity or organization in society might engage in—for instance, employing workers, emitting pollutants, or selling information.

Thus, the anti-commandeering principle does not threaten the scores of federal laws that regulate the states' behavior when they act in a proprietary role. Such "generally applicable legislation"—like the Fair Labor Standards Act (FLSA), which imposes minimum-wage and maximum-hour requirements on all employers in the United States of a certain size, whether public or private—does not "commandeer" the states because it does not command them to implement, administer, or enforce federal law. Rather, it requires state governments to themselves adhere to federal law, just like the private employers also subject to the law. Statutes like the FLSA treat the states as *objects* of federal regulation, not as governmental tools for the implementation of a federal legislative program.

Again, the Supreme Court upheld the constitutionality of applying such a generally applicable law to the states in *Garcia*. And the Court's opinions in *New York* and *Printz* (announcing and applying the anti-commandeering principle) were careful to distinguish *Garcia*, thus preserving the validity of its precise holding. Moreover, the Court subsequently reaffirmed Congress's authority to regulate the states' proprietary activity in *Reno v. Condon*, 528 U.S. 141 (2000). As the Court explained in *Condon*, the federal statute at issue there (the Driver's Privacy Protection Act) was constitutional because it "regulates the States as the owners of data bases," not "in their sovereign capacity to regulate their own citizens."

b. *Prohibitions vs. commands to act*

A second important limitation on the anti-commandeering principle is that it only forbids federal laws that command state governments to take *affirmative steps* in regulating or governing their residents. It does not extend to mere prohibitions: federal commands that states *not* regulate in a particular fashion. This must be so, because otherwise the anti-commandeering principle would swallow up the doctrine of preemption, a rule dictated by the text of the Constitution itself.

The Supremacy Clause of Article VI provides as follows:

"This Constitution, and the Laws of the United States which shall be made in Pursuance thereof; and all Treaties made, or which shall be made, under the Authority of the United States, shall be the supreme Law of the Land; and the Judges in every State shall be bound thereby, any Thing in the Constitution or Laws of any State to the Contrary notwithstanding."

Since the dawn of the Republic, this language has been understood as dictating that, when federal law and a state law conflict, the state law is inoperable, at least to the extent of the conflict. A federal statute that preempts state law— most obviously, when it does so through an express preemption clause[17]—is, in essence, a command by Congress that the states *not* regulate or govern in a

---

[17] To illustrate, consider the following express preemption clause contained in the federal Food Drug and Cosmetic Act concerning nonprescription drugs, codified at 21 U.S.C. §379r(a): "Except as provided in subsection (b), (c)(1), (d), (e), or (f), no State or political subdivision of a State may establish or continue in effect any requirement—(1) that relates to the regulation of a drug that is not subject to the requirements of section 353(b)(1) or 353(f)(1)(A) of this title; and (2) that is different from or in addition to, or that is otherwise not identical with, a requirement under this chapter, the Poison Prevention Packaging Act of 1970 or the Fair Packaging and Labeling Act." This provision *commands* states and their political subdivisions *not* to impose certain regulations. And it plainly applies to states in their *sovereign* capacities. Nonetheless, it is not a commandeering, because it merely *forbids* the states from taking certain actions, rather than commanding that they affirmatively act according to federal directives.

particular way. Thus, if the anti-commandeering principle and the doctrine of preemption are to coexist, the former can only apply to directives requiring the states affirmatively to act. Federal commands that states *not* regulate in a particular way cannot amount to a commandeering.

This distinction between prohibitions and mandates to take affirmative acts may be somewhat artificial, especially at the edges. Prohibitions can often be re-characterized (or re-conceptualized) as commands to act, and vice-versa. Still, the action-inaction distinction is generally respected in law, and it accurately captures the Court's various articulations of the anti-commandeering principle—statements that presumably were crafted with the implications for preemption in mind. For instance, the Court stated in *Condon* that the Driver's Privacy Protection Act did not commandeer the states because "[i]t does not require the South Carolina Legislature to enact any laws or regulations, and it does not require state officials to assist in the enforcement of federal statutes regulating private individuals." Similarly, the Court in both *New York* and *Printz* phrased the anti-commandeering principle as prohibiting the federal government from "compel[ling] the States to enact or administer a federal regulatory program." As such, this action-prohibition distinction sets an important boundary between unconstitutional commandeerings and the permissible preemption of state law.

c. *Commands, enticements, and coercion*

A final limitation on the anti-commandeering principle (one already covered in the material addressing the spending power) is that, though Congress cannot *command* the states to take affirmative steps to govern in a particular fashion, nothing precludes it from *encouraging* states through the enticement of federal dollars. The General Welfare Clause grants Congress the authority to "provide for the common Defence and general Welfare of the United States." Congress can use this spending power to offer funding to state governments with certain strings attached, requiring states to govern or regulate in particular ways to qualify for the federal funding.

To be sure, Congress's spending program must meet the requirements spelled out in *South Dakota v. Dole*, 483 U.S. 203 (1987): it must promote the "general welfare"; the spending conditions must be germane to the purposes of the spending program; the conditions must be unambiguous (so the states can fully appreciate the obligations they are accepting); and the conditions cannot induce the states to act unconstitutionally. But assuming these requirements are satisfied, nothing prevents Congress from achieving indirectly (through conditional spending) what would constitute an impermissible commandeering if pursued directly through compulsion. As the Court explained in *New York*, when Congress employs such a "permissible method of encouraging a State to conform to federal policy choices, the residents of the State retain the ultimate decision as to whether or not the State will comply."

Critical to the constitutionality of such conditional spending, of course, is that the states' acceptance of the strings attached to the federal dollars is *voluntary*. If the conditions operated as commands—such that the states had no real choice but to comply with the conditions—they would constitute a commandeering (at least insofar as those conditions required states to take affirmative steps in their sovereign capacities). "Coercive" conditions attached to federal spending programs are effectively mandates, and thus violate the anti-commandeering principle if the other elements of the doctrine apply.

4. Coercion and commandeering after *NFIB v. Sebelius*

As discussed in Chapter 10, Court's decision in *NFIB v. Sebelius* invalidated a portion of the Affordable Care Act's expansion of the Medicaid program on the ground that it coerced the states and thus exceeded Congress's spending power. It is important to see, though, that a federal statute's exceeding the spending power *in itself* would not render the statute unconstitutional. A federal statute might exceed Congress's spending authority but nonetheless be constitutional if it fits within one of Congress's other enumerated powers. Thus, the ultimate constitutional problem with the ACA's Medicaid expansion was that it *commandeered* the states. In the words of the Chief Justice, it "require[d] the States to govern according to Congress' instructions."

Of course, the ACA did not formally require the states to do anything with respect to Medicaid. As a formal matter, the states were free to walk away from the program if they so desired. But the Court nonetheless concluded the conditions Congress had attached to the states' existing Medicaid funds were effectively commands because, given the practical realities facing the states, they had no "real choice" but to accept Congress's conditions. The ACA only offered the states a choice "in theory," not "in fact." If the states lack the practical ability to say no, the federal law's conditions must be viewed as commands. And if those commands require the states to take affirmative acts in their sovereign capacities, the federal law violates the anti-commandeering principle (despite its being dressed in the garb of conditional spending).

Applying this rule, the ACA's Medicaid expansion provisions were unconstitutional due to the confluence of two features: (1) the ACA made the continuance of funding for a preexisting, distinct program (pre-ACA Medicaid) dependent on the states' compliance with the conditions of a new program (the ACA's Medicaid expansion); *and* (2) the amount of money the states stood to lose from the preexisting program was *huge*. If Congress had simply presented a new program, offering the states staggering amounts of money but with conditions attached, it would not have been coercive. Likewise, had the amount of preexisting program funds not been so substantial (those in the pre-ACA Medicaid program), the newly attached conditions would not have been coercive. (This was the case in *South Dakota v. Dole*, for instance, where Congress placed new conditions on a preexisting spending program.) It was the confluence of *both* of these features that led the Court to conclude that the

ACA's Medicaid expansion was coercive, and thus unconstitutional as applied to the states' preexisting Medicaid programs.

To follow this through, because the conditions were coercive, this meant they were commands, not merely inducements, and thus constituted *regulations*—mandatory norms of conduct. And as regulations, they violated the anti-commandeering principle because they directed the states, in their sovereign capacities, affirmatively to govern their residents according to federal instructions. That is the precise definition of an impermissible commandeering, no different than the problem in *New York* and *Printz*.

5. Prohibiting states from repealing regulations

As *New York* makes clear, a federal law directing the states to enact legislation violates the anti-commandeering principle. But suppose most states presently have in force laws that forbid a particular activity (such as gambling on sporting events), and Congress then enacts a statute forbidding states from repealing those laws. Does such a federal statute likewise amount to an unconstitutional commandeering of the states? The Supreme Court answered yes in *Murphy v. NCAA*, 138 S. Ct. 1461 (2018). As a logical matter, there is no meaningful difference between a federal statute that requires states to regulate in a particular manner and one that forbids states from repealing laws that already do so. In either case, the federal statute operates to command the states to legislate as Congress sees fit.

At issue in *Murphy* was the Professional and Amateur Sports Protection Act (PASPA). PASPA did not make gambling on sports a federal crime, but instead made it unlawful for a state "to sponsor, operate, advertise, promote, license, or authorize by law or compact . . . a lottery, sweepstakes, or other betting, gambling, or wagering scheme based . . . on" competitive sporting events. PAPSA exempted states that, at the time of its enactment, permitted sports gambling as a matter of state law. But that category consisted of only one state: Nevada. This meant that all other states were effectively required by PAPSA to keep in place their laws criminalizing sports gambling. The New Jersey legislature enacted a statute legalizing sports gambling in the state (at specific locations), and the United States and the NCAA sued to prevent New Jersey's legalization from going into effect.

The Supreme Court held that, by forbidding states from repealing their laws that proscribed sports gambling, PAPSA constituted an impermissible commandeering. It effectively commanded the states to legislate affirmatively, and to regulate their citizens (in their sovereign capacities) according to Congress's instructions—no differently than how the Low-Level Radioactive Waste Policy Amendments had done so in *New York*. In the Court's words, PAPSA

> "unequivocally dictates what a state legislature may and may not do. . . .
> [S]tate legislatures are put under the direct control of Congress. It is as if

federal officers were installed in state legislative chambers and were armed with the authority to stop legislators from voting on any offending proposals. A more direct affront to state sovereignty is not easy to imagine."

* * *

PROBLEMS ON THE ANTI-COMMANDEERING PRINCIPLE

In each of the following circumstances, please assess whether the federal statute at issue violates the anti-commandeering principle and, where applicable, whether the state law is consistent with the structural principles of federalism.

1. A federal statute requires all employers with at least 50 employees, including state and local governments, to provide their full-time employees with minimally adequate health insurance.

2. A federal law requires all state governments to criminalize the possession of marijuana within their borders (under state law).

3. A federal law requires all state and local law enforcement officers to enforce the federal Controlled Substances Act (CSA) within the state's borders.

4. An existing federal law (the CSA) criminalizes the possession of marijuana anywhere in the country. By voter initiative, the State of Washington decriminalizes the possession of marijuana under state law. The federal government continues to enforce the CSA against those possessing marijuana within the State of Washington.

5. A federal law criminalizes the possession of marijuana. By voter initiative, the State of Colorado decriminalizes the possession of marijuana by enacting a law which states as follows: "No person shall be penalized, by any governmental authority, for the possession of marijuana in this state."

6. A federal statute provides that if a state government does not regulate the emission of greenhouse gases within its borders precisely as dictated by Congress in the Clean Air Act, any state regulation on the subject will be preempted by federal law (which is enforced by the federal Environmental Protection Agency).

7. A federal law requires that all vehicles used for business purposes in the United States by organizations employing at least 100 employees have a fuel efficiency standard of at least 30 miles per gallon. The statute applies to state and local governments that own vehicles and use those vehicles in their operations.

8. A federal statute forbids states (including state courts) from imposing tort liability on any firearms manufacturer for any incident of violence perpetrated by a person by using one of the manufacturer's firearms.

* * *

B. Congress's Abrogation of States' Sovereign Immunity

Another important limit on Congress's capacity to regulate state governments concerns Congress's authority to abrogate the states' sovereign immunity. A principal means by which Congress regulates activities is by enacting statutes that make parties who engage in certain conduct subject to private suits brought by persons injured by that conduct. For example, the federal Age Discrimination in Employment Act (ADEA) provides that "[i]t shall be unlawful for an employer to fail or refuse to hire or to discharge any individual or otherwise discriminate against any individual with respect to his compensation, terms, conditions, or privileges of employment, because of such individual's age." The ADEA further states that "[a]ny person aggrieved may bring a civil action in any court of competent jurisdiction for such legal or equitable relief as will effectuate the purposes of this chapter." Thus, one way Congress might regulate the conduct of state governments is make them amenable to private, unconsenting suits for damages.

But this enforcement mechanism runs headlong into the Constitution's protection of the states' sovereign immunity. The states' immunity from unconsenting private suits is protected in part by the Eleventh Amendment, but it extends farther than that. The Eleventh Amendment addresses the federal courts' jurisdiction to adjudicate unconsenting actions against states. But state governments also generally enjoy immunity (as independent sovereigns) from unconsenting suits in other forums, such as their own state courts or federal tribunals other than Article III courts. In certain circumstances, Congress can use its legislative powers to abrogate (or pierce) this immunity and subject the states to private unconsenting suits. But the Constitution places tight constraints on this authority, permitting Congress to do so only in narrow circumstances.

Again, the Eleventh Amendment provides states with immunity from private unconsenting suits filed in federal court. But Congress may abrogate this immunity through legislation that constitutes a valid exercise of the power granted by §5 of the Fourteenth Amendment. For instance, Title VII of the Civil Rights Act of 1964 forbids all employers—including state governments—from discriminating on the basis of race in the terms and conditions of employment. Title VII includes a private right of action, which permits a victim of employment discrimination to sue the employer for damages and other forms of relief. In *Fitzpatrick v. Bitzer*, 427 U.S. 445 (1976), the Supreme Court held that, as applied to state governments, Title VII is within the legislative power granted to Congress by §5 of the Fourteenth Amendment, and thus validly abrogated states' sovereign immunity.

In addition, states lack immunity from suits to which they implicitly consented by entering the Union. Again, the idea is that "the plan of the Convention" was for states to be amenable to certain kinds lawsuits, and the Eleventh Amendment did nothing to disturb this arrangement. Thus, for example, Congress may enact statutes subjecting states to private, unconsenting suits in connection with bankruptcy proceedings, *see Central Va. Community College v. Katz*, 546 U. S. 356, 379 (2006), or its efforts to build and keep a national military, *see Torres v. Texas Dept. of Public Safety*, No. 20–603 (2022).

The protection conveyed to states by the Eleventh Amendment only applies in federal court, but the Constitution's constraint on Congress's capacity to abrogate states' sovereign immunity is not so limited. As the Court held in *Alden v. Maine*, 527 U.S. 706 (1999), it operates as a limit on Congress's regulation of the states more generally, regardless of the forum in which a suit against a state might be brought. In *Alden*, the plaintiffs filed suit against the State of Maine in Maine *state* court for the state's alleged violations of the federal Fair Labor Standards Act (FLSA). The Eleventh Amendment was inapplicable because the action had been filed in state court. Further, the text of the FLSA clearly subjected the states to private unconsenting suits for retrospective relief. But the Supreme Court held that Congress's attempt in the FLSA to abrogate the states' sovereign immunity was unconstitutional. Though the FLSA was valid legislation under the commerce power, it could not be justified as valid legislation under §5 of the Fourteenth Amendment. As a result, Congress could not render states liable to private unconsenting suits for violations of the FLSA, regardless of where those suits might be brought.

In a sense, the principle recognized in *Alden* extends the immunity provided by the Eleventh Amendment: state governments enjoy immunity from private unconsenting suits brought under federal statutes in state court, just as they do in federal court. But more accurately, this immunity is unrelated to the Eleventh Amendment (which is really a regulation of the federal judiciary's subject matter jurisdiction). The constraint recognized in *Alden* is better understood a limit on Congress's legislative powers—a limit on how Congress can use its enumerated powers to regulate the actions of state governments. In this sense, it operates much like the anti-commandeering principle, grounded not in any particular textual provision of the Constitution but in the Constitution's overarching structure of dual sovereignty. Just as the anti-commandeering principle forbids Congress from commanding states to take affirmative steps to govern their citizens according to federal directives, so, too, is Congress forbidden—unless acting pursuant to §5 of the Fourteenth Amendment, or with respect to a matter on which the states' have surrendered their immunity pursuant to the "plan of the Convention"—from subjecting state governments to private unconsenting suits, regardless of the court in which the claim is filed.

* * *

QUESTION: Congress enacts the Family and Medical Leave Act (FMLA). The Act entitles eligible employees to take up to 12 work weeks of unpaid leave annually for any of several reasons, including the onset of a "serious health condition" in an employee's spouse, child, or parent. It creates a private right of action to seek both equitable relief and money damages against any employer (including a state government) "in any Federal or State court of competent jurisdiction" for violations of the Act. Plaintiff is an employee of the State of Nevada. She alleges that, in violation of the FMLA, the state deprived her of leave to care for her father for ten weeks during her father's serious illness and eventual death. She sues the state in Nevada state court, seeking $50,000 in damages. Under Nevada state law, the state is immune from private unconsenting suits for damages in Nevada state court. Can the state court adjudicate Plaintiff's suit?

ANSWER: Yes. *See Nevada Dept. of Human Resources v. Hibbs*, 538 U.S. 721 (2003). First, state courts are courts of general jurisdiction, and thus have subject matter jurisdiction over all claims, regardless of the source of law creating the cause of action. Plaintiff's claim under the FMLA is created by federal law, but state courts have jurisdiction to hear federal claims (unless Congress by statute has made federal jurisdiction exclusive). Indeed, state courts are generally *obligated* to hear federal claims brought before them. Second, the FMLA Is within Congress's §5 power, because it is "congruent" and "proportional" to the constitutional violations—gender discrimination in violation of the Equal Protection Clause—that Congress sought to remedy. The Act combats the general, discriminatory assumption that women will care for ill family members, regardless of the impact on their finances or their careers. Third, because the FMLA is valid §5 legislation, it abrogates the states' sovereign immunity, assuming the statute's language subjecting the states to private unconsenting suits is clear and unambiguous. Thus, the FMLA forces the states to stand suit against private unconsenting actions, for whatever relief afforded by the FMLA, in state or federal court. As a result, the Nevada state court has subject matter jurisdiction to adjudicate Plaintiff's action against the State of Nevada.

* * *

C.   The Principle of Equal State Sovereignty

A third limitation on Congress's power to enact laws regulating the actions of states is the "fundamental principle of equal sovereignty." In general terms, absent an exceptional justification, Congress cannot single out a subset of states for differential treatment, forcing them to endure significant burdens not borne by other states.

This principle was decisive in *Shelby County v. Holder*, 570 U.S. 529 (2013), which concerned the constitutionality of a central provision of the Voting Rights Act. Section 5 of the Voting Rights Act subjects so-called "covered jurisdictions" throughout the U.S. to a "preclearance procedure" if they seek to change their election laws. Specifically, covered jurisdictions are not permitted to change any aspect of their election laws without first receiving the approval of either (a) a special three-judge federal district court, or (b) the Voting Rights Division of the U.S. Department of Justice. Section 4 of the Voting Rights Act, in turn, specified which jurisdictions are subject to §5's preclearance procedure.

Congress originally enacted the Voting Rights Act in 1965, not long after the "Bloody Sunday" march across the Edmund Pettus Bridge in Selma,

Alabama. Section 4's coverage formula turned on voter registration and participation numbers current in 1965; it captured jurisdictions, almost exclusively in the deep South, with a recent and ongoing history of racial discrimination in voting. Due to this discrimination, these jurisdictions had lower rates of voter registration and participation and contained significant racial disparities.

Congress subsequently re-enacted the Voting Rights Act several times, most recently in 2006. In doing so, however, Congress did not update the terms of §4's coverage formula. Instead, Congress continued to base the formula on 40-year-old data concerning voter registration and participation. As a result, as late as 2013, the jurisdictions captured by §4 (and thus subject to §5's preclearance requirement) were largely the same as those in 1965. To be sure, the record amassed by Congress in reenacting the Voting Rights Act in 2006 demonstrated ongoing problems of racial discrimination in voting, including discrimination in the covered jurisdictions. But Congress did not actually update §4's formula so as to reflect the changed circumstances.

In 2013, Alabama remained a covered jurisdiction under §4, and this meant Shelby County, Alabama, was subject to §5's preclearance provision. The county challenged the application §5 to its election laws on the ground that Congress's continued reliance on §4's outdated coverage formula rendered it unconstitutional. By a 5-to-4 vote, the Supreme Court agreed.

Writing for the Court, Chief Justice Roberts explained that the Voting Rights Act "imposes current burdens and must be justified by current needs." Specifically, "a departure from the fundamental principle of equal sovereignty requires a showing that a statute's disparate geographic coverage is sufficiently related to the problem that it targets." The states retain broad autonomy under the Constitution in structuring their governments and pursuing legislative objectives, including "the power to regulate elections." And the "fundamental principle of equal sovereignty" is highly pertinent in assessing Congress's disparate treatment of the states.

To the Court, the Voting Rights Act sharply departed from these basic principles. It required states to beseech the federal government for permission to implement laws that they would otherwise have the right to enact and execute on their own. And despite the nation's tradition of equal sovereignty, the Act applied to only nine States (and some additional counties located in other states). In 1966, such an "uncommon exercise of congressional power" could be justified by "exceptional conditions"; the "blight of racial discrimination in voting" had "infected the electoral process in parts of our country for nearly a century."

Nearly 50 years later, the Court reasoned, matters had changed. Largely because of the Voting Rights Act, "[v]oter turnout and registration rates" in covered jurisdictions "now approach parity. Blatantly discriminatory evasions of federal decrees are rare. And minority candidates hold office at unprecedented levels." The tests and devices that previously blocked ballot access had been forbidden nationwide for over 40 years. Yet the Act had not eased §5's restrictions or narrowed the scope of §4's coverage formula along the way. Instead, those extraordinary and unprecedented features had been reauthorized as if nothing had changed.

The Court thus concluded that §4's formula was now unconstitutional. When originally enacted, the coverage formula was "rational in both practice and theory": it looked at both the cause and effect of racial discrimination in voting, and it tailored its remedy of preclearance to those jurisdictions exhibiting both. But in 2013, §4 was based on decades-old data and eradicated practices. It captured states due to events in the 1960s and early 1970s. In assessing the current need for preclearance, the history since 1965 could not be ignored. If Congress wishes to divide the states—and single out specific jurisdictions for significant burdens—it must identify those jurisdictions on a basis that makes sense given current conditions. Regardless of how one looked at the legislative record compiled by Congress in reenacting the Voting Rights Act in 2006, no one could fairly say that it showed anything approaching the "pervasive," "flagrant," "widespread," and "rampant" discrimination that clearly distinguished the covered jurisdictions from the rest of the nation in 1965.

More generally, *Shelby County* held that a federal statute treating the states differently—singling out particular jurisdictions for disfavored treatment—is presumptively invalid. Such a statute might still be constitutional, but a "departure from the fundamental principle of equal sovereignty requires a showing that a statute's disparate geographic coverage is sufficiently related to the problem that it targets." The 2006 reenactment of the Voting Rights Act failed this test, rendering §4's coverage formula—the trigger for preclearance under §5 of the Act—unconstitutional.

PART IV

THE SEPARATION OF POWERS

CHAPTER 13
THE POWERS OF THE PRESIDENT

A. Introduction

We now turn to an examination of the powers of the Executive Branch and its head, the President. In doing so, our focus shifts from questions about the "vertical" separation of authority (between the federal government and the states) to the "horizontal" distribution of powers among the three branches of the national government. To be sure, earlier chapters have touched on these issues. The justiciability doctrines of standing and political questions, as well as the foundational principle that federal courts have the power of judicial review, certainly concern the separation of national powers; they address what is appropriate for the federal judiciary to decide and what, instead, must be left to the elected branches. But for the principles, rules, and doctrines covered in the following three chapters, separation-of-powers questions are more plainly front and center.

1. The "separation of powers" and "checks and balances"

Two stock phrases are often used to describe the Constitution's arrangement of the three branches of the federal government, phrases that may be familiar. One is the "separation of powers"; the other is a "system of checks and balances." Though these phrases are sometimes used interchangeably, they refer to different phenomena—and a moment of reflection reveals there is some tension between the two. The idea of *separated* powers implies that each branch of government has its own, distinct sphere—legislative, executive, or judicial—and each is autonomous in its respective sphere. The idea of checks and balances, by contrast, implies a degree of intermingling and overlapping power, a system in which unilateral action by any one branch is unusual (if not nonexistent). Each branch works to check the powers of the others.

Despite this tension, it is fair to say that, depending on the precise circumstance, the Constitution embraces *both* ideas. First, the Constitution provides for several interbranch checks on the exercise of governmental power. Consider the following list, containing just a few examples:

* The President is granted the power to veto legislation passed by Congress—and Congress then has the power to override the President's veto.

* Through the power of judicial review, the Supreme Court can invalidate national legislation, or executive action, as unconstitutional or

otherwise inconsistent with federal law (at least as applied in a particular case).

* The President, officers in the Executive Branch, and federal judges may be impeached and removed from office by the House of Representatives and the Senate through the process of impeachment.

* The Senate must confirm the appointments of all principal executive officers and Article III judges.

* Congress can regulate and define the jurisdiction of the federal courts.

At the same time, the Constitution also calls for the *separation* of governmental power. As many Supreme Court decisions attest, the Constitution generally requires each branch to perform the function assigned to it. Consider the first sentences of Articles I, II, and III. Those texts expressly assign the legislative power to Congress, the executive power to the President, and the judicial power to the Supreme Court and those lower federal courts that Congress chooses to create. Moreover, it is a essential axiom of constitutional law that no branch can "unduly interfere" with another's constitutionally assigned duties. Conversely, no branch is permitted to give away its constitutionally assigned power to another branch.

Thus, despite the tension between these two animating ideas—the separation of powers and checks and balances—our Constitution embodies a mixture of the two. This—along with the unavoidable fact that the Constitution only speaks in broad outlines—has left the law in this area relatively indefinite. The case law is sparse, as these sorts of disputes are often resolved through politics rather than litigation. And this means that the Supreme Court decisions that do exist are exceptionally important.

2. General principles

There is a final point about this material that warrants mention before delving into the details. A common complaint about existing constitutional law governing the separation of powers is that it is difficult to locate general principles of broad application—that the doctrinal rules do not seem to be much more than a grab bag of various holdings from specific cases. There are two responses.

First, that observation has some validity. There have been relatively few litigated cases resulting in court-made constitutional doctrine that we typically recognize as such. Instead, many of these interbranch struggles about the scope of the branches' respective powers—particularly the struggles between the President and Congress—have been resolved through the political process. Thus, the residuum of relevant judicial decisions is thin.

Second, if one wanted to give some shape to the area, it is fair to say that *most* separation of powers controversies fall into one of two basic categories. One category is those cases where a very specific textual provision in the

Constitution is implicated. In these sorts of disputes, the Supreme Court has generally required a rather fastidious adherence to the precise wording of the Constitution. (Cases like *INS v. Chadha*, *Clinton v. New York*, and *Bowsher v. Synar* would be good examples.) A second category comprises those cases governed by general separation-of-powers principles: the basic ideas that each branch must perform its assigned function, and that no branch can unduly interfere with another. (The cases addressing the removal of federal officers, such as *Morrison v. Olson* and *Seila Law v. CFPB*, are illustrative.) In these instances, the law is necessarily fuzzier, as the guiding sources of law are less clearly defined.

B.   The Framework for Understanding Executive Power

1. Article II

We start with the basic framework for understanding the powers of the President. The decision most associated with this framework is the Steel Seizure Case, *Youngstown Sheet & Tube Co. v. Sawyer*, 343 U.S. 579 (1952). More specifically, it is Justice Jackson's concurring opinion in *Youngstown* that has endured as the precedent with far more influence than the majority opinion authored by Justice Black.

The first sentence of Article II provides that "[t]he executive Power shall be vested in a President of the United States of America." Thus, just as Article I vests the legislative power in Congress, Article II vests the executive power in the President. What does the "executive power" entail? At least in general terms, it means the power to *enforce* or *administer* federal law. It is distinguishable from the legislative power, which is the power to *make law*—to prescribe the generally applicable rules that govern behavior, rules that are then to be enforced, administered, or executed. The executive power is likewise distinguishable from the judicial power, which is the power to adjudicate disputes about the specific application of those rules to particular persons or entities in the context of a case or controversy.

Thus, the President is clearly vested with the power to execute, to administer, and to enforce the laws that have been duly enacted by Congress. Indeed, another clause—perhaps the most important clause in Article II—imposes on the President a constitutional *obligation* to ensure that the laws of the United States are adequately enforced. This is the Take Care Clause of Article II, §3: "[The President] shall take Care that the Laws be faithfully executed."

A crucial question, then, is whether the President has any power *beyond* that of executing those laws duly enacted by Congress. There are two parts to the answer. First, the President does have some powers (other than to execute federal law) that are granted *directly by the Constitution*, and thus that the President can exercise absent any statute from Congress. For example, Article II, §2 states that "[t]he President shall be Commander in Chief of the Army and Navy of the United States." The President needs no statutorily conferred power to exercise this authority (though Congress must have *created* an Army and Navy for this authority to mean anything practically). Likewise, Article II grants the President the pardon power (to grant pardons for federal criminal offenses) and the recognition power (to recognize foreign governments).

Second, the President also enjoys some residuum of "inherent executive power," power that inheres in being the head of the Executive Branch or which is implicit in the granting of these specific powers. The scope of these inherent powers is unclear, as they (by definition) are not spelled out expressly in the Constitution. But plainly *some* power inheres in the office of President—power that entitles the President to take actions that go beyond directly enforcing the laws of the United States or performing one of the other, expressly specified powers delineated in Article II. The authority to keep certain communications confidential, for instance, is considered an inherent presidential power.

But the vast, vast majority of the Executive Branch's actions constitute the administration or enforcement of federal statutes enacted by Congress. In these instances, the President—usually through his agents, such as the heads of executive agencies and departments—is exercising power that has been granted to him or her by Congress through duly enacted statutes. In such instances, the relevant constitutional question does not turn on the powers granted by Article II, but whether Congress had the authority to enact the statute being enforced. But presidential power questions, as such, arise when the President is doing something else—taking action that has not been clearly authorized by a federal statute. In such instances, the President must justify his actions either through a specific grant of power from the Constitution or in the office's inherent authority. *Youngstown* is perhaps the leading example in our nation's history of how these disputes play out, and it continues to provide the framework by which questions of presidential power are analyzed.

2. The Steel Seizure Case: *Youngstown*

Youngstown belongs in the pantheon of great constitutional cases with *Marbury* and *McCulloch*. In April 1952, President Truman issued Executive Order 10340, which directed the Secretary of Commerce (at the time, Charles Sawyer) to seize control of the nation's steel mills. An Executive Order is an order by the President instructing the Executive Branch to take certain action that the President believes is within the Executive Branch's statutory or constitutional authority. Executive orders are official documents, numbered consecutively, through which the President manages the operations of the federal government. Modern presidents have issued hundreds of such orders over the course of their presidencies.

Executive orders look very much like statutes, with separate sections, declared purposes, and definitions. President Truman issued Executive Order 10340 because the U.S. was in the midst of the Korean War and he perceived a national emergency if steel production screeched to a halt. The United

Steelworkers of America had announced they would soon go on strike. This would have shuttered the mills, and ongoing steel production was (at least in the mind of President Truman) vital to the war effort. Not only were thousands of American troops in harm's way on the Korean Peninsula, but the war was the principal flashpoint in the Cold War with the Soviet Union. The President concluded that a disruption in domestic steel production would constitute a national emergency. The question presented was whether the President had the authority to direct the federal government to seize the mills in this fashion. As you read the opinion, consider the following questions:

1. On what precise basis did the President claim he had the authority to seize the steel mills?

2. What is "executive power," and what does it mean to "take care that the law be faithfully executed"? Why do these powers necessarily depend on Congress?

3. Can the President *ever* act without Congress first enacting a federal statute? If so, when, and under what authority?

4. According to Justice Jackson's concurrence, when is the President's claim to constitutional authority at its strongest? When is it at its weakest? Why?

5. Exactly why was Executive Order 10340 unconstitutional? What provision in the Constitution did it violate?

Youngstown Sheet & Tube Co. v. Sawyer
343 U.S. 579 (1952)

JUSTICE BLACK delivered the opinion of the Court.

We are asked to decide whether the President was acting within his constitutional power when he issued an order directing the Secretary of Commerce to take possession of and operate most of the Nation's steel mills. The mill owners argue that the President's order amounts to law-making, a legislative function which the Constitution has expressly confided to the Congress and not to the President. The Government's position is that the order was made on findings of the President that his action was necessary to avert a national catastrophe which would inevitably result from a stoppage of steel production, and that in meeting this grave emergency the President was acting within the aggregate of his constitutional powers as the Nation's Chief Executive and the Commander in Chief of the Armed Forces of the United States. The issue emerges here from the following series of events:

In the latter part of 1951, a dispute arose between the steel companies and their employees over terms and conditions that should be included in new collective bargaining agreements. Long-continued conferences failed to resolve the dispute. On December 18, 1951, the employees' representative, United Steelworkers of America, C.I.O., gave notice of an intention to strike when the existing bargaining agreements expired on

December 31. The Federal Mediation and Conciliation Service then intervened in an effort to get labor and management to agree. This failing, the President on December 22, 1951, referred the dispute to the Federal Wage Stabilization Board to investigate and make recommendations for fair and equitable terms of settlement. This Board's report resulted in no settlement. On April 4, 1952, the Union gave notice of a nation-wide strike called to begin at 12:01 a.m. April 9. The indispensability of steel as a component of substantially all weapons and other war materials led the President to believe that the proposed work stoppage would immediately jeopardize our national defense and that governmental seizure of the steel mills was necessary in order to assure the continued availability of steel. Reciting these considerations for his action, the President, a few hours before the strike was to begin, issued Executive Order 10340. The order directed the Secretary of Commerce to take possession of most of the steel mills and keep them running. The Secretary immediately issued his own possessory orders, calling upon the presidents of the various seized companies to serve as operating managers for the United States. They were directed to carry on their activities in accordance with regulations and directions of the Secretary. The next morning the President sent a message to Congress reporting his action. Twelve days later he sent a second message. Congress has taken no action.

Obeying the Secretary's orders under protest, the companies brought proceedings against him in the District Court. Their complaints charged that the seizure was not authorized by an act of Congress or by any constitutional provisions. The District Court was asked to declare the orders of the President and the Secretary invalid and to issue preliminary and permanent injunctions restraining their enforcement. Opposing the motion for preliminary injunction, the United States asserted that a strike disrupting steel production for even a brief period would so endanger the well-being and safety of the Nation that the President had "inherent power" to do what he had done—power "supported by the Constitution, by historical precedent, and by court decisions." The Government also contended that in any event no preliminary injunction should be issued because the companies had made no showing that their available legal remedies were inadequate or that their injuries from seizure would be irreparable. Holding against the Government on all points, the District Court on April 30 issued a preliminary injunction restraining the Secretary from "continuing the seizure and possession of the plants . . . and from acting under the purported authority of Executive Order No. 10340." On the same day the Court of Appeals stayed the District Court's injunction. Deeming it best that the issues raised be promptly decided by this Court, we granted certiorari on May 3 and set the cause for argument on May 12.

Two crucial issues have developed: First. Should final determination of the constitutional validity of the President's order be made in this case which has proceeded no further than the preliminary injunction stage? Second. If so, is the seizure order within the constitutional power of the President?

* * *

II

The President's power, if any, to issue the order must stem either from an act of Congress or from the Constitution itself. There is no statute that expressly authorizes the President to take possession of property as he did here. Nor is there any act of Congress to which our attention has been directed from which such a power can fairly be implied. Indeed, we do not understand the Government to rely on statutory authorization for this seizure. There are two statutes which do authorize the President to take both personal and real property under certain conditions. However, the Government admits that these conditions were not met and that the President's order was not rooted in either of the statutes. The Government refers to the seizure provisions of one of these statutes as "much too cumbersome, involved, and time-consuming for the crisis which was at hand."

Moreover, the use of the seizure technique to solve labor disputes in order to prevent work stoppages was not only unauthorized by any congressional enactment; prior to this controversy, Congress had refused to adopt that method of settling labor disputes. When the Taft-Hartley Act was under consideration in 1947, Congress rejected an amendment which would have authorized such governmental seizures in cases of emergency. Apparently it was thought that the technique of seizure, like that of compulsory arbitration, would interfere with the process of collective bargaining. Consequently, the plan Congress adopted in that Act did not provide for seizure under any circumstances. Instead, the plan sought to bring about settlements by use of the customary devices of mediation, conciliation, investigation by boards of inquiry, and public reports. In some instances temporary injunctions were authorized to provide cooling-off periods. All this failing, unions were left free to strike after a secret vote by employees as to whether they wished to accept their employers' final settlement offer.

It is clear that if the President had authority to issue the order he did, it must be found in some provision of the Constitution. And it is not claimed that express constitutional language grants this power to the President. The contention is that presidential power should be implied from the aggregate of his powers under the Constitution. Particular reliance is placed on provisions in Article II which say that "The executive Power shall be vested in a President . . ."; that "he shall take Care that the Laws be faithfully executed"; and that he "shall be Commander in Chief of the Army and Navy of the United States."

The order cannot properly be sustained as an exercise of the President's military power as Commander in Chief of the Armed Forces. The Government attempts to do so by citing a number of cases upholding broad powers in military commanders engaged in day-to-day fighting in a theater of war. Such cases need not concern us here. Even though "theater of war" be an expanding concept, we cannot with faithfulness to our constitutional system hold that the Commander in Chief of the Armed Forces has the ultimate power as such to take possession of private property in order to keep labor disputes from stopping production. This is a job for the Nation's lawmakers, not for its military authorities.

Nor can the seizure order be sustained because of the several constitutional provisions that grant executive power to the President. In the framework of our Constitution, the President's power to see that the laws are faithfully executed refutes the idea that he is to be a lawmaker. The Constitution limits his functions in the lawmaking process to the recommending of laws he thinks wise and the vetoing of laws he thinks bad. And the Constitution is neither silent nor equivocal about who shall make laws which the President is to execute. The first section of the first article says that "All legislative Powers herein granted shall be vested in a Congress of the United States." After granting many powers to the Congress, Article I goes on to provide that Congress may "make all Laws which shall be necessary and proper for carrying into Execution the foregoing Powers, and all other Powers vested by this Constitution in the Government of the United States, or in any Department or Officer thereof."

The President's order does not direct that a congressional policy be executed in a manner prescribed by Congress—it directs that a presidential policy be executed in a manner prescribed by the President. The preamble of the order itself, like that of many statutes, sets out reasons why the President believes certain policies should be adopted, proclaims these policies as rules of conduct to be followed, and again, like a statute, authorizes a government official to promulgate additional rules and regulations consistent with the policy proclaimed and needed to carry that policy into execution. The power of Congress to adopt such public policies as those proclaimed by the order is beyond question. It can authorize the taking of private property for public use. It can make laws regulating the relationships between employers and employees, prescribing rules designed to settle labor disputes, and fixing wages and working conditions in certain fields of our economy. The Constitution does not subject this lawmaking power of Congress to presidential or military supervision or control.

It is said that other Presidents without congressional authority have taken possession of private business enterprises in order to settle labor disputes. But even if this be true, Congress has not thereby lost its exclusive constitutional authority to make laws necessary and proper to carry out the powers vested by the Constitution "in the Government of the United States, or any Department or Officer thereof."

The Founders of this Nation entrusted the lawmaking power to the Congress alone in both good and bad times. It would do no good to recall the historical events, the fears of power and the hopes for freedom that lay behind their choice. Such a review would but confirm our holding that this seizure order cannot stand.

MR. JUSTICE JACKSON, concurring in the judgment and opinion of the Court. . . .

A judge, like an executive adviser, may be surprised at the poverty of really useful and unambiguous authority applicable to concrete problems of executive power as they actually present themselves. Just what our forefathers did envision, or would have envisioned had they foreseen modern conditions, must be divined from materials almost as enigmatic as the dreams Joseph was called upon to interpret for Pharaoh. A century and a half of partisan debate and scholarly speculation yields no net result but only supplies more or less apt quotations from respected sources on each side of any question. They largely cancel each other. And court decisions are indecisive because of the judicial practice of dealing with the largest questions in the most narrow way.

The actual art of governing under our Constitution does not and cannot conform to judicial definitions of the power of any of its branches based on isolated clauses or even single Articles torn from context. While the Constitution diffuses power the better to secure liberty, it also contemplates that practice will integrate the dispersed powers into a workable government. It enjoins upon its branches separateness but interdependence, autonomy but reciprocity. Presidential powers are not fixed but fluctuate, depending upon their disjunction or conjunction with those of Congress. We may well begin by a somewhat over-simplified grouping of practical situations in which a President may doubt, or others may challenge, his powers, and by distinguishing roughly the legal consequences of this factor of relativity.

1. When the President acts pursuant to an express or implied authorization of Congress, his authority is at its maximum, for it includes all that he possesses in his own right plus all that Congress can delegate. In these circumstances, and in these only, may he be said (for what it may be worth) to personify the federal sovereignty. If his act is held unconstitutional under these circumstances, it usually means that the Federal Government as an undivided whole lacks power. A seizure executed by the President pursuant to an Act of Congress would be supported by the strongest of presumptions and the widest latitude of judicial interpretation, and the burden of persuasion would rest heavily upon any who might attack it.

2. When the President acts in absence of either a congressional grant or denial of authority, he can only rely upon his own independent powers, but there is a zone of twilight in which he and Congress may have concurrent authority, or in which its distribution is uncertain. Therefore, congressional inertia, indifference or quiescence may sometimes, at least as a practical matter, enable, if not invite, measures on independent presidential responsibility. In this area, any actual test of

power is likely to depend on the imperatives of events and contemporary imponderables rather than on abstract theories of law.

3. When the President takes measures incompatible with the expressed or implied will of Congress, his power is at its lowest ebb, for then he can rely only upon his own constitutional powers minus any constitutional powers of Congress over the matter. Courts can sustain exclusive presidential control in such a case only by disabling the Congress from acting upon the subject. Presidential claim to a power at once so conclusive and preclusive must be scrutinized with caution, for what is at stake is the equilibrium established by our constitutional system.

Into which of these classifications does this executive seizure of the steel industry fit? It is eliminated from the first by admission, for it is conceded that no congressional authorization exists for this seizure. That takes away also the support of the many precedents and declarations which were made in relation, and must be confined, to this category.

Can it then be defended under flexible tests available to the second category? It seems clearly eliminated from that class because Congress has not left seizure of private property an open field but has covered it by three statutory policies inconsistent with this seizure. In cases where the purpose is to supply needs of the Government itself, two courses are provided: one, seizure of a plant which fails to comply with obligatory orders placed by the Government; another, condemnation of facilities, including temporary use under the power of eminent domain. The third is applicable where it is the general economy of the country that is to be protected rather than exclusive governmental interests. None of these were invoked. In choosing a different and inconsistent way of his own, the President cannot claim that it is necessitated or invited by failure of Congress to legislate upon the occasions, grounds and methods for seizure of industrial properties.

This leaves the current seizure to be justified only by the severe tests under the third grouping, where it can be supported only by any remainder of executive power after subtraction of such powers as Congress may have over the subject. In short, we can sustain the President only by holding that seizure of such strike-bound industries is within his domain and beyond control by Congress. Thus, this Court's first review of such seizures occurs under circumstances which leave presidential power most vulnerable to attack and in the least favorable of possible constitutional postures. . . .

The Solicitor General seeks the power of seizure in three clauses of the Executive Article, the first reading, "The executive Power shall be vested in a President of the United States of America." Lest I be thought to exaggerate, I quote the interpretation which his brief puts upon it: "In our view, this clause constitutes a grant of all the executive powers of which the Government is capable." If that be true, it is difficult to see

300

why the forefathers bothered to add several specific items, including some trifling ones.

The example of such unlimited executive power that must have most impressed the forefathers was the prerogative exercised by George III, and the description of its evils in the Declaration of Independence leads me to doubt that they were creating their new Executive in his image. Continental European examples were no more appealing. And if we seek instruction from our own times, we can match it only from the executive powers in those governments we disparagingly describe as totalitarian. I cannot accept the view that this clause is a grant in bulk of all conceivable executive power but regard it as an allocation to the presidential office of the generic powers thereafter stated.

The clause on which the Government next relies is that "The President shall be Commander in Chief of the Army and Navy of the United States." These cryptic words have given rise to some of the most persistent controversies in our constitutional history. . . . Nothing in our Constitution is plainer than that declaration of a war is entrusted only to Congress. Of course, a state of war may in fact exist without a formal declaration. But no doctrine that the Court could promulgate would seem to me more sinister and alarming than that a President whose conduct of foreign affairs is so largely uncontrolled, and often even is unknown, can vastly enlarge his mastery over the internal affairs of the country by his own commitment of the Nation's armed forces to some foreign venture. I do not, however, find it necessary or appropriate to consider the legal status of the Korean enterprise to discountenance argument based on it. . . . .

The third clause in which the Solicitor General finds seizure powers is that "he shall take Care that the Laws be faithfully executed . . . ." That authority must be matched against words of the Fifth Amendment that "No person shall be . . . deprived of life, liberty or property, without due process of law . . . ." One gives a governmental authority that reaches so far as there is law, the other gives a private right that authority shall go no farther. These signify about all there is of the principle that ours is a government of laws, not of men, and that we submit ourselves to rulers only if under rules.

The Solicitor General lastly grounds support of the seizure upon nebulous, inherent powers never expressly granted but said to have accrued to the office from the customs and claims of preceding administrations. The plea is for a resulting power to deal with a crisis or an emergency according to the necessities of the case, the unarticulated assumption being that necessity knows no law.

Loose and irresponsible use of adjectives colors all nonlegal and much legal discussion of presidential powers. "Inherent" powers, "implied" powers, "incidental" powers, "plenary" powers, "war" powers and "emergency" powers are used, often interchangeably and without fixed or ascertainable meanings. . . .

The essence of our free Government is "leave to live by no man's leave, underneath the law"—to be governed by those impersonal forces which we call law. Our Government is fashioned to fulfill this concept so far as humanly possible. The Executive, except for recommendation and veto, has no legislative power. The executive action we have here originates in the individual will of the President and represents an exercise of authority without law. No one, perhaps not even the President, knows the limits of the power he may seek to exert in this instance and the parties affected cannot learn the limit of their rights. We do not know today what powers over labor or property would be claimed to flow from Government possession if we should legalize it, what rights to compensation would be claimed or recognized, or on what contingency it would end. With all its defects, delays and inconveniences, men have discovered no technique for long preserving free government except that the Executive be under the law, and that the law be made by parliamentary deliberations.

Such institutions may be destined to pass away. But it is the duty of the Court to be last, not first, to give them up.

CHIEF JUSTICE VINSON, with whom JUSTICE REED and JUSTICE MINTON join, dissenting.

The President of the United States directed the Secretary of Commerce to take temporary possession of the Nation's steel mills during the existing emergency because "a work stoppage would immediately jeopardize and imperil our national defense and the defense of those joined with us in resisting aggression, and would add to the continuing danger of our soldiers, sailors and airmen engaged in combat in the field."

In passing upon the question of Presidential powers in this case, we must first consider the context in which those powers were exercised. Those who suggest that this is a case involving extraordinary powers should be mindful that these are extraordinary times. A world not yet recovered from the devastation of World War II has been forced to face the threat of another and more terrifying global conflict.

In 1950, when the United Nations called upon member nations "to render every assistance" to repel aggression in Korea, the United States furnished its vigorous support. For almost two full years, our armed forces have been fighting in Korea, suffering casualties of over 108,000 men. Hostilities have not abated. The "determination of the United Nations to continue its action in Korea to meet the aggression" has been reaffirmed. Congressional support of the action in Korea has been manifested by provisions for increased military manpower and equipment and for economic stabilization, as hereinafter described. Alert to our responsibilities, which coincide with our own self preservation through mutual security, Congress has enacted a large body of implementing legislation. As an illustration of the magnitude of the over-all program,

Congress has appropriated $130 billion for our own defense and for military assistance to our allies since the June, 1950, attack in Korea.

The President has the duty to execute the foregoing legislative programs. Their successful execution depends upon continued production of steel and stabilized prices for steel. Accordingly, when the collective bargaining agreements between the Nation's steel producers and their employees, represented by the United Steel Workers, were due to expire on December 31, 1951, and a strike shutting down the entire basic steel industry was threatened, the President acted to avert a complete shutdown of steel production. . . .

Plaintiffs do not remotely suggest any basis for rejecting the President's finding that any stoppage of steel production would immediately place the Nation in peril. At the time of seizure there was not, and there is not now, the slightest evidence to justify the belief that any strike will be of short duration. The Union and the steel companies may well engage in a lengthy struggle. Plaintiff's counsel tells us that "sooner or later" the mills will operate again. That may satisfy the steel companies and, perhaps, the Union. But our soldiers and our allies will hardly be cheered with the assurance that the ammunition upon which their lives depend will be forthcoming—"sooner or later," or, in other words, "too little and too late."

Accordingly, if the President has any power under the Constitution to meet a critical situation in the absence of express statutory authorization, there is no basis whatever for criticizing the exercise of such power in this case. . . .

Focusing now on the situation confronting the President on the night of April 8, 1952, we cannot but conclude that the President was performing his duty under the Constitution to "take Care that the Laws be faithfully executed"—a duty described by President Benjamin Harrison as "the central idea of the office." The President reported to Congress the morning after the seizure that he acted because a work stoppage in steel production would immediately imperil the safety of the Nation by preventing execution of the legislative programs for procurement of military equipment. And, while a shutdown could be averted by granting the price concessions requested by plaintiffs, granting such concessions would disrupt the price stabilization program also enacted by Congress. Rather than fail to execute either legislative program, the President acted to execute both. . . .

Faced with the duty of executing the defense programs which Congress had enacted and the disastrous effects that any stoppage in steel production would have on those programs, the President acted to preserve those programs by seizing the steel mills. There is no question that the possession was other than temporary in character and subject to congressional direction—either approving, disapproving or regulating the manner in which the mills were to be administered and returned to the owners. The President immediately informed Congress of his action and clearly stated his intention to abide by the legislative will. No basis for claims of arbitrary action, unlimited powers or dictatorial usurpation of congressional power appears from the facts of this case. On the contrary, judicial, legislative and executive precedents throughout our history demonstrate that in this case the President acted in full conformity with his duties under the Constitution.

* * *

Notes on *Youngstown Sheet & Tube Co. v. Sawyer*

1. ***The majority opinion***: Justice Black authored the opinion for the Court, which held that Executive Order 10340 was unconstitutional as exceeding the President's authority. He started with the essential postulate that any action taken by the President—just like any action taken by Congress or the federal judiciary—must be authorized by the Constitution. There must be some constitutional grant of authority that justifies the President's action, whether that grant of authority is express or implicit. Here, the government pointed to three provisions in Article II: those providing that "the executive Power shall be vested in a President"; that "he shall take Care that the Laws be faithfully executed"; and that he "shall be Commander in Chief of the Army and Navy of the United States." According to the Court, the first two could not justify the President's seizure order because Congress had not enacted a law granting the President the authority to take the action at issue. Thus, the executive order could not possibly constitute a use of "the executive Power" or represent the President's efforts to "take Care that the Laws be faithfully executed." No federal law existed that could be "executed" in this fashion.

This left the President's commander-in-chief power. And on that point, the Court explained that, though the precise contours of that power have not been judicially defined, it could not possibly extend this far—into the regulation of domestic economic matters—without threatening the foundational norms established in the Constitution:

> "Even though 'theater of war' be an expanding concept, we cannot with faithfulness to our constitutional system hold that the Commander in Chief of the Armed Forces has the ultimate power as such to take possession of private property in order to keep labor disputes from stopping production. This is a job for the Nation's lawmakers, not for its military authorities."

Hence, there was no Article II power that granted the President the authority to seize the mills, rendering the order unconstitutional—no matter how essential the President thought it to meet a national emergency.

2. ***Justice Jackson's three categories***: Though it was merely a concurrence for one justice, Justice Jackson's *Youngstown* opinion has become the most influential. Jackson set out an elegant (if someone simplistic) framework for analyzing assertions of presidential power, and it has become the prism through which most such questions have been evaluated ever since. Jackson

stated that there are essentially three sorts of circumstances in which the President seeks to exercise his authority, what he called "a somewhat over-simplified grouping of practical situations." One category describes when the President's authority is at its apex; one describes his power at its lowest ebb; and one falls between. Different situations may not fit neatly into one of these three boxes, but the three categories offer a helpful way of thinking about the President's power in any particular situation.

a. *Category 1*: Category 1 is where the President's authority at its apex, when he acts with Congress's authorization. "When the President acts pursuant to an express or implied authorization of Congress, his authority is at its maximum, for it includes all that he possesses in his own right plus all that Congress can delegate." In this category, the President "personifies federal sovereignty." This captures the vast, vast majority of the Executive Branch's actions—actions enforcing or administering a federal law that Congress has charged the President with implementing. To be sure, disputes often arise as to whether Congress has actually delegated the particular authority in question—that is, whether the relevant statute actually gives the President the power he seeks to exercise. (For instance, whether the Clean Air Act actually gives the Administrator of the Environmental Protection Agency the authority to regulate greenhouse gases, rather than just airborne pollutants that pose a more immediate risk to human health.) But these are probably better understood as questions of statutory interpretation rather than the scope of the President's authority under Article II.

If the actions of the Executive Branch are clearly authorized by statute, can they nonetheless be unconstitutional? Absolutely, if Congress lacks the authority to enact the statute the President is seeking to enforce or implement. Consider *United States v. Lopez*. Recall that it was federal prosecutors—federal officers within the Department of Justice, a part of the Executive Branch—who prosecuted Rodrigo Lopez for violating the Gun-Free School Zones Act. Though the GFSZA might have been unconstitutional, it was only after Lopez was prosecuted that the constitutionality of the GFSZA became a live, litigable controversy. In essence, the government's actions were ultimately unconstitutional not simply because the GFSZA exceeded Congress's enumerated powers, but because the Executive Branch attempted to enforce the statute.

b. *Category 2*: Jackson's second category encompasses those circumstances where Congress has neither authorized nor forbidden the President's action. Justice Jackson refers to this area as "a zone of twilight": "When the President acts in the absence of either a congressional grant or denial of authority, he can only rely upon his own independent powers, but there is a zone of twilight in which he and Congress may have concurrent authority, or in which its distribution is uncertain." In these instances, as Jackson explained, the answer will be unclear. Justice Frankfurter likewise noted (in his separate concurring opinion) that history and tradition can be very important in these instances, and that can include precedent from outside the judicial process.

c. *Category 3*: Finally, the Jackson's third category describes instances in which the President's authority is at its nadir. "When the President takes measures incompatible with the expressed or implied will of Congress, his power is at its lowest ebb, for then he can rely only upon his own constitutional powers minus any constitutional powers of Congress over the matter." The President is on weakest constitutional ground when he is *defying* the will of Congress—when he ignores or violates the terms of a federal statute.

What historical examples might fall into this category? The George W. Bush administration's clandestine wiretapping of phone calls involving American citizens in the U.S. was arguably one. A plausible reading of the Foreign Intelligence Surveillance Act (FISA) meant that the Executive Branch was prohibited from taking such actions without first obtaining a warrant from the FISA court. And some members of the Bush Administration believed that Congress lacked the authority to prevent the President from doing so, even if that was the best reading of the FISA. Another example would be the Reagan administration's secret funding of the Contra rebels in Nicaragua during the 1980s. After it became public that the CIA conducted a number of sabotage operations aimed at the Nicaraguan government without receiving consent in advance from congressional intelligence committees, Congress enacted the Boland Amendment. The Boland Amendment prohibited the federal government from providing military support "for the purpose of overthrowing the Government of Nicaragua." Members of the Executive Branch—notably, John Poindexter and Oliver North, working through the National Security Administration—nonetheless funneled millions of dollars to the Contras.

Assuming a federal law clearly prohibits the act in question, are there any circumstances in which the President's action would nonetheless be constitutional? Yes, if the statute itself is unconstitutional because it impermissibly interferes with the President's authority. In other words, Congress may lack the power to enact the statute because it unconstitutionally interferes with the President's constitutional authority. As Justice Jackson noted in his *Youngstown* concurrence, "[c]ourts can sustain exclusive presidential control in such a case only by disabling the Congress from acting upon the subject." It must be an area that the Constitution has vested *exclusively* in the President, such that Congress's attempt to restrain the President is unconstitutional. A good example is the Tenure in Office Act of 1867, which purported to prevent President Andrew Johnson from firing any cabinet member, including the Secretary of War, without Congress's consent. This was almost certainly an unconstitutional interference with the President's authority to remove a principal officer (as Chapter 14 will discuss).

3. *Categorizing Executive Order 10340*: In which of these three categories did Executive Order 10340 belong? First, this was not a situation where

Congress had expressly authorized the President's action. President Truman conceded this point. Thus, to be constitutional, the seizure had to be an action that (a) Congress had *implicitly* authorized, (b) fell into the "zone of twilight" but was nonetheless permissible, or (c) contravened a federal statute, but was nonetheless permissible because Congress had attempted to encroach on powers resting exclusively with the President.

The Court concluded that Congress had *disapproved* of this action by the President, placing the matter in Category 3. As Justice Jackson wrote in his concurrence, "[i]t seems clearly eliminated from that class [in which Congress has not acted] because Congress has not left seizure of private property an open field but has covered it by three statutory policies inconsistent with the seizure." Or consider this passage from Justice Frankfurter's concurring opinion: "A proposal that the President be given powers to seize plants to avert a shutdown where the 'health or safety' of the nation was endangered, was thoroughly canvassed by Congress and rejected." The majority opinion was less definitive, but it drew the same conclusion: "[T]he use of the seizure technique to solve labor disputes in order to prevent work stoppages was not only unauthorized by congressional enactment; prior to this controversy, Congress had refused to adopt that method of settling labor disputes."

Thus, six justices in *Youngstown* believed that Congress had acted *affirmatively* to preclude the President from seizing the mills. And given this conclusion, the executive order could have been constitutional only if Congress's prohibiting the President from doing so was an unconstitutional interference with the President's constitutional authority.

4. *The relevant presidential powers*: Again, the Court's majority opinion concluded that Executive Order 10340 exceeded the President's constitutional powers because it could not be justified by the three provisions plausibly supporting it: the Vesting Clause of Article II, §1, clause 1 ("The executive Power shall be vested in a President of the United States of America"); the Take Care Clause of Article II, §3 ("[The President] shall take Care that the Laws be faithfully executed"); or the commander-in-chief power of Article II, §2, clause 1 ("The President shall be Commander in Chief of the Army and Navy of the United States, and of the Militia of the several States, when called into the actual Service of the United States"). The Court held that, in light of Congress's failure to enact a statute authorizing the President to take this action—indeed, its having tacitly prohibited such action—none of these powers gave the President the authority to seize the mills.

Justice Jackson reached this conclusion by reference to Congress's constitutional authority, specified in Article I, §8, clauses 12 and 13, "to raise and support Armies" and "to provide and maintain a Navy." That is, although *commanding* the armed forces is the President's responsibility, funding and providing for it are Congress's, and Executive Order 10340 fell into the latter category. "While Congress cannot deprive the President of the command of the army and navy, only Congress can provide him an army or navy to command." Justice Douglas instead reasoned that the seizure order was a "taking" of private property that, by the terms of the Fifth Amendment, would require "just compensation." Such compensation requires funding, and only Congress has the authority appropriate federal spending. Consequently, the order was necessarily legislative in nature.

The dissenters did not really take issue with the majority's premises, but instead with its conclusion that the action was legislative rather than executive in nature. They contended that this was an execution of Congress's general endorsement (through legislation) of the Korean War. In other words, Congress *had* authorized the President's actions (implicitly) by funding the war effort. It was this legislative program—the war on the Korean Peninsula—that the President was effectively executing. Thus, to the dissent, the dispute belonged in Category 1, not Category 3.

5. *A spectrum rather than categories*: Though Justice Jackson's concurrence has been extremely influential, the three categories it referenced, by Jackson's own admission, were "a somewhat over-simplified grouping." Not every action taken by the Executive Branch will fit neatly into one of these boxes. The Supreme Court acknowledged this in *Dames & Moore v. Regan*, 453 U.S. 654 (1981), a case in which the plaintiff had challenged the President's authority to enter into an agreement with the Iranian government to end the crisis of American hostages being held at the U.S. embassy in Tehran. In *Dames & Moore*, the Court noted that, instead of thinking of the President's actions as falling into one of the three distinct categories, it is more accurate to consider them as existing along a spectrum—from express congressional authorization at one end, to clear congressional prohibition at the other:

> "Justice Jackson himself recognized that his three categories represented 'a somewhat over-simplified grouping,' and it is doubtless the case that executive action in any particular instance falls not neatly in one of three pigeonholes, but rather at some point along a spectrum running from explicit congressional authorization to explicit congressional prohibition."

Courts and commentators continue to refer to Justice Jackson's three categories, and they are still helpful as archetypes. But in most cases, the notion of a spectrum of congressional authorization will be more accurate.

*   *   *

PROBLEMS ON CATEGORIZING ASSERTIONS OF EXECUTIVE POWER

The single most famous (and most frequently cited) Supreme Court opinion on the powers of the President is Justice Jackson's concurrence in *Youngstown*. There, Justice Jackson explained that every assertion of authority by the President falls into one of three categories: (1) where the President's power is at its apex, (2) a "twilight zone," in which the President's authority is uncertain, or (3) where the President's power is at its lowest ebb.

In each of the following scenarios (some of which may be familiar), please determine in which of these three categories the assertion of executive power belongs (and why).

1. An Assistant U.S. Attorney in Texas prosecutes Rodrigo Lopez in federal district court for possessing a gun in a school zone in violation of the Gun Free School Zones Act.

2. In 2016, the Internal Revenue Service audits the tax return of a taxpayer, determines that she has failed obtain minimally adequate health coverage, and assesses a tax deficiency. The IRS orders her to pay the deficiency.

3. A federal statute directs the State Department to record the place of birth as "Israel" on the passport of any American citizen born in Jerusalem who so requests. The State Department refuses to do so and will only record the place of birth as "Jerusalem."

4. In September 2001, Congress enacts a resolution entitled the "Authorization for the Use of Military Force" (AUMF), which authorizes the President to conduct military operations against al Qaeda and its allies. In 2013, the President commits thousands of U.S. troops to military actions against ISIL (or ISIS) in Iraq, Syria, and Libya, citing the AUMF as congressional authorization for the action.

5. Congress enacts a law making any person who enters the country without proper immigration documents "deportable," providing that such persons "shall be deported." (Roughly 11 million such individuals currently reside in the U.S.) Congress appropriates sufficient funds for the Department of Homeland Security (and Immigration and Customs Enforcement) to deport roughly 400,000 persons per year. The President issues an executive statement declaring that undocumented individuals who arrived in the U.S. before age 16, have continuously resided in the U.S. since 2007, have obtained a high school degree (or its equivalent), and have not committed a felony will not be deported within the next five years (provided they do not commit a crime).

* * *

C. The Recognition Power

Youngstown involved three of the most significant powers that Article II grants the President: the power to execute federal law (from the Vesting Clause), the power to "take care" that federal law is faithfully executed (from the Take Care Clause), and the commander-in-chief power. Again, more than 99 percent of actions of the President (or the Executive Branch) involve the execution of federal law, so the Vesting and Take Care Clauses are plainly the most important in understanding the President's role in our constitutional system. The commander-in-chief power is also significant, given the consequences of military actions. But there have been few litigated controversies about the scope of this power, so there is almost no case law on the subject.

Article II grants the President only a handful of other powers. One is the so-called "recognition power": the authority to recognize foreign sovereigns. The Supreme Court addressed the scope of this authority in *Zivotofsky v. Kerry*, 576 U.S. 1 (2015). As discussed in Chapter 6, the dispute in *Zivotofsky* concerned the constitutionality of §214(d) of the Foreign Relations Authorization Act, Fiscal Year 2003, which addressed the place of birth to be recorded for American citizens born in Jerusalem. Section 214(d) directed the Secretary of State, when requested by a citizen or the citizen's parent or guardian, to record the place of birth as "Israel." For many years, the State Department (a part of the Executive Branch) directed its employees to record the place of birth of such citizens simply as "Jerusalem" (in order to remain formally neutral as to which country exercises sovereignty over Jerusalem).

After Zivotofsky was born in Jerusalem, his parents sought to have "Israel" denominated on his passport under the terms of §214(d). The government refused, and Zivotofsky sued. The lower courts held that they could not decide the matter on the ground it presented a nonjusticiable "political question." In *Zivotofsky v. Clinton*, the Supreme Court reversed those holdings, concluding that the dispute was justiciable. On remand, the D.C. Circuit declared §214(d) unconstitutional. And on a second appeal, the Supreme Court affirmed.

In a 5-to-4 decision, the Court concluded that the President's authority to grant formal recognition to a foreign sovereign is *exclusive*. Under the *Youngstown* framework, if the President's action is "incompatible with the expressed or implied will of Congress," the President "can rely [for his authority] only upon his own constitutional powers minus any constitutional powers of Congress over the matter." The President's asserted power must be both "exclusive" and "conclusive" on the issue; his actions must rest on a power the Constitution grants the President alone.

Applying this framework, the Court explained that the Reception Clause of Article II, §3 directs that the President "shall receive Ambassadors and other public Ministers." At the time of the founding, receiving an ambassador was considered tantamount to recognizing the sending state's sovereignty. The Court thus found it logical to infer that the Reception Clause acknowledged the President's power to recognize other nations. This inference was supported by the President's additional Article II powers: to negotiate treaties and to nominate the nation's ambassadors and dispatch other diplomatic agents. Although the ratification of a treaty and the confirmation of ambassadors require Senate approval, Congress lacks the authority to initiate these actions without the President's involvement. Moreover, the President, unlike Congress, has the power to open diplomatic channels simply by engaging in direct diplomacy with foreign heads of state and their ministers. The Constitution thus assigns to the President, and not Congress, the means to recognize a sovereign unilaterally.

To the Court, functional considerations also suggested that the President's recognition power is exclusive. The nation must "speak . . . with one voice" regarding which governments are legitimate in the eyes of the United States, and only the President has the characteristic of unity at all times. And unlike Congress, the President is capable of engaging in the delicate and often secret diplomatic contacts that may lead to recognition, and is better positioned to take the decisive action necessary to recognize other nations. To be sure, under basic separation of powers principles, Congress has substantial authority regarding many policy determinations that precede and follow an act of recognition; the President's recognition determination is thus only one part of a political process. But a fair reading of relevant precedent illustrated the Court had long considered recognition to be the exclusive prerogative of the President.

At the same time, the Court took pains to emphasize that its decision in *United States v. Curtiss-Wright Export Corp.*, 299 U.S. 304 (1936), does *not* support the broader notion that the Constitution gives the President *alone* the authority to determine the nation's foreign policy. Congress possesses considerable authority relevant to international commerce, foreign relations, and the exercise of military power, and the President is not free from the ordinary checks from Congress merely because foreign affairs are at issue. Still, it is for the President alone to make the specific decision of what foreign power the Executive Branch will formally recognize as legitimate.

Because the recognition power is exclusive to the President, §214(d) was unconstitutional because it impermissibly infringed on the Executive Branch's decision to withhold recognition with respect to Jerusalem. The statute forced the President (acting through the Secretary of State) to denominate citizens born in Jerusalem as being born in Israel when, as a matter of U.S. policy, neither Israel nor any other country was acknowledged as being sovereign over Jerusalem. If the recognition power means anything, it must mean the President not only makes the initial, formal recognition determination, but may also maintain that determination in his agent's statements. If Congress could alter the President's statements on matters of recognition, or force him to contradict them, Congress would effectively exercise the recognition power. As *Youngstown* makes clear, "exclusive" Presidential power "disabl[es] the Congress from acting upon the subject." If Congress cannot enact a statute effecting the formal recognition of a foreign nation, it likewise cannot force the President to contradict his prior recognition determination in an official document issued by the Secretary of State.

D.   The Pardon Power

Article II, §2, clause 1 provides that the President "shall have power to grant reprieves and pardons for offenses against the United States, except in cases of impeachment." This is another of the few authorities granted exclusively to the President, precluding congressional interference. As the Court explained in *United States v. Klein*, 80 U.S. (13 Wall.) 128 (1871), Congress cannot limit the President's grant of an amnesty or pardon, but it can grant other or further amnesties itself. While some pardons have been litigated, the Court has consistently refused to limit the President's discretion in issuing them. Thus, there are virtually no limits to the President's decision to grant a reprieve or a pardon.

By its terms, the pardon power only extends to reprieves and pardons "for offenses against the United States." Thus, it does not include state-law offenses. For instance, the President could not pardon a person for committing a crime under New York law. (This is one reason some states initiated their own prosecutions against persons tied to President Trump's 2016 campaign.) It also does not extend to *civil* cases. An "offense against the United States" refers only to *crimes*. Thus, a pardon power cannot relieve a person of civil liability. Likewise, the pardon power—by its express terms—does not empower the President to shield an official from impeachment or conviction on articles of impeachment. To be clear, an officer who is impeached and removed from office might subsequently be charged with federal crimes, and the President could grant a pardon or reprieve from those criminal charges. But the President has no authority to shield an officer from the impeachment process.

A pardon completely eliminates the legal effects of a criminal conviction. As the Supreme Court explained in *Ex parte Garland*, 71 U.S. (4 Wall.) 333 (1866),

> "If granted before conviction, it prevents any of the penalties and disabilities consequent upon conviction from attaching [thereto]; if granted after conviction, it removes the penalties and disabilities, and restores him to all his civil rights; it makes him, as it were, a new man, and gives him a new credit and capacity. . . . A pardon reaches both the punishment prescribed for the offence and the guilt of the offender . . . so that in the eye of the law the offender is as innocent as if he had never committed the offence."

The President can grant a reprieve or pardon for any federal crime that has already been committed, even if the offender has not yet been convicted. Indeed, a pardon may be granted to a person who has not yet been charged, and for crimes that may never be investigated. But the pardon cannot operate prospectively; that is, the President could not immunize a person from prosecution for acts the individual has not yet committed. The power to grant such immunity would effectively grant the President the power to repeal federal law, at least with respect to the covered individuals, usurping the legislative authority Article I grants exclusively to Congress.

As explained, a presidential pardon can completely eliminate the effect of a criminal conviction, such that the offender is viewed by the law as if the conviction had never occurred. But the President can also use the pardon power to grant a lesser reprieve, such as to reduce the offender's sentence. For example, in *Biddle v. Perovich*, 274 U.S. 480 (1927), the Supreme Court upheld the President's use of the pardon power to commute the punishment of an offender who had been sentenced to death to the lesser sentence of life in prison. Further, the pardon can come with strings attached. In *Schick v. Reed*, 419 U.S. 256 (1974), the Court held that the President could reduce an offender's sentence from death to life in prison on the condition that the offender would never be eligible for parole, even though (under extant federal law) an offender could not be sentenced to life without the possibility of parole.

Moreover, a pardon is valid even if it is rejected by the pardoned individual. As Justice Oliver Wendell Holmes explained in *Biddle*, a pardon "is not a private act of grace from an individual happening to possess power. It is a part of the constitutional scheme." Thus, presidential pardons have been used for the broader purpose of calming the political waters after tumultuous times for the Republic. As Alexander Hamilton argued in The Federalist No. 74, "in seasons of insurrection or rebellion there are often critical moments when a well-timed offer of pardon to the insurgents or rebels may restore the tranquility of the commonwealth; and which, if suffered to pass unimproved, it may never be possible afterwards to recall." Presidents have sought to use the pardon power to mitigate the effects of major crises: President George Washington granted amnesties to those who participated in the Whiskey Rebellion; Presidents Abraham Lincoln and Andrew Johnson issued amnesties to those who fought for the Confederacy during the Civil War; and Presidents Ford and Carter granted amnesties to Vietnam-era draft evaders.

Could the President pardon herself, effectively creating immunity from prosecution for federal crimes committed while in office? A self-pardon is not precluded by the text of the Constitution. And in 1974, some of President Nixon's lawyers argued it would be constitutional. But a broader reading of the Constitution, and the general principles and traditions of American law, suggest it would be constitutionally questionable. A self-pardon would seem to contradict the basic axioms that a person should not be a judge in his own case, that the rule of law is supreme, and that the President is not above the law.

E. Presidential Immunities or Privileges

In addition to conferring on the President various powers, Article II grants the President various immunities or privileges inherent in the executive function. There is no textual provision for these immunities or privileges, but the Supreme Court has found them implicit in the Constitution's design.

1. Immunity from suit

Given his place in the constitutional scheme, the President is *absolutely immune* from suits for damages attributable to actions taken in his official capacity as President. The crucial case is *Nixon v. Fitzgerald*, 457 U.S. 731 (1982). There, a management analyst in the Air Force was discharged as part of a reduction in force, and he sued President Nixon in federal district court for damages, asserting he had been terminated in retaliation for his testimony before Congress. The Supreme Court concluded that the suit could not go forward, as the President "is entitled to absolute immunity from damages liability predicated on his official acts. We consider this immunity a functionally mandated incident of the President's unique office, rooted in the constitutional tradition of the separation of powers and supported by our history." Given the singular importance of the President's duties, diversion of his energies by concern with private lawsuits would raise unique risks to the effective functioning of government.

> "In view of the visibility of his office and the effect of his actions on countless people, the President would be an easily identifiable target for suits for civil damages. Cognizance of this personal vulnerability frequently could distract a President from his public duties, to the detriment of not only the President and his office but also the Nation that the Presidency was designed to serve.

Though separation-of-powers principles do not bar every exercise of jurisdiction over the President, the Court emphasized in *Fitzgerald* that a district court—before exercising jurisdiction—must balance the constitutional weight of the interest to be served against the dangers of intrusion on the functions of the Executive Branch. The exercise of jurisdiction is not warranted in cases merely presenting private suits for damages based on a President's official acts. Moreover, "[i]n view of the special nature of the President's constitutional office and functions," it was "appropriate to recognize absolute Presidential immunity from damages liability for acts within the 'outer perimeter' of his official responsibility."

By contrast, the Supreme Court held in *Clinton v. Jones*, 520 U.S. 681 (1997), that the President is *not* constitutionally entitled to the postponement of civil litigation until he leaves office when the suit is based on actions occurring before being President. The Court reasoned that the principal rationale for immunity from damages actions for official acts—*i.e.*, to enable the performance of designated functions without the fear that a particular decision might give rise to personal liability—did not support immunity for *unofficial* conduct. Any immunities afforded by the Constitution are grounded in the nature of the function performed, not the identity of the actor performing it.

Nor would these sorts of lawsuits place unacceptable burdens on the President. There was little historical support for such fears, given the paucity of suits against sitting Presidents for their private actions. And it was already "settled" that "the Judiciary may severely burden the Executive Branch by reviewing the legality of the President's official conduct, and may direct appropriate process to the President himself." It must follow that federal courts have the power to determine the legality of the President's *unofficial* conduct.

Neither *Fitzgerald* nor *Jones* (nor any other decision) resolves whether a sitting President can be *criminally* prosecuted while in office. The current position of the Department of Justice is that this would unduly interfere with the President's Article II responsibilities, and thus violate separation-of-powers principles. (This was why Robert Mueller did not pursue a criminal prosecution of President Trump in his investigation of the 2016 campaign.) But this position is controversial. In all events, the Constitution clearly permits the criminal prosecution of the President after she leaves office. Indeed, the text of Article I, §3, clause 7 expressly contemplates the possibility:

> "Judgment in Cases of Impeachment shall not extend further than to removal from Office, and disqualification to hold and enjoy any Office of honor, Trust, or Profit under the United States; but the Party convicted shall nevertheless be liable and subject to Indictment, Trial, Judgment, and Punishment, according to Law."

Likewise, the President is plainly subject to judicial process, such as being required to respond to a subpoena or to other judicial orders. This was a crucial aspect of the Supreme Court's recent decisions in *Trump v. Vance*, 140 S. Ct. 2412 (2020), and *Trump v. Mazars USA LLP*, 140 S. Ct. 2019 (2020), which both concerned subpoenas of the financial records of the President while he was in office. The Court cautioned, though, that district courts must carefully consider the separation-of-powers implications of issuing or enforcing a subpoena against a sitting President.

Finally, the President is often sued in his *official* capacity in lawsuits seeking an injunction to forbid or require the President to take certain actions in his execution of federal law. *See, e.g., Trump v. Hawaii*, 138 S. Ct. 2392 (2018); *Boumediene v. Bush*, 553 U.S. 723 (2008). These lawsuits do not implicate the immunity recognized in *Fitzgerald*, as an action against the President in his official capacity (for injunctive relief) practically functions as an action against the federal government and not the President personally.

2. Executive privilege

In addition to these immunities, the Supreme Court has conclusively held that Article II entitles the President to keep certain communications within the Executive Branch confidential. In *United States v. Nixon*, 418 U.S. 683 (1974), the Supreme Court recognized that this "executive privilege" is inherent in the executive power granted to the President by the Vesting and Take Care Clauses. To responsibly discharge the obligations imposed by Article II, the President needs confidentiality in communications to ensure robust, candid discussions that will produce the best decisions.

Nonetheless, *Nixon* made clear that this privilege is not absolute. The President's need for secrecy must be balanced against the other interests at stake. Indeed, the Court ultimately held in *Nixon* that the President's claim to executive privilege was outweighed by the judicial system's need for the communications in dispute (the Watergate tapes) in the prosecution of criminal offenses (of other conspirators to the burglary of the Democratic headquarters in the Watergate Hotel). Thus, any assertion of executive privilege must be evaluated on a case-by-case basis.

What criteria are relevant in making such case-by-case judgments? The Court has suggested that assertions of executive privilege are more likely to be sustained when there is a greater need for secrecy in communications—for example, in matters of foreign policy or intelligence gathering. Similarly, communications by the President himself are more likely to be privileged, as are the President's communications with close advisors. On the other hand, the justification for disclosure—that is, for overcoming the assertion of the privilege—will be stronger when the communications are needed in a criminal (rather than a civil) matter.

CHAPTER 14

THE APPOINTMENT AND REMOVAL OF FEDERAL OFFICERS

The power to appoint and remove "Officers of the United States" lies at the core of the power to the execute the law. At first blush, the various constitutional rules governing such appointments and removals may seem arcane. But they have a huge impact on the functioning of the federal government. At bottom, the question is one of *control*: controlling—or at least influencing—those who execute, implement, or apply federal law.

It's easy to appreciate why Congress might have concerns about the President having an unfettered power to appoint and remove federal officers. Congress's broad delegations of policymaking discretion in statutes, as a practical matter, grant thousands of officials in the Executive Branch substantial policymaking authority. On a daily basis, these federal officers make their own decisions (within the bounds of the relevant statute) as to how to apply or implement federal law. And the President will likely have a particular agenda for the exercise of that discretion—an agenda that might diverge from Congress's. Naturally, Congress will want *its* intentions respected in the fleshing out of statutory gaps or ambiguities.

Alternatively, Congress might simply want a particular federal officer to be insulated from political pressure, whether that pressure comes from the President or someone else. Consider the Chair of the Board of Governors of the Federal Reserve System. Congress (for understandable, nonpartisan reasons) might want to prevent the President from being able to fire the Chair of the Fed at will. With such a power, the President could potentially manipulate U.S. monetary policy for political gain, stimulating the economy in advance of an election to aid her reelection chances (but harming the nation's long-term economic health). Congress might therefore seek to insulate the Fed Chair from being fired by the President so the officer has greater policymaking autonomy.

But these congressional objectives raise important constitutional questions. As we have seen, Article II, §3 charges the President with the obligation to "take Care" that federal law is faithfully executed. And the President's capacity to fulfill this obligation logically includes (at least to some degree) hiring people who will do the job well and terminating those who are not. It is difficult for the President to ensure federal law is being faithfully executed without the capacity to control those officers administering and executing that law.

By way of comparison, consider the CEO of a publicly traded company, who is held accountable by the company's shareholders and board of directors. Suppose the CEO is deprived of the capacity to remove the company's vice presidents—its CFO or CIO or whomever—even when those officers fail to carry out the CEO's specific instructions for company strategy. Such a state of affairs would make it quite difficult for the CEO to fulfill her obligations to the shareholders and the board. In the same way, the insulation of various federal officers from the President's control could impair the President's capacity to take care that federal law is faithfully executed—at least in terms of how the President views such faithful execution.

This is the constitutional tension regarding the appointment and removal of federal officers. Congress may have entirely legitimate and public-spirited reasons to insulate various officers from presidential control, or from political pressure more generally. But the President is the one who bears the constitutionally assigned obligation to execute federal law. Thus, the question is how the Constitution accommodates these competing pressures in the operation of modern American government.

A.   The Appointments Clause

1. "Officers of the United States" vs. mere employees

The powers to appoint and remove federal officers, though functionally related, are governed by distinct constitutional provisions and doctrines. There is no text in the Constitution that specifically addresses the power to remove officers from their offices. By contrast, Article II, §2, clause 2 addresses the appointment of officers in fine detail:

> "[The President] shall nominate, and by and with the Advice and Consent of the Senate, shall appoint Ambassadors, other public Ministers and Consuls, Judges of the supreme Court, and all other Officers of the United States, whose Appointments are not herein otherwise provided for, and which shall be established by law; but the Congress may by Law vest the Appointment of such inferior Officers, as they think proper, in the President alone, in the Courts of Law, or in the Heads of Departments."

An important initial question is to whom this clause applies. By its terms, it only governs the appointment of "officers of the United States." Who falls into this category? How do we distinguish an "officer"—whose appointment will be governed by Article II—from a "mere employee," whose appointment will not carry any constitutional significance? The Supreme Court recently addressed this question in *Lucia v. SEC*, 138 S. Ct. 2044 (2018). At issue was the constitutionality of the appointment of administrative law judges in the Securities and Exchange Commission, an executive agency charged with enforcing federal securities law. As you read the opinion, please consider the following questions:

1. Exactly how were the ALJs within the SEC appointed?

2. Why did the constitutionality of their mode of appointment turn on whether they were "employees" or "officers"?

3. Why was it unnecessary that the ALJs be appointed by the President with the advice and consent of the Senate? (Would that method of appointment have been necessary for the SEC Commissioners themselves? Why or why not?)

Lucia v. SEC
138 S. Ct. 2044 (2018)

JUSTICE KAGAN delivered the opinion of the Court.

The Appointments Clause of the Constitution lays out the permissible methods of appointing "Officers of the United States," a class of government officials distinct from mere employees. This case requires us to decide whether administrative law judges (ALJs) of the Securities and Exchange Commission (SEC or Commission) qualify as such "Officers." In keeping with *Freytag v. Commissioner*, 501 U.S. 868 (1991), we hold that they do.

I

The SEC has statutory authority to enforce the nation's securities laws. One way it can do so is by instituting an administrative proceeding against an alleged wrongdoer. By law, the Commission may itself preside over such a proceeding. But the Commission also may, and typically does, delegate that task to an ALJ. The SEC currently has five ALJs. Other staff members, rather than the Commission proper, selected them all.

An ALJ assigned to hear an SEC enforcement action has extensive powers—the "authority to do all things necessary and appropriate to discharge his or her duties" and ensure a "fair and orderly" adversarial proceeding. Those powers "include, but are not limited to," supervising discovery; issuing, revoking, or modifying subpoenas; deciding motions; ruling on the admissibility of evidence; administering oaths; hearing and examining witnesses; generally "[r]egulating the course of" the proceeding and the "conduct of the parties and their counsel"; and imposing sanctions for "[c]ontemptuous conduct" or violations of procedural requirements. As that list suggests, an SEC ALJ exercises authority "comparable to" that of a federal district judge conducting a bench trial. *Butz v. Economou*, 438 U.S. 478, 513 (1978).

After a hearing ends, the ALJ issues an "initial decision." That decision must set out "findings and conclusions" about all "material issues of fact [and] law"; it also must include the "appropriate order, sanction, relief, or denial thereof." The Commission can then review the ALJ's decision, either upon request or *sua sponte*. But if it opts against review, the Commission "issue[s] an order that the [ALJ's] decision has become final." At that point, the initial decision is "deemed the action of the Commission."

This case began when the SEC instituted an administrative proceeding against petitioner Raymond Lucia and his investment company. Lucia marketed a retirement savings strategy called "Buckets of Money." In the SEC's view, Lucia used misleading slideshow presentations to deceive prospective clients. The SEC charged Lucia under the Investment Advisers Act, and assigned ALJ Cameron Elliot to adjudicate the case. After nine days of testimony and argument, Judge Elliot issued an initial decision concluding that Lucia had violated the Act and imposing sanctions, including civil penalties of $300,000 and a lifetime bar from the investment industry. In his decision, Judge Elliot made factual findings about only one of the four ways the SEC thought Lucia's slideshow misled investors. The Commission thus remanded for fact-finding on the other three claims, explaining that an ALJ's "personal experience with the witnesses" places him "in the best position to make findings of fact" and "resolve any conflicts in the evidence." Judge Elliot then made additional findings of deception and issued a revised initial decision, with the same sanctions.

On appeal to the SEC, Lucia argued that the administrative proceeding was invalid because Judge Elliot had not been constitutionally appointed. According to Lucia, the Commission's ALJs are "Officers of the United States" and thus subject to the Appointments Clause. Under that Clause, Lucia noted, only the President, "Courts of Law," or "Heads of Departments" can appoint "Officers." And none of those actors had made Judge Elliot an ALJ. To be sure, the Commission itself counts as a "Head of Department." But the Commission had left the task of appointing ALJs, including Judge Elliot, to SEC staff members. As a result, Lucia contended, Judge Elliot lacked constitutional authority to do his job. . . .

II

The sole question here is whether the Commission's ALJs are "Officers of the United States" or simply employees of the Federal Government. The Appointments Clause prescribes the exclusive means of appointing "Officers." Only the President, a court of law, or a head of department can do so.[3] And as all parties agree, none of those actors appointed Judge Elliot before he heard Lucia's case; instead, SEC staff members gave him an ALJ slot. So if the Commission's ALJs are constitutional officers, Lucia raises a valid Appointments Clause claim.

---

[3] That statement elides a distinction, not at issue here, between "principal" and "inferior" officers. See *Edmond v. United States*, 520 U.S. 651, 659–660 (1997). Only the President, with the advice and consent of the Senate, can appoint a principal officer; but Congress (instead of relying on that method) may authorize the President alone, a court, or a department head to appoint an inferior officer. Both the Government and Lucia view the SEC's ALJs as inferior officers and acknowledge that the Commission, as a head of department, can constitutionally appoint them.

The only way to defeat his position is to show that those ALJs are not officers at all, but instead non-officer employees—part of the broad swath of "lesser functionaries" in the Government's workforce. *Buckley v. Valeo*, 424 U.S. 1, 126, n.162 (1978). For if that is true, the Appointments Clause cares not a whit about who named them. See *United States v. Germaine*, 99 U.S. 508, 510 (1879).

Two decisions set out this Court's basic framework for distinguishing between officers and employees. *Germaine* held that "civil surgeons" (doctors hired to perform various physical exams) were mere employees because their duties were "occasional or temporary" rather than "continuing and permanent." *Id.*, at 511–512. Stressing "ideas of tenure [and] duration," the Court there made clear that an individual must occupy a "continuing" position established by law to qualify as an officer. *Id.*, at 511. *Buckley* then set out another requirement, central to this case. It determined that members of a federal commission were officers only after finding that they "exercis[ed] significant authority pursuant to the laws of the United States." 424 U.S., at 126. The inquiry thus focused on the extent of power an individual wields in carrying out his assigned functions.

Both the *amicus* and the Government urge us to elaborate on *Buckley*'s "significant authority" test, but another of our precedents makes that project unnecessary. The standard is no doubt framed in general terms, tempting advocates to add whatever glosses best suit their arguments. And maybe one day we will see a need to refine or enhance the test *Buckley* set out so concisely. But that day is not this one, because in *Freytag v. Commissioner*, 501 U.S. 868 (1991), we applied the unadorned "significant authority" test to adjudicative officials who are near-carbon copies of the Commission's ALJs. As we now explain, our analysis there (sans any more detailed legal criteria) necessarily decides this case.

The officials at issue in *Freytag* were the "special trial judges" (STJs) of the United States Tax Court. The authority of those judges depended on the significance of the tax dispute before them. In "comparatively narrow and minor matters," they could both hear and definitively resolve a case for the Tax Court. *Id.*, at 873. In more major matters, they could preside over the hearing, but could not issue the final decision; instead, they were to "prepare proposed findings and an opinion" for a regular Tax Court judge to consider. *Ibid.* The proceeding challenged in *Freytag* was a major one, involving $1.5 billion in alleged tax deficiencies. See *id.*, at 871, n.1. After conducting a 14-week trial, the STJ drafted a proposed decision in favor of the Government. A regular judge then adopted the STJ's work as the opinion of the Tax Court. See *id.*, at 872. The losing parties argued on appeal that the STJ was not constitutionally appointed.

This Court held that the Tax Court's STJs are officers, not mere employees. Citing *Germaine,* the Court first found that STJs hold a continuing office established by law. They serve on an ongoing, rather than a "temporary [or] episodic[,] basis"; and their "duties, salary, and means of appointment" are all specified in the Tax Code. *Ibid.* The Court then considered, as *Buckley* demands, the "significance" of the "authority" STJs wield. 501 U.S., at 881. In addressing that issue, the Government had argued that STJs are employees, rather than officers, in all cases (like the one at issue) in which they could not "enter a final decision." *Ibid.* But the Court thought the Government's focus on finality "ignore[d] the significance of the duties and discretion that [STJs] possess." *Ibid.* Describing the responsibilities involved in presiding over adversarial hearings, the Court said: STJs "take testimony, conduct trials, rule on the admissibility of evidence, and have the power to enforce compliance with discovery orders." *Id.,* at 881–882. And the Court observed that "[i]n the course of carrying out these important functions, the [STJs] exercise significant discretion." *Id.,* at 882. That fact meant they were officers, even when their decisions were not final.[4]

Freytag says everything necessary to decide this case. To begin, the Commission's ALJs, like the Tax Court's STJs, hold a continuing office established by law. See *id.,* at 881. Indeed, everyone here—Lucia, the Government, and the *amicus*—agrees on that point. Far from serving temporarily or episodically, SEC ALJs "receive[ ] a career appointment." And that appointment is to a position created by statute, down to its "duties, salary, and means of appointment." *Freytag,* 501 U.S., at 878.

Still more, the Commission's ALJs exercise the same "significant discretion" when carrying out the same "important functions" as STJs do. Both sets of officials have all the authority needed to ensure fair and orderly adversarial hearings—indeed, nearly all the tools of federal trial judges. Consider in order the four specific (if overlapping) powers *Freytag* mentioned. First, the Commission's ALJs (like the Tax Court's STJs) "take testimony." 501 U.S., at 881. More precisely, they "[r]eceiv[e] evidence" and "[e]xamine witnesses" at hearings, and may also take pre-hearing depositions. Second, the ALJs (like STJs) "conduct trials." 501 U.S., at 882. As detailed earlier, they administer oaths, rule on motions, and generally "regulat[e] the course of" a hearing, as well as the conduct of parties and counsel. Third, the ALJs (like STJs) "rule on the admissibility of evidence." 501 U.S., at 882. They thus

---

[4] The Court also provided an alternative basis for viewing the STJs as officers. "Even if the duties of [STJs in major cases] were not as significant as we . . . have found them," we stated, "our conclusion would be unchanged." *Freytag,* 501 U.S., at 878. That was because the Government had conceded that in minor matters, where STJs could enter final decisions, they had enough "independent authority" to count as officers. And we thought it made no sense to classify the STJs as officers for some cases and employees for others. Justice SOTOMAYOR relies on that back-up rationale in trying to reconcile *Freytag* with her view that "a prerequisite to officer status is the authority" to issue at least some "final decisions." But *Freytag* has two parts, and its primary analysis explicitly rejects Justice SOTOMAYOR's theory that final decisionmaking authority is a *sine qua non* of officer status. As she acknowledges, she must expunge that reasoning to make her reading work.

critically shape the administrative record (as they also do when issuing document subpoenas). And fourth, the ALJs (like STJs) "have the power to enforce compliance with discovery orders." 501 U.S., at 882. In particular, they may punish all "[c]ontemptuous conduct," including violations of those orders, by means as severe as excluding the offender from the hearing. So point for point—straight from *Freytag*'s list—the Commission's ALJs have equivalent duties and powers as STJs in conducting adversarial inquiries.

And at the close of those proceedings, ALJs issue decisions much like that in *Freytag*—except with potentially more independent effect. As the *Freytag* Court recounted, STJs "prepare proposed findings and an opinion" adjudicating charges and assessing tax liabilities. 501 U.S., at 873. Similarly, the Commission's ALJs issue decisions containing factual findings, legal conclusions, and appropriate remedies. And what happens next reveals that the ALJ can play the more autonomous role. In a major case like *Freytag*, a regular Tax Court judge must always review an STJ's opinion. And that opinion counts for nothing unless the regular judge adopts it as his own. By contrast, the SEC can decide against reviewing an ALJ decision at all. And when the SEC declines review (and issues an order saying so), the ALJ's decision itself "becomes final" and is "deemed the action of the Commission." That last-word capacity makes this an *a fortiori* case: If the Tax Court's STJs are officers, as *Freytag* held, then the Commission's ALJs must be too.

For all the reasons we have given, and all those *Freytag* gave before, the Commission's ALJs are "Officers of the United States," subject to the Appointments Clause. . . .

* * *

Notes on *Lucia v. SEC*

1. ***"Officers" vs. "employees"***: If the individual in question is not an "officer of the United States" under Article II, but instead a "mere employee," the method appointment is not subject to the strictures of the Appointments Clause. As the Court explained in *Lucia* (relying on the 1976 decision in *Buckley v. Valeo*, 424 U.S. 1 (1978)), an "officer" is an appointee who "hold[s] a continuing office authorized by law" and who "exercise[es] significant authority pursuant to the laws of the United States." The Court in *Lucia* did not further elucidate this standard, but instead relied heavily on its prior decision in *Freytag v. Commissioner*, 501 U.S. 868 (1991). In *Freytag*, the Court held that Special Trial Judges of the Tax Court (a non-Article III court) were "officers" rather than employees. In particular, those judges (1) "hold a continuing office established by law," serving "on an ongoing, rather than a temporary" or episodic basis, as "their duties, salary, and means of appointment are all specified in the Tax Code"; and (2) "[i]n the course of carrying out these important functions, the [STJs] exercise significant discretion": they "take testimony, conduct trials, rule on the admissibility of evidence, and have the power to enforce compliance with discovery orders." Thus, even though the STJs' decisions were not

final, the judges were still "officers" given the nature of their offices and the significance of the discretion they exercised. In *Lucia*, the Court concluded the SEC ALJs were nearly identical in relevant respects to the Tax Court's STJs—and that their decisions could be final—making it "an *a fortiori* case."

2. *Persons serving in the legislative branch*: Importantly, persons serving in the legislative branch are not "officers of the United States" under the Appointments Clause. This means Senators, Members of the House of Representatives, and any persons hired to assist them in carrying out their legislative responsibilities. We know this largely because the Constitution provides for their appointment through other means—namely, elections. Legislative officials create (or help create) federal law. This role includes the creation of federal offices other than those specified in the Constitution, and enacting laws that provide the funds for those officers to act and carry out various executive functions. But those in the legislative branch cannot be involved in the application, implementation, or enforcement of federal law—in other words, the work of "officers of the United States."

* * *

2. "Inferior" and "principal" (or "superior") officers

In addition to distinguishing "officers" from "employees," the Appointments Clause draws a line between so-called "inferior" officers and all other federal officers. The clause states that Congress, if it chooses, "may by Law vest the Appointment of such inferior Officers, as they think proper, in the President alone, in the Courts of Law, or in the Heads of Departments." But with respect to "all other Officers"— "principal" or "superior" officers—there is only one constitutional choice: the President "shall nominate, and, by and with the Advice and Consent of the Senate, shall appoint" them. (If Congress does not specify how an officer is to be appointed in the relevant statute, nomination by the President with Senate confirmation is the default; the other methods of appointment only come into play if Congress so directs by statute.) Hence, a second critical issue is how to distinguish "principal" from "inferior" officers.

The Supreme Court recently addressed this question in *United States v. Arthrex*, 141 S. Ct. 1970 (2021). At issue was the method of appointment for Administrative Patent Judges (APJs) within the Patent and Trademark Office (PTO). The APJs conducted adversarial proceedings for challenging the validity of an existing patent before the Patent Trial and Appeal Board (PTAB), proceedings known as "inter partes review." The APJs were appointed by the Secretary of Commerce, the head of an executive department. Thus, the appointment of the APJs was consistent with the Appointments Clause only if they were "inferior" officers. As you read *Arthrex*, please consider the following questions:

1. Were the Administrative Patent Judges "officers of the United States"? Why or why not?

2. What does the Court determine is critical in discerning whether a particular officer is "inferior" or "principal"? Why? What is the underlying rationale for this test?

3. Was the constitutional problem the manner in which the APJs were appointed? Or was it that, in inter partes review proceedings, the APJs issued "final decisions," unreviewable by anyone else within the Executive Branch? Or was it both? How would you describe the constitutional violation?

4. In a portion of the opinion omitted from this excerpt, the Court addressed the remedial question: how to render the relevant provisions of the America Invents Act constitutional. Given the Act's infirmity, how could the statutory scheme have been made constitutional? Was there more than one possibility?

United States v. Arthrex
141 S. Ct. 1970 (2021)

CHIEF JUSTICE ROBERTS delivered the opinion of the Court.

The validity of a patent previously issued by the Patent and Trademark Office can be challenged before the Patent Trial and Appeal Board, an executive tribunal within the PTO. The Board, composed largely of Administrative Patent Judges appointed by the Secretary of Commerce, has the final word within the Executive Branch on the validity of a challenged patent. Billions of dollars can turn on a Board decision.

Under the Constitution, "[t]he executive Power" is vested in the President, who has the responsibility to "take Care that the Laws be faithfully executed." Art. II, §1, cl. 1; §3. The Appointments Clause provides that he may be assisted in carrying out that responsibility by officers nominated by him and confirmed by the Senate, as well as by other officers not appointed in that manner but whose work, we have held, must be directed and supervised by an officer who has been. §2, cl. 2. The question presented is whether the authority of the Board to issue decisions on behalf of the Executive Branch is consistent with these constitutional provisions.

I

A

. . . The present [patent] system is administered by the Patent and Trademark Office (PTO), an executive agency within the Department of Commerce "responsible for the granting and issuing of patents" in the name of the United States. Congress has vested the "powers and duties" of the PTO in a sole Director appointed by the President with the advice and consent of the Senate. As agency head, the Director "provid[es] policy direction and management supervision" for PTO officers and employees.

This suit centers on the Patent Trial and Appeal Board (PTAB), an executive adjudicatory body within the PTO established by the Leahy-Smith America Invents Act of 2011. The PTAB sits in panels of at least three members drawn from the Director, the Deputy Director, the Commissioner for Patents, the Commissioner for Trademarks, and more than 200 Administrative Patent Judges (APJs). The Secretary of Commerce appoints the members of the PTAB (except for the Director), including the APJs at issue in this dispute. Like the 1790 Patent Board, the modern Board decides whether an invention satisfies the standards for patentability on review of decisions by primary examiners.

Through a variety of procedures, the PTAB can also take a second look at patents previously issued by the PTO. One such procedure is inter partes review. Established in 2011, inter partes review is an adversarial process by which members of the PTAB reconsider whether existing patents satisfy the novelty and nonobviousness requirements for inventions. Any person—other than the patent owner himself—can file a petition to institute inter partes review of a patent. The Director can institute review only if, among other requirements, he determines that the petitioner is reasonably likely to prevail on at least one challenged patent claim. Congress has committed the decision to institute inter partes review to the Director's unreviewable discretion. By regulation, the Director has delegated this authority to the PTAB itself.

The Director designates at least three members of the PTAB (typically three APJs) to conduct an inter partes proceeding. The PTAB then assumes control of the process, which resembles civil litigation in many respects. The PTAB must issue a final written decision on all of the challenged patent claims within 12 to 18 months of institution. A party who disagrees with a decision may request rehearing by the PTAB.

The PTAB is the last stop for review within the Executive Branch. A party dissatisfied with the final decision may seek judicial review in the Court of Appeals for the Federal Circuit. At this stage, the Director can intervene before the court to defend or disavow the Board's decision. The Federal Circuit reviews the PTAB's application of patentability standards *de novo* and its underlying factual determinations for substantial evidence. Upon expiration of the time to appeal or termination of any appeal, "the Director shall issue and publish a certificate canceling any claim of the patent finally determined to be unpatentable, confirming any claim of the patent determined to be patentable, and incorporating in the patent by operation of the certificate any new or amended claim determined to be patentable." §318(b).

B

Arthrex, Inc. develops medical devices and procedures for orthopedic surgery. In 2015, it secured a patent on a surgical device for reattaching soft tissue to bone without tying a knot, U. S. Patent No. 9,179,907 ('907 patent). Arthrex soon claimed that Smith & Nephew, Inc. and Arthro-Care Corp. (collectively, Smith & Nephew) had infringed the '907 patent, and the dispute eventually made its way to inter partes review in the PTO. Three APJs formed the PTAB panel that conducted the proceeding and ultimately concluded that a prior patent application "anticipated" the invention claimed by the '907 patent, so that Arthrex's patent was invalid.

On appeal to the Federal Circuit, Arthrex raised for the first time an argument premised on the Appointments Clause of the Constitution. That Clause specifies how the President may appoint officers who assist him in carrying out his responsibilities. *Principal* officers must be appointed by the President with the advice and consent of the Senate, while *inferior* officers may be appointed by the President alone, the head of an executive department, or a court. Art. II, §2, cl. 2. Arthrex argued that the APJs were principal officers and therefore that their appointment by the Secretary of Commerce was unconstitutional. . . . We granted those petitions to consider whether the PTAB's structure is consistent with the Appointments Clause. . . .

II

A

The President is "responsible for the actions of the Executive Branch" and "cannot delegate [that] ultimate responsibility or the active obligation to supervise that goes with it." *Free Enterprise Fund* v. *Pulic Company Accounting Oversight Bd.*, 561 U.S. 477, 496–497 (2010). The Framers recognized, of course, that "no single person could fulfill that responsibility alone, [and] expected that the President would rely on subordinate officers for assistance." *Seila Law LLC* v. *Consumer Financial Protection Bureau*, 591 U.S. ___ (2020) (plurality opinion).

Today, thousands of officers wield executive power on behalf of the President in the name of the United States. That power acquires its legitimacy and accountability to the public through "a clear and effective chain of command" down from the President, on whom all the people vote. *Free Enterprise Fund,* 561 U. S., at 498. James Madison extolled this "great principle of unity and responsibility in the Executive department," which ensures that "the chain of dependence [will] be preserved; the lowest officers, the middle grade, and the highest, will depend, as they ought, on the President, and the President on the community." 1 Annals of Cong. 499 (1789).

The Appointments Clause provides:

"[The President] shall nominate, and by and with the Advice and Consent of the Senate, shall appoint Ambassadors, other public Ministers and Consuls, Judges of the supreme Court, and all other Officers of the United States, whose Appointments are not herein otherwise provided for, and which shall be established by Law: but Congress may by Law vest the Appointment of such inferior Officers, as they think proper, in the President alone, in the Courts of Law, or in the Heads of Departments." Art. II, §2, cl. 2.

Assigning the nomination power to the President guarantees accountability for the appointees' actions because the "blame of a bad nomination would fall upon the president singly and absolutely." The Federalist No. 77, p. 517 (J. Cooke ed. 1961) (A. Hamilton). As Hamilton wrote, the "sole and undivided responsibility of one man will naturally beget a livelier sense of duty and a more exact regard to reputation." *Id.*, No. 76, at 510–511. The Appointments Clause adds a degree of accountability in the Senate, which shares in the public blame "for both the making of a bad appointment and the rejection of a good one." *Edmond* v. *United States*, 520 U.S. 651, 660 (1997).

Only the President, with the advice and consent of the Senate, can appoint noninferior officers, called "principal" officers as shorthand in our cases. The "default manner of appointment" for inferior officers is also nomination by the President and confirmation by the Senate. *Id.*, at 660. But the Framers foresaw that "when offices became numerous, and sudden removals necessary, this mode might be inconvenient." *United States* v. *Germaine*, 99 U.S. 508, 510 (1879). Reflecting this concern for "administrative convenience," the Appointments Clause permits Congress to dispense with joint appointment, but only for inferior officers. *Edmond,* 520 U.S., at 660. Congress may vest the appointment of such officers "in the President alone, in the Courts of Law, or in the Heads of Departments."

B

Congress provided that APJs would be appointed as inferior officers, by the Secretary of Commerce as head of a department. The question presented is whether the nature of their responsibilities is consistent with their method of appointment. As an initial matter, no party disputes that APJs are officers—not "lesser functionaries" such as employees or contractors—because they "exercis[e] significant authority pursuant to the laws of the United States." *Buckley* v. *Valeo*, 424 U.S. 1, 126 (1976); see *Lucia* v. *SEC*, 585 U.S. ___ (2018). APJs do so when reconsidering an issued patent, a power that (the Court has held) involves the adjudication of public rights that Congress may appropriately assign to executive officers rather than to the Judiciary.

The starting point for each party's analysis is our opinion in *Edmond.* There we explained that "[w]hether one is an 'inferior' officer depends on whether he has a superior" other than the President. 520 U.S., at 662. An inferior officer must be "directed and supervised at some level by others who were appointed by Presidential nomination with the advice and consent of the Senate." *Id.,* at 663.

In *Edmond,* we applied this test to adjudicative officials within the Executive Branch—specifically, Coast Guard Court of Criminal Appeals judges appointed by the Secretary of Transportation. We held that the judges were inferior officers because they were effectively supervised by a combination of Presidentially nominated and Senate confirmed officers in the Executive Branch: first, the Judge Advocate

General, who "exercise[d] administrative oversight over the Court of Criminal Appeals" by prescribing rules of procedure and formulating policies for court-martial cases, and could also "remove a Court of Criminal Appeals judge from his judicial assignment without cause"; and second, the Court of Appeals for the Armed Forces, an executive tribunal that could review the judges' decisions under a *de novo* standard for legal issues and a deferential standard for factual issues. *Id.,* at 664–665. "What is significant," we concluded, "is that the judges of the Court of Criminal Appeals have no power to render a final decision on behalf of the United States unless permitted to do so by other Executive officers." *Id.,* at 665.

Congress structured the PTAB differently, providing only half of the "divided" supervision to which judges of the Court of Criminal Appeals were subject. *Id.,* at 664. Like the Judge Advocate General, the PTO Director possesses powers of "administrative oversight." *Ibid.* The Director fixes the rate of pay for APJs, controls the decision whether to institute inter partes review, and selects the APJs to reconsider the validity of the patent. 35 U. S. C. §§3(b)(6), 6(c), 314(a). The Director also promulgates regulations governing inter partes review, issues prospective guidance on patentability issues, and designates past PTAB decisions as "precedential" for future panels. §§3(a)(2)(A), 316(a)(4). He is the boss, except when it comes to the one thing that makes the APJs officers exercising "significant authority" in the first place—their power to issue decisions on patentability. *Buckley,* 424 U.S., at 126. In contrast to the scheme approved by *Edmond,* no principal officer at any level within the Executive Branch "direct[s] and supervise[s]" the work of APJs in that regard. 520 U.S., at 663.

Edmond goes a long way toward resolving this dispute. What was "significant" to the outcome there—review by a superior executive officer—is absent here: APJs have the "power to render a final decision on behalf of the United States" without any such review by their nominal superior or any other principal officer in the Executive Branch. *Id.,* at 665. The only possibility of review is a petition for rehearing, but Congress unambiguously specified that "[o]nly the Patent and Trial Appeal Board may grant rehearings." §6(c). Such review simply repeats the arrangement challenged as unconstitutional in this suit.

This "diffusion of power carries with it a diffusion of accountability." *Free Enterprise Fund,* 561 U.S., at 497. The restrictions on review relieve the Director of responsibility for the final decisions rendered by APJs purportedly under his charge. . . .

The Government and Smith & Nephew assemble a catalog of steps the Director might take to affect the decisionmaking process of the PTAB, despite his lack of any statutory authority to review its decisions. The Government reminds us that it is the Director who decides whether to initiate inter partes review. The Director can also designate the APJs who will decide a particular case and can pick ones predisposed to his views. And the Director, the Government asserts, can even vacate his institution decision if he catches wind of an unfavorable ruling on the way. The "proceeding will have no legal consequences" so long as the Director jumps in before the Board issues its final decision.

If all else fails, the Government says, the Director can intervene in the rehearing process to reverse Board decisions. The Government acknowledges that only the PTAB can grant rehearing under §6(c). But the Director, according to the Government, could manipulate the composition of the PTAB panel that acts on the rehearing petition. For one thing, he could "stack" the original panel to rehear the case with additional APJs assumed to be more amenable to his preferences. For another, he could assemble an entirely new panel consisting of himself and two other officers appointed by the Secretary—in practice, the Commissioner for Patents and the APJ presently designated as Chief Judge—to decide whether to overturn a decision and reach a different outcome binding on future panels. The Government insists that the Director, by handpicking (and, if necessary, repicking) Board members, can indirectly influence the course of inter partes review.

That is not the solution. It is the problem. The Government proposes (and the dissents embrace) a roadmap for the Director to evade a statutory prohibition on review without having him take responsibility for the ultimate decision. Even if the Director succeeds in procuring his preferred outcome, such machinations blur the lines of accountability demanded by the Appointments Clause. The parties are left with neither an impartial decision by a panel of experts nor a transparent decision for which a politically accountable officer must take responsibility. And the public can only wonder "on whom the blame or the punishment of a pernicious measure, or series of pernicious measures ought really to fall." The Federalist No. 70, at 476 (A. Hamilton).

The Government contends that the Director may respond after the fact by removing an APJ "from his judicial assignment without cause" and refusing to designate that APJ on *future* PTAB panels. *Edmond,* 520 U.S., at 664. Even assuming that is true, reassigning an APJ to a different task going forward gives the Director no means of countermanding the final decision already on the books. Nor are APJs "meaningfully controlled" by the threat of removal from federal service entirely, *Seila Law,* 591 U.S., at ___, because the Secretary can fire them after a decision only "for such cause as will promote the efficiency of the service," 5 U. S. C. §7513(a). In all the ways that matter to the parties who appear before the PTAB, the buck stops with the APJs, not with the Secretary or Director.

Review outside Article II—here, an appeal to the Federal Circuit—cannot provide the necessary supervision. While the duties of APJs "partake of a Judiciary quality as well as Executive," APJs are still exercising executive power and must remain "dependent upon the President." 1 Annals of Cong., at 611–612 (J. Madison). The activities of executive officers may "take 'legislative' and 'judicial' forms, but they are exercises of—indeed, under our constitutional structure they *must be* exercises of—the 'executive Power,'" for which the President is ultimately responsible. *Arlington* v. *FCC*, 569 U.S. 290, 305, n.4 (2013).

Given the insulation of PTAB decisions from any executive review, the President can neither oversee the PTAB himself nor "attribute the Board's failings to those whom he *can* oversee." *Free Enterprise Fund,* 561 U.S., at 496. APJs accordingly exercise power that conflicts with the design of the Appointments Clause "to preserve political accountability." *Edmond,* 520 U.S., at 663.

The principal dissent dutifully undertakes to apply the governing test from *Edmond,* but its heart is plainly not in it. For example, the dissent rejects any distinction between "inferior-officer power" and "principal-officer power," but *Edmond* calls for exactly that: an appraisal of how much power an officer exercises free from control by a superior. The dissent pigeonholes this consideration as the sole province of the Vesting Clause, but *Edmond* recognized the Appointments Clause as a "significant structural safeguard[ ]" that "preserve[s] political accountability" through direction and supervision of subordinates—in other words, through a chain of command. 520 U.S., at 659, 663. The dissent would have the Court focus on the location of an officer in the agency "organizational chart," but as we explained in *Edmond,* "[i]t is not enough that other officers may be identified who formally maintain a higher rank, or possess responsibilities of a greater magnitude," 520 U.S., at 662–663. The dissent stresses that "at least two levels of authority" separate the President from PTAB decisions, but the unchecked exercise of executive power by an officer buried many layers beneath the President poses more, not less, of a constitutional problem. Conspicuously absent from the dissent is any concern for the President's ability to "discharge his own constitutional duty of seeing that the laws be faithfully executed." *Myers* v. *United States*, 272 U.S. 52, 135 (1926). . . .

C

History reinforces the conclusion that the unreviewable executive power exercised by APJs is incompatible with their status as inferior officers. Since the founding, principal officers have directed the decisions of inferior officers on matters of law as well as policy. Hamilton articulated the principle of constitutional accountability underlying such supervision in a 1792 Treasury circular. Writing as Secretary of the Treasury to the customs officials under his charge, he warned that any deviations from his instructions "would be subversive of uniformity in the execution of the laws." 3 Works of Alexander Hamilton 557 (J. Hamilton ed. 1850). "The power to superintend," he explained, "must imply a right to judge and direct," thereby ensuring that "the responsibility for a wrong construction rests with the head of the department, when it proceeds from him." *Id.,* at 559. . . .

Congress has carried the model of principal officer review into the modern administrative state. As the Government forthrightly acknowledged at oral argument, it "certainly is the norm" for principal officers to have the capacity to review decisions made by inferior adjudicative officers. The Administrative Procedure Act, from its inception, authorized agency heads to review such decisions. 5 U. S. C. §557(b). And "higher-level agency reconsideration" by the agency head is the standard way to maintain political accountability and effective oversight for adjudication that takes place outside the confines of §557(b). To take one example recently discussed by this Court in *Free Enterprise Fund,* the Public Company Accounting Oversight Board can issue sanctions in disciplinary proceedings, but such sanctions are reviewable by its superior, the Securities and Exchange Commission.

The Government and Smith & Nephew point to a handful of contemporary officers who are appointed by heads of departments but who nevertheless purportedly exercise final decisionmaking authority. Several examples, however, involve inferior officers whose decisions a superior executive officer can review or implement a system for reviewing. For instance, the special trial judges in *Freytag* v. *Commissioner,* 501 U.S. 868 (1991), may enter a decision on behalf of the Tax Court—whose members are nominated by the President and confirmed by the Senate, 26 U. S. C. §7443(b)—but only "subject to such conditions and review as the court may provide." §7443A(c). And while the Board of Veteran Affairs does make the final decision within the Department of Veteran Affairs, its decisions are reviewed by the Court of Appeals for Veterans Claims, an Executive Branch entity. . . .

* * *

We hold that the unreviewable authority wielded by APJs during inter partes review is incompatible with their appointment by the Secretary to an inferior office. The principal dissent repeatedly charges that we never say whether APJs are principal officers who were not appointed in the manner required by the Appointments Clause, or instead inferior officers exceeding the permissible scope of their duties under that Clause. But both formulations describe the same constitutional violation: Only an officer properly appointed to a principal office may issue a final decision binding the Executive Branch in the proceeding before us.

In reaching this conclusion, we do not attempt to "set forth an exclusive criterion for distinguishing between principal and inferior officers for Appointments Clause purposes." *Edmond,* 520 U.S., at 661. Many decisions by inferior officers do not bind the Executive Branch to exercise executive power in a particular manner, and we do not address supervision outside the context of adjudication. Here, however, Congress has assigned APJs "significant authority" in adjudicating the public rights of private parties, while also insulating their decisions from review and their offices from removal. . . .

JUSTICE THOMAS, with whom JUSTICE BREYER, JUSTICE SOTOMAYOR, and JUSTICE KAGAN join, dissenting.

For the very first time, this Court holds that Congress violated the Constitution by vesting the appointment of a federal officer in the head of a department. Just who are these "principal" officers that Congress unsuccessfully sought to smuggle into the Executive Branch without Senate confirmation? About 250 administrative patent judges who sit at the bottom of an organizational chart, nestled under at least two levels of authority. Neither our precedent nor the original understanding of the Appointments Clause requires Senate confirmation of officers inferior to not one, but *two* officers below the President. . . .

[I]nterpreting the Appointments Clause to bar any nonprincipal officer from taking "final" action poses serious line-drawing problems. The majority assures that not every decision by an inferior officer must be reviewable by a superior officer. But this sparks more questions than it answers. Can a line prosecutor offer a plea deal without sign off from a principal officer? If faced with a life-threatening scenario, can an FBI agent use deadly force to subdue a suspect? Or if an inferior officer temporarily fills a vacant office tasked with making final decisions, do those decisions violate the Appointments Clause? And are courts around the country supposed to sort through lists of each officer's (or employee's) duties, categorize each one as principal or inferior, and then excise any that look problematic?

Beyond those questions, the majority's nebulous approach also leaves open the question of how much "principal officer power" someone must wield before he becomes a principal officer. What happens if an officer typically engages in normal inferior-officer work but also has several principal-officer duties? Is he a hybrid officer, properly appointed for four days a week and improperly appointed for the fifth? And whatever test the Court ultimately comes up with to sort through these difficult questions, are we sure it is encapsulated in the two words "inferior officer"? . . .

*   *   *

Notes on *United States v. Arthrex*

1. *The line between "principal" and "inferior" officers*: Whether a particular officer is "principal" or "inferior" can determine whether a given statutory scheme—such as that for inter partes review under the PTAB—is constitutional. When the officer in question is "principal," the only constitutionally permissible method of appointment is nomination by the President with Senate confirmation. *See* Art. II, §2, clause 2. What made the Administrative Patent Judges (APJs) principal officers? Critical to the judgment in *Arthrex* was that Congress had granted the APJs the power to render a final decision on behalf of the United States without any review by a superior executive officer:

"APJs have the 'power to render a final decision on behalf of the United States' without any such review by their nominal superior or any other principal officer in the Executive Branch. The only possibility of review is a petition for rehearing, but Congress unambiguously specified that '[o]nly the Patent and Trial Appeal Board may grant rehearings.' §6(c). Such review simply repeats the arrangement challenged as unconstitutional in this suit."

Because Congress had given the APJs the authority in inter partes review proceedings to render final decisions on behalf of the Executive Branch on the validity of challenged patents, they were necessarily *principal* officers.

2. *Distinguishing* Arthrex *from* Edmond: The Court's decision in *Arthrex* relied heavily on *Edmond*, one of its only other cases exploring the boundary between principal and inferior officers. *Edmond* concluded that the civilian members of the Coast Guard Court of Criminal Appeals (a court within the military justice system) were "inferior" officers. The critical difference between the ALJs in *Arthrex* and the Coast Guard judges in *Edmond*—at least according to the Court in *Arthrex*—was that the decisions of the Coast Guard Court of Criminal Appeals were reviewable by the Court of Appeals for the Armed Forces, a tribunal *within* the Executive Branch. In this way, the officers had "no power to render a final decision on behalf of the United States unless permitted to do so by other Executive officers." To be sure, the decisions of the PTAB in inter partes review proceedings were subject to rehearing—but only by the PTAB itself. And though the PTAB's decisions could be reviewed by the U.S. Court of Appeals for the Federal Circuit, this was *judicial* review, conducted by the judiciary, outside the Executive Branch. The PTAB's decisions thus were the Executive Branch's final word on the validity of challenged patents. This authority, concluded the Court, made them principal officers.

3. *Influence that fell short of the necessary review*: Notice that the Director of the Patent and Trademark Office—a principal officer, nominated by the President with Senate confirmation—had all sorts of practical means to *influence* the decisions of the PTAB in inter partes review proceedings. Consider the following:

* In each case, the Director decides whether to initiate inter partes review in the first instance.

* The Director designates the APJs who will decide a particular case (and thus can pick APJs predisposed to her views).

* The Director can vacate her initial decision to institute inter partes review if she catches wind of an unfavorable ruling from the PTAB on the way.

* The Director can intervene in the rehearing process to reverse PTAB decisions, and could manipulate the composition of the PTAB panel acting on the rehearing petition.

To the Court, though, these levers were insufficient to render the APJs "inferior." None of these mechanisms gave the Director—or any other principal officer—the authority to actually *review* (or countermand) the PTAB's decisions before they became the Executive Branch's final word on the matter. And this "unreviewable authority wielded by APJs during inter partes review" meant the APJs occupied "principal offices."

4. ***The precise nature of the constitutional problem***: Notice that there is no constitutional problem, in itself, in Congress granting APJs the authority to render unreviewable decisions on behalf of the Executive Branch. Nor is there necessarily a constitutional problem in the Secretary of Commerce appointing the APJs. The constitutional problem stemmed from Congress choosing to do *both*. Thus, Congress could create a scheme under which the APJs rendered final, unreviewable decisions in inter partes review proceedings so long as the APJs were nominated by the President and confirmed by the Senate. Alternatively, Congress could create a scheme where the APJs were appointed by the Secretary of Commerce so long as their decision were reviewable by a principal officer before binding the Executive Branch. What Congress could not do is what it did in the America Invents Act: give "principal officer" authority to officers who had been appointed by the head of a department. As the Court explained (in responding to Justice Thomas's dissent):

> "The principal dissent repeatedly charges that we never say whether APJs are principal officers who were not appointed in the manner required by the Appointments Clause, or instead inferior officers exceeding the permissible scope of their duties under that Clause. But both formulations describe the same constitutional violation: Only an officer properly appointed to a principal office may issue a final decision binding the Executive Branch in the proceeding before us."

This logic was reflected in Part III of Chief Justice Roberts's opinion, where he described the appropriate remedy for the Act's constitutional flaw. Though the Court described the scheme as a "violation of the Appointments Clause," its solution was *not* to mandate a different method of appointment for the APJs. Instead—invoking the rule that, when a court finds a statutory provision unconstitutional, it must preserve as much of the statute as possible—it held that "[d]ecisions by APJs must be subject to review by the Director" of the PTO. With such a mechanism for review, the PTAB's decisions would no longer be final, making the APJs "inferior officers." As such, their appointment by the Secretary of Commerce would be consistent with the Appointments Clause.

5. ***Future line-drawing problems?***: The *Arthrex* Court said it was not "attempt[ing] to set forth an exclusive criterion for distinguishing between principal and inferior officers for Appointments Clause purposes." In particular, it noted that "[m]any decisions by inferior officers do not bind the Executive Branch to exercise executive power in a particular manner, and we do not address supervision outside the context of adjudication." Nonetheless, the dissenters argued that the Court's rule—focusing on whether the officer has the authority to make final decisions for the Executive Branch—will inevitably create line-drawing problems. There may be hundreds (or thousands) of decisions made by inferior officers on a daily basis that effectively bind the Executive Branch. Are these all unconstitutional? Does it depend on whether a principal officer has the formal authority to countermand those decisions, even if such review almost never occurs? It seems unlikely *Arthrex* will be the final word on what distinguishes principal from inferior officers.

6. *What constitutes a "court of law"?*: If an officer is inferior, Congress may (by law) vest the officer's appointment "in the President alone, in the Courts of Law, or in the Heads of Departments." It is simple enough to discern the meaning of "the President alone." But what qualifies as a "court of law"? Clearly, an Article III court (the Supreme Court, a federal court of appeals, or a federal district court) qualifies. But what about other federal adjudicative bodies that are not part of the Article III judiciary? In *Freytag*, the Supreme Court held that so-called "Article I courts" (such as the Tax Court) can be "courts of law" under the Appointments Clause. Whether a court is sufficiently "judicial" to qualify as a "court of law" depends on the court's precise operation. In *Freytag*, the Court reasoned that the Tax Court

> "was established by Congress to interpret and apply the Internal Revenue Code in disputes between taxpayers and the Government. By resolving these disputes, the court exercises a portion of the judicial power of the United States. . . . It is neither advocate nor rulemaker. As an adjudicative body, it construes statutes passed by Congress and regulations promulgated by the Internal Revenue Service. It does not make political decisions.

> "The Tax Court's function and role in the federal judicial scheme closely resemble those of the federal district courts, which indisputably are 'Courts of Law.' Furthermore, the Tax Court exercises its judicial power in much the same way as the federal district courts exercise theirs. It has authority to punish contempts by fine or imprisonment; to grant certain injunctive relief; to order the Secretary of the Treasury to refund an overpayment determined by the court; and to subpoena and examine witnesses, order production of documents, and administer oaths. All these powers are quintessentially judicial in nature.

> "The Tax Court remains independent of the Executive and Legislative Branches. Its decisions are not subject to review by either the Congress or the President. Nor has Congress made Tax Court decisions subject to review in the federal district courts. Rather, like the judgments of the district courts, the decisions of the Tax Court are appealable only to the regional United States courts of appeals, with ultimate review in this Court. The courts of appeals, moreover, review those decisions 'in the same manner and to the same extent as decisions of the district courts in civil actions tried without a jury.'"

7. *What constitutes a "head of department"?*: It is also permissible for Congress to vest the appointment of inferior officers in "heads of departments." Who fits within this term? First, the "head" of a department is the officer in charge of that department, sitting atop its organizational chart. If an officer reports to someone else in the same department, she cannot be the "head." (The "head" can be multiple people, however, who act in concert as a collective "head." This describes the Securities and Exchange Commission (SEC), whose five commissioners are collectively the "head" of that agency.) Second, a "department" is something similar to a cabinet-level department. The cabinet-level departments are (in order of their heads' succession to the Presidency) the Department of State, the Department of the Treasury, the Department of Defense, the Department of Justice, the Department of the Interior, the Department of Agriculture, the Department of Commerce, the Department of Labor, the Department of Health and Human Services, the Department of Housing and Urban Development, the Department of Transportation, the Department of Energy, the Department of Education, the Department of Veterans Affairs, and the Department of Homeland Security. The secretaries of these Departments are clearly "heads of departments," but there are likely others who qualify. (The Court discussed these additional possibilities in *Freytag*, without definitively resolving the question.) So "heads of departments" likely includes (1) all heads of cabinet-level departments, and (2) the heads of similarly significant departments and agencies (such as the SEC, the Federal Communications Commission, and the Federal Trade Commission). It does *not* include lesser bureaus, agencies, commissions, or regional offices.

8. *The role of Congress in the appointment of federal officers*: A final point concerns the role of Congress in the appointment of federal officers. Of course, Congress always creates the office at issue through legislation, and Congress often specifies by statute how the officer is to be appointed. (If Congress fails to specify a mechanism for appointment, then the default is nomination by the President, with the advice and consent of the Senate.) But Congress cannot be involved after that; it cannot play a role in the selection of individuals to fill specific offices. There simply is no place in the Appointments Clause for the congressional appointment of federal officers (other than the Senate's role of advice and consent). The sum total of all permissible means of appointment are (1) by the President, with the advice and consent of the Senate; (2) by a court of law; (3) by a head of a department; or (4) by the President alone. Thus, in *Buckley v. Valeo*, the Supreme Court invalidated a statute that permitted members of Congress to appoint members of the Federal Election Commission.

More broadly, separation-of-powers principles preclude Congress from playing any role in the execution of federal law. Congress's constitutional role is to *enact* federal laws—to create and structure federal offices and enact the laws to be enforced and applied by federal officers. After that, Congress's role is to exercise oversight and enact new legislation. If Congress dislikes how the

Executive Branch is implementing federal law, it can revise the relevant statutes so as to more specifically direct or specify those actions. But Congress can play no role itself in the execution of an existing federal statute.

* * *

PROBLEMS ON THE APPOINTMENT OF FEDERAL OFFICERS

In each of the following scenarios, please evaluate whether the relevant appointment provision is constitutional. If there is additional information you think necessary to answer the question, explain what that information is and how it would affect your analysis.

1. By statute, the administrative assistant to the director of the Antitrust Division of the Department of Justice is appointed by the head of human resources for the Department of Justice. (As a matter of organizational structure, the director of the Antitrust Division reports to the Attorney General, who in turn reports to the President.) The administrative assistant handles scheduling, filing, and similar tasks.

2. When Senator John Kerry assumed the office of Secretary of State in 2013, Massachusetts Governor Deval Patrick unilaterally appointed William Cowan to replace Kerry as a U.S. Senator for Massachusetts. Why was Governor Patrick's appointment of Cowan appointment consistent with Article II, §2, clause 2? (It might help to review the Seventeenth Amendment.)

3. A federal statute creates a new office (known as "Vaccine Czar") who is to report to Congress regularly on the state of coronavirus vaccine production and distribution. The Vaccine Czar will report regularly to Congress, to assist members of Congress in discharging their responsibilities as legislators. The Czar is to be appointed by the Speaker of the House of Representatives.

4. A federal statute provides that the Commissioner of the Food and Drug Administration is to be nominated by the President and confirmed by the Senate. The FDA sits within the Department of Health and Human Services (HHS), and the Commissioner reports to the Secretary of HHS. The FDA is responsible for the administration of all federal laws concerning the safety and efficacy of all pharmaceuticals and medical devices marketed in the United States. Many of the Commissioner's decisions are the final word for the Executive Branch, unreviewable by the Secretary of HHS.

5. A statute provides that the FDA Commissioner is appointed by the Secretary of Health and Human Services.

6. The Center for Biologics Evaluation and Research constitutes a division within the FDA. The Director of Center for Biologics Evaluation and Research makes a range of significant policy decisions in the implementation of various federal statutes. By statute, the Director is appointed by the Commissioner of the FDA.

7. Assistant U.S. Attorneys conduct criminal prosecutions on behalf of the federal government. In doing this work, they regularly enter into plea agreements (and make decisions in the course of trials) that bind the Executive Branch. Their work is generally subject to the review of the U.S. Attorney for the district in which they work—the

principal officer to whom they report—but their everyday decisions bind the United States without ever being reviewed. Assistant U.S. Attorneys are appointed by the Attorney General of the United States, the head of the Department of Justice.

* * *

B.   The Removal of Federal Officers

1. *Myers v. United States* and *Humphrey's Executor*

In contrast to the Appointments Clause, there is no express provision in the Constitution addressing the removal of federal officers. Instead, removal issues are governed by the more general, non-textual principles relating to the separation of national powers. In *Myers v. United States*, 272 U.S. 52 (1926), the Supreme Court held that the President's power to remove federal officers is inherent in Article II's vesting in him "the executive Power." Specifically, the

> "power of removal is incident to the power of appointment, not to the power of advising and consenting to appointment, and when the grant of the executive power is enforced by the express mandate to take care that the laws be faithfully executed, it emphasizes the necessity for including within the executive power as conferred the exclusive power of removal."

Myers invalidated a statute under which the President was permitted to remove a postmaster from office only if the Senate consented to the removal. *Myers* thus established that a statute requiring congressional consent to the President's removal of an officer is unconstitutional.

Myers was somewhat unusual, in that the statute at issue attempted to retain for Congress a role in the removal of particular officers. More common have been statutes limiting the circumstances in which the President—or a high-level Executive Branch official acting on the President's behalf—can remove an officer. The Supreme Court confronted this more typical situation in *Humphrey's Executor*, 295 U.S. 602 (1935). At issue in was President Franklin Delano Roosevelt's removal of Humphrey from his position as a Federal Trade Commissioner before his term expired. The FTC was charged by statute with enforcing the laws of fair competition in private industry (such as the federal antitrust laws). Under the Federal Trade Act—the statute that created the FTC and specified the terms under which commissioners would be appointed and removed—FTC commissioners were to serve seven-year terms, and the President could remove a commissioner from office prior to the expiration of his term only "for inefficiency, neglect of duty, or malfeasance in office." This meant the President could not remove a commissioner at will; a mere difference in policy or political ideology was insufficient to meet this standard. But this was why Roosevelt wanted to remove Humphrey, who had been appointed by President Hoover and opposed Roosevelt's New Deal initiatives.

Of course, Congress had placed the limitation in the FTA precisely to prevent this sort of removal. Congress sought to insulate the FTC's policymaking from the political pressures imposed by the President; it wanted the FTC to act "independently." (Independence, in this context, means independence from direct presidential control, the sort of control that would obtain if the heads could be removed by the President at will. This is why the FTC is considered an "independent agency.") Hence, the constitutional stakes in *Humphrey's Executor* were substantial. At issue was not simply FDR's removal of Humphrey but the constitutionality of independent agencies more generally. Beyond the FTC, this included the Federal Communications Commission (FCC), the SEC, the Food and Drug Administration (FDA), the Consumer Product Safety Commission (CPSC), Federal Elections Commission (FEC), and the Federal Reserve Board, among others—a large swath of the modern federal government.

Against this backdrop, the Supreme Court held that the restriction Congress had placed on the removal of FTC commissioners was constitutional. Specifically, the Court explained that the FTC commissioners were not "purely executive," but instead also acted in a quasi-legislative, quasi-judicial manner. Further, Congress had sound reasons to insulate FTC commissioners from presidential and political pressure. As a result, the limitation did not violate separation-of-powers principles.

2. *Morrison v. Olsen*

At issue in *Morrison v. Olsen*, 487 U.S. 654 (1988), was a provision in the Ethics in Government Act that created the Office of the Independent Counsel. The purpose of the independent counsel was to investigate alleged wrongdoing by high-level officials in the Executive Branch. (This statute, which has since expired, operated differently than the process by which Robert Mueller was appointed as a special counsel within the Department of Justice to investigate potential wrongdoing by President Trump and his associates related to the 2016 campaign. Mueller and his investigation were, at all times, supervised by the Department of Justice, and thus operated within the traditional framework for the appointment, supervision, and removal of Executive Branch officers.)

Under the Ethics in Government Act, if the Attorney General found sufficient grounds to warrant further investigation, she was to forward that finding to a Special Division of the U.S. Court of Appeals for the District of Columbia. That court would then appoint an independent counsel to investigate the alleged wrongdoing. Once appointed, the independent counsel could only be removed by the Attorney General "for good cause." This was a significant limitation on the President's capacity to remove, similar to the limitation at issue in *Humphrey's Executor*. It restricted removal to grounds such as failure to follow the law, dereliction of duty, or mental or physical incapacity. Specifying that removal must be executed by the Attorney General (as opposed to the President himself) was not a significant a limitation because the Attorney General serves at the will of the President. Hence, if the President wanted the independent counsel removed, he could demand it of the Attorney General, and then fire the Attorney General if she failed to carry out the President's wishes.

The Court in *Morrison* held this removal limitation was constitutional:

"[T]he independent counsel is an inferior officer under the Appointments Clause, with limited jurisdiction and tenure and lacking policymaking or significant administrative authority. Although the counsel exercises no small amount of discretion and judgment in deciding how to carry out his or her duties under the Act, we simply do not see how the President's need to control the exercise of that discretion is so central to the functioning of the Executive Branch as to require as a matter of constitutional law that the counsel be terminable at will by the President. . . . We do not think that this limitation as it presently stands sufficiently deprives the President of control over the independent counsel to interfere impermissibly with his constitutional obligation to ensure the faithful execution of the laws."

3. *Free Enterprise Fund v. PCAOB*

The first Roberts Court decision addressing the constitutionality of a removal limitation came in *Free Enterprise Fund v. PCAOB*, 561 U.S. 477 (2010). Following the dramatic collapse of some major U.S. corporations (such as Enron and MCI) involving accounting fraud, Congress enacted the Sarbanes-Oxley Act of 2002. Among other things, the Act created the Public Company Accounting Oversight Board (PCAOB), a new body within the SEC. The Act granted the Board broad authority to regulate the nation's accounting firms. As relevant here, the Act specified that members of the PCAOB could only be removed by the SEC, and only "for good cause shown." And SEC Commissioners—the officers with the authority to remove members of the PCAOB—were themselves protected by a "for cause" removal limitation. Thus, the Act placed members of the PCAOB within a double-layered "for cause" removal protection.

To the Court, this multilevel protection rendered the President's capacity to control members of the PCAOB too attenuated, and thus violated Article II:

"Since 1789, the Constitution has been understood to empower the President to keep these officers accountable—by removing them from office, if necessary. This Court has determined, however, that this authority is not without limit. In *Humphrey's Executor* v. *United States*, we held that Congress can, under certain circumstances, create independent agencies run by principal officers appointed by the President, whom the President may not remove at will but only for good cause. Likewise, in *United States v. Perkins* and *Morrison v. Olson*, the Court sustained similar restrictions on the power of principal executive officers—themselves responsible to the President—to remove their own inferiors. . . .

"[This] is a new situation not yet encountered by the Court. The question is whether these separate layers of protection may be combined. May the President be restricted in his ability to remove a principal officer, who is in turn restricted in his ability to remove an inferior officer, even though that inferior officer determines the policy and enforces the laws of the United States?

"[S]uch multilevel protection from removal is contrary to Article II's vesting of the executive power in the President. The President cannot 'take Care that the Laws be faithfully executed' if he cannot oversee the faithfulness of the officers who execute them. Here the President cannot remove an officer who enjoys more than one level of good-cause protection, even if the President determines that the officer is neglecting his duties or discharging them improperly. That judgment is instead committed to another officer, who may or may not agree with the President's determination, and whom the President cannot remove simply because that officer disagrees with him. This contravenes the President's 'constitutional obligation to ensure the faithful execution of the laws.'"

4. Two recent statements: *Seila Law* and *Collins v. Yellen*

In 2020, the Roberts Court decided its second important case involving Congress' capacity to fetter the President's power to remove executive officers. The case involved the Consumer Financial Protection Bureau (CFPB), which was the brainchild of Senator Elizabeth Warren. In the wake of the 2008 meltdown of the financial system, Congress enacted the Dodd-Frank Act, which created the CFPB and gave the Bureau responsibility for enforcing 18 different federal statutes related to ensuring "all consumers have access to markets for consumer financial products and services and that markets for consumer financial products and services are fair, transparent, and competitive." The CFPB was to be headed by a single director, who could only be removed by the President for "inefficiency, neglect of duty, or malfeasance in office." As you read *Seila Law*, please consider the following questions:

1. How was the position of Director of the CFPB different from the position of a Federal Trade Commissioner at issue in *Humphrey's Executor*? How was it different from the position of the independent counsel at issue in *Morrison v. Olson*?

2. How does the classification of the office at issue as "principal" or "inferior" affect the constitutionality of a limitation on the removal of that officer?

3. After *Seila Law*, how would you phrase the rule for when Congress, consistent with the separation of powers, can impose a limitation on the President's capacity to remove an executive officer?

Seila Law LLC v. Consumer Financial Protection Bureau
140 S. Ct. 2183 (2020)

CHIEF JUSTICE ROBERTS delivered the opinion of the Court.

In the wake of the 2008 financial crisis, Congress established the Consumer Financial Protection Bureau (CFPB), an independent regulatory agency tasked with ensuring that consumer debt products are safe and transparent. In organizing the CFPB, Congress deviated from the structure of nearly every other independent administrative agency in our history. Instead of placing the agency under the leadership of a board with multiple members, Congress provided that the CFPB would be led by a single Director, who serves for a longer term than the President and cannot be removed by the President except for inefficiency, neglect, or malfeasance. The CFPB Director has no boss, peers, or voters to report to. Yet the Director wields vast rulemaking, enforcement, and adjudicatory authority over a significant portion of the U. S. economy. The question before us is whether this arrangement violates the Constitution's separation of powers.

Under our Constitution, the "executive Power"—all of it—is "vested in a President," who must "take Care that the Laws be faithfully executed." Art. II, § 1, cl. 1; *id.*, § 3. Because no single person could fulfill that responsibility alone, the Framers expected that the President would rely on subordinate officers for assistance. Ten years ago, in *Free Enterprise Fund v. Public Company Accounting Oversight Bd.*, we reiterated that, "as a general matter," the Constitution gives the President "the authority to remove those who assist him in carrying out his duties." "Without such power, the President could not be held fully accountable for discharging his own responsibilities; the buck would stop somewhere else."

The President's power to remove—and thus supervise—those who wield executive power on his behalf follows from the text of Article II, was settled by the First Congress, and was confirmed in the landmark decision *Myers v. United States*, 272 U.S. 52 (1926). Our precedents have recognized only two exceptions to the President's unrestricted removal power. In *Humphrey's Executor v. United States*, 295 U.S. 602 (1935), we held that Congress could create expert agencies led by a group of principal officers removable by the President only for good cause. And in *United States v. Perkins*, 116 U.S. 483 (1886), and *Morrison v. Olson*, 487 U.S. 654 (1988), we held that Congress could provide tenure protections to certain inferior officers with narrowly defined duties.

We are now asked to extend these precedents to a new configuration: an independent agency that wields significant executive power and is run by a single individual who cannot be removed by the President unless certain statutory criteria are met. We decline to take that step. While we need not and do not revisit our prior decisions allowing certain limitations on the President's removal power, there are compelling reasons not to extend those precedents to the novel context of an independent agency led by a single Director. Such an agency lacks a foundation in historical practice and clashes with constitutional structure by concentrating power in a unilateral actor insulated from Presidential control.

We therefore hold that the structure of the CFPB violates the separation of powers. We go on to hold that the CFPB Director's removal protection is severable from the other statutory provisions bearing on the CFPB's authority. The agency may therefore continue to operate, but its Director, in light of our decision, must be removable by the President at will.

I

A

In the summer of 2007, then-Professor Elizabeth Warren called for the creation of a new, independent federal agency focused on regulating consumer financial products. . . . That proposal soon met its moment. Within months of Professor Warren's writing, the subprime mortgage market collapsed, precipitating a financial crisis that wiped out over $10 trillion in American household wealth and cost millions of Americans their jobs, their retirements, and their homes. In the aftermath, the Obama administration embraced Professor Warren's recommendation. Through the Treasury Department, the administration encouraged Congress to establish an agency with a mandate to ensure that "consumer protection regulations" in the financial sector "are written fairly and enforced vigorously." . . .

In 2010, Congress acted on these proposals and created the Consumer Financial Protection Bureau (CFPB) as an independent financial regulator within the Federal Reserve System. Dodd-Frank Wall Street Reform and Consumer Protection Act (Dodd-Frank). Congress tasked the CFPB with "implement[ing]" and "enforc[ing]" a large body of financial consumer protection laws to "ensur[e] that all consumers have access to markets for consumer financial products and services and that markets for consumer financial products and services are fair, transparent, and competitive." 12 U. S. C. § 5511(a). Congress transferred the administration of 18 existing federal statutes to the CFPB, including the Fair Credit Reporting Act, the Fair Debt Collection Practices Act, and the Truth in Lending Act. In addition, Congress enacted a new prohibition on "any unfair, deceptive, or abusive act or practice" by certain participants in the consumer-finance sector. § 5536(a)(1)(B). Congress authorized the CFPB to implement that broad standard (and the 18 pre-existing statutes placed under the agency's purview) through binding regulations.

Congress also vested the CFPB with potent enforcement powers. The agency has the authority to conduct investigations, issue subpoenas and civil investigative demands, initiate administrative adjudications, and prosecute civil actions in federal court. To remedy violations of federal consumer financial law, the CFPB may seek restitution, disgorgement, and injunctive relief, as well as civil penalties of up to $1,000,000 (inflation adjusted) for each day that a violation occurs. Since its inception, the CFPB has obtained over $11 billion in relief for over 25 million consumers, including a $1 billion penalty against a single bank in 2018.

The CFPB's rulemaking and enforcement powers are coupled with extensive adjudicatory authority. The agency may conduct administrative proceedings to "ensure or enforce compliance with" the statutes and regulations it administers. 12 U. S. C. § 5563(a). When the CFPB acts as an adjudicator, it has "jurisdiction to grant any appropriate legal or equitable relief." The "hearing officer" who presides over the proceedings may issue subpoenas, order depositions, and resolve any motions filed by the parties. At the close of the proceedings, the hearing officer issues a "recommended decision," and the CFPB Director considers that recommendation and "issue[s] a final decision and order."

Congress's design for the CFPB differed from the proposals of Professor Warren and the Obama administration in one critical respect. Rather than create a traditional independent agency headed by a multimember board or commission, Congress elected to place the CFPB under the leadership of a single Director. The CFPB Director is appointed by the President with the advice and consent of the Senate. The Director serves for a term of five years, during which the President may remove the Director from office only for "inefficiency, neglect of duty, or malfeasance in office." §§ 5491(c)(1), (3).

Unlike most other agencies, the CFPB does not rely on the annual appropriations process for funding. Instead, the CFPB receives funding directly from the Federal Reserve, which is itself funded outside the appropriations process through bank assessments. Each year, the CFPB requests an amount that the Director deems "reasonably necessary to carry out" the agency's duties, and the Federal Reserve grants that request so long as it does not exceed 12% of the total operating expenses of the Federal Reserve (inflation adjusted). In recent years, the CFPB's annual budget has exceeded half a billion dollars.

B

Seila Law LLC is a California-based law firm that provides debt-related legal services to clients. In 2017, the CFPB issued a civil investigative demand to Seila Law to determine whether the firm had "engag[ed] in unlawful acts or practices in the advertising, marketing, or sale of debt relief services." The demand (essentially a subpoena) directed Seila Law to produce information and documents related to its business practices.

Seila Law asked the CFPB to set aside the demand, objecting that the agency's leadership by a single Director removable only for cause violated the separation of powers. The CFPB declined to address that claim and directed Seila Law to comply with the demand.

When Seila Law refused, the CFPB filed a petition to enforce the demand in the District Court. In response, Seila Law renewed its defense that the demand was invalid and must be set aside because the CFPB's structure violated the Constitution. . . .

* * *

III

We hold that the CFPB's leadership by a single individual removable only for inefficiency, neglect, or malfeasance violates the separation of powers.

A

Article II provides that "[t]he executive Power shall be vested in a President," who must "take Care that the Laws be faithfully executed." Art. II, §1, cl. 1; id., §3. The entire "executive Power" belongs to the President alone. But because it would be "impossib[le]" for "one man" to "perform all the great business of the State," the Constitution assumes that lesser executive officers will "assist the supreme Magistrate in discharging the duties of his trust." 30 Writings of George Washington 334 (J. Fitzpatrick ed. 1939).

These lesser officers must remain accountable to the President, whose authority they wield. As Madison explained, "[I]f any power whatsoever is in its nature Executive, it is the power of appointing, overseeing, and controlling those who execute the laws." That power, in turn, generally includes the ability to remove executive officials, for it is "only the authority that can remove" such officials that they "must fear and, in the performance of [their] functions, obey." *Bowsher*, 478 U.S., at 726.

The President's removal power has long been confirmed by history and precedent. It "was discussed extensively in Congress when the first executive departments were created" in 1789. *Free Enterprise Fund*, 561 U.S., at 492. "The view that 'prevailed, as most consonant to the text of the Constitution' and 'to the requisite responsibility and harmony in the Executive Department,' was that the executive power included a power to oversee executive officers through removal." *Ibid.* (quoting Letter from James Madison to Thomas Jefferson (June 30, 1789). The First Congress's recognition of the President's removal power in 1789 "provides contemporaneous and weighty evidence of the Constitution's meaning," *Bowsher*, 478 U.S., at 723, and has long been the "settled and well understood construction of the Constitution," *Ex parte Hennen*, 13 Pet. 230, 259 (1839).

The Court recognized the President's prerogative to remove executive officials in *Myers v. United States*, 272 U.S. 52. Chief Justice Taft, writing for the Court, conducted an exhaustive examination of the First Congress's determination in 1789, the views of the Framers and their contemporaries, historical practice, and our precedents up until that point. He concluded that Article II "grants to the President" the "general administrative control of those executing the laws, including the power of appointment *and removal* of executive officers." *Id.*, at 163–164 (emphasis added). Just as the President's "selection of administrative officers is essential to the execution of the laws by him, so must be his power of removing those for whom he cannot continue to be responsible." *Id.*, at 117. "[T]o hold otherwise," the Court reasoned, "would make it impossible for the President . . . to take care that the laws be faithfully executed." *Id.*, at 164.

We recently reiterated the President's general removal power in *Free Enterprise Fund*. "Since 1789," we recapped, "the Constitution has been understood to empower the President to keep these officers accountable—by removing them from office, if necessary." 561 U.S., at 483. Although we had previously sustained congressional limits on that power in certain circumstances, we declined to extend those limits to "a new situation not yet encountered by the Court"—an official insulated by two layers of for-cause removal protection. *Id.*, at 483, 514. In the face of that novel impediment to the President's oversight of the Executive Branch, we adhered to the general rule that the President possesses "the authority to remove those who assist him in carrying out his duties." *Id.*, at 513–514.

Free Enterprise Fund left in place two exceptions to the President's unrestricted removal power. First, in *Humphrey's Executor*, decided less than a decade after *Myers*, the Court upheld a statute that protected the Commissioners of the FTC from removal except for "inefficiency, neglect of duty, or malfeasance in office." 295 U.S. at 620. In reaching that conclusion, the Court stressed that Congress's ability to impose such removal restrictions "will depend upon the character of the office." 295 U.S. at 631.

Because the Court limited its holding "to officers of the kind here under consideration," *id.*, at 632, the contours of the *Humphrey's Executor* exception depend upon the characteristics of the agency before the Court. Rightly or wrongly, the Court viewed the FTC (as it existed in 1935) as exercising "no part of the executive power." *Id.*, at 628. Instead, it was "an administrative body" that performed "specified duties as a legislative or as a judicial aid." *Ibid.* It acted "as a legislative agency" in "making investigations and reports" to Congress and "as an agency of the judiciary" in making recommendations to courts as a master in chancery. *Ibid.* "To the extent that [the FTC] exercise[d] any executive *function*[,] as distinguished from executive power in the constitutional sense," it did so only in the discharge of its "quasi-legislative or quasi-judicial powers." *Ibid.* (emphasis added).

The Court identified several organizational features that helped explain its characterization of the FTC as non-executive. Composed of five members—no more than three from the same political party—the Board was designed to be "non-partisan" and to "act with entire impartiality." *Id.*, at 624. The FTC's duties were "neither political nor executive," but instead called for "the trained judgment of a body of experts" "informed by experience." *Id.*, at 624. And the Commissioners' staggered, seven-year terms enabled the agency to accumulate technical expertise and avoid a "complete change" in leadership "at any one time." *Ibid.*

In short, *Humphrey's Executor* permitted Congress to give for-cause removal protections to a multimember body of experts, balanced along partisan lines, that performed legislative and judicial functions and was said not to exercise any executive power. . . . While recognizing an exception for multimember bodies with "quasi-judicial" or "quasi-legislative" functions, *Humphrey's Executor* reaffirmed the core holding of *Myers* that the President has "unrestrictable power . . . to remove purely executive officers." 295 U.S. at 632. The Court acknowledged that between purely executive officers on the one hand, and officers that closely resembled the FTC Commissioners on the other, there existed "a field of doubt" that the Court left "for future consideration." *Ibid.*

We have recognized a second exception for inferior officers in two cases, *United States v. Perkins* and *Morrison v. Olson.* In *Perkins*, we upheld tenure protections for a naval cadet-engineer. 116 U.S. at 485. And, in *Morrison*, we upheld a provision granting good-cause tenure protection to an independent counsel appointed to investigate and prosecute particular alleged crimes by high-ranking Government officials. 487 U.S. at 662–663, 696–697. Backing away from the reliance in *Humphrey's Executor* on the concepts of "quasi-legislative" and "quasi-judicial" power, we viewed the ultimate question as whether a removal restriction is of "such a nature that [it] impede[s] the President's ability to perform his constitutional duty." 487 U.S. at 691. Although the independent counsel was a single person and performed "law enforcement functions that typically have been undertaken by officials within the Executive Branch," we concluded that the removal protections did not unduly interfere with the functioning of the Executive Branch because "the independent counsel [was] an inferior officer under the Appointments Clause, with limited jurisdiction and tenure and lacking policymaking or significant administrative authority." *Ibid.*

These two exceptions—one for multimember expert agencies that do not wield substantial executive power, and one for inferior officers with limited duties and no policymaking or administrative authority—"represent what up to now have been the outermost constitutional limits of permissible congressional restrictions on the President's removal power." *PHH*, 881 F.3d at 196 (Kavanaugh, J., dissenting) (internal quotation marks omitted).

B

Neither *Humphrey's Executor* nor *Morrison* resolves whether the CFPB Director's insulation from removal is constitutional. Start with *Humphrey's Executor*. Unlike the New Deal-era FTC upheld there, the CFPB is led by a single Director who cannot be described as a "body of experts" and cannot be considered "non-partisan" in the same sense as a group of officials drawn from both sides of the aisle. Moreover, while the staggered terms of the FTC Commissioners prevented complete turnovers in agency leadership and guaranteed that there would always be some Commissioners who had accrued significant expertise, the CFPB's single-Director structure and five-year term guarantee abrupt shifts in agency leadership and with it the loss of accumulated expertise.

In addition, the CFPB Director is hardly a mere legislative or judicial aid. Instead of making reports and recommendations to Congress, as the 1935 FTC did, the Director possesses the authority to promulgate binding rules fleshing out 19 federal statutes, including a broad prohibition on unfair and deceptive practices in a major segment of the U.S. economy. And instead of submitting recommended dispositions to an Article III court, the Director may unilaterally issue final decisions awarding legal and equitable relief in administrative adjudications. Finally, the Director's enforcement authority includes the power to seek daunting monetary penalties against private parties on behalf of the United States in federal court—a quintessentially executive power not considered in *Humphrey's Executor*.

The logic of *Morrison* also does not apply. Everyone agrees the CFPB Director is not an inferior officer, and her duties are far from limited. Unlike the independent counsel, who lacked policymaking or administrative authority, the Director has the sole responsibility to administer 19 separate consumer-protection statutes that cover everything from credit cards and car payments to mortgages and student loans. It is true that the independent counsel in *Morrison* was empowered to initiate criminal investigations and prosecutions, and in that respect wielded core executive power. But that power, while significant, was trained inward to high-ranking Governmental actors identified by others, and was confined to a specified matter in which the Department of Justice had a potential conflict of interest. By contrast, the CFPB Director has the authority to bring the coercive power of the state to bear on millions of private citizens and businesses, imposing even billion-dollar penalties through administrative adjudications and civil actions.

In light of these differences, the constitutionality of the CFPB Director's insulation from removal cannot be settled by *Humphrey's Executor* or *Morrison* alone.

C

The question instead is whether to extend those precedents to the "new situation" before us, namely an independent agency led by a single Director and vested with significant executive power. We decline to do so. Such an agency has no basis in history and no place in our constitutional structure.

1

"Perhaps the most telling indication of [a] severe constitutional problem" with an executive entity "is [a] lack of historical precedent" to support it. An agency with a structure like that of the CFPB is almost wholly unprecedented.

After years of litigating the agency's constitutionality, the Courts of Appeals, parties, and amici have identified "only a handful of isolated" incidents in which Congress has provided good-cause tenure to principal officers who wield power alone rather than as members of a board or commission. "[T]hese few scattered examples"—four to be exact—shed little light. *NLRB v. Noel Canning*, 573 U.S. 513, 538 (2014). . . . With the exception of the one-year blip for the Comptroller of the Currency, these isolated examples are modern and contested. And they do not involve regulatory or enforcement authority remotely comparable to that exercised by the CFPB. The CFPB's single-Director structure is an innovation with no foothold in history or tradition.

2

In addition to being a historical anomaly, the CFPB's single-Director configuration is incompatible with our constitutional structure. Aside from the sole exception of the Presidency, that structure scrupulously avoids concentrating power in the hands of any single individual.

"The Framers recognized that, in the long term, structural protections against abuse of power were critical to preserving liberty." *Bowsher*, 478 U.S., at 730. Their solution to governmental power and its perils was simple: divide it. To prevent the "gradual concentration" of power in the same hands, they enabled "[a]mbition . . . to counteract ambition" at every turn. The Federalist No. 51, p. 349 (J. Cooke ed. 1961) (J. Madison). At the highest level, they "split the atom of sovereignty" itself into one Federal Government and the States. *Gamble v. United States*, 139 S. Ct. 1960, 1968 (2019). They then divided the "powers of the new Federal Government into three defined categories, Legislative, Executive, and Judicial." *Chadha*, 462 U.S., at 951.

They did not stop there. Most prominently, the Framers bifurcated the federal legislative power into two Chambers: the House of Representatives and the Senate, each composed of multiple Members and Senators. Art. I, §§ 2, 3.

The Executive Branch is a stark departure from all this division. The Framers viewed the legislative power as a special threat to individual liberty, so they divided that power to ensure that "differences of opinion" and the "jarrings of parties" would "promote deliberation and circumspection" and "check excesses in the majority." See The Federalist No. 70, at 475 (A. Hamilton). By contrast, the Framers thought it necessary to secure the authority of the Executive so that he could carry out his unique responsibilities. As Madison put it, while "the weight of the legislative authority requires that it should be . . . divided, the weakness of the executive may require, on the other hand, that it should be fortified." *Id.*, No. 51, at 350.

The Framers deemed an energetic executive essential to "the protection of the community against foreign attacks," "the steady administration of the laws," "the protection of property," and "the security of liberty." *Id.*, No. 70, at 471. Accordingly, they chose not to bog the Executive down with the "habitual feebleness and dilatoriness" that comes with a "diversity of views and opinions." *Id.*, at 476. Instead, they gave the Executive the "[d]ecision, activity, secrecy, and dispatch" that "characterise the proceedings of one man." *Id.*, at 472.

To justify and check that authority—unique in our constitutional structure—the Framers made the President the most democratic and politically accountable official in Government. Only the President (along with the Vice President) is elected by the entire Nation. And the President's political accountability is enhanced by the solitary nature of the Executive Branch, which provides "a single object for the jealousy and watchfulness of the people." *Id.*, at 479. The President "cannot delegate ultimate responsibility or the active obligation to supervise that goes with it," because Article II "makes a single President responsible for the actions of the Executive Branch." *Free Enterprise Fund*, 561 U.S., at 496–497.

The resulting constitutional strategy is straightforward: divide power everywhere except for the Presidency, and render the President directly accountable to the people through regular elections. In that scheme, individual executive officials will still wield significant authority, but that authority remains subject to the ongoing supervision and control of the elected President. Through the President's oversight, "the chain of dependence [is] preserved," so that "the lowest officers, the middle grade, and the highest" all "depend, as they ought, on the President, and the President on the community." 1 Annals of Cong. 499 (J. Madison).

The CFPB's single-Director structure contravenes this carefully calibrated system by vesting significant governmental power in the hands of a single individual accountable to no one. The Director is neither elected by the people nor meaningfully controlled (through the threat of removal) by someone who is. The Director does not even depend on Congress for annual appropriations. Yet the Director may unilaterally, without meaningful supervision, issue final regulations, oversee adjudications, set enforcement priorities, initiate prosecutions, and determine what penalties to impose on private parties. With no colleagues to persuade, and no boss or electorate looking over her shoulder, the Director may dictate and enforce policy for a vital segment of the economy affecting millions of Americans.

The CFPB Director's insulation from removal by an accountable President is enough to render the agency's structure unconstitutional. But several other features of the CFPB combine to make the Director's removal protection even more problematic. In addition to lacking the most direct method of presidential control—removal at will—the agency's unique structure also forecloses certain indirect methods of Presidential control.

Because the CFPB is headed by a single Director with a five-year term, some Presidents may not have any opportunity to shape its leadership and thereby influence its activities. A President elected in 2020 would likely not appoint a CFPB Director until 2023, and a President elected in 2028 may never appoint one. That means an unlucky

President might get elected on a consumer-protection platform and enter office only to find herself saddled with a holdover Director from a competing political party who is dead set against that agenda. To make matters worse, the agency's single-Director structure means the President will not have the opportunity to appoint any other leaders—such as a chair or fellow members of a Commission or Board—who can serve as a check on the Director's authority and help bring the agency in line with the President's preferred policies.

The CFPB's receipt of funds outside the appropriations process further aggravates the agency's threat to Presidential control. The President normally has the opportunity to recommend or veto spending bills that affect the operation of administrative agencies. And, for the past century, the President has annually submitted a proposed budget to Congress for approval. Presidents frequently use these budgetary tools "to influence the policies of independent agencies." But no similar opportunity exists for the President to influence the CFPB Director. Instead, the Director receives over $500 million per year to fund the agency's chosen priorities. And the Director receives that money from the Federal Reserve, which is itself funded outside of the annual appropriations process. This financial freedom makes it even more likely that the agency will "slip from the Executive's control, and thus from that of the people." *Free Enterprise Fund*, 561 U.S., at 499.

3

Amicus raises three principal arguments in the agency's defense. At the outset, amicus questions the textual basis for the removal power and highlights statements from Madison, Hamilton, and Chief Justice Marshall expressing "heterodox" views on the subject. But those concerns are misplaced. It is true that "there is no 'removal clause' in the Constitution," but neither is there a "separation of powers clause" or a "federalism clause." These foundational doctrines are instead evident from the Constitution's vesting of certain powers in certain bodies. As we have explained many times before, the President's removal power stems from Article II's vesting of the "executive Power" in the President. *Free Enterprise Fund*, 561 U.S., at 483. As for the opinions of Madison, Hamilton, and Chief Justice Marshall, we have already considered the statements cited by amicus and discounted them in light of their context (Madison), the fact they reflect initial impressions later abandoned by the speaker (Hamilton), or their subsequent rejection as ill-considered dicta (Chief Justice Marshall).

Next, amicus offers a grand theory of our removal precedents that, if accepted, could leave room for an agency like the CFPB—and many other innovative intrusions on Article II. According to amicus, *Humphrey's Executor* and *Morrison* establish a general rule that Congress may impose "modest" restrictions on the President's removal power, with only two limited exceptions. Congress may not reserve a role for itself in individual removal decisions (as it attempted to do in *Myers* and *Bowsher*). And it may not eliminate the President's removal power altogether (as it effectively did in *Free Enterprise Fund*). Outside those two situations, amicus argues, Congress is generally free to constrain the President's removal power.

But text, first principles, the First Congress's decision in 1789, *Myers*, and *Free Enterprise Fund* all establish that the President's removal power is the rule, not the exception. While we do not revisit *Humphrey's Executor* or any other precedent today, we decline to elevate it into a freestanding invitation for Congress to impose additional restrictions on the President's removal authority.

Finally, amicus contends that if we identify a constitutional problem with the CFPB's structure, we should avoid it by broadly construing the statutory grounds for removing the CFPB Director from office. The Dodd-Frank Act provides that the Director may be removed for "inefficiency, neglect of duty, or malfeasance in office." 12 U. S. C. § 5491(c)(3). In amicus' view, that language could be interpreted to reserve substantial discretion to the President.

We are not persuaded. For one, *Humphrey's Executor* implicitly rejected an interpretation that would leave the President free to remove an officer based on disagreements about agency policy. *See* 295 U.S., at 619, 625–626. In addition, while both amicus and the House of Representatives invite us to adopt whatever construction would cure the constitutional problem, they have not advanced any workable standard derived from the statutory language. Amicus suggests that the proper standard might permit removals based on general policy disagreements, but not specific ones; the House suggests that the permissible bases for removal might vary depending on the context and the Presidential power involved. They do not attempt to root either of those standards in the statutory text. Further, although nearly identical language governs the removal of some two-dozen multimember independent agencies, amicus suggests that the standard should vary from agency to agency, morphing as necessary to avoid constitutional doubt. We decline to embrace such an uncertain and elastic approach to the text. . . .

As we explained in *Free Enterprise Fund*, "One can have a government that functions without being ruled by functionaries, and a government that benefits from expertise without being ruled by experts." *Ibid.* While "[n]o one doubts Congress's power to create a vast and varied federal bureaucracy," the expansion of that bureaucracy into new territories the Framers could scarcely have imagined only sharpens our duty to ensure that the Executive Branch is overseen by a President accountable to the people. *Ibid.*

* * *

A decade ago, we declined to extend Congress's authority to limit the President's removal power to a new situation, never before confronted by the Court. We do the same today. In our constitutional system, the executive power belongs to the President, and that power generally includes the ability to supervise and remove the agents who wield executive power in his stead. While we have previously upheld limits on the President's removal authority in certain contexts, we decline to do so when it comes to principal officers who, acting alone, wield significant executive power. The Constitution requires that such officials remain dependent on the President, who in turn is accountable to the people.

* * *

Notes on *Seila Law v. CFPB*

1. *A new framework after* **Seila Law**: Given its recency, the ultimate impact of *Seila Law* remains unclear. But the decision appears to have established a new framework for analyzing limitations imposed by Congress on the President's removal of executive officers. Though *Seila Law* did not expressly overrule any decisions, it construed narrowly the Court's precedent holding such limitations constitutional. In a critical passage, the Court characterized *Humphrey's Executor* and *Morrison v. Olson* as follows:

> "These two exceptions—one for multimember expert agencies that do not wield substantial executive power, and one for inferior officers with limited duties and no policymaking or administrative authority—represent what up to now have been the outermost constitutional limits of permissible congressional restrictions on the President's removal power."

Following *Seila Law*, removal limitations appear to be presumptively unconstitutional, such that they will only be permissible if they fit within one of these two "exceptions": the *Humphrey's Executor* exception, for positions on a "multimember expert agency" that does not "wield substantial executive power"; or the *Morrison v. Olsen* exception, for inferior officers who have only be given "limited duties and no policymaking or administrative authority." *Seila Law* suggests that any other limitation will violate Article II.

Notice that the *Humphrey's Executor* exception, as phrased by the Court, applies to any officer who is a member of a "multimember expert agency" that does not "wield substantial executive power." This includes principal officers, as Federal Trade Commissioners (such as Humphrey) fit that definition under *Arthrex*; the FTC has the authority to issue final decisions for the federal government that are not subject to review by any other officer in the Executive Branch. But presumably this exception also applies to *inferior* officers who are members of multimember expert agencies not wielding "substantial executive power." Such a restriction would only represent *less* of incursion on the President's authority to execute federal law.

2. *An application (and arguable extension) of* **Seila Law**: In 2021, the Court decided *Collins v. Yellen*, which concerned a constraint on the President's power to remove the Director of the Federal Housing Finance Agency (FHFA). Congress created the FHFA as part of the Housing and Economic Recovery Act of 2008. The agency supervises the Federal National Mortgage

Association (Fannie Mae) and the Federal Home Loan Mortgage Corporation (Freddie Mac), two of the nation's leading sources of mortgage financing. As with the CFPB, Congress structured the FHFA such that it was headed by a single director whom the President could only remove "for cause."

In an opinion by Justice Alito, the Court held that the Act's for-cause restriction on the President's capacity to remove the FHFA Director was unconstitutional. The Court found the removal restriction indistinguishable from that invalidated in *Seila Law*: "The FHFA (like the CFPB) is an agency led by a single Director, and the Recovery Act (like the Dodd-Frank Act) restricts the President's removal power." Importantly, the Court noted that the fact that the FHFA's authority might be more limited than the CFPB's was immaterial:

"We have noted differences between these two agencies. But the nature and breadth of an agency's authority is not dispositive in determining whether Congress may limit the President's power to remove its head. The President's removal power serves vital purposes even when the officer subject to removal is not the head of one of the largest and most powerful agencies. The removal power helps the President maintain a degree of control over the subordinates he needs to carry out his duties as the head of the Executive Branch, and it works to ensure that these subordinates serve the people effectively and in accordance with the policies that the people presumably elected the President to promote. In addition, because the President, unlike agency officials, is elected, this control is essential to subject Executive Branch actions to a degree of electoral accountability. At-will removal ensures that 'the lowest officers, the middle grade, and the highest, will depend, as they ought, on the President, and the President on the community.' 1 Annals of Cong. 499 (1789) (J. Madison). These purposes are implicated whenever an agency does important work, and nothing about the size or role of the FHFA convinces us that its Director should be treated differently from the Director of the CFPB. . . . Courts are not well-suited to weigh the relative importance of the regulatory and enforcement authority of disparate agencies, and we do not think that the constitutionality of removal restrictions hinges on such an inquiry."

Concurring only in the judgment—purely based on *stare decisis*—Justice Kagan took issue with what she argued was the Court's expansion of *Seila Law*'s rationale. Critical to *Seila Law*, she contended, was the fact that the CFPB wielded "significant executive power." But the Court's opinion in *Collins v. Yellen* appeared to abandon this limiting feature of *Seila Law*'s holding:

"Again and again, *Seila Law* emphasized that its rule was limited to single-director agencies 'wield[ing] significant executive power.' To take *Seila Law* at its word is to acknowledge where it left off: If an agency did not exercise 'significant executive power,' the constitutionality of a removal restriction would remain an open question. But today's majority careens right past that boundary line. Without even mentioning *Seila Law*'s 'significant executive power' framing, the majority announces that, actually, 'the constitutionality of removal restrictions' does not 'hinge[]' on 'the nature and breadth of an agency's authority.' Any 'agency led by a single Director,' no matter how much executive power it wields, now becomes subject to the requirement of at-will removal."

Thus, after *Collins v. Yellen* any removal restriction on the director of a single-headed executive agency is apparently unconstitutional. And this must mean that the "*Morrison v. Olsen* exception" (for inferior officers with only "limited duties and no policymaking or administrative authority") cannot apply to the *directors* of agencies, even if the agencies they direct do not wield "significant executive power."

3. *The role of Congress in the removal of officers*: Bowsher v. Synar: A separate question is whether Congress can play any role in the removal of federal executive officers. That is, can Congress reserve to itself some authority in removing executive officers from their offices? The clear answer, going back to *Myers*, is no—other than through the mechanism of impeachment and conviction. Congress's role in the Constitution's scheme of separated powers is to enact legislation, the laws for the Executive Branch to enforce. Congress itself can play no role in the *administration* or *execution* of those laws. If Congress disagrees with how a law is being implemented, it can enact new legislation that directs the Executive Branch to execute the law in a particular way. But Congress cannot grant itself any role in removing an executive officer (which is really a part of implementing or executing federal law).

This means an officer who is removable by Congress (other than by impeachment) cannot have any responsibility for executing federal law. This was the holding of *Bowsher v. Synar*, 478 U.S. 714 (1986), which concerned the constitutionality of the Gramm-Rudman-Hollings Act. Under the Act, the Comptroller General (the head of the General Accounting Office, now known as the Government Accountability Office) played a small role in the Act's implementation. And the Comptroller General was removable by Congress by joint resolution. *Bowsher* held this scheme was unconstitutional: Because the Comptroller General was removable by Congress, it violated separation-of-powers principles for him to have any role in the execution of federal law.

4. *The Tenure of Office Act of 1867*: Perhaps the most famous removal controversy in U.S. history was never actually litigated. After President Lincoln was assassinated in April 1865, Vice President Andrew Johnson became President. Johnson was a pro-Union Democrat; Lincoln had selected him as a running mate to balance out the ticket. Following the Confederacy's surrender, Johnson and Congress (controlled by northern Republicans) clashed incessantly. Johnson was lenient to the former confederates, while the Republican Congress sought to radically reconstruct the South.

The War Department was crucial to post-Civil War policy, as the Union army was largely responsible for implementing the Reconstruction Acts. And Congress (rightfully) believed President Johnson was undermining Reconstruction policy through his half-hearted implementation of these statutes. President Johnson thus collided frequently with the Secretary of War, Edwin Stanton, a Lincoln appointee. To protect Stanton and other cabinet members, Congress enacted the Tenure of Office Act of 1867. The Act prohibited the President from unilaterally removing any members of his cabinet, including the Secretary of War. President Johnson violated the Act by firing Secretary Stanton, and he was immediately impeached by the House of Representatives.

Was the Tenure of Office Act of 1867 constitutional? No, at least under current understandings of Article II. The Secretary of War (now the Secretary of Defense) is clearly a principal officer, and the position clearly falls outside the exception created by *Humphey's Executor*. Though the matter was never litigated, most everyone has assumed the Act was unconstitutional. Indeed, the Supreme Court has alluded to this fact in its own opinions. *See Free Enterprise Fund v. PCAOB*, 561 U.S. 477, 494 n.3 (2010) (the Tenure of Office Act of 1867 "was widely regarded as unconstitutional and void (as it is universally regarded today)").

* * *

PROBLEMS ON THE REMOVAL OF FEDERAL OFFICERS

In each of the following situations, please assess whether the relevant removal provision is constitutional. If there is any additional information necessary to answer the question, please explain what that information is and how it would affect your analysis.

1. A statute provides that the Solicitor General (who is nominated by the President and confirmed by the Senate) may only be removed from office by the Attorney General of the United States. No provision of law permits the President to directly remove the Solicitor General from office. (The Attorney General is removable at will by the President.) The Solicitor General is an attorney within the Department of Justice and reports to the Attorney General.

2. Congress enacts a statute providing that the President may not remove the Secretary of State from office except for "good cause," which is further defined as "physical or mental incapacity, incompetence, neglect of duty, or malfeasance in office." The Secretary of State is the head of the State Department, a cabinet-level executive department.

3. Congress enacts a statute providing that the President may not remove the Commissioner of Internal Revenue from office except for "good cause," which is further defined as "physical or mental incapacity, incompetence, neglect of duty, or malfeasance in office." The IRS is a division within the Department of Treasury, and the IRS Commissioner reports to the Secretary of the Treasury. The Secretary of Treasury is the head of the Treasury Department, a cabinet-level executive department.

4. Suppose the Act creating the Securities and Exchange Commission (SEC) provides that SEC commissioners cannot be removed from office except for "physical or mental incapacity, incompetence, neglect of duty, or malfeasance in office." The SEC is an independent agency and does not sit within any executive department. It has the responsibility to enforce a wide range of federal securities laws. Its decisions are not reviewable by another other officer within the Executive Branch.

5. Suppose the Federal Trade Commission were headed by a single director (rather than five commissioners). Would the removal limitation upheld in *Humphrey's Executor* then be unconstitutional?

*   *   *

REVIEW ESSAY QUESTION 2

The Board of Patent Appeals and Interferences (BPAI) is composed of several administrative patent judges within the Patent and Trademark Office (PTO). The judges sit in panels of three and, so sitting, constitute the BPAI in a given case. (Although the Director of the PTO, the Commissioner for Patents, and the Commissioner for Trademarks can sit on such panels, the panels typically consist of three administrative patent judges. Sitting on such panels is one of several job duties of the Director of the PTO, who oversees all of the other administrative and executive functions of the office.) The decisions rendered by these three-judge panels are final for the PTO, though such decisions may ultimately be reversed on rehearing. (This is unusual). Pursuant to this authority, the patent judges run trials, take evidence, rule on admissibility, and compel compliance with discovery orders.

Patent judges are not members of the federal judiciary appointed according to Article III. Instead, they are administrative law judges, discharging the statutory obligations of the PTO. (There is nothing constitutionally problematic in this *per se*, though there are constitutional limits on the power that non-Article III judges can wield. Federal administrative agencies can enforce federal statutes through a variety of means, including administrative adjudication.) The PTO itself is part of the Department of Commerce. Indeed, the PTO Director is formally known as the "Under Secretary of Commerce for Intellectual Property and Director of the United States Patent and Trademark Office." 35 U.S.C. § 3(a). Thus, the Patent Director reports to the Secretary of Commerce, and she is subject to the Secretary's oversight.

The provision of federal law creating and defining the duties of these patent judges is 35 U.S.C. § 6(a), which provides as follows:

> There shall be in the United States Patent and Trademark Office a Board of Patent Appeals and Interferences. The Director, the Commissioner for Patents, the Commissioner for Trademarks, and the administrative patent judges shall constitute the Board. The administrative patent judges shall be persons of competent legal knowledge and scientific ability who are appointed by the Director [of the PTO].

Is §6(a) constitutional? Why or why not? On what facts or conclusions does the relevant analysis turn?

CHAPTER 15
OTHER SEPARATION OF POWERS PRINCIPLES

The preceding two chapters addressed two foundational aspects of the separation of national powers: the authority granted to the President by Article II and the rules regarding the appointment and removal of "Officers of the United States." This chapter takes up three other separation-of-powers issues: the nondelegation doctrine, the legislative veto, and the line-item veto.

A. The Nondelegation Doctrine

1. Legislative delegations generally

Generally speaking, if the President is implementing a federal statute, his actions will be consistent with the separation of powers. Such executive action falls into the first category of Justice Jackson's taxonomy, where the President's power is at its apex. At the same time, there are important constitutional limits on what powers Congress can confer on the President. Most obviously, Congress cannot give the President a power that Congress itself lacks in the first place, such as the authority to regulate activities exceeding Congress's enumerated powers. Likewise, Congress cannot grant the President the authority to violate individual constitutional rights, such as the protections for free speech or the free exercise of religion.

The nondelegation doctrine concerns a similar problem, but its logical converse. Congress runs afoul of the nondelegation doctrine when it gives away *too much* of its authority—authority the Constitution requires Congress itself to exercise. The rules prescribed by the Constitution for the separation of powers can be violated not just when one branch seeks to aggrandize its authority at the expense of another. They are also transgressed when one branch gives away its authority in a manner that contravenes the constitutional design.

The nondelegation doctrine concerns the degree of discretion—some call it lawmaking authority, others call it judgment exercised in law enforcement or execution—that Congress can delegate to another branch (typically the Executive Branch). In essence, it concerns the *specificity with which Congress must legislate*: the level of detail Congress must include in a statute to constrain the Executive Branch's discretion in its enforcement of the law.

Article I, § 1, clause 1—the substantive provision that comes first in the Constitution—grants the entirety of the legislative power to Congress: "All legislative Powers herein granted shall be vested in a Congress of the United

States." But times have changed since 1788. For the nation's first 150 years, almost all American law was *state* law; federal law was the exception. That grew less true over the course of the twentieth century. Federal law is no longer so unusual. Broad federal regulatory schemes cover many (if not most) areas of human activity, and Congress has created a vast federal bureaucracy of administrative agencies and executive departments to implement these schemes. For instance, the EPA administers the Clean Air Act and the Clean Water Act; the Food and Drug Administration administers the Food, Drug and Cosmetic Act; the Department of Labor administers the Fair Labor Standards Act; the Internal Revenue Service administers the Internal Revenue Code; the Department of Homeland Security enforces the nation's immigration laws; and so on.

These departments and agencies—through enforcement actions, adjudications, rulemakings, and other administrative processes—set out the terms by which these federal statutes are to be enforced or implemented. These rules, regulations, and enforcement decisions grow out of their authority to enforce specific federal statutes. Every statute necessarily leaves some gaps or ambiguities, some discretion in how they are to be enforced. But in filling out these gaps, agencies and departments are acting pursuant to authority granted by Congress in a federal statute. No agency or executive department can act without prior authorization from a statute enacted by Congress—except in those rare circumstances in which the action is pursuant to an authority granted specifically to the President by the Constitution (such as the commander-in-chief, pardon, or recognition power).

As a formal matter, these agency rules, regulations, and enforcement decisions are gap-filling measures; they clarify what a statute means in specific contexts. For example, when the FDA determines that nicotine is a drug, and that cigarettes constitute drug-delivery devices, it is not enacting a new federal law; it is interpreting and implementing an existing statute (the Food, Drug and Cosmetic Act) that grants the FDA the authority to regulate "drugs" and "devices." These regulations are not the same as statutes. Instead, they are promulgated pursuant to the Executive Branch's authority to *enforce* or *implement* (and not to *create*) federal statutes.

Still, as a practical matter—so long as these various regulations or discretionary enforcement decisions fall within the authority granted to the agency by the relevant statute—they operate very much like law. Thus, executive agencies and departments effectively exercise a large degree of policymaking authority, if not formal lawmaking power. For example, the Department of Homeland Security can make it more difficult for migrants coming to the U.S. to obtain asylum by promulgating a rule—pursuant to DHS's authority to enforce the Immigration and Naturalization Act—requiring such migrants, when they have crossed through another country before coming to the U.S., to have sought and been denied asylum by that other country. And the Executive Branch's exercise this sort of policymaking authority is generally not a constitutional problem. If it were, much of what the federal government does would be unconstitutional.

Indeed, it is important to see that some measure of policymaking discretion in the enforcement of law is *inescapable*. Even if Congress were to legislate in excruciating detail, statutes will always have some ambiguity in their terms; all language does. And so long as statutes contain some ambiguity, the enforcement of those statutes will include discretionary policymaking. The nondelegation doctrine does not forbid statutory delegations of policymaking authority; prohibiting them would be impossible. Rather, it places a *limit* on them. The relevant question is whether the delegation is *excessive*: does the statute at issue cross the line and violate the command in Article I, §1, clause 1 that the legislative power be exercised by *Congress*, not the Executive Branch?

2. The inevitability of legislative delegations

When a federal statute leaves discretion to the Executive Branch in deciding exactly what to regulate or how to regulate it, it clearly cedes power to the President and other executive officers. In tens of thousands of statutes, Congress has legislated in broad terms, granting this discretion. An important question is *why*. Presumably, Congress wants to preserve its own power, to retain the ability to influence policy outcomes. And these broad delegations are gifts of power to the Executive Branch. Why would Congress do this? There are at least four basic reasons:

(1) *Time*: Congress lacks sufficient time to write statutes that specify in minute detail how extraordinarily complex regulatory programs are to be administered.

(2) *Expertise*: Members of Congress are generalists (though they hire some specialists to serve on their personal and committee staffs), whereas agencies are filled with thousands of expert civil servants whose careers are devoted to the subject at issue. Thus, it can make more sense for experts to fill in details than for Congress to do so in the text of the statute.

(3) *Flexibility*: Broad delegations can be interpreted differently over time, as technology, knowledge, and circumstances evolve. This permits flexibility, avoiding the problem of freezing regulation to the state of affairs at the time a statute is enacted.

(4) *Political cost-shifting*: By legislating in broad terms—but not resolving all of the details—members of Congress can take credit for addressing problems without making the tough political calls necessary to the implementation of a statute.

Thus, there are important reasons these delegations exist, and modern government could not function without them. But they create some constitutional tension. The Constitution vests the lawmaking power in *Congress*, subject to the specific political accountability shouldered by House of Representatives and the Senate. Executive departments and agencies also face political pressures, and they are politically accountable to some degree (through presidential elections). But that accountability works quite differently. To the extent administrative agencies are effectively creating federal law, they are doing so subject to a different constellation of political forces than the Constitution contemplates for lawmaking. Moreover, as a purely textual matter, the Constitution dictates that the legislative power belongs to Congress, not the President.

3. The constitutional limit

To appreciate the contours of the nondelegation doctrine, consider the Supreme Court's decision in *Whitman v. American Trucking Association*, 531 U.S. 457 (2001). In *Whitman*, the Court confronted a nondelegation challenge to an important provision in the Clean Air Act, §109(b)(1), which states that the Administrator of the Environmental Protection Agency (EPA) shall set "ambient air quality standards the attainment and maintenance of which in the judgment of the Administrator, based in [the] criteria [documents of §108] and allowing an adequate margin of safety, are requisite to protect the public health." The EPA Administrator had invoked this authority to impose limits on the emission of air particulate matter (or soot)—limits that would have a significant impact on the trucking industry, whose diesel engines generate tons of particulate matter annually. The D.C. Circuit had held that §109(b)(1) violated the nondelegation doctrine, and the government appealed to the Supreme Court. As you read *Whitman*, please consider the following questions:

1. After concluding that §109(b)(1) violated the nondelegation doctrine, what remedy had the court of appeals ordered? Why did the Supreme Court conclude this was inappropriate?

2. What is the constitutional standard for when a federal statute's delegation is unconstitutionally excessive? Is it lenient or exacting?

3. What outcome does the Court reach in applying that standard to §109(b)(1)? Why? Of what significance was the Solicitor General's construction of the statute?

4. What is the principal difference between Justice Stevens's and Justice Scalia's description of legislative delegations? Is this just a semantic difference? Or does it reveal an important substantive difference?

Whitman v. American Trucking Ass'ns, Inc.
531 U.S. 457 (2001)

JUSTICE SCALIA delivered the opinion of the Court.

* * *

III

Section 109(b)(1) of the [Clean Air Act] instructs the EPA to set "ambient air quality standards the attainment and maintenance of which in the judgment of the Administrator, based on [the] criteria [documents of §108] and allowing an adequate margin of safety, are requisite to protect the public health." 42 U.S.C. §7409(b)(1). The Court of Appeals held that this section as interpreted by the Administrator did not provide an "intelligible principle" to guide the EPA's exercise of authority in setting NAAQS. "[The] EPA," it said, "lack[ed] any determinate criteria for drawing lines. It has failed to state intelligibly how much is too much." The court hence found that the EPA's interpretation (but not the statute itself) violated the nondelegation doctrine. We disagree.

In a delegation challenge, the constitutional question is whether the statute has delegated legislative power to the agency. Article I, § 1, of the Constitution vests "[a]ll legislative Powers herein granted ... in a Congress of the United States." This text permits no delegation of those powers, *Loving v. United States*, 517 U.S. 748, 771 (1996), and so we repeatedly have said that when Congress confers decisionmaking authority upon agencies Congress must "lay down by legislative act an intelligible principle to which the person or body authorized to [act] is directed to conform." *J.W. Hampton, Jr., & Co. v. United States*, 276 U.S. 394, 409 (1928). We have never suggested that an agency can cure an unlawful delegation of legislative power by adopting in its discretion a limiting construction of the statute. Both *Fahey v. Mallonee*, 332 U.S. 245, 252–253 (1947), and *Lichter v. United States*, 334 U.S. 742, 783 (1948), mention agency regulations in the course of their nondelegation discussions, but *Lichter* did so because a subsequent Congress had incorporated the regulations into a revised version of the statute, and *Fahey* because the customary practices in the area, implicitly incorporated into the statute, were reflected in the regulations, 332 U.S., at 250. The idea that an agency can cure an unconstitutionally standardless delegation of power by declining to exercise some of that power seems to us internally contradictory. The very choice of which portion of the power to exercise—that is to say, the prescription of the standard that Congress had omitted—would itself be an exercise of the forbidden legislative authority. Whether the statute delegates legislative power is a question for the courts, and an agency's voluntary self-denial has no bearing upon the answer.

We agree with the Solicitor General that the text of § 109(b)(1) of the CAA at a minimum requires that "[f]or a discrete set of pollutants and based on published air quality criteria that reflect the latest scientific knowledge, [the] EPA must establish uniform national standards at a level that is requisite to protect public health from the adverse effects of the pollutant in the ambient air." Requisite, in turn, "mean[s] sufficient, but not more than necessary." These limits on the EPA's discretion are strikingly similar to the ones we approved in *Touby v. United States*, 500 U.S. 160 (1991), which permitted the Attorney General to designate a drug as a controlled substance for purposes of criminal drug enforcement if doing so was "necessary to avoid an imminent hazard to the public safety." *Id.*, at 163. They also resemble the Occupational Safety and Health Act of 1970 provision requiring the agency to "set the standard which most adequately assures, to the extent feasible, on the basis of the best available evidence, that no employee will suffer any impairment of health"—which the Court upheld in *Industrial Union Dept., AFL-CIO v. American Petroleum Institute*, 448 U.S. 607, 646 (1980), and which even then-Justice Rehnquist, who alone in that case thought the statute violated the nondelegation doctrine, see *id.*, at 671 (opinion concurring in judgment), would have upheld if, like the statute here, it did not permit economic costs to be considered. See *American Textile Mfrs. Institute, Inc. v. Donovan*, 452 U.S. 490, 545 (1981) (Rehnquist, J., dissenting).

The scope of discretion §109(b)(1) allows is in fact well within the outer limits of our nondelegation precedents. In the history of the Court we have found the requisite "intelligible principle" lacking in only two statutes, one of which provided literally no guidance for the exercise of discretion, and the other of which conferred authority to regulate the entire economy on the basis of no more precise a standard than stimulating the economy by assuring "fair competition." See *Panama Refining Co. v. Ryan*, 293 U.S. 388 (1935); *A.L.A. Schechter Poultry Corp. v. United States*, 295 U.S. 495 (1935). We have, on the other hand, upheld the validity of §11(b)(2) of the Public Utility Holding Company Act of 1935, which gave the Securities and Exchange Commission authority to modify the structure of holding company systems so as to ensure that they are not "unduly or unnecessarily complicate[d]" and do not "unfairly or inequitably distribute voting power among security holders." *American Power & Light Co. v. SEC*, 329 U.S. 90, 104 (1946). We have approved the wartime conferral of agency power to fix the prices of commodities at a level that "'will be generally fair and equitable and will effectuate the [in some respects conflicting] purposes of th[e] Act.'" *Yakus v. United States*, 321 U.S. 414, 420, 423–426 (1944). And we have found an "intelligible principle" in various statutes authorizing regulation in the "public interest." See, e.g., *National Broadcasting Co. v. United States*, 319 U.S. 190, 225–226 (1943) (Federal Communications Commission's power to regulate airwaves); *New York Central Securities Corp. v. United States*, 287 U.S. 12, 24–25 (1932) (Interstate Commerce Commission's power to approve railroad consolidations). In short, we have "almost never felt qualified to second-guess Congress regarding the permissible degree of policy judgment that can be left to those executing or applying the law." *Mistretta v. United States*, 488 U.S. 361, 416 (1989) (Scalia, J., dissenting); see *id.*, at 373 (majority opinion).

It is true enough that the degree of agency discretion that is acceptable varies according to the scope of the power congressionally conferred. See *Loving v. United States*, 517 U.S., at 772–773; *United States v. Mazurie*, 419 U.S. 544, 556–557 (1975). While Congress need not provide any direction to the EPA regarding the manner in which it is to define "country elevators," which are to be exempt from new-stationary-source regulations governing grain elevators, see 42 U.S.C. §7411(i), it must provide substantial guidance on setting air standards that affect the entire national economy. But even in sweeping regulatory schemes we have never demanded, as the Court of Appeals did here, that statutes provide a "determinate criterion" for saying "how much [of the regulated harm] is too much." 175 F.3d, at 1034. In *Touby*, for example, we did not require the statute to decree how "imminent" was too imminent, or how "necessary" was necessary enough, or even—most relevant here— how "hazardous" was too hazardous. 500 U.S., at 165–167. Similarly, the statute at issue in *Lichter* authorized agencies to recoup "excess profits" paid under wartime Government contracts, yet we did not insist that Congress specify how much profit was too much. 334 U.S., at 783– 786. It is therefore not conclusive for delegation purposes that, as respondents argue, ozone and particulate matter are "nonthreshold" pollutants that inflict a continuum of adverse health effects at any airborne concentration greater than zero, and hence require the EPA to make judgments of degree. "[A] certain degree of discretion, and thus of lawmaking, inheres in most executive or judicial action." *Mistretta v. United States*, supra, at 417 (Scalia, J., dissenting); see 488 U.S., at 378–379 (majority opinion). Section 109(b)(1) of the CAA, which to repeat we interpret as requiring the EPA to set air quality standards at the level that is "requisite"—that is, not lower or higher than is necessary—to protect the public health with an adequate margin of safety, fits comfortably within the scope of discretion permitted by our precedent.

We therefore reverse the judgment of the Court of Appeals remanding for reinterpretation that would avoid a supposed delegation of legislative power. It will remain for the Court of Appeals—on the remand that we direct for other reasons—to dispose of any other preserved challenge to the NAAQS under the judicial-review provisions contained in 42 U.S.C. §7607(d)(9).

* * *

JUSTICE STEVENS, with whom JUSTICE SOUTER joins, concurring in part and concurring in the judgment.

Section 109(b)(1) delegates to the Administrator of the Environmental Protection Agency (EPA) the authority to promulgate national ambient air quality standards (NAAQS). In Part III of its opinion, the Court convincingly explains why the Court of Appeals erred when it concluded that §109 effected "an unconstitutional delegation of legislative power." *American Trucking Assns., Inc. v. EPA*, 175 F.3d 1027, 1033 (C.A.D.C.1999) (per curiam). I wholeheartedly endorse the Court's result and endorse its explanation of its reasons, albeit with the following caveat.

The Court has two choices. We could choose to articulate our ultimate disposition of this issue by frankly acknowledging that the power delegated to the EPA is "legislative" but nevertheless conclude that the delegation is constitutional because adequately limited by the terms of the authorizing statute. Alternatively, we could pretend, as the Court does, that the authority delegated to the EPA is somehow not "legislative power." Despite the fact that there is language in our opinions that supports the Court's articulation of our holding, I am persuaded that it would be both wiser and more faithful to what we have actually done in delegation cases to admit that agency rulemaking authority is "legislative power."[18]

The proper characterization of governmental power should generally depend on the nature of the power, not on the identity of the person exercising it. See Black's Law Dictionary 899 (6th ed.1990) (defining "legislation" as, *inter alia*, "[f]ormulation of rule[s] for the future"); 1 K. Davis & R. Pierce, Administrative Law Treatise § 2.3, p. 37 (3d ed. 1994) ("If legislative power means the power to make rules of conduct that bind everyone based on resolution of major policy issues, scores of agencies exercise legislative power routinely by promulgating what are candidly called 'legislative rules'"). If the NAAQS that the EPA promulgated had been prescribed by Congress, everyone would agree that those rules would be the product of an exercise of "legislative power." The same characterization is appropriate when an agency exercises rulemaking authority pursuant to a permissible delegation from Congress.

My view is not only more faithful to normal English usage, but is also fully consistent with the text of the Constitution. In Article I, the Framers vested "All legislative Powers" in the Congress, Art. I, § 1, just as in Article II they vested the "executive Power" in the President, Art. II, § 1. Those provisions do not purport to limit the authority of either recipient of power to delegate authority to others. Surely the authority granted to members of the Cabinet and federal law enforcement agents is properly characterized as "Executive" even though not exercised by the President.

It seems clear that an executive agency's exercise of rulemaking authority pursuant to a valid delegation from Congress is "legislative." As long as the delegation provides a sufficiently intelligible principle, there is nothing inherently unconstitutional about it. Accordingly, . . . I would hold that when Congress enacted §109, it effected a constitutional delegation of legislative power to the EPA.

* * *

Notes on *Whitman v. American Trucking Ass'ns, Inc.*

1. ***The appropriate remedy for an unconstitutional delegation***: In *Whitman*, the D.C. Circuit had held that §109(b)(1) violated the nondelegation

---

[18] See *Mistretta v. United States*, 488 U.S. 361, 372 (1989) ("[O]ur jurisprudence has been driven by a practical understanding that in our increasingly complex society . . . Congress simply cannot do its job absent an ability to delegate power."). See also *Loving v. United States*, 517 U.S. 748, 758 (1996) ("[The nondelegation] principle does not mean . . . that only Congress can make a rule of prospective force"); 1 K. Davis & R. Pierce, Administrative Law Treatise § 2.6, p. 66 (3d ed. 1994) ("Except for two 1935 cases, the Court has never enforced its frequently announced prohibition on congressional delegation of legislative power").

doctrine. But instead of invalidating the provision as unconstitutional, it remanded the case to the EPA to devise a narrower construction of its own discretion under the Clean Air Act. The first step in the Supreme Court's analysis was to explain that, even if §109(b)(1) had violated the nondelegation doctrine (which it did not), a remand to the EPA would have been an inappropriate remedy. The point of the nondelegation doctrine is that *Congress* must be the one that provides sufficient detail in its legislation to guide the Executive Branch in its enforcement. Thus, requiring the relevant administrative agency to devise a rule that limits its *own* discretion does nothing to cure the constitutional problem. Here, if §109(b)(1) had violated the nondelegation doctrine, the EPA would still have been exercising an impermissible degree of discretion in deciding how to limit its own discretion; the agency's tying its own hands could not have solved the problem, because how the agency decided to tie its own hands would have been another exercise of the same, excessive discretion. If a statute violates the nondelegation doctrine, only Congress—by enacting a more specific statute—can remedy the constitutional infirmity.

2. *The "intelligible principle" standard*: In its analysis on the merits, the Supreme Court in *Whitman* surveyed the nondelegation decisions that had come before and articulated the legal standard for what the nondelegation doctrine requires: Congress must set down "an intelligible principle" in the statute to guide the Executive Branch's execution of the law. And that standard is quite deferential. As the Court explained,

> "in the history of the Court we have found the requisite 'intelligible principle' lacking in only two statutes, one of which provided literally no guidance for the exercise of discretion, and the other of which conferred authority to regulate the entire economy on the basis of no more precise a standard than stimulating the economy by assuring 'fair competition.'"

Applying this standard, the Court concluded that §109(b)(1) did not impermissibly delegate too much discretion to the EPA. First, as a matter of statutory interpretation, the Court adopted the construction of the statute urged by the Solicitor General, under which "requisite" meant "sufficient, but not more than necessary," to protect the public health. This narrowed the authority conferred by §109(b)(1) from readings that might have given the EPA virtually limitless discretion. Second, the Court concluded that §109(b)(1) (so construed) was "well within the outer limits of our nondelegation precedents." In doing so, the Court surveyed a litany of broad statutory delegations it had previously upheld, many of which were extraordinarily broad. Consider the following:

* *American Power & Light Co. v. SEC*, 329 U.S. 90, 104 (1946): The statute directed the agency to ensure that holding companies are not "unduly or unnecessarily complicate[d]" and do not "unfairly or inequitably distribute voting power among security holders."

* *Yakus v. United States,* 321 U.S. 414 (1944): The statute required the agency to fix prices at a level that "will be generally fair and equitable and will effectuate the purposes of the Act."

* *National Broadcasting Co. v. United States,* 319 U.S. 190 (1943): The statute required the agency to regulate broadcasting "in the public interest."

* *Touby v. United States,* 500 U.S. 160 (1991): The statute permitted the Attorney General to designate a drug a controlled substance when she deemed it "necessary to avoid an imminent hazard to the public safety."

The Court in *Whitman* reasoned that, if these delegations complied with the "intelligible principle" standard, so did §109(b)(1).

3. *"The scope of the power congressionally conferred"*: An important doctrinal point is that nondelegation doctrine analysis depends not just on the amount of discretion conferred on the Executive Branch, but also on the nature of the authority to which that discretion applies. As the Court observed in *Whitman*, Congress could likely grant EPA unlimited discretion in deciding what constitutes a "country elevator" subject to the Clean Air Act without running afoul of the nondelegation doctrine, as the scope of that authority is quite narrow. But Congress must be more specific when the discretion concerns the emission of any airborne pollutant from *any stationary source* in the U.S. In other words, when the scope of the authority is substantial, then greater precision is necessary to meet the "intelligible principle" standard. Still, the level of precision required is not terribly demanding, even in a provision like §109(b)(1). Requiring only an "intelligible principle" is a lenient test, one that only two statutes have ever failed at the Court.

4. *The role of the judiciary in policing congressional delegations*: Perhaps the reason the Court has been deferential to Congress in this area—and invalidated only two statutes on nondelegation grounds—concerns the appropriate judicial role, and the difficulty in discovering a "judicially manageable standard" for policing statutory delegations. The problem for the Court in more aggressively enforcing the nondelegation doctrine is that it would require the justices to draw a very difficult line. Every law delegates authority to the Executive Branch; discretion is inherent in executing the law. How does a court decide exactly when the delegation has gone too far?

* * *

4. A nondelegation doctrine revival?

The Supreme Court's 2019 decision in *Gundy v. United States,* 139 S. Ct. 2116, rejected a claim that a provision in the Sex Offender Registration and Notification Act (SORNA) amounted to an unconstitutionally excessive delegation. But there was no controlling majority opinion, and four of the justices signaled in *Gundy* an interest in reviving the nondelegation doctrine as a meaningful constraint on the way Congress legislates.

At issue in *Gundy* was a SORNA provision now codified at 34 U.S.C. §20913. It requires "sex offenders" (defined elsewhere in the Act) to register with every state in which they reside or work "before completing a sentence of imprisonment with respect to the offense giving rise to the registration requirement" (or, if the offender is not sentenced to prison, "not later than [three] business days after being sentenced"). And §20913(d) addresses the "[i]nitial registration of sex offenders unable to comply with subsection (b)." (Sex offenders who, before SORNA was enacted, had committed their offenses and completed their sentences—so-called "pre-Act offenders"—would naturally be "unable to comply with" §20913(b)'s requirement.) The provision states: "The Attorney General shall have the authority to specify the applicability of the requirements of this subchapter to sex offenders convicted before the enactment of this chapter . . . and to prescribe rules for the registration of any such sex offenders and for other categories of sex offenders who are unable to comply with subsection (b)." Gundy contended that §20913(d) amounted to an unconstitutional legislative delegation because it granted the Attorney General unconstrained discretion to decide whether or how the registration requirements would apply to sex offenders who could not comply with §20913(b).

Writing for a four-justice plurality, Justice Kagan explained that

"a nondelegation inquiry always begins (and often almost ends) with statutory interpretation. The constitutional question is whether Congress has supplied an intelligible principle to guide the delegee's use of discretion. So the answer requires construing the challenged statute to figure out what task it delegates and what instructions it provides. Only after a court has determined a challenged statute's meaning can it decide whether the law sufficiently guides executive discretion to accord with Article I. And indeed, once a court interprets the statute, it may find that the constitutional question all but answers itself."

Applying that approach to SORNA's §20913, the plurality concluded it easily passed constitutional muster:

"§20913(d) does not give the Attorney General anything like the 'unguided' and 'unchecked' authority that Gundy says. The provision, in Gundy's view, 'grants the Attorney General plenary power to determine SORNA's applicability to pre-Act offenders—to require them to register, or not, as she sees fit, and to change her policy for any reason and at any time.' If that were so, we would face a nondelegation question. But it is not. This Court has already interpreted §20913(d) to say something different—to require the Attorney General to apply SORNA to all pre-Act offenders as soon as feasible. . . . The text, considered alongside its context, purpose, and history, makes clear that the Attorney General's discretion extends only to considering and addressing feasibility issues. Given that statutory meaning, Gundy's constitutional claim must fail. Section 20913(d)'s delegation falls well within permissible bounds."

Because Justice Alito concurred only in the judgment, Justice Kagan's opinion was not an opinion for the Court. Alito's brief concurrence stated that

"since 1935, the Court has uniformly rejected nondelegation arguments and has upheld provisions that authorized agencies to adopt important rules pursuant to extraordinarily capacious standards. If a majority of this Court were willing to reconsider the approach we have taken for the past 84 years, I would support that effort. But because a majority is not willing to do that, it would be freakish to single out the provision at issue here for special treatment. Because I cannot say that the statute lacks a discernable standard that is adequate under the approach this Court has taken for many years, I vote to affirm."

Justice Gorsuch, joined by Chief Justice Roberts and Justice Thomas, dissented, concluding that the discretion §20913(d) conferred on the Attorney General was beyond the constitutional pale:

"SORNA leaves the Attorney General free to impose on 500,000 pre-Act offenders all of the statute's requirements, some of them, or none of them. The Attorney General may choose which pre-Act offenders to subject to the Act. And he is free to change his mind at any point or over the course of different political administrations. In the end, there isn't a single policy decision concerning pre-Act offenders on which Congress even tried to speak, and not a single other case where we have upheld executive authority over matters like these on the ground they constitute mere 'details.' This much appears to have been deliberate, too. Because members of Congress could not reach consensus on the treatment of pre-Act offenders, it seems this was one of those situations where they found it expedient to hand off the job to the executive and direct there the blame for any later problems that might emerge.

"Nor can SORNA be described as an example of conditional legislation subject to executive fact-finding. To be sure, Congress could have easily written this law in that way. It might have required all pre-Act offenders to register, but then given the Attorney General the authority to make case-by-case exceptions for offenders who do not present an 'imminent hazard to the public safety' comparable to that posed by newly released post-Act offenders. It could have set criteria to inform that determination, too, asking the executive to investigate, say, whether an offender's risk of recidivism correlates with the time since his last offense, or whether multiple lesser offenses indicate higher or lower risks than a single greater offense.

"But SORNA did none of this. Instead, it gave the Attorney General unfettered discretion to decide which requirements to impose on which pre-

Act offenders. . . . If the separation of powers means anything, it must mean that Congress cannot give the executive branch a blank check to write a code of conduct governing private conduct for a half-million people."

The Supreme Court heard arguments in *Gundy* before the Senate had confirmed Justice Kavanaugh, so it decided the case with eight justices. But Kavanaugh has subsequently indicated his sympathies with Justice Gorsuch's *Gundy* dissent. In *Paul v. United States*, 140 S. Ct. 342 (2019), Kavanaugh authored a statement regarding the denial of a writ of certiorari, noting that

"JUSTICE GORSUCH's scholarly analysis of the Constitution's nondelegation doctrine in his *Gundy* dissent may warrant further consideration in future cases. JUSTICE GORSUCH's opinion built on views expressed by then-Justice Rehnquist some 40 years ago in *Industrial Union Dept., AFL–CIO v. American Petroleum Institute*, 448 U. S. 607, 685–686 (1980) (Rehnquist, J., concurring in judgment). In that case, Justice Rehnquist opined that major national policy decisions must be made by Congress and the President in the legislative process, not delegated by Congress to the Executive Branch. . . . Like Justice Rehnquist's opinion 40 years ago, JUSTICE GORSUCH's thoughtful *Gundy* opinion raised important points that may warrant further consideration in future cases."

Given Justice Gorsuch's *Gundy* dissent (joined by the Chief Justice and Justice Thomas), Justice Alito's concurrence in *Gundy*, and Justice Kavanaugh's statement in *Paul*, there now appears to be a majority—not counting Justice Barrett—interested in reinvigorating the nondelegation doctrine as a more stringent limit on Congress's legislative authority.

B.   The Legislative Veto

1. Introduction

Another important separation-of-powers controversy concerned the "legislative veto." To understand the question it posed, it is important to see its relationship to legislative delegations. Again, statutes granting the Executive Branch broad discretion in their enforcement are inevitable; Congress has no choice but to delegate a great deal of gap-filling responsibilities and enforcement discretion. This means, as a practical matter, executive agencies have substantial policymaking authority. A natural question, then, is what tools Congress might deploy to defend and preserve its constitutional prerogatives. One solution Congress devised starting in the 1930s was the so-called "legislative veto." A legislative veto is a mechanism (written into a statute) that permits Congress—or even just a part of Congress, such as one house or a particular committee or subcommittee—to "veto" particular administrative decisions made by the Executive Branch in enforcing or implementing federal law.

*   *   *

As originally enacted in 1976, the National Emergency Powers Act specified that the President shall have certain powers if he officially declares a "national emergency" within the meaning of the statute. (President Trump declared a national emergency under this Act with respect to the immigration situation at the southern border.) But §202(a)(1) of the Act also contained the following provision: "Any national emergency declared by the President in accordance with this title shall terminate if . . . Congress terminates the emergency by concurrent resolution." This clause created a *legislative veto* provision: It granted Congress a mechanism by which it could block or veto a decision by the Executive Branch on how to implement a statute without passing a new federal statute.

To be clear, Congress can always block the President's decisions on the execution of federal law by *enacting a new statute*. For instance, Congress could enact a statute that plainly provides that an increase in the volume of persons seeking entry into the country can never constitute a "national emergency" for purposes of National Emergency Powers Act. Such a statute, of course, would need to be lawfully enacted pursuant to the rules specified in Article I, §7: passage by both the House of Representatives and the Senate, presentment to the President, and either signed by the President or (following a presidential veto) re-passage by both the House and the Senate by two-thirds majorities. What makes a legislative veto different is that it grants Congress a power to block an Executive Branch's enforcement decision through a mechanism short of enacting a new federal statute.

* * *

Such statutory veto provisions appeared in various forms. Sometimes the veto was to be exercised by both the Senate and the House jointly; sometimes by just one chamber; sometimes by the relevant committee or subcommittee; sometimes it only applied to regulations surpassing a certain threshold (*e.g.*, regulations that would impose more than $10 million in costs on private industry). What all legislative veto provisions had in common is that they preserved for Congress (or some portion of Congress) a power to block particular decisions by the Executive Branch in the implementation of federal law—without requiring Congress to follow the constitutionally prescribed process for enacting a new federal statute. Administrative actions taken by the Executive Branch subject to a legislative veto would only go into effect if they were not vetoed by the relevant congressional actor or body.

2. The demise of the legislative veto

Legislative vetoes made a great deal of practical sense as a means for Congress to retain some control over the Executive Branch's discretionary decisions in the implementation of federal law. But the Supreme Court—in one of the more important separation-of-powers decisions in U.S. history—held in *INS v. Chadha*, 462 U.S. 919 (1983), that legislative vetoes are categorically unconstitutional. At issue in *Chadha* was §244(c)(2) of the Immigration and

Naturalization Act, which permitted one house of Congress to reject the decision of the Attorney General to suspend the deportation of a removable alien. As you read *Chadha*, please consider the following questions:

1. How, exactly, did the legislative veto provision in the INA operate? Why did the Supreme Court conclude that the exercise of the veto was "legislative in nature"? What was the significance of that conclusion?

2. How did the legislative veto violate the Constitution? What constitutional provisions did it contravene?

3. What alternatives does *Chadha* leave open to Congress to accomplish the same basic objective of retaining some control over how the Executive Branch administers or executes federal statutes like the INA?

INS v. Chadha
462 U.S. 919 (1983)

CHIEF JUSTICE BURGER delivered the opinion of the Court.

[This case] presents a challenge to the constitutionality of the provision in §244(c)(2) of the Immigration and Nationality Act, authorizing one House of Congress, by resolution, to invalidate the decision of the Executive Branch, pursuant to authority delegated by Congress to the Attorney General of the United States, to allow a particular deportable alien to remain in the United States.

I

Chadha is an East Indian who was born in Kenya and holds a British passport. He was lawfully admitted to the United States in 1966 on a nonimmigrant student visa. His visa expired on June 30, 1972. On October 11, 1973, the District Director of the Immigration and Naturalization Service ordered Chadha to show cause why he should not be deported for having "remained in the United States for a longer time than permitted." Pursuant to §242(b) of the Immigration and Nationality Act (Act), a deportation hearing was held before an Immigration Judge on January 11, 1974. Chadha conceded that he was deportable for overstaying his visa, and the hearing was adjourned to enable him to file an application for suspension of deportation under § 244(a)(1) of the Act. Section 244(a)(1), at the time in question, provided: . . .

> "the Attorney General may, in his discretion, suspend deportation and adjust the status to that of an alien lawfully admitted for permanent residence, in the case of an alien who applies to the Attorney General for suspension of deportation and . . . is deportable under any law of the United States except the provisions specified in paragraph (2) of this subsection; has been physically present in the United States for a continuous period of not less than seven years immediately preceding the date of such application, and proves that during all of such period he was and is a person of good moral character; and is a person whose deportation would, in the opinion of the Attorney General,

result in extreme hardship to the alien or to his spouse, parent, or child, who is a citizen of the United States or an alien lawfully admitted for permanent residence."

After Chadha submitted his application for suspension of deportation, the deportation hearing was resumed on February 7, 1974. On the basis of evidence adduced at the hearing, affidavits submitted with the application, and the results of a character investigation conducted by the INS, the Immigration Judge, on June 25, 1974, ordered that Chadha's deportation be suspended. The Immigration Judge found that Chadha met the requirements of 244(a)(1): he had resided continuously in the United States for over seven years, was of good moral character, and would suffer "extreme hardship" if deported.

Pursuant to §244(c)(1) of the Act, the Immigration Judge suspended Chadha's deportation and a report of the suspension was transmitted to Congress. Section 244(c)(1) provides:

> "Upon application by any alien who is found by the Attorney General to meet the requirements of subsection (a) of this section the Attorney General may in his discretion suspend deportation of such alien. If the deportation of any alien is suspended under the provisions of this subsection, a complete and detailed statement of the facts and pertinent provisions of law in the case shall be reported to the Congress with the reasons for such suspension."

Once the Attorney General's recommendation for suspension of Chadha's deportation was conveyed to Congress, Congress had the power under §244(c)(2) of the Act to veto the Attorney General's determination that Chadha should not be deported. Section 244(c)(2) provides: . . .

> "[I]f during the session of the Congress at which a case is reported, or prior to the close of the session of the Congress next following the session at which a case is reported, either the Senate or the House of Representatives passes a resolution stating in substance that it does not favor the suspension of such deportation, the Attorney General shall thereupon deport such alien or authorize the alien's voluntary departure at his own expense under the order of deportation in the manner provided by law. If, within the time above specified, neither the Senate nor the House of Representatives shall pass such a resolution, the Attorney General shall cancel deportation proceedings." . . .

On December 12, 1975, Representative Eilberg, Chairman of the Judiciary Subcommittee on Immigration, Citizenship, and International Law, introduced a resolution opposing "the granting of permanent residence in the United States to [six] aliens," including Chadha. The resolution was referred to the House Committee on the Judiciary. On December 16, 1975, the resolution was discharged from further consideration by the House Committee on the Judiciary and submitted to the House of Representatives for a vote. The resolution had not been printed and was not made available to other Members of the House prior to or at the time it was voted on. So far as the record before us shows, the House consideration of the resolution was based on Representative Eilberg's statement from the floor that

> "[i]t was the feeling of the committee, after reviewing 340 cases, that the aliens contained in the resolution [Chadha and five others] did not meet these statutory requirements, particularly as it relates to hardship; and it is the opinion of the committee that their deportation should not be suspended."

The resolution was passed without debate or recorded vote. Since the House action was pursuant to §244(c)(2), the resolution was not treated as an Art. I legislative act; it was not submitted to the Senate or presented to the President for his action.

After the House veto of the Attorney General's decision to allow Chadha to remain in the United States, the Immigration Judge reopened the deportation proceedings to implement the House order deporting Chadha. . . . On November 8, 1976, Chadha was ordered deported pursuant to the House action. . . . After full briefing and oral argument, the Court of Appeals held that the House was without constitutional authority to order Chadha's deportation; accordingly it directed the Attorney General "to cease and desist from taking any steps to deport this alien based upon the resolution enacted by the House of Representatives.". . .

III

A

We turn now to the question whether action of one House of Congress under § 244(c)(2) violates strictures of the Constitution. . . . [T]he fact that a given law or procedure is efficient, convenient, and useful in facilitating functions of government, standing alone, will not save it if it is contrary to the Constitution. Convenience and efficiency are not the primary objectives—or the hallmarks—of democratic government, and our inquiry is sharpened, rather than blunted, by the fact that congressional veto provisions are appearing with increasing frequency in statutes which delegate authority to executive and independent agencies: "Since 1932, when the first veto provision was enacted into law, 295 congressional veto-type procedures have been inserted in 196 different statutes as follows: from 1932 to 1939, five statutes were affected; from 1940–49, nineteen statutes; between 1950-59, thirty-four statutes; and from 1960–69, forty-nine. From the year 1970 through 1975, at least one hundred sixty-three such provisions were included in eighty-nine laws." Abourezk, The Congressional Veto: A Contemporary Response to Executive Encroachment on Legislative Prerogatives, 52 Ind. L. Rev. 323, 324 (1977).

JUSTICE WHITE undertakes to make a case for the proposition that the one-House veto is a useful "political invention," and we need not challenge that assertion. We can even concede this utilitarian argument, although the long-range political wisdom of this "invention" is arguable. It has been vigorously debated, and it is instructive to compare the views of the protagonists. But policy arguments supporting even useful "political inventions" are subject to the demands of the Constitution, which defines powers and, with respect to this subject, sets out just how those powers are to be exercised.

Explicit and unambiguous provisions of the Constitution prescribe and define the respective functions of the Congress and of the Executive in the legislative process. Since the precise terms of those familiar provisions are critical to the resolution of these cases, we set them out verbatim. Article I provides:

"All legislative Powers herein granted shall be vested in a Congress of the United States, which shall consist of a Senate and House of Representatives." Art. I, § 1.

"Every Bill which shall have passed the House of Representatives and the Senate, shall, before it becomes a law, be presented to the President of the United States." Art. I, 7, cl. 2.

"Every Order, Resolution, or Vote to which the Concurrence of the Senate and House of Representatives may be necessary (except on a question of Adjournment) shall be presented to the President of the United States; and before the Same shall take Effect, shall be approved by him, or being disapproved by him, shall be repassed by two thirds of the Senate and House of Representatives, according to the Rules and Limitations prescribed in the Case of a Bill." Art. I, § 7, cl. 3.

These provisions of Art. I are integral parts of the constitutional design for the separation of powers. We have recently noted that "[t]he principle of separation of powers was not simply an abstract generalization in the minds of the Framers: it was woven into the document that they drafted in Philadelphia in the summer of 1787." *Buckley v. Valeo*, 424 U.S. at 124. Just as we relied on the textual provision of Art. II, § 2, cl. 2, to vindicate the principle of separation of powers in *Buckley*, we see that the purposes underlying the Presentment Clauses, Art. I, § 7, cls. 2, 3, and the bicameral requirement of Art. I, § 1, and § 7, cl. 2, guide our resolution of the important question presented in these cases. The very structure of the Articles delegating and separating powers under Arts. I, II, and III exemplifies the concept of separation of powers, and we now turn to Art. I.

B

The Presentment Clauses

The records of the Constitutional Convention reveal that the requirement that all legislation be presented to the President before becoming law was uniformly accepted by the Framers. Presentment to the President and the Presidential veto were considered so imperative that the draftsmen took special pains to assure that these requirements could

376

not be circumvented. During the final debate on Art. I, § 7, cl. 2, James Madison expressed concern that it might easily be evaded by the simple expedient of calling a proposed law a "resolution" or "vote," rather than a "bill." As a consequence, Art. I, § 7, cl. 3 was added. . . .

C

Bicameralism

The bicameral requirement of Art. I, §§ 1, 7, was of scarcely less concern to the Framers than was the Presidential veto, and indeed the two concepts are interdependent. By providing that no law could take effect without the concurrence of the prescribed majority of the Members of both Houses, the Framers reemphasized their belief, already remarked upon in connection with the Presentment Clauses, that legislation should not be enacted unless it has been carefully and fully considered by the Nation's elected officials. In the Constitutional Convention debates on the need for a bicameral legislature, James Wilson, later to become a Justice of this Court, commented:

"Despotism comes on mankind in different shapes, sometimes in an Executive, sometimes in a military, one. Is there danger of a Legislative despotism? Theory & practice both proclaim it. If the Legislative authority be not restrained, there can be neither liberty nor stability; and it can only be restrained by dividing it within itself, into distinct and independent branches. In a single house there is no check but the inadequate one of the virtue & good sense of those who compose it."

Hamilton argued that a Congress comprised of a single House was antithetical to the very purposes of the Constitution. Were the Nation to adopt a Constitution providing for only one legislative organ, he warned:

"[W]e shall finally accumulate, in a single body, all the most important prerogatives of sovereignty, and thus entail upon our posterity one of the most execrable forms of government that human infatuation ever contrived. Thus we should create in reality that very tyranny which the adversaries of the new Constitution either are, or affect to be, solicitous to avert." The Federalist No. 22 . . . .

IV

The Constitution sought to divide the delegated powers of the new Federal Government into three defined categories, Legislative, Executive, and Judicial, to assure, as nearly as possible, that each branch of government would confine itself to its assigned responsibility. The hydraulic pressure inherent within each of the separate Branches to exceed the outer limits of its power, even to accomplish desirable objectives, must be resisted.

Although not "hermetically" sealed from one another, *Buckley v. Valeo*, 424 U.S. at 121, the powers delegated to the three Branches are functionally identifiable. When any Branch acts, it is presumptively exercising the power the Constitution has delegated to it. When the Executive acts, he presumptively acts in an executive or administrative capacity as defined in Art. II. And when, as here, one House of Congress purports to act, it is presumptively acting within its assigned sphere.

Beginning with this presumption, we must nevertheless establish that the challenged action under §244(c)(2) is of the kind to which the procedural requirements of Art. I, § 7, apply. Not every action taken by either House is subject to the bicameralism and presentment requirements of Art. I. Whether actions taken by either House are, in law and fact, an exercise of legislative power depends not on their form, but upon "whether they contain matter which is properly to be regarded as legislative in its character and effect."

Examination of the action taken here by one House pursuant to §244(c)(2) reveals that it was essentially legislative in purpose and effect. In purporting to exercise power defined in Art. I, § 8, cl. 4, to "establish an uniform Rule of Naturalization," the House took action that had the purpose and effect of altering the legal rights, duties, and relations of persons, including the Attorney General, Executive Branch officials and Chadha, all outside the Legislative Branch. Section 244(c)(2) purports to authorize one House of Congress to require the Attorney General to deport an individual alien whose deportation otherwise would be canceled under §244. The one-House veto operated in these cases to overrule the Attorney General and mandate Chadha's deportation; absent the House action, Chadha would remain in the United States. Congress has acted, and its action has altered Chadha's status.

The legislative character of the one-House veto in these cases is confirmed by the character of the congressional action it supplants. Neither the House of Representatives nor the Senate contends that, absent the veto provision in §244(c)(2), either of them, or both of them acting together, could effectively require the Attorney General to deport an alien once the Attorney General, in the exercise of legislatively delegated authority, had determined the alien should remain in the United States. Without the challenged provision in §244(c)(2), this could have been achieved, if at all, only by legislation requiring deportation. Similarly, a veto by one House of Congress under §244(c)(2) cannot be justified as an attempt at amending the standards set out in §244(a)(1), or as a repeal of §244 as applied to Chadha. Amendment and repeal of statutes, no less than enactment, must conform with Art. I. . . .

Finally, we see that, when the Framers intended to authorize either House of Congress to act alone and outside of its prescribed bicameral legislative role, they narrowly and precisely defined the procedure for such action. There are four provisions in the Constitution, explicit and unambiguous, by which one House may act alone with the unreviewable force of law, not subject to the President's veto:

  (a) The House of Representatives alone was given the power to initiate impeachments. Art. I, § 2, cl. 5;

(b) The Senate alone was given the power to conduct trials following impeachment on charges initiated by the House, and to convict following trial. Art. I, § 3, cl. 6;

(c) The Senate alone was given final unreviewable power to approve or to disapprove Presidential appointments. Art. II, § 2, cl. 2;

(d) The Senate alone was given unreviewable power to ratify treaties negotiated by the President. Art. II, 2, cl. 2.

Clearly, when the Draftsmen sought to confer special powers on one House, independent of the other House, or of the President, they did so in explicit, unambiguous terms. These carefully defined exceptions from presentment and bicameralism underscore the difference between the legislative functions of Congress and other unilateral but important and binding one-House acts provided for in the Constitution. These exceptions are narrow, explicit, and separately justified; none of them authorize the action challenged here. On the contrary, they provide further support for the conclusion that congressional authority is not to be implied, and for the conclusion that the veto provided for in §244(c)(2) is not authorized by the constitutional design of the powers of the Legislative Branch.

Since it is clear that the action by the House under §244(c)(2) was not within any of the express constitutional exceptions authorizing one House to act alone, and equally clear that it was an exercise of legislative power, that action was subject to the standards prescribed in Art. I. The bicameral requirement, the Presentment Clauses, the President's veto, and Congress' power to override a veto were intended to erect enduring checks on each Branch and to protect the people from the improvident exercise of power by mandating certain prescribed steps. To preserve those checks, and maintain the separation of powers, the carefully defined limits on the power of each Branch must not be eroded. To accomplish what has been attempted by one House of Congress in this case requires action in conformity with the express procedures of the Constitution's prescription for legislative action: passage by a majority of both Houses and presentment to the President.

The veto authorized by §244(c)(2) doubtless has been in many respects a convenient shortcut; the "sharing" with the Executive by Congress of its authority over aliens in this manner is, on its face, an appealing compromise. In purely practical terms, it is obviously easier for action to be taken by one House without submission to the President; but it is crystal clear from the records of the Convention, contemporaneous writings, and debates that the Framers ranked other values higher than efficiency. The records of the Convention and debates in the states preceding ratification underscore the common desire to define and limit the exercise of the newly created federal powers affecting the states and the people. There is unmistakable expression of a determination that legislation by the national Congress be a step-by-step, deliberate and deliberative process.

The choices we discern as having been made in the Constitutional Convention impose burdens on governmental processes that often seem clumsy, inefficient, even unworkable, but those hard choices were consciously made by men who had lived under a form of government that permitted arbitrary governmental acts to go unchecked. There is no support in the Constitution or decisions of this Court for the proposition that the cumbersomeness and delays often encountered in complying with explicit constitutional standards may be avoided, either by the Congress or by the President. With all the obvious flaws of delay, untidiness, and potential for abuse, we have not yet found a better way to preserve freedom than by making the exercise of power subject to the carefully crafted restraints spelled out in the Constitution.

*   *   *

Notes on *INS v. Chadha*

1. *The lawmaking process prescribed by Article I, §7*: The Court began its analysis in *Chadha* by discussing the importance of the Constitution's "finely wrought and exhaustively considered procedure" for enacting federal legislation, focusing specifically on the Presentment Clauses and the bicameralism requirement. The Presentment Clauses appear in Article I, §7. Clause 2 states that "[e]very Bill which shall have passed the House of Representatives and the Senate, shall, before it become a Law, be presented to the President of the United States." Clause 3 provides that "[e]very Order, Resolution, or Vote to which the Concurrence of the Senate and House of Representatives may be necessary (except on a question of Adjournment) shall be presented to the President of the United States." The bicameralism requirement also appears in Article I, §7, and it dictates that every bill, order, resolution, or vote—to become a valid federal statute—must pass both the House of Representatives and the Senate. One house alone is insufficient.

As a matter of constitutional structure, these provisions are not mere formalities. The President plays an important role in lawmaking as a brake on the national legislature. The President is the only elected official who represents the nation as a whole. And the President constitutes another branch that must either concur or, with a veto, be overridden by a supermajority. The bicameralism requirement is likewise substantively important—as times when those houses are controlled by different parties illustrate. The House is more politically accountable, more representative of the nation as a whole, and therefore more prone to swings in popular opinion. With six-year terms and equal state representation, the Senate is less accountable to current popular opinion. Though both are elected bodies with representation from all fifty states, the nature of their political accountability differs.

In all events, under the terms of Article I, §7, if the House resolution that ordered Chadha deported counted constitutionally as *legislation*, it needed to comply with this "finely wrought procedure": to be passed by both the House and Senate and be presented to the President for his signature or veto. There are no exceptions to this process for the enactment of federal statutes.

2. *The nature of the resolution*: The Court's next step was to identify the nature of the House resolution rejecting the suspension of Chadha's deportation. (If the resolution was *legislative* in character, it was unconstitutional. But if it were something other than legislation, it might still be permissible.) The justices had little difficulty concluding that the resolution was, in fact, a legislative act. Its purpose and impact revealed its legislative character:

> "In purporting to exercise power defined in Art. I, §8, cl. 4 to 'establish an uniform Rule of Naturalization,' the House took action that had the purpose and effect of altering the legal rights, duties and relations of persons, including the Attorney General, Executive Branch officials and Chadha, all outside the legislative branch."

Altering the legal rights of persons outside the legislative branch is the essence of legislation; this is what federal statutes do. Federal laws set down rules of conduct that govern the behavior of those outside Congress.

Importantly, not all actions taken by Congress or its members are necessarily legislative in nature. Suppose the Senate Majority Leader offered another senator a plum committee chair if she supported a particular judicial nominee. Naming a senator to a committee chair would not be "legislative action" for constitutional purposes, as it does not affect anyone's legal rights outside the legislative branch; it only affects the internal organization of Congress itself. The same would be true if a congressional committee decided to conduct hearings on a particular subject. But the resolution passed by the House of Representatives regarding Chadha *was* legislative in character: it affected the legal rights or duties of Chadha, the Attorney General, and other Executive Branch officials, all persons outside Congress.

The Court then invoked an additional reason the resolution must have been legislative. Without §244(c)(2), how could Congress have changed Chadha's immigration status? Only by enacting a new statute—specifically, a private bill ordering Chadha's deportation. To be valid, such a statute would have needed to have been passed by both houses and signed by the President (or passed by two-thirds majorities in the House and Senate after a presidential veto). The fact that Chadha would have stayed in the country absent the House's resolution—and that Congress could have otherwise produced this outcome only by enacting a new statute—revealed that the House's resolution must have been legislative in nature.

3. *The logic of* **expressio unius**: Finally, the Court discussed the specific provisions in the Constitution permitting one house of Congress to act unilaterally, without presentment or bicameralism: Article I, §2, clause 5 grants the House of Representatives the power to impeach; Article I, §3, clause 6 grants the Senate the power to try all impeachments; Article II, §2, clause 2 grants the Senate the power to give its advice and consent on presidential appointments; and Article II, §2, clause 2 grants the Senate the power to ratify all treaties.[19] From this list, the Court inferred that the circumstances in which one house can act unilaterally are carefully circumscribed and delineated—and thus the Constitution should not be construed to permit any *other* such circumstances. This is the traditional interpretive canon of *expressio unius est exclusio alterius*: the expression of one implies the exclusion of others.

All of this pointed the Court to its ultimate conclusion: the legislative veto was unconstitutional. The resolution concerning Chadha was legislative in nature, and federal legislation must be enacted pursuant to the "finely wrought procedure" set out in Article I, §7, which includes both bicameral passage and presentment to the President. Because the resolution rejecting the suspension of Chadha's deportation had been passed only by the House of Representatives, and had never been presented to the President, it could not, consistent with the Constitution, have legal force. More generally, *any* legislative veto—any provision permitting Congress (or a portion thereof) to alter federal law without duly following the procedure set out in Article I, §7—is unconstitutional.

4. *Formalism and functionalism in separation of powers disputes*: It is worth noting the stark difference in approach between the majority opinion in *Chadha* and Justice White's dissent. The majority focused on the specific, formal requirements of Article I, §7. Because the legislative veto was legislative in nature, and it did not comply with the exact procedure set out in the Constitution's text, it was unconstitutional.

By contrast, Justice White focused on the broader purposes of the Constitution's separation of powers, starting from the pragmatic premise that the world has changed dramatically since 1789. In particular, the Executive Branch has grown dramatically, and Congress no longer has any choice but to legislate in capacious terms. This means Congress must delegate a great deal of policymaking authority to executive agencies and departments. To Justice White, the legislative veto was simply a means for Congress to *preserve* its constitutional role—indeed, the role the Framers envisioned—given modern realities. The legislative veto facilitated Congress's retaining its constitutional powers, not aggrandizing them. Indeed, a constitutional system in which Congress has the authority to enact legislative vetoes (in White's view) was much closer to the balance of power among the branches envisioned by the Framers than the system created by the majority's opinion.

Justice White's reasoning in *Chadha* was functionalist or pragmatic, rather than formalistic. It was more concerned with the broad purposes of the

---

[19] There are a few other such provisions in the Constitution the Court did not mention, but which only concern Congress's internal operations. Examples include judging the qualifications of fellow members, the House of Representatives' choosing the Speaker, and each house determining its rules of proceeding.

Constitution than with ensuring a strict, formal adherence to its specific provisions. In this way, the disagreement between the majority and the dissent was as much about interpretive methodology as it was about the legislative veto. Justice White asserted the Court should discern the basic objectives of the Constitution's structure and assesses each dispute against these objectives. By contrast, the majority believed the Court's job is simply to enforce the specific textual directives of the Constitution.

5. *Post-Chadha alternatives to the legislative veto*: Since *Chadha*, the legislative veto generally—and not just in the form at issue in *Chadha*—has been unconstitutional. But this does not mean Congress is powerless to restrain the Executive Branch, or to influence the enforcement of statutes Congress has enacted. There are several mechanisms Congress can still invoke to steer the Executive Branch in its implementation of federal law:

* It can reject Executive Branch decisions through the enactment of new federal statutes.

* It can enact more detailed legislation in the first instance, thereby limiting the Executive Branch's discretion in enforcement.

* It can conduct oversight hearings (in committees and subcommittees) that apply pressure on the Executive Branch, communicating the manner in which Congress would like to see federal statutes implemented.

* It can include sunset provisions in statutes, such that laws will expire on a certain date and continue in force beyond then only if Congress reenacts them.

* It can choose not to appropriate funds for the enforcement of certain agency rules or regulations.

* It can threaten agencies and departments with budget reductions if they do not enforce federal statutes consistent with Congress's expectations.

* It can appeal to the media and to the public to bring attention to how the Executive Branch is implementing a statute.

* Members can lobby and informally exert political pressure.

There are likely several other strategies. But after *Chadha*, the legislative veto is no longer a constitutional option.

* * *

PROBLEMS ON LEGISLATIVE VETOES

1. In January 2023 the House of Representatives and the Senate both pass the American Jobs Act of 2023, a bill appropriating nearly $1 trillion over ten years to expand and repair various aspects of the nation's infrastructure. After passing both houses, the bill is presented the President, who signs the bill into law. Under the terms of the Act, state and local governments are to apply to the Secretary of Transportation to receive

funding appropriated by the Act for projects that meet the prerequisites specified by the statute. The Act vests the ultimate decision of whether to fund a proposed project in the Secretary of Transportation (the head of the Department of Transportation, a cabinet-level executive department). The Act further specifies that, once the Secretary makes a determination to provide funds to a proposed infrastructure project, the Secretary shall report this determination to Congress. The Act states that the Secretary's funding decision shall be final unless—within 30 of receiving the Secretary's report—both the House and the Senate adopt a resolution stating that the project shall not be funded.

    a. Was the process by which the American Jobs Act of 2023 was enacted consistent with the Constitution? Why or why not?

    b. Is the content of the American Jobs Act of 2023 consistent with the Constitution? Why or why not?

2. The facts are the same as in (1), except that, in order to block the determination of the Secretary of Transportation to fund an infrastructure project, the resolution must be passed by two-thirds majorities in both the House of Representatives and the Senate. Would this procedure be consistent with the Constitution?

3. The facts are the same as in (1), except that, in order to block the determination of the Secretary of Transportation to fund an infrastructure project, the resolution—after it is passed by both the House of Representatives and the Senate—must be presented to the President, and the resolution will not block the Secretary's funding decision unless the resolution is signed by the President within ten days of being presented to him (not counting Sundays).

4. The facts are the same as in (1), except that Congress has no authority to block a determination by the Secretary of Transportation to fund a proposal. Nonetheless, under the terms of the Act, the Secretary of Transportation's determination cannot become final (and legally enforceable) unless he reports his determination to Congress. Further, no funds for a project can be transferred from the U.S. Treasury until 30 days have elapsed from the date of the Secretary's report to Congress.

*   *   *

C.   The Line-Item Veto

1. Overview

A "line-item veto" is an authority of the executive to veto "line items" (or specific provisions) within a larger statute. For example, suppose the legislature passes a bill containing 378 distinct provisions. A line-item veto would permit the executive to cancel out some of those provisions without rejecting the bill in its entirety. Those items not cancelled would become law, while the cancelled items would not. Most state constitutions grant the state's governor some form of line-item veto authority. For instance, Article 4, §10(e) of the California Constitution provides as follows:

"The Governor may reduce or eliminate one or more items of appropriation while approving other portions of a bill. The Governor shall append to the bill a statement of the items reduced or eliminated with the reasons for the action. The Governor shall transmit to the house originating the bill a copy of the statement and reasons. Items reduced or eliminated shall be separately reconsidered and may be passed over the Governor's veto in the same manner as bills."

In considering the constitutionality of a *federal* line-item veto, it is important to understand the relevant political incentives. Why would Congress—which clearly stands to lose authority if the President has a line-item veto power—create such a mechanism? (The Line Item Veto Act of 1996 was enacted by a Republican Congress, granting additional power to a Democratic President, Bill Clinton.) Crudely put, it is a convenient way for members of Congress to have their cake and eat it too. Most members face pressures to vote for spending directed to their own states or districts, but also face a political cost if they help create huge national budget deficits. The line-item veto offered a partial solution to this dilemma: members could vote for their favorite spending projects, but then—if they were later removed from the bill—blame the President. They could claim credit for voting for items important to their constituencies, but then rely on the President to keep the budget manageable.

2. The Line Item Veto Act of 1996: *Clinton v. New York*

The specific procedure set out by the Line Item Veto Act of 1996 was as follows. After Congress enacted a bill to which the Act applied, and the President signed that bill into law, the President had five days in which to "cancel in whole" any of the following: (a) any dollar amount of discretionary budget authority; (b) any item of new direct spending; or (c) any "limited tax benefit." The Act directed the President, in identifying items for cancellation, to consider the legislative history, purposes, and other relevant information about such items. To cancel an item, the President was required to find that the cancellation would (1) reduce the federal budget deficit, (2) not impair any essential government functions, and (3) not harm the national interest. Following the cancellation of an item, the President was required to send a special message to Congress informing it of the cancellation. Congress could then reverse the cancellation through a "disapproval bill." Such a disapproval bill was simply a new piece of legislation, and thus subject to the requirements of bicameralism and presentment to the President, just like any other federal statute.

In *Clinton v. New York*, 524 U.S. 417 (1998), the Supreme Court concluded that the procedural device created by the Line Item Veto Act was inconsistent with Article I, §7. That is, like the legislative veto, it failed to follow the "finely wrought, exhaustively considered procedure" for the enactment of federal legislation required by the Constitution. When the President canceled an item under the Line Item Veto Act, the statute that ultimately became federal law—the original budget bill passed by Congress, less the line items that had been cancelled by the President—had never passed the House or the Senate or been presented to the President. What ultimately became part of the U.S. Code as a statute had not complied with the Constitution's bicameralism and presentment requirements. Though the original budget bill when passed by Congress and presented to the President complied with these requirements, the content of that bill differed from what ultimately became federal law (after the cancellations).

The Court reasoned that the President has the constitutional authority to sign a bill into law or to return it *in full* to Congress. But there is no provision in the Constitution for the partial repeal or amendment of legislation presented to the President. And we should take this silence as determinative—as the equivalent of an express prohibition—because this process for the enacting federal statutes was a central point of debate at the Constitutional Convention.

As the Court noted, there were three differences between President's veto power under Article I, §7 and the line-item cancellation power the Act purported to confer. First, the constitutional return (*i.e.*, a presidential veto) takes place *before* a bill becomes law, while the line-item veto specified in the Act took place after. Second, the constitutional return is of the *entire bill*, while the line-item veto was a cancellation of only a part. Third, the Constitution expressly authorizes the President to play a role in the enactment of statutes, but it is silent on the President's unilateral role in the repeal or amendment of statutes that have already become law. The Act's line-item veto procedure was therefore inconsistent with Article I, §7, which sets out the *exclusive* means by which a federal statute is to come into being.

3. The related matter of presidential signing statements

In a sense, a line-item veto seems functions much like an official statement issued by the President when he signs a bill into law in which the President indicates he has constitutional qualms about a provision in the law. Consider, for instance, President Obama's statement concerning the omnibus spending bill he signed into law in 2013. There, the President identified several sections of the statute he would not enforce because he thought they were unconstitutional. Is such a signing statement distinguishable from a line-item veto of the sort that was declared unconstitutional in *Clinton v. New York*?

There are at least two important differences. First, in the case of the cancellations authorized by the Line Item Veto Act, what would have formally become federal law would not have included the items the President had cancelled. Through cancellation, these provisions would have been removed from the statute. In contrast, the items identified by the President in a signing statement formally remain a part of the statute. They are part of the U.S. Code; they are just quite unlikely to be enforced or observed by the President, at least so long as he remains in office. But they are officially federal law.

Second, the Line Item Veto Act's cancellation mechanism would have empowered the President to remove items from a bill for almost any reason. In contrast, Presidents have historically only used signing statements to lodge *constitutional* objections to statutory provisions. In essence, signing statements alert the public that, in the President's judgment, certain aspects of the statute are unconstitutional. Recall Presidents must take an oath to uphold the Constitution, and thus arguably are constitutionally *obligated* to reach her their own independent conclusions on such matters. If the President sincerely believes that a provision of federal law is unconstitutional, she arguably is *required* to refrain from implementing it. The signing statement just makes this constitutional determination public.

If the President believes a bill contains unconstitutional provisions, what else might she do (other than sign it into law and issue a signing statement)? She could veto the bill in full. Many have argued that this is the only constitutional option. The problem with this solution is its impracticality. When Congress enacts a bill spanning several hundred pages, should the President really be required to veto the entire bill if she believes only a single provision is unconstitutional? There are sound arguments on both sides, and the answer remains unresolved. The important point here is that presidential signing statements raise issues distinct from the line-item veto mechanism invalidated in *Clinton v. New York*.

*   *   *

PROBLEMS ON THE LINE-ITEM VETO

Please evaluate whether the following alternatives would be constitutional in light of the Supreme Court's decision in *Clinton v. New York*.

1. For the next fiscal year, Congress does not enact one single budget and appropriations bill, appropriating funds (and tax relief) in thousands of different line items of one bill. Instead, it splits the omnibus bill into roughly 12,000 separate bills, each of which is separately passed by the House of Representatives and the Senate. The President signs all but two of these bills into law. The President vetoes the remaining two, both of which concern items of discretionary spending.

2. For the next fiscal year, Congress enacts one huge budget and appropriations bill (the Omnibus Budget and Reconciliation Act), containing thousands of different line items of federal spending. The last provision contained in that bill states as follows:

   § 6001 Presidential discretion

   If the President concludes that the Government's failure to execute or implement any item of discretionary spending in this law would (1) decrease the federal deficit, (2) not impair any essential Governmental function, and (3) not harm the national interest, he may decide not to execute or implement that provision.

The President signs the Omnibus Budget and Reconciliation Act into law. Later, the President decides that two items of federal spending contained in the Act meet the criteria set out in §6001 and directs the relevant executive departments not to spend the appropriated funds.

3. For the next fiscal year, Congress enacts one huge budget and appropriations bill (the Omnibus Budget and Reconciliation Act), containing thousands of different line-items of federal spending. One provision contained somewhere in the middle of that bill states as follows:

> § 4233 Status of Jerusalem
>
> The Department of State shall spend $100,000 in order to inform affected individuals that any American citizen born in the City of Jerusalem may have the words "Jerusalem, Israel" recorded as her or his place of birth on any official document issued by the United States Government.

The President signs the Omnibus Budget and Reconciliation Act into law but believes §4233 is unconstitutional. As a result, the President orders the Secretary of State not to enforce §4233.

PART V

THE STRUCTURAL CONSTRAINTS ON THE STATES

CHAPTER 16
FEDERAL IMMUNITY AND PREEMPTION

A.   Introduction

The last three chapters examined the "horizontal" separation of powers among the three branches of the federal government. We now revisit the "vertical" separation of authority between the federal government and the states, but from a new perspective. The doctrines and principles relating to federalism addressed in prior chapters concerned the structural limits on the *national* government—the breadth of the federal judicial power and Congress's legislative authority. Here we address issues of federalism as they concern the Constitution's structural limits on state and local governments—constraints designed to protect the interests of the nation as a whole from the parochial, self-interested acts of the states or their political subdivisions.

It is worth remembering that one of the principal reasons the Framers gathered in Philadelphia in the summer of 1787 was to address this precise problem. Under the Articles of Confederation, the states were largely behaving as independent nations, regulating interstate and international commerce in ways that harmed each other and the collective interests of the nation. Such inefficiencies in commercial law were the central reason the Framers lodged the commerce power in the federal government; the states were regulating commerce in ways that perhaps benefitted them individually but dragged down the national economy. The Constitution created a new framework for resolving these issues.

But the root of the problem did not disappear. Nor could it ever fully disappear, because it stems from a structural reality endemic to any federal system—a reality evident, for instance, in *McCulloch v. Maryland*. Specifically, state officials only have an electoral incentive to represent the interests of their own constituents, the voters who live in their states. They have no incentive to protect the interests of out-of-state residents or of the nation as a whole. As a result, states are perpetually enacting laws that benefit themselves (or particular economic interests within their borders) at the expense of other states. And these parochial laws create economic inefficiencies, and thus tend to drag down the economic well-being of the nation as a whole.

This is the essential, intractable problem to which the constitutional principles in this area respond. On the one hand, the states are independent sovereigns, and thus have the authority to enact laws to promote the health and welfare of their residents. (This is their so-called "police power," a power reserved to the states and denied to the federal government.) On the other hand, if left to their own devices, states will inevitably harm the collective interests of the U.S. as a whole. They will enact laws with "negative externalities" and "spillover effects" that impose costs on the residents of other states and bring down the collective welfare of the nation.

The Constitution thus contains several important, union-preserving provisions and doctrines that place structural limits on the states. The next three chapters will take up the six most significant such restrictions: (1) the doctrine of federal immunity, (2) the federal preemption of state law under the Supremacy Clause, (3) the dormant Commerce Clause, (4) the Privileges and Immunities Clause of Article IV, (5) the Privileges or Immunities Clause of the Fourteenth Amendment, and (6) the Full Faith and Credit Clause.

B. Federal Immunity from State Taxes or Regulations

Prior chapters have discussed the immunity state governments enjoy from federal regulation. Recall that the anti-commandeering principle protects the states from being subjected to federal laws that command them to take affirmative steps to govern their residents according to particular instructions. The Constitution likewise forbids Congress (as part of its otherwise permissible enactment of legislation) from abrogating states' sovereign immunity from suit, except through legislation validly enacted pursuant to §5 of the Fourteenth Amendment. And the principle of equal state sovereignty dictates that, absent an exceptional justification, Congress cannot single out a subset of states for unfavorable treatment.

The topic here is the flip side of that coin: the federal government's immunity from state regulation or taxation. Historically, the law in this area has been called "intergovernmental immunity," as the immunities were understood to be reciprocal. But that is no longer accurate (if it ever really was). As we have seen, the federal government can regulate the states in all sorts of ways. Thus, the Supreme Court's recent decisions have referred to the rules in this field as "federal immunity doctrine." Stated simply, that doctrine forbids state or local governments from either (1) directly regulating or taxing the federal government or its instrumentalities, or (2) imposing regulations or taxes that discriminate against the federal government.

This doctrine has deep roots in constitutional history, and it effectuates an important structural principle. Recall that in *McCulloch v. Maryland* the Supreme Court invalidated Maryland's tax on the Bank of the United States, an instrumentality of the federal government. *McCulloch* held that Maryland's tax was inconsistent with the structure of government established by the Constitution, as it would have allowed a state to inhibit (or even nullify) the implementation of a valid federal law. Permitting states to veto or impede national law would contravene an essential premise of the federal system created by the Constitution. (Of course, states can control the enactment and implementation of their *own* laws, but they have no license to control the operation of federal law, even within their own borders.) Were states permitted to "opt out" of (or nullify) federal law, the United States could hardly operate as a single nation; purportedly *national* law—despite being validly enacted by Congress—would only consist of those statutes each state chose to accept.

Federal immunity doctrine effectuates this basic precept. But the scope of the doctrine has evolved, containing more detail than that articulated by Chief Justice Marshall in *McCulloch*. In digesting this material, it is important to keep two distinctions in mind: (a) that between state regulations or taxes imposed *directly* on the federal government or its instrumentalities, and those whose impact on the federal government is only indirect; and (b) that between state laws that treat all persons or entities equally, and those that discriminate against the federal government or its agents.

1. Waivers of federal immunity by Congress

Federal immunity is a species of *sovereign* immunity, as the United States is entitled to the doctrine's protections due to its identity as the national government. Thus, like other forms of sovereign immunity, the federal government can partially or fully waive it. If Congress, by statute, has spoken precisely to the question—by expressly granting or withholding immunity from state taxes or regulations as it concerns the federal government's own instrumentalities, agents, or contractors—the statute settles the matter. The purpose of the doctrine is to protect the interests of the nation as a whole. So if Congress decides to waive that immunity, the structural problem identified in *McCulloch* dissolves: a political body properly situated to protect the national interest has granted its imprimatur. The concerns typically triggered by state taxes or regulations affecting the federal government no longer exist if they have been blessed by Congress, as such taxes or regulations—by definition—are consistent with the interests of the United States.

Like other waivers concerning structural constitutional principles, however, Congress's waiver of the protectios of federal immunity doctrine must be "clear and unambiguous." As the Supreme Court explained recently in *United States v. Washington*, No. 21–404, slip op. at 6 (June 21, 2022), "[w]e will find that Congress has authorized regulation that would otherwise violate the Federal Government's intergovernmental immunity only when and to the extent there is a clear congressional mandate. In other words, Congress must provide clear and unambiguous authorization for this kind of state regulation."

2. Taxes or regulations imposed directly on the United States

Assuming Congress has not spoken directly to the issue, the federal immunity doctrine imposes two constraints on state taxes and regulations. First, states may not *directly* tax or regulate the federal government or its instrumentalities. Here, the question concerns the *legal incidence* of the tax or regulation: the party formally taxed or regulated by the state law. What matters is not who practically feels the pinch of the regulation or tax, but the party on whom it is *legally* imposed.

For instance, California cannot impose a property tax on the federal government, payable by the United States, for its ownership of the building that houses the United States Court of Appeals for the Ninth Circuit in San Francisco. (And this is true even if California imposes an identical property tax on *all* properties located in in the state, regardless of who owns them.) But California *can* impose an income tax on the federal government's employees who work for the Ninth Circuit, as the legal incidence of that tax falls on private individuals, not the United States itself. (That is, it is private individuals who are legally obligated to pay the California personal income tax, not their employers.) To be sure, California's taxation of the federal government's employees is apt to increase the federal government's costs in conducting its business; a state income tax reduces employee's after-tax income, and thus likely has the economic effect of requiring employers to pay their employees higher wages. But if the *legal* incidence of a state tax falls on a private individual—and not the federal government—it does not violate this prong of the federal immunity doctrine.

Indeed, a state does not impose a tax directly on the United States when it taxes private contractors who are performing services for the federal government, even if the federal government has pledged to reimburse those contractors for any costs related to the contract—including their state tax liabilities. The relevant question is not who bears the *economic* incidence of the tax or regulation, but who is legally required to make payment or to conform their actions to the regulation. As the Supreme Court explained in *South Carolina v. Baker*, 485 U.S. 505 (1988), "the States can never tax the United States directly but can tax any private parties with whom it does business, even though the financial burden falls on the United States." *Id.* at 523. And this rule applies identically whether the state law is a tax or a regulation, as "state taxes and regulations are subject to the same restrictions under the federal immunity doctrine." *North Dakota v. United States*, 495 U.S. 423, 454 n.3 (1990).

3. Taxes or regulations that discriminate against the United States

The second strand of the doctrine provides that states are also forbidden from imposing regulations or taxes that discriminate against the federal government. For instance, states are permitted to regulate the occupational safety of workplaces operated by private employers (assuming Congress has not preempted such regulation by federal statute). But states cannot impose more onerous regulations on private firms because they do business with the U.S. Department of Defense or U.S. Immigration and Customs Enforcement (ICE). Such regulations would impermissibly discriminate against the United States.

In recent years, this aspect of the federal immunity doctrine has commonly arisen in the context of state personal income taxes. Through 4 U.S.C. §111,

Congress has authorized states to impose nondiscriminatory taxes on the compensation paid to persons working for the federal government. And the Supreme Court has construed §111 as codifying the federal immunity doctrine as it applies to the taxation of individuals employed by the United States. Thus, cases arising under §111 have effectively determined the scope of the federal immunity doctrine, at least with respect to state personal income taxes.

A recent example is *Dawson v. Steager*, 139 S. Ct. 698 (2019). At issue was a provision of West Virginia's personal income tax that exempted from taxation the pension benefits paid to certain former West Virginia state law enforcement employees. The exemption did not apply to *all* former West Virginia law enforcement employees; but it also did not apply to *any* formal federal law enforcement employees. The question presented was whether this difference in tax treatment—between certain retired state and federal law enforcement employees—amounted to impermissible discrimination. As you read *Dawson*, please consider the following questions:

1. What were the possible groups of West Virginia taxpayers with whom the former federal law enforcement employees were "similarly situated"?

2. To which group of West Virginia taxpayers did the Court think it proper to compare the former federal law enforcement employees? Why? And why did this matter?

3. How significant was this difference in treatment, considering the full population of the former federal employees residing in West Virginia (and thus subject to the state's personal income tax)? Of what relevance was the magnitude of the difference in treatment?

4. Was it motivated by a hostility to the federal government (such as that at issue in *McCulloch*, when Maryland was clearly hostile to the Bank of the United States)? Did that matter? That is, of what relevance was the West Virginia legislature's purpose in adopting the challenged tax exemption?

Dawson v. Steager
139 S. Ct. 698 (2019)

JUSTICE GORSUCH delivered the opinion of the Court.

If you spent your career as a state law enforcement officer in West Virginia, you're likely to be eligible for a generous tax exemption when you retire. But if you served in federal law enforcement, West Virginia will deny you the same benefit. The question we face is whether a State may discriminate against federal retirees in that way.

For most of his career, James Dawson worked in the U.S. Marshals Service. After he retired, he began looking into the tax treatment of his pension. It turns out that his home State, West Virginia, doesn't tax the pension benefits of certain former state law enforcement employees.

But it does tax the benefits of all former federal employees. So Mr. Dawson brought this lawsuit alleging that West Virginia violated 4 U.S.C. §111. In that statute, the United States has consented to state taxation of the "pay or compensation" of "officer[s] or employee[s] of the United States," but only if the "taxation does not discriminate against the officer or employee because of the source of the pay or compensation." §111(a).

Section 111 codifies a legal doctrine almost as old as the Nation. In *McCulloch v. Maryland*, 4 Wheat. 316 (1819), this Court invoked the Constitution's Supremacy Clause to invalidate Maryland's effort to levy a tax on the Bank of the United States. Chief Justice Marshall explained that "the power to tax involves the power to destroy," and he reasoned that if States could tax the Bank they could "defeat" the federal legislative policy establishing it. *Id.,* at 431–432. For the next few decades, this Court interpreted *McCulloch* "to bar most taxation by one sovereign of the employees of another." *Davis v. Michigan Dept. of Treasury*, 489 U.S. 803, 810 (1989). In time, though, the Court softened its stance and upheld neutral income taxes—those that treated federal and state employees with an even hand. So eventually the intergovernmental tax immunity doctrine came to be understood to bar only *discriminatory* taxes. It was this understanding that Congress "consciously . . . drew upon" when adopting §111 in 1939. *Davis*, 489 U.S., at 813.

It is this understanding, too, that has animated our application of §111. Since the statute's adoption, we have upheld an Alabama income tax that did not discriminate on the basis of the source of the employees' compensation. *Jefferson County v. Acker*, 527 U.S. 423 (1999). But we have invalidated a Michigan tax that discriminated "in favor of retired state employees and against retired federal employees." *Davis*, 489 U.S., at 814. We have struck down a Kansas law that taxed the retirement benefits of federal military personnel at a higher rate than state and local government retirement benefits. *Barker v. Kansas*, 503 U.S. 594, 599 (1992). And we have rejected a Texas scheme that imposed a property tax on a private company operating on land leased from the federal government, but a "less burdensome" tax on property leased from the State. *Phillips Chemical Co. v. Dumas Indep. Sch. Dist.*, 361 U.S. 376 (1960).

Mr. Dawson's own attempt to invoke §111 met with mixed success. A West Virginia trial court found it "undisputed" that "there are no significant differences between Mr. Dawson's powers and duties as a U.S. Marshal and the powers and duties of the state and local law enforcement officers" that West Virginia exempts from income tax. In the trial court's judgment, the State's statute thus represented "precisely the type of favoritism" §111 prohibits. But the West Virginia Supreme Court of Appeals saw it differently. In reversing, the court emphasized that relatively few state employees receive the tax break denied Mr. Dawson. The court stressed, too, that the statute's "intent . . . was to give a benefit to a narrow class of state retirees," not to harm federal retirees. . . .

We believe the state trial court had it right. A State violates §111 when it treats retired state employees more favorably than retired federal employees and no "significant differences between the two classes" justify the differential treatment. *Davis*, 489 U.S., at 814–816. Here, West Virginia expressly affords state law enforcement retirees a tax benefit that federal retirees cannot receive. And before us everyone accepts the trial court's factual finding that there aren't any "significant differences" between Mr. Dawson's former job responsibilities and those of the tax-exempt state law enforcement retirees. Given all this, we have little difficulty concluding that West Virginia's law unlawfully "discriminate[s]" against Mr. Dawson "because of the source of [his] pay or compensation," just as §111 forbids.

The State offers this ambitious rejoinder. Even if its statute favors some state law enforcement retirees, the favored class is very small. Most state retirees are treated no better than Mr. Dawson. And this narrow preference, the State suggests, should be permitted because it affects so few people that it couldn't meaningfully interfere with the operations of the federal government.

We are unpersuaded. Section 111 disallows *any* state tax that discriminates against a federal officer or employee—not just those that seem to us especially cumbersome. Nor are we inclined to accept West Virginia's invitation to adorn §111 with a new and judicially manufactured qualification that cannot be found in its text. In fact, we have already refused an almost identical request. In *Davis,* we rejected Michigan's suggestion that a discriminatory state income tax should be allowed to stand so long as it treats federal employees or retirees the same as "the vast majority of voters in the State." 489 U.S., at 815 n.4. We rejected, too, any suggestion that a discriminatory tax is permissible so long as it "does not interfere with the Federal Government's ability to perform its governmental functions." *Id.,* at 814. In fact, as long ago as *McCulloch,* Chief Justice Marshall warned against enmeshing courts in the "perplexing" business, "so unfit for the judicial department," of attempting to delineate "what degree of taxation is the legitimate use, and what degree may amount to the abuse of power." 4 Wheat., at 430.

That's not to say the breadth or narrowness of a state tax exemption is irrelevant. Under §111, the scope of a State's tax exemption may affect the scope of its resulting duties. So if a State exempts from taxation all state employees, it must likewise exempt all federal employees. Conversely, if the State decides to exempt only a narrow subset of state retirees, the State can comply with §111 by exempting only the comparable class of federal retirees. But the narrowness of a discriminatory state tax law has never been enough to render it necessarily lawful.

With its primary argument lost, the State now proceeds more modestly. Echoing the West Virginia Supreme Court of Appeals, the State argues that we should uphold its statute because it isn't intended to harm federal retirees, only to help certain state retirees. But under the terms of §111, the "State's interest in adopting the discriminatory tax, no matter how substantial, is simply irrelevant." *Davis*, 489 U.S., at 816. We can safely assume that discriminatory laws like West Virginia's are almost always enacted with the purpose of benefiting state employees rather than harming their federal counterparts. Yet that wasn't enough to save the state statutes in *Davis, Barker,* or *Phillips,* and it can't be enough here. Under §111 what matters isn't the intent lurking behind the law but whether the letter of the law "treat[s] those who deal with" the federal government "as well as it treats those with whom [the State] deals itself." *Phillips Chemical Co.*, 361 U.S., at 385.

If treatment rather than intent is what matters, the State suggests that it should still prevail for other reasons. Section 111 prohibits "discriminat[ion]," something we've often described as treating similarly situated persons differently. And before us West Virginia insists that even if retired U.S. Marshals and tax-exempt state law enforcement retirees had similar job responsibilities, they aren't "similarly situated" for other reasons. Put another way, the State contends that the difference in treatment its law commands doesn't qualify as unlawful discrimination because it is "directly related to, and justified by," a lawful and "significant difference" between the two classes. *Davis*, 489 U.S., at 816.

In approaching this argument, everyone before us agrees on at least one thing. Whether a State treats similarly situated state and federal employees differently depends on how the State has defined the favored class. See *id.*, at 817. So if the State defines the favored class by reference to job responsibilities, a similarly situated federal worker will be one who performs comparable duties. But if the State defines the class by reference to some other criteria, our attention should naturally turn there. If a State gives a tax benefit to all retirees over a certain age, for example, the comparable federal retiree would be someone who is also over that age.

So how has West Virginia chosen to define the favored class in this case? The state statute singles out for preferential treatment retirement plans associated with West Virginia police, firefighters, and deputy sheriffs. See W. Va. Code Ann. §11–21–12(c)(6). The distinguishing characteristic of these plans is the nature of the jobs previously held by retirees who may participate in them; thus, a similarly situated federal retiree is someone who had similar job responsibilities to a state police officer, firefighter, or deputy sheriff. The state trial court correctly focused on this point of comparison and found no "significant differences" between Mr. Dawson's former job responsibilities as a U.S. Marshal and those of the state law enforcement retirees who qualify for the tax exemption. Nor did the West Virginia Supreme Court of Appeals upset this factual finding. So looking to how the State has chosen to define its favored class only seems to confirm that it has treated similarly situated persons differently because of the source of their compensation.

Of course, West Virginia sees it otherwise. It accepts (for now) that its statute distinguishes between persons based on their former job duties. It accepts, too, the trial court's finding that Mr. Dawson's former job responsibilities are materially identical to those of state retirees who qualify for its tax exemption. But, the State submits, Mr. Dawson's former job responsibilities are *also* similar to those of other state law enforcement retirees who *don't* qualify for its tax exemption. And, the State insists, the fact that it treats federal retirees no worse than (some) similarly situated state employees should be enough to save its statute.

But this again mistakes the nature of our inquiry. Under §111, the relevant question isn't whether federal retirees are similarly situated to state retirees who *don't* receive a tax benefit; the relevant question is whether they are similarly situated to those who *do.* So, for example, in *Phillips* we compared the class of federal lessees with the *favored* class of state lessees, even though the State urged us to focus instead on the disfavored class of private lessees. In *Davis,* we likewise rejected the State's effort to compare the class of federal retirees with state residents who did not benefit from the tax exemption rather than those who did.

At this point the State is left to play its final card. Now, it says, maybe the real distinction its statute draws isn't based on former job duties at all. Maybe its statute actually favors certain state law enforcement retirees only because their pensions are less generous than those of their federal law enforcement counterparts. At the least, the State suggests, we should remand the case to the West Virginia courts to explore this possibility.

The problem here is fundamental. While the State was free to draw whatever classifications it wished, the statute it enacted does not classify persons or groups based on the relative generosity of their pension benefits. Instead, it extends a special tax benefit to retirees who served as West Virginia police officers, firefighters, or deputy sheriffs—and it categorically denies that same benefit to retirees who served in similar federal law enforcement positions. Even if Mr. Dawson's pension turned out to be *identical* to a state law enforcement officer's pension, the law as written would deny him a tax exemption. West Virginia's law thus discriminates "because of the source of . . . compensation or pay" in violation of §111. Whether the unlawful classification found in the text of a statute might serve as some sort of proxy for a lawful classification hidden behind it is neither here nor there. No more than a beneficent legislative intent, an implicit but lawful distinction cannot save an express and unlawful one. . . .

* * *

Notes on *Dawson v. Steager*

1. ***Distinguishing the two strands of the doctrine***: Unlike Maryland in *McCulloch*, West Virginia had not attempted to impose a tax directly on the federal government or one of its instrumentalities. Thus, West Virginia's tax did not implicate the first strand of the federal immunity doctrine. Rather, the tax implicated the second prong, which forbids state regulations or taxes that discriminate against the federal government. Congress has codified this command (as it concerns state personal income taxes) in 4 U.S.C. §111, which states that the "United States consents to the taxation of pay or compensation for personal service as an officer or employee of the United States . . . by a duly constituted taxing authority having jurisdiction, if the taxation does not discriminate against the officer or employee because of the source of the pay or compensation." Thus, the questions whether West Virginia's tax violated §111 and whether it violated the federal immunity doctrine were one and the same.

2. ***The irrelevance of the law's purpose or the magnitude of the discrimination***: Notice that it did not matter whether West Virginia intended to discriminate against the federal government. As Justice Gorsuch wrote for the Court, "[u]nder §111 what matters isn't the intent lurking behind the law but whether the letter of the law treats those who deal with the federal government as well as it treats those with whom [the State] deals itself." The relevant question is whether the state tax discriminates against federal employees in practical effect. Likewise, notice that the degree to which West Virginia's tax favored the retired state law enforcement officers relative to their federal counterparts was beside the point. The federal immunity doctrine (and thus §111) proscribes *all* discrimination against the United States, no matter how trivial: "Section 111 disallows *any* state tax that discriminates against a federal officer or employee—not just those that seem to us especially cumbersome."

3. ***Discerning discrimination against federal employees in a state tax statute***: In determining whether a state or local tax impermissibly discriminates against federal employees, the first step is to identify the class of taxpayers who are favored by the tax. As the Court explains, "if the State defines the favored class by reference to job responsibilities, a similarly situated federal worker will be one who performs comparable duties. But if the State defines the class by reference to some other criteria, our attention should naturally turn there." The West Virginia tax at issue in *Dawson* "single[d] out for preferential treatment retirement plans associated with West Virginia police, firefighters, and deputy sheriffs," so what mattered was the nature of the jobs these state employees held. As a result, to be constitutional, the tax needed to treat the pension benefits of federal government employees who had held similar jobs no less favorably. But the trial court had found, as a factual matter, that there were "no 'significant differences'" between Mr. Dawson's former job responsibilities as a U.S. Marshal and those of the state law enforcement retirees who qualify for the tax exemption." Given how West Virginia had defined

the favored class, the tax thus "treated similarly situated persons differently because of the source of their compensation."

4. *Other disfavored state employees*: Notice, too, that it does not matter whether the disfavored federal employees are *also* similarly situated to other state employees who do not receive the favorable state tax treatment. In *Dawson*, for example—in addition to performing responsibilities nearly identical to those in the favored group of state police, firefighters, and deputy sheriffs—the job of a U.S. Marshal was nearly identical to other West Virginia law enforcement employees who did *not* receive the tax exemption. But that was immaterial. As Justice Gorsuch noted, "the relevant question isn't whether federal retirees are similarly situated to state retirees who *don't* receive a tax benefit; the relevant question is whether they are similarly situated to those who *do*." Thus, if the federal employees are similarly situated to the state employees who are treated more favorably by the state tax or regulation, the state has violated the tax immunity doctrine—even if there are *other* state employees, similarly situated to the federal employees, who also are disfavored by the challenged provision.

5. *The singling out of private contractors performing work for the federal government*: In 2018, Washington enacted a workers' compensation law that applied only to certain workers at a federal facility in the State who were "engaged in the performance of work, either directly or indirectly, for the United States." Wash. Rev. Code §51.32.187(1)(b). The law did not apply to federal government employees, but it did apply to private contractors performing work for the federal government. In *United States v. Washington,* No. 21–404 (June 21, 2022), the Supreme Court invalidated the statute:

> "[A] state law discriminates against the Federal Government or its contractors if it singles them out for less favorable treatment, or if it regulates them unfavorably on some basis related to their governmental status. Washington's law violates these principles by singling out the Federal Government for unfavorable treatment. On its face, the law applies only to a 'person, including a contractor or subcontractor, who was engaged in the performance of work, either directly or indirectly, for the United States.' §51.32.187(1)(b). The law thereby explicitly treats federal workers differently than state or private workers. And, in doing so, the law imposes upon the Federal Government costs that state or private entities do not bear. The law consequently violates the Supremacy Clause." Slip op. at 5–6 (internal quotations, citations, and alterations omitted).

C.   Preemption

1. The constitutional foundations of preemption

The basic principle that a valid federal law displaces conflicting state law—in the sense that a court, when forced to choose, must apply the federal law rather than the state law—has been a part of our constitutional fabric since the Republic came into being. This axiom derives directly from the text of the Supremacy Clause, found in Article VI, clause 2:

> "The Constitution, and the Laws of the United States which shall be made in Pursuance there of; and all Treaties made, or which shall be made, under the Authority of the United States, shall be the supreme Law of the Land; and the Judges in every State shall be bound thereby, any Thing in the Constitution or Laws of any State to the Contrary notwithstanding."

We encountered the Supremacy Clause in prior chapters. For instance, it is arguably involved whenever the question presented is whether a state law violates the federal Constitution: The Constitution supersedes conflicting state laws—and the federal judiciary has the authority to so hold, as the Court held long ago in *Fletcher v. Peck*. But the term "preemption" typically refers to when a state law conflicts with a sub-constitutional federal law—a federal statute or administrative regulation (which is just a more detailed elaboration of the meaning of a federal statute).

Preemption is essentially a conflicts-of-law rule. When federal and state law conflict in a given case, the court must apply the federal law (assuming, of course, the federal law is valid). As we have seen, Congress's legislative authority is limited; any statute it enacts must be within its enumerated powers. But so long as Congress acts pursuant to those powers, it can completely displace state law addressing the same subject. A preempting federal statute effectively tells the states, "You are prohibited from enacting or enforcing any state law that does X, Y, or Z."

This is why federal statutes commanding states *not* to regulate in a particular manner are not impermissible commandeerings. For if the anti-commandeering principle extended to these sorts of commands, it would swallow the doctrine of preemption. Like impermissible commandeerings, federal statutes preempting state law operate exclusively on the states and their political subdivisions, and they regulate state and local governments in their sovereign capacities. But the Supreme Court's anti-commandeering decisions, such as *New York v. United States* and *Printz v. United States*, have not cast any doubt on the doctrine of preemption. (Indeed, in *New York* itself the Court upheld another provision of the challenged federal statute as a valid preemption of state law.) Nor could they, as the central idea of federal preemption is dictated by the text of the Supremacy Clause. The critical distinction—between preemption on the one hand, and unconstitutional commandeering on the other—is that a commandeering requires states to act *affirmatively*, to take action with the machinery of the state. The federal preemption of state law, by contrast, amounts to a prohibition; it is a command to the states not to act.

2. The different bases for preemption

In its opinions, the Supreme Court has described instances of preemption as falling into four different categories based on the nature of the alleged conflict between federal law and state law. But these categories have no independent legal significance. They are simply different ways of describing how Congress might express its intent to displace state law. All that matters in a preemption dispute—"the ultimate touchstone," in the Court's phrasing—is whether Congress's purpose was to displace the type of state law at issue. The map below defines the four different categories of preemption as they are commonly understood and how they relate to one another.

MAP OF THE FEDERAL PREEMPTION OF STATE LAW

EXPRESS PREEMPTION

In the text of the statute, Congress explicitly states its intent to displace state law

Example: §10 of the Federal Boat Safety Act
"Unless permitted by the Secretary under section 4305 of this title, a State or political subdivision of a State may not establish, continue in effect, or enforce a law or regulation establishing a recreational vessel or associated equipment performance or other safety standard or imposing a requirement for associated equipment . . . that is not identical to a regulation prescribed under 4302 of this title."
Question: Does the preemption clause in the statute dictate preemption of the state law at issue?

IMPLIED PREEMPTION

No express statement in the statute regarding preemption

IMPLIED CONFLICT

Federal and state law conflict with each other in some way

IMPLIED FIELD

Congress has enacted a regulatory scheme so comprehensive that it is clear that Congress intended to displace all state law in that field

IMPOSSIBILITY

It is impossible to comply with both federal and state law
Question: Is it actually impossible to comply with both federal and state law?

OBSTACLE or "FRUSTRATION OF PURPOSE"

It is possible to comply with both federal and state law, but state law stands as an obstacle to the accomplishments of the federal statute's objectives
Question: Do the structure and implicit purposes of the federal statute indicate Congress's intent to displace the state law at issue

To be clear, these categories are not mutually exclusive. For instance, a state law is displaced under field preemption when the federal statute has so occupied the relevant field that it is clear Congress's intent was to displace all state laws on the same subject. But a conclusion that a federal law displaces a state law based on field preemption necessarily also means that one of Congress's purposes in legislating in that field was to displace all state law on the subject. In this sense, when there is field preemption, there will also be obstacle (or "frustration of purpose") preemption, at least in this limited sense.

The larger point is that these categories of preemption have no independent legal significance. Instead, they are merely different ways of describing how Congress can express its purpose (in a statute) to displace state law. So if a state law is preempted, it does not matter *how* it is preempted. Whether by express preemption or implied field preemption or implied obstacle preemption, the practical result the same: the court will apply the federal law and ignore the state law.

3. The "touchstone" in every preemption case: Congress's purpose

The critical question in every preemption case—really the *only* question—is whether (or to what extent) Congress intended the federal law at issue to displace the particular state law being invoked. Preemption is considered an aspect of constitutional law because it derives from the Supremacy Clause; and the principle that federal law displaces conflicting state law is an essential postulate of our constitutional structure. But whether a particular federal law has preemptive force in any given circumstance depends entirely on the specific state and federal laws drawn into question.

Thus, every preemption case is really a question of statutory interpretation. Preemption disputes present two basic inquiries. First, what does the state or local law at issue actually do? One cannot discern whether Congress has intended to displace a given state law without first ascertaining what that state law requires. Second, in enacting the federal statute that arguably preempts that state law, what did Congress intend with respect to the operation of such state laws? More pointedly, did Congress intend for such state laws to *supplement* the federal statute, such that both could be given full force? Or did Congress intend for such state laws to be displaced—replaced by the requirements of the federal statute? These are not questions of *constitutional* interpretation. (The constitutional aspect of preemption is well settled.) Instead, these are questions concerning the best understandings of the state and federal laws at issue—namely, whether such understandings put them in conflict.

4. The presumption against preemption

Preemption cases, by their nature, are almost always just illustrations. Rarely do they involve overarching principles. One exception is the issue of how willing courts should be to conclude that the state law in question is preempted. Should federal courts generally be disposed in favor of finding federal preemption? Or should they instead be presumptively inclined to hold against preemption so as to protect the independent policymaking authority of the states? Given the modern breadth of Congress's enumerated powers, the federal government can regulate most human activities. Perhaps, then, it is important to protect states' policy choices, at least at the margin, by placing a thumb on the scale against federal preemption.

For many years, the Supreme Court has taken this view, at least in its pronouncements. The Court has often articulated a general presumption against preemption, at least with respect to activities historically regulated by the states. (In areas where there is no such history—such as immigration and naturalization, which have historically been regulated by the federal government more than the states—there is no such presumption.) The ultimate practical effect of this presumption, however, is unclear.

There are strong and weak presumptions in the interpretation of statutes, and the importance of the presumption depends on how clear one finds Congress's intent. A strong presumption against preemption would demand that Congress make its intent to preempt state law unmistakably clear, construing any ambiguity against preemption. But that is not how the Court has deployed this presumption. Rather, its impact has been weaker, applicable where Congress's intent cannot be gleaned after applying the traditional tools of statutory construction. Thus, it is unclear how much the presumption has mattered. Over the past 40 years, in its scores of preemption cases, the Supreme Court has ruled in favor of preemption more often than not.

5. An example of federal preemption: *PG&E*

A relatively straightforward illustration of how federal preemption operates is *PG&E v. State Energy Resources Conservation and Development Comm'n*, 461 U.S. 190 (1983). Congress has enacted several statutes regulating nuclear power plants and the production of nuclear energy in great detail. Those statutes—in addition to comprehensively regulating the safety of nuclear facilities—also have the general purpose of promoting nuclear energy. In 1976, the California adopted a law that conditioned the construction of new nuclear power plants on the State Energy Resources Conservation and Development Commission first concluding that adequate storage facilities and means of disposal were available for nuclear waste. Two large utilities—PG&E and Southern California Edison—challenged the California law claiming that it was preempted. As you read the opinion, please consider the following questions:

1. What were the alternative theories put forward by the utilities as to why California's law was preempted? On what did these theories depend?

2. Had Congress stated anything expressly in the relevant statutes about the preemption of state law? How did that factor into the Court's analysis?

3. Is this a case of *field* preemption? How would you describe the relevant "field"?

4. Of what relevance was California's purpose in enacting the 1976 amendments to the Warren-Alquist Act? Will the purpose of a state law always be relevant in determining whether it is preempted? Why was it relevant here?

5. Why did the California law not conflict with the federal statutes' regulation of the disposal of nuclear waste? How could the laws be reconciled?

6. Why didn't California's law frustrate the federal statutes' clear purpose of promoting the expansion of nuclear energy?

7. In light of the Court's holding that the 1976 amendments to the Warren-Alquist Act, what sorts of state laws *would* be preempted by Congress's statutes regulating the production of nuclear energy?

PG&E v. State Energy Resources Cons. & Dev. Comm'n
461 U.S. 190 (1983)

JUSTICE WHITE delivered the opinion of the Court.

The turning of swords into plowshares has symbolized the transformation of atomic power into a source of energy in American society. To facilitate this development the Federal Government relaxed its monopoly over fissionable materials and nuclear technology, and in its place, erected a complex scheme to promote the civilian development of nuclear energy, while seeking to safeguard the public and the environment from the unpredictable risks of a new technology. Early on, it was decided that the States would continue their traditional role in the regulation of electricity production. The interrelationship of federal and state authority in the nuclear energy field has not been simple; the federal regulatory structure has been frequently amended to optimize the partnership.

This case emerges from the intersection of the Federal Government's efforts to ensure that nuclear power is safe with the exercise of the historic state authority over the generation and sale of electricity. At issue is whether provisions in the 1976 amendments to California's Warren-Alquist Act, Cal. Pub. Res. Code Ann. §§25524.1(b) and 25524.2, which condition the construction of nuclear plants on findings by the State Energy Resources Conservation and Development Commission that adequate storage facilities and means of disposal are available for nuclear waste, are pre-empted by the Atomic Energy Act of 1954, 68 Stat. 919, as amended, 42 U. S. C. §2011 *et seq.*

I

A nuclear reactor must be periodically refueled and the "spent fuel" removed. This spent fuel is intensely radioactive and must be carefully stored. The general practice is to store the fuel in a water-filled pool at the reactor site. For many years, it was assumed that this fuel would be reprocessed; accordingly, the storage pools were designed as short-term holding facilities with limited storage capacities. As expectations for reprocessing remained unfulfilled, the spent fuel accumulated in the storage pools, creating the risk that nuclear reactors would have to be shut down. This could occur if there were insufficient room in the pool to store spent fuel and also if there were not enough space to hold the entire fuel core when certain inspections or emergencies required unloading of the reactor. In recent years, the problem has taken on special urgency. Some 8,000 metric tons of spent nuclear fuel have already accumulated, and it is projected that by the year 2000 there will be some 72,000 metric tons of spent fuel. Government studies indicate that a number of reactors could be forced to shut down in the near future due to the inability to store spent fuel.

There is a second dimension to the problem. Even with water pools adequate to store safely all the spent fuel produced during the working lifetime of the reactor, permanent disposal is needed because the wastes will remain radioactive for thousands of years. A number of long-term nuclear waste management strategies have been extensively examined. These range from sinking the wastes in stable deep seabeds, to placing the wastes beneath ice sheets in Greenland and Antarctica, to ejecting the wastes into space by rocket. The greatest attention has been focused on disposing of the wastes in subsurface geologic repositories such as salt deposits. Problems of how and where to store nuclear wastes has engendered considerable scientific, political, and public debate. There are both safety and economic aspects to the nuclear waste issue: first, if not properly stored, nuclear wastes might leak and endanger both the environment and human health; second, the lack of a long-term disposal option increases the risk that the insufficiency of interim storage space for spent fuel will lead to reactor shutdowns, rendering nuclear energy an unpredictable and uneconomical adventure.

The California laws at issue here are responses to these concerns. In 1974, California adopted the Warren-Alquist State Energy Resources Conservation and Development Act, Cal. Pub. Res. Code Ann. 25000-25986. The Act requires that a utility seeking to build in California any electric power generating plant, including a nuclear powerplant, must apply for certification to the State Energy Resources Conservation and Development Commission (Energy Commission). The Warren-Alquist Act was amended in 1976 to provide additional state regulation of new nuclear powerplant construction.

Two sections of these amendments are before us. Section 25524.1(b) provides that before additional nuclear plants may be built, the Energy Commission must determine on a case-by-case basis that there will be "adequate capacity" for storage of a plant's spent fuel rods "at the time such nuclear facility requires such . . . storage." The law also requires that each utility provide continuous, on-site, "full core reserve storage capacity" in order to permit storage of the entire reactor core if it must be removed to permit repairs of the reactor. In short, § 25524.1(b) addresses the interim storage of spent fuel.

Section 25524.2 deals with the long-term solution to nuclear wastes. This section imposes a moratorium on the certification of new nuclear plants until the Energy Commission "finds that there has been developed and that the United States through its authorized agency has approved and there exists a demonstrated technology or means for the disposal of high-level nuclear waste." "Disposal" is defined as a "method for the permanent and terminal disposition of high-level nuclear waste." §§25524.2(a), (c). Such a finding must be reported to the state legislature, which may nullify it.

In 1978, petitioners Pacific Gas & Electric Co. and Southern California Edison Co. filed this action in the United States District Court, requesting a declaration that numerous provisions of the Warren-Alquist Act, including the two sections challenged here, are invalid under the Supremacy Clause because they are pre-empted by the Atomic Energy Act. . . .

III

It is well established that within constitutional limits Congress may pre-empt state authority by so stating in express terms. Absent explicit pre-emptive language, Congress' intent to supersede state law altogether may be found from a " 'scheme of federal regulation . . . so pervasive as to make reasonable the inference that Congress left no room for the States to supplement it,' because 'the Act of Congress may touch a field in which the federal interest is so dominant that the federal system will be assumed to preclude enforcement of state laws on the same subject,' or because 'the object sought to be obtained by the federal law and the character of obligations imposed by it may reveal the same purpose.'" *Fidelity Federal Savings & Loan Assn. v, De la Cuesta*, 458 U.S. 141, 153 (1982) (quoting *Rice v. Santa Fe Elevator Corp.*, 331 U.S. 218, 230 (1947)). Even where Congress has not entirely displaced state regulation in a specific area, state law is pre-empted to the extent that it actually conflicts with federal law. Such a conflict arises when "compliance with both federal and state regulations is a physical impossibility," *Florida Lime & Avocado Growers, Inc. v. Paul*, 373 U.S. 132, 142–143 (1963), or where state law "stands as an obstacle to the accomplishment and execution of the full purposes and objectives of Congress." *Hines v. Davidowitz*, 312 U.S. 52, 67 (1941).

Petitioners, the United States, and supporting *amici,* present three major lines of argument as to why § 25524.2 is pre-empted. First, they submit that the statute—because it regulates construction of nuclear plants and because it is allegedly predicated on safety concerns—ignores the division between federal and state authority created by the Atomic Energy Act, and falls within the field that the Federal Government has preserved for its own exclusive control. Second, the statute, and the judgments that underlie it, conflict with decisions concerning the nuclear waste disposal issue made by Congress and the Nuclear Regulatory Commission. Third, the California statute frustrates the federal goal of developing nuclear technology as a source of energy. We consider each of these contentions in turn.

A

Even a brief perusal of the Atomic Energy Act reveals that, despite its comprehensiveness, it does not at any point expressly require the States to construct or authorize nuclear powerplants or prohibit the States from deciding, as an absolute or conditional matter, not to permit the construction of any further reactors. Instead, petitioners argue that the Act is intended to preserve the Federal Government as the sole regulator of all matters nuclear, and that § 25524.2 falls within the scope of this impliedly pre-empted field. But as we view the issue, Congress, in passing the 1954 Act and in subsequently amending it, intended that the Federal Government should regulate the radiological safety aspects involved in the construction and operation of a nuclear plant, but that the States retain their traditional responsibility in the field of regulating electrical utilities for determining questions of need, reliability, cost, and other related state concerns.

Need for new power facilities, their economic feasibility, and rates and services, are areas that have been characteristically governed by the States. Justice Brandeis once observed that the "franchise to operate a public utility . . . is a special privilege which . . . may be granted or withheld at the pleasure of the State." *Frost v. Corporation Comm'n*, 278 U.S. 515, 534 (1929) (dissenting opinion). "The nature of government regulation of private utilities is such that a utility may frequently be required by the state regulatory scheme to obtain approval for practices a business regulated in less detail would be free to institute without any approval from a regulatory body." *Jackson v. Metropolitan Edison Co.*, 419 U.S. 345, 357 (1974). With the exception of the broad authority of the Federal Power Commission, now the Federal Energy Regulatory Commission, over the need for and pricing of electrical power transmitted in interstate commerce, these economic aspects of electrical generation have been regulated for many years and in great detail by the States. As we noted in *Vermont Yankee Nuclear Power Corp. v. NRDC*, 435 U.S. 519, 550 (1978): "There is little doubt that under the Atomic Energy Act of 1954, state public utility commissions or similar bodies are empowered to make the initial decision regarding the need for power." Thus, "Congress legislated here in a field which the States have traditionally occupied. . . . So we start with the assumption that the historic police powers of the States were not to be superseded by the Federal Act unless that was the clear and manifest purpose of Congress." *Rice v. Santa Fe Elevator Corp., supra*, at 230.

The Atomic Energy Act must be read, however, against another background. . . . Until 1954, . . . the use, control, and ownership of nuclear technology remained a federal monopoly. The Atomic Energy Act of 1954, 42 U.S.C. §2011 *et seq.*, grew out of Congress' determination that the national interest would be best served if the Government encouraged the private sector to become involved in the development of atomic energy for peaceful purposes under a program of federal regulation and licensing. The Act implemented this policy decision by providing for licensing of private construction, ownership, and operation of commercial nuclear power reactors. The AEC, however, was given exclusive jurisdiction to license the transfer, delivery, receipt, acquisition, possession, and use of nuclear materials. Upon these subjects, no role was left for the States.

The Commission, however, was not given authority over the generation of electricity itself, or over the economic question whether a particular plant should be built. We observed in *Vermont Yankee* that "[t]he Commission's prime area of concern in the licensing context, . . . is national security, public health, and safety." The Nuclear Regulatory Commission (NRC), which now exercises the AEC's regulatory authority, does not purport to exercise its authority based on economic considerations, and has recently repealed its regulations concerning the financial qualifications and capabilities of a utility proposing to construct and operate a nuclear powerplant. In its notice of rule repeal, the NRC stated that utility financial qualifications are only of concern to the NRC if related to the public health and safety. It is almost inconceivable that Congress would have left a regulatory vacuum; the only reasonable inference is that Congress intended the States to continue to make these judgments. Any doubt that ratemaking and plant-need questions were to remain in state hands was removed by § 271, which provided:

> "Nothing in this chapter shall be construed to affect the authority or regulations of any Federal, State or local agency with respect to the generation, sale, or transmission of electric power produced through the use of nuclear facilities licensed by the Commission."

. . . [F]rom the passage of the Atomic Energy Act in 1954, through several revisions, and to the present day, Congress has preserved the dual regulation of nuclear-powered electricity generation: the Federal Government maintains complete control of the safety and "nuclear" aspects of energy generation; the States exercise their traditional authority over the need for additional generating capacity, the type of generating facilities to be licensed, land use, ratemaking, and the like.

The above is not particularly controversial. But deciding how §25524.2 is to be construed and classified is a more difficult proposition. At the outset, we emphasize that the statute does not seek to regulate the construction or operation of a nuclear powerplant. It would clearly be impermissible for California to attempt to do so, for such regulation, even if enacted out of nonsafety concerns, would nevertheless directly conflict with the NRC's exclusive authority over plant construction and operation. Respondents appear to concede as much. Respondents do broadly argue, however, that although safety regulation of nuclear plants by States is forbidden, a State may completely prohibit new construction until its safety concerns are satisfied by the Federal Government. We reject this line of reasoning. State safety regulation is not preempted only when it conflicts with federal law. Rather, the Federal

Government has occupied the entire field of nuclear safety concerns, except the limited powers expressly ceded to the States. When the Federal Government completely occupies a given field or an identifiable portion of it, as it has done here, the test of pre-emption is whether "the matter on which the State asserts the right to act is in any way regulated by the Federal Act." *Rice v. Santa Fe Elevator Corp.*, 331 U.S., at 236. A state moratorium on nuclear construction grounded in safety concerns falls squarely within the prohibited field. Moreover, a state judgment that nuclear power is not safe enough to be further developed would conflict directly with the countervailing judgment of the NRC that nuclear construction may proceed notwithstanding extant uncertainties as to waste disposal. A state prohibition on nuclear construction for safety reasons would also be in the teeth of the Atomic Energy Act's objective to insure that nuclear technology be safe enough for widespread development and use—and would be pre-empted for that reason.

That being the case, it is necessary to determine whether there is a nonsafety rationale for §25524.2. California has maintained, and the Court of Appeals agreed, that §25524.2 was aimed at economic problems, not radiation hazards. The California Assembly Committee on Resources, Land Use, and Energy, which proposed a package of bills including § 25524.2, reported that the waste disposal problem was "largely economic or the result of poor planning, *not* safety related." The Committee explained that the lack of a federally approved method of waste disposal created a "clog" in the nuclear fuel cycle. Storage space was limited while more nuclear wastes were continuously produced. Without a permanent means of disposal, the nuclear waste problem could become critical, leading to unpredictably high costs to contain the problem or, worse, shutdowns in reactors. "Waste disposal *safety*," the Reassessment Report notes, "is not directly addressed by the bills, which ask only that a method [of waste disposal] be chosen and accepted by the federal government."

The Court of Appeals adopted this reading of §25524.2. Relying on the Reassessment Report, the court concluded:

> "[S]ection 25524.2 is directed towards purposes other than protection against radiation hazards. While Proposition 15 would have required California to judge the safety of a proposed method of waste disposal, section 25524.2 leaves that judgment to the federal government. California is concerned not with the adequacy of the method, but rather with its existence." 659 F. 2d, at 925.

Our general practice is to place considerable confidence in the interpretations of state law reached by the federal courts of appeals. Petitioners and *amici* nevertheless attempt to upset this interpretation in a number of ways. First, they maintain that § 25524.2 evinces no concern with the economics of nuclear power. The statute states that the "development" and "existence" of a permanent disposal technology approved by federal authorities will lift the moratorium; the statute does not provide for considering the economic costs of the technology

411

selected. This view of the statute is overly myopic. Once a technology is selected and demonstrated, the utilities and the California Public Utilities Commission would be able to estimate costs; such cost estimates cannot be made until the Federal Government has settled upon the method of long-term waste disposal. Moreover, once a satisfactory disposal technology is found and demonstrated, fears of having to close down operating reactors should largely evaporate.

Second, it is suggested that California, if concerned with economics, would have banned California utilities from building plants outside the State. This objection carries little force. There is no indication that California utilities are contemplating such construction; the state legislature is not obligated to address purely hypothetical facets of a problem. . . .

Although these specific indicia of California's intent in enacting §25524.2 are subject to varying interpretation, there are two further reasons why we should not become embroiled in attempting to ascertain California's true motive. First, inquiry into legislative motive is often an unsatisfactory venture. *United States v. O'Brien*, 391 U.S. 367, 383 (1968). What motivates one legislator to vote for a statute is not necessarily what motivates scores of others to enact it. Second, it would be particularly pointless for us to engage in such inquiry here when it is clear that the States have been allowed to retain authority over the need for electrical generating facilities easily sufficient to permit a State so inclined to halt the construction of new nuclear plants by refusing on economic grounds to issue certificates of public convenience in individual proceedings. In these circumstances, it should be up to Congress to determine whether a State has misused the authority left in its hands.

Therefore, we accept California's avowed economic purpose as the rationale for enacting §25524.2. Accordingly, the statute lies outside the occupied field of nuclear safety regulation.

B

Petitioners' second major argument concerns federal regulation aimed at the nuclear waste disposal problem itself. It is contended that §25524.2 conflicts with federal regulation of nuclear waste disposal, with the NRC's decision that it is permissible to continue to license reactors, notwithstanding uncertainty surrounding the waste disposal problem, and with Congress' recent passage of legislation directed at that problem.

Pursuant to its authority under the Act, the AEC, and later the NRC, promulgated extensive and detailed regulations concerning the operation of nuclear facilities and the handling of nuclear materials. The following provisions are relevant to the spent fuel and waste disposal issues in this case. To receive an NRC operating license, one must submit a safety analysis report, which includes a "radioactive waste handling syste[m]." 10 CFR §50.34(b)(2)(i), (ii) (1982). The regulations specify general design criteria and control requirements for fuel storage and handling and radioactive waste to be stored at the reactor site. 10 CFR pt. 50, App. A, Criteria 60-64, p. 412 (1982). In addition, the NRC has promulgated detailed regulations governing storage and disposal away from the reactor. 10 CFR pt. 72 (1982). NRC has also promulgated procedural requirements covering license applications for disposal of high-level radioactive waste in geologic repositories. 10 CFR pt. 60 (1982).

Congress gave the Department of Energy the responsibility for "the establishment of temporary and permanent facilities for storage, management, and ultimate disposal of nuclear wastes." 42 U.S.C. §7133(a)(8)(C). No such permanent disposal facilities have yet been licensed, and the NRC and the Department of Energy continue to authorize the storage of spent fuel at reactor sites in pools of water. In 1977, the NRC was asked by the Natural Resources Defense Council to halt reactor licensing until it had determined that there was a method of permanent disposal for high-level waste. The NRC concluded that, given the progress toward the development of disposal facilities and the availability of interim storage, it could continue to license new reactors.

The NRC's imprimatur, however, indicates only that it is safe to proceed with such plants, not that it is economically wise to do so. Because the NRC order does not and could not compel a utility to develop a nuclear plant, compliance with both it and §25524.2 is possible. Moreover, because the NRC's regulations are aimed at insuring that plants are safe, not necessarily that they are economical, §25524.2 does not interfere with the objective of the federal regulation.

Nor has California sought through §25524.2 to impose its own standards on nuclear waste disposal. The statute accepts that it is the federal responsibility to develop and license such technology. As there is no attempt on California's part to enter this field, one which is occupied by the Federal Government, we do not find § 25524.2 pre-empted any more by the NRC's obligations in the waste disposal field than by its licensing power over the plants themselves. . . .

C

Finally, it is strongly contended that §25524.2 frustrates the Atomic Energy Act's purpose to develop the commercial use of nuclear power. It is well established that state law is pre-empted if it "stands as an obstacle to the accomplishment and execution of the full purposes and objectives of Congress." *Hines v. Davidowitz*, 312 U.S., at 67.

There is little doubt that a primary purpose of the Atomic Energy Act was, and continues to be, the promotion of nuclear power. The Act itself states that it is a program "to encourage widespread participation in the development and utilization of atomic energy for peaceful purposes to the maximum extent consistent with the common defense and security and with the health and safety of the public." 42 U.S.C. §2013(d). The House and Senate Reports confirmed that it was "a major policy goal of the United States" that the involvement of private industry would "speed the further development of the peaceful uses of atomic energy." The same purpose is manifest in the passage of the Price-Anderson Act, 42 U.S.C. §2210, which limits private liability from a nuclear accident. The Act was passed "[i]n order to protect the public and to encourage the development of the atomic energy industry." 42 U.S.C. §2012(i). . . .

[However,] the promotion of nuclear power is not to be accomplished "at all costs." The elaborate licensing and safety provisions and the continued preservation of state regulation in traditional areas belie that. Moreover, Congress has allowed the States to determine—as a matter of economics—whether a nuclear plant vis-a-vis a fossil fuel plant should be built. The decision of California to exercise that authority does not, in itself, constitute a basis for pre-emption. Therefore, while the argument of petitioners and the United States has considerable force, the legal reality remains that Congress has left sufficient authority in the States to allow the development of nuclear power to be slowed or even stopped for economic reasons. Given this statutory scheme, it is for Congress to rethink the division of regulatory authority in light of its possible exercise by the States to undercut a federal objective. The courts should not assume the role which our system assigns to Congress.

*   *   *

Notes on *PG&E v. State Energy Resources Cons. & Dev. Comm'n*

1. *Express preemption*: The first question in any preemption case is whether the relevant federal statute contains an express preemption clause. If, as the Supreme Court has stated on several occasions, "the purpose of Congress is the ultimate touchstone in every preemption case," then the federal statute's *express statement* about preemption is the most direct evidence of that purpose. An example is the following clause contained in the Employee Retirement Income Security Act of 1974 (ERISA), 29 U.S.C §1144(a): "[T]he provisions of this subchapter and subchapter III shall supersede any and all State laws insofar as they may now or hereafter relate to any employee benefit plan." Another example is §10 of the Federal Boat Safety Act:

> "Unless permitted by the Secretary under section 4305 of this title, a State or political subdivision of a State may not establish, continue in effect, or enforce a law or regulation establishing a recreational vessel or associated equipment performance or other safety standard or imposing a requirement for associated equipment . . . that is not identical to a regulation prescribed under section 4302 of this title."

Both clauses expressly dictate that a certain category of state laws are "superseded" or cannot be "established" or "enforced." Thus, express preemption analysis is relatively straightforward: we only need to determine whether the state law at issue falls within the scope of the clause's text.

Neither the Atomic Energy Act nor any other federal statute relevant in *PG&E* contained a preemption clause, so the utilities could not contend that the California law was *expressly* preempted. Instead, they posited arguments of implied preemption: (1) that federal law had occupied the relevant "field," leaving no room for supplementing state legislation, and (2) that California's law conflicted with (and frustrated the purposes of) the Atomic Energy Act and other federal statutes.

2. *The forms of state law subject to preemption*: At issue in *PG&E* were California's 1976 amendments to its the Warren-Alquist Act, a state statute. But preemption analysis does not turn on the form of state law being challenged; any type of state law will be preempted if it conflicts with valid federal law. This means state common-law rules of liability (imposed, for instance, as a matter of state tort law), state constitutional rules, and local or municipal ordinances (which, under the Supremacy Clause, are just another form of state law). Again, the text of Article VI mandates that federal law is supreme, "any Thing in the Constitution or Laws of any State to the Contrary notwithstanding."

3. *Field preemption*: So-called "field preemption" is a form of implied preemption by which Congress has indicated its purpose to displace all state law in a particular field. As the Court explained in *PG&E*,

> "Congress' intent to supersede state law altogether may be found from a scheme of federal regulation . . . so pervasive as to make reasonable the inference that Congress left no room for the States to supplement it, because the Act of Congress may touch a field in which the federal interest is so dominant that the federal system will be assumed to preclude enforcement of state laws on the same subject, or because the object sought to be obtained by the federal law and the character of obligations imposed by it may reveal the same purpose."

The relevant "field" can be narrow or broad, depending on how Congress has written the federal statute at issue. What matters is whether Congress has intended to leave any room in that field for state law to supplement the federal scheme.

In *PG&E*, the Court recognized that federal statutes preempted state law in a specific field: "the Federal Government maintains complete control of the safety and 'nuclear' aspects of energy generation." As a result, any state law seeking to regulate the *safety* of nuclear power plants was subject to field preemption. But the Court rejected the utilities' broader claim of field preemption regarding "all matters nuclear." Instead, the Court concluded that the Atomic Energy Act plainly evinced Congress's intent that states still be permitted to "exercise their traditional authority over the need for additional generating capacity, the type of generating facilities to be licensed, land use, rate-making, and the like." This meant state laws regulating the construction of new generation plants for *economic* (and not safety) reasons fell outside the field fully occupied by federal law. And because the Court ultimately accepted "California's avowed economic purpose as the rationale for enacting §25524.2," the statute fell "outside the occupied field of nuclear safety regulation."

4. *"Savings" clauses*: Just as a federal statute can contain an express preemption clause, it also can contain a so-called "savings" clause: a provision that expressly "saves" a certain category of state laws from federal preemption. For example, ERISA's savings clause provides (among other things) that "nothing in this subchapter shall be construed to exempt or relieve any person from any law of any State which regulates insurance, banking, or securities." 29 U.S.C. §1144(b)(2)(A). Likewise, the Federal Boat Safety Act states that "[c]ompliance with this chapter or standards, regulations, or orders prescribed under this chapter does not relieve a person from liability at common law or under State law." 46 U.S.C. §4311(g). Thus, whether a particular state law is preempted can often turn on whether Congress has expressly "saved" it through such statutory language.

5. *Preemption via non-regulation*: At a conceptual level, federal preemption concerns the authority of Congress—when validly acting within its enumerated powers—to dictate how a particular activity is to be regulated, and thus to forbid the enforcement of any conflicting state regulation. Preempting federal regulation typically comes in the form of affirmative federal rules. (For example, in *PG&E*, the Atomic Energy Act provided the exclusive rules concerning the safety of nuclear power generation.) But Congress can also decide that the preempting federal rule is one of *non*-regulation. That is, Congress can use its enumerated powers to determine that a given field of activity should be left entirely *un*regulated. For example, Congress might conclude that state laws regulating the price of milk have generally harmed consumer welfare, and thus enact a statute that forbids states from enacting or enforcing such regulations. The federal statute might not replace the state laws with any affirmative federal milk price regulation; it might just mandate a federal rule of *non*-regulation. As the Supreme Court explained in *Arkansas Elec. Cooperative Corp. v. Arkansas Public Serv. Comm'n*, 461 U.S. 375 (1983), "a federal decision to forgo regulation in a given area may imply an authoritative federal determination that the area is best left *un*regulated, and in that event would have as much pre-emptive force as a decision *to* regulate." *Id.* at 384. Leaving an area of activity entirely unregulated is simply another possible federal policy choice, and thus can have just as much preemptive force as any other policy choice embodied in a federal statute.

6. *Obstacle (or "frustration of purpose") preemption*: The most difficult form of preemption analysis involves discerning whether a particular state law "stands as an obstacle to the accomplishment and execution of the full purposes and objectives of Congress." *Hines v. Davidowitz*, 312 U.S. 52, 67 (1941). Such analysis is always detailed and intensely case-specific; it depends on precisely how the state law operates, as well as the exact language of the relevant federal statute.

The utilities made two obstacle preemption arguments in *PG&E*. First, the utilities contended that Congress had determined, as expressed in the federal statutory scheme, that the construction of nuclear power plants should move forward notwithstanding any state concerns about waste disposal. Specifically, the federal Nuclear Regulatory Commission—pursuant to its authority under the Atomic Energy Act—had resolved that it could continue to license new plants despite the waste issue. And Congress had recently enacted legislation regulating the safe disposal of nuclear waste. A state law that restricted the construction of new plants based on the waste issue, contended the utilities, frustrated this purpose of going forward with new plants independent of the waste question. The Court rejected this argument. As Justice White's opinion for the Court reasoned, the NRC's willingness to license new plants "indicates only that it is safe to proceed with such plants, not that it is economically wise to do so." Further, because the federal regulation of waste disposal was "aimed at insuring that plants are safe, not necessarily that they are economical," California's law—which sought to promote the state's economic concerns, not those concerning the safety of waste disposal—did "not interfere with the objective of the federal regulation."

Second, the utilities contended California's law stood as an obstacle to "the Atomic Energy Act's purpose to develop the commercial use of nuclear power." In the utilities' view, the AEA expressed Congress's essential purpose to promote nuclear power, and California's law—by blocking some plants that would otherwise be built—frustrated that objective. The Court rejected this argument, too. Justice White's opinion conceded that "a primary purpose of the Atomic Energy Act was, and continues to be, the promotion of nuclear power." But the AEA had not dictated that this objective was to be pursued "at all costs." Instead, Congress had deliberately "left sufficient authority in the States to allow the development of nuclear power to be slowed or even stopped for economic reasons." Given that Congress had "allowed the States to determine—as a matter of economics—whether a nuclear plant vis-a-vis a fossil fuel plant should be built," it was simply not the case that any state law standing as an obstacle to the construction of new nuclear power plants frustrated the purposes of the AEA.

7. *State laws leaving an activity or field unregulated*: Again, Congress's decision (by statute) to leave a particular activity or field unregulated can preempt state law regulating that same activity. But a state's decision to leave an activity unregulated (as a matter of state law) *cannot* be preempted. Only *affirmative* state laws—laws imposing legal obligations—are susceptible to federal preemption. When a state fails to regulate an activity, there is nothing for federal law to preempt. That is, the Supremacy Clause dictates that, when confronted with conflicting state and federal laws, courts must apply the federal law; but if there is no applicable state law, a court simply applies the federal law. Preemption simply is not relevant in such circumstances.

This can be confusing when a state law purports to render it "legal" to engage in certain activity, especially when the state enacts a law repealing a prior prohibition. Consider the scores of state laws repealing criminal prohibitions on the personal possession and use of marijuana. These laws have rendered it legal, as a matter of state law, to engage in that activity, though the possession and use of marijuana remains a federal crime under the Controlled Substances Act (as *Gonzales v. Raich* illustrated). But the Controlled Substances Act does not preempt these state repealing laws. Though state laws legalizing the possession and use of marijuana might in some sense "frustrate the purposes" of federal law—as they take away the *state* legal penalty for engaging in such conduct—they do not *conflict* with the CSA in the relevant sense. State law does not "conflict" with federal law when it fails to regulate activity as federal statutes do; for purposes of preemption, only state laws that *regulate* an activity can create an actual conflict. So a state's decision *not* to regulate an activity (as a matter of state law) cannot "stand as an obstacle to the accomplishment and execution of the full purposes and objectives of Congress" in a way that counts for purposes of preemption.

Another way to see this is by remembering what the anti-commandeering principle forbids. Recall that Congress cannot direct states to govern their residents in a particular way, according to Congress's instructions. If a state's decision *not* to regulate a particular activity could be preempted by a federal law regulating that same activity—on the ground that the state's failure to do so "frustrates the purposes" of federal law—the necessary implication would be that federal law *requires* states to enact laws regulating the activity as Congress sees fit. But that is precisely what the anti-commandeering principle forbids. For example, by enacting the Controlled Substances Act, Congress cannot command states to criminalize the same behavior as a matter of state law. And this is true whether the federal command comes in the form of a dictate to enact a new state statute, or instead a dictate forbidding states from repealing an existing one. Either way, Congress cannot command states to affirmatively govern their citizens in a particular way. Thus, a state's decision to leave a particular activity unregulated (as a matter of state law) cannot be preempted.

*   *   *

PROBLEMS ON PREEMPTION

1. A state law requires any lawn mower sold in the state to meet a specified minimum level of fuel efficiency. A new federal statute requires all power equipment sold in the United States, including lawn mowers, to be labeled with energy efficiency stickers to permit purchasers to make informed choices when buying such equipment. The statute contains no provision expressly referring to the preemption of state law. Assume no other federal statute or administrative regulation addresses the energy efficiency

of power equipment. Which of the following would be the state's best argument for the continuing validity of its law?

(a) Congress cannot preempt state laws requiring a specified minimum level of fuel efficiency for lawn mowers, because the use of such equipment is a wholly local event and thus beyond the authority vested in Congress by the Commerce Clause.

(b) The state law is unaffected by the federal statute, because Congress did not expressly prohibit state laws requiring power equipment to meet specified levels of fuel efficiency.

(c) The purpose of the state law is consistent with the purpose of the federal statute, enforcement of the state law would not interfere with the full execution of the federal statute, and there is no evidence that Congress intended to preclude the states from enacting supplemental laws on the subject.

(d) There is a very strong presumption that a specific state law on a subject normally within the state's legislative authority prevails over a more general federal statute, because the Constitution reserves to the states primary authority over matters affecting public health, welfare, and safety.

2. Suppose the federal Fair Labor Standards Act (FLSA) provides that, whenever a non-management employee works more than 40 hours in a seven-day week, the employer must pay the employee "overtime wages." The FLSA further defines "overtime wages" as "a minimum of 150 percent of the employee's normal hourly wage rate." The City of Los Angeles has recently enacted an ordinance dictating that the "overtime wage rate" for all "essential workers" employed in the city shall be "200 percent of the employee's normal hourly wage rate." An "essential worker" in Los Angeles was paid only 150 percent of her hourly wage rate for working overtime; she sued her employer, asserting a claim under the city ordinance. Could the employer successful contend, as a defense, that the Los Angeles ordinance is preempted by the FLSA? Why or why not?

3. The federal Age Discrimination in Employment Act (ADEA) makes it unlawful "to fail or refuse to hire or to discharge any individual or otherwise discriminate against any individual with respect to his compensation, terms, conditions, or privileges of employment, because of such individual's age." Suppose that, under the terms of the ADEA, such discrimination is only actionable if the employee subjected to the discrimination is "at least 40 years of age." Suppose further that Connecticut enacts a state law forbidding *all* age discrimination in employment, so long as the employee is at least 18 years old. If a 38-year-old employee sues her employer under the state law, could the employer successfully assert, as a defense, that Connecticut's law is preempted by the ADEA? Why or why not?

4. Suppose Congress enacts the following provision as part of a statutory scheme regulating interstate transportation: "No State or political subdivision of a State shall enact or enforce any law or regulation related to a price, route, or service of any motor carrier with respect to the transportation of property."

a. Does the federal statute regulate states in their *sovereign* capacities?

b. Does the federal statute *command* the states to govern in a particular way?

c. Does the federal statute violate the anti-commandeering principle? Why or why not?

5. The federal Partial Birth Abortion Act of 2003 (PBAA), *inter alia*, provides as follows: "Any physician who, in or affecting interstate or foreign commerce, knowingly performs a partial-birth abortion and thereby kills a human fetus shall be fined under this title or imprisoned not more than 2 years, or both." Other provisions of the PBAA define what constitutes a prohibited "partial-birth abortion." In November 2022, the voters of California approve a ballot initiative that amends the state constitution to provide as follows: "The right to terminate a pregnancy prior to the completion of the sixth month of pregnancy is a fundamental constitutional right. It shall be legal for any person to obtain—and any medical professional to perform—an abortion up until this moment in pregnancy, regardless of the method used. (This includes so-called 'partial-birth abortions.')" Does federal law preempt California's constitutional amendment? Does it matter that the California law at issue is a constitutional amendment rather than a state statute? If you were an attorney for the State of California, what federal constitutional arguments might you raise in defense of the California law?

* * *

REVIEW ESSAY QUESTION 3

Suppose Congress enacts a federal statute containing the following provisions:

§1: The Supreme Court shall have the power to prescribe general rules of practice and procedure and rules of evidence for cases filed in federal district courts.

§2: Such rules shall not abridge, enlarge or modify any substantive right. All laws in conflict with such rules shall be of no further force or effect after such rules have taken effect.

Pursuant to the statute, the Supreme Court promulgates a rule (governing all actions filed in federal district court) regarding service of process. Specifically, the rule states that it shall be a valid method of service of process to leave the court summons and a copy of the complaint at the defendant's dwelling or usual place of abode with a person of suitable age and discretion who resides there.

Plaintiff files a complaint asserting a state-law claim against an estate in federal district court seeking more than $75,000. The plaintiff and the estate are citizens of different states. Assume that the claim will be governed by State A estate law, and that State A law provides that, in any suit seeking recovery from an estate, the executor of the estate must be personally served with process; leaving process with someone other than the executor is insufficient.

Plaintiff follows the rule promulgated by the Supreme Court and serves process by leaving the summons and a copy of the complaint with the executor's spouse at the home where they reside together. The defendant (the executor of the estate) timely files a motion to dismiss for insufficient service of process.

A. What arguments could the executor plausibly assert as to why the rule promulgated by the Supreme Court is unconstitutional? Do you think those arguments are likely to succeed? Explain.

B. Assume *arguendo* that the rule promulgated by the Supreme Court is constitutional. Should the district court apply the federal rule or the state rule in deciding whether service of process was sufficient in this case? Explain.

* * *

SUGGESTED ANALYSIS

A. The Supreme Court's rule has been promulgated pursuant to a statute enacted by Congress. Thus, one plausible constitutional challenge to the rule would be that Congress lacks the authority to enact the statute. Further, this statute plainly *delegates* authority to the Supreme Court. So another plausible constitutional challenge is that the statute violates separation of powers principles by unconstitutionally delegating legislative power to the judicial branch.

Rule statement: Congress may only enact statutes that are within its enumerated powers—powers that are granted, either expressly or implicitly, by the Constitution. Article I, §8, clause 9 grants Congress the authority "[t]o constitute Tribunals inferior to the Supreme Court"—that is, to create lower federal courts. In addition, the Necessary and Proper Clause grants the Congress the power to "[t]o make all Laws which shall be necessary and proper for carrying into Execution for the foregoing powers," which includes the power to create lower federal courts. As interpreted in *McCulloch v. Maryland*, the Necessary and Proper Clause gives Congress the authority to enact laws not just "absolutely necessary" to carry out its other enumerated powers, but any laws that are "appropriate" or "conducive" to the effectuation of those powers.

Application: This statute appears to fall well within Congress's enumerated power to make those laws "necessary and proper" to the creation of lower federal courts. Article I, §8, clause 9 plainly grants Congress the authority to create federal district courts. Once created, those district courts (like all courts) need rules to govern practice and procedure regarding litigation that occurs within them. This statute merely creates such rules. To be sure, it does so indirectly, by delegating the authority to specify the content of those rules to the Supreme Court. But that fact goes to whether the *delegation* is permissible; it does not in any way undermine the idea that the activity regulated by this statute (practice and procedure in federal district courts) is within Congress's power to regulate.

No other enumerated power seems particularly promising as a source of authority for this statute. The activity being regulated—legal practice in federal district courts—would not appear to be "economic or commercial in nature," such that it could be justified under the Commerce Clause, though such an argument does not seem crazy. (Nor is it a regulation of a use of a channel of interstate commerce, an instrumentality of interstate commerce, or a person or thing in interstate commerce.) But all Congress needs is one enumerated power to justify the statute. And its power to constitute lower federal courts, combined with the Necessary and Proper Clause, seems to provide that justification.

Rule statement: Even if a federal statute is within the authority granted to Congress by the Constitution, it will still be unconstitutional if it violates the principles that govern the separation of national powers. One such principle is that Congress may not delegate its legislative authority to another branch, as the Constitution vests the legislative power in Congress alone. In practice, this means no law enacted by Congress can constitute an excessive delegation, in violation of the nondelegation doctrine. The nondelegation doctrine requires that, in delegating discretion in the implementation or execution of a federal law, Congress must establish an "intelligible principle" to guide the exercise of that discretion. Whether a given delegation meets this standard depends both on the amount of specificity in the standard guiding the discretion and the amount of authority at issue. The broader the authority conferred by the statute, the greater the specificity in the standard necessary to constitute an "intelligible principle." By the same token, the "intelligible principle" standard remains quite deferential. The Supreme Court has only invalidated two federal statutes in American history on the ground that they violated the nondelegation doctrine.

Application: This statute plainly delegates a fair degree of authority to the Supreme Court. It gives the Court the "power to prescribe general rules of practice and procedure and rules of evidence for cases filed in federal district courts." Further, it only limits this authority by requiring that "[s]uch rules shall not abridge, enlarge or modify any substantive right." Still, this would seem to be within the bounds of the nondelegation doctrine. First, the authority delegated only concerns the "rules of practice and procedure and rules of evidence for cases filed in federal district courts." Those are important, to be sure, but it is nothing like setting air quality standards for the entire United States, in the regulation of all emitters of pollutants, as the Clean Air Act does (and which survived a nondelegation challenge). Further, the statute would seem to cabin the Court's discretion in fairly meaningful ways: (1) the rules the Court prescribes must be rules of practice, procedure, or evidence, so their scope is not terribly broad; and (2) they cannot "abridge, enlarge or modify *any* substantive right" (emphasis added). These are not tight constraints, but they would appear to limit the Court's discretion more than many of the statutes that have been upheld against a nondelegation challenge. For these reasons, it seems that though a nondelegation challenge is plausible, this statute contains an "intelligible principle" to guide the Supreme Court's discretion, and thus is constitutional.

Rule statement: One might also challenge this delegation, not because it confers an excessive degree of discretion, but because it confers on the judicial branch a power that Article III does not permit. Article III only permits federal courts to decide "cases" or "controversies." This means that there must be actual adversarial parties to a live legal dispute that falls within the federal courts' subject matter jurisdiction. Further, the Supreme Court can only decide matters "originally"—brough to it in the first instance—that are part of its "original jurisdiction." The Constitution does not anywhere mention a "rule making" function for the federal courts generally, or the Supreme Court in particular.

Application: It is true that Article III does not seem to grant this sort of authority to the federal courts, or the Supreme Court in particular. But there are three important matters to note. First, the Supreme Court is not acting on its own under this statute, but instead pursuant to an express delegation from Congress. And that delegation, as discussed above, would seem to be within constitutional bounds. Second, it is undoubtedly unconstitutional for a federal court to decide a legal dispute that is not a "case" or "controversy" within the meaning of Article III. But what this statute asks the Supreme Court to resolve are not legal disputes, but the ground rules for litigation in the district courts. So the precedent limiting the federal courts' authority (regarding standing, or the Court's original jurisdiction, or even advisory opinions) are not perfectly analogous. Finally, and perhaps most important, if Congress were not to have enacted this statute, district courts would (by necessity) need to devise rules to run their courtrooms; they could not let litigation unfold as a rule-less affair. So all this statute really does is permit the Supreme Court to promulgate rules that make all of those rules—which would exist anyway, in one form or another—uniform throughout the federal courts. If federal courts will be making these rules regardless, then giving the Supreme Court this authority (which is really just the authority to make those rules consistent) would not seem to be a violation of Article III. As a result, the statute would not seem to violate separation of powers principles.

Another note: One might also argue that the Supreme Court's rule is unconstitutional because it goes beyond the delegation (or statutory authorization) granted by Congress. We might typically think of this as a statutory, rather than a constitutional, problem, because it concerns what the statute permits. But it also might be characterized as a constitutional challenge, because if the Court's rule flouts Congress's intent—or indeed disobeys Congress's command that no rule promulgated by the Court "abridge, enlarge or modify any substantive right"—then arguably the Court would be exercising legislative power that Congress had not, in fact, delegated. And this might be considered a separation of powers problem.

But as the Supreme Court held in *Hanna v. Plumer*, 380 U.S. 460 (1965), rules specifying something as "procedural" as the means for serving process do not "abridge, enlarge or modify any substantive right," and thus are within this statute's authorization. Still, it is a nice insight to spot this issue, and to note that it arguably has constitutional implications.

B. When one party asserts that a court should apply state law, while the other party contends that the issue is controlled by a valid federal law, the issue is one of preemption—more specifically, whether the federal law preempts the state law at issue.

Rule statement: The doctrine of preemption, grounded in the Supremacy Clause of Article VI, dictates that when federal and state law conflict, a court must apply the federal law. The touchstone in every preemption case is Congress's intent. More specifically, what did Congress intend when enacting the federal statute at issue with respect to the continued operation of state law? Did Congress intend for this sort of state law to continue in operation (so as to supplement or complement federal law)? Or did Congress intend for federal law to displace this sort of state law, rendering it inoperative (at least on the facts of the case at hand)? Congress might express this intent in several different ways. It might do so expressly, through an express preemption provision. Or it might do so impliedly—by occupying the relevant field, by making it impossible to comply with federal and state law simultaneously, or by having a clear purpose for the federal statute that would be frustrated by application of the state statute in these circumstances.

Application: The rule promulgated by the Supreme Court fairly clearly preempts the state law regarding service of process in suits against an estate. First, the federal statute contains an express preemption clause: "All laws in conflict with such rules shall be of no further force or effect after such rules have taken effect." If we conclude that the federal and state laws are in conflict, at least as applied in this case, the statute itself dictates that the state law would be preempted. Second, even without the express preemption clause, the federal rule (which is presumably valid, for the reasons discussed in Part A) would plainly be frustrated by the application of the state law in this instance. The federal rule provides that service of process is proper when the summons and complaint are delivered at the defendant's place of abode to person of suitable age and discretion who resides there. Thus, the *purpose* of the rule is that render this form of service of process *proper*. But the state law makes this form of service *improper*—it flatly undercuts the purpose of the rule. Further, this is an affirmative state rule, not merely a state decision *not* to regulate a given activity. Were it to apply, the state law would forbid the plaintiff from continuing with the lawsuit, at least until the service of process defect had been cured. (And if the statute of limitations had run on the relevant claim, it would forbid the plaintiff from pursuing the claim altogether.) Thus, through either express or implied preemption, this state law is preempted, such that the district court should apply the federal rule and deny the executor's motion to dismiss for insufficient service of process.

CHAPTER 17
THE DORMANT COMMERCE CLAUSE

A. Introduction

Another important structural constraint on the actions of state and local governments is the dormant Commerce Clause. The Commerce Clause provides that "[t]he Congress shall have Power . . . [t]o regulate Commerce . . . among the several States." As we saw in Chapter 9, this language grants Congress the authority to enact federal legislation regulating interstate commerce. But for at least 170 years, the Supreme Court has also understood the clause as containing a *negative* implication: absent express congressional authorization, states are prohibited from taking actions that discriminate against or unduly burden interstate commerce.

To be sure, there are exceptions to this general principle. But the core purpose of the dormant Commerce Clause is to prohibit states from engaging in *economic protectionism*: governmental actions intended to improve the competitive position of in-state economic interests vis-à-vis out-of-state economic interests merely because they are in-state. The animating idea is that protectionism—though perhaps beneficial to the state taking the protectionist action—harms the nation as a whole. Protectionism creates trade barriers that necessarily result in inefficiencies, increasing the costs of production or consumption for reasons unrelated to the underlying value of the relevant activity.

The ensuing sections explore the details of dormant Commerce Clause doctrine. Here is a quick summary of the main points:

* Assuming the challenged state or local law or action is subject to dormant Commerce Clause scrutiny, the first question is whether the law or action discriminates against interstate commerce. A law might discriminate on its face, by expressly drawing a distinction based on geographic origin. Or the law might be neutral on its face (with respect to geographic origin) but have a discriminatory purpose of favoring intrastate commerce—and sometimes the law's practical effects on interstate commerce can reveal this protectionist purpose. Regardless, the crucial first question is whether the law discriminates against interstate commerce.

* If a state or local law so discriminates, it is virtually *per se* unconstitutional. It will be constitutional only if it furthers a legitimate, non-protectionist state interest, and the state has no practicable, nondiscriminatory alternatives for pursuing that interest.

* Even if the state or local law does not discriminate against interstate commerce, one still has to ask whether the law places an "undue burden" on interstate commerce. This requires the application of an *ad hoc* balancing test, weighing the burden on interstate commerce against the law's purported local benefits. If the burden on interstate commerce is "clearly excessive," the law violates the dormant Commerce Clause. (This test is quite deferential.)

* The dormant Commerce Clause also *categorically* forbids states from enacting laws that regulate or tax commercial activity occurring entirely in another state. Such "extraterritorial" state legislation is unconstitutional *per se*.

* There are three circumstances in which the dormant Commerce Clause does not apply: (1) Congress—by actively invoking its power to regulate interstate commerce—can authorize the state action at issue; (2) a state or local law that discriminates in favor of itself (as an economic enterprise)—at least with respect to a traditional governmental function (like trash collection)—does not "discriminate against interstate commerce" in the relevant sense; and (3) state or local government actions as a "market participant"—as opposed to the imposer of a regulation or tax— are exempt from dormant Commerce Clause scrutiny.

A majority of litigated dormant Commerce Clause cases turn on whether the challenged state action discriminates against interstate commerce. This is because (1) very few discriminatory laws are *necessary* to the achievement of a non-protectionist purpose, and (2) the Supreme Court has not invalidated a state or local law on the ground that it imposed an "undue burden" on interstate commerce in more than 30 years.

B.   The Scope of the Dormant Commerce Clause

A threshold question is when, exactly, the dormant Commerce Clause applies. Some governmental actions, by their nature, are exempt from dormant Commerce Clause scrutiny.

1. Only a constraint for state and local governments

The dormant Commerce Clause only limits state and local governmental action. It is a negative inference drawn from the positive grant of authority to Congress to regulate interstate commerce. Early in U.S. history, many viewed Congress's authority to regulate interstate commerce as *exclusive*, such that states had no power to regulate or tax activities considered "interstate commerce." This cramped conception of the states' legislative authority has long since been abandoned (as it would leave the states' precious little legislative authority, given the modern breadth of "interstate commerce"). But the principle that the dormant Commerce Clause only restrains state and local governments remains. Indeed, the purpose of the doctrine is to protect the nation's collective interests from the parochial actions of the states. It operates on the states' inherent political incentive to pursue their own constituents' interests at the expense of the welfare of persons outside the state.

2. Coterminous in breadth with Congress's commerce power

The scope of the dormant Commerce Clause—in terms of the state and local government actions to which it applies—is identical to that of Congress's commerce power. If the activity is one Congress could regulate under its commerce power, then a state or local government's regulation of that activity is subject to the strictures of the dormant Commerce Clause. This question arose in *Philadelphia v. New Jersey*, 437 U.S. 617 (1978) (explored further below). New Jersey barred the importation of solid waste for disposal in the state, and it contended its law was not even subject to the dormant Commerce Clause because garbage is essentially valueless, such that its importation did not constitute "commerce." The Supreme Court easily rejected this view. As Congress plainly could have used its commerce power to enact a statute regulating the relevant activity—the transportation of solid waste across state borders for disposal in landfills—New Jersey's law was subject to the dormant Commerce Clause.

In practice, this question rarely arises. Most dormant Commerce Clause challenges involve state or local laws that tax or regulate activities that are economic or commercial in nature, such that they are subject to the clause's strictures.

3. Congressional authorization

Because the dormant Commerce Clause is a negative inference drawn from a grant of power to Congress, Congress can effectively "switch off" its constraints by expressly authorizing the state or local action at issue. The dormant Commerce Clause limits states when Congress's commerce power has remained *dormant* with respect to the states' authority to burden interstate commerce. When Congress actively uses its commerce power to authorize state or local governments to regulate or tax in ways that would otherwise violate the clause, the clause's constraints dissolve. In those instances, Congress has deployed its commerce power to create a federal statutory scheme within which such state or local burdens on interstate commerce are permissible.

A nice illustration is *Prudential Insurance v. Benjamin*, 328 U.S. 408 (1946). At issue was a South Carolina tax on insurance premiums that applied only to insurers incorporated outside South Carolina. The tax required Prudential, a New Jersey corporation, to pay a 3 percent exaction on all premiums it collected from South Carolina customers. By contrast, insurers incorporated in South Carolina were exempt from the tax. South Carolina's tax plainly discriminated against interstate commerce. Thus, if the dormant Commerce Clause applied, the tax was almost certainly unconstitutional.

But Congress had enacted the McCarran Act, which provided that states were entitled to regulate and tax insurance companies however they saw fit, including by discriminating against out-of-state insurers. In relevant part, the McCarran Act provided:

> "The Congress hereby declares that the continued regulation and taxation by the several States of the business of insurance is in the public interest, and that silence on the part of the Congress shall not be construed to impose any barrier to the regulation or taxation of such business by the several States."

Congress thus had used its commerce power to *approve* state discrimination against interstate commerce in this context. The McCarran Act's command that "silence on the part of the Congress shall not be construed to impose any barrier to the regulation or taxation of such business by the several States" was a clear statement by Congress that courts should not apply the dormant Commerce Clause to laws like South Carolina's. Of course, the McCarran Act (like all federal statutes) needed to fall within Congress's enumerated powers. But that was no difficulty: the Act regulated the sale of insurance, a plainly commercial activity.

C.   Discrimination Against Interstate Commerce

When evaluating a state or local law subject to the constraints of the dormant Commerce Clause, the first question is whether the law discriminates against interstate commerce. There are two ways a state or local law might so discriminate. First, the law might discriminate on its face by drawing, in its text, a geographic distinction, treating commerce that crosses state lines less favorably than commerce that stays within one state. Second, the state or local government might have enacted the law with a discriminatory purpose: a purpose of favoring in-state economic interests at the expense of out-of-state interests. (And this underlying purpose, at least in some circumstances, might be evident from the law's discriminatory effects.) Either way, what matters is whether the state or local government has discriminated against interstate commerce. If so, its action is presumptively unconstitutional and will only be upheld if it can withstand "the most rigorous scrutiny." Absent such discrimination, the applicable judicial review is quite deferential: the law will be invalid only if the burden it imposes on interstate commerce is "clearly excessive" relative to its purported benefits.

Given this doctrinal framework, much turns on whether the challenged law is deemed to discriminate against interstate commerce. The following sections explore the various aspects of this inquiry.

1. Blatant discrimination: *Philadelphia v. New Jersey*

An example of a state law that plainly discriminated against interstate commerce is New Jersey's ban on the importation of garbage invalidated by the Supreme Court in *Philadelphia v. New Jersey*. The discrimination was easy to spot because the disadvantageous treatment of commerce crossing state lines (relative to commerce occurring entirely within one state) was obvious on the face of the statute. The challenged New Jersey law expressly prohibited the importation of most solid or liquid waste collected or generated outside New Jersey. In this way, the statute drew a geographic distinction between waste generated in New Jersey and elsewhere. The City of Philadelphia, which lies just across the Delaware River from New Jersey—and which shipped much of its garbage into New Jersey to be deposited in privately operated landfills— claimed that New Jersey's law violated the dormant Commerce Clause. As you read the Court's opinion, please consider the following questions:

1. What were New Jersey's asserted governmental interests in enacting chapter 363? Were those interests legitimate for purposes of the dormant Commerce Clause?

2. Did New Jersey have other, nondiscriminatory means of pursuing these interests? If so, what were they?

3. More generally, what is revealed by the existence of (unenacted) alternative, nondiscriminatory means for the state to pursue the same objectives? What does their existence suggest?

4. Under the test articulated by the Court, could a state law discriminating against interstate commerce *ever* be consistent with the dormant Commerce Clause? Why or why not?

Philadelphia v. New Jersey
437 U.S. 617 (1978)

MR. JUSTICE STEWART delivered the opinion of the Court.

A New Jersey law prohibits the importation of most "solid or liquid waste which originated or was collected outside the territorial limits of the State." In this case we are required to decide whether this statutory prohibition violates the Commerce Clause of the United States Constitution.

I

The statutory provision in question [ch. 363] . . . provides:

> "No person shall bring into this State any solid or liquid waste which originated or was collected outside the territorial limits of the State, except garbage to be fed to swine in the State of New Jersey, until the commissioner [of the State Department of Environmental Protection] shall determine that such action can be permitted without endangering the public health, safety and welfare and has promulgated regulations permitting and regulating the treatment and disposal of such waste in this State."

Apart from [some] narrow exceptions, New Jersey closed its borders to all waste from other States.

Immediately affected by these developments were the operators of private landfills in New Jersey, and several cities in other States that had agreements with these operators for waste disposal. They brought suit against New Jersey and its Department of Environmental Protection in state court, attacking the statute and regulations . . . .

III

A

Although the Constitution gives Congress the power to regulate commerce among the States, many subjects of potential federal regulation under that power inevitably escape congressional attention "because of their local character and their number and diversity." *South Carolina State Highway Dept. v. Barnwell Bros., Inc.,* 303 U.S. 177, 185. In the absence of federal legislation, these subjects are open to control by the States so long as they act within the restraints imposed by the Commerce Clause itself. The bounds of these restraints appear nowhere in the words of the Commerce Clause, but have emerged gradually in the decisions of this Court giving effect to its basic purpose. That broad purpose was well expressed by Mr. Justice Jackson:

> "This principle that our economic unit is the Nation, which alone has the gamut of powers necessary to control of the economy, including the vital power of erecting customs barriers against foreign competition, has as its corollary that the states are not separable economic units. As the Court said in *Baldwin* v. *Seelig,* 294 U. S. [511], 527, 'what is ultimate is the principle that one state in its dealings with another may not place itself in a position of economic isolation.'"

The opinions of the Court through the years have reflected an alertness to the evils of "economic isolation" and protectionism, while at the same time recognizing that incidental burdens on interstate commerce may be unavoidable when a State legislates to safeguard the health and safety of its people. Thus, where simple economic protectionism is effected by state legislation, a virtually *per se* rule of invalidity has been erected. The clearest example of such legislation is a law that overtly blocks the flow of interstate commerce at a State's borders. But where other legislative objectives are credibly advanced and there is no patent discrimination against interstate trade, the Court has adopted a much more flexible approach, the general contours of which were outlined in *Pike v. Bruce Church, Inc.,* 397 U.S. 137, 142:

> "Where the statute regulates evenhandedly to effectuate a legitimate local public interest, and its effects on interstate commerce are only incidental, it will be upheld unless the burden imposed on such commerce is clearly excessive in relation to the putative local benefits. . . . If a legitimate local purpose is found, then the question becomes one of degree. And the extent of the burden that will be tolerated will of course depend on the nature of the local interest involved, and on whether it could be promoted as well with a lesser impact on interstate activities."

The crucial inquiry, therefore, must be directed to determining whether ch. 363 is basically a protectionist measure, or whether it can fairly be viewed as a law directed to legitimate local concerns, with effects upon interstate commerce that are only incidental.

The purpose of ch. 363 is set out in the statute itself as follows:

> "The Legislature finds and determines that . . . the volume of solid and liquid waste continues to rapidly increase, that the treatment and disposal of these wastes continues to pose an even greater threat to the quality of the environment of New Jersey, that the available and appropriate land fill sites within the State are being diminished, that the environment continues to be threatened by the treatment and disposal of waste which originated or was collected outside the State, and that the public health, safety and welfare require that the treatment and disposal within this State of all wastes generated outside of the State be prohibited."

The New Jersey Supreme Court accepted this statement of the state legislature's purpose. The state court additionally found that New Jersey's existing landfill sites will be exhausted within a few years; that to go on using these sites or to develop new ones will take a heavy environmental toll, both from pollution and from loss of scarce open lands; that new techniques to divert waste from landfills to other methods of disposal and resource recovery processes are under development, but that these changes will require time; and finally, that "the extension of the lifespan of existing landfills, resulting from the exclusion of out-of-state waste, may be of crucial importance in preventing further virgin wetlands or other undeveloped lands from being devoted to landfill purposes." Based on these findings, the court concluded that ch. 363 was designed to protect, not the State's economy, but its environment, and that its substantial benefits outweigh its "slight" burden on interstate commerce. . . .

[Any] dispute about ultimate legislative purpose need not be resolved, because its resolution would not be relevant to the constitutional issue to be decided in this case. Contrary to the evident assumption of the state court and the parties, the evil of protectionism can reside in legislative means as well as legislative ends. Thus, it does not matter whether the ultimate aim of ch. 363 is to reduce the waste disposal costs of New Jersey residents or to save remaining open lands from pollution, for we assume New Jersey has every right to protect its residents' pocketbooks as well as their environment. And it may be assumed as well that New Jersey may pursue those ends by slowing the flow of *all* waste into the State's remaining landfills, even though interstate commerce may incidentally be affected. But whatever New Jersey's ultimate purpose, it may not be accomplished by discriminating against articles of commerce coming from outside the State unless there is some reason, apart from their origin, to treat them differently. Both on its face and in its plain effect, ch. 363 violates this principle of nondiscrimination.

The Court has consistently found parochial legislation of this kind to be constitutionally invalid, whether the ultimate aim of the legislation was to assure a steady supply of milk by erecting barriers to allegedly ruinous outside competition, or to create jobs by keeping industry within the State, or to preserve the State's financial resources from depletion by fencing out indigent immigrants. In each of these cases, a presumably legitimate goal was sought to be achieved by the illegitimate means of isolating the State from the national economy.

Also relevant here are the Court's decisions holding that a State may not accord its own inhabitants a preferred right of access over consumers in other States to natural resources located within its borders. These cases stand for the basic principle that a "State is without power to prevent privately owned articles of trade from being shipped and sold in interstate commerce on the ground that they are required to satisfy local demands or because they are needed by the people of the State." *Foster-Fountain Packing Co. v. Haydel, supra,* at 10.

The New Jersey law at issue in this case falls squarely within the area that the Commerce Clause puts off limits to state regulation. On its face, it imposes on out-of-state commercial interests the full burden of conserving the State's remaining landfill space. It is true that in our previous cases the scarce natural resource was itself the article of commerce, whereas here the scarce resource and the article of commerce are distinct. But that difference is without consequence. In both instances, the State has overtly moved to slow or freeze the flow of commerce for protectionist reasons. It does not matter that the State has shut the article of commerce inside the State in one case and outside the State in the other. What is crucial is the attempt by one State to isolate itself from a problem common to many by erecting a barrier against the movement of interstate trade. . . .

The New Jersey statute is not [a permissible] quarantine law. There has been no claim here that the very movement of waste into or through New Jersey endangers health, or that waste must be disposed of as soon and as close to its point of generation as possible. The harms caused by waste are said to arise after its disposal in landfill sites, and at that point, as New Jersey concedes, there is no basis to distinguish out-of-state waste from domestic waste. If one is inherently harmful, so is the other. Yet New Jersey has banned the former while leaving its landfill sites open to the latter. The New Jersey law blocks the importation of waste in an obvious effort to saddle those outside the State with the entire burden of slowing the flow of refuse into New Jersey's remaining landfill sites. That legislative effort is clearly impermissible under the Commerce Clause of the Constitution.

Today, cities in Pennsylvania and New York find it expedient or necessary to send their waste into New Jersey for disposal, and New Jersey claims the right to close its borders to such traffic. Tomorrow, cities in New Jersey may find it expedient or necessary to send their waste into Pennsylvania or New York for disposal, and those States might then claim the right to close their borders. The Commerce Clause will protect New Jersey in the future, just as it protects her neighbors now, from efforts by one State to isolate itself in the stream of interstate commerce from a problem shared by all.

* * *

Notes on *Philadelphia v. New Jersey*

1. ***A "virtually per se" rule against laws that discriminate against interstate commerce***: New Jersey's professed purposes for enacting chapter 363 were (1) to prevent environmental harm, (2) to preserve the disappearing space in the state's landfills, and (3) to preserve the state's aesthetics. These were plainly legitimate, non-protectionist interests. Nonetheless, the Court concluded that the statute violated the Commerce Clause because it treated *interstate* commerce—the traffic of waste from one state to another—less favorably than *intrastate* commerce—the traffic of waste entirely within New Jersey. (One could also think of the law this way: it permitted New Jersey landfill operators to do business with customers seeking to dump waste generated in New Jersey but forbid them from doing business with customers seeking to dump waste generated outside the state.) New Jersey's law discriminated against interstate commerce, and state laws discriminating against interstate commerce are virtually *per se* unconstitutional.

2. ***The applicable test for discriminatory state or local actions***: "Virtually *per se* unconstitutional" does not mean *always* unconstitutional. But such laws face a very stiff test. To be constitutional, such a law must survive "the most rigorous scrutiny": (1) it must further a legitimate, non-protectionist governmental objective; and (2) it must be narrowly tailored to achieving this non-protectionist objective—that is, the state must lack any practicable, non-discriminatory alternatives for achieving that interest. New Jersey's articulated purposes were legitimate and unrelated to economic protectionism: to preserve its environment, the health of its citizens, and the state's aesthetics. But New Jersey had alternative, nondiscriminatory ways to pursue these objectives. Out-of-state garbage is biologically and aesthetically indistinguishable from garbage generated within New Jersey. Thus, New Jersey could have simply limited the amount of garbage that could be dumped in landfills in the state, regardless of where it was generated. Or it could have imposed a tax on the disposal of solid waste in the state, setting the rate at a level that would have achieved the desired reduction. Regardless, it clearly wasn't *necessary* for New Jersey to discriminate against interstate commerce to achieve its professed goal of reducing the amount of waste dumped in the state's landfills.

3. ***Why require the state to demonstrate the lack of practicable, non-discriminatory alternatives?***: It is instructive to consider what justifies the applicable doctrinal test. Why ask whether the state has any practicable, non-discriminatory alternatives for pursuing its legitimate objectives? First, the answer might illuminate ways that the state could achieve the same goals without disadvantaging interstate commerce. Second (and relatedly), the existence of such alternatives suggests the state's professed purposes may be insincere, or at least incomplete. It reveals that, among the possibilities, the state *chose* a discriminatory one—perhaps precisely because one of its (unstated) goals was to benefit in-state interests, to the detriment of out-of-state interests.

4. *Another example of facial discrimination*: At issue in *Hughes v. Oklahoma*, 441 U.S. 322 (1979), was a state law that forbade the transport outside the state of minnows captured in Oklahoma if done to sell them in another state. Oklahoma's asserted interest was ecological: to preserve the state's dwindling minnow population. This was clearly a legitimate, non-protectionist goal. But Oklahoma's law facially discriminated against interstate commerce: the transport of Oklahoma minnows for sale within Oklahoma was legal, but their transport for sale outside the state was proscribed. Moreover, Oklahoma's discrimination was hardly necessary to achieve its stated objective. Had Oklahoma been truly (or exclusively) interested in protecting its minnow population, there was no reason only to limit the fishing of persons who intended to sell the minnows outside the state; Oklahoma could have reduced minnow fishing in a geographically neutral way. For instance, it could have placed limits on *all* persons procuring minnows in the state, regardless of where they planned to sell them. Given the existence of such practicable, nondiscriminatory alternatives, the law violated the Commerce Clause.

5. *City (as opposed to state) discrimination against interstate commerce*: At issue in *Dean Milk Co. v. City of Madison*, 340 U.S. 349 (1951), was an ordinance enacted by the City of Madison, Wisconsin, which made it unlawful to sell any pasteurized milk within Madison's city limits unless the milk had been processed and bottled at an approved pasteurization plant within a radius of five miles from the city center. Dean Milk was an Illinois company that sought to sell milk in Madison, but its two pasteurization plants were located in northern Illinois, more than 60 miles away. The ordinance facially discriminated on the basis of geographic origin; it drew a line five miles around Madison and forbid the sale of any milk pasteurized beyond that line. But unlike the laws at issue in *Philadelphia v. New Jersey* and *Hughes v. Oklahoma*, Madison's law harmed both in-state and out-of-state interests: the ordinance favored *Madison* milk producers to the detriment of all other producers (both inside and outside Wisconsin).

The Supreme Court concluded that the ordinance—despite harming some in-state producers—discriminated against interstate commerce; those advantaged by the ordinance were exclusively Wisconsin producers, and all out-of-state producers were disadvantaged. And because the ordinance was discriminatory, it could only withstand Commerce Clause scrutiny if Madison had a legitimate, non-protectionist interest supporting it, and no practicable nondiscriminatory means of accomplishing that interest. Madison defended its law on the ground it protected the health and safety of its residents: while the city could inspect and ensure quality control in pasteurization plants within five miles of the city center, it argued it could not afford to do so for plants beyond that radius. But the city clearly could have pursued that interest through nondiscriminatory means. First, it could have charged those companies bringing milk into Madison the cost incurred by the city in sending Madison officials to conduct inspections of their pasteurization facilities. Second, it could have banned milk pasteurized in plants not conforming to health standards as rigorous as Madison's and verify the reliability of inspections by public health officials in other jurisdictions. Either of these alternatives would have assured the same level of health and safety for the milk, but without closing the Madison market to out-of-state producers.

Given these practicable alternatives for ensuring the safety of milk sold in the city, we might be suspicious about Madison's *true* reasons for enacting the ordinance. It seems likely that least one of the city's (unstated) goals was to protect local milk producers from out-of-area competition. This is precisely the sort of economic protectionism the dormant Commerce Clause forbids.

6. Discrimination against interstate commerce that is nonetheless constitutional: Another small fish case, *Maine v. Taylor*, 477 U.S. 131 (1986), involved live baitfish—specifically, "golden shiners." Maine enacted a law prohibiting the importation of live baitfish into the state, and Taylor was caught trying to import 158,000 live golden shiners into the state. As in *Hughes*, the state's asserted justification was ecological. Testimony presented at trial indicated that imported live baitfish posed two significant threats to Maine's fisheries. First, three types of parasites common in out-of-state baitfish would have placed at risk Maine's native wild fish population. Second, nonnative species inadvertently included in shipments of live baitfish had the potential to harm the state's aquatic ecology by competing for food or habitat, preying on native species, or disrupting the environment in other ways. The Court upheld Maine's law because—though it plainly discriminated against interstate commerce—Maine had no practicable, nondiscriminatory means to prevent these harms. According to expert testimony, the size of the baitfish and the quantities of the shipments made inspection for commingled species impossible. And an examination for parasites would require killing the fish themselves, making it an impractical alternative. *Maine v. Taylor* is thus the truly exceptional case, the sole modern Supreme Court decision to uphold a state law discriminating against interstate commerce on the ground that the law was narrowly tailored to achieve a non-protectionist state interest.

*   *   *

2. Discriminatory purpose

Again—assuming the dormant Commerce Clause applies—the threshold question is whether the challenged law discriminates against interstate commerce. In *Philadelphia v. New Jersey*, *Hughes v. Oklahoma*, *Dean Milk*, and

Maine v. Taylor, that question was straightforward: the challenged laws drew explicit geographic distinctions, textually discriminating against activity that crossed state lines. Sometimes the discrimination is more subtle: the law contains no geographic distinction on its face, but it was enacted with a protectionist *purpose*. Here, the trick lies in discerning when such latent discrimination is afoot, a question that always depends on the particular facts and circumstances of the case. The relevant question is whether the law's purpose is to advantage in-state economic interests vis-à-vis out-of-state interests (even if it also has other, non-protectionist purposes).

The Supreme Court's decision in *Bacchus Imports, Ltd. v. Dias*, 468 U.S. 263 (1984), is illustrative. As you read *Bacchus*, please consider the following questions:

1. Did the text of the challenged Hawai'i liquor tax draw any distinction based on geographic origin?

2. Why did the Court conclude that the tax scheme discriminated against interstate commerce? What was the evidence regarding the Hawai'i legislature's purpose?

3. Why couldn't Hawai'i's tax scheme survive the "rigorous scrutiny" applicable to discriminatory laws? Can any state law found to have such a discriminatory purpose survive such scrutiny?

4. The plaintiffs in *Bacchus* (Bacchus Imports and Eagle Distributors) were liquor wholesalers residing in Hawai'i. How could they—as Hawai'i residents—assert a claim under the dormant Commerce Clause (which protects *interstate* commerce)?

Bacchus Imports, Ltd. v. Dias
468 U.S. 263 (1984)

JUSTICE WHITE delivered the opinion of the Court.

Appellants challenge the constitutionality of the Hawaii liquor tax, which is a 20% excise tax imposed on sales of liquor at wholesale. Specifically at issue are exemptions from the tax for certain locally produced alcoholic beverages. The Supreme Court of Hawaii upheld the tax. . . . We noted probable jurisdiction and now reverse.

I

The Hawaii liquor tax was originally enacted in 1939 to defray the costs of police and other governmental services that the Hawaii Legislature concluded had been increased due to the consumption of liquor. At its inception the statute contained no exemptions. However, because the legislature sought to encourage development of the Hawaiian liquor industry, it enacted an exemption for okolehao from May 17, 1971, until June 20, 1981, and an exemption for fruit wine from May 17, 1976, until June 30, 1981. Okolehao is a brandy distilled from the root of the ti plant, an indigenous shrub of Hawaii. The only fruit wine manufactured

436

in Hawaii during the relevant time was pineapple wine. Locally produced sake and fruit liqueurs are not exempted from the tax.

Appellants—Bacchus Imports, Ltd., and Eagle Distributors, Inc.—are liquor wholesalers who sell to licensed retailers. They sell the liquor at their wholesale price plus the 20% excise tax imposed by § 244–4, plus a one-half percent tax imposed by Haw. Rev. Stat. § 237–13. Pursuant to Haw. Rev. Stat. § 40–35, which authorizes a taxpayer to pay taxes under protest and to commence an action in the Tax Appeal Court for the recovery of disputed sums, the wholesalers initiated protest proceedings and sought refunds of all taxes paid. . . .

[The] Supreme Court of Hawaii [rejected the Commerce Clause challenge]. . . . [It] held that the tax did not illegally discriminate against interstate commerce because "[the] incidence of the tax . . . is on wholesalers of liquor in Hawaii and the ultimate burden is borne by consumers in Hawaii."

III

A cardinal rule of Commerce Clause jurisprudence is that "[n]o State, consistent with the Commerce Clause, may 'impose a tax which discriminates against interstate commerce . . . by providing a direct commercial advantage to local business.'" *Boston Stock Exchange v. State Tax Comm'n*, 429 U.S. 318, 329 (1977). Despite the fact that the tax exemption here at issue seems clearly to discriminate on its face against interstate commerce by bestowing a commercial advantage on okolehao and pineapple wine, the State argues—and the Hawaii Supreme Court held—that there is no improper discrimination. . . .

B

The State contends that a more flexible approach, taking into account the practical effect and relative burden on commerce, must be employed in this case because (1) legitimate state objectives are credibly advanced, (2) there is no patent discrimination against interstate trade, and (3) the effect on interstate commerce is incidental. On the other hand, it acknowledges that where simple economic protectionism is effected by state legislation, a stricter rule of invalidity has been erected.

A finding that state legislation constitutes "economic protectionism" may be made on the basis of either discriminatory purpose or discriminatory effect. Examination of the State's purpose in this case is sufficient to demonstrate the State's lack of entitlement to a more flexible approach permitting inquiry into the balance between local benefits and the burden on interstate commerce. The Hawaii Supreme Court described the legislature's motivation in enacting the exemptions as follows:

"The legislature's reason for exempting 'ti root okolehao' from the 'alcohol tax' was to 'encourage and promote the establishment of a new industry,' and the exemption of 'fruit wine manufactured in the State from products grown in the State' was intended 'to help' in stimulating 'the local fruit wine industry.'"

Thus, we need not guess at the legislature's motivation, for it is undisputed that the purpose of the exemption was to aid Hawaiian industry. Likewise, the effect of the exemption is clearly discriminatory, in that it applies only to locally produced beverages, even though it does not apply to all such products. Consequently, as long as there is some competition between the locally produced exempt products and nonexempt products from outside the State, there is a discriminatory effect.

No one disputes that a State may enact laws pursuant to its police powers that have the purpose and effect of encouraging domestic industry. However, the Commerce Clause stands as a limitation on the means by which a State can constitutionally seek to achieve that goal. One of the fundamental purposes of the Clause "was to insure . . . against discriminating State legislation." *Welton v. Missouri*, 91 U.S. 275, 280 (1876). In *Welton,* the Court struck down a Missouri statute that "discriminat[ed] in favor of goods, wares, and merchandise which are the growth, product, or manufacture of the State, and against those which are the growth, product, or manufacture of other states or countries." *Id.,* at 277. Similarly, in *Walling v. Michigan*, 116 U.S. 446, 455 (1886), the Court struck down a law imposing a tax on the sale of alcoholic beverages produced outside the State, declaring:

"A discriminating tax imposed by a State operating to the disadvantage of the products of other States when introduced into the first mentioned State, is, in effect, a regulation in restraint of commerce among the States, and as such is a usurpation of the power conferred by the Constitution upon the Congress of the United States."

More recently, in *Boston Stock Exchange v. State Tax Comm'n*, 429 U.S. 318, 329 (1977), the Court struck down a New York law that imposed a higher tax on transfers of stock occurring outside the State than on transfers involving a sale within the State. We observed that competition among the States for a share of interstate commerce is a central element of our free-trade policy but held that a State may not tax interstate transactions in order to favor local businesses over out-of-state businesses. Thus, the Commerce Clause limits the manner in which States may legitimately compete for interstate trade, for "in the process of competition no State may discriminatorily tax the products manufactured or the business operations performed in any other State." *Id.,* at 337. It is therefore apparent that the Hawaii Supreme Court erred in concluding that there was no improper discrimination against interstate commerce merely because the burden of the tax was borne by consumers in Hawaii.

The State attempts to put aside this Court's cases that have invalidated discriminatory state statutes enacted for protectionist purposes. The State would distinguish these cases because they all involved attempts "to enhance thriving and substantial business enterprises at the expense of any foreign competitors." Hawaii's attempt, on the other hand, was "to subsidize nonexistent (pineapple wine) and financially troubled (okolehao) liquor industries peculiar to Hawaii." However, we perceive no principle of Commerce Clause jurisprudence supporting a distinction between thriving and struggling enterprises under these circumstances, and the State cites no authority for its proposed distinction. In either event, the legislation constitutes "economic protectionism" in every sense of the phrase. It has long been the law that States may not "build up [their] domestic commerce by means of unequal and oppressive burdens upon the industry and business of other States." *Guy v. Baltimore*, 100 U.S. 434, 443 (1880). Were it otherwise, "the trade and business of the country [would be] at the mercy of local regulations, having for their object to secure exclusive benefits to the citizens and products of particular States." *Id.*, at 442. It was to prohibit such a "multiplication of preferential trade areas" that the Commerce Clause was adopted. *Dean Milk Co. v. Madison*, 340 U.S. 349, 356 (1951). Consequently, the propriety of economic protectionism may not be allowed to hinge upon the State's—or this Court's—characterization of the industry as either "thriving" or "struggling."

We also find unpersuasive the State's contention that there was no discriminatory intent on the part of the legislature because "the exemptions in question were not enacted to discriminate against foreign products, but rather, to promote a local industry." If we were to accept that justification, we would have little occasion ever to find a statute unconstitutionally discriminatory. Virtually every discriminatory statute allocates benefits or burdens unequally; each can be viewed as conferring a benefit on one party and a detriment on the other, in either an absolute or relative sense. The determination of constitutionality does not depend upon whether one focuses upon the benefited or the burdened party. A discrimination claim, by its nature, requires a comparison of the two classifications, and it could always be said that there was no intent to impose a burden on one party, but rather the intent was to confer a benefit on the other. Consequently, it is irrelevant to the Commerce Clause inquiry that the motivation of the legislature was the desire to aid the makers of the locally produced beverage rather than to harm out-of-state producers.

We therefore conclude that the Hawaii liquor tax exemption for okolehao and pineapple wine violated the Commerce Clause because it had both the purpose and effect of discriminating in favor of local products.

*　　*　　*

Notes on *Bacchus Imports, Ltd. v. Dias*

1. *Taxes imposed on a state's own residents*: Notice again that Hawai'i's tax was imposed only on Hawai'i residents (wholesalers) and not on any nonresident individuals or entities. But that did not immunize the tax from invalidation under the dormant Commerce Clause. Because the purpose of the tax was to give a competitive advantage to in-state products (namely, okolehao and pineapple wine), it discriminated against interstate commerce. Indeed, the entire reason these two products were singled out was that they were produced almost exclusively in Hawai'i. Given that Hawai'i lacked a non-protectionist justification for the tax, it was necessarily unconstitutional. And although the persons who most acutely felt the dormant Commerce Clause injury were out-of-state producers of beverages competing with okolehao and pineapple wine, the Hawai'i wholesalers plainly had suffered an injury-in-fact sufficient for standing, as they were required to pay the unconstitutional tax.

2. *Another example of discriminatory purpose*: Another frequently cited case involving a state's discriminatory purpose is *Baldwin v. G.A.F. Seelig, Inc.*, 294 U.S. 511 (1935). At issue was a New York law concerning the resale of milk in New York by milk dealers. The law prohibited the sale in New York of milk that had been purchased (at wholesale) at a price lower than that currently prevailing for New York milk producers. G.A.F. Seelig had purchased milk in Vermont at a lower price than New York milk producers were charging, rendering it illegal for G.A.F. Seelig to sell that milk at retail in New York. The effect of the law was to eliminate any competitive advantage for dairy farmers outside New York, farmers who were able to produce their milk at a lower cost than New York dairies. There was no plausible explanation for the law other than as an attempt to protect New York dairy farmers from out-of-state competition (in sales to New York consumers). The Supreme Court concluded the law discriminated against interstate commerce, even though it drew no geographic distinction on its face.

Again, a state or local law that discriminates against interstate commerce is not *automatically* unconstitutional. Rather, such laws are "virtually *per se* invalid" and still might be saved if the state has no other practicable means of achieving the law's non-protectionist objectives. (Recall *Maine v.* Taylor.) But when a state has enacted a law for a protectionist purpose, surviving this scrutiny is impossible. Once it is established that the law seeks to favor in-state economic interests, there is no way for the state justify the law as pursuing a legitimate, non-protectionist objective. In *G.A.F. Seelig*, for instance, the Court concluded that the real object of New York's law (obviously enough) was to protect New York dairy farmers. This protectionist goal meant New York had no basis on which to defend the law under "rigorous scrutiny." In other words, a protectionist purpose renders a state or local law *per se* invalid under the Commerce Clause.

3. *When discriminatory purpose can be inferred from discrimination "in practical effect"*: The Supreme Court has sometimes declared that state or local laws can discriminate against interstate commerce "in practical effect." But these statements need to be contextualized. State laws are not discriminatory (in the relevant sense) merely because they have a disparate, unfavorable impact on out-of-state commercial interests. Almost every state law regulating in the commercial sphere will have some ripple effects beyond the enacting state's borders. And those ripple effects often disproportionately impact out-of-state businesses. These sorts of "practical effects," by themselves, do not make the law "virtually *per se*" unconstitutional. Instead, the Court's decisions stand for a much more modest proposition: In particular circumstances, a state law's practical effects on interstate commerce (vis-à-vis intrastate commerce) can reveal an underlying protectionist *purpose*.[20] A comparison of two important decisions illustrates the point.

a. *Hunt v. Washington State Apple Advertising Commission*, 423 U.S. 333 (1977): At issue in *Hunt* was a North Carolina statute concerning the labeling of closed containers of apples sold in the state. The law required all containers to bear no grade other than that applicable under the U.S. Department of Agriculture's grading system. This meant no *state* grade could appear on a closed container. Washington state apple growers protested because they had created a grading system superior to the USDA's, one that had gained widespread acceptance throughout the country. And compliance with North Carolina's law would impose significant costs on Washington growers, forcing them (1) to alter their preprinted containers that displayed the Washington state grades, (2) to repack the apples that were shipped to North Carolina into boxes displaying only the USDA grade, or (3) to discontinue altogether the use of the preprinted containers displaying the Washington state grades. North Carolina's law thus disadvantaged interstate commerce in two ways: it increased the costs of doing business in North Carolina for Washington apple growers (while leaving North Carolina apple growers unaffected), and it stripped from the Washington growers a competitive advantage they had earned through their own inspection and grading system.

Citing these practical effects, the Supreme Court held the law discriminated against interstate commerce. North Carolina's asserted interest was to protect its citizens from confusion and deception in the marketing of food, a legitimate, non-protectionist interest. But North Carolina had a range of non-discriminatory ways to pursue that goal. (For example, it could have required the USDA grade *in addition* to any state grade, rather than banning the appearance of additional grades.) Moreover, North Carolina's law did not appear actually to further this interest. Removing information of more sophisticated grades actually made it more likely that consumers might be confused or deceived. (Only apple dealers, not consumers, see the closed containers of apples, and they are not confused by the appearance of multiple grades.) When a state's law does not actually further the interest it has asserted, a reasonable inference is that the stated objective was not the law's true purpose. Instead, the state's purpose appeared discriminatory: to protect North Carolina growers from out-of-state competition. Even if the Court did not advert to this

---

[20] It could also be that the law's practical effects are so significant that the law imposes an "undue burden" on interstate commerce—one that is clearly excessive in comparison to its putative benefits. This prong of dormant Commerce Clause doctrine is explored further below.

discriminatory purpose in its opinion, the "practical effects" to which the Court objected made North Carolina's protectionist intent fairly obvious.

b. ***Exxon Corp. v. Governor of Maryland***: A superficially similar case—but where the Court found no dormant Commerce Clause violation—is *Exxon Corp. v. Governor of Maryland*, 437 U.S. 117 (1978). At issue was a Maryland statute enacted after the 1973 oil crisis, a crisis that produced severe gasoline shortages. Maryland's law prohibited any producer or refiner of petroleum products from operating a retail service station in the state. In essence, the statute required companies either to be in the production business or the retail business, but not both; no producer or refiner could also be a retailer. Maryland defended the law on the ground that, during gas shortages, retail service stations owned by producers or refiners had received preferential treatment. Those stations had received more gasoline—and sooner—than the independent retailers. The statute was therefore "designed to correct the inequities in the distribution and pricing of gasoline" in times of shortage.

The face of the statute contained no geographic distinctions; the law instead discriminated against producers and refiners. But Exxon claimed that the statute discriminated against interstate commerce because there were no oil producers or refiners located in Maryland, so the law's restriction fell exclusively on out-of-state companies. Meanwhile, a majority of the independent petroleum retailers doing business in Maryland—the businesses standing to gain market share due to the law—were Maryland businesses.

Nonetheless, the Court concluded that this disparate impact—favorable to in-state firms and disadvantageous to out-of-state firms—did not constitute "discrimination against interstate commerce." Such an effect "alone does not lead, either logically or as a practical matter, to a conclusion that the State is discriminating against interstate commerce at the retail level." To the Court, the disproportionate impact of Maryland's law on out-of-state businesses was inadvertent, a happenstance given the state residence of the affected firms. "The fact that the burden of a state regulation falls on some interstate companies does not, by itself, establish a claim of discrimination against interstate commerce."

c. ***Reconciling*** Hunt ***and*** Exxon: What distinguishes *Hunt* from *Exxon*? The best explanation is that the practical effects of the North Carolina revealed an unmistakable purpose of economic protectionism, while Maryland's law did not. The nature of the North Carolina statute's discriminatory impact strongly suggested that the state's true objective was to benefit North Carolina apple growers at the expense of out-of-state competitors. By contrast, the Maryland law seemed genuinely aimed at achieving its professed, non-protectionist goal: the equitable distribution of gasoline to all retailers in times of shortage. True enough, the majority of independent gasoline retailers operating in Maryland were Maryland-based businesses, but many (more than 40 percent) were not. Moreover, only a small proportion of gasoline retail outlets in the state (roughly

10 percent) were owned by firms like Exxon that also engaged in production and refining. Thus, economic protectionism hardly seemed to explain why the Maryland legislature had enacted the law. All things considered, Maryland's statute would have been a strange (and relatively ineffective) means of favoring in-state firms.

Taken together, *Hunt* and *Exxon* reveal that the Court's references to "discrimination in practical effect" do *not* mean that every state or local law that has a disparate, negative impact on out-of-state economic interests "discriminates against interstate commerce" in the relevant sense. Instead, such these effects can constitute evidence of such discrimination, but only when they reveal the law has a protectionist purpose.

This understanding is confirmed by *Minnesota v. Clover Leaf Creamery Co.*, 449 U.S. 456 (1981), which the Court handed down shortly after *Hunt* and *Exxon*. At issue was a Minnesota law banning the sale of milk in plastic nonreturnable, nonrefillable containers, but permitting such sales in other nonreturnable, nonrefillable containers, such as paperboard cartons. As the Court explained, "plastic resin, the raw material used for making plastic nonreturnable milk jugs, is produced entirely by non-Minnesota firms, while pulpwood, used for making paperboard, is a major Minnesota product." Thus, Minnesota pulpwood producers were "likely to benefit significantly from the Act at the expense of out-of-state firms." Still, the Court found that Minnesota's law did "not effect simple protectionism, but regulates evenhandedly by prohibiting all milk retailers from selling their products in plastic, nonreturnable milk containers, without regard to whether the milk, the containers, or the sellers are from outside the State." Critically, the Court reasoned that a

> "nondiscriminatory regulation serving substantial state purposes is not invalid simply because it causes some business to shift from a predominantly out-of-state industry to a predominantly in-state industry. Only if the burden on interstate commerce clearly outweighs the State's legitimate purposes does such a regulation violate the Commerce Clause."

*   *   *

3. Discrimination in favor of the government itself

Each dormant Commerce Clause case discussed above involved a state or local law allegedly discriminating in favor of in-state *private* firms or consumers—for instance, the Hawai'ian producers of pineapple wine in *Bacchus*, the New Jersey generators of trash in *Philadelphia v. New Jersey*, and the North Carolina apple farmers in *Hunt*. But what if the local law does not favor any in-state private actors, and instead only favors the state or local government itself? For example, suppose a city constructs a solid waste processing facility and enacts an ordinance requiring all trash generated in the city to be processed at the city-owned facility. (Suppose, too, the city charges fees for that processing, which are steeper than those charged by private, out-of-state facilities.) The ordinance plainly disadvantages out-of-state sellers (the out-of-state waste processors) relative to an in-state seller (the city government) in the sale of a commercial service. But it treats all *private* entities in the relevant market equally, whether in-state or out-of-state. Does this sort of law violate the dormant Commerce Clause?

The Supreme Court confronted this precise question in *United Haulers Ass'n, Inc. v. Oneida-Herkimer Solid Waste Mgmt. Auth.*, 550 U.S. 330 (2007). As you read the Court's opinion, please consider the following:

1. Did the challenged "flow control" ordinances discriminate among waste processors? If so, was the discrimination based on geographic origin?

2. Would the result in *United Haulers* have been different if the ordinances had mandated that all solid waste generated in Oneida and Herkimer Counties be processed at a particular privately-owned facility? Exactly how would the analysis have changed?

3. Of what significance was the fact that the Court considered waste processing a "traditional governmental function"? How would the analysis have changed if the regulated activity had *not* been a "traditional governmental function"?

4. In a sentence, how would you summarize the holding of *United Haulers*? How does *United Haulers* alter the definition of "discrimination against interstate commerce" under the Commerce Clause doctrine?

United Haulers Ass'n v. Oneida-Herkimer Solid Waste Mgmt.
550 U.S. 330 (2007)

CHIEF JUSTICE ROBERTS delivered the opinion of the Court.

"Flow control" ordinances require trash haulers to deliver solid waste to a particular waste processing facility. In *C & A Carbone, Inc. v. Clarkstown*, 511 U.S. 383 (1994), this Court struck down under the Commerce Clause a flow control ordinance that forced haulers to deliver waste to a particular *private* processing facility. In this case, we face flow control ordinances quite similar to the one invalidated in *Carbone*. The only salient difference is that the laws at issue here require haulers to bring waste to facilities owned and operated by a state-created public benefit corporation. We find this difference constitutionally significant. Disposing of trash has been a traditional government activity for years, and laws that favor the government in such areas—but treat every private business, whether in-state or out-of-state, exactly the same—do not discriminate against interstate commerce for purposes of the Commerce Clause. . . .

I

Located in central New York, Oneida and Herkimer Counties span over 2,600 square miles and are home to about 306,000 residents. Traditionally, each city, town, or village within the Counties has been responsible for disposing of its own waste. Many had relied on local landfills, some in a more environmentally responsible fashion than others.

By the 1980's, the Counties confronted what they could credibly call a solid waste "crisis." Many local landfills were operating without permits and in violation of state regulations. Sixteen were ordered to close and remediate the surrounding environment, costing the public tens of millions of dollars. These environmental problems culminated in a federal cleanup action against a landfill in Oneida County; the defendants in that case named over 600 local businesses and several municipalities and school districts as third-party defendants.

The "crisis" extended beyond health and safety concerns. The Counties had an uneasy relationship with local waste management companies, enduring price fixing, pervasive overcharging, and the influence of organized crime. Dramatic price hikes were not uncommon: In 1986, for example, a county contractor doubled its waste disposal rate on six weeks' notice.

Responding to these problems, the Counties requested and New York's Legislature and Governor created the Oneida-Herkimer Solid Waste Management Authority (Authority), a public benefit corporation. The Authority is empowered to collect, process, and dispose of solid waste generated in the Counties. To further the Authority's governmental and public purposes, the Counties may impose "appropriate and reasonable limitations on competition" by, for instance, adopting "local laws requiring that all solid waste . . . be delivered to a specified solid waste management-resource recovery facility."

In 1989, the Authority and the Counties entered into a Solid Waste Management Agreement, under which the Authority agreed to manage all solid waste within the Counties. Private haulers would remain free to pick up citizens' trash from the curb, but the Authority would take over the job of processing the trash, sorting it, and sending it off for disposal. To fulfill its part of the bargain, the Authority agreed to purchase and develop facilities for the processing and disposal of solid waste and recyclables generated in the Counties.

The Authority collected "tipping fees" to cover its operating and maintenance costs for these facilities. The tipping fees significantly exceeded those charged for waste removal on the open market, but they allowed the Authority to do more than the average private waste disposer. In addition to landfill transportation and solid waste disposal, the fees enabled the Authority to provide recycling of 33 kinds of materials, as well as composting, household hazardous waste disposal, and a number of other services. If the Authority's operating costs and debt service were not recouped through tipping fees and other charges, the agreement provided that the Counties would make up the difference.

As described, the agreement had a flaw: Citizens might opt to have their waste hauled to facilities with lower tipping fees. To avoid being stuck with the bill for facilities that citizens voted for but then chose not to use, the Counties enacted "flow control" ordinances requiring that all solid waste generated within the Counties be delivered to the Authority's processing sites. Private haulers must obtain a permit from the Authority to collect waste in the Counties. Penalties for non-compliance with the ordinances include permit revocation, fines, and imprisonment.

Petitioners are United Haulers Association, Inc., a trade association made up of solid waste management companies, and six haulers that operated in Oneida and Herkimer Counties when this action was filed. In 1995, they sued the Counties and the Authority under 42 U.S.C. § 1983, alleging that the flow control laws violate the Commerce Clause by discriminating against interstate commerce. They submitted evidence that without the flow control laws and the associated $86-per-ton tipping fees, they could dispose of solid waste at out-of-state facilities for between $37 and $55 per ton, including transportation. . . .

II

A

To determine whether a law violates [the] so-called "dormant" aspect of the Commerce Clause, we first ask whether it discriminates on its face against interstate commerce. In this context, "'discrimination' simply means differential treatment of in-state and out-of-state economic interests that benefits the former and burdens the latter." *Oregon Waste Systems, Inc. v. Department of Environmental Quality of Ore.*, 511 U.S. 93, 99 (1994). Discriminatory laws motivated by "simple economic protectionism" are subject to a "virtually *per se* rule of invalidity," *Philadelphia v. New Jersey*, 437 U.S. 617, 624 (1978), which can only be overcome by a showing that the State has no other means to advance a legitimate local purpose.

* * *

C

The flow control ordinances in this case benefit a clearly public facility, while treating all private companies exactly the same. . . . [S]uch flow control ordinances do not discriminate against interstate commerce for purposes of the dormant Commerce Clause.

Compelling reasons justify treating these laws differently from laws favoring particular private businesses over their competitors. "Conceptually, of course, any notion of discrimination assumes a comparison of substantially similar entities." *General Motors Corp. v. Tracy*, 519 U.S. 278, 298 (1997). But States and municipalities are not private businesses—far from it. Unlike private enterprise, government is vested with the responsibility of protecting the health, safety, and welfare of its citizens. These important responsibilities set state and local government apart from a typical private business.

Given these differences, it does not make sense to regard laws favoring local government and laws favoring private industry with equal skepticism. As our local processing cases demonstrate, when a law favors in-state business over out-of-state competition, rigorous scrutiny is appropriate because the law is often the product of "simple economic protectionism." *Wyoming v. Oklahoma*, 502 U.S. 437, 454 (1992). Laws favoring local government, by contrast, may be directed toward any number of legitimate goals unrelated to protectionism. Here the flow control ordinances enable the Counties to pursue particular policies with respect to the handling and treatment of waste generated in the Counties, while allocating the costs of those policies on citizens and businesses according to the volume of waste they generate.

The contrary approach of treating public and private entities the same under the dormant Commerce Clause would lead to unprecedented and unbounded interference by the courts with state and local government. The dormant Commerce Clause is not a roving license for federal courts to decide what activities are appropriate for state and local government to undertake, and what activities must be the province of private market competition. In this case, the citizens of Oneida and Herkimer Counties have chosen the government to provide waste management services, with a limited role for the private sector in arranging for transport of waste from the curb to the public facilities. The citizens could have left the entire matter for the private sector, in which case any regulation they undertook could not discriminate against interstate commerce. But it was also open to them to vest responsibility for the matter with their government, and to adopt flow control ordinances to support the government effort. It is not the office of the Commerce Clause to control the decision of the voters on whether government or the private sector should provide waste management services. "The Commerce Clause significantly limits the ability of States and localities to regulate or otherwise burden the flow of interstate commerce, but it does not elevate free trade above all other values." *Maine v. Taylor*, 477 U.S., at 151.

We should be particularly hesitant to interfere with the Counties' efforts under the guise of the Commerce Clause because "[w]aste disposal is both typically and traditionally a local government function." 261 F.3d, at 264 (case below) (Calabresi, J., concurring). Congress itself has recognized local government's vital role in waste management, making clear that "collection and disposal of solid wastes should continue to be primarily the function of State, regional, and local agencies." Resource Conservation and Recovery Act of 1976, 42 U.S.C. § 6901(a)(4). The policy of the State of New York favors "displac[ing] competition with regulation or monopoly public control" in this area. We may or may not agree with that approach, but nothing in the Commerce Clause vests the responsibility for that policy judgment with the Federal Judiciary.

Finally, it bears mentioning that the most palpable harm imposed by the ordinances—more expensive trash removal—is likely to fall upon the very people who voted for the laws. Our dormant Commerce Clause cases often find discrimination when a State shifts the costs of regulation to other States, because when "the burden of state regulation falls on interests outside the state, it is unlikely to be alleviated by the operation of those political restraints normally exerted when interests within the state are affected." *Southern Pacific Co. v. Arizona ex rel. Sullivan*, 325 U.S. 761, 767–768, n.2 (1945). Here, the citizens and businesses of the Counties bear the costs of the ordinances. There is no reason to step in and hand local businesses a victory they could not obtain through the political process.

We hold that the Counties' flow control ordinances, which treat in-state private business interests exactly the same as out-of-state ones, do not "discriminate against interstate commerce" for purposes of the dormant Commerce Clause. . . .

* * *

Notes on *United Haulers Ass'n v. Oneida-Herkimer Solid Waste Mgmt.*

1. *An additional wrinkle in defining "discrimination against interstate commerce"*: *United Haulers* adds an important detail to the definition of "discrimination against interstate commerce." Only state or local laws that favor in-state *private* actors (at the expense of out-of-state actors) are "discriminatory" in the relevant sense. Thus, if the flow control ordinances had required all solid waste produced in the counties to be processed at facilities in the counties—whether those facilities were public or private—the ordinances would have been "discriminatory" and virtually *per se* invalid. (Indeed, they would have been indistinguishable from the ordinance invalidated in *Dean Milk* requiring all milk sold in Madison to be processed at a Madison milk-processing facility). But the ordinances in *United Haulers* "treat[ed] in-state private business interests exactly the same as out-of-state ones"; the discrimination favored *government-owned* facilities. To be sure, the ordinances drew a geographic distinction, and they plainly favored the local seller. But they left all private facilities (in-state and out-of-state) equally disfavored. As Chief Justice Roberts succinctly wrote, "[t]he flow control ordinances in this case benefit a clearly public facility, while treating all private companies exactly the same. . . . [S]uch flow control ordinances do not discriminate against interstate commerce for purposes of the dormant Commerce Clause."

2. *"Typical and traditional governmental functions"*: In reaching its conclusion, the *United Haulers* Court noted that the judiciary "should be particularly hesitant to interfere with the Counties' efforts under the guise of the Commerce Clause because waste disposal is both typically and traditionally a local government function." The Court did not say this was *necessary* to its holding, but it certainly seemed relevant. So when a state or local government discriminates in favor of itself in the provision of a service that is a "typical and traditional governmental function," the law does not discriminate against interstate commerce in the relevant sense. If such discrimination occurs with respect to a service that is *not* a "typical and traditional governmental function," it might still be nondiscriminatory under the dormant Commerce Clause. (After all, *United Haulers* states that the "dormant Commerce Clause is not a roving license for federal courts to decide what activities are appropriate for state and local government to undertake, and what activities must be the province of private market competition.") But the answer seems less clear.

3. *State tax schemes that discriminate in favor of the state's own municipal bonds*: The principal means by which state and local governments finance long-term capital projects is by issuing bonds: securitized debt instruments by which the purchasers of the bonds effectively lend money to the bond issuer in exchange for regular interest payments and the repayment of the principal upon redemption of the bond. Over 50,000 state and local governments in the U.S. have the authority to issue bonds for public projects, and the current value of such bonds exceeds $1 trillion.

The State of Kentucky (like most states) imposes a personal income tax, and it generally dictates that interest earned by a taxpayer (including the interest earned from bonds) is income subject to taxation. But Kentucky exempts from its tax any interest earned from a bond issued by a state or local government located in Kentucky. By contrast, the interest earned on bonds issued by out-of-state governments, or by any private issuer (in-state or out-of-state), is subject to Kentucky's income tax. Some Kentucky residents who earned interest on state and local bonds issued in other states—and who thus were taxed by Kentucky on that interest—challenged Kentucky's scheme as violating the Commerce Clause.

In *Department of Revenue of Kentucky v. Davis*, 553 U.S. 328 (2008), the Supreme Court (relying on *United Haulers*) held that the distinction drawn in Kentucky's tax code—though clearly discriminating based on geographic origin with respect to a commercial activity—did not constitute "discrimination against interstate commerce." In the opinion's critical passages, Justice Souter wrote as follows:

"In *United Haulers,* we explained that a government function is not susceptible to standard dormant Commerce Clause scrutiny owing to its likely motivation by legitimate objectives distinct from the simple economic protectionism the Clause abhors. This logic applies with even greater force to laws favoring a State's municipal bonds, given that the issuance of debt securities to pay for public projects is a quintessentially public function. . . . By issuing bonds, state and local governments spread the costs of public projects over time, much as one might buy a house with a loan subject to monthly payments. Bonds place the cost of a project on the citizens who benefit from it over the years, and they allow for public work beyond what current revenues could support. Bond proceeds are thus the way to shoulder the cardinal civic responsibilities listed in *United Haulers*: protecting the health, safety, and welfare of citizens. It should go without saying that the apprehension in *United Haulers* about 'unprecedented . . . interference' with a traditional government function is just as warranted here, where the Davises would have us invalidate a century-old taxing practice, presently employed by 41 States, and affirmatively supported by all of them.

"In fact, this emphasis on the public character of the enterprise supported by the tax preference is just a step in addressing a fundamental element of dormant Commerce Clause jurisprudence, the principle that 'any notion of discrimination assumes a comparison of substantially similar entities.' *United Haulers*, 550 U.S., at 342. In *Bonaparte v. Tax Court*, 104 U.S. 592 (1882), a case involving the Full Faith and Credit Clause, we held that a foreign State is properly treated as a private entity with respect to state-issued bonds that have traveled outside its borders. Viewed through this lens, the Kentucky tax scheme parallels the ordinance upheld in *United Haulers:* it 'benefit[s] a clearly public [issuer, that is, Kentucky], while treating all private [issuers] exactly the same.' 550 U.S., at 342. There is no forbidden discrimination because Kentucky, as a public entity, does not have to treat itself as being 'substantially similar' to the other bond issuers in the market.

"Thus, *United Haulers* provides a firm basis for reversal. Just like the ordinances upheld there, Kentucky's tax exemption favors a traditional government function without any differential treatment favoring local entities over substantially similar out-of-state interests. This type of law does 'not "discriminate against interstate commerce" for purposes of the dormant Commerce Clause.' *Id.* at 345."

* * *

PROBLEMS ON DISCRIMINATION AGAINST INTERSTATE COMMERCE

Please explain whether the governmental action at issue discriminates against interstate commerce (for purposes of dormant Commerce Clause analysis).

1. A state law forbids the transportation, for commercial purposes, of old growth redwood trees out of the state if they have been harvested in the state. The state legislature's stated purpose for the law is to protect the state's ecological heritage.

2. A city ordinance requires all large employers located in the city (defined as those with at least 100 employees whose principal place of employment is within the city limits) to ensure that at least 50 percent of their employees are residents of the city. The law's stated purpose is to decrease the city's unemployment rate.

3. A new California law imposes a 10 percent sales tax on all nuts sold at retail in the state. The stated purpose of the law is to reduce the number of dangerous health incidents related to nut allergies, especially among children. The law exempts almonds from the new nut tax. (A recent study shows that 98 percent of almonds consumed in the United States are grown in California.)

4. A state law imposes a premium tax on all car insurance policies sold in the state. The measure of the tax is 5 percent of the annual premium if the policy is sold by an insurance company headquartered in the state, and it is 10 percent of the annual premium if it is sold by a company headquartered outside the state.

5. A state law forbids the sale of herbal supplements that are "unsafe for human consumption." The state Department of Public Health is empowered to enforce the law. In the 10 years since the law has gone into effect, the Department of Public Health has successfully forced the recall of 138 herbal supplements, prohibiting their sale within the state. All 138 of these supplements were manufactured by companies headquartered outside the state.

6. A state imposes a 25 percent sales tax on all "sugary" soft drinks (defined with reference to grams of sugar or sugar equivalent per serving). The purpose of the law, as stated in the bill's preamble, is "to reduce the state's level of childhood obesity, and to improve public health." During the final debate on the bill in the state assembly, a state legislator argues that "this will be a significant benefit to the state's health, and it will cost no jobs. There are no soft drink manufacturers in the state that would be affected by this law. They are all located elsewhere."

7. In 2024, San Benito County operates several COVID vaccination clinics at various locations. The clinics administer booster shots targeted to the coronavirus variants presently in widest circulation. The county charges $5 for each vaccination, though persons with annual incomes under $50,000 are exempt from the charge. Most San Benito County residents receive their vaccinations at a Walgreens or CVS pharmacy—businesses that are incorporated in Delaware and have their headquarters in Illinois and Rhode Island, respectively. A new San Benito County ordinance forbids any medical provider (including pharmacies) other than the county-run clinics from administering COVID vaccinations in the county.

* * *

D. Undue Burdens on Interstate Commerce

The discussion to this point has focused on state or local discrimination against interstate commerce. But even when state or local law does not so discriminate, it will nonetheless violate the dormant Commerce Clause if it places an "undue burden" on interstate commerce. Importantly, though, the judicial scrutiny this test entails is quite deferential. It is rare that a law deemed not discriminate against interstate commerce will violate the Commerce Clause.

1. The *Pike* balancing test

The seminal case articulating the relevant Commerce Clause standard for nondiscriminatory state and local laws is *Pike v. Bruce Church*, 397 U.S. 137 (1970). There, the Supreme Court explained that

"[w]here the statute regulates even-handedly to effectuate a legitimate local public interest, and its effects on interstate commerce are only incidental, it will be upheld unless the burden imposed on such commerce is clearly excessive in relation to the putative local benefits. If a legitimate local purpose is found, then the question becomes one of degree. And the extent of the burden that will be tolerated will of course depend on the nature of the local interest involved, and on whether it could be promoted as well with a lesser impact on interstate activities."

Thus, the relevant question in such cases is whether the burden a law places on interstate commerce is "clearly excessive" relative to its asserted local benefits. But it is a bit unclear exactly how a court is to conduct this balancing. Consider Justice Scalia's critique: "This process is ordinarily called 'balancing,' but the scale analogy is not really appropriate, since the interests on both sides are incommensurate. It is more like judging whether a particular line is longer than a particular rock is heavy." *Bendix Autolite Corp. v. Midwesco Enterprises*, 486 U.S. 888 (1988) (Scalia, J., concurring in the judgment). Still, the *Pike* balancing test remains a part of current law.

2. An example of *Pike* balancing: *Kassel*

A good case for exploring the *Pike* balancing test is *Kassel v. Consolidated Freightways*, 450 U.S. 662 (1981). At issue was an Iowa statute that prohibited the use of so-called "doubles"—trucks with two trailer compartments—that exceeded 60 feet in length. Single-trailer trucks could be up to 55 feet. And the statute contained an exception, at a local government's option, for Iowa cities that bordered other states, which permitted 65-foot doubles; those cities were authorized to adopt truck length limitations identical to their bordering states.

Iowa's law burdened interstate commerce by significantly increasing the operating costs of interstate trucking companies that ran trucks through Iowa. All states surrounding Iowa had laws permitting 65-foot doubles, and most interstate trucking fleets using Iowa's highways employed 65-foot doubles. Iowa's law therefore forced trucking companies to adjust in one of four ways: (1) to use 55-foot singles; (2) to use 60-foot doubles; (3) to detach the two trailers (that made up the 65-foot doubles) and shuttle them through Iowa separately; or (4) to divert their 65-foot doubles around Iowa and through neighboring states (such as Missouri or Minnesota).

Notably, the extent of the Iowa law's burden on interstate commerce depended on the laws of the surrounding states. If Iowa's limit on the length of doubles had been identical to the other states' limits, there would have been no burden; there was nothing particularly costly about Iowa's 60-foot limit in the abstract. Rather, the problem came from the Iowa law's interaction with the laws of the surrounding states—and Iowa's geographic significance to interstate truck traffic.

The principal interest Iowa asserted in defense of the law was highway safety. According to Iowa, 65-foot doubles were more dangerous, as they are more difficult to pass, take longer to clear intersections, can back up only short distances, are more likely to jackknife, and are more likely to rear-end other vehicles. But the district court found that Iowa's 60-foot limit did not actually improve road safety; 65-foot doubles were, in fact, just as safe as 55-foot singles or 60-foot doubles. Thus, the law's purported safety benefits—at least according to the district court's findings—were illusory. Indeed, Iowa's law was likely to *aggravate* safety problems for the nation as a whole. It would naturally lead to more truck miles driven, either by breaking up doubles into singles within Iowa or by requiring longer routes for truckers who were forced to circumvent Iowa. All else being equal, more miles driven by trucks would mean more accidents. As to the law's burden on interstate commerce, the record showed that the compliance costs for the trucking industry would be close to $12.6 million annually. The Supreme Court thus concluded that the burden was "clearly excessive" in relation to the law's (nonexistent) safety benefits.

Notice that *Pike* "balancing" might be fairly easy if the law's benefits are illusory. Once the Court upheld the district court's conclusion that the 60-foot limit on the length of doubles made Iowa's roads (if anything) *less* safe, the *Pike* test was bound to invalidate the law if the costs imposed on interstate commerce were non-trivial. But what about cases that are not so simple? Suppose limiting doubles to 60 feet actually made highways in Iowa somewhat safer. How should a court weigh this gain in safety against the burden imposed on interstate commerce? Again, this is unclear. As Justice Scalia rightly noted, the problem is one of incommensurability: the *Pike* test essentially asks courts to balance apples and oranges. As a matter of institutional competence, it is odd for the judiciary (as opposed to the political branches) to be balancing these sorts of interests against one another. This is the principal reason the Supreme Court has only rarely invoked the *Pike* test to invalidate a law—indeed, not once since 1991.

3. *Pike* balancing and the "smoking out" of protectionist purposes

One way to understand the *Pike* test (at least in some cases) is as a mechanism for "smoking out" an underlying protectionist purpose. If a law's benefits are small or nonexistent, but the burdens imposed on interstate commerce are substantial, one might wonder whether its *real* goal is to favor in-state interests at the expense of out-of-state competitors. Then-Justice Rehnquist made this point in his *Kassel* dissent: "The purpose of the 'sensitive consideration' referred to [in *Pike*] is . . . to determine if the asserted justification, although rational, is merely a pretext for discrimination against interstate commerce." The logical response to Rehnquist—at least in *Kassel* itself—was that Iowa's justifications for its law seemed to be just such "pretext for discrimination." It protected Iowa citizens from a cost of being a part of the national economy—increased truck traffic—and sought to shift that cost onto neighboring states. Indeed, the law's local option provision made it clear that Iowa aimed (to the extent possible) to capture the benefit of interstate trucking where the destination was in-state, but divert the traffic that was only passing through Iowa to other destinations. In this sense, the law was similar to that invalidated in *Philadelphia v. New Jersey*. Like New Jersey, Iowa was trying to wall itself off from a particular sort of negative-value item; the state's intent was to benefit in-staters relative to out-of-staters with respect to an undesirable byproduct of an interstate commercial activity.

4. *Pike* and unclogging the channels of interstate commerce

A context in which the Supreme Court has been particularly sensitive to "undue burdens" on interstate commerce is where a state or local law has functioned to clog the channels of interstate commerce. Consider *Southern Pacific v. Arizona*, 325 U.S. 761 (1945). At issue was the Arizona Train Limit Law, which made it "unlawful for any person or corporation to operate within the state a railroad train of more than fourteen passenger or seventy freight cars." Surrounding states either imposed no train-length limits or had limits that were much more lenient. Arizona's law thus "impose[d] a serious burden on the interstate commerce conducted by appellant. It materially impede[d] the movement of appellant's interstate trains through that state and interpose[d] a substantial obstruction to the . . . adequate, economical and efficient railway transportation service." Given this burden, the Court invalidated the law. The statute imposed substantial costs on the interstate operation of trains, while affording only a "slight and dubious advantage, if any, over unregulated train lengths" in safety (Arizona's asserted interest).

Similarly, *Bibb v. Navajo Freight Lines, Inc.*, 359 U.S. 520 (1959), concerned an Illinois statute that required truck operators to use a specific type of rear fender mudguard on their vehicles. The Illinois law made the industry-standard mudguard (which was legal in 45 states) illegal on Illinois highways. It also made it illegal to drive the same truck in Illinois and Arkansas. Because mudguards were generally welded onto trucks, and because trucks were constantly crossing state borders, the costs imposed by Illinois's law on interstate trucking companies were "massive," and thus "clearly excessive" in comparison to its purported safety benefits. As the Court explained, a "State which insists on a design out of line with the requirements of almost all the other States may sometimes place a great burden of delay and inconvenience on those interstate motor carriers entering or crossing its territory." In some instances, such an idiosyncratic requirement "may be so compelling that the innovating State need not be the one to give way." But in *Bibb*, "balanced against the clear burden on commerce," the asserted safety benefits were "far too inconclusive to make this mudguard meet that test."

There was no clear indication in either *Southern Pacific* or *Bibb* that the state laws had been enacted for a protectionist purpose. Still, they created out-of-step rules that, in practical operation, placed significant burdens on interstate commerce while producing only marginal local benefits. (The same was arguably true of Iowa's law invalidated in *Kassel*.) But it remains unclear how much (or what kind) of a burden on interstate commerce will be "excessive."

Indeed, the overwhelming majority of state and local laws imposing significant costs on interstate commerce are perfectly constitutional. Thus, the *Pike* test—though still a part of the dormant Commerce Clause—remains an enigma.

E. Extraterritorial State Legislation

Another well-established principle of constitutional law is that states may not legislate "extraterritorially." That is, a basic premise of the Constitution's federal structure is that states generally can only regulate or tax activities occurring within their borders.[21]

One might understand this principle as simply a structural inference implicit in the Constitution's design (similar to the federal immunity doctrine first recognized in *McCulloch*). But several modern Supreme Court's decisions have located this principle in the dormant Commerce Clause. As the Court has explained, the "Commerce Clause precludes the application of a state statute to commerce that takes place wholly outside of the State's borders, whether or not the commerce has effects within the State." *Healy v. Beer Institute, Inc.*, 491 U.S. 324, 336 (1989). Likewise, the "Commerce Clauses forbid[s] the States to tax extraterritorial values"—that is, transactions, income, or property arising or located in another state. *MeadWestvaco Corp. v. Illinois Dept. of Rev.*, 553 U.S. 16, 19 (2008).[22]

Courts have generally treated this "extraterritoriality principle" as a distinct strand of the dormant Commerce Clause, independent of its prohibitions on laws discriminating against or unduly burdening interstate commerce. Thus, a state or local law violates the Commerce Clause *per se*—regardless of any other circumstances—if it regulates or taxes commercial activities occurring entirely outside the enacting state.

For instance, suppose the Texas legislature enacted a statute making it a crime for anyone to perform an abortion within 350 miles of the Texas border. And suppose Texas attempted to apply this law to an Arizona physician who provided an abortion in Tucson, Arizona, to a resident of Arizona. Texas's attempt to apply its law extraterritorially—to the actions of Arizona residents taking place in Arizona—would be unconstitutional. It would exceed Texas's legislative jurisdiction. Similarly, if California attempted to tax the income of a Texas resident that she earned while performing services in Georgia, the tax

---

[21] The Supreme Court has not definitively resolved the degree to which states are constitutionally permitted to regulate the conduct of their own citizens while they are temporarily outside their state of residence. This question will likely grow more significant after the Court's overruling of *Roe v. Wade* in *Dobbs v. Jackson Women's Health Org.*, No. 19–1392 (2022).

[22] States may constitutionally tax 100 percent of their residents' income, regardless of where it is earned. But this is based on the principle that a person enjoys and consumes her income in her state of residence, so the value being taxed is within the taxing state.

would be unconstitutional, and for the same reason. States are generally limited to taxing those activities that occur within their borders.

Importantly, the mere fact that a state or local law *affects* activities taking place in other states does not render that law unconstitutionally "extraterritorial." In today's integrated economy, *every* state or local law will have some ripple effects that extend beyond that state's borders. For example, California Health & Safety Code §119406(a) provides that "all cartridges for electronic cigarettes and solutions for filling or refilling an electronic cigarette shall be in child-resistant packaging." No doubt, some (and probably most) of the manufacturers selling electronic cigarettes and cartridges in California package their products in other states. Thus, §119406(a) has a *practical effect* on activity occurring elsewhere, as it proximately causes those manufacturers (that are packaging their products in, say, Kentucky) to do so in a way that complies with the law's child-resistance requirements. But the precise activity §119406(a) regulates is the sale *in California* of "cartridges for electronic cigarettes and solutions for filling or refilling an electronic cigarette." (Section 119406 does not make it unlawful for manufacturers to package their products in non-compliant packaging; it is perfectly lawful for them to do so, so long as they do not then sell those products in California.) As a result, §119406(a) does not regulate extraterritorially. To be clear, these extraterritorial effects would be relevant to the *Pike* balancing test, as any effect of a state law on interstate commerce is pertinent to determining whether it imposes an "undue burden." But the impact of a state's law beyond its borders, by itself, cannot render that law unconstitutionally "extraterritorial."

By contrast, a state law that has the practical effect of *regulating* activity occurring in another state—making that extraterritorial activity *unlawful*—is unconstitutional, even if it formally only regulates conduct occurring within the enacting state. For example, consider a New York statute that required all sellers of alcohol, on the first day of each month, to post the prices the sellers would charge in New York for their products that month, affirming they would not charge lower prices for those products in any adjoining states during the same month. The law forbade sellers from deviating from their posted prices (or their price affirmations) for the duration of the month.

Though this statute formally regulated activity occurring only in New York—sales in New York and the affirmations made to the New York state government—its practical effect was to regulate transactions occurring wholly outside the state. Once a seller had posted its New York prices, the statute made it unlawful for the seller to sell one of its products in, say, Connecticut at a price below its New York posted price. The law's practical effect was not just to *affect* conduct in Connecticut, but to render such conduct *unlawful*. This sort of law is impermissibly "extraterritorial" under the dormant Commerce Clause because it has the practical effect of *regulating* (that is, controlling) activity occurring entirely in another state. *See Brown-Forman Distillers Corp.*

456

v. New York State Liquor Auth., 476 U.S. 573 (1986). As the Supreme Court explained in *Healy*,

> "a statute that directly controls commerce occurring wholly outside the boundaries of a State exceeds the inherent limits of the enacting State's authority and is invalid regardless of whether the statute's extraterritorial reach was intended by the legislature. The critical inquiry is whether the practical effect of the regulation is to control conduct beyond the boundaries of the State." 491 U.S., at 336.

A related but distinct question is whether a state has a legitimate interest in influencing or altering behavior occurring in other states, especially when that behavior is lawful in those states. For example, suppose California enacts a statute that forbids the sale of pork products in California when the pigs producing the meat have not been housed with particular space allowances. Suppose 99.9 percent of the pork consumed in California is raised outside the state, and there is no established link between the space allowances and the health or safety of the pork. Instead, California's avowed purpose is to pressure out-of-state pig farmers into adopting practices that conform to California's views of animal welfare. (And that pressure is likely to succeed, given that 13 percent of the pork consumed in the U.S. is purchased by Californians.)

California's law does not violate the dormant Commerce Clause's extraterritoriality principle because it only regulates activities occurring within the state: sales of pork meat to California consumers. But under *Pike v. Bruce Church*, is it legitimate for California to seek to alter behavior occurring in other states—behavior that is perfectly lawful in those states? If not, California's law would likely impose an "undue burden" on interstate commerce: the costs it would entail pork producers would be substantial (in the billions of dollars), while the putative benefits (after setting aside the concern for animal welfare in other states) would be nearly nonexistent. The Supreme Court will take up this precise question this coming fall. *See National Pork Producers Council v. Ross*, 142 S. Ct. 1413 (2022).

F.   The Market Participant Exception

At the core of the market participant exception is the following principle: when a state or local government acts as a *participant in a market*—as a buyer or provider of goods or services—the dormant Commerce Clause simply does not constrain its actions. The dormant Commerce Clause is addressed to when a state *regulates* or *taxes* activities affecting interstate commerce. (Regulation and taxation entail a state's *sovereign* power, to coercively prescribe norms of conduct or collect revenue, with sanctions attached to the failure to adhere to those instructions.) If a state or local government's action is *proprietary*—as a buyer or seller of goods or services—it falls outside the purview of the dormant Commerce Clause.

A straightforward example—and one of the first Supreme Court decisions to apply it—is *Reeves v. Stake*, 447 U.S. 429 (1980). South Dakota owned and operated its own cement plant, which it built in the early 1900s. During a cement shortage in the 1970s, the state decided to favor its own residents (as cement customers) over out-of-state customers. Thus, the plant adopted a policy of first filling the orders of South Dakotans (and those customers with long-term contracts), selling whatever cement remained on a first-come first-served basis. A Wyoming company that had purchased cement from the plant for several years was suddenly unable to purchase cement from South Dakota, and it claimed the preference for in-state customers violated the dormant Commerce Clause. As you read *Reeves*, please consider the following questions:

1. Did South Dakota's policy regarding the sale of cement from the plant discriminate against interstate commerce? Was it protectionist?

2. In what sense was South Dakota a "market participant"? How does market participation differ from other state activities, which are subject to dormant Commerce Clause scrutiny?

3. Can you think of other, more common forms of market participation (other than manufacturing and selling cement) in which state or local governments routinely engage? Do states tend to discriminate against interstate commerce in these contexts? If so, how?

Reeves, Inc., v. Stake
447 U.S. 429 (1980)

MR. JUSTICE BLACKMUN delivered the opinion of the Court.

The issue in this case is whether, consistent with the Commerce Clause, the State of South Dakota, in a time of shortage, may confine the sale of the cement it produces solely to its residents.

I

In 1919, South Dakota undertook plans to build a cement plant. . . . The plant, however, located at Rapid City, soon produced more cement than South Dakotans could use. Over the years, buyers in no less than nine nearby States purchased cement from the State's plant. Between 1970 and 1977, some 40% of the plant's output went outside the State.

The plant's list of out-of-state cement buyers included petitioner Reeves, Inc. Reeves is a ready-mix concrete distributor organized under Wyoming law and with facilities in Buffalo, Gillette, and Sheridan, Wyoming. From the beginning of its operations in 1958, and until 1978, Reeves purchased about 95% of its cement from the South Dakota plant. In 1977, its purchases were $1,172,000. In turn, Reeves has supplied three northwestern Wyoming counties with more than half their ready-mix concrete needs. For 20 years the relationship between Reeves and the South Dakota cement plant was amicable, uninterrupted, and mutually profitable.

As the 1978 construction season approached, difficulties at the plant slowed production. Meanwhile, a booming construction industry spurred demand for cement both regionally and nationally. The plant found itself unable to meet all orders. Faced with the same type of "serious cement shortage" that inspired the plant's construction, the Commission "reaffirmed its policy of supplying all South Dakota customers first and to honor all contract commitments, with the remaining volume allocated on a first come, first served basis."

Reeves, which had no pre-existing long-term supply contract, was hit hard and quickly by this development. On June 30, 1978, the plant informed Reeves that it could not continue to fill Reeves' orders, and on July 5, it turned away a Reeves truck. Unable to find another supplier, Reeves was forced to cut production by 76% in mid-July.

On July 19, Reeves brought this suit against the Commission, challenging the plant's policy of preferring South Dakota buyers, and seeking injunctive relief.

II

A

Alexandria Scrap concerned a Maryland program designed to remove abandoned automobiles from the State's roadways and junkyards. To encourage recycling, a "bounty" was offered for every Maryland-titled junk car converted into scrap. Processors located both in and outside Maryland were eligible to collect these subsidies. The legislation, as initially enacted in 1969, required a processor seeking a bounty to present documentation evidencing ownership of the wrecked car. This requirement however, did not apply to "hulks," inoperable automobiles over eight years old. In 1974, the statute was amended to extend documentation requirements to hulks, which comprised a large majority of the junk cars being processed. Departing from prior practice, the new law imposed more exacting documentation requirements on out-of-state than in-state processors. By making it less remunerative for suppliers to transfer vehicles outside Maryland, the reform triggered a "precipitate decline in the number of bounty-eligible hulks supplied to appellee's [Virginia] plant from Maryland sources." 426 U.S., at 801. Indeed, "[t]he practical effect was substantially the same as if Maryland had withdrawn altogether the availability of bounties on hulks delivered by unlicensed suppliers to licensed non-Maryland processors." *Id.*, at 803, n.13.

Invoking the Commerce Clause, a three-judge District Court struck down the legislation. It observed that the amendment imposed "substantial burdens upon the free flow of interstate commerce," and reasoned that the discriminatory program was not the least disruptive means of achieving the State's articulated objective.

This Court reversed. It recognized the persuasiveness of the lower court's analysis if the inherent restrictions of the Commerce Clause were deemed applicable. In the Court's view, however, *Alexandria Scrap* did not involve "the kind of action with which the Commerce Clause is concerned." 426 U.S., at 805. Unlike prior cases voiding state laws inhibiting interstate trade, "Maryland has not sought to prohibit the flow of hulks, or to regulate the conditions under which it may occur. Instead, it has entered into the market itself to bid up their price," "as a purchaser, in effect, of a potential article of interstate commerce," and has restricted "its trade to its own citizens or businesses within the State."

Having characterized Maryland as a market participant, rather than as a market regulator, the Court found no reason to "believe the Commerce Clause was intended to require independent justification for [the State's] action." The Court couched its holding in unmistakably broad terms. "Nothing in the purposes animating the Commerce Clause prohibits a State, in the absence of congressional action, from participating in the market and exercising the right to favor its own citizens over others." *Id.*, at 810.

B

The basic distinction drawn in *Alexandria Scrap* between States as market participants and States as market regulators makes good sense and sound law. As that case explains, the Commerce Clause responds principally to state taxes and regulatory measures impeding free private trade in the national marketplace. There is no indication of a constitutional plan to limit the ability of the States themselves to operate freely in the free market. The precedents comport with this distinction.

* * *

III

South Dakota, as a seller of cement, unquestionably fits the "market participant" label more comfortably than a State acting to subsidize local scrap processors. Thus, the general rule of *Alexandria Scrap* plainly applies here. Petitioner argues, however, that the exemption for marketplace participation necessarily admits of exceptions. While conceding that possibility, we perceive in this case no sufficient reason to depart from the general rule.

A

In finding a Commerce Clause violation, the District Court emphasized "that the Commission . . . made an election to become part of the interstate commerce system." The gist of this reasoning, repeated by petitioner here, is that one good turn deserves another. Having long exploited the interstate market, South Dakota should not be permitted to withdraw from it when a shortage arises. This argument is not persuasive. It is somewhat self-serving to say that South Dakota has "exploited" the interstate market. An equally fair characterization is that neighboring States long have benefited from South Dakota's foresight and industry. Viewed in this light, it is not surprising that *Alexandria*

Scrap rejected an argument that the 1974 Maryland legislation challenged there was invalid because cars abandoned in Maryland had been processed in neighboring States for five years. As in *Alexandria Scrap*, we must conclude that "this chronology does not distinguish the case, for Commerce Clause purposes, from one in which a State offered [cement] only to domestic [buyers] from the start." 426 U.S., at 809.

Our rejection of petitioner's market-exploitation theory fundamentally refocuses analysis. It means that to reverse we would have to void a South Dakota "residents only" policy even if it had been enforced from the plant's very first days. Such a holding, however, would interfere significantly with a State's ability to structure relations exclusively with its own citizens. It would also threaten the future fashioning of effective and creative programs for solving local problems and distributing government largesse. A healthy regard for federalism and good government renders us reluctant to risk these results.

"To stay experimentation in things social and economic is a grave responsibility. Denial of the right to experiment may be fraught with serious consequences to the Nation. It is one of the happy incidents of the federal system that a single courageous State may, if its citizens choose, serve as a laboratory; and try novel social and economic experiments without risk to the rest of the country." *New State Ice Co. v. Liebmann*, 285 U.S. 262, 311 (1932) (Brandeis, J., dissenting).

B

Undaunted by these considerations, petitioner advances four more arguments for reversal:

First, petitioner protests that South Dakota's preference for its residents responds solely to the "non-governmental objectiv[e]" of protectionism. Therefore, petitioner argues, the policy is *per se* invalid.

We find the label "protectionism" of little help in this context. The State's refusal to sell to buyers other than South Dakotans is "protectionist" only in the sense that it limits benefits generated by a state program to those who fund the state treasury and whom the State was created to serve. Petitioner's argument apparently also would characterize as "protectionist" rules restricting to state residents the enjoyment of state educational institutions, energy generated by a state-run plant, police and fire protection, and agricultural improvement and business development programs. Such policies, while perhaps "protectionist" in a loose sense, reflect the essential and patently unobjectionable purpose of state government-to serve the citizens of the State.[23]

---

[23] Petitioner would distinguish *Alexandria Scrap* as involving state legislation designed to advance the nonprotectionist goal of environmentalism. This characterization is an oversimplification. The challenged feature of the Maryland program—the discriminatory documentation requirement—was not aimed at improving the environment; indeed, by decreasing the profit margin a hulk supplier could expect to receive if he delivered to the most accessible recycling plant, it is likely that the amendment somewhat set back the goal of encouraging hulk

461

Second, petitioner echoes the District Court's warning: "If a state in this union were allowed to hoard its commodities or resources for the use of their own residents only, a drastic situation might evolve. For example, Pennsylvania or Wyoming might keep their coal, the northwest its timber, and the mining states their minerals. The result being that embargo may be retaliated by embargo and commerce would be halted at state lines." This argument, although rooted in the core purpose of the Commerce Clause, does not fit the present facts. Cement is not a natural resource, like coal, timber, wild game, or minerals. It is the end product of a complex process whereby a costly physical plant and human labor act on raw materials. South Dakota has not sought to limit access to the State's limestone or other materials used to make cement. Nor has it restricted the ability of private firms or sister States to set up plants within its borders. Moreover, petitioner has not suggested that South Dakota possesses unique access to the materials needed to produce cement.[24] Whatever limits might exist on a State's ability to invoke the *Alexandria Scrap* exemption to hoard resources which by happenstance are found there, those limits do not apply here.

---

processing. The stated justification for the discriminatory regulation—reducing payments to out-of-state processors for recycling of hulks abandoned outside Maryland—was not even mentioned by the Court in rebuffing the Virginia processor's Commerce Clause challenge. Indeed, the central point of the Court's analysis was that demonstration of an "independent justification" was unnecessary to sustain the State's program. At bottom, the discrimination challenged in *Alexandria Scrap* was motivated by the same concern underlying South Dakota's resident-preference policy—a desire to channel state benefits to the residents of the State supplying them. If some underlying "commendable as well as legitimate" purpose, 426 U.S., at 809, is also required, it is certainly present here. In establishing the plant, South Dakota sought the most unstartling governmental goal: improvement of the quality of life in that State by generating a supply of a previously scarce product needed for local construction and governmental improvements. A cement program, to be sure, may be a somewhat unusual or unorthodox way in which to utilize state funds to improve the quality of residents' lives. But "[a] State's project is as much a legitimate governmental activity whether it is traditional, or akin to private enterprise, or conducted for profit. . . . A State may deem it as essential to its economy that it own and operate a railroad, a mill, or an irrigation system as it does to own and operate bridges, street lights, or a sewage disposal plant. What might have been viewed in an earlier day as an improvident or even dangerous extension of state activities may today be deemed indispensable." *New York v. United States*, 326 U.S., at 591 (dissenting opinion).

[24] Nor has South Dakota cut off access to its own cement altogether, for the policy does not bar resale of South Dakota cement to out-of-state purchasers. Although the out-of-state buyer in the secondary market will undoubtedly have to pay a markup not borne by South Dakota competitors, this result is not wholly unjust. There should be little question that South Dakota at least could exact a premium on out-of-state purchases to compensate it for the State's investment and risk in the plan. If one views the added markup paid by out-of-state buyers to South Dakota middlemen as the rough equivalent of this "premium," the challenged program equates with a permissible result. The "bottom line" of the scheme closely parallels the result in *Alexandria Scrap*: out-of-state concrete suppliers are not removed from the market altogether; to compete successfully with in-state competitors, however, they must achieve additional efficiencies or exploit natural advantage such as their location to offset the incremental advantage channeled by the State's own market behavior to in-state concrete suppliers.

Third, it is suggested that the South Dakota program is infirm because it places South Dakota suppliers of ready-mix concrete at a competitive advantage in the out-of-state market; Wyoming suppliers, such as petitioner, have little chance against South Dakota suppliers who can purchase cement from the State's plant and freely sell beyond South Dakota's borders.

The force of this argument is seriously diminished, if not eliminated by several considerations. The argument necessarily implies that the South Dakota scheme would be unobjectionable if sales in other States were totally barred. It therefore proves too much, for it would tolerate even a greater measure of protectionism and stifling of interstate commerce than the challenge system allows. Nor is it to be forgotten that *Alexandria Scrap* approved a state program that "not only . . . effectively protect[ed] scrap processors with existing plants in Maryland from the pressures of competitors with nearby out-of-state plants, but [that] implicitly offer[ed] to extend similar protection to any competitor . . . willing to erect a scrap processing facility within Maryland's boundaries." Finally, the competitive plight of out-of-state ready-mix suppliers cannot be laid solely at the feet of South Dakota. It is attributable as well to their own States' not providing or attracting alternative sources of supply and to the suppliers' own failure to guard against shortages by executing long-term supply contracts with the South Dakota plant.

In its last argument, petitioner urges that, had South Dakota not acted, free market forces would have generated an appropriate level of supply at free market prices for all buyers in the region. Having replaced free market forces, South Dakota should be forced to replicate how the free market would have operated under prevailing conditions.

This argument appears to us to be simplistic and speculative. The very reason South Dakota built its plant was because the free market had failed adequately to supply the region with cement. There is no indication, and no way to know, that private industry would have moved into petitioner's market area, and would have ensured a supply of cement to petitioner either prior to or during the 1978 construction season. Indeed, it is quite possible that petitioner would never have existed—far less operated successfully for 20 years—had it not been for South Dakota cement.

C

We conclude, then, that the arguments for invalidating South Dakota's resident-preference program are weak at best. Whatever residual force inheres in them is more than offset by countervailing considerations of policy and fairness. Reversal would discourage similar state projects, even though this project demonstrably has served the needs of state residents and has helped the entire region for more than a half century. Reversal also would rob South Dakota of the intended benefit of its foresight, risk, and industry. Under these circumstances, there is no reason to depart from the general rule of *Alexandria Scrap*.

*   *   *

Notes on Reeves v. Stake

1. *The significance of market participation*: Had the preference for South Dakota residents in *Reeves* constituted a regulation of private conduct, it plainly would have violated the Commerce Clause: it blatantly discriminated against interstate commerce, and its goal was to favor in-state over out-of-state economic interests. But because the state was acting as a market participant, its policy was constitutional. South Dakota was selling cement. It was *not* prohibiting anyone else from building cement plants; nor was it coercively directing all private cement sellers in South Dakota to favor in-state purchasers over out-of-state purchasers. Thus, even though South Dakota's purpose was clearly to favor in-state economic actors, there was no constitutional problem. Stated simply, the dormant Commerce Clause only constrains state and local governments when they are acting in their *sovereign* capacities.

2. *What exactly constitutes "market participation"?*: A state or local government acts as a "market participant" when it buys or provides goods or services.[25] (When a state provides a good or service, it often sells it for a price—such as when it charges a fee for a physician visit at a state-run health clinic. But a state is still acting as a market participant when it decides to provide that good or service for free; it is just a "sale" at a price of $0.) For example, the Supreme Court has held that a state acts as a market participant when it purchases abandoned, inoperable automobiles (as discussed in *Reeves*), sells cement (at issue in *Reeves*), sells timber, or employs workers. As the Court explained in *Department of Rev. of Ky. v. Davis*, the exception involves circumstances in which states

> "go beyond regulation and themselves participate in the market so as to exercise the right to favor their own citizens over others. Thus, the 'market-participant' exception reflects a basic distinction . . . between States as market participants and States as market regulators, there being no indication of a constitutional plan to limit the ability of the States themselves to operate freely in the free market."

---

[25] There must also be an existing *market* for the good or service the state is buying or selling. That is, there must be private buyers or sellers of that same good or service, other than the government itself. For example, there is no "market" for the provision of business licenses; only the government can provide them. So when a state "sells" a license to a business (in exchange for a business registration fee), it is not acting as a market participant; it is acting in its sovereign capacity as a regulator of business activity. Typically, it is easy to discern whether a market exists for the good or service the state is buying or providing. Such markets clearly exist for such things like cement, higher education, health care, and waste disposal. But some cases may be more difficult—for instance, when the good or service has historically been provided by both private and public actors, but so happens only to be provided by the state presently. The Supreme Court has yet to explain precisely where this line falls.

3. *The exception's limit:* South-Central Timber Development v. Wunnicke: There is an important limit to the market participant exception, revealed by the Court's decision in *South Central Timber Development v. Wunnicke*, 467 U.S. 82 (1984). At issue was Alaska's sale of 49 million board feet of raw timber. As a condition of the sale, Alaska required any purchaser to commit to having a specified percentage of the timber processed in Alaska. The state proffered three purposes for the condition: (1) to protect Alaska's timber processing industry; (2) to promote new industries; and (3) to derive revenue from all timber resources in the state.

A plurality of justices concluded this condition violated the dormant Commerce Clause because it was plainly discriminatory and it fell outside the market participant exception. In doing so, it drew the following line:

> "The limit of the market-participation doctrine must be that it allows a State to impose burdens on commerce within the market in which it is a participant, but allows it to go no further. The State may not impose conditions, whether by statute, regulation, or contract, that have a substantial regulatory effect outside of that particular market."

In other words, states may only impose conditions *in the market in which they actually participate*. The doctrine doesn't immunize "downstream" regulations that apply to subsequent transactions—transactions occurring in markets in which the state itself is not participating. In *South-Central Timber*, Alaska was participating in the raw timber market, but its condition operated in the timber processing market. Thus, the condition was "downstream" from the market in which Alaska was participating; it concerned subsequent activity in a different market. As such, it fell outside the market participant exception.

Lying behind *South-Central Timber* is the following logic. If the theory of the market participant exception is that the state is entitled to act like any other entity when acting as a buyer or provider of goods or services, then the analogy also has a limit. Generally, private market participants have no concern for what happens subsequent to their market participation. (For example, someone who sells a used cell phone on eBay generally does not place any conditions on the purchaser's subsequent use of that phone.) Thus, to the extent Alaska *did* care about what happened after it sold its timber, that concern stemmed more from its status as a *sovereign* than as a seller in the raw timber market. Downstream restrictions thus more closely resemble *regulation* than market participation, and thus should be treated as such for purposes of the dormant Commerce Clause.

4. *The implications of the regulation-market participation distinction*: Importantly, the fact that a state's action falls outside the market participant exception does not necessarily render it unconstitutional. Rather, it means that the condition must be analyzed as a *regulation*, subject to typical dormant Commerce Clause scrutiny. Applying that analysis, Alaska's condition in *South Central Timber* was plainly impermissible. It was facially discriminatory, requiring a certain percentage of timber processing to occur in Alaska. As a discriminatory regulation, it was "virtually *per se*" invalid. It would have only been permissible if Alaska could demonstrate (a) a legitimate, non-protectionist interest for the law, and (b) the lack of any practicable, non-discriminatory means to accomplish that interest. Here, Alaska had conceded that its goal was to favor the Alaska timber processing industry—a protectionist objective that is verboten under the dormant Commerce Clause.

* * *

QUESTION: A state owned and operated an electric power system, which included a nuclear power plant. To ensure the availability of sites for the disposal of spent fuel from the nuclear power plant, the state refused to supply electric power to out-of-state purchasers residing in states that do not accept spent fuel from the plant for storage or disposal. Assume no federal statute applies. Which of the following is the strongest argument that the state's action is constitutional?

(A) A state may condition the sale to out-of-state purchasers of any products produced in that state on the willingness of those purchasers to bear their fair share of the environmental costs of producing those products.

(B) The generation of electricity is intrastate by nature and therefore subject to plenary state control.

(C) The state itself owns and operates the power system, and therefore its refusal to supply power to out-of-state purchasers is not subject to the strictures of the dormant Commerce Clause.

(D) The state's action is rationally related to the health, safety, and welfare of its citizens.

ANSWER: The best choice is (C). Choice (A) fails because it goes beyond the market-participant exception and states a rule that is too broad. A state may condition *its own sale* to out-of-state purchasers of goods or services on those purchasers' willingness to bear their fair share of the environmental costs. (Indeed, a state could simply refuse to sell to out-of-state purchasers altogether.) But a state may not so condition sales to out-of-state purchasers "of *any* products produced in the state." To do so is to go well beyond those transactions in which the state is itself a participant, and to regulate transactions between private parties. And when a state *regulates*, any action that discriminates against out-of-state purchasers will be virtually *per se* unconstitutional. Answer (B) does not work because the scope of the dormant Commerce Clause is the same as that of Congress's authority to enact legislation under the commerce power. At issue in this question are sales of electricity—activity that is plainly "economic or commercial in nature." Congress could regulate this activity using its commerce power (under *Lopez*'s third category as an activity "substantially affecting interstate commerce). As a result, a state's actions in relation to that activity are subject to the strictures of the dormant Commerce Clause (assuming the state's actions are not otherwise exempt from dormant Commerce Clause review). In this way, the generation of electricity is hardly "subject to plenary state control." Answer (D) fails because it is not the *strongest* argument that the state's action is constitutional. This would be a good argument if the only claim that out-of-state purchasers could raise would be that the state's action violated the Due Process Clause or the Equal Protection Clause. Under either of those provisions, for this sort of law, the relevant scrutiny would be mere rational basis, and the state would only have to show that the law was rationally related to a legitimate state interest (such as the health, safety, and welfare of its citizens). But this state action appears to discriminate against interstate commerce, thus potentially triggering a more searching constitutional examination. Merely showing that the law has a rational basis will generally not be enough. Thus, (C) is the best choice. The state is acting as a seller of electricity, meaning its action falls under the market-participant exception. This means the dormant Commerce Clause will not apply, despite the state's discrimination against out-of-state purchasers.

* * *

CONCLUDING PROBLEMS ON THE DORMANT COMMERCE CLAUSE

In each of the following circumstances, please evaluate whether you believe the law in question violates the dormant Commerce Clause. In each case, please identify the precise rationale for your conclusion.

1. A California statute imposes a 5% sales tax on all wine sold within the state. The statute also imposes an additional 2.5% surtax on all wine produced in vineyards outside of California. California justifies the additional surtax on the ground that the out-of-state wines use more of the state's public resources (such as causing additional traffic on the state's highways) in bringing them to stores for sale.

2. A California statute imposes an inspection fee on all milk producers who wish to sell their products in state. The fee is measured in each case to equal the cost to the state in conducting an inspection of the products. In practice, the fee imposed on out-of-state producers is often twice the fee for in-state producers, due to the costs of state officials traveling to the production sites to conduct the inspections.

3. Due to the increase in wildfire danger, a new California statute forbids the sale or use of fireworks within the state. There are no significant firework manufacturers in California, so the economic impact of the statute (on fireworks producers) is felt is almost entirely outside the state.

4. A federal statute forbids the transportation of solid waste across any state border.

5. Santa Clara County operates a landfill. Residents of the county may dump any nonhazardous solid waste at the dump, and they are permitted two trips to the dump each year free of charge. Non-residents may also dump solid waste at the landfill, but

they are charged by the weight of the waste, with the typical truck-full of waste costing $150 to dump.

6. The City of San Francisco wishes to invest millions of dollars in the creation of temporary housing for the unhoused in the city, as well as to dramatically expand the city's provision of mental health services and substance abuse treatment for city residents who cannot afford them. To finance these initiatives, the city has instituted a new 10 percent sales tax that applies exclusively to the provision of hotel rooms and rental cars in the city.

7. The Washington state legislature enacts a new statute imposing a "financial services windfall profits tax." The provision imposes a 1 percent surtax on the revenues of any bank doing business in Washington. The tax applies only to the revenues attributable to a bank's operations in Washington. The tax only applies to banks with total global revenues exceeding $1 billion. All banks doing business in Washington with $1 billion in global revenue are incorporated and headquartered in other states. (There are several banks incorporated and headquartered in Washington, but their global revenues are less than $1 billion.)

8. The State of New York has adopted a new statute regarding the registration of firms to do business in the state. (Registration is necessary to lawfully sell goods or services to customers in the state.) As a condition of registration, a firm (as part of its health insurance package) must cover gender-affirming medical care for its employees and their dependents. Further, the firm must attest that it covers (and will continue to cover) such treatment for *all* of its U.S.-based employees, regardless of where they are employed.

CHAPTER 18

OTHER STRUCTURAL CONSTRAINTS ON THE STATES

A.   The Privileges and Immunities Clause of Article IV

Another important structural limitation on state governments is the Privileges and Immunities Clause of Article IV, §2. Two clauses in the Constitution refer to the "privileges" and "immunities" of citizenship. One appears in the Fourteenth Amendment, alongside the Equal Protection and Due Process Clauses. The other—addressed here—is located in Article IV.

Article IV contains several provisions concerning interstate comity. Article IV, §1 includes the Full Faith and Credit Clause, which generally requires each state to recognize the valid judgments of other states' courts. Article IV, § 2, clause 3 contains the infamous Fugitive Slave Clause, which mandated that forbid states from freeing an escaped slave from their enslavement, and mandated that all such slaves "shall be delivered up on claim of the party to whom such service or labor is due." Article IV, § 2, clause 1 contains the Extradition Clause: "A Person charged in any State with Treason, Felony, or other Crime, who shall flee from Justice, and be found in another State, shall on demand of the executive Authority of the State from which he fled, be delivered up, to be removed to the State having Jurisdiction of the Crime." Each of these clauses shares a common purpose of requiring the states to respect each other's legal processes (for better and, sometimes, for worse).

Likewise, the Privileges and Immunities Clause of Article IV, §2 constrains the states' capacity to discriminate against citizens of other states. It is partly a *structural* provision, aimed at limiting the degree to which states can favor (or not favor) their own residents. But accomplishes this structural objective by providing an individual right: it protects citizens from discrimination based on their state residence, at least in many circumstances.

1.   The basic protection: being treated as a "welcome guest"

A classic case applying Article IV, §2 is *Toomer v. Witsell*, 334 U.S. 385 (1948). At issue were license fees that South Carolina charged for the privilege of shrimping in the state's coastal waters. South Carolina imposed an annual fee of $25 per boat for state residents and $2,500 per boat for nonresidents. Several Georgia commercial shrimp fishermen challenged the scheme under the Privileges and Immunities Clause of Article IV. As you read the Court's opinion, please consider the following questions:

1. What exactly is the protection provided by the Privileges and Immunities Clause of Article IV? When will a state government's discrimination against nonresidents nonetheless be constitutional?

2. What was the "privilege" or "immunity" at issue in *Toomer*? Why was it one of the privileges or immunities protected by the clause?

3. Once the Court determined that South Carolina's license scheme was subject to scrutiny under the Privileges and Immunities Clause, what doctrinal test did the Court apply to determine whether the scheme was permissible? Why did the state's scheme fail that test?

Toomer v. Witsell
334 U.S. 385 (1948)

MR. CHIEF JUSTICE VINSON delivered the opinion of the Court.

This is a suit to enjoin as unconstitutional the enforcement of several South Carolina statutes governing commercial shrimp fishing in the three-mile maritime belt off the coast of that State. Appellants, who initiated the action, are five individual fishermen, all citizens and residents of Georgia, and a non-profit fish dealers' organization incorporated in Florida. Appellees are South Carolina officials charged with enforcement of the statutes. . . .

The fishery which South Carolina attempts to regulate by the statutes in question is part of a larger shrimp fishery extending from North Carolina to Florida. Most of the shrimp in this area are of a migratory type, swimming south in the late summer and fall and returning northward in the spring. Since there is no federal regulation of the fishery, the four States most intimately concerned have gone their separate ways in devising conservation and other regulatory measures. While action by the States has followed somewhat parallel lines, efforts to secure uniformity throughout the fishery have by and large been fruitless. Because of the integral nature of the fishery, many commercial shrimpers, including the appellants, would like to start trawling off the Carolinas in the summer and then follow the shrimp down the coast to Florida. Each State has been desirous of securing for its residents the opportunity to shrimp in this way, but some have apparently been more concerned with channeling to their own residents the business derived from local waters. Restrictions on non-resident fishing in the marginal sea, and even prohibitions against it, have now invited retaliation to the point that the fishery is effectively partitioned at the state lines; bilateral bargaining on an official level has come to be the only method whereby any one of the States can obtain for its citizens the right to shrimp in waters adjacent to the other States.

* * *

The statutes appellants challenge relate to shrimping during the open season in the three-mile belt: Section 3300 of the South Carolina Code provides that the waters in that area shall be "a common for the people of the State for the taking of fish." . . . Section 3379, as amended in 1947, requires payment of a license fee of $25 for each shrimp boat owned by a resident, and of $2,500 for each one owned by a non-resident. . . . Violation of the fishing laws entails suspension of the violator's license as well as a maximum of a $1,000 fine, imprisonment for a year, or a combination of a $500 fine and a year's imprisonment. . . .

Appellants' most vigorous attack is directed at §3379 which, as amended in 1947, requires non-residents of South Carolina to pay license fees one hundred times as great as those which residents must pay. The purpose and effect of this statute, they contend, is not to conserve shrimp, but to exclude non-residents and thereby create a commercial monopoly for South Carolina residents. As such, the statute is said to violate the privileges and immunities clause of Art. IV, §2, of the Constitution and the equal protection clause of the Fourteenth Amendment.

Article IV, §2, so far as relevant, reads as follows: "The Citizens of each State shall be entitled to all Privileges and Immunities of Citizens in the several States." The primary purpose of this clause, like the clauses between which it is located—those relating to full faith and credit and to interstate extradition of fugitives from justice—was to help fuse into one Nation a collection of independent, sovereign States. It was designed to insure to a citizen of State A who ventures into State B the same privileges which the citizens of State B enjoy. For protection of such equality the citizen of State A was not to be restricted to the uncertain remedies afforded by diplomatic processes and official retaliation. "Indeed, without some provision of the kind removing from the citizens of each State the disabilities of alienage in the other States, and giving them equality of privilege with citizens of those States, the Republic would have constituted little more than a league of States; it would not have constituted the Union which now exists." *Paul v. Virginia*, 8 Wall. 168, 180 (1868).

In line with this underlying purpose, it was long ago decided that one of the privileges which the clause guarantees to citizens of State A is that of doing business in State B on terms of substantial equality with the citizens of that State.

Like many other constitutional provisions, the privileges and immunities clause is not an absolute. It does bar discrimination against citizens of other States where there is no substantial reason for the discrimination beyond the mere fact that they are citizens of other States. But it does not preclude disparity of treatment in the many situations where there are perfectly valid independent reasons for it. Thus the inquiry in each case must be concerned with whether such reasons do exist and whether the degree of discrimination bears a close relation to them. The inquiry must also, of course, be conducted with due regard for the principle that the States should have considerable leeway in analyzing local evils and in prescribing appropriate cures.

With these factors in mind. we turn to a consideration of the constitutionality of §3379.

By that statute South Carolina plainly and frankly discriminates against non-residents, and the record leaves little doubt but that the discrimination is so great that its practical effect is virtually exclusionary. This the appellees do not seriously dispute. Nor do they argue that since the statute is couched in terms of residence it is outside the scope of the privileges and immunities clause, which speaks of citizens. Such an argument, we agree, would be without force in this case.

As justification for the statute, appellees urge that the State's obvious purpose was to conserve its shrimp supply, and they suggest that it was designed to head off an impending threat of excessive trawling. The record casts some doubt on these statements. But in any event, appellees' argument assumes that any means adopted to attain valid objectives necessarily squares with the privileges and immunities clause. It overlooks the purpose of that clause, which, as indicated above, is to outlaw classifications based on the fact of non-citizenship unless there is something to indicate that non-citizens constitute a peculiar source of the evil at which the statute is aimed.

In this connection appellees mention, without further elucidation, the fishing methods used by non-residents, the size of their boats, and the allegedly greater cost of enforcing the laws against them. One statement in the appellees' brief might also be construed to mean that the State's conservation program for shrimp requires expenditure of funds beyond those collected in license fees—funds to which residents and not non-residents contribute. Nothing in the record indicates that non-residents use larger boats or different fishing methods than residents, that the cost of enforcing the laws against them is appreciably greater, or that any substantial amount of the State's general funds is devoted to shrimp conservation. But assuming such were the facts, they would not necessarily support a remedy so drastic as to be a near equivalent of total exclusion. The State is not without power, for example, to restrict the type of equipment used in its fisheries, to graduate license fees according to the size of the boats, or even to charge non-residents a differential which would merely compensate the State for any added enforcement burden they may impose or for any conservation expenditures from taxes which only residents pay. We would be closing our eyes to reality, we believe, if we concluded that there was a reasonable relationship between the danger represented by non-citizens, as a class, and the severe discrimination practiced upon them.

Thus, § 3379 must be held unconstitutional unless commercial shrimp fishing in the maritime belt falls within some unexpressed exception to the privileges and immunities clause. [The Court concluded that no such exception applied here.]

* * *

Thus we hold that commercial shrimping in the marginal sea, like other common callings, is within the purview of the privileges and immunities clause. And since we have previously concluded that the reasons advanced in support of the statute do not bear a reasonable relationship to the high degree of discrimination practiced upon citizens of other States, it follows that § 3379 violates Art. IV, § 2, of the Constitution. . . .

*　　*　　*

Notes on *Toomer v. Witsell*

1. ***The nature of the clause's guarantee***: The Privileges and Immunities Clause of Article IV protects nonresident citizens against discrimination based on their status as nonresidents. But it does not guarantee any particular constellation of substantive rights. For example, a state that denies *everyone* within its borders a privilege or immunity covered by the clause would not violate the Privileges and Immunities Clause. Rather, the clause generally requires the equal treatment of residents and nonresidents with respect to those rights covered by the clause. As the Court stated in *Toomer*, the clause "was designed to insure to a citizen of State A who ventures into State B the same privileges which the citizens of State B enjoy."

2. ***The constitutional right to travel***: The Constitution protects a so-called "right to travel," but it does so in a complicated way. As explained in the next section, there are three distinct strands of this "right to travel," each with a different scope and constitutional source. First, there is a right to move physically across state borders. This might be a right protected by the Due Process Clause, the Privileges or Immunities Clause of the Fourteenth Amendment, or simply an inference drawn from the Constitution's structure as a whole. Regardless, states are generally prohibited from restricting a person's physical movement from state to state.

Second, there is the right to visit another state as a nonresident and be treated as a "welcome guest." This is the aspect protected by the Privileges and Immunities Clause of Article IV. The Georgia shrimpers in *Toomer* were presumptively entitled to visit South Carolina to pursue a common calling without suffering discrimination due to their status as nonresidents.

Third, the Constitution protects the right of U.S. citizens to migrate from one state to another and not suffer any discrimination due to being a *new* state resident. This aspect of the right to travel is explored in *Saenz v. Roe*, 526 U.S. 489 (1999), and is protected by the Privileges or Immunities Clause of the Fourteenth Amendment. It generally forbids discrimination based on the duration of citizens' residency in the state.

3. ***The "privileges and immunities" protected by Article IV, §2***: What are the "privileges and "immunities" to which the Privileges and Immunities Clause of Article IV applies? The Supreme Court has defined them in various

ways: as those rights that are "fundamental to the promotion of interstate harmony"; those rights "bearing upon the vitality of the Nation as a single entity"; and those rights "sufficiently basic to the livelihood of the Nation." The most famous statement comes from Justice Bushrod Washington's opinion in *Corfield v. Coryell*, 6 Fed. Cas. 546 (1823). It stated that the clause protects

> "the right of a citizen of one state to pass through or reside in any other state, for purposes of trade . . . or otherwise, to claim the benefit of the writ of habeas corpus; to institute and maintain actions of any kind in the courts of the state; to take, hold, and dispose of property; and an exemption from higher taxes or impositions than are paid by other citizens of the state."

Historically, the right most frequently vindicated under Article IV has been the right "to pursue a common calling"—to pursue employment, conduct business, or otherwise earn a living. This was the "privilege" at issue in *Toomer*, as the Georgia shrimpers were pursuing the common calling of commercial fishing. This was also the privilege at issue in *Austin v. New Hampshire*, 420 U.S. 656 (1975), where the plaintiff sought to practice law, and in *Building Trades & Construction Trades Council v. Camden*, 465 U.S. 208 (1984) (explored below), where the plaintiffs sought construction jobs. The clause also protects the right of access to a state's courts; the right to make and enforce contracts; the right to acquire, hold, and dispose of property; and the right to fully enjoy those liberties protected elsewhere in the Constitution. (For instance, a state could not provide greater and lesser degrees of the free exercise of religion depending on a person's state residence. *See Doe v. Bolton*, 410 U.S. 179 (1973).)

4. *Rights not protected by Article IV*: Some rights fall outside the protections of the Privileges and Immunities Clause, such that a state's discrimination against nonresidents with respect to them will be constitutional. As the Court explained in *Baldwin v. Fish and Game Commission*, 436 U.S. 371 (1978), "[o]nly with respect to those 'privileges' and 'immunities' bearing upon the vitality of the Nation as a single entity must the State treat all citizens, resident and nonresident, equally." *Baldwin* held this standard did not encompass recreational elk hunting. Thus, the Court rejected a challenge by nonresidents to a Montana recreational hunting license scheme that charged nonresidents substantially more, and on more restrictive terms:

> "Appellants' interest in sharing this limited resource on more equal terms with Montana residents simply does not fall within the purview of the Privileges and Immunities Clause. Equality in access to Montana elk is not basic to the maintenance or well-being of the Union. Appellants do not—and cannot—contend that they are deprived of a means of a livelihood by the system or of access to any part of the State to which they may seek to travel. We do not decide the full range of activities that are sufficiently basic to the livelihood of the Nation that the States may not interfere with a nonresident's participation therein without similarly interfering with a resident's participation. Whatever rights or activities may be 'fundamental'

under the Privileges and Immunities Clause, we are persuaded, and hold, that elk hunting by nonresidents in Montana is not one of them."

The result in *Baldwin* almost certainly would have been different if the elk hunting at issue had been *commercial*. (In that case, it likely would have been considered a "common calling.") But recreational activities fall outside the scope of the clause. More recently, the Supreme Court held in *McBurney v. Young*, 569 U.S. 221 (2013), that a Virginia law that permitted Virginia citizens to make Freedom of Information Act requests from the state government—but denied that opportunity to nonresidents—was consistent with the clause. To the Court, "the right to access public information on equal terms with citizens of the Commonwealth" was not a privilege or immunity covered by the clause.

5. *"Citizens"*: There is a substantial overlap in the prohibitions of the Privileges and Immunities Clause of Article IV and the dormant Commerce Clause. Indeed, plaintiffs often raise both claims when challenging a state or local law that arguably discriminates against nonresidents. But there are also important differences. One difference concerns who is protected. The Privileges and Immunities Clause protects "citizens," a term that only includes natural persons. Thus, neither the Washington Apple Commission nor the Dean Milk Company could have brought claims under the Privileges and Immunities Clause. While corporations are "persons" under the Constitution, only human beings are "citizens" under Article IV. (But notice that corporations and other entities are "citizens" for purposes of diversity jurisdiction under Article III.)

6. *The applicable standard of scrutiny*: State laws that discriminate against nonresidents with respect to a privilege or immunity protected by the clause trigger a form of "intermediate" scrutiny: to nonetheless be constitutional, the law must (a) advance a "substantial" state interest, and (b) be "substantially related" to that interest. The first part of this test concerns the *weight* of the relevant state interest, while the second concerns the "fit" between the means employed (*i.e.*, the challenged law) and the objective the state is pursuing. The Supreme Court has also phrased the second part of the test this way: "nonresidents must somehow be shown to constitute a peculiar source of the evil at which the statute is aimed." In other words, the state cannot disadvantage nonresidents merely because it is politically convenient to do so. But notice that laws discriminating against nonresidents with respect to protected privileges or immunities can still be constitutional—provided they survive this intermediate level of scrutiny.

7. *Permissible discrimination against nonresidents*: The Privileges and Immunities Clause *constrains* state discrimination against nonresidents, but it is far from absolute. In several contexts, a state's favoring its own residents is plainly permissible. Indeed, such discrimination is often necessary for states to retain their independent identities as states. As the Court explained in *Baldwin*:

"It has not been suggested . . . that state citizenship or residency may never be used by a State to distinguish among persons. Suffrage, for example, always has been understood to be tied to an individual's identification with a particular State. No one would suggest that the Privileges and Immunities Clause requires a State to open its polls to a person who declines to assert that the State is the only one where he claims a right to vote. The same is true as to qualification for an elective office of the State. Nor must a State always apply all its laws or all its services equally to anyone, resident or nonresident, who may request it so to do. Some distinctions between residents and nonresidents merely reflect the fact that this is a Nation composed of individual States, and are permitted."

* * *

2. City-level discrimination and market participation

The text of Article IV, §2 makes clear that it applies to discrimination by *states* against citizens of other *states*: "The Citizens of each State shall be entitled to all Privileges and Immunities of Citizens in the several States." But what if the challenged law was enacted by a city or municipal government? And what if the discrimination is based not on state residency, but on *city* residency? Does the clause apply in those circumstances? Further, is there a "market participant" exception to Article IV, §2, just as there is to the dormant Commerce Clause? The Supreme Court addressed each of these questions in *Building Trades & Constr. Council v. Camden*, 465 U.S. 208 (1984). As you read *Camden*, please consider the following questions:

1. Why was Camden's hiring preference treated no differently—at least for purposes of the Privileges and Immunities Clause—than if it had it been enacted by the State of New Jersey?

2. Did Camden's hiring preference discriminate against some New Jersey citizens? Did that matter? Why or why not?

3. Is there a "market participant exception" to the Privileges and Immunities Clause? Why or why not?

4. What was that relevance of the fact that Camden was providing these jobs itself, through the spending of its own funds? At what point in the constitutional analysis would that fact be relevant, if at all?

5. Did the Court decide that Camden's hiring preference was unconstitutional? If not, what exactly did it hold?

Building Trades & Constr. Council v. Camden
465 U.S. 208 (1984)

JUSTICE REHNQUIST delivered the opinion of the Court.

A municipal ordinance of the city of Camden, New Jersey, requires that at least 40% of the employees of contractors and subcontractors working on city construction projects be Camden residents. Appellant, the United Building and Construction Trades Council of Camden County and Vicinity (Council), challenges that ordinance as a violation of the Privileges and Immunities Clause, Art. IV, § 2, cl. 1, of the United States Constitution. The Supreme Court of New Jersey rejected appellant's privileges and immunities attack on the ground that the ordinance discriminates on the basis of municipal, not state, residency. The court decline[d] to apply the Privileges and Immunities Clause in the context of a municipal ordinance that has identical effects upon out-of-state citizens and New Jersey citizens not residing in the locality. We conclude that the challenged ordinance is properly subject to the strictures of the Clause. We therefore reverse the judgment of the Supreme Court of New Jersey and remand the case for a determination of the validity of the ordinance under the appropriate constitutional standard.

On August 28, 1980, the Camden City Council . . . adopted an ordinance setting minority hiring "goals" on all public works contracts. The ordinance also created a hiring preference for Camden residents . . . . As subsequently amended, the ordinance requires that, on all construction projects funded by the city: "The developer/contractor, in hiring for jobs, shall make every effort to employ persons residing within the City of Camden but, in no event, shall less than forty percent (40%) of the entire labor force be residents of the City of Camden." The contractor is also obliged to ensure that any subcontractors working on such projects adhere to the same requirement. . . . Appellant, an association of labor organizations representing private employees in the building and construction trades in various New Jersey counties, . . . challenged state approval of the resident-hiring quota as ultra vires, and as unconstitutional under the Commerce Clause and the Privileges and Immunities Clause of Art. IV of the United States Constitution and under the Fourteenth Amendment's Equal Protection Clause.

We noted probable jurisdiction. Since the Council filed its appeal, however, there have been two significant changes in the posture of the case. First, the Court decided *White v. Massachusetts Council of Construction Employers, Inc.*, 460 U.S. 204 (1983), which held that an executive order of the Mayor of Boston, requiring that at least 50% of all jobs on construction projects funded in whole or in part by city funds be filled by bona fide city residents, was immune from scrutiny under the Commerce Clause because Boston was acting as a market participant, rather than as a market regulator. In light of the decision in *White*, appellant has abandoned its Commerce Clause challenge to the Camden ordinance.

Second, in July, 1983, Camden amended its affirmative action plan. The . . . scope of the ordinance was clarified. It now applies to any construction project "which is funded in whole or in part with City funds or funds which the City expends or administers in accordance with the terms of a grant." Finally, the 40% resident-hiring requirement was changed from a strict "quota" to a "goal" with which developers and contractors must make "every good faith effort" to comply.

Because of these changes, the only question left for our consideration is whether the Camden ordinance, as now written, violates the Privileges and Immunities Clause. We first address the argument, accepted by the Supreme Court of New Jersey, that the Clause does not even apply to a municipal ordinance such as this. Two separate contentions are advanced in support of this position: first, that the Clause only applies to laws passed by a State and, second, that the Clause only applies to laws that discriminate on the basis of state citizenship.

The first argument can be quickly rejected. The fact that the ordinance in question is a municipal, rather than a state, law does not somehow place it outside the scope of the Privileges and Immunities Clause. . . . [A] municipality is merely a political subdivision of the State from which its authority derives. *Trenton v. New Jersey*, 262 U.S. 182, 187 (1923). It is as true of the Privileges and Immunities Clause as of the Equal Protection Clause that what would be unconstitutional if done directly by the State can no more readily be accomplished by a city deriving its authority from the State. *Memorial Hospital v. Maricopa County*, 415 U.S. 250, 256 (1974); *Avery v. Midland County*, 390 U.S. 474, 480–481 (1968). Thus, even if the ordinance had been adopted solely by Camden, and not pursuant to a state program or with state approval, the hiring preference would still have to comport with the Privileges and Immunities Clause.

The second argument merits more consideration. The New Jersey Supreme Court concluded that the Privileges and Immunities Clause does not apply to an ordinance that discriminates solely on the basis of municipal residency. The Clause is phrased in terms of state citizenship, and was designed "to place the citizens of each State upon the same footing with citizens of other States, so far as the advantages resulting from citizenship in those States are concerned." *Paul v. Virginia*, 8 Wall. 168, 180 (1869).

"The primary purpose of this clause, like the clauses between which it is located—those relating to full faith and credit and to interstate extradition of fugitives from justice—was to help fuse into one Nation a collection of independent, sovereign States. It was designed to insure to a citizen of State A who ventures into State B the same privileges which the citizens of State B enjoy. For protection of such equality, the citizen of State A was not to be restricted to the uncertain remedies afforded by diplomatic processes and official retaliation."

Toomer v. Witsell, 334 U.S. 385, 395 (1948). Municipal residency classifications, it is argued, simply do not give rise to the same concerns.

We cannot accept this argument. We have never read the Clause so literally as to apply it only to distinctions based on state citizenship. For example, in *Mullaney v. Anderson*, 342 U.S. 415, 419–420 (1952), the Court held that the Alaska Territory had no more freedom to discriminate against those not residing in the Territory than did any State to favor its own citizens. And despite some initial uncertainty, it is now established that the terms "citizen" and "resident" are "essentially interchangeable," *Austin v. New Hampshire*, 420 U.S. 656, 662, n.8 (1975), for purposes of analysis of most cases under the Privileges and Immunities Clause. A person who is not residing in a given State is *ipso facto* not residing in a city within that State. Thus, whether the exercise of a privilege is conditioned on state residency or on municipal residency, he will just as surely be excluded.

Given the Camden ordinance, an out-of-state citizen who ventures into New Jersey will not enjoy the same privileges as the New Jersey citizen residing in Camden. It is true that New Jersey citizens not residing in Camden will be affected by the ordinance as well as out-of-state citizens. And it is true that the disadvantaged New Jersey residents have no claim under the Privileges and Immunities Clause. *Slaughter-House Cases*, 16 Wall. 36, 77 (1873). But New Jersey residents at least have a chance to remedy at the polls any discrimination against them. Out-of-state citizens have no similar opportunity, *Austin v. New Hampshire*, supra, at 662, and they must not "be restricted to the uncertain remedies afforded by diplomatic processes and official retaliation." *Toomer v. Witsell*, supra, at 395.[9] We conclude that Camden's ordinance is not immune from constitutional review at the behest of out-of-state residents merely because some instate residents are similarly disadvantaged.

Application of the Privileges and Immunities Clause to a particular instance of discrimination against out-of-state residents entails a two-step inquiry. As an initial matter, the Court must decide whether the ordinance burdens one of those privileges and immunities protected by

---

[9] The dissent suggests that New Jersey citizens not residing in Camden will adequately protect the interests of out-of-state residents and that the scope of the Privileges and Immunities Clause should be measured in light of this political reality. What the dissent fails to appreciate is that the Camden ordinance at issue in this case was adopted pursuant to a comprehensive, statewide program applicable in all New Jersey cities. The Camden resident-preference ordinance has already received state sanction and approval, and every New Jersey city is free to adopt a similar protectionist measure. Some have already done so. Thus, it is hard to see how New Jersey residents living outside Camden will protect the interests of out-of-state citizens.

More fundamentally, the dissent's proposed blanket exemption for all classifications that are less than statewide would provide States with a simple means for evading the strictures of the Privileges and Immunities Clause. Suppose, for example, that California wanted to guarantee that all employees of contractors and subcontractors working on construction projects funded in whole or in part by state funds are state residents. Under the dissent's analysis, the California Legislature need merely divide the State in half, providing one resident-hiring preference for northern Californians on all such projects taking place in northern California, and one for southern Californians on all projects taking place in southern California. State residents generally would benefit from the law at the expense of out-of-state residents; yet, the law would be immune from scrutiny under the Clause simply because it was not phrased in terms of *state* citizenship or residency. Such a formalistic construction would effectively write the Clause out of the Constitution.

the Clause. *Baldwin v. Montana Fish and Game Comm'n*, 436 U.S. 371, 383 (1978). Not all forms of discrimination against citizens of other States are constitutionally suspect.

"Some distinctions between residents and nonresidents merely reflect the fact that this is a Nation composed of individual States, and are permitted; other distinctions are prohibited because they hinder the formation, the purpose, or the development of a single Union of those States. Only with respect to those 'privileges' and 'immunities' bearing upon the vitality of the Nation as a single entity must the State treat all citizens, resident and nonresident, equally."

Ibid. As a threshold matter, then, we must determine whether an out-of-state resident's interest in employment on public works contracts in another State is sufficiently "fundamental" to the promotion of interstate harmony so as to "fall within the purview of the Privileges and Immunities Clause." *Id.* at 388.

Certainly, the pursuit of a common calling is one of the most fundamental of those privileges protected by the Clause. Many, if not most, of our cases expounding the Privileges and Immunities Clause have dealt with this basic and essential activity. Public employment, however, is qualitatively different from employment in the private sector; it is a subspecies of the broader opportunity to pursue a common calling. We have held that there is no fundamental right to government employment for purposes of the Equal Protection Clause. *Massachusetts Bd. of Retirement v. Murgia*, 427 U.S. 307, 313 (1976) (per curiam). And in *White*, we held that, for purposes of the Commerce Clause, everyone employed on a city public works project is, "in a substantial if informal sense, 'working for the city.'"

It can certainly be argued that, for purposes of the Privileges and Immunities Clause, everyone affected by the Camden ordinance is also "working for the city," and therefore has no grounds for complaint when the city favors its own residents. But we decline to transfer mechanically into this context an analysis fashioned to fit the Commerce Clause. Our decision in *White* turned on a distinction between the city acting as a market participant and the city acting as a market regulator. The question whether employees of contractors and subcontractors on public works projects were or were not, in some sense, working for the city was crucial to that analysis. The question had to be answered in order to chart the boundaries of the distinction. But the distinction between market participant and market regulator relied upon in *White* to dispose of the Commerce Clause challenge is not dispositive in this context. The two Clauses have different aims, and set different standards for state conduct.

The Commerce Clause acts as an implied restraint upon state regulatory powers. Such powers must give way before the superior authority of Congress to legislate on (or leave unregulated) matters involving interstate commerce. When the State acts solely as a market participant, no conflict between state regulation and federal regulatory authority can arise. The Privileges and Immunities Clause, on the other hand, imposes a direct restraint on state action in the interests of interstate harmony. *Hicklin v. Orbeck*, supra, at 523–524; *Ward v. Maryland*, supra, at 430; *Paul v. Virginia*, 8 Wall. at 180. This concern with comity cuts across the market regulator-market participant distinction that is crucial under the Commerce Clause. It is discrimination against out-of-state residents on matters of fundamental concern which triggers the Clause, not regulation affecting interstate commerce. Thus, the fact that Camden is merely setting conditions on its expenditures for goods and services in the marketplace does not preclude the possibility that those conditions violate the Privileges and Immunities Clause.

In *Hicklin v. Orbeck*, we struck down as a violation of the Privileges and Immunities Clause an "Alaska Hire" statute containing a resident-hiring preference for all employment related to the development of the State's oil and gas resources. Alaska argued in that case that, "because the oil and gas that are the subject of Alaska Hire are owned by the State, this ownership, of itself, is sufficient justification for the Act's discrimination against nonresidents, and takes the Act totally without the scope of the Privileges and Immunities Clause." *Id.* at 528. We concluded, however, that the State's interest in controlling those things it claims to own is not absolute. "Rather than placing a statute completely beyond the Clause, a State's ownership of the property with which the statute is concerned is a factor—although often the crucial factor—to be considered in evaluating whether the statute's discrimination against noncitizens violates the Clause." *Id.* at 529. Much the same analysis, we think, is appropriate to a city's efforts to bias private employment decisions in favor of its residents on construction projects funded with public moneys. The fact that Camden is expending its own funds or funds it administers in accordance with the terms of a grant is certainly a factor—perhaps the crucial factor—to be considered in evaluating whether the statute's discrimination violates the Privileges and Immunities Clause. But it does not remove the Camden ordinance completely from the purview of the Clause.

In sum, Camden may, without fear of violating the Commerce Clause, pressure private employers engaged in public works projects funded in whole or in part by the city to hire city residents. But that same exercise of power to bias the employment decisions of private contractors and subcontractors against out-of-state residents may be called to account under the Privileges and Immunities Clause. A determination of whether a privilege is "fundamental" for purposes of that Clause does not depend on whether the employees of private contractors and subcontractors engaged in public works projects can or cannot be said to be "working for the city." The opportunity to seek employment with such private employers is "sufficiently basic to the livelihood of the Nation," *Baldwin v. Montana Fish and Game Comm'n*, as to fall within the purview of the Privileges and Immunities Clause even though the contractors and subcontractors are themselves engaged in projects funded in whole or part by the city.

The conclusion that Camden's ordinance discriminates against a protected privilege does not, of course, end the inquiry. We have stressed in prior cases that, "[l]ike many other constitutional provisions, the privileges and immunities clause is not an absolute." *Toomer v. Witsell*, 334 U.S. at 396. It does not preclude discrimination against citizens of other States where there is a "substantial reason" for the difference in treatment. "[T]he inquiry in each case must be concerned with whether such reasons do exist and whether the degree of discrimination bears a close relation to them." *Ibid.* As part of any justification offered for the discriminatory law, nonresidents must somehow be shown to "constitute a peculiar source of the evil at which the statute is aimed." *Id.* at 398.

The city of Camden contends that its ordinance is necessary to counteract grave economic and social ills. Spiralling unemployment, a sharp decline in population, and a dramatic reduction in the number of businesses located in the city have eroded property values and depleted the city's tax base. The resident-hiring preference is designed, the city contends, to increase the number of employed persons living in Camden and to arrest the "middle-class flight" currently plaguing the city. The city also argues that all non-Camden residents employed on city public works projects, whether they reside in New Jersey or Pennsylvania, constitute a "source of the evil at which the statute is aimed." That is, they "live off" Camden without "living in" Camden. Camden contends that the scope of the discrimination practiced in the ordinance, with its municipal residency requirement, is carefully tailored to alleviate this evil without unreasonably harming nonresidents, who still have access to 60% of the available positions.

Every inquiry under the Privileges and Immunities Clause "must . . . be conducted with due regard for the principle that the States should have considerable leeway in analyzing local evils and in prescribing appropriate cures." *Toomer v. Witsell, supra,* at 396. This caution is particularly appropriate when a government body is merely setting conditions on the expenditure of funds it controls. The Alaska Hire statute at issue in *Hicklin v. Orbeck* swept within its strictures not only contractors and subcontractors dealing directly with the State's oil and gas; it also covered suppliers who provided goods and services to those contractors and subcontractors. We invalidated the Act as "an attempt to force virtually all businesses that benefit in some way from the economic ripple effect of Alaska's decision to develop its oil and gas resources to bias their employment practices in favor of the State's residents." *Id.* at 531. No similar "ripple effect" appears to infect the Camden ordinance. It is limited in scope to employees working directly on city public works projects.

Nonetheless, we find it impossible to evaluate Camden's justification on the record as it now stands. No trial has ever been held in the case.

No findings of fact have been made. The Supreme Court of New Jersey certified the case for direct appeal after the brief administrative proceedings that led to approval of the ordinance by the State Treasurer. It would not be appropriate for this Court either to make factual determinations as an initial matter or to take judicial notice of Camden's decay. We, therefore, deem it wise to remand the case to the New Jersey Supreme Court. That court may decide, consistent with state procedures, on the best method for making the necessary findings.

* * *

Notes on *Building Trades & Constr. Council v. Camden*

1. *Local or municipal discrimination*: Camden argued that its hiring ordinance was immune from Privileges and Immunities Clause scrutiny because it was a *city* ordinance (rather than a state law), and because it discriminated in favor of *city* (rather than state) residents. The Supreme Court rejected both arguments. First, "that the ordinance in question is a municipal, rather than a state, law does not somehow place it outside the scope of the Privileges and Immunities Clause. . . . [A] municipality is merely a political subdivision of the State from which its authority derives." Second, like the dormant Commerce Clause, the Privileges and Immunities Clause applies as much to municipal-residence discrimination as to state-residence discrimination. To be sure, other New Jersey residents also suffered from Camden's discrimination (just as most Wisconsin milk producers were disadvantaged by Madison's ordinance in *Dean Milk*). But only New Jersey residents benefited, and all residents of other states were disadvantaged. Moreover, as the Court explained in a footnote, exempting geographic discrimination that is short of coterminous with the state's borders would open the door for states to devise ingenious ways to evade the clause's strictures.

2. *Did Camden's ordinance concern a "privilege" or "immunity" protected by Article IV, §2?*: A critical question in *Camden* was whether the city's ordinance discriminated with respect to a "privilege" or "immunity" protected by the clause. Clearly employment (or the "pursuit of a common calling") constitutes such a right. But this case involved "a subspecies of the broader opportunity to pursue a common calling"—namely, "employment on public works contracts in another State." Ultimately, the Court concluded that public employment, funded by the state, was a "common calling" under Article IV:

"A determination of whether a privilege is 'fundamental' for purposes of that Clause does not depend on whether the employee of private contractors or subcontractors engaged in public works projects can or cannot be said to be 'working for the city.' The opportunity to seek employment with such employers is 'sufficiently basic to the livelihood of the Nation' as to fall within the Privileges and Immunities Clause."

3. *Market participation and Article IV*: In reaching this conclusion, the Court explained that, in contrast to the dormant Commerce Clause, the

Privileges and Immunities Clause contains no "market participant" exception. Why? Market participation is exempt from Commerce Clause scrutiny because the purpose of that clause is to constrain states' authority to *regulate* or *tax* the activities of private actors; when states act as market participants, they are not acting as sovereigns, using coercive governmental power to regulate or tax. By contrast, the Privileges and Immunities Clause is a restraint on *all* state actions—whether they constitute regulation, taxation, or proprietary activities. Article IV constrains a state's authority to draw distinctions based on state residence, full stop. Thus, whether a state is acting as a market participant, a regulator, or something else is immaterial to whether it actions are subject to the Privileges and Immunities Clause.

4. *But market participation can still be relevant to Privileges and Immunities Clause analysis*: Nevertheless, the Court in *Camden* emphasized that, if the government is acting as a market participant, this may be quite important to the Privileges and Immunities Clause question: "The fact that Camden is expending its own funds or funds it administers in accordance with the terms of a grant is certainly a factor—perhaps the crucial factor—to be considered in evaluating whether the statue's discrimination violates the Clause." More specifically, the Court suggested that the fact that Camden was spending its own money might be critical in evaluating the "substantiality" of the city's interest and the "fit" between that interest and the challenged law:

> "Every inquiry under the Privileges and Immunities clause must be conducted with due regard for the principle that the states should have considerable leeway in analyzing local evils and in prescribing appropriate cures. *This caution is particularly appropriate when a government body is merely setting the conditions on the expenditure of funds it controls*." (Emphasis added).

Thus, the fact that a state or city is acting as a market participant does not immunize its actions from Privileges and Immunities Clause review. But it might weigh heavily in evaluating whether the city's reasons for so discriminating are "substantial," and whether those reasons would be "substantially furthered" by the discrimination at issue.

5. *The provision of "public benefits" exclusively to state residents*: It is important to keep in mind that the Privileges and Immunities Clause of Article IV does not prohibit states from limiting most publicly-funded benefits only to their own residents. This sort of discrimination is quite familiar; states provide a range of state-funded benefits exclusively to residents: cash assistance, unemployment insurance, subsidized health insurance, public education, and driver's licenses, to name a few. The Supreme Court explained this point in *Martinez v. Bynum*, 461 U.S. 321 (1983), a case involving Texas's refusal to provide free primary and secondary education to persons other than *bona fide* Texas residents:

"A bona fide residence requirement, appropriately defined and uniformly applied, furthers the substantial state interest in assuring that services provided for its residents are enjoyed only by residents. Such a requirement with respect to attendance in public free schools . . . does not burden or penalize the constitutional right of interstate travel, for any person is free to move to a State and to establish residence there. A bona fide residence requirement simply requires that the person *does* establish residence before demanding the services that are restricted to residents."

Likewise, in *Vlandis v. Kline*, 412 U.S. 441 (1973), the Court "fully recognize[d] that a State has a legitimate interest in protecting and preserving the quality of its colleges and universities and the right of its own bona fide residents to attend such institutions on a preferential tuition basis." *See also Starns v. Malkerson*, 401 U.S. 985 (1971) (affirming a lower court judgment permitting Minnesota to require students at the University of Minnesota to reside in the state for at least a year before qualifying for the lower in-state tuition rate).

The essential justification for sustaining the constitutionality of such favoritism for a state's own residents is that it permits states to limit the "benefits generated by a state program to those who fund the state treasury and whom the State was created to serve," whether those benefits are "the enjoyment of state educational institutions, energy generated by a state-run plant, police and fire protection, [or] agricultural improvement and business development programs." *Reeves, Inc. v. Stake*, 447 U.S. 429, 442 (1980). The Constitution permits this kind of discrimination precisely because it favors those citizens who have principally paid for the benefits.

* * *

B. The Privileges or Immunities Clause of the Fourteenth Amendment

The other clause in the Constitution protecting citizens' "privileges" and "immunities" is the Privileges or Immunities Clause of the Fourteenth Amendment. Like Article IV, §2, this clause proscribes a form of discrimination against "outsiders," with the goal of promoting national unity. But the rights protected by the two clauses are quite different. While the clause in Article IV protects a citizen's right to visit other states as a "welcome visitor" by constraining discrimination based on state residence, the Privileges or Immunities Clause of the Fourteenth Amendment protects a citizen's right to establish residency in a new state: the right to interstate migration.

1. The *Slaughter-House Cases*

Shortly after the Civil War, the nation ratified the Fourteenth Amendment. This was one of the three Reconstruction Amendments—amendments added to the Constitution during Reconstruction (the others being the Thirteenth and the Fifteenth Amendments). As a matter of constitutional law, the single most significant provision in the Reconstruction Amendments is the second sentence of §1 of the Fourteenth Amendment, which provides as follows:

> "No state shall make or enforce any law which shall abridge the privileges or immunities of citizens of the United States; nor shall any state deprive any person of life, liberty, or property, without due process of law; nor deny to any person within its jurisdiction the equal protection of the laws."

The first major Supreme Court decision interpreting this provision was the *Slaughter-House Cases*, 83 U.S. 36 (1873). (Chapter 19 will explore the *Slaughter-House* decision in more detail.) As pertinent here, the plaintiffs argued that the Privileges or Immunities Clause of the Fourteenth Amendment made the protections of the Bill of Rights—the individual rights protected by the Constitution's first eight amendments—applicable to the states. Specifically, they contended these rights were "privileges or immunities of the United States," such that no state could deprive persons of them without violating the Fourteenth Amendment. (Prior to the Civil War, the Bill of Rights was understood only to constrain the actions of the federal government.)

In the *Slaughter-House Cases*, the Court rejected this argument, concluding that the scope of the Privileges or Immunities Clause of the Fourteenth Amendment was much narrower. Specifically, it held the clause only protects those rights that derive exclusively from the existence of the *national* government, and thus not any rights historically protected by the states. So if the right had traditionally been protected by state law—for instance, a person's basic civil liberties—it could not be a "privilege or immunity" protected by the Fourteenth Amendment. Under this reading, what rights did the Privileges or Immunities Clause protect? The *Slaughter-House* opinion explained as follows:

> "[W]e venture to suggest some which owe their existence to the Federal government, its National character, its Constitution, or its laws. One of these is well described in the case of *Crandall v. Nevada*. . . . It is said to be the right of the citizen of this great country, protected by implied guarantees of its Constitution, to come to the seat of government to assert any claim he may have upon that government, to transact any business he may have with it, to seek its protection, to share its offices, to engage in administering its functions. He has the right of free access to its seaports, through which all operations of foreign commerce are conducted, to the subtreasuries, land offices, and courts of justice in the several States. Another privilege of a citizen of the United States is to demand the care and protection of the Federal government over his life, liberty, and property when on the high seas or within the jurisdiction of a foreign government. [The] right to peaceably assemble and petition for redress of grievances, the privilege of the writ of habeas corpus, are rights of the citizen guaranteed by the Federal Constitution. The right to use the navigable waters of the United States, however they may penetrate the territory of the several States, all rights secured to

our citizens by treaties with foreign nations, are dependent upon citizenship of the United States, and not citizenship of a State."

These are rights that, by their nature, owe their existence to there being a national government. And it is a rather paltry list—at least when considering that the Fourteenth Amendment was intended to codify in the Constitution the outcome of the Civil War. (Hence, the dissent in *Slaughter-House* accused the majority of effectively reading the Privileges or Immunities Clause out of the Constitution.)

Given this narrow reading—one that remains good law today—the Privileges or Immunities Clause of the Fourteenth Amendment seemed to lack much importance to constitutional law. (Indeed, the Supreme Court invalidated only one state law as violating the clause between 1873 and 1999, and it overruled that decision within ten years.) In 1999, though, the Court gave the clause new life.

2. The right to interstate migration

In *Saenz v. Roe*, 526 U.S. 489 (1999), the Supreme Court invalidated a law under the Privileges or Immunities Clause of the Fourteenth Amendment for the first time in more than fifty years. At issue was a durational residency requirement imposed by California to qualify for cash assistance under the Temporary Assistance for Needy Families (TANF) program. Clearly, California could restrict eligibility for cash assistance payments (coming from the state's treasury) to California residents without violating Article IV, §2. But California's law did more. It provided that, if a California resident had been a state resident for less than a year, they would receive the level of cash assistance they would have received in the state from which they migrated (assuming that state offered a smaller benefit than California's). Only after a year of residing in California would they be treated the same as other California residents, entitled to the full amount of TANF assistance. Thus, the California scheme discriminated *among* California residents based on their duration of state residency. As you read *Saenz*, please consider the following questions:

1. Why wasn't §11450.03 of the California Welfare and Institutions Code subject to scrutiny under the Privileges and Immunities Clause of Article IV, §2? How was the discrimination at issue in *Saenz* different from that covered by the Privileges and Immunities Clause of Article IV, §2?

2. In what way did §11450.03 interfere with the constitutionally protected "right to travel"? Which aspect of the right to travel did it implicate?

3. What level of scrutiny did the Supreme Court apply to §11450.03 once the Court determined that the law impinged on this aspect of the right to travel? How did the Court justify this level of scrutiny?

4. What state interest did California assert in defending the constitutionality of §11450.03? Why was this interest insufficient to sustain the law?

Why did California not defend the law on the ground that it deterred indigent persons from migrating to California?

5. What was the "privilege or immunity" vindicated by the Court in *Saenz*?

6. How did the Court in *Saenz* distinguish the other ways in which states have historically required individuals to reside in the state for a certain period of time before being eligible for a benefit (such as reduced tuition at a state-run, public university)?

Saenz v. Roe
526 U.S. 489 (1999)

JUSTICE STEVENS delivered the opinion of the Court.

In 1992, California enacted a statute limiting the maximum welfare benefits available to newly arrived residents. The scheme limits the amount payable to a family that has resided in the State for less than 12 months to the amount payable by the State of the family's prior residence. [The question] presented by this case [is] whether the 1992 statute was constitutional when it was enacted . . . .

I

California is not only one of the largest, most populated, and most beautiful States in the Nation; it is also one of the most generous. Like all other States, California has participated in several welfare programs authorized by the Social Security Act and partially funded by the Federal Government. Its programs, however, provide a higher level of benefits and serve more needy citizens than those of most other States. In one year the most expensive of those programs, Aid to Families with Dependent Children (AFDC), which was replaced in 1996 with Temporary Assistance to Needy Families (TANF), provided benefits for an average of 2,645,814 persons per month at an annual cost to the State of $2.9 billion. In California the cash benefit for a family of two—a mother and one child—is $456 a month, but in the neighboring State of Arizona, for example, it is only $275.

In 1992, in order to make a relatively modest reduction in its vast welfare budget, the California Legislature enacted §11450.03 of the state Welfare and Institutions Code. That section sought to change the California AFDC program by limiting new residents, for the first year they live in California, to the benefits they would have received in the State of their prior residence. . . .

On December 21, 1992, three California residents who were eligible for AFDC benefits filed an action in the Eastern District of California challenging the constitutionality of the durational residency requirement in §11450.03. Each plaintiff alleged that she had recently moved to California to live with relatives in order to escape abusive family circumstances. One returned to California after living in Louisiana for seven years, the second had been living in Oklahoma for six weeks and the third came from Colorado. Each alleged that her monthly AFDC grant for the ensuing 12 months would be substantially lower under §11450.03 than if the statute were not in effect. Thus, the former residents of Louisiana and Oklahoma would receive $190 and $341 respectively for a family of three even though the full California grant was $641; the former resident of Colorado, who had just one child, was limited to $280 a month as opposed to the full California grant of $504 for a family of two.

II

On April 1, 1997, the [] respondents filed this action in the Eastern District of California . . . . The District Court issued a temporary restraining order and certified the case as a class action. [District Court Judge Levi made] certain additional comments on the parties' factual contentions. He noted that the State did not challenge plaintiffs' evidence indicating that, although California benefit levels were the sixth highest in the Nation in absolute terms, when housing costs are factored in, they rank 18th; that new residents coming from 43 States would face higher costs of living in California; and that welfare benefit levels actually have little, if any, impact on the residential choices made by poor people. On the other hand, he noted that the availability of other programs such as homeless assistance and an additional food stamp allowance of $1 in stamps for every $3 in reduced welfare benefits partially offset the disparity between the benefits for new and old residents. Notwithstanding those ameliorating facts, the State did not disagree with plaintiffs' contention that §11450.03 would create significant disparities between newcomers and welfare recipients who have resided in the State for over one year.

The State relied squarely on the undisputed fact that the statute would save some $10.9 million in annual welfare costs—an amount that is surely significant even though only a relatively small part of its annual expenditures of approximately $2.9 billion for the entire program. It contended that this cost saving was an appropriate exercise of budgetary authority as long as the residency requirement did not penalize the right to travel. The State reasoned that the payment of the same benefits that would have been received in the State of prior residency eliminated any potentially punitive aspects of the measure. Judge Levi concluded, however, that the relevant comparison was not between new residents of California and the residents of their former States, but rather between the new residents and longer term residents of California. He therefore again enjoined the implementation of the statute.

Without finally deciding the merits, the Court of Appeals affirmed his issuance of a preliminary injunction. . . . We now affirm.

III

The word "travel" is not found in the text of the Constitution. Yet the "constitutional right to travel from one State to another" is firmly embedded in our jurisprudence. *United States* v. *Guest*, 383 U.S. 745, 757 (1966). Indeed, as Justice Stewart reminded us in *Shapiro*

489

v. *Thompson*, 394 U.S. 618 (1969), the right is so important that it is "assertable against private interference as well as governmental action ... a virtually unconditional personal right, guaranteed by the Constitution to us all." *Id.*, at 643 (concurring opinion).

In *Shapiro*, we reviewed the constitutionality of three statutory provisions that denied welfare assistance to residents of Connecticut, the District of Columbia, and Pennsylvania, who had resided within those respective jurisdictions less than one year immediately preceding their applications for assistance. Without pausing to identify the specific source of the right, we began by noting that the Court had long "recognized that the nature of our Federal Union and our constitutional concepts of personal liberty unite to require that all citizens be free to travel throughout the length and breadth of our land uninhibited by statutes, rules, or regulations which unreasonably burden or restrict this movement." *Id.*, at 629. We squarely held that it was "constitutionally impermissible" for a State to enact durational residency requirements for the purpose of inhibiting the migration by needy persons into the State.[11] We further held that a classification that had the effect of imposing a penalty on the exercise of the right to travel violated the Equal Protection Clause "unless shown to be necessary to promote a *compelling* governmental interest," *id.*, at 634, and that no such showing had been made.

In this case California argues that §11450.03 was not enacted for the impermissible purpose of inhibiting migration by needy persons and that, unlike the legislation reviewed in *Shapiro,* it does not penalize the right to travel because new arrivals are not ineligible for benefits during their first year of residence. California submits that, instead of being subjected to the strictest scrutiny, the statute should be upheld if it is supported by a rational basis and that the State's legitimate interest in saving over $10 million a year satisfies that test. . . . The debate about the appropriate standard of review, together with the potential relevance of the federal statute, persuades us that it will be useful to focus on the source of the constitutional right on which respondents rely.

IV

The "right to travel" discussed in our cases embraces at least three different components. It protects the right of a citizen of one State to enter and to leave another State, the right to be treated as a welcome visitor rather than an unfriendly alien when temporarily present in the

---

[11] "We do not doubt that the one-year waiting-period device is well suited to discourage the influx of poor families in need of assistance. . . . But the purpose of inhibiting migration by needy persons into the State is constitutionally impermissible." 394 U.S., at 629. "Thus, the purpose of deterring the in-migration of indigents cannot serve as justification for the classification created by the one-year waiting period . . . . If a law has 'no other purpose . . . than to chill the assertion of constitutional rights by penalizing those who choose to exercise them, then it [is] patently unconstitutional.' *United States* v. *Jackson*, 390 U.S. 570, 581 (1968)." *Id.*, at 631.

second State, and, for those travelers who elect to become permanent residents, the right to be treated like other citizens of that State.

It was the right to go from one place to another, including the right to cross state borders while en route, that was vindicated in *Edwards v. California*, 314 U.S. 160 (1941), which invalidated a state law that impeded the free interstate passage of the indigent. We reaffirmed that right in *United States* v. *Guest*, 383 U.S. 745 (1966), which afforded protection to the "right to travel freely to and from the State of Georgia and to use highway facilities and other instrumentalities of interstate commerce within the State of Georgia." *Id.,* at 757. Given that §11450.03 imposed no obstacle to respondents' entry into California, we think the State is correct when it argues that the statute does not directly impair the exercise of the right to free interstate movement. For the purposes of this case, therefore, we need not identify the source of that particular right in the text of the Constitution. The right of "free ingress and regress to and from" neighboring States, which was expressly mentioned in the text of the Articles of Confederation,[13] may simply have been "conceived from the beginning to be a necessary concomitant of the stronger Union the Constitution created." *Id.,* at 758.

The second component of the right to travel is, however, expressly protected by the text of the Constitution. The first sentence of Article IV, §2, provides: "The Citizens of each State shall be entitled to all Privileges and Immunities of Citizens in the several States." Thus, by virtue of a person's state citizenship, a citizen of one State who travels in other States, intending to return home at the end of his journey, is entitled to enjoy the "Privileges and Immunities of Citizens in the several States" that he visits. This provision removes "from the citizens of each State the disabilities of alienage in the other States." *Paul* v. *Virginia,* 8 Wall. 168, 180 (1869). It provides important protections for nonresidents who enter a State whether to obtain employment, *Hicklin v. Orbeck,* 437 U.S. 518 (1978), to procure medical services, *Doe v. Bolton,* 410 U.S. 179, 200 (1973), or even to engage in commercial shrimp fishing, *Toomer v. Witsell,* 334 U.S. 385 (1948). Those protections are not "absolute," but the Clause "does bar discrimination against citizens of other States where there is no substantial reason for the discrimination beyond the mere fact that they are citizens of other States." *Id.,* at 396. There may be a substantial reason for requiring the nonresident to pay more than the resident for a hunting license, see *Baldwin v. Fish and Game Comm'n, Mont.,* 436 U.S. 371, 390–391 (1978), or to enroll in the state university, see *Vlandis* v. *Kline,* 412 U.S. 441, 445 (1973), but our cases have not identified any acceptable reason for qualifying the protection afforded by the Clause for "the citizen of State A who ventures

---

[13] "The 4th article, respecting the extending the rights of the Citizens of each State, throughout the United States . . . is formed exactly upon the principles of the 4th article of the present Confederation." 3 Records of the Federal Convention of 1787, p. 112 (M. Farrand ed. 1966). Article IV of the Articles of Confederation provided that "the people of each State shall have free ingress and regress to and from any other State."

into State B to settle there and establish a home." *Zobel,* 457 U.S., at 74 (O'Connor, J., concurring in judgment). Permissible justifications for discrimination between residents and nonresidents are simply inapplicable to a nonresident's exercise of the right to move into another State and become a resident of that State.

What is at issue in this case, then, is this third aspect of the right to travel—the right of the newly arrived citizen to the same privileges and immunities enjoyed by other citizens of the same State. That right is protected not only by the new arrival's status as a state citizen, but also by her status as a citizen of the United States.[15] That additional source of protection is plainly identified in the opening words of the Fourteenth Amendment:

"All persons born or naturalized in the United States, and subject to the jurisdiction thereof, are citizens of the United States and of the State wherein they reside. No State shall make or enforce any law which shall abridge the privileges or immunities of citizens of the United States."

Despite fundamentally differing views concerning the coverage of the Privileges or Immunities Clause of the Fourteenth Amendment, most notably expressed in the majority and dissenting opinions in the *Slaughter-House Cases,* 16 Wall. 36 (1873), it has always been common ground that this Clause protects the third component of the right to travel. Writing for the majority in the *Slaughter-House Cases,* Justice Miller explained that one of the privileges conferred by this Clause "is that a citizen of the United States can, of his own volition, become a citizen of any State of the Union by a *bona fide* residence therein, with the same rights as other citizens of that State." *Id.,* at 80. Justice Bradley, in dissent, used even stronger language to make the same point:

"The states have not now, if they ever had, any power to restrict their citizenship to any classes or persons. A citizen of the United States has a perfect constitutional right to go to and reside in any State he chooses, and to claim citizenship therein, and an equality of rights with every other citizen; and the whole power of the nation is pledged to sustain him in that right. He is not bound to cringe to any superior, or to pray for any act of grace, as a means of enjoying all the rights and privileges enjoyed by other citizens." *Id.,* at 112–113.

---

[15] The Framers of the Fourteenth Amendment modeled this Clause upon the "Privileges and Immunities" Clause found in Article IV. Cong. Globe, 39th Cong., 1st Sess., 1033–1034 (1866) (statement of Rep. Bingham). In *Dred Scott* v. *Sandford,* 19 How. 393 (1857), this Court had limited the protection of Article IV to rights under state law and concluded that free blacks could not claim citizenship. The Fourteenth Amendment overruled this decision. The Amendment's Privileges and Immunities Clause and Citizenship Clause guaranteed the rights of newly freed black citizens by ensuring that they could claim the state citizenship of any State in which they resided and by precluding that State from abridging their rights of national citizenship.

That newly arrived citizens "have two political capacities, one state and one federal," adds special force to their claim that they have the same rights as others who share their citizenship. Neither mere rationality nor some intermediate standard of review should be used to judge the constitutionality of a state rule that discriminates against some of its citizens because they have been domiciled in the State for less than a year. The appropriate standard may be more categorical than that articulated in *Shapiro*, but it is surely no less strict.

V

Because this case involves discrimination against citizens who have completed their interstate travel, the State's argument that its welfare scheme affects the right to travel only "incidentally" is beside the point. Were we concerned solely with actual deterrence to migration, we might be persuaded that a partial withholding of benefits constitutes a lesser incursion on the right to travel than an outright denial of all benefits. See *Dunn v. Blumstein*, 405 U.S. 330, 339 (1972). But since the right to travel embraces the citizen's right to be treated equally in her new State of residence, the discriminatory classification is itself a penalty.

It is undisputed that respondents and the members of the class that they represent are citizens of California and that their need for welfare benefits is unrelated to the length of time that they have resided in California. We thus have no occasion to consider what weight might be given to a citizen's length of residence if the bona fides of her claim to state citizenship were questioned. Moreover, because whatever benefits they receive will be consumed while they remain in California, there is no danger that recognition of their claim will encourage citizens of other States to establish residency for just long enough to acquire some readily portable benefit, such as a divorce or a college education, that will be enjoyed after they return to their original domicile. See, *e.g., Sosna* v. *Iowa*, 419 U.S. 393 (1975); *Vlandis* v. *Kline*, 412 U.S. 441 (1973).

The classifications challenged in this case—and there are many—are defined entirely by (a) the period of residency in California and (b) the location of the prior residences of the disfavored class members. The favored class of beneficiaries includes all eligible California citizens who have resided there for at least one year, plus those new arrivals who last resided in another country or in a State that provides benefits at least as generous as California's. Thus, within the broad category of citizens who resided in California for less than a year, there are many who are treated like lifetime residents. And within the broad sub-category of new arrivals who are treated less favorably, there are many smaller classes whose benefit levels are determined by the law of the States from whence they came. To justify §11450.03, California must therefore explain not only why it is sound fiscal policy to discriminate against those who have been citizens for less than a year, but also why it is permissible to apply such a variety of rules within that class.

These classifications may not be justified by a purpose to deter welfare applicants from migrating to California for three reasons. First, although it is reasonable to assume that some persons may be motivated to move for the purpose of obtaining higher benefits, the empirical evidence reviewed by the District Judge, which takes into account the high cost of living in California, indicates that the number of such persons is quite small—surely not large enough to justify a burden on those who had no such motive. Second, California has represented to the Court that the legislation was not enacted for any such reason. Third, even if it were, as we squarely held in *Shapiro* v. *Thompson,* 394 U.S. 618 (1969), such a purpose would be unequivocally impermissible.

Disavowing any desire to fence out the indigent, California has instead advanced an entirely fiscal justification for its multitiered scheme. The enforcement of §11450.03 will save the State approximately $10.9 million a year. The question is not whether such saving is a legitimate purpose but whether the State may accomplish that end by the discriminatory means it has chosen. An evenhanded, across-the-board reduction of about 72 cents per month for every beneficiary would produce the same result. But our negative answer to the question does not rest on the weakness of the State's purported fiscal justification. It rests on the fact that the Citizenship Clause of the Fourteenth Amendments expressly equates citizenship with residence: "That Clause does not provide for, and does not allow for, degrees of citizenship based on length of residence." *Zobel*, 457 U.S., at 69. It is equally clear that the Clause does not tolerate a hierarchy of 45 subclasses of similarly situated citizens based on the location of their prior residence.[20] Thus §11450.03 is doubly vulnerable: Neither the duration of respondents' California residence, nor the identity of their prior States of residence, has any relevance to their need for benefits. Nor do those factors bear any relationship to the State's interest in making an equitable allocation of the funds to be distributed among its needy citizens. As in *Shapiro*, we reject any contributory rationale for the denial of benefits to new residents:

"But we need not rest on the particular facts of these cases. Appellants' reasoning would logically permit the State to bar new residents from schools, parks, and libraries or deprive them of police and fire protection. Indeed it would permit the State to apportion all benefits and services according to the past tax contributions of its citizens." 394 U.S., at 632–633.

In short, the State's legitimate interest in saving money provides no justification for its decision to discriminate among equally eligible citizens.

---

[20] See Cohen, *Discrimination Against New State Citizens: An Update*, 11 Const. Comm. 73, 79 (1994) ("[J]ust as it would violate the Constitution to deny these new arrivals state citizenship, it would violate the Constitution to concede their citizenship in name only while treating them as if they were still citizens of other states").

* * *

Citizens of the United States, whether rich or poor, have the right to choose to be citizens "of the State wherein they reside." U.S. Const., Amdt. 14, §1. The States, however, do not have any right to select their citizens.[27] The Fourteenth Amendment, like the Constitution itself, was, as Justice Cardozo put it, "framed upon the theory that the peoples of the several states must sink or swim together, and that in the long run prosperity and salvation are in union and not division." *Baldwin* v. *G. A. F. Seelig, Inc.,* 294 U.S. 511, 523 (1935).

*   *   *

Notes on *Saenz v. Roe*

1. *The constitutional right to travel*: As Justice Stevens's opinion for the Court in *Saenz* explains, the Constitution protects a so-called "right to travel." But that right is not a singular right; it consists of three distinct strands.

a. *The right to move across state borders*: One aspect of the constitutional right to travel is that recognized in cases such as *Edwards v. California*, 314 U.S. 160 (1941): the right to move throughout the country physically unimpeded, or the right to cross state borders. The Court in *Edwards* invalidated a California law that made it unlawful to bring an indigent person into the state. A prior decision, *Crandall v. Nevada*, 73 U.S. 35 (1868), had invalidated a tax on any person leaving Nevada via common carrier. The precise textual basis for this component of the right to travel is uncertain. It could be a fundamental right as a matter of due process; it could be protected by the Privileges or Immunities Clause; or it could simply inhere in the Constitution's federal structure. But as the Court observed in *Saenz*, "we need not identify the source of that particular right in the text of the Constitution. The right of free ingress and regress to and from neighboring States . . . may simply have been conceived from the beginning to be a necessary concomitant of the stronger Union the Constitution created."

b. *The right to be treated as a welcome guest*: The second aspect of the right to travel is that protected by the Privileges and Immunities Clause of Article IV, §2. Again, this is the right, as a citizen of one state, to enjoy those privileges and immunities protected by the clause when visiting another state. It is not absolute, but states generally cannot discriminate against nonresidents unless (1) they have a substantial reason for doing so, and (2) the discrimination is substantially related to that objective.

---

[27] As Justice Jackson observed, "it is a privilege of citizenship of the United States, protected from state abridgment, to enter any State of the Union, either for temporary sojourn or for the establishment of permanent residence therein and for gaining resultant citizenship thereof. If national citizenship means less than this, it means nothing." *Edwards* v. *California*, 314 U.S. 160, 183 (1941) (concurring opinion).

c. *The right to interstate migration*: *Saenz v. Roe* implicated the third aspect of the constitutional right to travel: "for those travelers who elect to become permanent residents, the right to be treated like other citizens of that State." This right stems distinctively from *national* citizenship, even under the narrow reading of the clause rendered in the *Slaughter-House Cases*: the right of any U.S. citizen to move to any state and become a citizen of that state. Discrimination against new residents because they recently resided elsewhere clearly burdens this right, and thus presumptively violates the Privileges or Immunities Clause of the Fourteenth Amendment.

2. *The appropriate level of scrutiny for discrimination based on duration of residency*: After finding that §11450.03 burdened the right to interstate migration, the Supreme Court needed to determine what level of judicial scrutiny was appropriate for state laws infringing on this right. The Court concluded it was the most exacting possible: strict scrutiny. "Neither mere rationality nor some intermediate standard of review should be used to judge the constitutionality of a state rule that discriminates against some of its citizens because they have been domiciled in the State for less than a year." The application of strict scrutiny will almost always result in the law being found unconstitutional. A law can survive such scrutiny only if the government can establish that (1) the law is supported by a compelling state interest, and (2) it is narrowly tailored (or necessary) to accomplishing that interest.

3. *Applying strict scrutiny in* Saenz: California could not defend §11450.03 on the ground that it sought to deter indigent persons from moving into the state; decisions like *Edwards* and *Crandall* had declared that goal constitutionally impermissible. California thus asserted that its purpose was to save money, as the provision reduced the state's annual TANF payments by roughly $11 million. The Court held this interest could not sustain the statute. No matter this interest's strength, the law surely was not *necessary* to achieve it. For instance, California could have adopted an across-the-board cut in its TANF benefits that drew no distinction based on duration of residency. That could have saved the state $11 million without burdening the right to interstate migration. Stated differently, discriminating against those citizens who had resided in the state for less than a year had virtually nothing to do with the interest California was supposedly pursuing.

4. *The need to identify "bona fide" citizens*: The Court's analysis in *Saenz* was simplified considerably by the fact that it was "undisputed that respondents and the members of the class that they represent are citizens of California." This meant the state was discriminating among its own citizens based on how long they had been citizens. Moreover, the Court assumed the plaintiffs would consume their TANF benefits entirely in California, and not take those benefits with them back to another state. In this sense, the benefit was not "readily portable."

The Court thus sidestepped whether states may—at least for purposes of distributing "readily portable benefits"—require persons to reside in the state for a certain period of time to demonstrate they are "bona fide citizens" of that state. In Justice Stevens's words, the case provided

> "no occasion to consider what weight might be given to a citizen's length of residence if the bona fides of her claim to state citizenship were questioned. Moreover, because whatever benefits they receive will be consumed while they remain in California, there is no danger that recognition of their claim will encourage citizens of other States to establish residency for just long enough to acquire some readily portable benefit, such as a divorce or a college education, that will be enjoyed after they return to their original domicile. See, *e.g., Sosna* v. *Iowa*, 419 U.S. 393 (1975); *Vlandis* v. *Kline*, 412 U.S. 441 (1973)."

Sosna involved a state's provision of a divorce decree. *Vlandis* involved a state's capacity to charge nonresidents higher tuition to attend a public university. In both cases, the Court upheld a state's authority to require a person to reside in the state for an extended period of time to obtain a "readily portable" state-provided benefit. If *Vlandis* and *Sosna* are to coexist with *Saenz*, the rationale must be that—at least with respect to these sorts of benefits—states can require a more stringent demonstration of residency before treating persons as "*bona fide* residents."

*   *   *

PROBLEMS ON PRIVILEGES AND IMMUNITIES

In each of the following circumstances, please assess whether the governmental action at issue violates the Privileges and Immunities Clause of Article IV or the Privileges or Immunities Clause of the Fourteenth Amendment.

1. A Hawai'i law provides that, to become a member of the Hawai'i Bar Association, an attorney must be a resident of Hawai'i. By law, an attorney must be a member of the Hawai'i Bar Association to make an appearance in a Hawai'i state court (though a judge, at her discretion, may grant permission to appear *pro hac vice* to members of other states' bar associations).

2. A New York City ordinance provides that only New York City residents may own more than two properties within the city with assessed values exceeding $5 million.

3. A Nevada law limits those eligible for the state's Medicaid program—a means-tested health insurance program for the indigent and disabled—to Nevada state residents.

4. The Fremont Union School District requires any student attending a high school within the district to be a resident of the district. (The school district spans Cupertino, Sunnyvale, and San Jose, and it is political subdivision of the State of California.) What if the district also required students to be U.S. citizens?

5. A California law requires a permit for an individual to camp overnight in a state park. The price of a permit for California residents is $10 per night; the price for nonresidents is $100 per night.

6. An Arizona law requires a license for hiking guides to lead tours of campers within the state. (The licensing scheme does not apply to guides who are merely leading friends or family.) The cost of obtaining such a license is $250 for Arizona residents and $500 for nonresidents.

7. A Texas law mandates that any person holding elected office in the state (for the State of Texas or for any local or municipal office) must be a Texas resident.

8. A new program adopted by Washington state provides cash assistance to tenants who are more than $4,000 behind in their payment of rent for their principal residence. The program was adopted to alleviate the economic burdens imposed by the coronavirus pandemic. To be eligible for the program, individuals must have been Washington residents (and remained Washington residents) since March 16, 2020, the date the governor first issued a shelter-in-place order.

9. The facts are the same as in (8), except that all Washington residents are eligible for the program. To prove their status as a Washington resident, an individual must present a government-issued photo identification, which can be either a driver's license or a state ID card. As a practical matter, given the operations of the Washington Department of Motor Vehicles, it takes a minimum of four weeks to obtain either of these forms of government-issued photo identification.

* * *

REVIEW ESSAY QUESTION 4

From September 2012 to August 2018, Student lived in Massachusetts. He graduated from college in 2016 and worked for two years as a paralegal in Boston. This past summer, he packed his things and moved to Los Angeles to attend law school at UCLA (a part of the public, University of California system). Annual tuition at UCLA School of Law is roughly $47,000 for California residents, but closer to $56,000 for nonresidents.

In moving to Los Angeles, Student fully intended to make California his permanent home, at least for the foreseeable future. He left no belongings in Massachusetts; he registered to vote, obtained a driver's license, and registered his car in California. He planned to work during his summers—and permanently following graduation—in Southern California. When Student received his tuition bill for his first semester of law school, however, he discovered that UCLA had charged him the higher, nonresident tuition. In doing so, the school was following several provisions set out in the California Education Code. The relevant sections state as follows:

§ 68017 "Resident" – A "resident" is a student who has residence, pursuant to Article 5 (commencing with § 68060) of this chapter in the state for more than one year immediately preceding the residence determination date.

§ 68018. "Nonresident" – A "nonresident" is a student who does not have residence in the state for more than one year immediately preceding the residence determination date.

§ 68050. Nonresident tuition – A student classified as a nonresident shall be required, except as otherwise provided in this part, to pay, in addition to other fees required by the institution, nonresident tuition.

Student has filed suit in the U.S. District Court for the Central District of California against the appropriate state official in her official capacity. In his complaint, Student seeks an injunction forbidding UCLA from charging him the higher rate of tuition. He argues that the discrimination against nonresidents in the relevant parts of the California Education Code is unconstitutional.

A. Can Student successfully argue that these provisions of the California Education Code violate the Commerce Clause? Explain.

B. Can Student successfully argue that these provisions of the California Education Code violate the Privileges and Immunities Clause of Article IV, §2? Explain.

C. Can Student successfully argue that these provisions of the California Education Code violate the Privileges or Immunities Clause of the Fourteenth Amendment? Explain.

*   *   *

SUGGESTED ANALYIS

A. An initial question to ask in any dormant Commerce Clause case is whether the challenged state law discriminates against interstate commerce. Laws that so discriminate are "virtually *per se* unconstitutional"; they will only be sustained if the state has a legitimate, non-protectionist purpose and no practicable, nondiscriminatory means of achieving that objective. If the law does not discriminate against interstate commerce, it will be permissible under the dormant Commerce Clause so long as it does not impose burdens on interstate commerce that are "clearly excessive" in relation to its putative local benefits.

California's statutory scheme seems to discriminate against interstate commerce. Persons crossing state lines to obtain a legal education are charged more than those persons who are from the state. The face of the statute dictates that intrastate commerce be treated more favorably than interstate commerce: it draws a distinction based on the geographic origin of the customer, a classic form of facial discrimination.

But the dormant Commerce Clause only constrains state and local governments when they impose regulations or taxes. That is, the dormant Commerce Clause does not constrain states when they act as *market participants*, entering a market as a buyer or provider of a good or service.

In this instance, California is not regulating or taxing. It is providing (or selling) a service: a graduate education. As such, it is acting as a market participant. (Indeed, there is a thriving market for legal education in California, with 18 ABA-accredited law schools, the majority of which are private, and a large number of California-accredited schools as well.) Because California is acting as a market participant, the dormant Commerce Clause is inapplicable. Student's dormant Commerce Clause claim necessarily fails on this ground.

B. The Privileges and Immunities Clause of Article IV presumptively prohibits discrimination by state or local governments against nonresidents based on their status as nonresidents. The clause prohibits such discrimination with respect to those "privileges" or "immunities" protected by the clause—rights that are "fundamental" within the meaning of Article IV. These are rights that, in words of the Court, bear "upon the vitality of the Nation as a single entity," such that equality in access to the privilege "basic to the maintenance or well-being of the Union." They include such rights as the right to pursue a common calling, to make and enforce contracts, to access the state's courts, and to acquire, hold, and dispose of property. When a state law discriminates against nonresidents with respect to such a "privilege" or "immunity," it will only be constitutional if it can survive a form of intermediate scrutiny: the state must have a substantial interest that supports the law, and the law must be substantially related to that interest. Stated differently, nonresidents must be a peculiar source of the evil the law seeks to remedy.

Here, it is clear that the statute discriminates against nonresidents. (It may also discriminate against California residents based on their duration of their residency in the state, a question explored below.) On its face, the scheme requires nonresidents to pay a higher rate of tuition. This is blatant discrimination against nonresidents.

The question, then, is whether access to a public legal education is a "privilege" or "immunity" protected by the clause. The answer seems unclear. It is not a trivial right, especially in light of the importance of a higher education to pursue one's livelihood in our modern economy. Most cases under Article IV, §2 have involved the right to pursue one's livelihood, a "common calling." Higher education, if nothing else, seems substantially more important than the right to recreational elk hunting, a privilege the Supreme Court has held is not "fundamental" for purposes of this clause. But this is a publicly subsidized benefit (the lower tuition at law school), *not* a regulation that somehow forbids the nonresident from doing something in the state. What is really at issue is the *additional subsidy* to tuition that the state provides only to its residents. Though the right to become a member of the state's bar association and be licensed to practice is clearly a "privilege" or "immunity" under the clause (as an example of the right to pursue a common calling or employment), the right to a publicly subsidized legal education (or really just one with a *larger* public subsidy) is not necessarily so.

But even if we assume *arguendo* that the subsidy for public legal education is indeed a "privilege" within the purview of the Privileges and Immunities Clause of Article IV, §2, it seems fairly clear that California's scheme would survive the applicable intermediate scrutiny. First, California would seem to have a substantial interest in limiting a publicly provided benefit (like the subsidized tuition rate) to its own residents. It is California's own funds that are providing the subsidized tuition, and a state has a substantial interest in limiting eligibility for a public benefit to those who actually contributed (through their tax dollars, or through their membership in the community) to the creation of that benefit. Thus, limiting the benefit to residents seems substantially related to that interest. States generally are not required to provide publicly funded benefits to nonresidents; they need not provide them cash assistance or health insurance or COVID vaccines. As the Supreme Court explained in *Martinez v. Bynum*, 461 U.S. 321 (1983), which upheld a Texas statute limiting enrollment in public elementary and secondary schools to state residents,

> "A bona fide residence requirement, appropriately defined and uniformly applied, furthers the substantial state interest in assuring that services provided for its residents are enjoyed only by residents. Such a requirement with respect to attendance in public free schools does not violate the Equal Protection Clause of the Fourteenth Amendment. It does not burden or penalize the constitutional right of interstate travel, for any person is free to move to a State and to establish residence there. A bona fide residence requirement simply requires that the person *does* establish residence before demanding the services that are restricted to residents."

Thus, even if a public graduate education in law would be considered a "privilege" or "immunity" under Article IV, §2, this discrimination in the tuition charged nonresidents would seem fully consistent with the Privileges and Immunities Clause of Article IV.

(Notice that it is unclear whether Student is actually a nonresident for constitutional purposes on these facts. California has attempted to define him as a nonresident by statute—at least for purposes of law school tuition—but the question is whether the Constitution permits California to do so. Thus, we still have to address the following question: if Student is actually a *resident*, is this discrimination constitutional?)

C. The Privileges or Immunities Clause of the Fourteenth Amendment generally prohibits a state from discriminating among its residents based on the duration of residency in the state. As the Court held in *Saenz v. Roe*, any such discrimination—with respect to any governmental rule or benefit—impinges on the right of interstate migration: the rights, as a citizen of the United States, to become a citizen of any state within the Union. Thus, any such discrimination is subject to strict scrutiny: the government's interest must be *compelling*, and the law must be *necessary* (or *narrowly* tailored) to achieve that compelling interest. When a person enters a state to access a "highly portable benefit," however—such as higher education or a divorce decree—a state may impose tests, for purposes of accessing that benefit, that ensure the individual is a *bona fide* resident. Hence, the Court has generally upheld state residency requirements for purposes of lower instate tuition at colleges and universities that require persons to have resided in the state for at least a year.

A difficult, threshold question is whether California's scheme actually discriminates *among* state residents (or instead just against nonresidents). To the extent it only discriminates against nonresidents, this is purely an Article IV question (addressed above), and the Privileges and Immunities Clause of the Fourteenth Amendment is irrelevant. But one could alternatively construe the scheme as *also* discriminating among California residents on the basis of duration of their residency—between those who have resided in California for more or less than a year following the residence determination date.

As a general matter, *Saenz* holds that *any* discrimination among residents based on the duration of residency is subject to strict scrutiny. And If this scheme were subjected to true strict scrutiny, it seems almost certainly unconstitutional. California's interest in preserving its subsidized legal education for those who have contributed to the public fisc may well be compelling—for being unable to do so may well lead to no state provision of important public goods (of which higher education would only be one). But it does not seem that this discrimination, at least in the way it is drawn, is *necessary* to achieve that end. There would seem to be other means to differentiate between those who have contributed to the benefit and those who have not. Again, the Court in *Saenz* seemed to indicate that treating new residents less favorably, purely because they are new residents, is nearly *per se* unconstitutional. Thus, if *Saenz* fully applied, then California's scheme would appear to be unconstitutional.

But the Court in *Saenz* was careful to distinguish cases in which states treated "new" residents (by deeming them nonresidents) unfavorably when they came to the state to obtain a "highly portable" benefit. Specifically, the Court stated that *Saenz* presented "no occasion to consider what weight might be given to a citizen's length of residence if the *bona fides* of her claim to state citizenship were questioned." More specifically, said the Court, because the welfare benefits at issue in *Saenz* would be consumed while the plaintiffs remained in California, there was "no danger that recognition of their claim will encourage citizens of other states to establish residency for just long enough to acquire some readily portable benefit, such as a divorce or a college education, that will be enjoyed after they return to their original domicile."

This seems to suggest that, when a newcomer comes to a state *for the purpose of obtaining a highly portable benefit* (such as a divorce decree or a higher education), the state has strong reasons to be skeptical of the newcomer's claim to be a resident of the state. Hence, in these circumstances—at least for purposes of distributing the highly portable benefit—it would be permissible, within reasonable bounds, for the state to treat the newcomer as a nonresident (rather than a new, *bona fide* resident of the state). If that is the case—and this definition of residence, at least for purposes of higher education tuition is reasonable—then there is no longer a Privileges or Immunities Clause question under the Fourteenth Amendment. Rather, it is an Article IV question: discrimination against a *nonresident* (discussed above).

The Court in *Saenz* was careful not to disturb its prior holdings regarding so-called "portable" benefits. One of those holdings was *Vlandis v. Kline*, 412 U.S. 441 (1973), in which the Court reasoned as follows:

> "We are aware, of course, of the special problems involved in determining the *bona fide* residence of college students who come from out of State to attend that State's public university. Our holding today should in no wise be taken to mean that Connecticut must classify the students in its university system as residents, for purposes of tuition and fees, just because they go to school there. Nor should our decision be

construed to deny a State the right to impose on a student, as one element in demonstrating *bona fide* residence, a reasonable durational residency requirement, which can be met while in student status. We fully recognize that a State has a legitimate interest in protecting and preserving the quality of its colleges and universities and the right of its own *bona fide* residents to attend such institutions on a preferential tuition basis. . . . The State can establish such reasonable criteria for in-state status as to make virtually certain that students who are not, in fact, bona fide residents of the State, but who have come there solely for educational purposes, cannot take advantage of the in-state rates."

Thus, despite *Saenz*, it seems states can take reasonable steps to treat newcomers as nonresidents with respect to highly portable benefits, including higher education. Of course, there must be some constitutional limit. At some point, the Constitution must require the state to treat the newcomer as a resident. But the discrimination here would seem to be reasonable, at least under existing precedent.

* * *

C. The Full Faith and Credit Clause

Article IV, § 1 contains another clause intended to constrain the actions of states in the interests of interstate comity: the Full Faith and Credit Clause. The text of that clause provides that "Full Faith and Credit shall be given in each State to the public Acts, Records, and judicial Proceedings of every other State." The clause generally requires each state to respect the public acts of the other states, particularly judgments entered by other states' courts. It serves "to alter the status of the several states as independent foreign sovereignties, each free to ignore obligations created under the laws or by the judicial proceedings of the others, and to make them integral parts of a single nation." *Milwaukee County v. M.E. White Co.*, 296 U.S. 268, 277 (1935).

Though the Full Faith and Credit Clause imposes this general obligation on the states, it operates quite differently with respect to (a) the final judgments of another state's courts, and (b) another state's statutes or other regulatory rules. As the Supreme Court has explained, "[w]hereas the full faith and credit command is exacting with respect to [a] final judgment . . . rendered by a court with adjudicatory authority over the subject matter and persons governed by the judgment, it is less demanding with respect to choice of laws." *Franchise Tax Bd. v. Hyatt*, 538 U.S. 488, 494 (2003). With respect to *judgments*, states are generally required to accept them almost unconditionally. But with respect to regulatory rules, the clause permits a state to apply its own laws (in deciding what law to apply to adjudicate a case) so long as that state has a sufficient, "minimum connection" with the dispute or the parties.

1. The obligation to credit the judgments of other states' courts

The Full Faith and Credit Clause "requires each State to recognize and give effect to valid judgments rendered by the courts of its sister States." *V.L. v.*

E.L., 136 S. Ct. 1017, 1020 (2016). Indeed, with respect to judgments, "the full faith and credit obligation is exacting." As the Court has stated on several occasions, "[a] final judgment in one State, if rendered by a court with adjudicatory authority over the subject matter and persons governed by the judgment, qualifies for recognition throughout the land." Thus, a state has no authority to disregard a judgment entered by another state's court "because it disagrees with the reasoning underlying the judgment or deems it to be wrong on the merits." As the Court explained in *Milliken v. Meyer*, 311 U.S. 457 (1940), the Full Faith and Credit Clause prohibits a state from reexamining "the merits of the cause of action, the logic or consistency of the decision, or the validity of the legal principles on which the judgment is based."

*   *   *

EXAMPLE

Suppose Plaintiff obtains a valid, final judgment against Defendant (a resident of Oregon) in a Washington state court. Suppose, however, that Defendant does not pay the judgment, and has no assets located in Washington. Plaintiff then brings an action in Oregon state court to enforce the judgment she obtained against Defendant in Washington (through the seizure of the defendant's property in Oregon). The Full Faith and Credit Clause requires the Oregon court to recognize the Washington court's judgment. Unless the Washington court's judgment was somehow jurisdictionally invalid, the Oregon court must accept it—even if the Oregon court strongly disagrees with the Washington court's decision on the merits.

*   *   *

More generally, the Full Faith and Credit Clause requires state courts to grant another state court's judgment the preclusive effect the judgment would receive in the rendering state's courts (the state in which the judgment was entered). For example, suppose Kansas courts recognize the doctrine of offensive nonmutual issue preclusion, a doctrine by which a plaintiff who was not a party to the first judgment can nonetheless use that judgment to establish an issue in an action against a defendant (who had the issue resolved against it in the first judgment). But suppose Missouri courts do not recognize this doctrine. If a Kansas state court judgment conclusively resolves an issue that meets the requirements of nonmutual offensive issue preclusion, and a plaintiff seeks to use that judgment offensively in an action in Missouri state court, the Missouri court must apply Kansas's rule of preclusion, even if the doctrine would be rejected as a matter of Missouri state law. "Full faith and credit" dictates granting a judgment from another state's court the full preclusive effect the judgment would receive in the state where it was rendered.

The only exception to this stringent rule regarding judgments is when the rendering court "did not have jurisdiction over the subject matter or the relevant parties." State courts are therefore entitled to inquire into the rendering court's jurisdiction before crediting the judgment. But that is *all* they may do.

Moreover, the jurisdictional inquiry in this context, as the Supreme Court has instructed, "is a limited one."

The scope of this rule was explored in the recent case of *V.L. v. E.L.* At issue was the validity of a Georgia superior court's judgment regarding a petition for adoption. The Georgia court had approved the adoption by a non-biological parent (V.L.) of two children, V.L. being half of a lesbian couple with the biological mother (E.L.). The couple lived in Alabama and, several years after the adoption, ended their relationship. A dispute then arose regarding each parent's time with the children, and V.L. petitioned an Alabama court for greater visitation, invoking her status as a legal parent. The Alabama Supreme Court refused to recognize the validity of the Georgia state court judgment validating the adoption, prompting V.L. to appeal to the Supreme Court. As you read the Court's *per curiam* opinion in *V.L.*, please consider the following questions:

1. What is the precise constitutional test for when the Full Faith and Credit Clause requires a state to recognize a judgment rendered by another state's court?

2. On what ground did the Alabama Supreme Court refuse to recognize the validity of the Georgia court's judgment of adoption? Why did this constitute reversible error?

3. How searching should a state court's inquiry be into the validity of another state court's judgment? What can it permissibly examine?

4. From the materials provided, do you believe the Georgia court's decision granting the adoption was incorrect as a matter of Georgia law? Was that relevant in the case before the Alabama Supreme Court? Why or why not?

V.L. v. E.L.
577 U.S. 464 (2016)

PER CURIAM.

A Georgia court entered a final judgment of adoption making petitioner V. L. a legal parent of the children that she and respondent E. L. had raised together from birth. V. L. and E. L. later separated while living in Alabama. V. L. asked the Alabama courts to enforce the Georgia judgment and grant her custody or visitation rights. The Alabama Supreme Court ruled against her, holding that the Full Faith and Credit Clause of the United States Constitution does not require the Alabama courts to respect the Georgia judgment. That judgment of the Alabama Supreme Court is now reversed by this summary disposition.

I

V. L. and E. L. are two women who were in a relationship from approximately 1995 until 2011. Through assisted reproductive technology, E. L. gave birth to a child named S. L. in 2002 and to twins named

N. L. and H. L. in 2004. After the children were born, V. L. and E. L. raised them together as joint parents.

V. L. and E. L. eventually decided to give legal status to the relationship between V. L. and the children by having V. L. formally adopt them. To facilitate the adoption, the couple rented a house in Alpharetta, Georgia. V. L. then filed an adoption petition in the Superior Court of Fulton County, Georgia. E. L. also appeared in that proceeding. While not relinquishing her own parental rights, she gave her express consent to V. L.'s adoption of the children as a second parent. The Georgia court determined that V. L. had complied with the applicable requirements of Georgia law, and entered a final decree of adoption allowing V. L. to adopt the children and recognizing both V. L. and E. L. as their legal parents.

V. L. and E. L. ended their relationship in 2011, while living in Alabama, and V. L. moved out of the house that the couple had shared. V. L. later filed a petition in the Circuit Court of Jefferson County, Alabama, alleging that E. L. had denied her access to the children and interfered with her ability to exercise her parental rights. She asked the Alabama court to register the Georgia adoption judgment and award her some measure of custody or visitation rights. The matter was transferred to the Family Court of Jefferson County. That court entered an order awarding V. L. scheduled visitation with the children.

E. L. appealed the visitation order to the Alabama Court of Civil Appeals. She argued, among other points, that the Alabama courts should not recognize the Georgia judgment because the Georgia court lacked subject-matter jurisdiction to enter it. The Court of Civil Appeals rejected that argument. It held, however, that the Alabama family court had erred by failing to conduct an evidentiary hearing before awarding V. L. visitation rights, and so it remanded for the family court to conduct that hearing.

The Alabama Supreme Court reversed. It held that the Georgia court had no subject-matter jurisdiction under Georgia law to enter a judgment allowing V. L. to adopt the children while still recognizing E. L.'s parental rights. As a consequence, the Alabama Supreme Court held Alabama courts were not required to accord full faith and credit to the Georgia judgment.

II

The Constitution provides that "Full Faith and Credit shall be given in each State to the public Acts, Records, and judicial Proceedings of every other State." U. S. Const., Art. IV, §1. That Clause requires each State to recognize and give effect to valid judgments rendered by the courts of its sister States. It serves "to alter the status of the several states as independent foreign sovereignties, each free to ignore obligations created under the laws or by the judicial proceedings of the others, and to make them integral parts of a single nation." *Milwaukee County* v. *M. E. White Co.*, 296 U.S. 268, 277 (1935).

With respect to judgments, "the full faith and credit obligation is exacting." *Baker* v. *General Motors Corp.*, 522 U.S. 222, 233 (1998). "A final judgment in one State, if rendered by a court with adjudicatory authority over the subject matter and persons governed by the judgment, qualifies for recognition throughout the land." *Ibid.* A State may not disregard the judgment of a sister State because it disagrees with the reasoning underlying the judgment or deems it to be wrong on the merits. On the contrary, "the full faith and credit clause of the Constitution precludes any inquiry into the merits of the cause of action, the logic or consistency of the decision, or the validity of the legal principles on which the judgment is based." *Milliken* v. *Meyer,* 311 U.S. 457, 462 (1940).

A State is not required, however, to afford full faith and credit to a judgment rendered by a court that "did not have jurisdiction over the subject matter or the relevant parties." *Underwriters Nat. Assurance Co.* v. *North Carolina Life & Accident & Health Ins. Guaranty Assn.,* 455 U.S. 691, 705 (1982). "Consequently, before a court is bound by [a] judgment rendered in another State, it may inquire into the jurisdictional basis of the foreign court's decree." *Ibid.* That jurisdictional inquiry, however, is a limited one. "[I]f the judgment on its face appears to be a 'record of a court of general jurisdiction, such jurisdiction over the cause and the parties is to be presumed unless disproved by extrinsic evidence, or by the record itself.'" *Milliken, supra,* at 462 (quoting *Adam* v. *Saenger,* 303 U.S. 59, 62 (1938)).

Those principles resolve this case. Under Georgia law, as relevant here, "[t]he superior courts of the several counties shall have exclusive jurisdiction in all matters of adoption." Ga. Code Ann. §19–8–2(a) (2015). That provision on its face gave the Georgia Superior Court subject-matter jurisdiction to hear and decide the adoption petition at issue here. The Superior Court resolved that matter by entering a final judgment that made V. L. the legal adoptive parent of the children. Whatever the merits of that judgment, it was within the statutory grant of jurisdiction over "all matters of adoption." *Ibid.* The Georgia court thus had the "adjudicatory authority over the subject matter" required to entitle its judgment to full faith and credit. *Baker, supra,* at 233.

The Alabama Supreme Court reached a different result by relying on Ga. Code Ann. §19–8–5(a). That statute states (as relevant here) that "a child who has any living parent or guardian may be adopted by a third party . . . only if each such living parent and each such guardian has voluntarily and in writing surrendered all of his or her rights to such child." The Alabama Supreme Court concluded that this provision prohibited the Georgia Superior Court from allowing V. L. to adopt the children while also allowing E. L. to keep her existing parental rights. It further concluded that this provision went not to the merits but to the Georgia court's subject-matter jurisdiction. In reaching that crucial second conclusion, the Alabama Supreme Court seems to have relied solely on the fact that the right to adoption under Georgia law is purely statutory, and "'[t]he requirements of Georgia's adoptions statutes are mandatory and must be strictly construed in favor of the natural parents.'" App. to Pet. for Cert. 23a–24a (quoting *In re Marks*, 300 Ga. App. 239, 243, 684 S. E. 2d 364, 367 (2009)).

That analysis is not consistent with this Court's controlling precedent. Where a judgment indicates on its face that it was rendered by a court of competent jurisdiction, such jurisdiction "is to be presumed unless disproved." *Milliken, supra*, at 462. There is nothing here to rebut that presumption. The Georgia statute on which the Alabama Supreme Court relied, Ga. Code Ann. §19–8–5(a), does not speak in jurisdictional terms; for instance, it does not say that a Georgia court "shall have jurisdiction to enter an adoption decree" only if each existing parent or guardian has surrendered his or her parental rights. Neither the Georgia Supreme Court nor any Georgia appellate court, moreover, has construed §19–8–5(a) as jurisdictional. That construction would also be difficult to reconcile with Georgia law. Georgia recognizes that in general, subject-matter jurisdiction addresses "whether a court has jurisdiction to decide a particular class of cases," *Goodrum* v. *Goodrum*, 283 Ga. 163, 657 S. E. 2d 192 (2008), not whether a court should grant relief in any given case. Unlike §19–8–2(a), which expressly gives Georgia superior courts "exclusive jurisdiction in all matters of adoption," §19–8–5(a) does not speak to whether a court has the power to decide a general class of cases. It only provides a rule of decision to apply in determining if a particular adoption should be allowed.

Section 19–8–5(a) does not become jurisdictional just because it is "mandatory" and "must be strictly construed." This Court "has long rejected the notion that all mandatory prescriptions, however emphatic, are properly typed jurisdictional." *Gonzalez* v. *Thaler*, 565 U.S. 134, ___ (2012) (slip op., at 10–11). Indeed, the Alabama Supreme Court's reasoning would give jurisdictional status to *every* requirement of the Georgia adoption statutes, since Georgia law indicates those requirements are all mandatory and must be strictly construed. *Marks, supra*, at 243, 684 S. E. 2d, at 367. That result would comport neither with Georgia law nor with common sense.

As Justice Holmes observed more than a century ago, "it sometimes may be difficult to decide whether certain words in a statute are directed to jurisdiction or to merits." *Fauntleroy* v. *Lum*, 210 U.S. 230, 234–235 (1908). In such cases, especially where the Full Faith and Credit Clause is concerned, a court must be "slow to read ambiguous words, as meaning to leave the judgment open to dispute, or as intended to do more than fix the rule by which the court should decide." *Id.*, at 235. That time-honored rule controls here. The Georgia judgment appears on its face to have been issued by a court with jurisdiction, and there is no established Georgia law to the contrary. It follows that the Alabama Supreme Court erred in refusing to grant that judgment full faith and credit.

*   *   *

2. State regulatory rules

While the Full Faith and Credit Clause's mandate that states recognize the judgments of other states is stringent, the clause is much less demanding with respect to choice-of-law questions. As the Supreme Court has explained, "the Full Faith and Credit Clause does not compel a state to substitute the statutes of other states for its own statutes dealing with a subject matter concerning which it is competent to legislate." *Franchise Tax Bd. v. Hyatt*, 538 U.S. 488, 494 (2003).

To be clear, "[i]n certain limited situations, the courts of one state must apply the statutory law of another State." For instance, in *Bradford Electric Co. v. Clapper*, 286 U.S. 145 (1932), the Supreme Court held that a federal court sitting in New Hampshire was required to apply Vermont law in an action between a Vermont employee and a Vermont employer arising out of a contract made in Vermont. But as the Court clarified in *Nevada v. Hall*, 440 U.S. 410, 422 (1979), the Full Faith and Credit Clause "does not require a State to apply another State's law in violation of its own legitimate public policy."

This issue was explored in some depth in *Pacific Employers Ins. Co. v. Industrial Accident Comm'n*, 306 U.S. 493 (1939). At issue was whether the Full Faith and Credit Clause precluded California from applying its own workmen's compensation act in the case of an injury suffered by a Massachusetts employee of a Massachusetts employer while in California in the course of his employment. Though the employer and employee had agreed to be bound by the laws of Massachusetts, the Supreme Court held that the Constitution did not forbid the California court from applying California substantive law to adjudicate the case. As the Court explained,

> "in the case of statutes, . . . the full faith and credit clause does not require one state to substitute for its own statute, applicable to persons and events within it, the conflicting statute of another state, even though that statute is of controlling force in the courts of the state of its enactment with respect to the same persons and events. . . . Although Massachusetts has an interest in safeguarding the compensation of Massachusetts employees while temporarily abroad in the course of their employment, and may adopt that policy for itself, that could hardly be thought to support an application of the full faith and credit clause which would override the constitutional authority of another state to legislate for the bodily safety and economic protection of employees injured within it. Few matters could be deemed more appropriately the concern of the state in which the injury occurs or more completely within its power."

Importantly, the Court in *Pacific Employers Insurance* distinguished *Clapper* on the ground that, in *Clapper*, "there was nothing in the New Hampshire statute, the decisions of its courts, or in the circumstances of the case to suggest that reliance on the provisions of the Vermont statute, as a defense to the New

Hampshire suit, was obnoxious to the policy of New Hampshire." By contrast, in *Pacific Employers Insurance* "California had its own scheme governing compensation for injuries in the State, and the California courts had found that the policy of that scheme would be frustrated were it denied enforcement." In short, the Full Faith and Credit Clause does not "enable one state to legislate for the other or to project its laws across state lines so as to preclude the other from prescribing for itself the legal consequences of acts within it."

* * *

REVIEW ESSAY QUESTION 5

Sebago Lake State Park is owned and operated by the State of Maine; it is located near Maine's border with New Hampshire. Under Maine Rev. Stat. §74–233, all persons visiting the park must pay a "tax" or "fee" at the time of their entry. The charge is $5 for Maine residents and $25 for nonresidents. Each day, several tour buses enter the park, carrying mostly (but not exclusively) persons who live outside Maine. As these buses enter the park (at its only point of entrance), the drivers are required to remit the amount dictated by §74–233 to the park ranger on duty, to cover the tax or fee due for the driver and the bus's passengers.

Dorothy Ferguson is a United States citizen who lives in New Hampshire. She earns her living by operating her own tour bus. In doing so, she frequently carries visitors into Sebago Lake State Park. Most of Ferguson's customers live outside Maine. As a tour bus operator, she has remitted the exactions mandated by §74–233 on hundreds of occasions.

Ferguson has recently filed a lawsuit in federal district court alleging that Maine Rev. Stat. §74–233 is unconstitutional. She seeks an injunction against its enforcement. Assume Ferguson's lawsuit is justiciable and the court has subject matter jurisdiction. Please objectively analyze what claims Ferguson could plausibly assert in challenging the constitutionality of Maine Rev. Stat. §74–233, and how the district court is likely to rule on those claims.

PART VI

AN INTRODUCTION TO INDIVIDUAL RIGHTS

CHAPTER 19
"INCORPORATION" OF THE BILL OF RIGHTS

To this point, our focus has been on the structure of government created by the Constitution: the rules it sets for the creation, execution, and application of law—whether by legislatures, executives, or courts at the federal, state, or local level. Here, the subject shifts to a qualitatively different issue: the Constitution's protection of individual rights. We now face a different sort of question: assuming the government is acting within the scope of a valid grant of power, has it nonetheless impermissibly infringed on a person's constitutionally protected rights?

*   *   *

EXAMPLE

The commerce power plainly grants Congress the authority to regulate virtually all the actions of television networks, newspapers, and commercial websites. These media companies are commercial enterprises, engaged in economic and commercial activity. Thus, most (if not all) of their activities "substantially affect interstate commerce," as that phrase has been construed in the Supreme Court's decisions. But the Free Speech Clause of the First Amendment limits how Congress can deploy that legislative power. So even if a federal statue falls within the commerce power, it may nonetheless violate the Constitution by "abridging the freedom of speech, or of the press." If a federal statute were to forbid the sale of newspapers containing editorials criticizing the government's policy with respect to Afghanistan, for instance, it would be within Congress's commerce power, but it would run afoul of the First Amendment. The statute would be consistent with Article I, but it nonetheless would be unconstitutional.

*   *   *

A.   The State Action Doctrine

A foundational point concerning constitutional law is this: with the sole exception of the Thirteenth Amendment, the Constitution only constrains the behavior of the government and government officials. Stated simply, *only the government (or persons exercising governmental authority) can violate the Constitution.*[26] A more accurate name for this principle would be the "government

---

[26] The Thirteenth Amendment is the one exception. The text of §1 of the Thirteenth Amendment provides that "[n]either slavery nor involuntary servitude, except as a punishment for crime whereof the party shall have been duly convicted, shall exist within the United States, or any place subject to their jurisdiction." By its express terms, the amendment forbids slavery,

action" doctrine. But because the earliest cases addressing the matter concerned state governments, it came to be known as the "state action" doctrine.

Recall that the state action doctrine was critical to the Supreme Court's decision in *United States v. Morrison*, 529 U.S. 598 (2000), holding that the civil remedy provision of the Violence Against Women Act (§13981) exceeded Congress's power under §5 of the Fourteenth Amendment. Section 13981 granted the survivors of gender-motivated violence a private right of action against the perpetrator, and one of the bases on which the government contended the statute was within Congress's enumerated powers was as "appropriate legislation" to "enforce" the Equal Protection Clause's prohibition of sex discrimination. But the perpetrators of gender-motivated violence—private individuals like Antonio Morrison—are legally incapable of violating the Equal Protection Clause. Only *governments* can violate the substantive prohibitions contained in the Fourteenth Amendment. Thus, the Court held §13981 was not "congruent" or "proportional" to the constitutional violations Congress was purportedly seeking to prevent or remedy.

To be clear, the Constitution empowers the federal government to enact laws, execute laws, and adjudicate cases regulating the actions of private persons. Thousands of federal statutes regulate private behavior; the Executive Branch enforces these laws against private individuals; and the federal courts hand down decisions settling the rights of private parties. So the Constitution obviously *empowers* the federal government to regulate private persons. But the Constitution *itself* does not constrain the actions of private persons.

*   *   *

QUESTION: Suppose Congress enacts a statute forbidding colleges and universities—whether public or private—from considering the race of applicants when making admissions decisions. Is the statute within Congress's enumerated powers?

ANSWER: Almost certainly. The provision of higher education—whether graduate or undergraduate—would seem to be "economic or commercial in nature." (Indeed, it is a multi-billion-dollar industry in the U.S., constituting a large portion of the nation's economy.) As such, a law that dictates the terms on which that product is offered to customers likely constitutes the regulation of an activity "substantially affecting" interstate commerce—and thus falls within Congress's commerce power.

QUESTION: If Santa Clara University, despite this statute, considered the race of an applicant in making an admissions decision, would it be acting unlawfully?

---

full stop. Any person—public or private—violates this provision if he enslaves another human being within the meaning of the amendment.

ANSWER: Yes. If a valid federal statute forbids an action, taking that action is unlawful. This is just as true for private actors as it is for state actors.

QUESTION: If Santa Clara University considered the race of an applicant in making an admissions decision, would it be acting unconstitutionally?

ANSWER: No. Santa Clara University—as a private entity—is *incapable* of violating the Constitution (unless it were to somehow violate the Thirteenth Amendment). And this is true even if the Fourteenth Amendment forbids colleges and universities from considering the race of their applicants in making admissions decisions.

QUESTION: If the University of California-Berkeley considered the race of an applicant in making an admissions decision, would it be acting unconstitutionally?

ANSWER: Quite possibly. The University of California is a part of the government, and thus a "state actor" for purposes of the state action doctrine. Thus, its actions are subject to the strictures of the Constitution, including the Fourteenth Amendment. The Supreme Court has interpreted the Equal Protection Clause of the Fourteenth Amendment as prohibiting the government from making any decisions based on race except in very rare circumstances. One such circumstance is when it is necessary to achieve a certain degree of diversity in higher education. *See Fisher v. University of Texas*, 136 S. Ct. 2198 (2016). But even admissions programs with this purpose are unconstitutional if they are not *necessary* to achieve that objective (and go no further).

* * *

In short, Congress can constitutionally enact statutes that regulate the behavior of private actors—indeed, that criminalize that behavior—such that private actors are federal law violators when they disobey the terms of those statues. But private persons cannot violate the Constitution. Only "state actors"— the government and persons cloaked with governmental authority—can act *unconstitutionally*.

B.   The Original Constitution and Individual Rights

Many of the Constitution's framers (including James Madison and Alexander Hamilton) rejected the idea of a dichotomy between the Constitution's structural provisions and its protection of individual rights. They felt the structure created by the Constitution would be sufficient to protect individual rights—and more, that the real purpose of the structure created by the Constitution was to accomplish just that. They opposed the Constitution's inclusion of a bill of rights because it might *weaken* the protection of individual liberty by implying (through the failure to enumerate every such right) the government had greater power to interfere with individual freedoms than the Constitution actually conferred.

But the Anti-Federalists were unpersuaded. They demanded the inclusion of a set of individual rights guarantees in the text of the Constitution. Thus, the addition of the Bill of Rights became an essential aspect of the compromise that led to ratification in those states where the vote was close—most notably, Virginia and New York. The conventions in these states voted to ratify the Constitution with the understanding that the first Congress would propose a bill of rights to be added as amendments. Madison, as a member of the first House of Representatives, drafted sixteen amendments. Twelve of those proposed amendments were passed by Congress according to the requirements of Article V, approved by two-thirds majorities in both the House of Representatives and the Senate. Ten of these proposed amendments were then ratified by three-fourths of the states as required by Article V. These first ten amendments to the Constitution are generally known as the Bill of Rights.

The original Constitution contains a handful of individual rights protections. These include the Privileges and Immunities Clause of Article IV, the Contracts Clause, and the prohibitions on *ex post facto* laws and bills of attainder. But these protections are paltry compared to those in the Bill of Rights.

C.   The Antebellum Period: *Barron v. Baltimore*

A careful reading of the Bill of Rights shows that none is expressly directed at state or local governments. None restricts the actions of "states" as such. This contrasts with the language of Article I, §10, which expressly directs certain prohibitions at the states. For instance, Article I, §10, clause 3 provides that "No State shall . . . pass any Bill of Attainder, ex post facto Law, or Law impairing the Obligation of Contracts, or grant any Title of Nobility." To the extent the provisions of the Bill of Rights are directed at a specific government, it is the *national* government. (The First Amendment, for example, directs its prohibitions specifically at Congress.)

Thus, an important early question was whether the Bill of Rights constrained the actions of state and local governments. The Supreme Court answered that question in *Barron v. Baltimore*, 32 U.S. (7 Pet.) 243 (1833). Barron owned a wharf in Baltimore harbor, and the City of Baltimore had diverted streams into the harbor in a manner that left a large deposit of silt near his wharf. This made the waters surrounding the wharf shallower—and the wharf less valuable—because it was inaccessible to larger ships. Barron claimed the city's actions were unconstitutional because they amounted to a "taking" of his property that, under the Fifth Amendment, required "just compensation."

The Takings Clause clearly constrains the actions of the federal government; Congress could not have taken Barron's property for public use without providing him just compensation. The pertinent question was whether the clause also applied to the City of Baltimore. And because the city was a political subdivision of the State of Maryland, the ultimate question was whether the Takings Clause applied to the states.

Writing for the Court, Chief Justice Marshall concluded that the individual rights protections contained in the Bill of Rights apply only to the federal government, and thus do not restrain the actions of state or local governments. At the time of ratification, the states were already governed by their own respective constitutions. The great object of the new federal Constitution, reasoned Marshall, was to set out the powers—and define the limits to those powers—resting in the "the general government." To be sure, some provisions in the original Constitution plainly apply to the states; Article 1, §10 contains several. But each of these provisions *expressly* identifies the states as the object of the relevant prohibition. For example, Article I, §10, clause 1 provides that "[n]o *State* shall enter into any Treaty, Alliance, or Confederation." And Article I, §10, clause 3 provides that "[n]o *State* shall, without the Consent of Congress, lay any duty of Tonnage, keep Troops, or Ships of War in time of Peace." The Court thus reasoned that, when the Constitution meant to impose limitations on the states, it did so expressly. Consequently, a constitutional provision phrased in general terms—without any specific reference as to which government it constrains—should logically be understood as applying only to the federal government.

Marshall tied this textual reading to the original understanding of those who participated in the Constitution's framing and ratification. The compromise between the proponents of the Constitution and the Anti-Federalists that produced the Bill of Rights concerned the powers of the *national* government, not those of the states. The Anti-Federalists were principally concerned about the authority to be exercised by the new national government, not that of the states. Thus, those involved in the creation of the Bill of Rights understood that it was designed to alleviate these Anti-Federalist fears by restraining the actions of the federal government, not those of the states.

D. The Civil War and the Reconstruction Amendments

Barron v. Baltimore cemented the antebellum understanding that the Constitution imposed almost no obligations on the states to respect individual rights. This was, of course, part of a broader ideological struggle concerning the power of the federal government and the independent sovereignty of the states. Many states adhered to the idea that the states were the only true sovereigns in our constitutional system (despite the Supreme Court's decision in *McCulloch v. Maryland*). Many people—particularly in the South—believed the states retained the authority to disobey the federal government when, in their view, it acted unconstitutionally, and that the states could unilaterally withdraw from the Union if they chose. (This was the constitutional theory that, in the minds of many southern statesmen, justified secession.)

This debate was obviously intertwined with the struggle over slavery and the need in the South to justify its position that federal government lacked the constitutional authority to prohibit slavery in the federal territories. (Recall that much of the land that is now part of the United States was, at that point, merely territories that had not yet achieved statehood.) The Civil War effectively resolved this dispute, establishing the superiority of federal government—that is, the superiority of those rights protected by federal law over the independent sovereignty of the states. In the aftermath of the Civil War, the nation adopted the Reconstruction Amendments: the Thirteenth, Fourteenth, and Fifteenth Amendments. These were the constitutional embodiment of the war's outcome. The Thirteenth Amendment constitutionalized President Lincoln's Emancipation Proclamation, and indeed went much further: "Neither slavery nor involuntary servitude, except as a punishment for crime whereof the party shall have been duly convicted, shall exist within the United States, or any place subject to their jurisdiction." The Fifteenth Amendment prohibited racial discrimination in voting: "The right of the citizens of the United States to vote shall not be denied or abridged by the United States or by any State on account of race, color, or previous condition of servitude."

The Fourteenth is easily the most complicated and far-reaching of the three Reconstruction Amendments. Section 1 guarantees some broadly worded, open-textured individual rights against encroachment by the *states*. This was a departure from the Bill of Rights, and in many respects effectuated a radical change in the structure of federalism: "No State shall make or enforce any law which shall abridge the privileges or immunities of the citizens of the United States; nor shall any State deprive any person of life, liberty, or property, without due process of law; nor deny to any person within its jurisdiction the equal protection of the law." Unlike the beginning of the First Amendment—which states that "Congress shall pass no law . . ."—this sentence begins "No *State*." It is an express protection of national rights against encroachments by the states or their political subdivisions.

It is this structural change, and the scope of the substantive rights that the Fourteenth Amendment has been construed to protect, that has fundamentally altered the nature of our Constitution. In many respects, it revolutionized our constitutional order, amounting to a sort of "second founding" of the Republic.

E.   The *Slaughter-House Cases*

The Fourteenth Amendment's principal architect, Representative John Bingham of Ohio, believed that an essential purpose of the amendment was to make the Bill of Rights applicable to the states. And this was the contention put forth by the plaintiffs in the *Slaughter-House Cases*, 83 U.S. 36 (1873), the first major case following the Fourteenth Amendment's ratification to test the amendment's scope. At issue was a New Orleans ordinance that had granted a local firm (the Crescent City Live-Stock Landing and Slaughter-House Company) a monopoly over the slaughterhouse business in the city. The ordinance required butchers in New Orleans—who to that point had operated their own slaughterhouses, or at least benefited from competition between a number of slaughterhouses—to rent space and pay a fee (set by regulation) to the Crescent City Company. Several butchers filed suit, claiming that the city's granting of a monopoly to Crescent City violated, among other things, the Privileges or Immunities Clause of the Fourteenth Amendment, pressing the argument that the Fourteenth Amendment made the protections contained in the Bill of Rights binding on the states.

The Supreme Court rejected that understanding of the Privileges or Immunities Clause, adopting a much narrower view of what it protects. In his opinion for a 5-to-4 Court, Justice Samuel Miller distinguished two forms of citizenship, and the rights that inhere in each. He reasoned that there is a critical difference between the "privileges or immunities" of the citizens of the United States and the "privileges or immunities" of the citizens of a state. While the first sentence of §1 of the Fourteenth Amendment specifically describes two types of citizenship—national and state—the Privileges or Immunities Clause only refers to "citizens of the United States." Justice Miller thus inferred that "[i]t is too clear for argument that the change in phraseology was adopted understandingly and with a purpose." And that purpose, according to the Court, was to specify that the Privilege or Immunities Clause only protected those privileges or immunities that are *distinctly national in character*—those that inhere *exclusively* in United States citizenship.

Justice Miller bolstered this textual argument with an appeal to the "absurd consequences" that would otherwise follow. He posited that, were the Court to adopt the plaintiffs' position, the result would be unthinkable. Recall that the *other* Privileges and Immunities Clause (appearing in Article IV, §2) covers, among other things, the right to pursue a vocation or a common calling, the right to hold and dispose of property, and the right of access to the courts. In *Slaughter-House*, Justice Miller concluded that this very broad set of rights—rights that had, from the birth of the Republic, always been protected exclusively by the states—must be considered the privileges or immunities of *state* citizenship. For if the Privileges or Immunities Clause of the Fourteenth Amendment had been intended to protect all of these rights, it would completely revolutionize the nation's system of government. It would transfer protection of all of these rights from state governments to the national government: to the federal courts through constitutional litigation, and to Congress through its power to enact legislation enforcing the Fourteenth Amendment under §5. To the Court, such a result was too extravagant to be entertained:

> "[W]hen, as in the case before us, these consequences are so serious, so far-reaching and pervading, so great a departure from the structure and spirit of our institutions; when the effect is to fetter and degrade the State governments by subjecting them to the Control of Congress, in the exercise of powers heretofore universally conceded to them of the most ordinary and fundamental character; when in fact it radically changes the whole theory of the relations of the State and Federal governments to each other and of both these governments to the people; the argument has a force that is irresistible, in the absence of language which expresses such a purpose too clearly to admit of doubt."

One might reasonably ask why this consequence would have been so absurd. Why had 620,000 Americans died—2 percent of the nation's population, and a much higher percentage of its adult males—if the Civil War did *not* radically change the relationship between the states and the federal government? Would we not *expect* these amendments to mark a "great departure from the structure and spirit of our institutions" as they existed before the war? Arguably, the more absurd consequence was that the nation had fought the Civil War without producing a dramatic constitutional break from its past.

Nonetheless, according to *Slaughter-House*, the Privileges or Immunities Clause of the Fourteenth Amendment only protected those "privileges or immunities" incident exclusively to United States citizenship—that is, rights that could only exist due to the existence of the federal government. What did this include? Justice Miller listed several such rights, and they are not terribly consequential:

* The right to come to the seat of government and to assert any claim upon that government.

* The right to transact business with the federal government.

* The right to hold office in the federal government.

* The right to seek the protection of the federal government.

* The right to engage in the administration of the federal government's functions.

* And the right of free access of the nation's seaports, subtreasuries, land offices, and federal courts.

What is wrong with this picture? A fundamental problem with the Court's analysis in *Slaughter-House* is that these rights must have existed prior to the ratification of the Fourteenth Amendment—for they existed (based on the Court's own reasoning) due to the existence of the national government. And if these rights already existed, and they were a product of *federal* law, then it was *already* impermissible for states to interfere with these rights under the Supremacy Clause. That is, even before ratification of the Fourteenth Amendment, a state's effort to interfere with, for example, a person's right to transact business with the federal government or to hold office in the federal government would have been preempted by federal law. Such state laws plainly would have frustrated the purpose of the federal laws enabling such business or creating such offices. And if these federal rights were *already* protected against state interference prior to the Civil War, then the Court's interpretation of the Privileges or Immunities Clause meant that the clause was largely meaningless. It essentially rendered the Privileges or Immunities Clause superfluous. (This was the principal argument advanced by Justice Stephen Field in his dissent.)

Thus, not only did *Slaughter-House* foreclose the possibility that the Privileges or Immunities Clause rendered the Bill of Rights applicable to states, but it nearly gutted the clause in its entirety. And this has had a lasting influence on the shape of constitutional law. To this day, the Privileges or Immunities Clause protects only a single right: the third aspect of the right to travel—the right of U.S. citizens to migrate from one state to another recognized in *Saenz v. Roe*, 526 U.S. 489 (1999). And though nearly every right specified in the first eight amendments to the Constitution has been incorporated via the Fourteenth Amendment so as to apply to the states, that process has taken place via the Due Process Clause, a development that has spawned several important consequences of its own.

F.   "Incorporation" via the Due Process Clause

The Court's holding in the *Slaughter-House Cases* that the protections of the Bill of Rights did not apply to the states was one that, in the long run, the American people were unwilling to accept. Indeed, shortly after the *Slaughter-House* decision, private business interests grew concerned about what they perceived as excessive regulation by state and local governments—regulation they thought should be unconstitutional. From this milieu emerged a new legal theory that might force states to respect the rights included in the Bill of Rights, but without asking the Court to overrule *Slaughter-House*. Specifically, litigants began arguing that various protections enumerated in the first ten amendments constituted aspects of the *process* that was *due*, and thus were subsumed within the *Due Process Clause* of the Fourteenth Amendment. And over time, the Court grew receptive to these arguments.

Only four years after the *Slaughter-House* decision, the Supreme Court suggested in *Munn v. Illinois*, 94 U.S. 113 (1877), that some state laws might be so unreasonable as to amount to a deprivation of due process: "Undoubtedly, in mere private contracts, relating to matters in which the public has no interest, what is reasonable must be ascertained judicially." And in 1897, for the first time, such a claim actually prevailed. In *Chicago, Burlington & Quincy R'wy Co. v. Chicago*, 166 U.S. 226 (1897), the Court held that the Due Process Clause of the Fourteenth Amendment prohibited the states from taking a person's property without just compensation. The Court concluded that the government's obligation to pay just compensation when taking private property was an aspect of the process that was constitutionally *due*. As a result, the Court made the Takings Clause of the Fifth Amendment applicable to the states via the Due Process Clause of the Fourteenth Amendment. Thus began the process of "incorporation"—the incorporation of the Bill of Rights into the Due Process Clause of the Fourteenth Amendment so as to apply to the actions of state and local governments.

The ensuing debate about how and whether to incorporate the various individual rights contained in the Bill of Rights featured a number of different facets. Perhaps the most basic of these questions concerned *which* rights should be incorporated: which of the protections enshrined in the first eight amendments to the Constitution are so significant that a state or local government's failure to respect them amounts to a denial of due process?

Over time, in various decisions, the Supreme Court phrased the relevant test in different ways, but each aimed at the same basic idea: whether the right is "of the very essence of a scheme of ordered liberty"; whether it is "so rooted in the traditions and conscience of our people as to be ranked as fundamental"; whether it is one of those "fundamental principles of liberty and justice which lie at the base of all our civil and political institutions"; whether it is "implicit in the concept of ordered liberty"; whether its denial "offends those cannons of decency and fairness which express the notions of justice of English-speaking peoples"; and whether the right is "basic in our system of jurisprudence." These formulations each embrace the same essential idea. And they focus on *American* traditions and notions of justice rather than the traditions or notions of justice among humanity more generally.

Surprisingly enough, this process of "incorporation" continues to this day. In *McDonald v. Chicago*, 561 U.S. 742 (2010), the Supreme Court held for the first time that the individual right to bear arms protected by the Second Amendment is "fundamental" as a matter of due process, and thus applicable to state and local governments. And in 2019, in *Timbs v. Indiana*, 139 S. Ct. 682, the Supreme Court held that the Eighth Amendment's prohibition on the imposition of "excessive fines" is likewise incorporated. As you read *Timbs*, please consider the following questions:

1. What standard does the Supreme Court apply in determining whether the Excessive Fines Clause should be incorporated? What evidence does the Court consult in applying this standard?

2. Why did the Court ultimately conclude that the Excessive Fines Clause was incorporated, and thus operates as a restriction on state and local governmental action?

3. Is there any difference in the content of a right's protections when it applies directly to the federal government as opposed to when the right applies (via incorporation through the Fourteenth Amendment) to a state or local government?

4. How does the approach embraced by Justice Thomas (and potentially Justice Gorsuch) differ from that articulated by the majority? How might that difference matter?

Timbs v. Indiana
139 S. Ct. 682 (2019)

Justice GINSBURG delivered the opinion of the Court.

Tyson Timbs pleaded guilty in Indiana state court to dealing in a controlled substance and conspiracy to commit theft. The trial court sentenced him to one year of home detention and five years of probation, which included a court-supervised addiction-treatment program. The sentence also required Timbs to pay fees and costs totaling $1,203. At the time of Timbs's arrest, the police seized his vehicle, a Land Rover SUV Timbs had purchased for about $42,000. Timbs paid for the vehicle with money he received from an insurance policy when his father died.

The State engaged a private law firm to bring a civil suit for forfeiture of Timbs's Land Rover, charging that the vehicle had been used to transport heroin. After Timbs's guilty plea in the criminal case, the trial court held a hearing on the forfeiture demand. Although finding that Timbs's vehicle had been used to facilitate violation of a criminal statute, the court denied the requested forfeiture, observing that Timbs had recently purchased the vehicle for $42,000, more than four times the maximum $10,000 monetary fine assessable against him for his drug conviction. Forfeiture of the Land Rover, the court determined, would be grossly disproportionate to the gravity of Timbs's offense, hence unconstitutional under the Eighth Amendment's Excessive Fines Clause. The Court of Appeals of Indiana affirmed that determination, but the Indiana Supreme Court reversed. . . [I]t held that the Excessive Fines Clause constrains only federal action and is inapplicable to state impositions. We granted certiorari.

The question presented: Is the Eighth Amendment's Excessive Fines Clause an "incorporated" protection applicable to the States under the Fourteenth Amendment's Due Process Clause? Like the Eighth Amendment's proscriptions of "cruel and unusual punishment" and "[e]xcessive bail," the protection against excessive fines guards against abuses of government's punitive or criminal-law-enforcement authority. This safeguard, we hold, is "fundamental to our scheme of ordered liberty," with "dee[p] root[s] in [our] history and tradition." *McDonald v. Chicago*, 561 U.S. 742, 767 (2010). The Excessive Fines Clause is therefore incorporated by the Due Process Clause of the Fourteenth Amendment.

I

A

When ratified in 1791, the Bill of Rights applied only to the Federal Government. *Barron v. Baltmore*, 7 Pet. 243 (1833). "The constitutional Amendments adopted in the aftermath of the Civil War," however, "fundamentally altered our country's federal system." *McDonald*, 561 U.S., at 754. With only "a handful" of exceptions, this Court has held that the Fourteenth Amendment's Due Process Clause incorporates the protections contained in the Bill of Rights, rendering them applicable to the States. A Bill of Rights protection is incorporated, we have explained, if it is "fundamental to our scheme of ordered liberty," or "deeply rooted in this Nation's history and tradition." *Id.,* at 767.

Incorporated Bill of Rights guarantees are "enforced against the States under the Fourteenth Amendment according to the same standards that protect those personal rights against federal encroachment." *Id.*, at 765. Thus, if a Bill of Rights protection is incorporated, there is no daylight between the federal and state conduct it prohibits or requires.

B

Under the Eighth Amendment, "[e]xcessive bail shall not be required, nor excessive fines imposed, nor cruel and unusual punishments inflicted." Taken together, these Clauses place "parallel limitations" on "the power of those entrusted with the criminal-law function of government." *Browning-Ferris Industries v. Kelco Disposal, Inc.*, 492 U.S. 257, 263 (1989). Directly at issue here is the phrase "nor excessive fines imposed," which "limits the government's power to extract payments, whether in cash or in kind, as punishment for some offense." *United States v. Bajakajian*, 524 U.S. 321, 327–328 (1998). The Fourteenth Amendment, we hold, incorporates this protection.

The Excessive Fines Clause traces its venerable lineage back to at least 1215, when Magna Carta guaranteed that "[a] Free-man shall not be amerced for a small fault, but after the manner of the fault; and for a great fault after the greatness thereof, saving to him his contenement." § 20, 9 Hen. III, ch. 14, in 1 Eng. Stat. at Large 5 (1225). As relevant here, Magna Carta required that economic sanctions "be proportioned to the wrong" and "not be so large as to deprive [an offender] of his livelihood." *Browning-Ferris*, 492 U.S., at 271.

Despite Magna Carta, imposition of excessive fines persisted. The 17th century Stuart kings, in particular, were criticized for using large fines to raise revenue, harass their political foes, and indefinitely detain those unable to pay. *E.g.,* The Grand Remonstrance ¶¶17, 34 (1641). When James II was overthrown in the Glorious Revolution, the attendant English Bill of Rights reaffirmed Magna Carta's guarantee by providing that "excessive Bail ought not to be required, nor excessive Fines imposed; nor cruel and unusual Punishments inflicted." 1 Wm. & Mary, ch. 2, §10, in 3 Eng. Stat. at Large 441 (1689).

Across the Atlantic, this familiar language was adopted almost verbatim, first in the Virginia Declaration of Rights, then in the Eighth Amendment, which states: "Excessive bail shall not be required, nor excessive fines imposed, nor cruel and unusual punishments inflicted."

Adoption of the Excessive Fines Clause was in tune not only with English law; the Clause resonated as well with similar colonial-era provisions. See, e.g., Pa. Frame of Govt., Laws Agreed Upon in England, Art. XVIII (1682) ("[A]ll fines shall be moderate, and saving men's contenements, merchandize, or wainage."). In 1787, the constitutions of eight States—accounting for 70% of the U.S. population—forbade excessive fines.

An even broader consensus obtained in 1868 upon ratification of the Fourteenth Amendment. By then, the constitutions of 35 of the 37

States—accounting for over 90% of the U.S. population—expressly prohibited excessive fines.

Notwithstanding the States' apparent agreement that the right guaranteed by the Excessive Fines Clause was fundamental, abuses continued. Following the Civil War, Southern States enacted Black Codes to subjugate newly freed slaves and maintain the prewar racial hierarchy. Among these laws' provisions were draconian fines for violating broad proscriptions on "vagrancy" and other dubious offenses. See, *e.g.*, Mississippi Vagrant Law, Laws of Miss. § 2 (1865). When newly freed slaves were unable to pay imposed fines, States often demanded involuntary labor instead. Congressional debates over the Civil Rights Act of 1866, the joint resolution that became the Fourteenth Amendment, and similar measures repeatedly mentioned the use of fines to coerce involuntary labor.

Today, acknowledgment of the right's fundamental nature remains widespread. As Indiana itself reports, all 50 States have a constitutional provision prohibiting the imposition of excessive fines either directly or by requiring proportionality. Indeed, Indiana explains that its own Supreme Court has held that the Indiana Constitution should be interpreted to impose the same restrictions as the Eighth Amendment.

For good reason, the protection against excessive fines has been a constant shield throughout Anglo-American history: Exorbitant tolls undermine other constitutional liberties. Excessive fines can be used, for example, to retaliate against or chill the speech of political enemies, as the Stuarts' critics learned several centuries ago. Even absent a political motive, fines may be employed "in a measure out of accord with the penal goals of retribution and deterrence," for "fines are a source of revenue," while other forms of punishment "cost a State money." *Harmelin v. Michigan*, 501 U.S. 957, 979, n.9 (1991) (opinion of Scalia, J.). This concern is scarcely hypothetical. See Brief for American Civil Liberties Union et al. as *Amici Curiae* 7 ("Perhaps because they are politically easier to impose than generally applicable taxes, state and local governments nationwide increasingly depend heavily on fines and fees as a source of general revenue.").

In short, the historical and logical case for concluding that the Fourteenth Amendment incorporates the Excessive Fines Clause is overwhelming. Protection against excessive punitive economic sanctions secured by the Clause is, to repeat, both "fundamental to our scheme of ordered liberty" and "deeply rooted in this Nation's history and tradition." *McDonald*, 561 U.S., at 767.

II

The State of Indiana does not meaningfully challenge the case for incorporating the Excessive Fines Clause as a general matter. Instead, the State argues that the Clause does not apply to its use of civil *in rem* forfeitures because, the State says, the Clause's specific application to such forfeitures is neither fundamental nor deeply rooted.

In *Austin v. United States*, 509 U.S. 602 (1993), however, this Court held that civil *in rem* forfeitures fall within the Clause's protection when they are at least partially punitive. *Austin* arose in the federal context. But when a Bill of Rights protection is incorporated, the protection applies "identically to both the Federal Government and the States." *McDonald*, 561 U.S., at 766 n.14. Accordingly, to prevail, Indiana must persuade us either to overrule our decision in *Austin* or to hold that, in light of *Austin,* the Excessive Fines Clause is not incorporated because the Clause's application to civil *in rem* forfeitures is neither fundamental nor deeply rooted. The first argument is not properly before us, and the second misapprehends the nature of our incorporation inquiry.

A

In the Indiana Supreme Court, the State argued that forfeiture of Timbs's SUV would not be excessive. It never argued, however, that civil *in rem* forfeitures were categorically beyond the reach of the Excessive Fines Clause. The Indiana Supreme Court, for its part, held that the Clause did not apply to the States at all, and it nowhere addressed the Clause's application to civil *in rem* forfeitures. Accordingly, Timbs sought our review of the question "[w]hether the Eighth Amendment's Excessive Fines Clause is incorporated against the States under the Fourteenth Amendment." In opposing review, Indiana attempted to reformulate the question to ask "[w]hether the Eighth Amendment's Excessive Fines Clause restricts States' use of civil asset forfeitures." And on the merits, Indiana has argued not only that the Clause is not incorporated, but also that *Austin* was wrongly decided. Respondents' "right, in their brief in opposition, to restate the questions presented," however, "does not give them the power to expand [those] questions." *Bray v. Alexandria Women's Health Clinic*, 506 U.S. 263, 279 n.10 (1993). That is particularly the case where, as here, a respondent's reformulation would lead us to address a question neither pressed nor passed upon below. We thus decline the State's invitation to reconsider our unanimous judgment in *Austin* that civil *in rem* forfeitures are fines for purposes of the Eighth Amendment when they are at least partially punitive.

B

As a fallback, Indiana argues that the Excessive Fines Clause cannot be incorporated if it applies to civil *in rem* forfeitures. We disagree. In considering whether the Fourteenth Amendment incorporates a protection contained in the Bill of Rights, we ask whether the right guaranteed—not each and every particular application of that right—is fundamental or deeply rooted.

Indiana's suggestion to the contrary is inconsistent with the approach we have taken in cases concerning novel applications of rights already deemed incorporated. For example, in *Packingham v. North Carolina*, 137 S. Ct. 1730 (2017), we held that a North Carolina statute prohibiting registered sex offenders from accessing certain common-place social media websites violated the First Amendment right to freedom of speech. In reaching this conclusion, we noted that the First Amendment's Free Speech Clause was "applicable to the States under the Due Process Clause of the Fourteenth Amendment." *Id.*, at 1733. We did not, however, inquire whether the Free Speech Clause's application specifically to social media websites was fundamental or deeply rooted. Similarly here, regardless of whether application of the Excessive Fines Clause to civil *in rem* forfeitures is itself fundamental or deeply rooted, our conclusion that the Clause is incorporated remains unchanged.

* * *

For the reasons stated, the judgment of the Indiana Supreme Court is vacated, and the case is remanded for further proceedings not inconsistent with this opinion.

JUSTICE GORSUCH, concurring.

The majority faithfully applies our precedent and, based on a wealth of historical evidence, concludes that the Fourteenth Amendment incorporates the Eighth Amendment's Excessive Fines Clause against the States. I agree with that conclusion. As an original matter, I acknowledge, the appropriate vehicle for incorporation may well be the Fourteenth Amendment's Privileges or Immunities Clause, rather than, as this Court has long assumed, the Due Process Clause. But nothing in this case turns on that question, and, regardless of the precise vehicle, there can be no serious doubt that the Fourteenth Amendment requires the States to respect the freedom from excessive fines enshrined in the Eighth Amendment.

JUSTICE THOMAS, concurring in the judgment.

I agree with the Court that the Fourteenth Amendment makes the Eighth Amendment's prohibition on excessive fines fully applicable to the States. But I cannot agree with the route the Court takes to reach this conclusion. Instead of reading the Fourteenth Amendment's Due Process Clause to encompass a substantive right that has nothing to do with "process," I would hold that the right to be free from excessive fines is one of the "privileges or immunities of citizens of the United States" protected by the Fourteenth Amendment. . . .

* * *

Notes on *Timbs v. Indiana*

1. The standard for whether a right is "fundamental" as a matter of due process (and thus incorporated): The Court in *Timbs* articulated and applied the well-established (if somewhat stripped-down) standard for whether a right contained in the Bill of Rights is "incorporated" into the Due Process Clause of the Fourteenth Amendment: "A Bill of Rights protection is incorporated . . . if it is 'fundamental to our scheme of ordered liberty,' or 'deeply rooted in this Nation's history and tradition.'" Thus, the *Timbs* opinion stated the test in the *disjunctive*: to be "fundamental" as a matter of due process, the right must *either* be "fundamental to our scheme of ordered liberty" *or* "deeply rooted in this Nation's history or tradition." The first prong focuses on the significance of the right, while the second centers on its historical protection in the United States. Notably, in *Dobbs v. Jackson Women's Health Org.*, No. 19–1392 (2022)—the recent decision overruling *Roe v. Wade*—the Court phrased the test in the *conjunctive*: to constitute a fundamental right under the Due Process Clause of the Fourteenth Amendment, the "right must be 'deeply rooted in this Nation's history and tradition' *and* 'implicit in the concept of ordered liberty.'" Slip op. at 5 (emphasis added). As a result, whether both prongs of this test must be satisfied, or instead only one, is unsettled.

But it's unclear whether this fine doctrinal point has much practical significance. While the two prongs of the test are conceptually distinct, they overlap substantially in their actual application. How does one demonstrate that a right is "fundamental" to America's scheme of ordered liberty? In many respects, it is by demonstrating that its recognition has "deep roots" in American history. Thus, predictably enough, no recent Supreme Court decision has held that a right satisfies one prong of this test without satisfying the other.

2. *Application of the standard in* Timbs: Applying this test, the Court had little difficulty concluding that the Eighth Amendment's prohibition on excessive fines was "fundamental" in the relevant sense, and thus applicable to the states. The Court relied on pre-constitutional English history, law in the American colonies and states contemporaneous with the framing of the Constitution, and the laws of the United States at the time of the framing and ratification of the Fourteenth Amendment. Writing for the Court, Justice Ginsburg concluded that "the historical and logical case for concluding that the Fourteenth Amendment incorporates the Excessive Fines Clause is overwhelming. Protection against excessive punitive economic sanctions secured by the Clause is . . . both 'fundamental to our scheme of ordered liberty' and 'deeply rooted in this Nation's history and tradition.'"

3. *What components of the Bill of Rights remain unincorporated?*: Over the past century, from 1897 through *Timbs*, the Supreme Court has held that nearly all of the liberties enumerated in the Bill of Rights are "fundamental" and thus protected by the Due Process Clause of the Fourteenth Amendment. Though incorporation has always been "selective" (evaluated right by right to determine whether each right is "fundamental") rather than "wholesale" (all of them incorporated, all at once), the Court has quite nearly arrived at the same place. After *Timbs*, only three provisions in the Bill of Rights remain unincorporated: (1) the Third Amendment privilege against being forced to quarter troops in one's home; (2) the Fifth Amendment right to indictment by a grand jury in criminal proceedings; and (3) the Seventh Amendment right to a jury in civil trials.

These rights might be incorporated in the future. Indeed, given the relevant standard—and the fact that these rights were important enough to be included in the Bill of Rights in 1791—there is a strong argument that each is either "fundamental to our scheme of ordered liberty" or "deeply rooted in this Nation's history and tradition." But under present law, these rights remain unenforceable against state or local governments.

4. *The content of incorporated rights: jot for jot?*: A subsidiary question raised by the process of "selective incorporation" is whether the content of each incorporated right is precisely the same when applied to state and local governments as when applied to the federal government. The Court's opinion in *Timbs* explains that the content is identical:

> "Incorporated Bill of Rights guarantees are enforced against the States under the Fourteenth Amendment according to the same standards that protect those personal rights against federal encroachment. Thus, if a Bill of Rights protection is incorporated, there is no daylight between the federal and state conduct it prohibits or requires."

For many years, a small exception to this rule concerned the unanimity of jury verdicts in criminal trials. The Sixth Amendment right to a jury, as applied to the federal government, requires the jury to be unanimous to justify a criminal conviction. But the Supreme Court held in *Apodaca v. Oregon*, 406 U.S. 404 (1972), that—while the right to a jury was "fundamental" (and thus incorporated)—the right to a *unanimous* jury verdict was not. In 2020, the Court eliminated this "daylight" in the scope of the right in federal and state court. In *Ramos v. Louisiana*, 140 S. Ct. 1390 (2020), the Court overruled *Apodaca* and held that the Sixth Amendment applies to the states no differently than to the federal government:

> "There can be no question . . . that the Sixth Amendment's unanimity requirement applies to state and federal criminal trials equally. This Court has long explained that the Sixth Amendment right to a jury trial is 'fundamental to the American scheme of justice' and incorporated against the States under the Fourteenth Amendment. This Court has long explained, too, that incorporated provisions of the Bill of Rights bear the same content when asserted against States as they do when asserted against the federal government. So if the Sixth Amendment's right to a jury trial requires a unanimous verdict to support a conviction in federal court, it requires no less in state court."

5. *Incorporation and Congress's §5 power*: Recall that §5 of the Fourteenth Amendment grants Congress the authority to enact "appropriate legislation" to "enforce" the amendment's substantive guarantees. Because the Court has now deemed all but three provisions of the Bill of Rights to be "fundamental" such that they are protected by the Due Process Clause, Congress has the authority under §5 to enact legislation to enforce all of these incorporated rights against encroachment by the states. Of course, as discussed in Chapter 11, any such legislation must be "congruent" and "proportional" to the constitutional violations Congress seeks to prevent or remedy. But assuming this requirement is satisfied, Congress can invoke the §5 power to enforce a wide variety of constitutional rights—such as the right to free speech, to the free exercise of religion, to keep and bear arms, or to be free from unreasonable searches and seizures. A federal statute protecting one of these rights (in a congruent and proportional way) is "appropriate legislation" to enforce the Due Process Clause of the Fourteenth Amendment.

6. *Revisiting* **Slaughter-House?**: Interestingly, Justice Thomas—both in *Timbs* and *McDonald*, the Second Amendment case—concurred only in the Court's judgment. He agreed that the rights in question are enforceable against the states, but he would overrule *Slaughter-House* and hold that these rights (like all the other provisions of the Bill of Rights) are "privileges or immunities" within the meaning of the Privileges or Immunities Clause of the Fourteenth Amendment. Justice Thomas has long argued that *substantive* rights have nothing to do with the *process* a person is due, and thus cannot be protected by the Due Process Clause. In his brief concurring opinion in *Timbs*, Justice Gorsuch indicated he might well agree: "As an original matter, I acknowledge, the appropriate vehicle for incorporation may well be the Fourteenth Amendment's Privileges or Immunities Clause, rather than, as this Court has long assumed, the Due Process Clause." But Justice Gorsuch was nonetheless willing to join the majority opinion in *Timbs*, leaving any reconsideration of *Slaughter-House* for another day.

CHAPTER 20
THE TAKINGS, CONTRACTS, AND EX POST FACTO CLAUSES

Though the Due Process Clause continues to protect various unenumerated "fundamental" rights—such as the right to engage in intimate relations in private and the right to marry, it is no longer understood to protect *economic* rights. The Supreme Court vigorously protected economic rights as a matter of due process—most notably, the right to contract—during the era of *Lochner v. New York*, 198 U.S. 45 (1905). For instance, the Court invalidated laws forbidding child labor, setting maximum hours for employees, and prescribing a minimum wage for workers. But that era collapsed during the New Deal. Due process challenges to laws regulating economic relations now receive mere "rational basis" review, meaning they are constitutional so long as they reasonably further a legitimate governmental interest.

The decline of economic rights under the Due Process Clause, however, has not left *all* economic rights constitutionally unprotected. Indeed, the Constitution contains important provisions specifically safeguarding certain economic or property-related liberties. Most notably, the Fifth Amendment's Takings Clause provides that the government cannot take a person's property without paying just compensation, and the Contracts Clause of Article I, §10 forbids state or local governments from enacting laws that impair contractual obligations. This chapter explores these two important constitutional protections (as well as the Constitution's Ex Post Facto Clauses).

A.   The Takings Clause

The final clause of the Fifth Amendment states: "nor shall private property be taken for public use, without just compensation." Given this phrasing, the Takings Clause *presumes* the government has the authority to take title to private property (for instance, through eminent domain). Thus, the taking of private property does not, by itself, violate the Takings Clause. Rather, the clause demands that, when such a taking occurs, the government pay the owner "just compensation."

The rationale of the Takings Clause is straightforward. First, if the government needs property for a public purpose, the public (as a whole) should bear the cost of acquiring it. It is unfair to force a single person (or a small handful of individuals) to bear such costs merely because she happens to own the property best suited for the public project. The cost should instead be borne collectively. Paying the owner just compensation for her property—and thus spreading the cost among the community's taxpayers—achieves that objective. Second, the just compensation requirement operates as a check on the governmental abuse, much as the Free Speech Clause protects political dissent. Without such a constraint, governments could selectively invoke eminent domain as a means of punishing political opponents. The Takings Clause thus complements the requirement that the government afford due process before depriving any person of their property.

The framework for analyzing Takings Clause problems involves three basic questions. The first is whether there has been a "taking." Takings can be "physical appropriations"—where the government takes possession or physically occupies private property, or where it authorizes a third party to do the same. Takings can also occur when the government restricts the owner's use of the property without physically appropriating it. These sorts of takings are more difficult to identify, as all regulations imposed on the uses of property reduce its value to some extent. The relevant question in these cases is whether the regulation has gone "too far." The second question is whether the taking was for a "public use." The government's confiscation of private property for *private* use is unconstitutional, period—even if just compensation is paid. Finally, the third question is whether the government (if it has taken private property) has paid the owner "just compensation." The following sections take up these three questions in turn.

1. Physical appropriations of property

The more straightforward type of taking is when the government "physically appropriates" private property: when the government—either itself, or someone the government has authorized—possesses or physically occupies the property. The quintessential example is when the government uses eminent domain to acquire title to the property. Such action is plainly a taking, and the government must pay the owner just compensation. But the definition of a "physical appropriation" extends much further. The physical occupation of private property constitutes a taking even if the government has not acquired ownership. For example, it might be accomplished through a regulation of the property that authorizes government officials to physically enter the property whenever the government pleases. Further, the physical occupation need not be by the government itself. For instance, if the government releases water from a dam, thereby flooding a landowner's property (which "physically occupies" that land), this will constitute a taking of the property, necessitating the payment of just compensation.

Doctrinally, physical appropriations of private property are takings *per se*. That is, the physical appropriation of property is a taking, full stop—even if the physical occupation is miniscule, and the impact on the property's value trivial. The extent of the appropriation will affect the calculation of "just compensation," but it does not bear on whether the government's action constitutes a taking. All physical appropriations, by definition, are takings.

a. *An example: Loretto v. Teleprompter Manhattan CATV Corp.*

The Court's decision in *Loretto v. Teleprompter Manhattan CATV Corp.*, 458 U.S. 419 (1982), is a nice illustration. A New York law provided that landlords were required to permit a cable television company to install cable facilities on their property. As authorized by the law, a private cable company installed a cable less than one-half inch in diameter and approximately 30 feet in length along the side of the building. The company also installed two silver boxes on the building's roof. The owner of the building challenged the installation of these items on her property as a taking without just compensation.

The government did not acquire any interest in the property, nor did the government itself occupy the property. The regulation merely authorized a third parties (cable companies) to permanently occupy the property with their cables and boxes. Further, the physical intrusion on the owner's property bordered on the negligible. Still, the Supreme Court concluded that the New York law effectuated a physical appropriation of the owner's property and thus constituted a taking *per se*. In the Court's words,

> "we have long considered a physical intrusion by government to be a property restriction of an unusually serious character for purposes of the Takings Clause. Our cases further establish that when the physical intrusion reaches the extreme form of a permanent physical occupation, a taking has occurred. In such a case, 'the character of the government action' not only is an important factor in resolving whether the action works a taking but also is determinative. . . . [W]hen the 'character of the governmental action' is a permanent physical occupation of property, our cases uniformly have found a taking to the extent of the occupation, without regard to whether the action achieves an important public benefit or has only minimal economic impact on the owner."

Loretto demonstrates that the extent of a physical appropriation is immaterial to whether a taking has occurred. The space occupied by the cable that ran along Jean Loretto's building was de minimis. But that was beside the point. Because the installation of the cable constituted a physical occupation of her property, it amounted to a taking of her property *per se*. *Loretto* also shows how it need not be the government that physically occupies or appropriates the property. The owner of the cable (Teleprompter Manhattan CATV Corp.) was not the government. What mattered was that the State of New York had authorized third parties to physically occupy private property. Thus, the occupation was accomplished by government action, making the appropriation a taking. (Had Teleprompter occupied Loretto's property without government authorization, it likely would have constituted a private trespass.)

b. *Physical appropriations of other forms of property*

Importantly, the government's appropriation of property constitutes a takings *per se* regardless of the type of property appropriated. For instance, the government's appropriation of intellectual property (such as a patent, copyright, or trademark) constitutes a taking, no different than the appropriation of land. Similarly, the physical appropriation of tangible personal property will constitute a taking. At issue in *Horne v. Department of Agriculture*, 569 U.S. 513 (2013), for example, was a U.S. Department of Agriculture California Raisin Marketing Order, under which raisin growers were required to set aside a percentage of their crop for the federal government, free of charge (at least in certain years). The government could then sell, allocate, or otherwise dispose of the raisins in ways it determined were best suited to maintaining an orderly raisin market. In the years at issue, the Hornes refused to set aside the raisins required by the marketing order, and government officials came to their farm and physically removed the raisins. The government contended there had not been a taking because the raisins were *personal* (and not real) property.

The Supreme Court disagreed. "Nothing in the text or history of the Takings Clause, or our precedents, suggests that the rule is any different when [there is an] appropriation of personal property. The Government has a categorical duty to pay just compensation when it takes your car, just as when it takes your home." This meant the marketing order effectuated a taking:

> "Actual raisins are transferred from the growers to the Government. Title to the raisins passes to the Raisin Committee. . . . The Committee disposes of what become its raisins as it wishes, to promote the purposes of the raisin marketing order. . . . The Government's formal demand that the Hornes turn over a percentage of their raisin crop without charge, for the Government's control and use, is of such a unique character that it is a taking without regard to other factors that a court might ordinarily examine."

c. *A more recent example: Cedar Point Nursery v. Hassid*

In June 2021, the Court decided an important Takings Clause dispute concerning a California law that granted labor union organizers access to private farms. The California Agricultural Labor Relations Board promulgated a regulation mandating that agricultural employers permit union organizers onto their premises "for the purpose of meeting and talking with employees and soliciting their support." Cal. Code Regs., tit. 8, §20900(e). The organizers could not engage in disruptive conduct, but they were free to meet with employees, and an employer's interference with organizers' right of access could amount to an unfair labor practice under California law. Two agricultural employers subject to the regulation—Cedar Point Nursery and Fowler Packing Company—challenged the regulation as a taking of property requiring just compensation. As you read *Cedar Point Nursery*, please consider the following questions:

1. California did not acquire title (or any other possessory interest) in the employers' properties. Nor did California transfer a possessory interest

to the labor organizers. Why, then, did the government's action still constitute a "physical appropriation" of property?

2. Did it matter that this taking was accomplished through a regulation? Why or why not?

3. If the California's access regulation had not constituted a "physical appropriation" of property, would it have necessarily not been a taking? Why or why not?

4. Does the Court hold that the California access regulation is unconstitutional? Explain.

5. What are the implications of the Court's opinion in *Cedar Point Nursery* for government regulations of public accommodations, such as those mandating that businesses not discriminate based of race, sex, religion, disability, sexual orientation, or gender identity? What are the implications for routine governmental safety and health inspections of private property?

Cedar Point Nursery v. Hassid
141 S. Ct. 2063 (2021)

CHIEF JUSTICE ROBERTS delivered the opinion of the Court.

A California regulation grants labor organizations a "right to take access" to an agricultural employer's property in order to solicit support for unionization. Agricultural employers must allow union organizers onto their property for up to three hours per day, 120 days per year. The question presented is whether the access regulation constitutes a *per se* physical taking under the Fifth and Fourteenth Amendments.

I

The California Agricultural Labor Relations Act of 1975 gives agricultural employees a right to self-organization and makes it an unfair labor practice for employers to interfere with that right. Cal. Lab. Code Ann. §§1152, 1153(a) (West 2020). The state Agricultural Labor Relations Board has promulgated a regulation providing, in its current form, that the self-organization rights of employees include "the right of access by union organizers to the premises of an agricultural employer for the purpose of meeting and talking with employees and soliciting their support." Cal. Code Regs., tit. 8, §20900(e). Under the regulation, a labor organization may "take access" to an agricultural employer's property for up to four 30-day periods in one calendar year. §§20900(e)(1)(A), (B). In order to take access, a labor organization must file a written notice with the Board and serve a copy on the employer. Two organizers per work crew (plus one additional organizer for every 15 workers over 30 workers in a crew) may enter the employer's property for up to one hour before work, one hour during the lunch break, and one hour after work. Organizers may not engage in disruptive conduct, but are otherwise free to meet and talk with employees as they wish. Interference with organizers' right of access may constitute an unfair labor practice, which can result in sanctions against the employer.

Cedar Point Nursery is a strawberry grower in northern California. It employs over 400 seasonal workers and around 100 full-time workers, none of whom live on the property. According to the complaint, in October 2015, at five o'clock one morning, members of the United Farm Workers entered Cedar Point's property without prior notice. The organizers moved to the nursery's trim shed, where hundreds of workers were preparing strawberry plants. Calling through bullhorns, the organizers disturbed operations, causing some workers to join the organizers in a protest and others to leave the worksite altogether. Cedar Point filed a charge against the union for taking access without giving notice. The union responded with a charge of its own, alleging that Cedar Point had committed an unfair labor practice.

Fowler Packing Company is a Fresno-based grower and shipper of table grapes and citrus. It has 1,800 to 2,500 employees in its field operations and around 500 in its packing facility. As with Cedar Point, none of Fowler's workers live on the premises. In July 2015, organizers from the United Farm Workers attempted to take access to Fowler's property, but the company blocked them from entering. The union filed an unfair labor practice charge against Fowler, which it later withdrew.

Believing that the union would likely attempt to enter their property again in the near future, the growers filed suit in Federal District Court against several Board members in their official capacity. The growers argued that the access regulation effected an unconstitutional *per se* physical taking under the Fifth and Fourteenth Amendments by appropriating without compensation an easement for union organizers to enter their property. They requested declaratory and injunctive relief prohibiting the Board from enforcing the regulation against them.

The District Court denied the growers' motion for a preliminary injunction and granted the Board's motion to dismiss. . . . A divided panel of the Court of Appeals for the Ninth Circuit affirmed.

II

A

The Takings Clause of the Fifth Amendment, applicable to the States through the Fourteenth Amendment, provides: "[N]or shall private property be taken for public use, without just compensation." The Founders recognized that the protection of private property is indispensable to the promotion of individual freedom. As John Adams tersely put it, "[p]roperty must be secured, or liberty cannot exist." Discourses on Davila, in 6 Works of John Adams 280 (C. Adams ed. 1851). This Court agrees, having noted that protection of property rights is "necessary to preserve freedom" and "empowers persons to shape and to plan their own destiny in a world where governments are always eager to do so for them." *Murr* v. *Wisconsin*, 582 U. S. ___, ___ (2017).

When the government physically acquires private property for a public use, the Takings Clause imposes a clear and categorical obligation to provide the owner with just compensation. The Court's physical takings jurisprudence is "as old as the Republic." The government commits a physical taking when it uses its power of eminent domain to formally condemn property. The same is true when the government physically takes possession of property without acquiring title to it. And the government likewise effects a physical taking when it occupies property—say, by recurring flooding as a result of building a dam. These sorts of physical appropriations constitute the "clearest sort of taking," *Palazzolo* v. *Rhode Island*, 533 U.S. 606, 617 (2001), and we assess them using a simple, *per se* rule: The government must pay for what it takes.

When the government, rather than appropriating private property for itself or a third party, instead imposes regulations that restrict an owner's ability to use his own property, a different standard applies. Our jurisprudence governing such use restrictions has developed more recently. Before the 20th century, the Takings Clause was understood to be limited to physical appropriations of property. In *Pennsylvania Coal Co.* v. *Mahon*, 260 U.S. 393 (1922), however, the Court established the proposition that "while property may be regulated to a certain extent, if regulation goes too far it will be recognized as a taking." *Id.*, at 415. This framework now applies to use restrictions as varied as zoning ordinances, *Village of Euclid* v. *Ambler Realty Co.*, 272 U.S. 365 (1926), orders barring the mining of gold, *United States* v. *Central Eureka Mining Co.*, 357 U.S. 155 (1958), and regulations prohibiting the sale of eagle feathers, *Andrus* v. *Allard*, 444 U.S. 51 (1979). To determine whether a use restriction effects a taking, this Court has generally applied the flexible test developed in *Penn Central*, balancing factors such as the economic impact of the regulation, its interference with reasonable investment-backed expectations, and the character of the government action.

Our cases have often described use restrictions that go "too far" as "regulatory takings." But that label can mislead. Government action that physically appropriates property is no less a physical taking because it arises from a regulation. That explains why we held that an administrative reserve requirement compelling raisin growers to physically set aside a percentage of their crop for the government constituted a physical rather than a regulatory taking. *Horne*, 576 U. S., at 361. The essential question is not . . . whether the government action at issue comes garbed as a regulation (or statute, or ordinance, or miscellaneous decree). It is whether the government has physically taken property for itself or someone else—by whatever means—or has instead restricted a property owner's ability to use his own property. Whenever a regulation results in a physical appropriation of property, a *per se* taking has occurred, and *Penn Central* has no place.

B

The access regulation appropriates a right to invade the growers' property and therefore constitutes a *per se* physical taking. The regulation grants union organizers a right to physically enter and occupy the growers' land for three hours per day, 120 days per year. Rather than restraining the growers' use of their own property, the regulation appropriates for the enjoyment of third parties the owners' right to exclude.

The right to exclude is "one of the most treasured" rights of property ownership. *Loretto* v. *Teleprompter Manhattan CATV Corp.*, 458 U. S. 419, 435 (1982). According to Blackstone, the very idea of property entails "that sole and despotic dominion which one man claims and exercises over the external things of the world, in total exclusion of the right of any other individual in the universe." 2 W. Blackstone, Commentaries on the Laws of England 2 (1766). In less exuberant terms, we have stated that the right to exclude is "universally held to be a fundamental element of the property right," and is "one of the most essential sticks in the bundle of rights that are commonly characterized as property." *Kaiser Aetna* v. *United States*, 444 U. S. 164, 176, 179–180 (1979).

Given the central importance to property ownership of the right to exclude, it comes as little surprise that the Court has long treated government-authorized physical invasions as takings requiring just compensation. The Court has often described the property interest taken as a servitude or an easement.

For example, in *United States* v. *Causby* we held that the invasion of private property by overflights effected a taking. 328 U. S. 256 (1946). The government frequently flew military aircraft low over the Causby farm, grazing the treetops and terrorizing the poultry. *Id.*, at 259. The Court observed that ownership of the land extended to airspace that low, and that "invasions of it are in the same category as invasions of the surface." *Id.*, at 265. Because the damages suffered by the Causbys "were the product of a direct invasion of [their] domain," we held that "a servitude has been imposed upon the land." *Id.*, at 265–266, 267.

We similarly held that the appropriation of an easement effected a taking in *Kaiser Aetna* v. *United States*. A real-estate developer dredged a pond, converted it into a marina, and connected it to a nearby bay and the ocean. 444 U. S., at 167. The government asserted that the developer could not exclude the public from the marina because the pond had become a navigable water. *Id.*, at 168. We held that the right to exclude "falls within [the] category of interests that the Government cannot take without compensation." *Id.*, at 180. After noting that "the imposition of the navigational servitude" would "result in an actual physical invasion of the privately owned marina" by members of the public, we cited *Causby* and *Portsmouth* for the proposition that "even if the Government physically invades only an easement in property, it must nonetheless pay just compensation." 444 U. S., at 180.

In *Loretto* v. *Teleprompter Manhattan CATV Corp.*, we made clear that a permanent physical occupation constitutes a *per se* taking regardless whether it results in only a trivial economic loss. New York adopted a law requiring landlords to allow cable companies to install equipment on their properties. 458 U. S., at 423. Loretto alleged that the installation of a ½-inch diameter cable and two 1½-cubic-foot boxes on her roof caused a taking. *Id.*, at 424. We agreed, stating that where government action results in a "permanent physical occupation of property, our cases uniformly have found a taking to the extent of the occupation, without regard to whether the action achieves an important public benefit or has only minimal economic impact on the owner." *Id.*, at 434–435. . . .

More recently, in *Horne* v. *Department of Agriculture*, we observed that "people still do not expect their property, real or personal, to be actually occupied or taken away." 576 U. S., at 361. The physical appropriation by the government of the raisins in that case was a *per se* taking, even if a regulatory limit with the same economic impact would not have been. *Id.*, at 362. "The Constitution," we explained, "is concerned with means as well as ends." *Id.*

The upshot of this line of precedent is that government-authorized invasions of property—whether by plane, boat, cable, or beachcomber—are physical takings requiring just compensation. As in those cases, the government here has appropriated a right of access to the growers' property, allowing union organizers to traverse it at will for three hours a day, 120 days a year. The regulation appropriates a right to physically invade the growers' property—to literally "take access," as the regulation provides. It is therefore a *per se* physical taking under our precedents. Accordingly, the growers' complaint states a claim for an uncompensated taking in violation of the Fifth and Fourteenth Amendments.

C

The Ninth Circuit saw matters differently, as do the Board and the dissent. In the decision below, the Ninth Circuit took the view that the access regulation did not qualify as a *per se* taking because, although it grants a right to physically invade the growers' property, it does not allow for permanent and continuous access "24 hours a day, 365 days a year." The dissent likewise concludes that the regulation cannot amount to a *per se* taking because it allows "access short of 365 days a year." That position is insupportable as a matter of precedent and common sense. There is no reason the law should analyze an abrogation of the right to exclude in one manner if it extends for 365 days, but in an entirely different manner if it lasts for 364.

To begin with, we have held that a physical appropriation is a taking whether it is permanent or temporary. Our cases establish that "compensation is mandated when a leasehold is taken and the government occupies property for its own purposes, even though that use is temporary." *Tahoe-Sierra*, 535 U. S., at 322. The duration of an appropriation—just like the size of an appropriation—bears only on the amount of compensation. For example, after finding a taking by physical invasion, the Court in *Causby* remanded the case to the lower court to determine "whether the easement taken was temporary or permanent," in order to fix the compensation due. 328 U. S., at 267–268.

To be sure, *Loretto* emphasized the heightened concerns associated with "[t]he permanence and absolute exclusivity of a physical occupation" in contrast to "temporary limitations on the right to exclude," and stated that "[n]ot every physical *invasion* is a taking." 458 U. S., at 435, n. 12. The latter point is well taken, as we will explain. But *Nollan* clarified that appropriation of a right to physically invade property may constitute a taking "even though no particular individual is permitted to station himself permanently upon the premises." 483 U. S., at 832.

Next, we have recognized that physical invasions constitute takings even if they are intermittent as opposed to continuous. *Causby* held that overflights of private property effected a taking, even though they occurred on only 4% of takeoffs and 7% of landings at the nearby airport. 328 U. S., at 259. And while *Nollan* happened to involve a legally continuous right of access, we have no doubt that the Court would have reached the same conclusion if the easement demanded by the Commission had lasted for only 364 days per year. After all, the easement was hardly continuous as a practical matter. As Justice Brennan observed in dissent, given the shifting tides, "public passage for a portion of the year would either be impossible or would not occur on [the Nollans'] property." 483 U. S., at 854. What matters is not that the easement notionally ran round the clock, but that the government had taken a right to physically invade the Nollans' land. And when the government physically takes an interest in property, it must pay for the right to do so. The fact that a right to take access is exercised only from time to time does not make it any less a physical taking. . . .

[The Board contends that the access regulation] fails to qualify as a *per se* taking because it "authorizes only limited and intermittent access for a narrow purpose." That position is little more defensible than the Ninth Circuit's. The fact that the regulation grants access only to union organizers and only for a limited time does not transform it from a physical taking into a use restriction. Saying that appropriation of a three hour per day, 120 day per year right to invade the growers' premises "does not constitute a taking of a property interest but rather . . . a mere restriction on its use, is to use words in a manner that deprives them of all their ordinary meaning." *Nollan*, 483 U. S., at 831.

The Board also takes issue with the growers' premise that the access regulation appropriates an easement. In the Board's estimation, the regulation does not exact a true easement in gross under California law because the access right may not be transferred, does not burden any particular parcel of property, and may not be recorded. This, the Board

540

says, reinforces its conclusion that the regulation does not take a constitutionally protected property interest from the growers. The dissent agrees, suggesting that the access right cannot effect a *per se* taking because it does not require the growers to grant the union organizers an easement as defined by state property law.

These arguments misconstrue our physical takings doctrine. As a general matter, it is true that the property rights protected by the Takings Clause are creatures of state law. But no one disputes that, without the access regulation, the growers would have had the right under California law to exclude union organizers from their property. And no one disputes that the access regulation took that right from them. The Board cannot absolve itself of takings liability by appropriating the growers' right to exclude in a form that is a slight mismatch from state easement law. Under the Constitution, property rights "cannot be so easily manipulated." *Horne*, 576 U. S., at 365.

Our decisions consistently reflect this intuitive approach. We have recognized that the government can commit a physical taking either by appropriating property through a condemnation proceeding or by simply "enter[ing] into physical possession of property without authority of a court order." *Dow*, 357 U. S., at 21. In the latter situation, the government's intrusion does not vest it with a property interest recognized by state law, such as a fee simple or a leasehold. Yet we recognize a physical taking all the same. Any other result would allow the government to appropriate private property without just compensation so long as it avoids formal condemnation. We have never tolerated that outcome. For much the same reason, in *Portsmouth*, *Causby*, and *Loretto* we never paused to consider whether the physical invasions at issue vested the intruders with formal easements according to the nuances of state property law (nor do we see how they could have). Instead, we followed our traditional rule: Because the government appropriated a right to invade, compensation was due. That same test governs here.

The Board and the dissent further contend that our decision in *PruneYard Shopping Center* v. *Robins*, 447 U.S. 74 (1980), establishes that the access regulation cannot qualify as a *per se* taking. There the California Supreme Court held that the State Constitution protected the right to engage in leafleting at the PruneYard, a privately owned shopping center. The shopping center argued that the decision had taken without just compensation its right to exclude. Applying the *Penn Central* factors, we held that no compensable taking had occurred. 447 U. S., at 83; cf. *Heart of Atlanta Motel, Inc.* v. *United States*, 379 U.S. 241, 261 (1964) (rejecting claim that provisions of the Civil Rights Act of 1964 prohibiting racial discrimination in public accommodations effected a taking).

The Board and the dissent argue that *PruneYard* shows that limited rights of access to private property should be evaluated as regulatory rather than *per se* takings. We disagree. Unlike the growers' properties, the PruneYard was open to the public, welcoming some 25,000 patrons a day. Limitations on how a business generally open to the public may treat individuals on the premises are readily distinguishable from regulations granting a right to invade property closed to the public. . . .

D

. . . . In "ordinary English" "appropriation" means "*taking* as one's own," 1 Oxford English Dictionary 587 (2d ed. 1989) (emphasis added), and the regulation expressly grants to labor organizers the "right to *take* access," Cal. Code Regs., tit. 8, §20900(e)(1)(C) (emphasis added). We cannot agree that the right to exclude is an empty formality, subject to modification at the government's pleasure. On the contrary, it is a "fundamental element of the property right," *Kaiser Aetna*, 444 U. S., at 179–180, that cannot be balanced away. Our cases establish that appropriations of a right to invade are *per se* physical takings, not use restrictions subject to *Penn Central*: "[W]hen [government] planes use private airspace to approach a government airport, [the government] is required to pay for that share no matter how small." *Tahoe-Sierra*, 535 U. S., at 322. And while *Kaiser Aetna* may have referred to the test from *Penn Central*, the Court concluded categorically that the government must pay just compensation for physical invasions. With regard to the complexities of modern society, we think they only reinforce the importance of safeguarding the basic property rights that help preserve individual liberty, as the Founders explained. . . .

III

The Board, seconded by the dissent, warns that treating the access regulation as a *per se* physical taking will endanger a host of state and federal government activities involving entry onto private property. That fear is unfounded.

First, our holding does nothing to efface the distinction between trespass and takings. Isolated physical invasions, not undertaken pursuant to a granted right of access, are properly assessed as individual torts rather than appropriations of a property right. This basic distinction is firmly grounded in our precedent. . . .

Second, many government-authorized physical invasions will not amount to takings because they are consistent with longstanding background restrictions on property rights. As we explained in *Lucas* v. *South Carolina Coastal Council*, the government does not take a property interest when it merely asserts a "pre-existing limitation upon the land owner's title." 505 U. S., at 1028–1029. For example, the government owes a landowner no compensation for requiring him to abate a nuisance on his property, because he never had a right to engage in the nuisance in the first place.

These background limitations also encompass traditional common law privileges to access private property. One such privilege allowed individuals to enter property in the event of public or private necessity. See Restatement (Second) of Torts §196 (1964) (entry to avert an imminent public disaster); §197 (entry to avert serious harm to a person, land, or chattels). The common law also recognized a privilege to enter property to effect an arrest or enforce the criminal law under certain circumstances. Because a property owner traditionally had no right to exclude an official engaged in a reasonable search, government searches that are consistent with the Fourth Amendment and state law cannot be said to take any property right from landowners.

Third, the government may require property owners to cede a right of access as a condition of receiving certain benefits, without causing a taking. In *Nollan*, we held that "a permit condition that serves the same legitimate police-power purpose as a refusal to issue the permit should not be found to be a taking if the refusal to issue the permit would not constitute a taking." 483 U. S., at 836. The inquiry, we later explained, is whether the permit condition bears an "essential nexus" and "rough proportionality" to the impact of the proposed use of the property. *Dolan*, 512 U. S., at 386, 391.

Under this framework, government health and safety inspection regimes will generally not constitute takings. When the government conditions the grant of a benefit such as a permit, license, or registration on allowing access for reasonable health and safety inspections, both the nexus and rough proportionality requirements of the constitutional conditions framework should not be difficult to satisfy. See, *e.g.*, 7 U.S.C. §136g(a)(1)(A) (pesticide inspections); 16 U.S.C. §823b(a) (hydroelectric project investigations); 21 U.S.C. §374(a)(1) (pharmaceutical inspections); 42 U.S.C. §2201(o) (nuclear material inspections). None of these considerations undermine our determination that the access regulation here gives rise to a *per se* physical taking. Unlike a mere trespass, the regulation grants a formal entitlement to physically invade the growers' land. Unlike a law enforcement search, no traditional background principle of property law requires the growers to admit union organizers onto their premises. And unlike standard health and safety inspections, the access regulation is not germane to any benefit provided to agricultural employers or any risk posed to the public. The access regulation amounts to simple appropriation of private property.

* * *

The access regulation grants labor organizations a right to invade the growers' property. It therefore constitutes a *per se* physical taking.

*   *   *

Notes on *Cedar Point Nursery v. Hassid*

1. *"Physical appropriations" of property as takings* per se: The Court in *Cedar Point Nursery* made clear that all physical appropriations of property effectuated by the government constitute takings *per se*, even if the government does not acquire title to the property (or transfer title to a third party). As the material below explores in greater detail, regulations of an owner's *use* of her property are generally subject to a balancing test (outlined in *Penn*

Central Transportation Co. v. New York, 438 U.S. 104 (1978)) to determine whether a taking has occurred. But if a regulation constitutes a "physical appropriation"—an appropriation of the owner's "right to exclude"—it categorically constitutes a taking. As the Court explained:

> "The essential question is not . . . whether the government action at issue comes garbed as a regulation (or statute, or ordinance, or miscellaneous decree). It is whether the government has physically taken property for itself or someone else—by whatever means—or has instead restricted a property owner's ability to use his own property. Whenever a regulation results in a physical appropriation of property, a *per se* taking has occurred, and *Penn Central* has no place."

2. *Why was California's regulation a "physical appropriation" of property?*: Section II-B of the opinion explains why, at least in the Court's view, California's regulation constituted a "physical appropriation" of property. Specifically, the regulation constituted more than just a "restrain[t on] the growers' use of their own property": it "appropriate[d] for the enjoyment of third parties the owners' right to exclude." Through its regulation, California had "appropriated a right of access to the growers' property, allowing union organizers to traverse it at will for three hours a day, 120 days a year." Thus, it appropriated "a right to physically invade the growers' property—to literally 'take access,' as the regulation provides."

Importantly, the Court explained that—at least in this respect—California's regulation amounted to a "government-authorized physical invasion," indistinguishable from several others that the Court had found to constitute takins *per se*. These included the government's use of the airspace just above an owner's property for overflights by military aircraft, *United States v. Causby*, 328 U.S. 256 (1946); an order that a real-estate developer open a waterway and marina to public access (because it connected to a nearby bay and the ocean), *Kaiser Aetna v. United States*, 444 U.S. 164 (1979); the law in *Loretto*, which forced apartment owners to allow cable companies to install coaxial cable and cable boxes in their buildings; and the physical taking of raisins from the Hornes.

3. *Regulations not constituting "physical appropriations"*: As the Court notes, when a property regulation does *not* effectuate a "physical appropriation"—when it merely "restrict[s] an owner's ability to use his own property"—the analysis is different. Generally, such regulations are subject to a three-part balancing test that examines "the economic impact of the regulation, its interference with reasonable investment-backed expectations, and the character of the government action." Only if the regulation "goes too far" (in light of these three considerations) will it be considered a taking of property. There is an exception, though, for regulations on use (short of physical appropriations") that deprive the owner of all "economically beneficial uses" of her property. Such regulations—because, in practice, they effectively operate as physical appropriations—are also considered takings *per se*. *See Lucas v. South Carolina Coastal Council*, 505 U.S. 1003 (1992) (discussed below).

4. *Distinguishing regulations on public accommodations*: Federal and state governments have long regulated "public accommodations"—businesses that are generally open to the public—mandating that they serve their customers in various ways or open their premises to various activities. For example, the Civil Rights Act of 1964 forbids restaurants, hotels, and various other businesses from discriminating based on race, and thus forces private property owners to grant access to their property. Similarly, California law requires certain private property owners (such as shopping malls and universities) to permit peaceful expressive activity on their property. The Supreme Court has long held that these sorts of regulations do not constitute takings. *See PruneYard Shopping Center v. Robins*, 447 U.S. 74 (1980). The opinion in *Cedar Point Nursery* distinguished these sorts of regulations from that granting union organizers access to farms: "Unlike the growers' properties, the [shopping mall] was open to the public, welcoming some 25,000 patrons a day. Limitations on how a business generally open to the public may treat individuals on the premises are readily distinguishable from regulations granting a right to invade property closed to the public." Thus, at least for now, the rule of *Cedar Point Nursery* only applies to property not open to the public.

5. *Governmental health and safety inspections*: A routine feature of modern government is that government officials routinely inspect private property (often without warning) to assess compliance with various health and safety regulations. County environmental health officials conduct spot inspections of restaurants to determine their adherence to food safety rules; federal Occupational Safety and Health Administration (OSHA) officials inspect workplaces for their compliance with federal statutes and regulations; city officers inspect buildings and construction sites for their compliance with various building codes; and so on. *Cedar Point Nursery* explains that regulations subjecting private property to these sorts of inspections will generally not constitute "physical appropriations." As the Court notes near the end of the opinion, "[w]hen the government conditions the grant of a benefit such as a permit, license, or registration on allowing access for reasonable health and safety inspections, both the nexus and rough proportionality requirements of the constitutional conditions framework should not be difficult to satisfy."

Notice, though, that such regulations must satisfy two conditions. First, the regulation must be imposed on the granting of "a benefit such as a permit, license, or registration." This seems to suggest that if the access is conditioned on a use of the property that is not a "benefit"—a use for which the owner should not need to seek permission from the government in the first instance—the regulation *would* be a taking *per se*. Second, such regulations must still be "reasonable"—they must have "an 'essential nexus' and 'rough proportionality' to the impact of the proposed use of the property." Thus, many worry that the long-term implications of *Cedar Point Nursery* pose a serious threat to many contemporary regulations that have long been considered constitutional.

* * *

2. Restrictions on the use of property

As *Loretto* and *Cedar Point Nursery* underscore, physical appropriations of private property are *always* takings. But other governmental actions can constitute takings as well. Specifically, regulations that restrict an owner's uses of her property can qualify as takings when they substantially diminish the property's value. For many years, the Supreme Court seemed to believe that a mere regulation of how one uses her property could *never* amount to a taking. But in *Pennsylvania Coal Co. v. Mahon*, 260 U.S. 393 (1922), the Court held that, at some point, a non-appropriating regulation can be so onerous that it operates as a "practical ouster of [the owner's] possession." In his opinion for the Court, however, Justice Holmes was maddeningly vague in identifying *when* such a taking occurs. He famously wrote that, "while property may be regulated to a certain extent, if regulation goes too far it will be recognized as a taking." Thus, the relevant question is whether a particular restriction on the use of one's property has gone "too far."

Subsequent decisions have added more detail to this principle. The two most important are *Lucas v. South Carolina Coastal Council*, 505 U.S. 1003 (1992), and *Penn Central Transportation Co. v. New York*, 438 U.S. 104, 124 (1978). *Lucas* addressed a regulation depriving the owner of all "economically beneficial or productive use" of his property. *Lucas* explains that, in such cases, the use restriction is a taking *per se*, no different than if the government physically appropriates the property. By contrast, *Penn Central* sets out the relevant test for analyzing non-appropriating regulations that leave some economically beneficial or productive uses in place. Under those circumstances, as *Penn Central* explains, a court must weigh several factors in determining whether the regulation "goes too far."

As you read *Lucas*, please consider the following questions:

1. Did the State of South Carolina take title or physically occupy the private landowner's property? How did that matter to the Takings Clause analysis?

2. Following South Carolina's enactment of the Beachfront Management Act, what could the owner do with his property? How did this affect its value?

3. Was the government's action in *Lucas* at taking *per se*, or a taking that depended on the evaluation of several factors? Why?

4. After *Lucas*, when will a regulation of property constitute a taking *per se*, regardless of what any other factors suggest?

Lucas v. South Carolina Coastal Council
505 U.S. 1003 (1992)

JUSTICE SCALIA, delivered the opinion of the Court.

In 1986, petitioner David H. Lucas paid $975,000 for two residential lots on the Isle of Palms in Charleston County, South Carolina, on which he intended to build single-family homes. In 1988, however, the South Carolina Legislature enacted the Beachfront Management Act, which had the direct effect of barring petitioner from erecting any permanent habitable structures on his two parcels. A state trial court found that this prohibition rendered Lucas's parcels "valueless." This case requires us to decide whether the Act's dramatic effect on the economic value of Lucas's lots accomplished a taking of private property under the Fifth and Fourteenth Amendments requiring the payment of "just compensation."

I

A

South Carolina's expressed interest in intensively managing development activities in the so-called "coastal zone" dates from 1977 when, in the aftermath of Congress's passage of the federal Coastal Zone Management Act of 1972, the legislature enacted a Coastal Zone Management Act of its own. In its original form, the South Carolina Act required owners of coastal zone land that qualified as a "critical area" (defined in the legislation to include beaches and immediately adjacent sand dunes) to obtain a permit from the newly created South Carolina Coastal Council (Council) prior to committing the land to a "use other than the use the critical area was devoted to on [September 28, 1977]."

In the late 1970's, Lucas and others began extensive residential development of the Isle of Palms, a barrier island situated eastward of the city of Charleston. Toward the close of the development cycle for one residential subdivision known as "Beachwood East," Lucas in 1986 purchased the two lots at issue in this litigation for his own account. No portion of the lots, which were located approximately 300 feet from the beach, qualified as a "critical area" under the 1977 Act; accordingly, at the time Lucas acquired these parcels, he was not legally obliged to obtain a permit from the Council in advance of any development activity. His intention with respect to the lots was to do what the owners of the immediately adjacent parcels had already done: erect singlefamily residences. He commissioned architectural drawings for this purpose.

The Beachfront Management Act brought Lucas's plans to an abrupt end. Under that 1988 legislation, the Council was directed to establish a "baseline" connecting the landwardmost "point[s] of erosion . . . during the past forty years" in the region of the Isle of Palms that includes Lucas's lots. In action not challenged here, the Council fixed this baseline landward of Lucas's parcels. That was significant, for under the Act construction of occupable improvements was flatly prohibited seaward of a line drawn 20 feet landward of, and parallel to, the baseline. The Act provided no exceptions.

B

Lucas promptly filed suit in the South Carolina Court of Common Pleas, contending that the Beachfront Management Act's construction bar effected a taking of his property without just compensation. Lucas did not take issue with the validity of the Act as a lawful exercise of South Carolina's police power, but contended that the Act's complete extinguishment of his property's value entitled him to compensation regardless of whether the legislature had acted in furtherance of legitimate police power objectives. Following a bench trial, the court agreed. Among its factual determinations was the finding that "at the time Lucas purchased the two lots, both were zoned for single-family residential construction and . . . there were no restrictions imposed upon such use of the property by either the State of South Carolina, the County of Charleston, or the Town of the Isle of Palms." The trial court further found that the Beachfront Management Act decreed a permanent ban on construction insofar as Lucas's lots were concerned, and that this prohibition "deprive[d] Lucas of any reasonable economic use of the lots, . . . eliminated the unrestricted right of use, and render[ed] them valueless." The court thus concluded that Lucas's properties had been "taken" by operation of the Act, and it ordered respondent to pay "just compensation" in the amount of $1,232,387.50. The Supreme Court of South Carolina reversed. . . .

III

A

Prior to Justice Holmes's exposition in *Pennsylvania Coal Co. v. Mahon,* 260 U.S. 393 (1922), it was generally thought that the Takings Clause reached only a "direct appropriation" of property, or the functional equivalent of a "practical ouster of [the owner's] possession," *Transportation Co. v. Chicago,* 99 U.S. 635, 642 (1879). Justice Holmes recognized in *Mahon,* however, that if the protection against physical appropriations of private property was to be meaningfully enforced, the government's power to redefine the range of interests included in the ownership of property was necessarily constrained by constitutional limits. If, instead, the uses of private property were subject to unbridled, uncompensated qualification under the police power, "the natural tendency of human nature [would be] to extend the qualification more and more until at last private property disappear[ed]." *Id.,* at 415. These considerations gave birth in that case to the oft-cited maxim that, "while property may be regulated to a certain extent, if regulation goes too far it will be recognized as a taking." *Ibid.*

Nevertheless, our decision in *Mahon* offered little insight into when, and under what circumstances, a given regulation would be seen as going "too far" for purposes of the Fifth Amendment. In 70-odd years of succeeding "regulatory takings" jurisprudence, we have generally eschewed any "set formula" for determining how far is too far, preferring to "engag[e] in . . . essentially ad hoc, factual inquiries." *Penn Central Transportation Co. v. New York*, 438 U.S. 104, 124 (1978). We have, however, described at least two discrete categories of regulatory action as compensable without case-specific inquiry into the public interest advanced in support of the restraint. The first encompasses regulations that compel the property owner to suffer a physical "invasion" of his property. In general (at least with regard to permanent invasions), no matter how minute the intrusion, and no matter how weighty the public purpose behind it, we have required compensation. For example, in *Loretto v. Teleprompter Manhattan CATV Corp.*, 458 U.S. 419 (1982), we determined that New York's law requiring landlords to allow television cable companies to emplace cable facilities in their apartment buildings constituted a taking, *id.,* at 435–440, even though the facilities occupied at most only 1½ cubic feet of the landlords' property, see *id.,* at 438, n. 16.

The second situation in which we have found categorical treatment appropriate is where regulation denies all economically beneficial or productive use of land. As we have said on numerous occasions, the Fifth Amendment is violated when land-use regulation "does not substantially advance legitimate state interests *or denies an owner economically viable use of his land.*" *Agins v. City of Tiburon*, 447 U.S. 255, 260 (1980).

We have never set forth the justification for this rule. Perhaps it is simply, as Justice Brennan suggested, that total deprivation of beneficial use is, from the landowner's point of view, the equivalent of a physical appropriation. "[F]or what is the land but the profits thereof[?]" 1 E. Coke, Institutes, ch. 1, § 1 (1st Am. ed. 1812). Surely, at least, in the extraordinary circumstance when *no* productive or economically beneficial use of land is permitted, it is less realistic to indulge our usual assumption that the legislature is simply "adjusting the benefits and burdens of economic life," *Penn Central,* 438 U.S. at 124, in a manner that secures an "average reciprocity of advantage" to everyone concerned, *Mahon,* 260 U.S. at 415. And the *functional* basis for permitting the government, by regulation, to affect property values without compensation—that "Government hardly could go on if to some extent values incident to property could not be diminished without paying for every such change in the general law," *id.,* at 413—does not apply to the relatively rare situations where the government has deprived a landowner of all economically beneficial uses.

On the other side of the balance, affirmatively supporting a compensation requirement, is the fact that regulations that leave the owner of land without economically beneficial or productive options for its use—typically, as here, by requiring land to be left substantially in its natural state—carry with them a heightened risk that private property is being pressed into some form of public service under the guise of mitigating serious public harm. As Justice Brennan explained: "From the government's point of view, the benefits flowing to the public from preservation of open space through regulation may be equally great as from creating a wildlife refuge through formal condemnation or increasing electricity production through a dam project that floods private property." *San Diego Gas & Elec. Co., supra,* at 652 (dissenting opinion). The many statutes on the books, both state and federal, that provide for the use of eminent domain to impose servitudes on private scenic lands preventing developmental uses, or to acquire such lands altogether, suggest the practical equivalence in this setting of negative regulation and appropriation.

We think, in short, that there are good reasons for our frequently expressed belief that when the owner of real property has been called upon to sacrifice *all* economically beneficial uses in the name of the common good, that is, to leave his property economically idle, he has suffered a taking.

B

The trial court found Lucas's two beachfront lots to have been rendered valueless by respondent's enforcement of the coastal-zone construction ban. Under Lucas's theory of the case, which rested upon our "no economically viable use" statements, that finding entitled him to compensation. Lucas believed it unnecessary to take issue with either the purposes behind the Beachfront Management Act, or the means chosen by the South Carolina Legislature to effectuate those purposes. The South Carolina Supreme Court, however, thought otherwise. In its view, the Beachfront Management Act was no ordinary enactment, but involved an exercise of South Carolina's "police powers" to mitigate the harm to the public interest that petitioner's use of his land might occasion. By neglecting to dispute the findings enumerated in the Act or otherwise to challenge the legislature's purposes, petitioner "concede[d] that the beach/dune area of South Carolina's shores is an extremely valuable public resource; that the erection of new construction, *inter alia,* contributes to the erosion and destruction of this public resource; and that discouraging new construction in close proximity to the beach/dune area is necessary to prevent a great public harm." In the court's view, these concessions brought petitioner's challenge within a long line of this Court's cases sustaining against Due Process and Takings Clause challenges the State's use of its "police powers" to enjoin a property owner from activities akin to public nuisances. See *Mugler v. Kansas,* 123 U.S. 623 (1887) (law prohibiting manufacture of alcoholic beverages); *Hadacheck v. Sebastian,* 239 U.S. 394 (1915) (law barring operation of brick mill in residential area); *Miller v. Schoene,* 276 U.S. 272 (1928) (order to destroy diseased cedar trees to prevent infection of nearby orchards); *Goldblatt c. Hempstead,* 369 U.S. 590 (1962) (law effectively preventing continued operation of quarry in residential area).

It is correct that many of our prior opinions have suggested that "harmful or noxious uses" of property may be proscribed by government regulation without the requirement of compensation. For a number of reasons, however, we think the South Carolina Supreme Court was too quick to conclude that that principle decides the present case. The "harmful or noxious uses" principle was the Court's early attempt to describe in theoretical terms why government may, consistent with the Takings Clause, affect property values by regulation without incurring an obligation to compensate—a reality we nowadays acknowledge explicitly with respect to the full scope of the State's police power. . . .

Where the State seeks to sustain regulation that deprives land of all economically beneficial use, we think it may resist compensation only if the logically antecedent inquiry into the nature of the owner's estate shows that the proscribed use interests were not part of his title to begin with. This accords, we think, with our "takings" jurisprudence, which has traditionally been guided by the understandings of our citizens regarding the content of, and the State's power over, the "bundle of rights" that they acquire when they obtain title to property. It seems to us that the property owner necessarily expects the uses of his property to be restricted, from time to time, by various measures newly enacted by the State in legitimate exercise of its police powers; "[a]s long recognized, some values are enjoyed under an implied limitation and must yield to the police power." *Mahon*, 260 U.S. at 413. And in the case of personal property, by reason of the State's traditionally high degree of control over commercial dealings, he ought to be aware of the possibility that new regulation might even render his property economically worthless (at least if the property's only economically productive use is sale or manufacture for sale). In the case of land, however, we think the notion pressed by the Council that title is somehow held subject to the "implied limitation" that the State may subsequently eliminate all economically valuable use is inconsistent with the historical compact recorded in the Takings Clause that has become part of our constitutional culture.

Where "permanent physical occupation" of land is concerned, we have refused to allow the government to decree it anew (without compensation), no matter how weighty the asserted "public interests" involved—though we assuredly *would* permit the government to assert a permanent easement that was a pre-existing limitation upon the landowner's title. We believe similar treatment must be accorded confiscatory regulations, *i.e.,* regulations that prohibit all economically beneficial use of land: Any limitation so severe cannot be newly legislated or decreed (without compensation), but must inhere in the title itself, in the restrictions that background principles of the State's law of property and nuisance already place upon land ownership. A law or decree with such an effect must, in other words, do no more than duplicate the result that could have been achieved in the courts—by adjacent landowners (or other uniquely affected persons) under the State's law of private nuisance, or by the State under its complementary power to abate nuisances that affect the public generally, or otherwise.

On this analysis, the owner of a lake bed, for example, would not be entitled to compensation when he is denied the requisite permit to engage in a land filling operation that would have the effect of flooding others' land. Nor the corporate owner of a nuclear generating plant, when it is directed to remove all improvements from its land upon discovery that the plant sits astride an earthquake fault. Such regulatory action may well have the effect of eliminating the land's only economically productive use, but it does not proscribe a productive use that was previously permissible under relevant property and nuisance principles. The use of these properties for what are now expressly prohibited purposes was *always* unlawful, and (subject to other constitutional limitations) it was open to the State at any point to make the implication of those background principles of nuisance and property law explicit. In light of our traditional resort to "existing rules or understandings that stem from an independent source such as state law" to define the range of interests that qualify for protection as "property" under the Fifth and Fourteenth Amendments, *Board of Regents v. Roth*, 408 U.S. 564, 577 (1972), this recognition that the Takings Clause does not require compensation when an owner is barred from putting land to a use that is proscribed by those "existing rules or understandings" is surely unexceptional. When, however, a regulation that declares "off-limits" all economically productive or beneficial uses of land goes beyond what the relevant background principles would dictate, compensation must be paid to sustain it. . . .

*   *   *

Notes on *Lucas v. South Carolina Coastal Council*

1. *A per se rule for regulations depriving the owner of all economically beneficial use*: The Court's decision in *Lucas* holds that a government regulation on the use of property "leave[s] the owner of land without economically beneficial or productive options for its use" is a taking *per se*. There is very little difference, reasoned the Court, between such a regulation and the use of eminent domain to take title to the property outright. In the *Lucas*-type scenario, the government's action is formally a regulation on the owner's use of the property (rather than a confiscation), but the practical effect is nearly indistinguishable.

2. *The complication of preexisting restraints on use*: There is considerable logic behind the rule announced in *Lucas*. It is hard to see much difference between (1) the Coastal Council using eminent domain to acquire title to Lucas's property (so it can ensure the property remains undeveloped)—which would plainly amount to a taking—and (2) the Council imposing a regulation on the property's use that ensures no owner will ever be able to develop the property. It seems sensible that the doctrinal result for the two cases is identical: a taking *per se* that requires just compensation.

The complication is that some uses of property have long been prohibited, and thus must be understood as restrictions inherent in the ownership rights Lucas acquired when he purchased the land. Suppose the lot Lucas purchased, under traditional applications of property law, would never have been suitable for development because any structure built on the lot would have been unsafe. Under those circumstances, would it have been a taking for the state to enforce its building code and forbid Lucas from constructing any habitable structures on his property, depriving him of all "economically beneficial uses"? The Court in *Lucas* said no, but it is unclear how we can parse such restrictions from those at issue in *Lucas* itself. As Justice Scalia wrote for the Court,

> "[a]ny limitation so severe cannot be newly legislated or decreed (without compensation), but must inhere in the title itself, in the restrictions that background principles of the State's law of property and nuisance already place upon land ownership. A law or decree with such an effect must, in other words, do no more than duplicate the result that could have been achieved in the courts—by adjacent landowners (or other uniquely affected persons) under the State's law of private nuisance, or by the State under its complementary power to abate nuisances that affect the public generally, or otherwise."

3. *Regulations leaving some economically beneficial or productive uses of the property*: When a use restriction leaves the owner with some economically beneficial uses for the affected property, the Supreme Court has applied a multifactor balancing test to determine whether the regulation so diminishes the value of the property that it goes "too far" and amounts to a taking. The critical case on this point is *Penn Central Transportation Co. v. New York*, in which a New York City preservation law designating the Grand Central Terminal building a "historic landmark." The law required the owner of a designated landmark to keep the building's exterior "in good repair" and to obtain approval from a city commission before making exterior alterations. A request for approval to build a multistory office building atop the terminal was denied by the commission because, in its view, the office tower would impair the aesthetic quality of the Terminal's "flamboyant Beaux Arts facade." Penn Central, the terminal's owner, contended this development restriction constituted a taking. The Supreme Court disagreed.

Justice Brennan's opinion for the Court concluded that the government may, as part of a comprehensive historic landmark preservation program, "place restrictions on the development of individual historic landmarks [without] effecting a 'taking.'" He conceded that the inquiry involved "essentially *ad hoc* factual inquiries" rather than "any 'set formula,'" but he nonetheless set forth a list of factors for courts to consider in balancing the public benefit of a use restriction against the private harm:

> "The economic impact of the regulation on the claimant and, particularly, the extent to which the regulation has interfered with distinct investment-backed expectations are, of course, relevant considerations. So, too, is the character of the governmental action. A 'taking' may more readily be found when the interference with property can be characterized as a physical

invasion by government than when interference arises from some public program adjusting the benefits and burdens of economic life to promote the common good."

Distinguishing *Mahon*, Justice Brennan explained that

"landmark laws are not like discriminatory, or 'reverse spot,' zoning: that is, a land use decision which arbitrarily singles out a particular parcel for different, less favorable treatment than the neighboring ones. In contrast to discriminatory zoning, [the law here] embodies a comprehensive plan to preserve structures of historic or aesthetic interest wherever they may be found in the city, [and] over 400 landmarks [have] been designated pursuant to this plan."

As a result, the interference with Penn Central's use of the terminal did not go "too far." Its use of the air space had not been completely forbidden, and Penn Central had exaggerated the economic impact of the law given that development rights on the restricted parcel were transferable to other, nearby parcels. The restrictions imposed on the use of the property were "substantially related to the promotion of the general welfare and not only permit reasonable beneficial use of the landmark site but afford [the owner] opportunities further to enhance not only the Terminal site proper but also other properties."

3. Special problems with particular types of takings

a. *Temporary takings (and temporary regulations)*

Suppose the government effectuates a taking of property in the constitutional sense, but the taking will only occur for a temporary period. Is that still a taking of property that requires just compensation? Alternatively, suppose the government imposes a use restriction that *might* constitute a taking, but the regulation is only of limited duration. Does the temporary nature of the use restriction affect whether the regulation constitutes a taking?

In *First English Evangelical Lutheran Church v. Los Angeles County*, 482 U.S. 304 (1987), the Supreme Court held that *if* the government's action constitutes a taking, the owner must be compensated for the duration of the taking, even if that taking turns out to be temporary. At issue in *First English* was a California use restriction that had been adjudicated to constitute a taking, and which the state had then decided to repeal. The Court explained that California could "elect to abandon its intrusion or discontinue regulations," but it was required to pay just compensation "for the period of time during which regulations deny a landowner all use of his land." If "the government's activities have already worked a taking of all use of property, no subsequent action by the government can relieve it of the duty to provide compensation for the period during which the taking was effective."

The analysis is different when a temporary use restriction is challenged as taking. At issue in *Tahoe–Sierra Preservation Council, Inc. v. Tahoe Regional*

Planning Agency, 535 U.S. 302 (2002), was a land use regulation that temporarily barred any construction—and thus, for a temporary period, deprived the owner of all economically beneficial uses of the property. (The legal question was different than that posed by *First English*, because in *First English* the regulation was already determined to be a taking, and the question was whether the government was required to pay just compensation for the duration of that taking.) In *Tahoe-Sierra*, the Court held that, even though the regulation (for its duration) deprived the owners of all economically beneficial uses of their property, it nonetheless was *not* a taking *per se* because the use restriction was temporary. Such regulations, held the Court, must be evaluated on a case-by-case basis under the *Penn Central* factors:

> "The ultimate constitutional question is whether the concepts of fairness and justice that underlie the Takings Clause will be better served [by] categorical rules or by a *Penn Central* inquiry into all the relevant circumstances in particular cases. [The] extreme categorical rule that any deprivation of all economic use, no matter how brief, constitutes a compensable taking surely cannot be sustained. [Such a] broad submission would apply to numerous normal delays in obtaining building permits, changes in zoning ordinances, variances, and the like, as well as to orders temporarily prohibiting access to crime scenes, businesses that violate health codes, [and] fire-damaged buildings. [Such] a rule would [require] changes in [practices] that have long been considered permissible exercises of the police power. [In] rejecting petitioners' *per se* rule, we do not hold that the temporary nature of a land-use restriction precludes finding that it effects a taking; we simply recognize that it should not be given exclusive significance one way or the other."

b. *Preexisting regulations*

What if an owner acquires property when the challenged regulation has already been imposed, such that her "expectations" should include the fact that the property is subject to the regulation? Does that mean the owner cannot challenge the regulation as a taking? The Court said no in *Palazzolo v. Rhode Island*, 533 U.S. 606 (2001). There, Rhode Island argued that the owner's taking claim should fail automatically, on the theory that the owner's property rights—and under *Penn Central*, his reasonable investment-backed expectations—were defined by the property's pre-acquisition restrictions. But the Court disagreed: "The State may not put so potent a Hobbesian stick into the Lockean bundle." The preexistence of the regulation was not, in itself, dispositive; "future generations, too, have a right to challenge unreasonable limitations on the use and value of land."

* * *

PROBLEMS ON IDENTIFYING A TAKING

In each of the following scenarios, please evaluate whether there has been a taking of private property for purposes of the Takings Clause. If there is additional information that is not provided that would affect your answer, please identify that information and how it would affect your response.

1. The Santa Clara County Health Department determines that it needs additional housing for persons who have tested positive for the coronavirus (who do not need to be hospitalized but cannot safely isolate at home without exposing others to the virus). The County thus invokes its eminent domain power to seize title to a privately-owned hotel near the San Jose International Airport, which it will use for this purpose.

2. The facts are the same as (1), except that, instead of operating the hotel itself, the County transfers ownership to a new private owner, who enters into a long-term contract with the County to operate it solely for public health purposes.

3. Owner lives in Half Moon Bay, in a large home next to the beach. The beach that runs in between the owner's property and ocean is public property. But due to the topography of the area, there is no feasible way for people to access the beach except to walk across a portion of Owner's property. The California Coastal Commission—a part of the California state government—imposes a public easement across Owner's property, between the hours of 7:00 am and 7:00 pm, for purposes of accessing the beach.

4. The California legislature determines that residential natural gas leaks are a significant danger to the public. It therefore enacts a law authorizing a private company to install and monitor the readings of natural gas detectors in every human dwelling in the state. The natural gas detectors are roughly a square foot in volume, and the average single-family home requires only one detector.

5. The California legislature determines that residential natural gas leaks are a significant danger to the public. It therefore enacts a law requiring every private property owner to install and monitor the readings of natural gas detectors in every human dwelling in the state.

6. Owner purchases a vacant tract of land in San Joaquin County for $30 million, on which she plans to build a new residential development containing 100 single-family houses. After she purchases the land, the State of California enacts a new law limiting development on land that previously was used for farming.

    a. As a result of the new law, Owner can only build 60 new houses in the development, and the land she purchased for $30 million is now only worth $20 million.

    b. As a result of the new law, Owner can only build 10 new houses in the development, and the land she purchased for $30 million is now only worth $5 million.

    c. As a result of the new law, Owner is not permitted to build any improvements on the property. She may visit it and camp on it, but she may not construct any permanent buildings on it.

d. As a result of the new law, Owner is not permitted to build any improvements on the property for the next two years; the law imposes a temporary moratorium on the construction of buildings on former farmland.

e. As a result of the new law, Owner can only build 10 new houses in the development, and the land she purchased for $30 million is now only worth $5 million. A court determines that the law amounts to a taking of Owner's property, requiring just compensation. Following that judgment, the California legislature repeals the law, permitting Owner to build the 100 homes she had originally planned.

f. As a result of the new law, Owner can only build 10 new houses in the development. But the law was enacted one year before Owner purchased the property, which she obtained for $5 million (rather than $30 million).

* * *

4. Land use "exactions": conditions on development

Most significant real estate developments or improvements to property in the United States require some sort of approval from a local governmental body, such as a land use commission, a city council, or a regional planning commission. Often, the relevant governmental body—in exchange for the owner's permission to pursue the development—requires the owner to take certain steps to mitigate the impact of the development on the community. These requirements are often called "exactions," as they exact something from the owner in exchange for the permission to develop or improve the property.

Exactions present tricky questions under the Takings Clause. On the one hand, the government cannot simply physically appropriate a person's property interests (such as by imposing a public easement over the property) without paying just compensation. On the other hand, the government has no obligation to permit an owner to develop or improve her property however she wishes. For example, if a particular neighborhood is zoned for residential use, a landowner has no entitlement to use her property in that neighborhood for commercial purposes. Or if a city has a height restriction on buildings, an owner has no right to construct a building that exceeds that limit. These sorts of zoning and land use regulations are perfectly constitutional. So what constitutional limits exist when the government asks a property owner to surrender something in exchange for permission to improve her property—permission the government is not obligated to grant in the first instance?

Roughly 30 years ago, the Supreme Court decided two important cases addressing this question that created a two-part test for determining when such "exactions" constitute a taking. At issue in *Nollan v. California Coastal Commission*, 483 U.S. 825 (1987), was a condition imposed on landowners seeking to replace a small home on their property with a larger, two-story house. The purpose of the existing development restriction (from which the owners sought an exemption) was to preserve the ocean views of homes further back from the coastline. The Commission approved the owners' application to build a two-story house, but on the condition that they allow the public to pass across their beachfront property (which was located between two public beaches).

The Court held that the Commission's proposed quid pro quo constituted a taking. First, the Court noted that a regulation directly imposing such a public easement on the owners' property would constitute a taking, as it would have amounted to a "permanent physical occupation." Second, the Court acknowledged that the Commission could have denied the permit entirely or imposed any number of other restrictions that "substantially advanced" the purpose of the development restriction (preserving the views of the coastline from homes further from the beach). But by conditioning the owners' development on the provision of an easement, the exaction lacked a sufficient connection to the Commission's interest in preserving those views:

> "It is quite impossible to understand how a requirement that people already on the public beaches be able to walk across the Nollans' property reduces any obstacles to viewing the beach created by the new house. [If California] wants an easement across the Nollans' property, it must pay for it. . . . [U]nless the permit condition serves the same governmental purpose as the development ban, the building restriction is not a valid regulation of land use but 'an out-and-out plan of extortion.'"

More specifically, an "essential nexus" must exist between the governmental interest supporting the use restriction and the exaction imposed on the owner for permission to develop the property. Absent such a nexus, the exaction constitutes a taking.

Seven years after *Nollan*, the Court further elucidated the relevant test in *Dolan v. City of Tigard*, 512 U.S. 374 (1994). A hardware store owner had applied to expand the size of her store in downtown Tigard, Oregon. The property on which the store sat lay next to a creek that was prone to flooding. The city conditioned approval of the owner's permit to expand the store on her dedicating a portion of her property for flood control and traffic improvements. With respect to flood control, the city required the owner to dedicate the flood plain portion of her property to the improvement of the drainage system along the creek. With respect to traffic concerns, the owner was required to dedicate a 15–foot strip adjoining the flood plain for a public pedestrian and bike path.

The Court first explained the basic framework for assessing exactions under the Takings Clause:

> "Under the well-settled doctrine of 'unconstitutional conditions,' the government may not require a person to give up a constitutional right—here the right to receive just compensation when property is taken for a public use—in exchange for a discretionary benefit conferred by the government where the property sought has little or no relationship to the benefit."

The first question is "whether [an] 'essential nexus' exists between the legitimate state interests and the permit condition exacted by the City." If such a nexus exists, the next question concerns the "degree of connection between the exactions and the projected impact of the proposed development." The Court explained that it had not reached this second question in *Nollan* "because we concluded that the connection did not meet even the loosest standard." Unlike in *Nollan*, the "essential nexus" requirement was easily met in *Dolan*: the conditions were directly connected to the reasons for the use restriction—namely, preventing flooding and avoiding traffic congestion in downtown Tigard.

The Court then addressed the second part of the test: "whether the degree of the exactions demanded by the city's permit conditions bear the required relationship to the projected impact of petitioner's proposed development." The Court noted that some state courts had accepted "very generalized statements as to the necessary connection between the required dedication and the proposed development." This approach, the Court concluded, was "too lax to adequately protect" the property interests at stake. Other state courts had required "a very exacting correspondence, described as the 'specifi[c] and uniquely attributable' test." This, too, was unacceptable to the Court: "We do not think the Federal Constitution requires such exacting scrutiny given the nature of the interests involved." The Court continued:

> "A number of state courts have taken an intermediate position, requiring the municipality to show a 'reasonable relationship' between the required dedication and the impact of the proposed development. [We] think the ['rough proportionality'] test adopted by a majority of the state courts is closer to the federal constitutional norm than either of those previously discussed. No precise mathematical calculation is required, but the City must make some sort of individualized determination that the required dedication is related both in nature and extent to the impact of the proposed development."

Applying that standard, the Court concluded that, although flood control was a valid governmental interest, the city had

> "never said why a public greenway, as opposed to a private one, was required in the interest of flood control. [It] is difficult to see why a recreational visitor's trampling along petitioner's floodplain easement are sufficiently related to the city's legitimate interest in reducing flooding problems along Fanno Creek. [Moreover,] the city must make some effort to quantify its findings in support of the dedication for the pedestrian/bicycle pathway beyond the conclusory statement that it would offset some of the traffic demand generated. [The] city's goals [are] laudable, but there are outer limits to how this may be done."

5. "Just compensation"

The Fifth Amendment does not forbid the government from taking private property. Rather, it demands that the owners of such property receive "just compensation." Fortunately, the question of what constitutes just compensation is simple: except in rare circumstances, just compensation equals the property's fair market value. As the Supreme Court explained in *United States v. Miller*, 317 U.S. 369, 373–374 (1943),

> "[s]uch compensation means the full and perfect equivalent in money of the property taken. The owner is to be put in as good position pecuniarily as he would have occupied if his property had not been taken. It is conceivable that an owner's indemnity should be measured in various ways depending upon the circumstances of each case and that no general formula should be used for the purpose. In an effort, however, to find some practical standard, the courts early adopted, and have retained, the concept of market value. The owner has been said to be entitled to the 'value,' the 'market value,' and the 'fair market value' of what is taken."

Importantly, this fair market value need not account for any "holdout" value in the property—its value as a necessary piece to a bigger puzzle. For instance, if the government needs to acquire 150 contiguous lots to construct a new transit hub, and it has acquired 149 of them, the final lot will suddenly become quite valuable to the government (due to its necessity to the project). But the government need not take this into account in its payment of compensation. What matters is the property's value *independent of* the government's planned use for it. Further, the relevant date for ascertaining the fair market value is the date on which the property is taken, not some other point in the course of the dispute.

6. "Public use"

The precise phrasing of the Takings Clause—"nor shall private property be taken for public use, without just compensation"—seems to presuppose that the government will only take private property for a public use. And indeed, the Supreme Court has interpreted the clause as imposing this requirement: any taking of property must be "for public use." A taking is flatly unconstitutional if it fails this requirement, even if the government pays the owner just compensation.

But what constitutes a "public use"? As the following case explores, the Court has interpreted this phrase capaciously, permitting a wide variety of uses that are intended to benefit the public. The decision in *Kelo v. City of New London*, 545 U.S. 469 (2005), was highly controversial, provoking a substantial nationwide backlash. But as Justice Stevens's opinion for the Court explains, it largely reiterated a well-established constitutional rule. As you read *Kelo*, please consider the following questions:

1. What was the "public use" that the City of New London was pursuing with its redevelopment plan and seizure of the properties at issue?

2. Does the "public use" requirement mean the government must obtain title to the property? That the public have access to the taken property? How would you define the phrase "public use," precisely?

3. What constitutional rule did the owners contend the Supreme Court should adopt in *Kelo*? Why did the Court reject that rule?

4. According to *Kelo*, how deferential should a reviewing court be to the government's assertion that the challenged taking furthers a "public use"? Why?

Kelo v. City of New London
545 U.S. 469 (2005)

JUSTICE STEVENS delivered the opinion of the Court.

In 2000, the city of New London approved a development plan that, in the words of the Supreme Court of Connecticut, was "projected to create in excess of 1,000 jobs, to increase tax and other revenues, and to revitalize an economically distressed city, including its downtown and waterfront areas." In assembling the land needed for this project, the city's development agent has purchased property from willing sellers and proposes to use the power of eminent domain to acquire the remainder of the property from unwilling owners in exchange for just compensation. The question presented is whether the city's proposed disposition of this property qualifies as a "public use" within the meaning of the Takings Clause of the Fifth Amendment to the Constitution.

I

The city of New London (hereinafter City) sits at the junction of the Thames River and the Long Island Sound in southeastern Connecticut. Decades of economic decline led a state agency in 1990 to designate the City a "distressed municipality." In 1996, the Federal Government closed the Naval Undersea Warfare Center, which had been located in the Fort Trumbull area of the City and had employed over 1,500 people. In 1998, the City's unemployment rate was nearly double that of the State, and its population of just under 24,000 residents was at its lowest since 1920.

These conditions prompted state and local officials to target New London, and particularly its Fort Trumbull area, for economic revitalization. To this end, respondent New London Development Corporation (NLDC), a private nonprofit entity established some years earlier to assist the City in planning economic development, was reactivated. In January 1998, the State authorized a $5.35 million bond issue to support the NLDC's planning activities and a $10 million bond issue toward the creation of a Fort Trumbull State Park. In February, the pharmaceutical company Pfizer Inc. announced that it would build a $300 million research facility on a site immediately adjacent to Fort

Trumbull; local planners hoped that Pfizer would draw new business to the area, thereby serving as a catalyst to the area's rejuvenation. After receiving initial approval from the city council, the NLDC continued its planning activities and held a series of neighborhood meetings to educate the public about the process. In May, the city council authorized the NLDC to formally submit its plans to the relevant state agencies for review. Upon obtaining state-level approval, the NLDC finalized an integrated development plan focused on 90 acres of the Fort Trumbull area.

The Fort Trumbull area is situated on a peninsula that juts into the Thames River. The area comprises approximately 115 privately owned properties, as well as the 32 acres of land formerly occupied by the naval facility (Trumbull State Park now occupies 18 of those 32 acres). The development plan encompasses seven parcels. Parcel 1 is designated for a waterfront conference hotel at the center of a "small urban village" that will include restaurants and shopping. This parcel will also have marinas for both recreational and commercial uses. A pedestrian "riverwalk" will originate here and continue down the coast, connecting the waterfront areas of the development. Parcel 2 will be the site of approximately 80 new residences organized into an urban neighborhood and linked by public walkway to the remainder of the development, including the state park. This parcel also includes space reserved for a new U. S. Coast Guard Museum. Parcel 3, which is located immediately north of the Pfizer facility, will contain at least 90,000 square feet of research and development office space. Parcel 4A is a 2.4-acre site that will be used either to support the adjacent state park, by providing parking or retail services for visitors, or to support the nearby marina. Parcel 4B will include a renovated marina, as well as the final stretch of the riverwalk. Parcels 5, 6, and 7 will provide land for office and retail space, parking, and water-dependent commercial uses.

The NLDC intended the development plan to capitalize on the arrival of the Pfizer facility and the new commerce it was expected to attract. In addition to creating jobs, generating tax revenue, and helping to "build momentum for the revitalization of downtown New London," the plan was also designed to make the City more attractive and to create leisure and recreational opportunities on the waterfront and in the park.

The city council approved the plan in January 2000, and designated the NLDC as its development agent in charge of implementation. The city council also authorized the NLDC to purchase property or to acquire property by exercising eminent domain in the City's name. The NLDC successfully negotiated the purchase of most of the real estate in the 90-acre area, but its negotiations with petitioners failed. As a consequence, in November 2000, the NLDC initiated the condemnation proceedings that gave rise to this case.

II

Petitioner Susette Kelo has lived in the Fort Trumbull area since 1997. She has made extensive improvements to her house, which she prizes for its water view. Petitioner Wilhelmina Dery was born in her Fort Trumbull house in 1918 and has lived there her entire life. Her husband Charles (also a petitioner) has lived in the house since they married some 60 years ago. In all, the nine petitioners own 15 properties in Fort Trumbull—4 in parcel 3 of the development plan and 11 in parcel 4A. Ten of the parcels are occupied by the owner or a family member; the other five are held as investment properties. There is no allegation that any of these properties is blighted or otherwise in poor condition; rather, they were condemned only because they happen to be located in the development area.

In December 2000, petitioners brought this action in the New London Superior Court. They claimed, among other things, that the taking of their properties would violate the "public use" restriction in the Fifth Amendment. After a 7-day bench trial, the Superior Court granted a permanent restraining order prohibiting the taking of the properties located in parcel 4A (park or marina support). It, however, denied petitioners relief as to the properties located in parcel 3 (office space).

After the Superior Court ruled, both sides took appeals to the Supreme Court of Connecticut. That court held, over a dissent, that all of the City's proposed takings were valid. It began by upholding the lower court's determination that the takings were authorized by chapter 132, the State's municipal development statute. That statute expresses a legislative determination that the taking of land, even developed land, as part of an economic development project is a "public use" and in the "public interest." Next, relying on cases such as *Hawaii Housing Authority v. Midkiff*, 467 U. S. 229 (1984), and *Berman v. Parker*, 348 U. S. 26 (1954), the court held that such economic development qualified as a valid public use under both the Federal and State Constitutions.

Finally, adhering to its precedents, the court went on to determine, first, whether the takings of the particular properties at issue were "reasonably necessary" to achieving the City's intended public use, and, second, whether the takings were for "reasonably foreseeable needs." The court upheld the trial court's factual findings as to parcel 3, but reversed the trial court as to parcel 4A, agreeing with the City that the intended use of this land was sufficiently definite and had been given "reasonable attention" during the planning process.

The three dissenting justices would have imposed a "heightened" standard of judicial review for takings justified by economic development. Although they agreed that the plan was intended to serve a valid public use, they would have found all the takings unconstitutional because the City had failed to adduce "clear and convincing evidence" that the economic benefits of the plan would in fact come to pass.

We granted certiorari to determine whether a city's decision to take property for the purpose of economic development satisfies the "public use" requirement of the Fifth Amendment.

III

Two polar propositions are perfectly clear. On the one hand, it has long been accepted that the sovereign may not take the property of A for the sole purpose of transferring it to another private party B, even though A is paid just compensation. On the other hand, it is equally clear that a State may transfer property from one private party to another if future "use by the public" is the purpose of the taking; the condemnation of land for a railroad with common-carrier duties is a familiar example. Neither of these propositions, however, determines the disposition of this case.

As for the first proposition, the City would no doubt be forbidden from taking petitioners' land for the purpose of conferring a private benefit on a particular private party. Nor would the City be allowed to take property under the mere pretext of a public purpose, when its actual purpose was to bestow a private benefit. The takings before us, however, would be executed pursuant to a "carefully considered" development plan. The trial judge and all the members of the Supreme Court of Connecticut agreed that there was no evidence of an illegitimate purpose in this case. Therefore, as was true of the statute challenged in *Midkiff*, the City's development plan was not adopted "to benefit a particular class of identifiable individuals."

On the other hand, this is not a case in which the City is planning to open the condemned land—at least not in its entirety—to use by the general public. Nor will the private lessees of the land in any sense be required to operate like common carriers, making their services available to all comers. But although such a projected use would be sufficient to satisfy the public use requirement, this "Court long ago rejected any literal requirement that condemned property be put into use for the general public." *Id.*, at 244. Indeed, while many state courts in the mid-19th century endorsed "use by the public" as the proper definition of public use, that narrow view steadily eroded over time. Not only was the "use by the public" test difficult to administer (*e.g.*, what proportion of the public need have access to the property? at what price?), but it proved to be impractical given the diverse and always evolving needs of society. Accordingly, when this Court began applying the Fifth Amendment to the States at the close of the 19th century, it embraced the broader and more natural interpretation of public use as "public purpose." Thus, in a case upholding a mining company's use of an aerial bucket line to transport ore over property it did not own, Justice Holmes' opinion for the Court stressed "the inadequacy of use by the general public as a universal test." *Strickley v. Highland Boy Gold Mining Co.*, 200 U. S. 527, 531 (1906). We have repeatedly and consistently rejected that narrow test ever since.

The disposition of this case therefore turns on the question whether the City's development plan serves a "public purpose." Without exception, our cases have defined that concept broadly, reflecting our longstanding policy of deference to legislative judgments in this field.

In *Berman v. Parker*, 348 U. S. 26 (1954), this Court upheld a redevelopment plan targeting a blighted area of Washington, D. C., in which most of the housing for the area's 5,000 inhabitants was beyond repair. Under the plan, the area would be condemned and part of it utilized for the construction of streets, schools, and other public facilities. The remainder of the land would be leased or sold to private parties for the purpose of redevelopment, including the construction of low-cost housing.

The owner of a department store located in the area challenged the condemnation, pointing out that his store was not itself blighted and arguing that the creation of a "better balanced, more attractive community" was not a valid public use. *Id.*, at 31. Writing for a unanimous Court, Justice Douglas refused to evaluate this claim in isolation, deferring instead to the legislative and agency judgment that the area "must be planned as a whole" for the plan to be successful. *Id.*, at 34. The Court explained that "community redevelopment programs need not, by force of the Constitution, be on a piecemeal basis—lot by lot, building by building." *Id.*, at 35. The public use underlying the taking was unequivocally affirmed:

> "We do not sit to determine whether a particular housing project is or is not desirable. The concept of the public welfare is broad and inclusive. . . . The values it represents are spiritual as well as physical, aesthetic as well as monetary. It is within the power of the legislature to determine that the community should be beautiful as well as healthy, spacious as well as clean, well-balanced as well as carefully patrolled. In the present case, the Congress and its authorized agencies have made determinations that take into account a wide variety of values. It is not for us to reappraise them. If those who govern the District of Columbia decide that the Nation's Capital should be beautiful as well as sanitary, there is nothing in the Fifth Amendment that stands in the way." *Id.*, at 33.

In *Hawaii Housing Authority v. Midkiff*, 467 U. S. 229 (1984), the Court considered a Hawaii statute whereby fee title was taken from lessors and transferred to lessees (for just compensation) in order to reduce the concentration of land ownership. We unanimously upheld the statute and rejected the Ninth Circuit's view that it was "a naked attempt on the part of the state of Hawaii to take the property of A and transfer it to B solely for B's private use and benefit." *Id.*, at 235. Reaffirming *Berman*'s deferential approach to legislative judgments in this field, we concluded that the State's purpose of eliminating the "social and economic evils of a land oligopoly" qualified as a valid public use. Our opinion also rejected the contention that the mere fact that the State immediately transferred the properties to private individuals upon condemnation somehow diminished the public character of the taking. "[I]t is only the taking's purpose, and not its mechanics," we explained, that matters in determining public use. *Id.*, at 244.

In that same Term we decided another public use case that arose in a purely economic context. In *Ruckelshaus v. Monsanto Co.*, 467 U. S. 986 (1984), the Court dealt with provisions of the Federal Insecticide, Fungicide, and Rodenticide Act under which the Environmental Protection Agency could consider the data (including trade secrets) submitted by a prior pesticide applicant in evaluating a subsequent application, so long as the second applicant paid just compensation for the data. We acknowledged that the "most direct beneficiaries" of these provisions were the subsequent applicants, *id.*, at 1014, but we nevertheless upheld the statute under *Berman* and *Midkiff.* We found sufficient Congress' belief that sparing applicants the cost of time-consuming research eliminated a significant barrier to entry in the pesticide market and thereby enhanced competition.

Viewed as a whole, our jurisprudence has recognized that the needs of society have varied between different parts of the Nation, just as they have evolved over time in response to changed circumstances. Our earliest cases in particular embodied a strong theme of federalism, emphasizing the "great respect" that we owe to state legislatures and state courts in discerning local public needs. For more than a century, our public use jurisprudence has wisely eschewed rigid formulas and intrusive scrutiny in favor of affording legislatures broad latitude in determining what public needs justify the use of the takings power.

IV

Those who govern the City were not confronted with the need to remove blight in the Fort Trumbull area, but their determination that the area was sufficiently distressed to justify a program of economic rejuvenation is entitled to our deference. The City has carefully formulated an economic development plan that it believes will provide appreciable benefits to the community, including—but by no means limited to—new jobs and increased tax revenue. As with other exercises in urban planning and development, the City is endeavoring to coordinate a variety of commercial, residential, and recreational uses of land, with the hope that they will form a whole greater than the sum of its parts. To effectuate this plan, the City has invoked a state statute that specifically authorizes the use of eminent domain to promote economic development. Given the comprehensive character of the plan, the thorough deliberation that preceded its adoption, and the limited scope of our review, it is appropriate for us, as it was in *Berman*, to resolve the challenges of the individual owners, not on a piecemeal basis, but rather in light of the entire plan. Because that plan unquestionably serves a public purpose, the takings challenged here satisfy the public use requirement of the Fifth Amendment.

To avoid this result, petitioners urge us to adopt a new bright-line rule that economic development does not qualify as a public use. Putting aside the unpersuasive suggestion that the City's plan will provide only purely economic benefits, neither precedent nor logic supports petitioners' proposal. Promoting economic development is a traditional and long-accepted function of government. There is, moreover, no principled way of distinguishing economic development from the other public purposes that we have recognized. In our cases upholding takings that facilitated agriculture and mining, for example, we emphasized the importance of those industries to the welfare of the States in question; in *Berman*, we endorsed the purpose of transforming a blighted area into a "well-balanced" community through redevelopment; in *Midkiff*, we upheld the interest in breaking up a land oligopoly that "created artificial deterrents to the normal functioning of the State's residential land market"; and in *Monsanto*, we accepted Congress' purpose of eliminating a "significant barrier to entry in the pesticide market." It would be incongruous to hold that the City's interest in the economic benefits to be derived from the development of the Fort Trumbull area has less of a public character than any of those other interests. Clearly, there is no basis for exempting economic development from our traditionally broad understanding of public purpose.

Petitioners contend that using eminent domain for economic development impermissibly blurs the boundary between public and private takings. Again, our cases foreclose this objection. Quite simply, the government's pursuit of a public purpose will often benefit individual private parties. For example, in *Midkiff*, the forced transfer of property conferred a direct and significant benefit on those lessees who were previously unable to purchase their homes. In *Monsanto*, we recognized that the "most direct beneficiaries" of the data-sharing provisions were the subsequent pesticide applicants, but benefiting them in this way was necessary to promoting competition in the pesticide market. The owner of the department store in *Berman* objected to "taking from one businessman for the benefit of another businessman," referring to the fact that under the redevelopment plan land would be leased or sold to private developers for redevelopment. Our rejection of that contention has particular relevance to the instant case: "The public end may be as well or better served through an agency of private enterprise than through a department of government—or so the Congress might conclude. We cannot say that public ownership is the sole method of promoting the public purposes of community redevelopment projects." *Id.*, at 33–34.

It is further argued that without a bright-line rule nothing would stop a city from transferring citizen A's property to citizen B for the sole reason that citizen B will put the property to a more productive use and thus pay more taxes. Such a one-to-one transfer of property, executed outside the confines of an integrated development plan, is not presented in this case. While such an unusual exercise of government power would certainly raise a suspicion that a private purpose was afoot, the hypothetical cases posited by petitioners can be confronted if and when they arise. They do not warrant the crafting of an artificial restriction on the concept of public use.

Alternatively, petitioners maintain that for takings of this kind we should require a "reasonable certainty" that the expected public benefits will actually accrue. Such a rule, however, would represent an even greater departure from our precedent. "When the legislature's purpose is legitimate and its means are not irrational, our cases make clear that empirical debates over the wisdom of takings—no less than debates over the wisdom of other kinds of socioeconomic legislation—are not to be carried out in the federal courts." *Midkiff*, 467 U. S., at 242–243. Indeed, earlier this Term we explained why similar practical concerns (among others) undermined the use of the "substantially advances" formula in our regulatory takings doctrine. *See Lingle v. Chevron U. S. A. Inc.*, 544 U. S. 528, 544 (2005). The disadvantages of a heightened form of review are especially pronounced in this type of case. Orderly implementation of a comprehensive redevelopment plan obviously requires that the legal rights of all interested parties be established before new construction can be commenced. A constitutional rule that required postponement of the judicial approval of every condemnation until the likelihood of success of the plan had been assured would unquestionably impose a significant impediment to the successful consummation of many such plans.

Just as we decline to second-guess the City's considered judgments about the efficacy of its development plan, we also decline to second-guess the City's determinations as to what lands it needs to acquire in order to effectuate the project. "It is not for the courts to oversee the choice of the boundary line nor to sit in review on the size of a particular project area. Once the question of the public purpose has been decided, the amount and character of land to be taken for the project and the need for a particular tract to complete the integrated plan rests in the discretion of the legislative branch." *Berman*, 348 U. S., at 35–36.

In affirming the City's authority to take petitioners' properties, we do not minimize the hardship that condemnations may entail, notwithstanding the payment of just compensation. We emphasize that nothing in our opinion precludes any State from placing further restrictions on its exercise of the takings power. Indeed, many States already impose "public use" requirements that are stricter than the federal baseline. Some of these requirements have been established as a matter of state constitutional law, while others are expressed in state eminent domain statutes that carefully limit the grounds upon which takings may be exercised. As the submissions of the parties and their amici make clear, the necessity and wisdom of using eminent domain to promote economic development are certainly matters of legitimate public debate. This Court's authority, however, extends only to determining whether the City's proposed condemnations are for a "public use" within the meaning of the Fifth Amendment to the Federal Constitution. Because over a century of our case law interpreting that provision dictates an affirmative answer to that question, we may not grant petitioners the relief that they seek.

* * *

Notes on *Kelo v. City of New London*

1. *"Public use" and "public purpose"*: In *Kelo*, the Supreme Court held (or reaffirmed) that, to satisfy the "public use" requirement, the public need not *own* the property taken. Nor need the property even be available for *use* by the public. Instead, the Fifth Amendment merely requires that the taking be for "a public purpose." Thus, the government can take property from one private party and transfer it to another private party so long as the *purpose* of that transfer is to benefit the public (and not a private party). As the Court explained, "a State may transfer property from one private party to another if future 'use by the public' is the purpose of the taking; the condemnation of land for a railroad with common-carrier duties is a familiar example." So there would have been a constitutional problem if the city had condemned the Fort Trumbull *for the purpose* of benefitting Pfizer. But because the city took the property to effectuate an "economic rejuvenation" of the area, and to "provide appreciable benefits to the community, including—but by no means limited to—new jobs and increased tax revenue," it was constitutionally permissible.

2. *Takings and economic development*: The Court had held on multiple occasions prior to *Kelo* (in cases like *Berman* and *Midkiff*) that the transfer of property from one private party to another can satisfy the "public use" requirement so long as the taking has a public purpose. And the Court had held that objectives like the elimination of blight, the more equitable distribution of property, and the operation of railroads or mines met this standard of "public purpose." Thus, the challengers in *Kelo* argued for a specific bright-line rule: that "economic development" cannot qualify as a "public use" because it is too prone to abuse. It is too easy, they argued, for governments to transfer property from A to B but then justify the transfer as furthering economic development. The Court rejected this proposed rule because, in its view, singling out economic development for disfavor (among the scores of possible public purposes) would be arbitrary. The Takings Clause requires a public purpose, but it makes no distinction among the various forms a public purpose might take.

3. *Deferential scrutiny of "public use"*: The Court in *Kelo* emphasized that judicial review of challenges to the taking of property on the ground that they violate the "public use" requirement should be deferential to the judgments of state and local governments:

"Viewed as a whole, our jurisprudence has recognized that the needs of society have varied between different parts of the Nation, just as they have evolved over time in response to changed circumstances. Our earliest cases in particular embodied a strong theme of federalism, emphasizing the 'great respect' that we owe to state legislatures and state courts in discerning local public needs. For more than a century, our public use jurisprudence has wisely eschewed rigid formulas and intrusive scrutiny in favor of affording legislatures broad latitude in determining what public needs justify the use of the takings power."

In other words, *Kelo* stands for the proposition that, unless it is clear the government's articulated public purpose is pretextual—and that the real purpose was to benefit a private party—courts should reject "public use" challenges.

4. *Revisiting* Kelo?: On July 2, 2021, the Supreme Court denied certiorari in *Eychaner v. City of Chicago*, 594 U.S. ___ (2021). At issue was Chicago's use of eminent domain to transfer a tract of land owned by Eychaner to the Blommer Chocolate Company. Blommer, which owned and operated a factory two blocks away, wanted the property "to create a buffer with nearby residential areas." Blommer initially offered Eychaner just under $1 million for the tract, which Eychaner refused. Two months later, the city notified Eychaner that it "planned to invoke its eminent domain power to transfer Eychaner's property to the company." Eychaner claimed the city's plan lacked a "public use." But Chicago argued that, if it did not transfer the property, "it may become a blighted area." The Illinois state courts rejected Eychaner's challenge, concluding that the Constitution permitted the city to "use the power of eminent domain to prevent future blight."

Justices Thomas, Gorsuch, and Kavanaugh dissented from the denial of certiorari. Justice Thomas authored an opinion (joined by Justice Gorsuch), asserting that *Kelo* should be overruled:

"This petition provides us the opportunity to correct the mistake the Court made in *Kelo*. There, the Court found the Fifth Amendment's 'public use' requirement satisfied when a city transferred land from one private owner to another in the name of economic development. That decision was wrong the day it was decided. And it remains wrong today. 'Public use' means something more than any conceivable 'public purpose.' The Constitution's text, the common-law background, and the early practice of eminent domain all indicate that the Takings Clause authorizes the taking of property only if the public has a right to employ it, not if the public realizes any conceivable benefit from the taking. Taking land from one private party to give to another rarely will be for 'public use.' The majority in *Kelo* strayed from the Constitution to diminish the right to be free from private takings."

*   *   *

CONCLUDING PROBLEMS ON THE TAKINGS CLAUSE

1. A city filed eminent domain proceedings in order to obtain 40 beach houses fronting a particularly attractive stretch of shoreline. As part of an elaborate plan to increase the city's tourist trade and revive the local economy, the city planned to sell the beach houses to a company that would demolish the houses and build a luxury hotel

in their place. The owners of the beach houses have challenged the city's exercise of eminent domain, contending only that the city's plan is unconstitutional. Will the owners of the beach houses be likely to prevail?

(a) No, because a property owner can challenge an exercise of eminent domain only on the ground of the sufficiency of the compensation.

(b) No, because the planned sale to the private developer to increase the tourist trade qualifies as a public use.

(c) Yes, because a public entity cannot seize the property of one person in order to transfer that property intact to other private parties.

(d) Yes, because the city's action would deprive the owners of all economically beneficial use of their property.

2. A consumer watchdog group presented petitions to the state legislature bearing the signatures of over 10,000 state residents complaining about the recent increases in the cost of cable television. A corporation that provides cable television services successfully persuaded the state legislature to grant it an exclusive right to install cable television lines in all multiple family dwellings in the state, in exchange for the corporation's promise to freeze cable television rates for the next four years. An owner of several large multifamily apartment buildings in the state brought an action challenging the constitutionality of the state legislation. The suit claimed that the space used by the corporation when it subsequently installed cable television lines in one of his apartment buildings amounted to a taking without just compensation. In this action, the owner will most likely be awarded:

(a) no relief, because easements for utility lines are presumed to be beneficial to the servient estate.

(b) no relief, because the legislation is merely a regulation of the use of property and not a taking.

(c) no relief, because the corporation is not a government entity.

(d) compensation for the value of property used by the corporation.

* * *

B. The Contracts Clause

1. Overview

The other significant constitutional provision aimed specifically at protecting economic or property rights is the Contracts Clause. Article I, §10, clause 1 provides that "[n]o State shall . . . pass any . . . Law impairing the Obligation of Contracts." Two important limits to the clause's protection spring straight from this text. First, the Contracts Clause only applies to *existing* contracts. It has no bearing on the regulation of contracts that have not yet been made. (In this respect, its protection is much narrower than the "right to contract" recognized as a matter of due process during the *Lochner* era, which was an expensive liberty to enter into contracts on the terms of one's choosing.) The Contracts Clause protects reliance interests, akin to the prohibition on *ex post facto* laws. It is a constraint on the legislative undoing of existing contractual obligations.

Second, the Contracts Clause does not apply to the federal government. By its terms, it applies only to states and their political subdivisions. A federal statute impairing contractual obligations could conceivably violate the Due Process Clause of the Fifth Amendment. Or, depending on the exact facts, such a statute might constitute a taking of property. But the federal government is constitutionally incapable of violating the Contracts Clause.

2. The current doctrinal framework

a. *A "substantial impairment"*

The Contracts Clause protects persons from the impairment of contracts by state governments. But almost every state law *affects* the terms of some existing contracts in some way. For example, a law that immediately requires all persons traveling on buses, trains, or airplanes to wear face masks alters the terms of thousands of existing contracts—for instance, contracts between rail passengers who had already purchased tickets and railroad operators. When these parties entered into their contract, the passenger was (implicitly) permitted to ride the train without a mask. But this alteration to the terms of the contract is quite small, and hence does not raise a Contracts Clause question. (If it did, then almost every state law would be susceptible to some sort of Contracts Clause challenge.) Thus, the relevant question is what sorts of interferences with contractual obligations cross the constitutional line.

The Supreme Court has explained that there are two essential steps to the applicable test. The threshold question is "whether the state law has operated as a substantial impairment of a contractual relationship." *Allied Structural Steel Co. v. Spannaus*, 438 U.S. 234, 244 (1978). And to answer this question, the Court has examined three factors: "the extent to which the law [1] undermines the contractual bargain, [2] interferes with a party's reasonable expectations, and [3] prevents the party from safeguarding or reinstating his rights." *Sveen v. Melin*, 138 S. Ct. 1815, 1822 (2018).

The Court's recent decision in *Sveen* is instructive. At issue was a Minnesota statute providing that "the dissolution or annulment of a marriage revokes any revocable[] beneficiary designation[] made by an individual to the individual's former spouse." The law effectively created a default rule in the event of divorce. If one spouse had made the other the beneficiary of a life insurance policy or similar asset, the Minnesota statute dictated that their divorce automatically revoked that beneficiary designation—on the theory that the policyholder would desire that result (but might forget to change the beneficiary). If the policyholder did not desire this change, she could re-designate the ex-spouse as the beneficiary following the divorce. A disappointed ex-spouse, Kaye Melin, was removed as the beneficiary of a life insurance policy as a result of a divorce from her ex-husband. Thus—by operation of Minnesota's law—she was not entitled to the policy's proceeds after her ex-husband's death. Melin challenged the law as a violation of the Contracts Clause.

The Supreme Court upheld Minnesota's statute on the ground that it did not "substantially impair pre-existing contractual arrangements." (Thus, the Court did not reach whether the statute would survive the scrutiny applicable under the Contracts Clause to laws constituting a "substantial impairment.") As the Court explained:

> "True enough that in revoking a beneficiary designation, the law makes a significant change. As Melin says, the 'whole point' of buying life insurance is to provide the proceeds to the named beneficiary. But three aspects of Minnesota's law, taken together, defeat Melin's argument that the change it effected 'severely impaired' her ex-husband's contract. First, the statute is designed to reflect a policyholder's intent—and so to support, rather than impair, the contractual scheme. Second, the law is unlikely to disturb any policyholder's expectations because it does no more than a divorce court could always have done. And third, the statute supplies a mere default rule, which the policyholder can undo in a moment. Indeed, Minnesota's revocation statute stacks up well against laws that this Court upheld against Contracts Clause challenges as far back as the early 1800s."

b. *Purely private contracts*

If the challenged state law (unlike in *Sveen*) constitutes a "substantial impairment" of an existing contractual relationship, then it will be subject to judicial scrutiny as to both the means it deploys and the ends it pursues. The precise nature of the applicable scrutiny is somewhat unclear, but one point is plain: the Supreme Court has applied much more exacting review to laws impairing contractual obligations when the government itself was a party to the contract (and thus stood to benefit from the impairment).

With respect to purely private contracts, "the Court has asked whether the state law is drawn in an 'appropriate' and 'reasonable' way to advance a 'significant and legitimate public purpose.'" *Sveen*, 138 S. Ct. at 1822. This is a more rigorous standard than mere rational basis review, which asks only if the law is reasonably related to a legitimate government purpose. But it also falls well short of strict scrutiny. Thus, the best characterization may be as some form of intermediate scrutiny (though the Court has never so labeled it). And the standard of scrutiny applied by the Court seems to have varied a bit from case to case, depending on the magnitude of the impairment on the parties' contractual relationship. Suffice it to say that, when a state law impairs a private contract, the state will need to demonstrate more than that its law is rationally related to a legitimate governmental interest in defending its constitutionality.

c. *Contracts to which the state itself is a party*

More clearly, the Court has applied something approaching strict scrutiny when a state law impairs the obligations of a *government* contract—a contract to which the government itself is a party. The critical case on this point is *United States Trust Co. v. New Jersey*, 431 U.S. 1 (1977). There, the Supreme Court held that such impairments must be "necessary to serve an important public purpose." As under the dormant Commerce Clause or the Due Process Clause, a standard of *necessity* with respect to the means embodied in the challenged law is quite difficult to satisfy. The reason for greater scrutiny when a law impairs a government contract is that it would simply be too tempting for a state or local government, when it no longer liked the terms of a contract, to renege on the deal by enacting a statute that altered its terms. Heightened scrutiny is a guard against this potential for governmental self-dealing.

B.   The Ex Post Facto Clauses

The Constitution contains two Ex Post Facto Clauses, one applying to the federal government and one to the states. In terms of their substantive prohibitions, the content of the two clauses is the same. Article I, §9, clause 3 states "[n]o . . . ex post facto Law shall be passed," a limitation that constrains Congress. Article I, §10, clause 1—the same clause containing the Contracts Clause—provides "[n]o State shall . . . pass any . . . ex post facto Law."

Ex post facto means "after the fact," so the essential function of the clauses is to proscribe laws that operate retroactively. Critically, though, the clauses only apply to *criminal* laws; they impose no limitation on the retroactive imposition of civil liability. Typically, whether a particular law is criminal or civil is fairly clear. For instance, if one of the punishments for violating the law is imprisonment, it is plainly criminal. But sometimes the matter is uncertain, and the inquiry turns principally on the legislature's intent. As the Supreme Court explained in *Kansas v. Hendricks*, 521 U.S. 346 (1997),

> "[t]he categorization of a particular proceeding as civil or criminal is first of all a question of statutory construction. We must initially ascertain whether the legislature meant the statute to establish 'civil' proceedings. If so, we ordinarily defer to the legislature's stated intent. . . . Although we recognize that a civil label is not always dispositive, we will reject the legislature's manifest intent only where a party challenging the statute provides the clearest proof that the statutory scheme is so punitive either in purpose or effect as to negate the State's intention to deem it 'civil.'" *Id.* at 362 (internal quotations and alterations omitted).

To be clear, there are some constitutional limitations on retroactive civil legislation. As we have seen, the Contracts Clause constrains the states' capacity to enact laws that retroactively alter the terms of contracts. The prohibitions on bills of attainder (likewise located in sections 9 and 10 of Article I) forbid the government from enacting laws that impose punishment on identifiable individuals (including punishment that would not be considered criminal). The Takings Clause limits the government's ability to interfere with a person's investments in property, a species of retroactive regulation. And under certain circumstances, the imposition of retroactive civil liability can be so fundamentally unfair as to violate the Due Process Clause.

But the Ex Post Facto Clauses only forbid laws that retroactively impose criminal liability. A law might do so in three basic ways:

*   It could make criminal an act that was innocent when it was committed.

*   It could increase the punishment for an act relative to the punishment that attached when the act was committed.

*   It could alter the rules of evidence so that a defendant could be convicted based on the existence of lesser proof, or eliminate a defense to liability, compared to when the act was committed.

The first category—the quintessential example of an *ex post facto* law—is the simplest. Suppose it was completely legal in July 2021 for a Texas physician to perform an abortion on a woman in the eighteenth week of pregnancy. Suppose the Texas legislature—in July 2022—enacts a law criminalizing the performance of such abortions, punishable by up to two years' imprisonment. If Texas attempted in October 2022 to prosecute a physician who performed such an abortion in July 2021, the prosecution would plainly violate the Ex Post Facto Clause. Texas would be applying a criminal law retroactively, attempting to make criminal an act that was innocent when committed. Texas could apply its new law *prospectively*, to any abortions performed after the law's passage, but not to those performed before.

The second category is also relatively straightforward, at least in theory. If the maximum punishment for armed robbery was 20 years in prison when the offense was committed—but the legislature amends the law between the commission of the offense and trial, and a court applies the new law to sentence the defendant to 30 years in prison—this would violate the Ex Post Facto Clause. The government has impermissibly increased the applicable punishment retroactively.

The third category is the most complicated. It can be difficult to distinguish a law that merely alters trial procedure (in a way that is entirely constitutional) from one that changes the evidence necessary to convict or eliminates a substantive defense. Consider *Carmell v. Texas*, 529 U.S.513 (2000), in which the defendant was convicted of multiple counts of sexual abuse and sexual assault. At the time of the offenses at issue, Texas law provided that a defendant could not be convicted based solely on the uncorroborated testimony of the victim unless the victim was less than 14 years old at the time of the offense. After the incidents at issue—but before the defendant's trial—Texas amended its law to permit convictions based on the uncorroborated testimony of victims who were younger that 18 at the time of the offense. The alleged victim in *Carmell* was between the age of 14 and 18 at the time of the offenses, and the defendant was convicted based solely on her uncorroborated testimony.

In a 5–4 decision, the Supreme Court held that Carmell's convictions violated the Ex Post Facto Clause. The Court explained that Justice Chase's seminal opinion in *Calder v. Bull*, 3 Dall. 386 (1798), had stated that "[e]very law that alters the legal rules of evidence, and receives less, or different, testimony, than the law required at the time of the commission of the offence, in order to convict the offender" constituted an "*ex post facto law*[], within the *words* and the *intent* of the prohibition." *Id.*, at 390. According to the Court, Texas's law "unquestionably" met this definition:

> "Under the law in effect at the time the acts were committed, the prosecution's case was legally insufficient and petitioner was entitled to a judgment of acquittal, unless the State could produce both the victim's testimony *and* corroborative evidence. The amended law, however, changed the quantum of evidence necessary to sustain a conviction; under the new law, petitioner could be (and was) convicted on the victim's testimony alone, without any corroborating evidence. Under any commonsense understanding of *Calder* . . . , [the new Texas law] plainly fits. Requiring only the victim's testimony to convict, rather than the victim's testimony plus other corroborating evidence is surely 'less testimony required to convict' in any straightforward sense of those words."

Recently, the most commonly litigated Ex Post Facto Clause issue has been whether a new law retroactively increased a defendant's sentence when the sentence was legally permissible (though perhaps less likely) under the old law. A good example is *Peugh v. United States*, 569 U.S. 530 (2013). Following a series of constitutional rulings (culminating in *United States v. Booker*, 543 U.S. 220 (2005)) holding that any fact increasing a defendant's maximum sentence must be found by a jury (rather than a judge), the U.S. Sentencing Guidelines—which guide the sentences imposed for federal convictions—became merely advisory (rather than mandatory). Still, federal district court judges were required to consult them, and the Guidelines exerted a considerable influence on the sentences actually imposed. The question in *Peugh* was whether the Ex Post Facto Clause forbid the court from applying a new version of the Guidelines retroactively (which increased the "advised" sentencing range), even though the court had full discretion to depart from the prescribed range. As you read *Peugh*, please consider the following questions:

1. What role did the Guidelines play in determining Peugh's sentence? Why did that matter?

2. Was it certain that the district court's application of the new version of the Guidelines had increased Peugh's sentence? Why or why not?

3. What rule did the Supreme Court apply to determine whether the application of the new version of the Guidelines impermissibly increased Peugh's sentence, and thus violated the Ex Post Facto Clause?

4. After *Peugh*, when will the retroactive application of a new version of the Guidelines *not* violate the Ex Post Facto Clause? Why?

Peugh v. United States
569 U.S. 530 (2013)

JUSTICE SOTOMAYOR delivered the opinion of the Court.

The Constitution forbids the passage of *ex post facto* laws, a category that includes "[e]very law that changes the punishment, and inflicts a greater punishment, than the law annexed to the crime, when committed." *Calder v. Bull*, 3 Dall. 386, 390 (1798). The U.S. Sentencing Guidelines set forth an advisory sentencing range for each defendant convicted in federal court. We consider here whether there is an *ex post facto* violation when a defendant is sentenced under Guidelines promulgated after he committed his criminal acts and the new version provides a higher applicable Guidelines sentencing range than the version in place at the time of the offense. We hold that there is.

I

Petitioner Marvin Peugh and his cousin, Steven Hollewell, ran two farming-related businesses in Illinois. Grainery, Inc., bought, stored, and sold grain; Agri-Tech, Inc., provided farming services to landowners and tenants. When the Grainery began experiencing cash-flow problems, Peugh and Hollewell engaged in two fraudulent schemes. . . . When their acts were uncovered, Peugh and Hollewell were charged with nine counts of bank fraud, in violation of 18 U.S.C. §1344. While Hollewell pleaded guilty to one count of check kiting, Peugh pleaded not guilty and went to trial, where he testified that he had not intended to defraud the banks. The jury found him guilty of five counts of bank fraud and acquitted him of the remaining counts.

At sentencing, Peugh argued that the *Ex Post Facto* Clause required that he be sentenced under the 1998 version of the Federal Sentencing Guidelines in effect at the time of his offenses, rather than under the 2009 version in effect at the time of sentencing. The two versions yielded significantly different results for Peugh's applicable Guidelines sentencing range. . . . [H]is sentencing range under the 1998 Guidelines was 30 to 37 months. The 2009 Guidelines in effect when Peugh was sentenced in May 2010 assigned more severe consequences to his acts. . . . Peugh's sentencing range rose under the 2009 Guidelines to 70 to 87 months. The low end of the 2009 Guidelines range was 33 months higher than the high end of the 1998 Guidelines range. . . .

II

[Our] decisions have clarified the role that the Guidelines play in sentencing procedures, both at the district court level and when sentences are reviewed on appeal. First, "a district court should begin all sentencing proceedings by correctly calculating the applicable Guidelines range. As a matter of administration and to secure nationwide consistency, the Guidelines should be the starting point and the initial benchmark." *Gall v. United States*, 552 U.S. 38, 49 (2007). The district court must then consider the arguments of the parties and the factors set forth in § 3553(a). The district court "may not presume that the Guidelines range is reasonable," *id.*, at 50; and it "may in appropriate cases impose a non-Guidelines sentence based on disagreement with the [Sentencing] Commission's views," *Pepper v. United States*, 562 U.S. ___ (2011). The district court must explain the basis for its chosen sentence on the record. *Gall*, 552 U.S., at 50. "[A] major departure [from the Guidelines] should be supported by a more significant justification than a minor one." *Ibid.*

On appeal, the district court's sentence is reviewed for reasonableness under an abuse-of-discretion standard. Failure to calculate the correct Guidelines range constitutes procedural error, as does treating the Guidelines as mandatory. The court of appeals may, but is not required to, presume that a within-Guidelines sentence is reasonable. The reviewing court may not apply a heightened standard of review or a presumption of unreasonableness to sentences outside the Guidelines range, although it "will, of course, take into account the totality of the circumstances, including the extent of any variance from the Guidelines range." *Gall*, 552 U.S. at 49–51. We have indicated that "a district court's decision to vary from the advisory Guidelines may attract greatest respect when" it is based on the particular facts of a case. *Kimbrough*, 552 U.S., at 109. Overall, this system "requires a court to give respectful consideration to the Guidelines," but it "permits the court to tailor the sentence in light of other statutory concerns as well." *Id.*, at 101. . . .

III

A

The Constitution prohibits both federal and state governments from enacting any "*ex post facto* Law." Art. I, § 9, cl. 3; Art. I, § 10. The phrase "'*ex post facto* law' was a term of art with an established meaning at the time of the framing." *Collins v. Youngblood*, 497 U.S. 37, 41 (1990). In *Calder v. Bull*, Justice Chase reviewed the definition that the term had acquired in English common law:

"1st. Every law that makes an action done before the passing of the law, and which was innocent when done, criminal; and punishes such action. 2d. Every law that aggravates a crime, or makes it greater than it was, when committed. 3d. Every law that changes the punishment, and inflicts a greater punishment, than the law annexed to the crime, when committed. 4th. Every law that alters the legal rules of evidence, and receives less, or different, testimony, than the law required at the time of the commission of the offence, in order to convict the offender." 3 Dall., at 390.

Building on Justice Chase's formulation of what constitutes an "*ex post facto* Law," our cases "have not attempted to precisely delimit the scope of this Latin phrase, but have instead given it substance by an accretion of case law." *Dobbert v. Florida*, 432 U.S. 282, 292 (1977).

At issue here is *Calder*'s third category of *ex post facto* laws, those that "chang[e] the punishment, and inflic[t] a greater punishment, than the law annexed to the crime, when committed." Peugh's claim is that the Clause was violated because the 2009 Guidelines call for a greater punishment than attached to bank fraud in 2000, when his crimes were completed. The Government counters that because the more punitive Guidelines applied at Peugh's sentencing were only advisory, there was no *ex post facto* problem.

Each of the parties can point to prior decisions of this Court that lend support to its view. On the one hand, we have never accepted the proposition that a law must increase the maximum sentence for which a defendant is eligible in order to violate the *Ex Post Facto* Clause. Moreover, the fact that the sentencing authority exercises some measure of discretion will also not defeat an *ex post facto* claim. On the other hand, we have made it clear that mere speculation or conjecture that a change in law will retrospectively increase the punishment for a crime will not suffice to establish a violation of the *Ex Post Facto* Clause. The touchstone of this Court's inquiry is whether a given change in law presents a "sufficient risk of increasing the measure of punishment attached to the covered crimes." *Garner*, 529 U.S., at 250. The question when a change in law creates such a risk is "a matter of degree"; the test cannot be reduced to a "single formula." *Morales,* 514 U.S., at 509.

B

The most relevant of our prior decisions for assessing whether the requisite degree of risk is present here is *Miller v. Florida*, 482 U.S. 423 (1987), in which this Court considered an *ex post facto* challenge to a sentencing guidelines scheme implemented by the State of Florida. Under Florida's system, a calculation under the guidelines yielded a presumptive sentencing range. This range was assumed to be appropriate, and the sentencing judge had discretion to fix a sentence within that range "without the requirement of a written explanation." If the court wished to depart from the guidelines range, however, it was required to give "clear and convincing reasons in writing for doing so." 482 U.S., at 426. A within-guidelines sentence was unreviewable; a non-guidelines sentence was subject to appellate review.

The petitioner in *Miller* had been sentenced under new guidelines that yielded a higher sentencing range than the guidelines that had been in place at the time of his crime, and he had received a sentence at the top of the new range. This Court found an *ex post facto* violation. We emphasized that in order to impose the petitioner's sentence under the pre-existing guidelines, the sentencing judge would have been required to provide clear and convincing reasons in writing for the departure, and the sentence would then have been reviewable on appeal. *Id.,* at 432. In contrast, because the sentence imposed was within the new guidelines range, it required no explanation and was unreviewable. *Id.,* at 432–433. The fact that Florida's guidelines "create[d] a high hurdle that must be cleared before discretion can be exercised" was sufficient to render the changed guidelines an *ex post facto* law. *Id.,* at 435.

Miller thus establishes that applying amended sentencing guidelines that increase a defendant's recommended sentence can violate the *Ex Post Facto* Clause, notwithstanding the fact that sentencing courts possess discretion to deviate from the recommended sentencing range. The sentencing scheme in *Miller* was designed to channel sentences for similarly situated offenders into a specified range. Its reason-giving requirements and standards of appellate review meant that while variation was possible, it was burdensome; and so in the ordinary case, a defendant would receive a within-guidelines sentence. Under the Florida system, therefore, an increase in the guidelines range applicable to an offender created a significant risk that he would receive a higher sentence. The same principles apply here.

The post-*Booker* federal sentencing scheme aims to achieve uniformity by ensuring that sentencing decisions are anchored by the Guidelines and that they remain a meaningful benchmark through the process of appellate review. As we have described, "district courts *must* begin their analysis with the Guidelines and remain cognizant of them throughout the sentencing process." *Gall,* 552 U.S., at 50, n.6. (emphasis added). Failing to calculate the correct Guidelines range constitutes procedural error. *Id.,* at 51. A district court contemplating a non-Guidelines sentence "must consider the extent of the deviation and ensure that the justification is sufficiently compelling to support the degree of the variance." *Id.,* at 50.

These requirements mean that "[i]n the usual sentencing, . . . the judge will use the Guidelines range as the starting point in the analysis and impose a sentence within the range." *Freeman v. United States,* 654 U.S. ___ (2011) (plurality opinion). Even if the sentencing judge sees a reason to vary from the Guidelines, "if the judge uses the sentencing range as the beginning point to explain the decision to deviate from it, *then the Guidelines are in a real sense the basis for the sentence." Ibid.* (emphasis added). That a district court may ultimately sentence a given defendant outside the Guidelines range does not deprive the Guidelines of force as the framework for sentencing. Indeed, the rule that an incorrect Guidelines calculation is procedural error ensures that they remain the starting point for every sentencing calculation in the federal system.

Similarly, appellate review for reasonableness using the Guidelines as a benchmark helps promote uniformity by "tend[ing] to iron out sentencing differences." *Booker*, 543 U.S., at 263. Courts of appeals may presume a within-Guidelines sentence is reasonable, and they may further "consider the extent of the deviation" from the Guidelines as part of their reasonableness review, *Gall*, 552 U.S., at 51. As in *Miller,* then, the post-*Booker* sentencing regime puts in place procedural "hurdle[s]" that, in practice, make the imposition of a non-Guidelines sentence less likely.

This is a more difficult case than *Miller,* because there are relevant differences between Florida's sentencing scheme and the current federal sentencing regime. The Florida Legislature had made a within-guidelines sentence unreviewable; whereas in the federal system, the courts of appeals may—but are not required to—presume that a within-Guidelines sentence is reasonable. And under Florida's scheme, a sentencing court departing from the guideline range was required to provide "clear and convincing" reasons for the departure; whereas this Court has not, post-*Booker,* applied such an exacting across-the-board standard of review to variances. Rather, we have held that a district court varying from the Federal Guidelines should provide an explanation adequate to the extent of the departure.

But . . . these differences are not dispositive. Although the federal system's procedural rules establish gentler checks on the sentencing court's discretion than Florida's did, they nevertheless impose a series of requirements on sentencing courts that cabin the exercise of that discretion. Common sense indicates that in general, this system will steer district courts to more within-Guidelines sentences.

Peugh points to considerable empirical evidence indicating that the Sentencing Guidelines have the intended effect of influencing the sentences imposed by judges. Even after *Booker* rendered the Sentencing Guidelines advisory, district courts have in the vast majority of cases imposed either within-Guidelines sentences or sentences that depart downward from the Guidelines on the Government's motion. In less than one-fifth of cases since 2007 have district courts imposed above- or below-Guidelines sentences absent a Government motion. Moreover, the Sentencing Commission's data indicate that when a Guidelines range moves up or down, offenders' sentences move with it.

The federal system adopts procedural measures intended to make the Guidelines the lodestone of sentencing. A retrospective increase in the Guidelines range applicable to a defendant creates a sufficient risk of a higher sentence to constitute an *ex post facto* violation. . . .

IV

The Government's principal argument that there is no constitutional violation in this case is that the Sentencing Guidelines lack sufficient legal effect to attain the status of a "law" within the meaning of the *Ex Post Facto* Clause. Whereas the pre-*Booker* Guidelines "ha[d] the force and effect of laws," the post-*Booker* Guidelines, the Government contends, have lost that status due to their advisory nature. . . .

The distinction that the Government draws is necessarily a fine one, because our precedents firmly establish that changes in law need not bind a sentencing authority in order to violate the *Ex Post Facto* Clause. So, for example, a law can run afoul of the Clause even if it does not alter the statutory maximum punishment attached to a crime. In *Lindsey v. Washington*, 301 U.S. 397, this Court considered an *ex post facto* challenge to a Washington law altering the statutory penalty for grand larceny from a range of 0 to 15 years' imprisonment to a mandatory term of 15 years' imprisonment. Although the upper boundary of the sentencing court's power to punish remained unchanged, it was enough that the petitioners were "deprived of all *opportunity* to receive a sentence which would give them freedom from custody and control prior to the expiration of the 15-year term." *Id.,* at 402 (emphasis added).

In addition, our cases make clear that "[t]he presence of discretion does not displace the protections of the *Ex Post Facto* Clause." *Garner,* 529 U.S., at 253. In a series of cases, for example, this Court has considered the validity under the *Ex Post Facto* Clause of state laws altering the terms on which discretionary parole or early release was available to prisoners. Although these cases reached differing conclusions with respect to whether there was an *ex post facto* violation, in none of them did we indicate that the mere fact that the prisoner was not guaranteed parole but rather received it at the will of the parole board was fatal to his claim.

The Government does not challenge these holdings but rather argues, in essence, that the Guidelines are too much like guideposts and not enough like fences to give rise to an *ex post facto* violation. It contrasts the Sentencing Guidelines with the Florida system at issue in *Miller,* which, the Government indicates, really did place "a substantial legislative constraint on the judge's exercise of sentencing discretion." But as we have explained at length, the difference between the federal system and the scheme the Court considered in *Miller* is one in degree, not in kind. The Florida system did not achieve its "binding legal effect" by mandating a within-guidelines sentence in every case. Rather, it achieved its "binding legal effect" through a set of procedural rules and standards for appellate review that, in combination, encouraged district courts to sentence within the guidelines. We have detailed all of the ways in which the federal sentencing regime after *Booker* does the same. . . .

On the Government's account, the Guidelines are just one among many persuasive sources a sentencing court can consult, no different from a "policy paper." The Government's argument fails to acknowledge, however, that district courts are not required to consult any policy paper in order to avoid reversible procedural error; nor must they "consider the extent of [their] deviation" from a given policy paper and "ensure that the justification is sufficiently compelling to support the degree of the variance," *Gall*, 552 U.S., at 50. Courts of appeals, in turn, are not permitted to presume that a sentence that comports with a particular policy paper is reasonable; nor do courts of appeals, in considering whether the district court's sentence was reasonable, weigh the extent of any departure from a given policy paper in determining whether the district court abused its discretion. It is simply not the case that the Sentencing Guidelines are merely a volume that the district court reads with academic interest in the course of sentencing.

Of course, . . . notwithstanding a rule that retrospective application of a higher Guidelines range violates the *Ex Post Facto* Clause, sentencing courts will be free to give careful consideration to the current version of the Guidelines as representing the most recent views of the agency charged by Congress with developing sentencing policy. But this does not render our holding "purely semantic." District courts must begin their sentencing analysis with the Guidelines in effect at the time of the offense and use them to calculate the sentencing range correctly; and those Guidelines will anchor both the district court's discretion and the appellate review process in all of the ways we have described. The newer Guidelines, meanwhile, will have the status of one of many reasons a district court might give for *deviating* from the older Guidelines, a status that is simply not equivalent for *ex post facto* purposes. . . .

* * *

"[T]he *Ex Post Facto* Clause forbids the [government] to enhance the measure of punishment by altering the substantive 'formula' used to calculate the applicable sentencing range." *Morales*, 514 U.S., at 505. That is precisely what the amended Guidelines did here. Doing so created a "significant risk" of a higher sentence for Peugh and offended "one of the principal interests that the *Ex Post Facto* Clause was designed to serve, fundamental justice," *Carmell*, 529 U.S., at 531. . . .

* * *

Notes on *Peugh v. United States*

1. *The continuing influence of Justice Chase's opinion in* **Calder v. Bull**: The Court's analysis in *Peugh* begins by quoting a famous paragraph from Justice Samuel Chase's opinion in *Calder v. Bull*. Though more than 220 years old (and an opinion for only a single justice), that opinion continues to frame the Court's approach to nearly all Ex Post Facto Clause problems. The paragraph quoted by Justice Sotomayor identified the four categories of laws that come within the clause's prohibitions. (The second category—for "[e]very law that aggravates a crime, or makes it greater than it was, when committed"—has proven largely redundant with the third category; in practice, laws that "aggravate" a crime typically increase the punishment for that crime.)

2. *A "sufficient risk of increasing the measure of punishment"*: Peugh was convicted of committing an act that was a crime at the time of commission, so the first category of *ex post facto* laws was not pertinent. Likewise, there had been no changes to the rules of evidence or available defenses (as was the case in *Carmell*). Instead, Peugh's case turned on whether the district court's application of the revised Guidelines "change[d] the punishment, and inflict[ed] a greater punishment, than the law annexed to the crime, when committed."

Critically, the fact that the Sentencing Guidelines are now merely *advisory*—such that district courts can impose sentences outside the prescribed range—was not dispositive. The Court's prior decision in *Miller v. Florida* had "establishe[d] that applying amended sentencing guidelines that increase a defendant's recommended sentence can violate the *Ex Post Facto* Clause, notwithstanding the fact that sentencing courts possess discretion to deviate from the recommended sentencing range." More broadly, it need not be *certain* that the application of the new law resulted in a stiffer punishment. Rather, the standard is whether application of the new law "presents a *sufficient risk* of increasing the measure of punishment attached to the covered crimes." (In other cases, the Court has phrased the test as whether application of the new law creates a "significant risk" of greater punishment.) And whether "a change in law creates such a risk is a matter of degree," such that "the test cannot be reduced to a single formula."

In *Peugh* itself, the Court concluded—given the practical impact of the Guidelines on federal sentences—that the district court's retroactive application of the revised Guidelines created a "sufficient" or "significant" risk of greater punishment. As Justice Sotomayor explained, "[t]he post-*Booker* federal sentencing scheme aims to achieve uniformity by ensuring that sentencing decisions are anchored by the Guidelines and that they remain a meaningful benchmark through the process of appellate review." Moreover, there was ample empirical evidence demonstrating that the Guidelines "have the intended effect of influencing the sentences imposed by judges. Even after *Booker* rendered the Sentencing Guidelines advisory, district courts have in the vast majority of cases imposed either within-Guidelines sentences or sentences that depart downward from the Guidelines on the Government's motion." Under these circumstances, the retroactive application of the revised Guidelines posed a "sufficient risk of a higher sentence to constitute an *ex post facto* violation."

3. *Reviving criminal jeopardy beyond the applicable limitations period*: Suppose the statute of limitations for a particular crime has expired, but the legislature amends the limitations period to render an already-expired prosecution timely. Would this resurrection of time-barred prosecutions violate the Ex Post Facto Clause? In *Stogner v. California*, 539 U.S. 607 (2003), the Supreme Court said yes. Stogner had allegedly committed acts of sex-related child abuse between 1955 and 1973, when the applicable statute of limitations was three years. In 1993, California amended the limitations period such that a prosecution would be timely if brought within a year of the acts being reported to the police, regardless of when the offense had been committed. In 1998, Stogner was convicted under the new statute of limitations.

The Supreme Court held Stogner's prosecution was unconstitutional. Writing for a five-justice majority, Justice Breyer explained that

> "a statute of limitations reflects a legislative judgment that, after a certain time, no quantum of evidence is sufficient to convict. And that judgment typically rests, in large part, upon evidentiary concerns—for example, concern that the passage of time has eroded memories or made witnesses or other evidence unavailable. Indeed, this Court once described statutes of limitations as creating 'a presumption which renders proof unnecessary.' *Wood v. Carpenter*, 101 U.S. 135, 139 (1879). Consequently, to resurrect a prosecution after the relevant statute of limitations has expired is to eliminate a currently existing conclusive presumption forbidding prosecution, and thereby to permit conviction on a quantum of evidence where that quantum, at the time the new law is enacted, would have been legally insufficient." *Id.* at 615–616.

Moreover, applying the new limitations period "threatens the kinds of harm that . . . the *Ex Post Facto* Clause seeks to avoid":

> "[E]xtending a limitations period after the State has assured a man that he has become safe from its pursuit . . . seems to most of us unfair and dishonest. . . . It has deprived the defendant of the fair warning that might have led him to preserve exculpatory evidence. And a Constitution that permits such an extension, by allowing legislatures to pick and choose when to act retroactively, risks both arbitrary and potentially vindictive legislation, and erosion of the separation of powers." *Id.* at 611.

Importantly, the Court limited its holding in *Stogner* to circumstances where the limitations period extant at the time of the offense had expired prior to its amendment, so the defendant was (at least for some time) "free and clear" of criminal jeopardy. It reserved the question whether extending the limitations period prior to its expiration would be impermissibly *ex post facto*.

* * *

PROBLEMS ON THE EX POST FACTO CLAUSES

In each of the following scenarios, please assess whether, in enacting the law at issue, the state has violated the *Ex Post Facto* Clause.

1. On May 1, Defendant takes a selfie in the voting booth while casting her vote for President. On May 10, the state legislature enacts a new law criminalizing the act of taking a photograph in a voting booth. On May 20, Defendant is arrested and charged with the offense of taking a photograph in a voting booth.

2. The facts are the same as in (1), except that the new law criminalizes possessing a photograph (including a digital image) taken inside a voting booth. Defendant

continues to possess her photograph from May 1 to May 20. On May 20, Defendant is arrested and charged with the offense of possessing such an image.

3. On May 1, the state legislature enacts a law criminalizing the act of taking a photograph in a voting booth, punishable by a sentence of between 6 and 12 months in prison. On May 10, Defendant takes a selfie in a voting booth and is arrested. On May 20, the state legislature amends the law so as to increase the punishment for the offense to a sentence of between 12 and 24 months in prison. On May 30, Defendant is convicted of taking a photograph in a voting booth and sentenced to 18 months in prison.

4. The facts are the same as in (3), except that, in applying the new sentencing range of 12 to 24 months, the court sentences defendant to 12 months in prison.

5. In 2021, Defendant commits first degree armed robbery in Santa Clara, California. At the time he committed the robbery, the offense was punishable by up to nine years in prison. (There was no minimum sentence.) In July 2022, the California legislature enacts a new statute—effective immediately—which imposes an automatic sentence of nine years' imprisonment for first degree armed robbery. Defendant goes to trial in October 2022, and the jury convicts him. The superior court judge applies the new California statute and sentences Defendant to nine years in prison.

6. In 2021, the state legislature enacts a law criminalizing the act of taking a photograph in a voting booth; the statute of limitations is one year. Later in 2021, after the legislature has enacted the law, Defendant takes a selfie in a voting booth. In 2023, the state legislature amends the law so as to permit prosecutions for the offense of taking a photograph in a voting booth if the prosecution was initiated within 100 days of the offense being reported to the police, regardless of when the photograph was taken. In 2024, a person reports that Defendant took a selfie in a voting booth in 2021. Defendant is prosecuted and convicted of the offense.

7. The facts are the same as in (5), except that the state legislature amends the statute of limitations for the offense in December 2021, after defendant had taken the selfie but before the one-year limitations period for her offense had expired.

APPENDIX

FINAL EXAM QUESTIONS

QUESTION 1

In January 2022, Congress passes (and the President signs into law) the "Coronavirus Surveillance and Protection Act" (or CSPA). The two most important sections of the CSPA provide as follows:

§1 Vaccination mandate

(a) All employers in the United States (including all state or local governments) that maintain or operate a sensitive work setting are hereby commanded to require each of their employees who work in those sensitive work settings to be fully vaccinated against COVID-19 no later than March 31, 2022 (unless the employee has a valid health or religious justification for not being vaccinated).

(b) For purposes of this Act, the term "sensitive work setting" includes all workplaces in the health care, education, government, and transportation sectors, as well as any other work settings determined to be sensitive by the Coronavirus Surveillance and Protection Board.

§2 Coronavirus Surveillance and Protection Board

(a) There shall be a five-member Coronavirus Surveillance and Protection Board (CSPB). The Board's one responsibility shall be to promulgate any regulations necessary to the implementation of §1 of this Act.

(b) The members of the Board shall be appointed by the Secretary of Health and Human Services and shall serve for five-year terms. The President may remove any member of the Board from office, but only for inefficiency, neglect of duty, or malfeasance in office.

(c) Any regulation promulgated by the Board shall become effective 30 days after its official publication. Such a regulation shall represent the final position of the United States unless—following its publication but before it becomes effective—the Secretary of Health and Human Services revises or rescinds it, in which case the Secretary's determination shall represent the final position of the United States.

The CSPB is situated within the Department of Health and Human Services (HHS). HHS is a cabinet-level executive department; the Secretary of HHS reports directly to the President and is removable at will by the President.

In response to the passage of the CSPA, the South Dakota legislature has enacted a statute entitled the "South Dakota Health Freedom Act." It provides as follows: "No South Dakota citizen shall be required—by any employer, school, university, government (including the federal government), or any other entity—to be vaccinated against COVID-19." Thus, despite employing thousands of employees in work settings that qualify as "sensitive" under §1 of the CSPA, the State of South Dakota has refused to require any of its employees to be vaccinated against COVID-19.

In April 2022, the United States files suit against the State of South Dakota in federal district court seeking an injunction that would require the state to comply with the CSPA. (The suit does not name any state officers as defendants in their official capacity; instead, it asserts the claim directly against the state itself.) South Dakota has timely filed a motion to dismiss, contending that the CSPA is unconstitutional (at least as applied to state governments).

Please disregard any issues regarding standing, ripeness, mootness, or the political questions doctrine.

A. Does §1 of the CSPA exceed Congress's legislative powers? Explain.

B. Does §1 of the CSPA violate any federalism-based constraint on how Congress can use its legislative powers? Explain.

C. Are the CSPA's provisions concerning the appointment and removal of the members of the CSPB constitutional? Explain.

D. Does the CSPA violate any other doctrines or principles concerning the separation of powers? Explain.

SUGGESTED ANALYSIS for QUESTION 1

A

Issue: Whether §1 of the CSPA either exceeds Congress's enumerated powers.

Rule statement: The Constitution enumerates several powers that Congress can use to enact legislation, but the only one that appears relevant here is the commerce power. The commerce power permits Congress to regulate three categories of activity. First, Congress can regulate the use of the channels of interstate commerce. Second, Congress can regulate or protect the instrumentalities of, or persons or things in, interstate commerce. Finally, Congress can regulate those activities having a substantial effect on interstate commerce. With respect to this third category—activities substantially affecting interstate commerce—the critical factor is whether the activity regulated by the statute is "economic or commercial in nature." If it is, the effect of the activity (in all its instances nationwide) can be aggregated, and it will almost certainly be considered to have a substantial effect on interstate commerce. The Supreme Court has also stated that three other factors should be assessed as part of the "substantial effects" inquiry: whether Congress has made findings about the activity's impact on interstate commerce; whether the connection between the activity and interstate commerce is attenuated; and whether the activity has historically been regulated primarily by the states (rather than the federal government). Lastly, even if the challenged provision standing alone (or its application in a given case) does not fit within the above framework when viewed in isolation, the provision might nonetheless be within Congress's commerce power if Congress had a reasonable basis for concluding that the provision was essential to render effective a broader regulatory scheme, which scheme itself (when considered as a whole) is within Congress's commerce power.

Application: The precise activity this statute regulates is the employment of persons who work in "sensitive work settings." The statute forbids employers from employing persons in such workplaces if they have not been vaccinated against COVID-19. This provision does not appear to be a regulation of the use of the channels of interstate commerce; it does not concern a channel through which interstate commerce is conducted (like a highway or navigable waterway). Nor does the statute appear to regulate or protect the instrumentalities of, or persons or things in, interstate commerce; it does not address instrumentalities, nor is it limited to regulating persons while they are "in" the stream of interstate commerce. Still, the activity of employing persons—whether in a sensitive work setting or otherwise—is clearly "economic or commercial" in nature. Employment is the payment of employees for the provision of services in the labor market. Thus, a statute that regulates the terms on which employment can occur is necessarily a regulation of economic or commercial activity. As a result, this statute is justifiable as a regulation of an activity that substantially affects interstate commerce. True enough, there do not appear to be any congressional findings regarding the impact of the activity on interstate commerce. But employment is not clearly an area in which states have historically been sovereign (like education or family law), nor is this activity's impact on interstate commerce especially attenuated. Regardless, these other three factors are of limited importance. By far the most important factor in determining whether a statute falls within *Lopez*'s third category is whether the activity the statute regulates is economic or commercial. Here, it plainly is.

Conclusion: The activity regulated by §1 of the CSPA is one that—because it is economic or commercial in nature—substantially affects interstate commerce, which means §1 is within Congress's commerce power.

B

Issue: Whether §1 of the CSPA violates any federalism-based constraint on how Congress can use its legislative powers?

Rule statement: The only federalism-based constraint on how Congress can use its legislative powers that might be relevant here is the anti-commandeering principle. The anti-commandeering principle forbids Congress from using its enumerated powers—even if Congress has the general authority to regulate the activity at issue—in a way that forces states to affirmatively act in their sovereign capacities (that is, to legislate, regulate, or otherwise govern). Congress cannot command the states to regulate or govern, in the form of affirmative acts, according to Congress's instructions. But Congress *can* command states to act through "generally applicable" legislation that regulates the actions of state and local governments in their *propriety* capacities. Proprietary activities are those that any entity might engage in (as opposed to activities that are distinctively governmental). Examples include federal statutes that regulate state and local governments as employers (*Garcia*) or collectors and disseminators of personal information (*Reno v. Condon*).

Application: The CSPA plainly commands state and local governments to take action: it commands them "to require each of their employees who work in those settings to be fully vaccinated against COVID-19 no later than March 31, 2022." But this command only regulates the actions of state and local governments in their *proprietary* capacities—as employers—through generally applicable legislation. The Act applies to *all* employers—public and private alike—who maintain or operate sensitive work settings. Critically, the CSPA does not command state or local governments to take any affirmative actions in their sovereign or governmental capacities: to regulate or legislate according to federal directives. Thus, the CSPA does not violate the anti-commandeering principle, as that principle does not forbid Congress from regulating the activities of state and local governments in their proprietary capacities.

Conclusion: The CSPA does not violate the anti-commandeering principle.

C

Issue: Whether the provisions of the CSPA concerning the appointment and removal of members of the Coronavirus Surveillance and Protection Board are constitutional.

1. *Appointment*

Rule statement: Under the Appointments Clause, all principal officers of the United States must be nominated by the President with confirmation by the Senate. So-called "inferior officers" can also be appointed in that way; but Congress can alternatively (if it so chooses) vest their appointment in the President alone, the head of a department, or a court of law. (Persons who do not exercise "significant authority" are "mere employees"—and not "officers"—such that their appointment is not subject to the requirements of the Appointments Clause.) A governmental official is an "officer of the United States" if she exercises "significant authority" while occupying a continuing office established by law. She is a "principal officer" if she has the authority to make decisions that are unreviewable by other executive officers, such that her decisions represent the final word for the Executive Branch. *See United States v. Arthrex.*

Application: Section 2(b) of the CSPA specifies that members of the Coronavirus Surveillance and Protection Board are to be appointed by the Secretary of Health and Human Services, the head of an executive department (HHS). This provision is constitutional if Board members are "inferior officers" or "mere employees," but it is unconstitutional if they are "principal officers." As decided in *Arthrex*, the critical factor in determining whether officers are "principal officers" is whether their decisions are binding on the Executive Branch, without being subject to review by a principal officer before becoming final. Here, the decisions of the Board (to issue rules or regulations implementing the CSPA) *are* subject to review and revision by the Secretary of HHS before becoming final. True enough, the Board's decisions can become final without the Secretary's review. But that can only occur if the Secretary decides not to review them; every rule or regulation issued by the Board is *subject* to the Secretary's review. This is the critical fact that was missing in *Arthrex*, and thus led the Court to conclude that the Administrative Patent Judges were principal officers. Thus, this scheme is distinguishable from that in *Arthrex*. Because the Board's decisions are subject to review by the Secretary (who is a principal officer, nominated by the President and confirmed by the Senate, and removable at will by the President), members of the Board are almost certainly inferior officers. As a result, their appointment by the Secretary comports with the Appointments Clause.

Conclusion: The appointment provision of the CSPA is constitutional.

2. *Removal*

Rule statement: Inherent in the powers granted the President by Article II—specifically through the Vesting and Take Care Clauses—is the power to remove executive officers from office. The power to remove executive officers is part of the power to see that federal law is faithfully executed. Nevertheless, the Constitution permits Congress to constrain the President's removal power (if it so chooses) when the constraint fits within one of two "exceptions." One exception comes from *Perkins* and *Morrison v. Olsen*, and it permits removal limitations on inferior officers who have limited jurisdiction and tenure and lack policymaking or significant administrative power. The other exception comes from *Humphrey's Executor*, and it permits removal limitations for officers (even if they are principal officers) who are members of a multimember body of experts who perform quasi-legislative and quasi-judicial functions—that is, "multimember expert agencies that do not wield substantial executive power." Constraints that go beyond these exceptions are presumptively unconstitutional; they are inconsistent with Article II and separation of powers principles.

Application: The CSPA places a significant constraint on the President's capacity to remove members of the Coronavirus Surveillance and Protection Board. It provides that they may be removed from office "only for inefficiency, neglect of duty, or malfeasance in office." But this removal limitation is likely constitutional, as it likely fits within the *Humphrey's Executor* exception. In several senses, the Board members are analogous to the Federal Trade Commissioners at issue in *Humphrey's Executor*: they are members of a five-member board, and they bring expertise to bear on very particular questions of workplace safety. More important, the Board probably does not "wield substantial executive power," as their decisions are reviewable by the Secretary of HHS before becoming final. Indeed, the limitation in *Humphrey's Executor* was permissible even though the FTC Commissioners were principal officers. Given that the members of the Board are almost certainly *inferior* officers (as discussed above), the intrusion on the President's authority to execute the law is *a fortiori* less significant than it was in *Humphrey's Executor*. This removal limitation probably would not fit within the exception recognized in *Perkins* and *Morrison v. Olsen*. These Board members pretty clearly have "policymaking or administrative authority" under the CSPA: they are given the authority to implement a reasonably significant statute, including determining which workplace settings are "sensitive" and thus covered by the mandate. The *Perkins* and *Morrison* exception applies to "inferior officers with limited duties and *no* policymaking or administrative authority." Thus, that exception seems inapposite here.

Conclusion: The removal provision of the CSPA is likely constitutional under the authority of *Humphrey's Executor*.

D

Issue: Whether the CSPA violates any other separation-of-powers doctrines or principles.

Rule statement: The only other separation-of-powers doctrine or principle that appears relevant to this fact pattern is the nondelegation doctrine. In enacting federal statutes, Congress may delegate broad authority to the Executive Branch in determining how the statute will be enforced or implemented. (Indeed, a large measure of delegation is unavoidable.) But Congress cannot simply give away its legislative power to the President. Under the nondelegation doctrine, federal statutes—at a minimum—must articulate an "intelligible principle" to guide the Executive Branch's enforcement. This is not a particularly demanding standard, but it must in some way constrain the Executive Branch. And the detail required varies depending on the breadth of the authority conferred by the statute: the more significant the statute at issue (in terms of the authority to be exercised by the Executive Branch), the more specific the statute must be to satisfy the "intelligible principle" requirement.

Application: Section 1(b) of the CSPA delegates fairly broad authority to the Coronavirus Surveillance and Protection Board. It gives the Board the authority to determine whether any workplace setting (beyond those specified in the CSPA) is subject to the vaccine mandate, and the only guidance the CSPA provides the Board in making such determinations is that they "shall be to best protect the public health." That is a fairly broad delegation of discretion. But it also is similar to many that the Supreme Court has upheld as satisfying the "intelligible principle" standard. (Several statutes upheld by the Supreme Court have only demanded that the relevant executive official devise rules that are consistent with the public interest and the purposes of the statute.) Moreover, the scope of the CSPA is narrow: it merely concerns which employers will be subject to the COVID-19 vaccine mandate for their employees. This is certainly important, but it is not nearly as broad as the authority conferred by thousands of other federal statutes, including the Clean Air Act (at issue in *Whitman v. American Trucking Associations*).

Conclusion: Though the legislative delegation in the CSPA to the Board to determine which workplace settings are "sensitive" is broad, it probably meets the "intelligible principle" standard as applied in the Court's prior decisions, and thus likely does not run afoul of the nondelegation doctrine.

QUESTION 2

It is November 2020. Because State A public health officials have taken aggressive steps from the beginning of the coronavirus pandemic, State A has consistently maintained lower-than-average infection rates among its residents. As infection rates have soared recently in other states, the State A legislature has just passed a bill containing two key sections. Those sections provide as follows:

§1 Entry of Nonresidents into State A

Beginning the day after this section becomes law, all nonresidents are prohibited from entering State A unless they can present proof that they have tested negative for the coronavirus within the past 48 hours. Persons unable to make such a demonstration shall be denied entry into State A. Any person found within State A who has entered the state without complying with this section will be required to leave State A immediately.

§2 Free Coronavirus Testing and COVID Treatments for State A Residents

The government of State A will henceforth provide free coronavirus testing and free COVID-19 therapeutic treatments (as prescribed by a competent physician) to all residents of State A. To establish residency for purposes of this section, a person must (a) produce documents (such as utility bills, bank statements, pay stubs, or the like) demonstrating that the individual has resided in State A for a minimum of 90 days; and (b) sign a pledge that they intend to reside in State A indefinitely. Persons unable to meet this requirement shall be considered, for purposes of this section, nonresidents.

You are a legal advisor to the governor of State A, who is concerned about the bill's constitutionality. To help her decide whether to sign the bill into law, the governor has asked you to address the two questions below. Please ignore any potential justiciability issues, as well as any possible claims under the Due Process Clause. Assume there is no federal statute that could preempt this law. And if there are any important facts you believe are relevant but not provided, please identify them and explain how they would affect your analysis.

A. If enacted, what plausible claims might be raised that §1 is unconstitutional? Do you think such challenges are likely to succeed? Explain.

B. If enacted, what plausible claims might be raised that §2 is unconstitutional? Do you think such challenges are likely to succeed? Explain.

SUGGESTED ANALYSIS for QUESTION 2

Both sections of the bill could plausibly be challenged as violating three constitutional provisions: (1) the dormant Commerce Clause, (2) the Privileges and Immunities Clause of Article IV, or (3) the Privileges and Immunities Clause of the Fourteenth Amendment.

Dormant Commerce Clause rule statement: The dormant Commerce Clause generally forbids states from imposing taxes or regulations that discriminate against or unduly burden interstate commerce. If a state law discriminates against interstate commerce—treating commercial activity crossing state lines less favorably than commercial activity that remains entirely within one state—it is virtually *per se* invalid. It will only be constitutional if the state has a legitimate, non-protectionist reason for the law, and the law is *necessary* to accomplish that objective (*i.e.*, the state has no practicable nondiscriminatory alternatives). If the law does not discriminate against interstate commerce, it will not violate the Commerce Clause so long as the burden it imposes on interstate commerce is not "clearly excessive" relative to its putative local benefits. Under the "market participant exception," when the state is not regulating or imposing a tax—when it is buying or providing a good or service in a market (like a private person in that market)—the dormant Commerce Clause does not apply. As a market participant, a state is entitled to discriminate in favor of its own residents and in favor of purely intrastate commerce.

Privileges and Immunities Clause of Article IV Rule statement: The Privileges and Immunities Clause of Article IV presumptively prohibits discrimination against citizens of other U.S. states based on their status as nonresidents. Thus, a threshold question under this clause is whether the law discriminates on the basis of state residency. Even if the law so discriminates, not all rights or privileges are protected by the clause. The clause only protects those rights considered "fundamental" for purposes of Article IV: "those privileges or immunities bearing upon the vitality of the Nation as a single entity," such that equality in access to the privilege "basic to the maintenance or well-being of the Union." If a law discriminates against nonresidents with respect to such a right, it is subject to an intermediate level of scrutiny: the state must have a substantial justification for the law, and the law must be "substantially related" to that justification. In other words, nonresidents must constitute a "peculiar source of the evil" at which the law is aimed.

Privileges or Immunities Clause of the Fourteenth Amendment rule statement: The Privileges or Immunities Clause of the Fourteenth Amendment generally prohibits a state from discriminating among its residents based on their duration of residency in the state. As the Court held in *Saenz v. Roe*, any such discrimination—with respect to any governmental rule or benefit—impinges on the right to interstate migration: the rights, as a citizen of the United States, to become a citizen of any state within the Union. Thus, such discrimination is subject to strict scrutiny: the government's interest must be *compelling*, and the law must be *necessary* (or narrowly tailored) to achieve that interest. When a person enters a state to access a "highly portable benefit," however—such as higher education or a divorce decree—a state may impose tests, for purposes of accessing that benefit, that ensure the individual is a *bona fide* resident. Hence, the Court has generally upheld state residency requirements for purposes of lower in-state tuition at colleges and universities that require persons to have resided in the state for at least a year.

A

Issue: Whether §1 would violate the dormant Commerce Clause.

Application: By forbidding the entry of any nonresident into the state unless she meets certain conditions, §1 plainly discriminates against interstate commerce. To be sure, many border crossings will be noncommercial in nature, but many—and perhaps most—will be commercial. Much interstate commercial activity is being halted, whereas §1 has no impact on commerce conducted entirely within State A. (This statute is analogous to that in *Philadelphia v. New Jersey*, which the Supreme Court held discriminated against interstate commerce.) Thus, to be consistent with the dormant Commerce Clause, §1 would need to withstand "rigorous scrutiny": State A would need a legitimate, non-protectionist purpose for the law, and the state could not have any nondiscriminatory alternatives for achieving that objective.

State A pretty clearly has a legitimate, non-protectionist objective: to prevent the further spread of the coronavirus within the state. This is a governmental objective of the highest order. But are there no alternative, nondiscriminatory means available for State A to achieve that objective? That is difficult to say, and dependent on facts not presented in the fact pattern. There *might* be such alternatives, such as requiring all persons coming from a state with a higher infection rate to quarantine themselves for a certain period of time after arriving in State A. (But this might be ineffective, as such quarantine requirements are very difficult to enforce.) It is unclear whether this fairly extreme measure of barring entry is *necessary*. But this is what would decide the question.

Issue: Whether §1 would violate the Privileges and Immunities Clause of Article IV.

Application: Section 1 plainly discriminates against nonresidents; it explicitly bars them from entering the state unless they can demonstrate they have tested negative for the virus within the last 48 hours. The next question is whether entry into the state is a "privilege" or "immunity" protected by the clause. It would seem to be, though we have not seen any cases addressing this precise question. Movement across a state border would seem to be "basic to the maintenance or well-being of the Union." Were states permitted to bar nonresidents from entry, the Union would hardly be a *nation*. Moreover, barring nonresidents from entering the state prevents them from pursuing all sorts of rights we know are protected by the clause, such as the right to pursue a common calling.

If movement into the state is a "privilege" protected by the clause, the question would be whether State A has a "substantial reason" for this measure, and whether the law is "substantially related" to it. Preventing the further spread of the coronavirus is unquestionably a "substantial reason"; it is hard to think of a more compelling governmental interest. But it is not obvious that this law would be "substantially related" to that objective. What reason is there, exactly, for singling out *nonresidents* crossing the border—as opposed to any person (including residents) coming from a jurisdiction with a high infection rate? Why shouldn't all persons crossing the border be required to show that they have tested negative? Perhaps because State A residents need to come home, and the better solution for them is to quarantine at home. But there are no facts here suggesting how residents are treated, so we are left to think that nonresidents are being singled out for unfavorable treatment, even though returning residents would be just as much of a threat to public health. Perhaps without a deeper understanding of the virus, it is hard to be sure that nonresidents are a "peculiar source of the evil" at which this statute is aimed. In all events, we know the virus is transmitted through human-to-human interaction, and it is given in the facts that infection rates are higher in other states. Thus, State A *might* have a decent argument that its discrimination against nonresidents in §1 survives intermediate scrutiny. But again, the question is ultimately why State A would treat nonresidents less favorably than residents in this respect.

Issue: Whether §1 would violate the Privileges or Immunities Clause of the Fourteenth Amendment.

Application: Section 1 discriminates against *nonresidents*. It draws no distinction *among* State A residents on the basis of the duration of their residency in State A. Hence, the Privileges or Immunities Clause of the Fourteenth Amendment poses no barrier to §1.

B

Issue: Whether §2 would violate the dormant Commerce Clause.

Application: Under §2 of the bill, State A would provide coronavirus testing and COVID-19 treatments to State A residents (under State A's definition of residency). The state would be providing services in the market, and not regulating or taxing. (There is a broader market in the provision of tests and therapeutics, with most being provided by private providers—private medical providers and hospitals.) Moreover, even if the state is the predominant provider of these services, the statute does not make nonresidents *ineligible* to receive them; it merely provides that only residents will receive them free of charge from the state government. That is, residents would receive a preference in *price* (or in receiving them in kind) directly from the state. As a result, the market participant exception applies. This means §2 is not subject to dormant Commerce Clause scrutiny.

Issue: Whether §2 would violate the Privileges and Immunities Clause of Article IV.

Application: There is no doubt that §2 discriminates against nonresidents; it limits the provision of tests and treatments to State A residents. (It might also discriminate against State A residents based on their duration of residency, an issue explored below.) But is the provision (through public funds) of free coronavirus testing and treatments for COVID-19 a "privilege" or "immunity" protected by the clause? Probably not. Though discrimination in the provision of public benefits by the state is not exempt from scrutiny under Article IV (*see Camden*), the fact that these are publicly funded benefits is important to the analysis. These are unlike the rights typically protected by the Clause, such as that to pursue employment or a common calling, the right to enter into contracts, the right to buy and sell property, or the right of access to the courts. The public provision of free tests and therapeutics are *state-provided benefits*, funded entirely by State A. It hardly seems necessary to the "vitality of the Nation as a whole" that each state provide such benefits to all comers, regardless of their state of residence. (Most modern state benefits, such as cash assistance, health insurance, public education, and the like are only provided to state residents.) Finally, even if these were considered "privileges" or "immunities" covered by Article IV, it would seem State A has a "substantial reason" for limiting these benefits to residents. Namely, State A residents have paid for these benefits with their tax dollars, and public benefit programs would need to be shut down (or much smaller) if nonresidents could "free ride" off of a state's generosity. Nonresidents thus likely constitute a "peculiar source of the evil" that limiting the benefits to State A residents seeks to address. Thus, despite the obvious discrimination against nonresidents, §2 seems consistent with the Privileges and Immunities Clause of Article IV.

Issue: Whether §2 would violate the Privileges or Immunities Clause of the Fourteenth Amendment.

Application: A difficult, threshold question is whether this provision discriminates at all *among* state residents (or instead just against nonresidents). To the extent it is discriminating only against nonresidents, this is purely an Article IV question (addressed above), and the Privileges and Immunities Clause of the Fourteenth Amendment is irrelevant. But one could alternatively construe this provision as *also* discriminating among State A residents on the basis of duration of residency—between those who have resided in State A for less than and more than 90 days. As a general matter, such discrimination should be subjected to strict scrutiny, and presumptively unconstitutional. But as the Court explained in *Saenz*, states are permitted to limit the provision of "highly portable" public benefits to "*bona fide* residents." The provision of free coronavirus tests and COVID treatments may well fall into this category. Certainly, with respect to the tests, it would be easy for nonresidents to come into the state, obtain the test, and quickly leave (in the span of a day, or even an hour). COVID treatment may involve a longer duration, but it also is potentially portable—especially since all residents would be eligible, regardless of means. Hence, under this carve-out, this discrimination likely withstands scrutiny under the Privileges or Immunities Clause of the Fourteenth Amendment, on the ground that it *really* constitutes discrimination against nonresidents (rather than among residents on the basis of duration of residency). That is, the Constitution may well permit states to treat persons who have "resided" in the state for less than 90 days as nonresidents for purposes of obtaining such highly portable benefits. (Recall that states are permitted to treat persons who have resided in the state for less than a year as nonresidents for purposes of receiving the benefit of lower in-state tuition at public colleges and universities.)

QUESTION 3

A newly enacted federal statute—the Racial Violence Compensation Act (or RVCA)—consists of the following four provisions:

§10 State Legislation

Every State, as a matter of state law, shall enact a statute creating a cause of action similar in kind to that specified in §30 of this Act.

§20 Consequences for States

Any state failing to carry out its obligations under §10 of this Act shall be ineligible for 10 percent of the federal funding to which it would otherwise be entitled under federal spending programs dedicated to enhancing the effectiveness of state and local police departments.

§30 Private Right of Action

A person who commits a crime of violence motivated by racial discrimination shall be liable to the party injured, in an action for the recovery of compensatory and punitive damages.

§40 States' Amenability to Suit

A private plaintiff whose rights are protected by this Act may sue a state government for appropriate relief, including damages, in a state or federal court of competent jurisdiction.

Five years ago, the voters of State X approved an amendment to the State X Constitution, which provides that "it shall be unconstitutional to consider a defendant's racial motivation or purpose in any lawsuit brought by a private plaintiff seeking to recover damages from the defendant for physical injuries."

Following a political rally in a city in State X (where both Plaintiff and Defendant reside), two private citizens—Plaintiff and Defendant—were embroiled in a heated argument, after which Defendant assaulted Plaintiff. Plaintiff then sued Defendant in federal district court, asserting a cause of action under §30 of the RVCA and alleging (with evidentiary support) that the assault was motivated by racial discrimination. Defendant subsequently moved for the district court to dismiss Plaintiff's suit on several legal grounds.

The district court denied Defendant's motion to dismiss, and Plaintiff prevailed at trial, obtaining a verdict against Defendant for $350,000 in damages. Defendant appealed the judgment, asserting a series of legal arguments as grounds for reversal. Assume that Defendant preserved each of these arguments at trial; that the case does not present a "political question"; and that intentional discrimination on the basis of race violates the Equal Protection Clause (which is part of §1 of the Fourteenth Amendment).

A. Is the court of appeals likely to rule in favor of Defendant on the ground that Plaintiff's suit is barred by the Eleventh Amendment? Explain.

B. Is the court of appeals likely to rule in favor of Defendant on the ground that the RVCA violates the structural principles of federalism? Explain.

C. Is the court of appeals likely to rule in favor of Defendant on the ground that the RVCA exceeds Congress's enumerated powers? Explain.

SUGGESTED ANALYSIS for QUESTION 3

A

Issue: Whether the Court of Appeals is likely to rule in favor of Defendant on the ground that Plaintiff's lawsuit is barred by the Eleventh Amendment.

Rule statement: The Eleventh Amendment precludes federal courts from exercising subject matter jurisdiction over unconsenting suits against state governments brought by private parties (or foreign governments or Indian tribes).

Application: In this case, the party sued was Defendant, a private person. The action has not been asserted against a state government. Thus, the Eleventh Amendment is beside the point, and Defendant's appeal on this ground should be rejected.

B

Issue: Whether the Court of Appeals is likely to rule in favor of Defendant on the ground that the RVCA violates the structural principles of federalism.

Rule statement: The structural principles of federalism (among other things) forbid Congress from using its enumerated powers to "commandeer" the states by forcing them to affirmatively act in their sovereign capacities (to legislate or regulate). (*See New York v. United States*, *Printz v. United States*, and *NFIB v. Sebelius*.) Congress may not command the states to regulate or govern, in the form of affirmative acts, according to Congress's instructions. The structural principles of federalism also forbid Congress from abrogating the states' sovereign immunity by forcing them to stand suit to unconsenting actions brought by private parties (except through legislation that is valid under §5 of the Fourteenth Amendment). (*See Alden v. Maine*.)

Application: Defendant has only been affected (or injured) by §30 of the RVCA, not any of its other provisions. Section 30 of the RVCA does not violate either of these structural principles of federalism. It does not command state governments to take any action, but only regulates the actions of private persons. Similarly, §30 subjects private persons to suit, not state governments. Because Plaintiff's suit relies only on §30—and §§10 and 40 are immaterial to Plaintiff's suit or Defendant's defense—Defendant has no colorable argument that the structural principles of federalism bar Plaintiff's suit.

C

(Defendant clearly has standing to challenge §30 in his appeal: Defendant was injured by §30's existence—as it produced a $350,000 judgment against Defendant; injury was caused by §30's existence; and declaring §30 unconstitutional would redress Defendant's harm.)

Issue: Whether the Court of Appeals is likely to rule in favor of Defendant on the ground that the RVCA exceeds Congress's enumerated powers.

Introduction: The three enumerated powers within which §30 might fit are the commerce power, the power granted by §5 of the Fourteenth Amendment, and the power granted by §2 of the Thirteenth Amendment.

Issue: Whether §30 constitutes a valid exercise of Congress's commerce power.

Rule statement: The commerce power permits Congress to regulate three categories of activity. First, Congress can regulate the use of the channels of interstate commerce. (This means any *use* of such channels, and not just regulations of the channels themselves. Second, Congress can regulate or protect the instrumentalities of, or persons or things in, interstate commerce. Finally, Congress can regulate those activities having a substantial effect on interstate commerce.

With respect to this third category—activities substantially affecting interstate commerce—the most important question is whether the regulated activity is "economic or commercial in nature." If so, the effect of the activity (in all its occurrences nationwide) can be aggregated, and it will almost certainly be considered to have a substantial effect on interstate commerce. The Supreme Court has also stated that three other factors should be assessed under this category: whether Congress has made findings about the activity's impact on interstate commerce; whether the connection between the activity and interstate commerce is attenuated; and whether the activity has historically been regulated primarily by the states.

Lastly, even if the challenged provision standing alone (or its application in a given case) does not fit within the above framework when viewed in isolation, the provision might nonetheless be within Congress's commerce power if Congress had a reasonable basis for concluding that the provision was essential to render effective a broader regulatory scheme, which scheme itself (when considered as a whole) is within Congress's commerce power.

Application: The precise activity §1 regulates is the commission of a racially motivated assault. This is not a regulation of the use of the channels of interstate commerce, nor is it a regulation or protection of an instrumentality of, or person or thing in, interstate commerce. With respect to the third category, this activity is *not* economic or commercial in nature. *Morrison* held that an act of gender-motivated violence was not economic or commercial in nature, and this activity is virtually identical in its nature. More broadly, *Morrison* held that §13981 of the Violence Against Women Act—a nearly identical statute—exceeded Congress's commerce power. Thus, it almost certainly follows that §30 exceeds Congress's commerce power; this statute is not distinguishable in any meaningful way from that in *Morrison* for purposes of the commerce power.

Issue: Does §30 fit within the power granted by §5 of the Fourteenth Amendment?

Rule statement: Section 5 of the Fourteenth Amendment permits Congress to enact legislation that is "appropriate" to the enforcement of the prohibitions of the Amendment. Those prohibitions include the Equal Protection Clause, which forbids states from discriminating on the basis of race. Section 5 legislation must be "congruent and proportional" to the constitutional prohibitions Congress seeks to enforce. As the Court held in

Morrison, legislation regulating the conduct of *private* persons is categorically *incongruent*, and thus beyond the §5 power.

Application: Section 30 of the RVCA regulates *private* conduct, just like §13981 of the Violence Against Women Act. It thus exceeds the power conferred by §5.

Issue: Does this fit within the power granted by §2 of the Thirteenth Amendment?

Rule statement: Section 2 of the Thirteenth Amendment grants Congress the authority to enact legislation appropriate to enforcing the prohibitions of the Thirteenth Amendment, which forbids slavery in the United States. The Supreme Court has interpreted §2 as permitting Congress to enact legislation—in addition to prohibiting slavery itself—that forbids any form of racial discrimination. Further, because the Thirteenth Amendment itself reaches private conduct, §2 permits Congress to regulate private behavior.

Application: Section 30 of the RVCA regulates racial discrimination: discrimination expressed through physical violence. Thus, even though it regulates private conduct, it almost certainly falls within Congress's power under §2 of the Thirteenth Amendment.

Conclusion: Defendant's argument that the RVCA exceeds Congress's enumerated powers should be rejected, as it falls within Congress's authority under §2 of the Thirteenth Amendment.

QUESTION 4

Congress enacts a new statute, the Animal Cruelty Prevention Act (ACPA). The operative section of the ACPA provides as follows: "It shall be unlawful for any person to travel to another state for purposes of participating in a staged fight between animals. Any violation of this provision shall be punishable by a $50,000 fine, a prison sentence of up to 5 years, or both." Other provisions of the ACPA make clear that "staged fights between animals" includes cockfights—fights between two roosters—and that the Act applies to fights staged for any purpose. (Assume that the vast majority of staged animal fights are organized for the entertainment of family and friends, and do not constitute commercial enterprises.)

Plaintiff is a citizen of State A who regularly travels to State B to participate in cockfights, where cockfights are legal under state law. Plaintiff files suit against the Attorney General of the United States (the federal officer responsible for enforcing the ACPA) in federal district court, seeking a permanent injunction against the ACPA's enforcement. In his complaint, Plaintiff asserts one claim: that the ACPA exceeds Congress's enumerated powers. Assume the case is justiciable.

How is the court likely to rule on Plaintiff's claim? Explain.

SUGGESTED ANALYSIS for QUESTION 4

Issue: All federal statutes enacted by Congress must be within Congress's enumerated powers to be constitutional. These powers include the taxing power, the spending power, the powers to regulate interstate and international commerce, the powers to enforce the Thirteenth, Fourteenth, and Fifteenth Amendments, and several others. In this case, the only enumerated power that seems likely to justify the Animal Cruelty Prevention Act (ACPA) is the interstate commerce power. This cannot be an exercise of the taxing power, as the Act imposes a penalty of imprisonment. (By definition, a tax can only raise revenue; if it renders any activity "unlawful," it cannot be a tax.) Nor is this statute spending federal funds, so it cannot fit within the spending power. Nor is there any constitutional right that the ACPA appears to be enforcing. Thus, if the ACPA is within Congress's authority, it would need to be under the commerce power.

Rule statement: The commerce power permits Congress to regulate three categories of activity. First, Congress can regulate the use of the channels of interstate commerce. (This means any *use* of such channels, and not just regulations of the channels themselves. For instance, long before the "switch in time" of 1937, the Supreme Court held in *United States v. Darby* that a statute forbidding the shipment in interstate commerce of items manufactured with child labor was a valid exercise of the commerce power.) Second, Congress can regulate or protect the instrumentalities of, or persons or things in, interstate commerce. Finally, Congress can regulate those activities having a substantial effect on interstate commerce.

With respect to this third category—activities substantially affecting interstate commerce—the most important question is whether the regulated activity is "economic or commercial in nature." If so, the effect of the activity (in all its instances nationwide) can be aggregated, and it will almost certainly be considered to have a substantial effect on interstate commerce. The Supreme Court has also stated that three other factors should be assessed under this category: whether Congress has made findings about the activity's impact on interstate commerce; whether the connection between the activity and interstate commerce is attenuated; and whether the activity has historically been regulated primarily by the states (rather than the federal government).

Lastly, even if the challenged provision standing alone (or its application in a given case) does not fit within the above framework when viewed in isolation, the provision might nonetheless be within Congress's commerce power if Congress had a reasonable basis for concluding that the provision was essential to render effective a broader regulatory scheme, which scheme itself (when considered as a whole) is within Congress's commerce power.

Application: Here, the ACPA seems to plainly fall into the first category outlined above—a regulation of the use of the channels of interstate commerce. The precise activity that the Act regulates is "travel[ling] to another state for purposes of participating in a staged fight between animals." Travel to another state—except perhaps for some very odd and unusual examples—*necessarily* involves the use of the channels of interstate commerce. To travel to another state, a person needs to travel on an interstate road or highway; ride on an interstate train; fly on an interstate airplane; travel on an interstate boat; or the like. Thus, although the Act does not regulate the channels of interstate commerce themselves (*e.g.*, the width of the highway), it *does* regulate the *use* of such channels. (To wit, the Act forbids that they be *used* as a means of attending an organized animal fight.) And that is all that is necessary. This means the ACPA is almost certainly within Congress's commerce power.

The Act might conceivably also be justifiable as a regulation of an activity substantially affecting interstate commerce. The problem, though, is that it is unclear whether the act of "travel[ling] to another state for purposes of participating in a staged fight between animals" is economic or commercial in nature. The Act does not regulate the *purchase* of such travel, which clearly is a commercial activity. Rather, it regulates the travel itself. (The fact that one generally would purchase such travel is not enough to make the travel itself economic or commercial in nature. One must generally purchase a gun to possess one, but that fact does not make the possession of a gun economic or commercial activity. *See Lopez.*) And the facts here indicate that the event to which the travel occurs is generally noncommercial. So it seems somewhat unlikely that the ACPA could fit within *Lopez*'s third category.

In all events, the Act seems to plainly regulate the use of the channels of interstate commerce, making it a valid exercise of Congress's commerce power. As result, the court should reject Plaintiff's claim that the Act exceeds Congress's enumerated powers.

QUESTION 5

Farms in State X produce 99 percent of the almonds consumed in the United States. In 2017, the State X legislature adopts the Almond Promotion Act (APA), which imposes two new mandates on all public, government-run school districts in State X when those districts purchase food for school-provided meals and snacks: (1) all nuts served in school meals shall be almonds, and (2) the only non-dairy milk substitute served in school meals shall be almond milk. The statute's preamble states that the purpose of the APA "is to promote the competitiveness and profitability of the state's almond industry, which is vital to the State X economy."

Acme Co. is a corporation that is incorporated in State Y and has its headquarters in State Y. Prior to 2017, Acme sold several million dollars of peanuts, cashews, and soy milk to State X school districts. Since the enactment of the APA, however, those sales have ceased, costing Acme roughly $15 million in lost revenue annually.

Acme files suit in federal district court against the Superintendent of Education for State X (the state officer responsible for implementing and enforcing the APA) in her official capacity. In its complaint, Acme contends that the APA violates the Privileges and Immunities Clause of Article IV, the Privileges or Immunities Clause of the Fourteenth Amendment, and the dormant Commerce Clause; it seeks damages for Acme's lost sales attributable to the APA. In response, the Superintendent has filed a motion to dismiss Acme's complaint on the ground that the district court lacks subject matter jurisdiction. (Assume the federal government does not operate any school districts.)

A. Should the district court grant the Superintendent's motion to dismiss? Explain.

B. Assume the district court (correctly or incorrectly) denies the Superintendent's motion to dismiss. How should the court rule on the merits of Acme's claims? Explain.

SUGGESTED ANALYSIS for QUESTION 5

A

Rule statement: The Eleventh Amendment deprives federal courts of subject matter jurisdiction over unconsenting suits brought by private parties against state governments. The doctrine of *Ex parte Young*, however, provides a means to avoid this jurisdictional barrier: the Eleventh Amendment does not apply when a plaintiff sues the state officer responsible for enforcing the challenged state law in her official capacity and only seeks prospective relief. Prospective relief includes an injunction or declaratory relief. It does not include damages, the quintessential form of retrospective relief. When a plaintiff sues a state officer for damages in an official-capacity suit, the action is considered a suit against the state itself, and thus is barred by the Eleventh Amendment.

Application: Acme has sued the Attorney General in her official capacity (consistent with the *Ex parte Young* exception). But it is seeking damages, rather than prospective relief (such as an injunction or a declaratory judgment). As such, the Eleventh Amendment applies to this action. There is no indication that the state has waived its Eleventh Amendment immunity in this case, either by statute or through its litigation conduct. Thus, the district court should grant the Attorney General's motion to dismiss, as the Eleventh Amendment deprives the court of subject matter jurisdiction over Acme's claim. (As to other aspects of the court's jurisdiction, Acme's claim falls within the subject matter jurisdiction of the district court with respect to the basis for the claims it has asserted. All three claims—that the APA violates the Privileges and Immunities Clause of Article IV, the Privileges or Immunities Clause of the Fourteenth Amendment, and the dormant Commerce Clause—"arise under" federal law. They are federal questions, claims created by the federal Constitution. Further, Acme has standing. Acme has an injury in fact from its lost revenue, which is a concrete and particularized injury, and which has actually occurred. This injury appears to have been caused by the APA. And damages compensating Acme for its losses would redress that injury by compensating it for its losses.)

B

1. The Privileges and Immunities Clause of Article IV

Rule statement: The Privileges and Immunities Clause of Article IV generally forbids discrimination on the basis of state residence, with respect to those "privileges" or "immunities" considered "fundamental" for purposes Article IV. (The discrimination need not necessarily appear on the face of the statute.) Only "citizens" are protected by the clause. And "citizens" only includes natural persons, and not legal entities (such as corporations).

Application: Acme is a corporation, and thus not a "citizen" within the meaning of Article IV. Thus, even if the APA discriminates against non-residents (which it might), Acme has no plausible claim under the clause.

2. The Privileges or Immunities Clause of the Fourteenth Amendment

Rule statement: The Privileges or Immunities Clause of the Fourteenth Amendment generally forbids a state from discriminating among its citizens based on the duration of their residency in the state. Such discrimination constitutes a burden on the right to interstate migration, a "privilege or immunity" protected by the clause. Any such discrimination (at least when imposed on *bona fide* state residents) is subject to strict scrutiny. As with Article IV, only "citizens" are protected by the clause. And "citizens" only includes natural persons, and not legal entities (such as corporations).

Application: Again, Acme is a corporation. Thus, it is not a "citizen" within the meaning of this clause, and therefore has no plausible claim under the clause. (Further, the APA does not appear to discriminate on the basis of the duration of residency. So even if Acme were a "citizen," it appears that its claim would be unavailing.)

3. The dormant Commerce Clause

Rule statement: The dormant Commerce Clause generally forbids state laws that discriminate against or unduly burden interstate commerce. It only constrains state or local regulations or taxes—acts that use the coercive power of the state. It does not constrain state or local governments acting as "market participants": as buyers or providers in a market for goods or services. When a state or local government acts as a market participant, it is free to favor intrastate commerce over interstate commerce, even when doing so is plainly motivated by economic protectionism.

Application: The APA contains two mandates: that all public, government-run school districts in State X—when those districts purchase food for school-provided meals and snacks—(1) serve only almonds when they are serving nuts of any sort, and (2) serve almond milk as the only non-dairy milk substitute. Critically, *the Act only addresses the purchasing of food by public, government-run school districts*. It merely sets rules for governmental bodies' market participation—buying in the market. Public school districts are political subdivisions of the state government. Hence, this Act only concerns market participation; it imposes no regulations (or taxes) on any private individuals or entities. As a result, under the market participant exception, the APA is fully consistent with the dormant Commerce Clause; it is exempt from dormant Commerce Clause scrutiny. It does not matter that the APA is plainly motivated by a protectionist purpose ("to promote the competitiveness and profitability of the state's almond industry"). Thus, Acme's dormant Commerce Clause claim, too, must fail.

In short, if the district court were to deny the Attorney General's motion to dismiss, it should reject all three of Acme's claims on the merits. Because Acme is not a "citizen," it cannot assert a claim under either the Privileges and Immunities Clause of Article IV or the Privileges or Immunities Clause of the Fourteenth Amendment. And because the Act only concerns the state's school districts' purchasing of food for school lunches, it falls within the market participant exception, and therefore does not violate the dormant Commerce Clause.

QUESTION 6

Congress enacted a statute requiring any "place of public accommodation" to permit its patrons to use those restrooms designated by the gender with which they most identify, regardless of the patrons' sex at birth. The statute defines "place of public accommodation" as any "business or commercial premise, store, hotel, inn, performance venue, restaurant, place of amusement or entertainment, or similar establishment generally open to the public." It further provides that any person unlawfully denied access to a restroom according to the terms of the statute is entitled to sue the violator for damages, an injunction, or both.

A law of the State of Suntopia requires that, on state-owned property, all persons must use the restroom designated by their sex at birth, regardless of their present gender identity.

Plaintiff, a transgender person who was born with male anatomy, attempted to use a female-designated restroom in a Suntopia state park. A Suntopia park employee denied Plaintiff access to the restroom on the ground that state law required Plaintiff to use the male-designated restroom.

Invoking the federal statute, Plaintiff has sued Suntopia's Director of State Parks, the official responsible for managing the state's parks, in federal district court. Plaintiff seeks an injunction requiring that she have access to the park's female-designated restrooms. The Suntopia Director of State Parks has filed a motion to dismiss.

Assume there are no standing problems, and that the lawsuit does not raise a nonjusticiable political question. Please provide an objective analysis of what constitutional arguments the Director of State Parks is likely to raise in the motion to dismiss, what arguments Plaintiff is likely to make in response, and how the district court is likely to rule on the motion.

SUGGESTED ANALYSIS for QUESTION 6

The fact pattern presents three issues worth addressing: whether the Eleventh Amendment bars the court from hearing Plaintiff's suit; whether the federal statute violates the anti-commandeering principle; and whether the federal statute is within Congress's enumerated powers.

1. The Eleventh Amendment

Rule statement: The Director might argue that this lawsuit, brought in federal court, is barred by the Eleventh Amendment. Under the Eleventh Amendment, federal courts lack subject matter jurisdiction over nonconsenting suits against state governments brought by private parties (provided the state does not waive or forfeit its immunity, by statute or by its conduct in the litigation). This immunity does not extend to suits brought against state officers (rather than the state government itself) in their official capacity, so long as the plaintiff seeks prospective relief (such as an injunction or a declaratory judgment). *See Ex parte Young.*

Application: Plaintiff has filed suit against the Director (a state officer) seeking an injunction, a form of prospective relief. As a result, the holding of *Ex Parte Young* controls, and the Eleventh Amendment is no barrier to federal court jurisdiction.

2. The anti-commandeering principle

Rule statement: Because this statute regulates the conduct of state governments, the Director might attempt to argue that is it constitutes an unconstitutional commandeering of the states. Under the anti-commandeering principle, Congress cannot force states to act affirmatively to regulate (*i.e.*, to enact or administer legislative or regulatory rules) in their capacities as sovereigns. But Congress can impose coercive regulation on the actions of state governments when those federal regulations are "generally applicable"—meaning they apply to states in their proprietary capacities (acting in a manner that private actors can also act).

Application: This federal statute applies to all entities—public or private—that maintain accommodations that are open to the public. States are regulated just as all other private actors. This is therefore "generally applicable" legislation, and the states are being regulated like all other proprietors of "places of amusement." Thus, the anti-commandeering principle does not forbid Congress from enacting this statute.

3. Congress's enumerated powers

The Director's principal argument will be that the federal statute exceeds Congress's enumerated powers. All federal legislation must be grounded in an affirmative grant of power to Congress. Here, there are two possible sources of congressional authority: the commerce power and Section 5 of the Fourteenth Amendment.

a. The Commerce Power

Rule statement: The commerce power permits Congress to regulate three categories of activity. First, Congress can regulate the use of the channels of interstate commerce.

(This means any *use* of such channels, and not just regulations of the channels themselves. For instance, long before the "switch in time" of 1937, the Supreme Court held in *United States v. Darby* that a statute forbidding the shipment in interstate commerce of items manufactured with child labor was a valid exercise of the commerce power.) Second, Congress can regulate or protect the instrumentalities of, or persons or things in, interstate commerce. Finally, Congress can regulate those activities having a substantial effect on interstate commerce.

With respect to this third category—activities substantially affecting interstate commerce—the most important question is whether the regulated activity is economic or commercial in nature. If it is, the effect of the activity (in all its instances nationwide) can be aggregated, and it will almost certainly be considered to have a substantial effect on interstate commerce. The Supreme Court has also stated that three other factors should be assessed under this category: whether Congress has made findings about the activity's impact on interstate commerce; whether the connection between the activity and interstate commerce is attenuated; and whether the activity has historically been regulated primarily by the states (rather than the federal government).

Lastly, even if the challenged provision standing alone (or its application in a given case) does not fit within the above framework when viewed in isolation, the provision might nonetheless be within Congress's commerce power if Congress had a reasonable basis for concluding that the provision was essential to render effective a broader regulatory scheme, which scheme itself (when considered as a whole) is within Congress's commerce power.

Application: The first step is to identify the regulated activity regulated. Here, that is the service of individuals in places of public accommodations, or perhaps the provision of restrooms accompanying that activity of hosting patrons. The vast bulk of the activities covered by the statute are economic or commercial in nature: restaurants, hotels, places of amusement, etc. The park being run by the state may or may not be commercial. Does the state charge for entry? Is it part of a broader commercial premise, or does it have commercial activities within it? What matters, though, is whether the activity *as Congress has defined it in the statute* is economic or commercial in nature. Here, it appears to be so, because that activity is the operation of a place of public accommodation.

To be sure, some of the instances of the activity within that category may not be. But *Raich* is instructive. It holds that Congress is not obligated to make exceptions for such noncommercial instances of the regulated activity, when that activity is generally economic or commercial in nature. Congress must still have a reasonable basis for concluding that reaching that activity is necessary to make the regulatory scheme function effectively. It is unclear whether that is the case here. Nonetheless, the operation of a park open to the public seems likely to be considered economic or commercial in nature. As a result, its regulation likely falls within the third category under *Lopez*, as an activity that substantially affects interstate commerce.

b. Section 5 of the Fourteenth Amendment

Rule statement: An alternative possible basis for the provision is §5 of the Fourteenth Amendment. Section 5 permits Congress to enact appropriate legislation to enforce the prohibitions of §1 of the Fourteenth Amendment, which includes the Due Process Clause. And the Due Process Clause of the Fourteenth Amendment protects a substantive right to privacy, which includes a host of important, life-defining choices. Hence, Congress may use §5 to enact "appropriate legislation" "to enforce" this constitutional right to privacy and personal autonomy.

Application: The choice of which gender to identify with might plausibly be among those "liberties" protected by the Due Process Clause. The Court has construed the clause as protecting certain "fundamental" rights of personal autonomy that could be analogous: the right to terminate a pregnancy prior to the fetus becoming viable; the right to engage in intimate behavior with another consenting adult in private; and the right to marry, regardless of the couple's respective genders. In declaring these rights constitutionally protected, the Court has held that they are central to one's identity, and thus too important for the government to interfere with without substantial justification.

The right to identify as a particular gender—or no gender at all—could be a similar right, and thus protected as "fundamental." And if so, then Congress would be empowered pursuant to §5 to enact legislation enforcing this right against state action interfering with this right. The law would not be within Congress's §5 power as applied to *private* operators of public accommodations. But the State of Suntopia is a state actor, and thus would potentially be violating the Fourteenth Amendment by requiring persons to use the restroom designated by their sex at birth, regardless of their present gender identity. Thus, the law—as applied here—could potentially be within Congress's §5 power.

4. Conclusion

On balance, the statute (as a regulation of the operations of public accommodations, almost all of which are economic or commercial in nature) would appear to fall within Congress's commerce power. There is also a plausible argument that the statute is also justifiable as within Congress's §5 power, at least as applied to state governments (including the State of Suntopia). For these reasons, the court should probably deny the Director's motion to dismiss.

QUESTION 7

State A recently enacted a statute regulating abortion. It requires (1) that any abortion performed in State A be performed by a physician who is a resident of State A, and (2) that any woman receiving an abortion performed in State A must be a resident of State A. State A is largely rural and sparsely populated, though the City of Metropolis, located in State B with a population of roughly 750,000, is located just 20 miles from the State B-State A border.

Plaintiff is a physician and a citizen of State B. Before the new State A law was enacted, Plaintiff regularly performed abortions at a family planning clinic in State A, where she practiced medicine six days each month. Roughly half of her patients at the State A clinic were residents of State A, and roughly half were residents of State B.

Plaintiff has filed suit in federal district court against State A's Attorney General, the official responsible for enforcing the state's abortion law. Plaintiff contends that the abortion law is unconstitutional, and she seeks an injunction against its enforcement and compensation for the medical fees she has been unable to collect from patients, insurers, and other payers since the law went into effect. The Attorney General has filed a motion to dismiss Plaintiff's suit.

Assume there are no standing problems, and that the lawsuit does not raise a nonjusticiable political question. Please provide your objective analysis of what constitutional arguments Plaintiff is likely to raise in her lawsuit, what constitutional arguments the Attorney General is likely to raise in the motion to dismiss, and how the district court is likely to rule in the case. (Assume Plaintiff does not make any claim regarding the constitutional right to obtain an abortion.)

SUGGESTED ANALYSIS for QUESTION 7

The fact pattern presents at least three principal issues—two to be raised by Plaintiff, and one by the Attorney General. Plaintiff can plausibly claim that the law violates the dormant Commerce Clause and the Privileges and Immunities Clause of Article IV. The Attorney General can argue that the Eleventh Amendment divests the district court of jurisdiction (at least in part).

1. The Dormant Commerce Clause

Issue: Because the statute forbids commercial activity crossing state lines (customers or physicians coming from outside the state to consume or provide services in the state), it may violate the dormant Commerce Clause.

Rule statement: A state law that discriminates against interstate commerce (assuming it does not fall within one of the DCC's exceptions) is subject to "rigorous scrutiny." This means the state (1) must have a legitimate, non-protectionist justification for the law, and (2) the state must lack any practicable nondiscriminatory alternatives to achieve that objective.

Application: Here, the law obviously discriminates against interstate commerce: commercial activity that crosses state lines (residents of State B seeking abortions in State A) are disfavored relative to intrastate commerce (residents in State A seeking abortions in State A). This is facial discrimination. And it is with respect to commerce, as most medical services are provided in a commercial setting. (Indeed, here Plaintiff was obtaining fees from the provision of these services). The law also discriminates against out-of-state providers, such as Plaintiff. Thus, the law is subject to "rigorous scrutiny." The state may well have legitimate, non-protectionist interests that support the law—namely, promoting patient health and protecting the potential life of the fetus. But this law is not *necessary* to furthering either interest: the residence of the patient or the physician seems irrelevant to those interests. Perhaps, with respect to patient health, the state believes its licensing of physicians is more rigorous. But (as in *Dean Milk*) there are practicable nondiscriminatory alternatives, such as requiring physicians who practice in the state to be licensed by the state. A complete bar to out-of-state residents is hardly *necessary*. Thus, both provisions in the law appear to violate the dormant Commerce Clause.

2. The Privileges and Immunities Clause of Article IV

Issue: By discriminating against out-of-state residents—both physicians and patients—the law may also violate the Privileges and Immunities Clause of Article IV.

Rule statement: The Privileges and Immunities Clause of Article IV presumptively proscribes state discrimination against nonresidents based on their state of residency. Only citizens are protected by the clause, and it only applies to discrimination with respect to rights considered "fundamental" in a particular sense—vital to the Nation's unity. One such privilege is that to pursue employment or a common calling. If the state so discriminates, its law is constitutional only if its objective is "substantial," and the law is "substantially related" to that objective. In other words, out-of-state residents must be a peculiar source of the harm.

Application: This law plainly discriminates against nonresidents wishing to perform abortions in State A. The practice of medicine would seem to be a common calling protected by the clause. Plaintiff is a citizen. Thus, State A's law can survive only if the state has a substantial interest, and the law is substantially related to that interest. Again, State A probably has two interests in this context, both of which might be considered substantial: protecting the health of the patient and preserving the life of the fetus. (Alternatively, one might characterize this latter interest in terms of ensuring the woman's choice is informed or stating the state's preference for childbirth over abortion.) The problem is that barring out-of-state physicians from performing abortions does not seem substantially related to either of these interests. If the state's concern is the quality of physicians licensed in other states, it would be easy enough to require them to be licensed in State A as well. And if the state simply is aiming to reduce the number of abortions, there is no reason to target those performed by out-of-state physicians. If the state has a moral objection to abortion, those performed by out-of-state physicians are no different than those performed by in-state physicians.

The statute might also violate the Privileges and Immunities Clause by requiring that the patient be a resident of State A. Because the right to an abortion (at least before viability) is fundamental for purposes of due process, it presumably is for the Privileges and Immunities Clause as well. And based on the same analysis as above, it does not appear that prohibiting out-of-state residents from obtaining abortions is substantially related to the state's relevant interests. It is unclear whether Plaintiff could raise this objection, as it would require third-party standing (the physician raising the constitutional rights of the patients). But the question asks us to assume there are no standing problems.

3. The Eleventh Amendment and state sovereign immunity

Issue: The court may lack jurisdiction because the state may have immunity from Plaintiff's suit under the Eleventh Amendment.

Rule statement: The Eleventh Amendment bars unconsenting suits against state governments in federal court brought by private parties. Under *Ex parte Young*, the Eleventh Amendment does not bar suits brought against state officers in their official capacities when the relief sought is purely prospective. A suit for retrospective relief (such as damages)—because the damages will be paid out of the state's treasury—will be deemed a suit against the state itself, and thus falls outside the rule of *Ex parte Young*.

Application: A portion of Plaintiff's suit will be barred by the Eleventh Amendment. The suit falls with *Ex parte Young* to the extent Plaintiff seeks an injunction against the Attorney General. An injunction is a form of prospective relief, and the Eleventh Amendment does not bar a federal court from adjudicating a suit against a state officer in her official capacity for prospective relief. But the claim seeking compensatory (and hence retrospective) relief in the form of lost medical fees is barred. Plaintiff seeks "compensation for the medical fees she has been unable to collect from patients, insurers, and other payers since the law went into effect." This is retrospective relief, and thus goes beyond what *Ex parte Young* permits. Because it seeks compensation—compensation that would be paid from the state's treasury—this claim will be treated as an action against the state itself under the Eleventh Amendment (even though the Attorney General is the named defendant). The district court thus lacks subject matter jurisdiction over her claim for compensation, so that aspect of her suit should be dismissed.